MORAL PHILOSOPHY for modern life

SECOND EDITION

Anthony Falikowski

SHERIDAN COLLEGE INSTITUTE OF
TECHNOLOGY AND ADVANCED LEARNING

PEARSON
Prentice
Hall

Toronto

National Library of Canada Cataloguing in Publication

Falikowski, Anthony, 1953–
    Moral Philosophy for Modern Life / Anthony Falikowski. — 2nd ed.

Includes index.
ISBN 0-13-123817-5

    1. Ethics. I. Title.

BJ1012.F344 2005   170   C2004-900842-0

ISBN 0-13-123817-5

Vice President, Editorial Director: Michael J. Young
Executive Acquisitions Editor: Christine Cozens
Marketing Manager: Ryan St. Peters
Developmental Editor: Paula Drùzga
Production Editor: Judith Scott
Copy Editor: Nadia Halim
Production Coordinator: Susan Johnson
Page Layout: Carolyn E. Sebestyen
Art Director: Mary Opper
Cover Design: Michelle Bellemare
Cover Image: Veer

4 5 6 DPC 10 09 08

Printed and bound in Canada.

Dedicated with love to Bubble-Wand, Scooter, Heddy, and Pie.
You know who you are...or do you really?

Contents

Note to the Instructor

Moral Philosophy for Modern Life, Second Edition, is designed as an introductory level textbook for post-secondary students. It can be used in moral philosophy, liberal arts, humanities, social science, general education, critical reasoning and generic skills courses, as well as in any vocational program of study containing an ethics component.

Moral Philosophy for Modern Life, Second Edition, offers beginners a comprehensive and integrated "outcomes-based" approach to the study of ethics. Adopting a learning-centred orientation, the book shifts attention away from simple coverage of theoretical content and places it on what students will know and be able to do as a result of their philosophical study. With this subtle but significant pedagogical shift, instructors using this text will feel more confident at course end that the stated exit competencies have been achieved by students. Students, on the other hand, will be able to use the pedagogical aids included in the text to make their education in ethics more self-directed. This book suits a student-centred paradigm of education, wherein instructors become more like mentors, facilitators, coaches or learning directors and less like experts or moral authorities on controversial ethical matters. Working together in partnership, students and instructors will be able to make great pedagogical gains.

Broad in its overall scope, *Moral Philosophy for Modern Life*, Second Edition, consists of three components: theories, skills and applications. Before starting the theory component, the "Preview and Introduction" of the book underscores the practicality of ethics by pointing to its therapeutic value and relevance for establishing an objective basis for moral criticism and social reform. Also, in the Preview and Introduction, students are invited to complete something I call the Moral Preference Indicator (MPI)—an informal self-diagnostic instrument to be used to help them identify their preferred ethical orientations to life. Students are asked to complete the MPI again after finishing the moral theory portion of the book to discover whether their ethical perspectives have changed as a result of critical thought and reflection.

In Part One, six of the historically most important approaches to morality are covered under the headings of Greek Virtue Ethics, Utilitarian Ethics, Deontological Ethics, Ethical Egoism, Existentialist Ethics and the Morality of Care. The works of Plato, Aristotle, Jeremy Bentham, John Stuart Mill, Immanuel Kant, John Rawls, Ayn Rand, Jean-Paul Sartre, Carol Gilligan and Nel Noddings are used as a theoretical springboard for moral application and analysis. Reviewing these philosophers and their moral perspectives will serve students well as they embark on the difficult task of grappling with matters of personal morality and decision making on controversial social issues. Suggested readings and source references throughout the text help to encourage further studies in ethical theory. Although the several classical and contemporary moral positions offered in this book provide students with a good start, they constitute only a small sample of the range of ideas in this field. A full treatment of all or even most moral positions would not be useful here, however, given the more practical, introductory focus of the book. As the proverbial saying goes, the longest journey must begin with the first step.

Part Two begins with another self-diagnostic, this time to assess reasoning skills. Once students discover how much work they need to do personally, they begin to develop those reasoning skills necessary for rational debate in matters of morality. For instance, they learn how to distinguish among factual statements, value judgments and conceptual claims. They learn to use processes of inductive and deductive logic, how to construct logical/practical syllogisms, how to test for the soundness of arguments and how to identify instances of fallacious and invalid reasoning. In addition, students master a seven-step procedure for ethical case-study analysis. With all of this "how to" learning behind them, students will be well prepared for critical analysis and objective evaluation of the issues discussed later in the book, not to mention all of those that will arise in their futures.

Part Three deals with contemporary moral issues. Outstanding readings selected for their relevance, interest value and readability are gathered together under the headings of Business Ethics, Health-Care Ethics, Professional Ethics, Sexual Ethics, Legal/Political Ethics and Global/Environmental Ethics. To facilitate critical evaluation of these readings, an Argument Analysis Worksheet is provided in Appendix Four. Critical analysis of the readings will offer students practice when it comes to applying ethical principles to real-world problems.

SPECIAL FEATURES OF *MORAL PHILOSOPHY FOR MODERN LIFE*

Comprehensive and Integrated Approach

As mentioned, this text takes a comprehensive and integrated approach to moral philosophy. Theories, reasoning skills and applications are combined to help students learn how to approach ethical decision making in a rational and informed fashion. Unlike "social issues" books that often omit theories or "theories" books that leave out applications, and unlike some "logic" and "critical reasoning" texts that focus on thinking processes and therefore neglect moral theories and/or applications altogether, *Moral Philosophy for Modern Life*, Second Edition, integrates all these components in a way that promotes students' moral understanding and furthers their abilities to deal with the moral complexities of everyday modern life.

Readability

Experience has taught me that in order to teach philosophy effectively, one must operate according to the KISS principle—"Keep it simple, Sylvia!" Philosophical ethics is difficult enough for students without confusing them with the use of unnecessarily convoluted language and incomprehensible vocabulary. Every effort has been made to make the writing style of *Moral Philosophy for Modern Life*, Second Edition, accessible to students. All too often people tell me that their first philosophy course was their last. When I ask why, they usually say that they could not understand the books and articles they were expected to read. The ideas seemed interesting enough; they just could not get past the awkward language and technical vocabulary. This text is written *not* to discourage students, but to encourage them with interesting ideas presented in an accessible and understandable way. A glossary and lists of key terms in every one of the theories and skills chapters help students identify and understand those concepts having particular importance (see my "Message to Students").

Built-in Student Study Guide

To help achieve learning-centred educational outcomes, *Moral Philosophy for Modern Life*, Second Edition, incorporates a built-in student study guide. The learning aids that are included help foster mastery of theoretical content, proficiency in critical thinking as well as the ability to deal with different moral problems using appropriate rational strategies. The inclusion of a built-in study guide means that students need not buy an extra workbook at additional cost. It is essential that students be able to grasp basic moral concepts, define theoretical terms and think critically, before engaging in more complex article and issue analysis.

The guide included in this book is intended as an optional aid, not as a required tool. Certain instructors may wish to integrate some, or all, of the elements of the guide into their lesson plans to complement their teaching. Others may wish to have students use the guide for self-directed study outside the classroom. Many aspects of the guide are suitable for tutorial sessions. Regardless of how it is used, the guide offers many individual and group learning opportunities. Instructors and students can use their own goals and preferences to determine how they will employ the guide.

The built-in study guide used in Parts One and Two of this book is based on the SQ3R method of learning. SQ3R stands for survey, question, read, recite and review. Chapters are designed so that students can

a. *survey* the content to be covered,
b. use Philosophical Focus *Questions* to direct their attention,
c. *read* the material presented, and
d. *recite* and *review* what was covered for self-testing.

As part of the built-in guide, you will find

- Chapter overviews
- Explicitly stated learning outcomes
- Philosophical focus questions
- Boldfacing
- A glossary
- A list of key terms
- Chapter end progress checks
- Summaries of major points

Details on how to use the various components of the SQ3R method of self-directed learning are included in my "Message to Students."

Moral Preference Indicator (MPI)

Moral Philosophy for Modern Life, Second Edition, contains a moral preference self-diagnostic. By completing the "Moral Preference Indicator" (MPI) found in the "Preview and Introduction," students are helped to identify their moral value preferences for ethical decision making and action. Students using the MPI will discover whether they prefer a moral perspective based on utilitarian, deontological, egoistic, feminine, existential or character-based virtue considerations. By completing the MPI a second time, after covering ethical theories in Part One, students can then determine whether or not they have changed their moral viewpoints following careful theoretical study and analysis.

Self-Diagnostic: Reasoning Skills Assessment

Part Two of the book starts with a reasoning skills level self-assessment. By completing this informal diagnostic and developmental tool, students get some preliminary indication of how good their current logical thinking skills are. This tool deals with such matters as inductive logic, deductive logic and frequently made logical mistakes stemming from fallacious reasoning. After finishing Part Two, students can return to the reasoning self-diagnostic to discover what progress has been made in their development as rational thinkers.

Biographical Briefs

Sometimes, a little knowledge about the philosophers themselves makes it easier to appreciate their writings. For this reason, "Biographical Briefs" are provided to put names and faces on the various moral theories discussed. These briefs will also help to place moral theories into a personal, historical context.

Back to the Source

Moral Philosophy for Modern Life, Second Edition, is written, in part, to decipher difficult and complex moral theories for beginning students in philosophy. Without some initial guidance, interpretation, and summary, the original works of the philosophers would be simply too imposing for many undergraduate students. Yet, to complete an introductory ethics course without having read any of the philosophers' actual works would seem inappropriate. For this reason, short excerpts are taken from original sources and presented in a feature called "Back to the Source." These sourceworks are highly aligned to the material in the chapter in which they are found. They will benefit students by giving them a philosophical sampling of the real thing, so to speak.

Philosophers at Work

This book encourages students not only to learn about moral philosophy but also to *do* a lot of moral philosophizing themselves. Philosophy is best understood not as a body of knowledge, but as an activity or method of thinking. With this in mind, students are given opportunities in the text to apply theories, test arguments, analyze ideas and interpret social issues from an ethical perspective. In this feature, students will be encouraged to engage in personal reflections and group discussions in class or in tutorial. They will also be helped to develop intellectual attitudes conducive to rational living.

Mindwork Meditations

Students using this text are encouraged to keep a personal journal. To facilitate making journal entries, they are provided with opportunities in the book for "Mindwork Meditations." Such meditations do not require a stilling or emptying of the mind, as in Eastern mysticism, but rather thought and mental activity relating to a problem, question or issue. Keeping a journal can be a wonderful way for students to record their thoughts, feelings and reflections during their philosophical quest in your course. They can volunteer to read their journal entries in class, submit them for evaluation or simply keep them as a personal record of their philosophical development as rational thinkers. How the journal is used is up to you and the members of your class.

Philosophical Focus Questions

Philosophical Focus Questions are included in the book as part of its built-in student study guide. These questions serve to direct students' attention to chapter content, which is essential to mastering designated learning outcomes. The focus questions can also serve as a basis of discussion and debate in classroom or tutorial sessions.

Practical Applications

Part Three of this book consists of articles relating to personal and contemporary socio-moral issues. The articles included have been selected for their clarity and relevance to modern life. Students should find them interesting and thought provoking and a good means by which to practise their moral reasoning skills—skills that will serve them well on their journeys into the moral domain of life.

Source References and Related Readings

For anyone wishing to pursue their interests in any topic covered in *Moral Philosophy for Modern Life*, Second Edition, source references and related readings are provided. These will assist students and instructors alike to find more information on topics that interest them.

Appendix 1: Answer Key

The answers to chapter-end "Progress Checks" are found in Appendix 1. They help to verify student understanding of course content.

Appendix 2: How to Write a Moral Position Paper

Probably the hardest task facing philosophical beginners is having to write their first thesis defence. Having opinions is one thing; rationally defending one's point of view with reasoned arguments is quite another. In Appendix 2, students are taken through a process of reasoning that shows them how to take contrasting viewpoints and objections into account, while defending their own moral positions in a formal, written format.

Appendix 3: Case Studies for Ethical Analysis

For those wishing to develop their moral-analytical reasoning skills when it comes to real-life moral dilemmas, case studies are provided for consideration.

Appendix 4: Argument Analysis Worksheet

A worksheet template is also provided to help with initial analysis and evaluation of readings found in this book.

Inspirational Quotations

Sprinkled throughout *Moral Philosophy for Modern Life* are thought-provoking quotations designed to inspire, uplift and sometimes to disturb and challenge. I hope you enjoy them as much as I enjoyed selecting them for your interest and personal reflection.

CHANGES TO THE SECOND EDITION

Previous users of the first edition of *Moral Philosophy for Modern Life* will notice a number of changes and improvements in this, the second edition. To begin with, three new ethical perspectives have been added to the "Classical and Contemporary Moral Theories" discussed in Part One: Ethical Egoism, Care-Based Morality, and Existentialist Ethics. This inclusion makes the theoretical component of the book much more substantial and has the added advantage of including female thinkers, proving once and for all that not all of philosophy has been conducted by "dead white males." Users of the book will be introduced to Ayn Rand's egoistic "virtue of selfishness" and the care-based feminine ethics of Carol Gilligan and Nel Noddings, two contemporary thinkers whose work on morality has been very influential in contemporary philosophical circles. The work of Jean-Paul Sartre will underscore some of the personal and existential dimensions of moral action and decision making. With the new inclusions for this text, female students and those individuals who tend to be suspicious of "systems of thought" should find moral philosophy a little more engaging. No doubt this will have pedagogical payoffs!

Part Two has also been substantially improved with new material. For instance, in the context of the distinction between factual statements and value judgments, the nature of conceptual claims is discussed. Conceptual claims are shown to be different from factual and normative ones. Subsequently, detailed methods of conceptual analysis are covered to help students deal with them when they arise in moral contexts. These methods will be useful when it comes to writing papers and critically evaluating scholarly articles. The precise methods of conceptual analysis to be discussed are drawn from the work of John Wilson.

In Part Two, the treatment of 'argument' has also been enhanced. For instance, students now learn not only that arguments are different from opinions, but that they are different from explanations as well. Furthermore, they learn to identify indicator words for premises and conclusions—the elements which in fact constitute arguments in everyday life. They also learn about unstated premises and conclusions, simple and complex arguments, how to express arguments in standard form and how to diagram arguments for analysis. These skills will prove to be invaluable when analyzing and evaluating the arguments expressed in articles presented in Part Three.

In keeping with the practical objectives of this text, an outline of a seven-step procedure for ethical case-study analysis has been added. Situations arise in modern life that require all of us, students included, to make moral sense of them. A method of case-study analysis, used originally in European business contexts and later adopted for training purposes by the American Philosophical Practitioners Association, will be offered to students for their use and consideration. The generic skills promoted here will serve students well in all areas of personal and professional life, wherever ethical issues arise. Designed to help students develop the ability to handle real-life moral dilemmas using a structured, rational process of thought, this material is an exciting addition to this second edition. A number of case studies are provided in Appendix Three in the event instructors wish to practise resolving moral dilemmas using the case-study methodology.

The changes to Part Three are significant as well. Articles in this section that were no longer relevant have been discarded and replaced with new ones of current interest. Those articles that might be considered "classics" have been left in, given their insightfulness either in understanding a particular issue, or because of their usefulness to students when it comes to developing their critical-analytical thinking skills.

All in all, I believe the changes to this second edition of *Moral Philosophy for Modern Life* are certain to make an already useful book even more so! I hope you agree.

Message to Students

As the author of *Moral Philosophy for Modern Life*, Second Edition, I would like to welcome you to the interesting and stimulating world of ethical inquiry. In this text, we will embark on a journey that will take us through some difficult and oftentimes uphill terrain. Energy and effort will be required to reach our ultimate destination of moral enlightenment, but, once we are on our way, the fruits of rational inquiry should quench our thirst for truth and understanding. I cannot guarantee that we will arrive at our final destination by term's end, but I can assure you the journey has the potential to be life transforming. This course in applied ethics could change your worldview forever—I mean this seriously! The timing could not be better; you are here and ready and your philosophy teacher has appeared. Let us join minds and accompany your course instructor as we set off together on a journey—one that will lead to your personal ethical illumination.

To help you find your way through the theoretical forests and over the cracks and fault lines in logic, a built-in study guide has been included as a convenient navigation device. This guide will enable you to master the various moral theories discussed, to practise logical and critical-analytical reasoning skills and to apply both theories and skills to real-world ethical problems. The study guide will assist you in your self-directed efforts to learn moral philosophy and to appreciate its relevance to everyday modern life.

The study guide in Parts One and Two of this text is based on the *SQ3R Method of Learning*. SQ3R is an acronym standing for *Survey, Question, Read, Recite and Review*. Part Three of this text, "Applying Ethics in the Real World," has its own distinct learning aid, namely an argument analysis template, which can be found in Appendix Four. First, let me take you through the SQ3R process used in Parts One and Two of this text. If you follow this system, it will help you master the content and skills targeted in the intended "learning outcomes" included in each chapter opener. In plain terms, you are more likely to pass the course and to do well! The steps are provided below.

(1) SURVEY THE CONTENT TO BE COVERED

Chapters One to Eleven begin with overviews that provide a preview of what is to be covered. By simply glancing at the headings, you can survey (S) the material you will be expected to master.

Look Over the Learning Outcomes

To make the overview and survey process easier, learning outcomes have been stated explicitly. By perusing them at the outset, you can discover what you will be expected to know and do. After completing a chapter, you should review the list of learning outcomes to ensure that you have assimilated the information and have developed the skills marked for mastery. If not, you can go back and review the appropriate sections of the chapter.

(2) DIRECT YOUR READING ATTENTION BY USING "PHILOSOPHICAL FOCUS QUESTIONS"

Each chapter in Parts One and Two contains Philosophical Focus Questions. These questions make up the "Q" portion of the SQ3R methodology. You should examine the questions before actually reading the main text of the chapter. As suggested by the heading itself, the questions serve to focus your attention while you read so that you will know what to look for and what is important. Your instructor may use these questions for classroom discussion. Concentrate on finding the answers to the focus questions while you read. This will help you prepare for discussions, whether they take place in regular classes or in tutorial sessions.

(3) READ THE CHAPTER

Once you have an idea of what is in the chapter and what to look for, go ahead and read. I caution you to be patient. Reading philosophy is not like reading the newspaper or comic strips. Do not be surprised if you find yourself reading the same paragraph or page over several times before you understand the meaning. You are being introduced to a new way of thinking and it has a technical vocabulary all its own. You are also being asked to think and to communicate with a level of precision and clarity that has likely never been demanded of you in your academic career until now. Try not to get discouraged. Like the saying goes, "anything worthwhile takes time."

Highlighted Key Terms

Given the inherent difficulty of philosophy, you should not be left to guess what is important. Just in case the Philosophical Focus Questions have not been a sufficient guide, key terms and concepts have been **boldfaced** to make clear what is especially significant and worth remembering. A list of boldfaced key terms is found just before the Progress Checks of each chapter in Parts One and Two.

Glossary

Because it would be unwieldy to include definitions of all the key terms contained in the main body of this text, I have included a glossary of the "most important" ones. These definitions, along with the other boldfaced terms and the focus questions, should enable you to pick out and to understand what is essential for mastery of the chapter.

(4) RECITE AND REVIEW

Progress Checks

After reading the chapter, you should start the recitation and review process by doing the Progress Check. Your mastery of the content is reflected in your ability to correctly answer questions contained in the check. Your responses to each of the progress checks can be verified by referring to the answer key in Appendix 1.

Summary of Major Points

Chapter summaries found in Parts One and Two also comprise the recitation and review component of the SQ3R methodology. You may examine them before and/or after doing the Progress Checks to consolidate learning and to make sure that outcomes have been achieved. Reviewing the summaries is something you should do at test time to maximize your chances for success.

Acknowledgments

The production of any book involves the hard work of many people in addition to the author. With this in mind, I would like to thank Christine Cozens, executive acquisitions editor, and Michael Young, vice-president, editorial director at Pearson Education Canada, for signing me to this project. Both individuals were extremely creative and accommodating in their efforts to address my personal concerns about embarking on yet another book project. Paula Drùzga, the developmental editor for the book, helped to get the revision process started by assisting me in incorporating the critical feedback I received regarding the first edition and preliminary drafts of the second. Judith Scott, production editor, and Nadia Halim, copy editor, looked after scheduling and manuscript quality. I wish to express my gratitude to them as well.

I would also like to thank all those who read and reviewed the text and rough drafts of this second edition of *Moral Philosophy for Modern Life*, especially Dr. Jean Saindon at York University, whose enthusiasm and strong interest in teaching philosophy came through clearly in his very useful critical remarks. Other reviewers I especially wish to thank include Sharon Lee, University of Waterloo; Elzbieta and Krzysztof Swiatek, Grant MacEwan College and Athabasca University respectively; Wendell Kisner, Grant MacEwan College; John Artibello, Centennial College; Susan Seguin, Mohawk College and Peter March, St. Mary's University. Finally, I would like to acknowledge the influence of Sam Mallin at York University, whose introduction to the Modes of Reasoning course offered there led me to a number of improvements and new inclusions in the second part of the text, dealing with logic and critical thinking. I would like to believe that the book is significantly better as a result.

The Practical Value of Philosophical Ethics

A number of years ago, a theatre arts student taking my moral philosophy course as a general education elective raised his hand in class. We had been discussing the ethics of abortion that day, and he was obviously very agitated and upset. When I called on him, he blurted out: "C'mon Tony, you've been studying this ethics stuff for years. You're the expert. Let's stop all of this arguing. It's driving me crazy. Just tell me, will you, is abortion right or wrong?"

As I think back to the painful experience of my theatre arts student, I cannot help but feel a little disturbed myself by the mental torment he was suffering. He was, apparently, experiencing considerable anxiety in his efforts to make the correct moral value judgment on the controversial issue of abortion. He knew that abortion was a serious matter and that it was important for him to take the right moral position on it; yet, he was uncertain about how to decide for himself. He wanted me to decide for him.

Like my theatre arts student, many others in society experience mental anguish when making important ethical decisions. Values must be championed, people must be confronted, principles must be defended, and sometimes difficult or unpleasant actions must be carried out. When there is much uncertainty or diversity of opinion, psychological tension can result. Moral doubt can be a significant source of stress in everyday life.

In their efforts to cope with this moral suffering of the mind, some individuals like my tormented student look to experts and gurus for answers. By placing faith in the judgment of others, people try to relieve themselves of the burden of having to decide for themselves. By granting moral authority to an ethics professor, a cult leader, a politician or a military officer, some attempt to escape from the personal responsibility of making moral decisions. If any wrong-doing or bad judgment arises as a result of the escape attempts, then the moral authorities are to blame, not the would-be moral escape artists.

Of course, it is possible that, in some cases, deferring to moral authority is little more than a veiled attempt to get off the moral hook of life. Perhaps the most obvious example of this is found in the war crimes trials that followed World War II. At that time, a number of senior German officers pleaded innocent to war crimes charges on the grounds that they were just obeying orders from the *Führer*. In their minds, they were not responsible. World opinion seems to suggest otherwise.

Another psychological strategy to relieve morally induced mental stress is to quit thinking and simply to conclude that all values are a matter of personal preference. Once this stance is adopted, there is no need whatsoever to agonize over moral matters. After all, on this account, no one person has the right to make a value judgment on the actions or character of another. As the saying goes, "different strokes for different folks." People just have different feelings and opinions about what is morally acceptable in any situation or given set of circumstances.

> *Vain is the word of a philosopher which does not heal any suffering of man. For just as there is no profit in medicine if it does not expel the diseases of the body, so there is no profit in philosophy either if it does not expel the suffering of the mind.*
>
> EPICURUS

Although this relativistic position is one that some might wish to defend and though it offers some degree of psychological solace, it is fraught with difficulties. If, for example, everybody is right and nobody is wrong, because rightness and wrongness are relative to the person, culture or generation, then opposite and conflicting positions could both be right at the same time—a proposition that does not make very much logical sense. Furthermore, if there is no objective way to decide matters of right and wrong or good and bad, then there would be no ethical basis for criticizing social policies or for improving society. Things like slavery, terrorism, child abuse or discrimination against women would have to be accepted on the grounds that, morally speaking, it is all a matter of personal opinion and how people feel at the time. What's right for a terrorist might be considered wrong for an expectant mother.

If we are not to abandon morality and the possibility of social progress, if we do not wish to wash our hands of moral responsibility or to escape from it by becoming mindless followers and sheep, we must look for adequate ways to make moral decisions for ourselves.

Fortunately, for us, a great many thinkers have grappled for centuries with the problems of ethical decision making. We need not bow down and worship these thinkers; nor do we have to accept unconditionally all of what they say to us. This would be mindless following again. As thoughtful and mature adults, what we can do is to consider intelligently the insights the thinkers have to offer and to evaluate their moral philosophies from a rational, objective perspective. We can decide which ideas have worth, which ones need alteration, and which ones must be rejected altogether. We can do all this if we choose to be free and independent thinkers ourselves, and if we assume at the outset that, when it comes to moral matters, debate is meaningful and that there are better and worse decisions to be made.

In Part One of *Moral Philosophy for Modern Life*, Second Edition, we will examine six classical and contemporary moral perspectives. They are either historically important and/or currently influential, impacting on our common-sense thinking about morality today. The classical perspectives to be covered include the virtue ethics of Plato and Aristotle, the utilitarian ethics of Jeremy Bentham and John Stuart Mill and the deontological duty and rights-based ethics of Immanual Kant and John Rawls. Though John Rawls only recently died, his "*A Theory of Justice*" has quickly become a classic in the field, and given how much Kant influenced Rawls, his work has been placed under the deontological heading and presented together with Kant's.

As for contemporary moral perspectives, we will bring several female thinkers into the discussion. We will examine Ayn Rand's notion of rational selfishness as she presents it in the context of ethical egoism. We will also look at feminine care-based ethics as offered up by Carol Gilligan and Nel Noddings. They both take issue with a purely rational morality for a variety of reasons. A final theory to be discussed will be the existentialist ethic of Jean-Paul Sartre. Contrary to some who believe that the godless universe of the atheistic existentialist is necessarily nihilistic or without value, Sartre illustrates how life continues to have value and meaning through active engagement in the world—even though there is no God to oversee worldly affairs.

Of course, in any introductory text on moral philosophy or applied ethics, not all moral perspectives can be covered. Space and time considerations make a complete and comprehensive treatment of all theories impractical. I have thus chosen to omit, for our immediate purposes, non-Western and religious ethical perspectives. By doing so, I am not suggesting that Eastern philosophy or Christian morality, for example, have less worth or justifiability than those Western, predominantly rational perspectives I have selected for treatment. Whether or not all of morality is completely rational, for instance, is a debatable point, as Gillian and Noddings remind us. So too is the notion of whether or not morality can make sense without the existence of a supreme being.

The theoretical questions just raised, though interesting and philosophically important, are beyond the scope of this more practical and applied introductory text. The ethical perspectives I have chosen for consideration simply suit us best for getting started with the business of having to make moral decisions in the real world. In my efforts to respect religious diversity and the pluralistic values of North American society, I have opted for a non-religious approach to practical ethics. Although people's religious and ethnic backgrounds differ in a multicultural society like ours, reason, or the ability to engage in rational inquiry, is the one common thread that binds us together as moral persons. After you have completed this introductory course in applied ethics, I invite you to revisit ethical theory by researching other moral perspectives not covered here. Think about what differences, if any, they would make to your practical day-to-day moral decision making.

Once we have completed our coverage of moral theories in Part One of the text, we will move on in Part Two to a treatment of logical and critical-analytical thinking skills necessary for effective ethical decision making. First, you will learn how science and philosophy handle matters of morality differently. You will learn that different kinds of claims can be made about morality and that some require special techniques of conceptual analysis. Further, you will discover how arguments differ from opinions and explanations and how arguments can be structured and evaluated. To assist you in making real-life moral decisions, an ethical case-study methodology will be introduced for your consideration and use. In addition to all of this, be prepared to learn about processes of inductive and deductive logic and how they function in the context of moral argument. Also, in Part Two, you will learn a kind of "logical self-defence" against irrationality and dishonest attempts to persuade. I will show you how to identify a number of in-

Hagar

Copyright © 1994 New York, NY: King Features Syndicate. Reprinted with special permission of King Features Syndicate.

formal logical fallacies — what I call "sleazy logic" — to protect yourself from the threat of nonsense, attack and diversionary tactics designed to manipulate.

In Part Three, we will use our newly acquired theoretical knowledge and critical analytical thinking skills to discuss selected ethical issues that dominate modern life. We will take our theoretical knowledge and reasoning skills and apply them to some of the most important and relevant issues of the day. This application will underscore the practical importance of ethics. You will come to appreciate how philosophical ethics can, in fact, have lasting personal value. By offering direction and providing a method for moral decision making, a study of applied ethics can relieve some of the suffering of the mind mentioned earlier—at least where moral uncertainty is concerned.

Before we move on to Part One and Plato to discover what practical wisdom he has to share with us, let us turn to the Moral Preference Indicator (MPI) which follows. By completing the MPI you will begin to identify some of your underlying beliefs and assumptions in regard to morality. After studying the philosophers, you may wish to complete the MPI again to determine if there has been a shift in your moral perspective or if your moral position has been strengthened.

THE MORAL PREFERENCE INDICATOR (MPI)

Aim

The purpose of the MPI is to help you identify your moral preferences in regard to the six classical and contemporary moral perspectives to be discussed in this book. Discovering your preferences and learning about other possibilities will help you to understand better the nature of moral disagreement and some of the reasons why people do not always see eye to eye on moral matters.

Once you have covered the six ethical perspectives addressed in Part One of *Moral Philosophy for Modern Life*, Second Edition, you should complete the MPI again to discover whether there has been a shift in your moral position. You may find that you have changed your moral point of view after some serious study and reflection.

For each number below, circle the option which best completes the sentence in your estimation. In other words, circle the letter next to the statement you agree with most. If you like all six statements, pick the one for which you have even the slightest preference. Pick only one. If you dislike all six statements, pick the statement you dislike least.

When it comes to morality, I believe

1. a. the ends justify the means

    b. the ends do not justify the means

    c. the end of morality is finding happiness through living the ethically good life

    d. rational self-interest is the best basis of morality

    e. the deepest moral insights must be expressed indirectly through art and metaphor etc., not by rational deductive logic

    f. emotional considerations should serve as the basis of morality

2. In my estimation,

    a.   virtue is its own reward

    b.   the right thing to do is to promote good consequences

    c.   the right thing to do is to do your duty

    d.   principles can sometimes get in the way of maintaining healthy relationships with people

    e.   we live in a godless universe, which means there is no objective basis for morality

    f.   morally requiring people to be altruistic transforms them into sacrificial animals

3. As I see it,

    a.   some actions are right or wrong in themselves

    b.   the rightness or wrongness of an action depends on its results

    c.   correct actions promote inner harmony

    d.   altruism encourages people to become parasites on others' goodwill

    e.   general systems and theories of morality are nonsense

    f.   moral decisions should be made on the basis of connection and relationship

4. On the subject of morality, my position is that

    a.   wrong-doing is essentially a product of ignorance

    b.   wrong-doing is essentially a violation of duty

    c.   wrong-doing is a failure to promote the common good

    d.   a collectivism which puts the group before the individual is dangerous

    e.   moral decisions are purely personal and subjective

    f.   care is more important than justice

5. Speaking from an ethical perspective, I would have to say that

    a.   we are morally obligated to fulfill our potentialities as persons

    b.   morality is a way of achieving human happiness

    c.   morality is about following rational principles

    d.   personal interests should override objective principles

    e.   life is art, morality the picture we paint

    f.   that which promotes human survival is good

6. According to my view of the world

    a.   if an action is morally unacceptable, then it is unacceptable for everyone

    b.   whether or not an action is morally acceptable depends on circumstances and people's wants

    c.   an action is morally acceptable if it promotes the development of our higher faculties

    d.   nothing has value in itself except life

    e.   taking responsibility for one's free choices should serve as the basis of morality

    f.   morality should reinforce ongoing relationships

7. The fundamental moral question is:

    a.   what is the good at which human behaviour aims?

    b.   how can we reduce suffering and promote human welfare?

    c.   what are my obligations?

    d.   for whom should I care?

    e.   what life should I create?

    f.   what is in my rational self-interest?

8. The basis of morality is:

    a.   character

    b.   utility (i.e., benefit, pleasure)

    c.   duty

    d.   life/survival

    e.   free and responsible action

    f.   persons in relation

9. The ultimate end of morality is:

    a.   the greatest happiness for the greatest number

    b.   justice

    c.   developing an appropriate lifestyle based on wisdom and moderation

    d.   harmony and social cooperation

    e.   creative authenticity/genuine self-expression

    f.   self-pride and productivity

10. Acting morally involves

    a.   doing what nature requires

    b.   the principle of respect for persons

    c.   a preliminary calculation of any action's pros and cons

    d.   treating others as equal partners or "traders"

    e.   accepting responsibility for humanity

    f.   recognizing our interdependence

11. Which option below captures best the central issues of morality?

    a.   pain and pleasure

    b.   freedom and responsibility

   c.   lifestyle and states of character

   d.   caring and being cared-for

   e.   authenticity and free choice

   f.   living for one's own happiness

12. Morality is

   a.   absolute

   b.   dependent upon people and circumstances

   c.   determined by our rational natures

   d.   an emotionally-based concept

   e.   a creation of the individual

   f.   something weak persons sometimes use against the strong

13. The best thing to do is

   a.   develop your potential as a human being

   b.   promote happiness

   c.   honour your obligations

   d.   look after others

   e.   find meaning and purpose in your life

   f.   live as fully conscious and aware human beings

14. Moral principles are

   a.   universal and unconditional

   b.   specific and conditional

   c.   self-referring, but applicable to others too

   d.   self-chosen and not prescriptive for everybody

   e.   sometimes an impediment to maintaining relationships

   f.   rational and serve to benefit the individual

15. A proper system of morality

   a   helps people to achieve their goals

   b   maintains fairness, equality, and freedom

   c   helps people to develop proper habits of conduct

   d   doesn't require people to act unnaturally

   e   is not a system at all, but unique to the individual

   f   does not romanticize rationality

Scoring Instructions

Below are six columns labelled with the names of the theories to be covered in Part One of *Moral Philosophy for Modern Life*. Down the left-hand side you will find numbers for the 15 statements you completed, each with options A through F. For each statement number, circle the letter which you selected. When you are finished, add the total number circled at the bottom of each column. The column with the highest total reflects your dominant moral preferences at this time. You can then plot your scores on the "Circular Scoring Graph for the Moral Preference Indicator." Shade it in as appropriate, given your results. The shaded graph will provide a circular profile of your moral preferences. Which perspective do you agree with least? Which perspective do you agree with most?

Scoring Sheet

Answers

Utilitarian	Deontologist	Virtue Moralist	Existentialist	Egoist	Care-Based Moralist
1. a	b	c	e	d	(f)
2. (b)	c	a	f	e	d
3. b	(a)	c	e	d	f
4. (c)	b	a	e	d	f
5. b	c	a	(e)	f	d
6. (b)	a	c	e	d	f
7. (b)	c	a	e	f	d
8. b	c	(a)	e	d	f
9. a	b	c	e	(f)	d
10. c	b	a	e	d	f
11. a	(b)	c	e	f	d
12. b	(a)	c	e	f	d
13. b	c	(a)	e	f	(d)
14. b	a	(c)	d	f	e
15. a	b	(c)	e	d	f

Totals 4___   3___   4___   1___   2___   2___

Plot your scores on "The Moral Preference Indicator." Shade in as required.

The Moral Preference Indicator

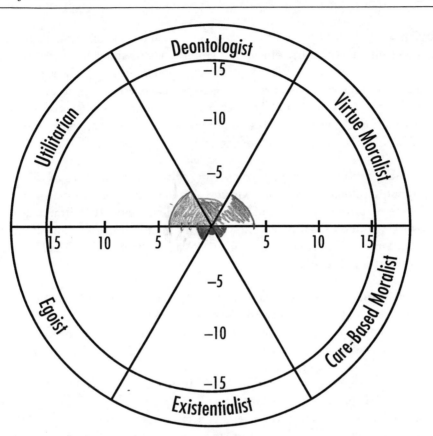

Explanation of Results

The statements contained in the MPI reflect six classical and contemporary ethical positions that have been identified in the history of moral philosophy. Any single statement in the indicator makes an assertion, claim or assumption consistent with a particular moral point of view: utilitarian, care-based, egoistic, existential, deontological or virtue-based. By graphing your results and reading the descriptions of the moral viewpoints below, you can now begin to identify your moral preferences in regard to ethical decision making.

Utilitarian: As a utilitarian, you do not believe that actions like abortion are right or wrong in themselves. For you, circumstances must be taken into account. In addition, the costs and benefits of alternative courses of action must be weighed before deciding what is the morally correct thing to do. At bottom, morality is about maximizing happiness and relieving human misery and pain; thus, an action is good or bad depending on the consequences for human welfare.

Deontologist: As a deontologist or duty-based ethicist, you believe that rational principles can be used to determine the morality of actions. Morality is not about making sure people are happy; it is about doing your duty. Rightness rules over goodness. Doing the right thing for the right reason is more important than maximizing pleasure, benefit or utility. Actions are based on prescriptive rules. If a rule is morally acceptable, then it applies to everyone consistently, fairly and unconditionally. People's rights cannot be bargained away or compromised through some kind of calculation of beneficial consequences.

Virtue Moralist: As a virtue moralist, you see morality largely in terms of self-realization. Morality is about developing appropriate virtues, attitudes, lifestyles and states of mind. The morally good life requires us to fulfill our function as human beings, to harmonize our "souls" or internal workings, and to seek moral knowledge through rational contemplation. Morality raises eternal questions like, "How should I live?" "What is the good life?" and "What kind of person should I strive to become?"

(Atheistic) Existentialist: As an existentialist who does not believe in God, there are for you no objective moral standards by which to govern one's behaviour. Moral decisions must be taken in a purely personal and subjective fashion, without any objective assurances. Though you accept nobody else's systems or rules, you still adhere to humanistic values of individuality, freedom, authenticity and responsibility.

Egoist: As an ethical egoist, you reject any sort of mysticism or blind faith in God. You also oppose emotionalism and/or subjective preference serving as the basis of any justified morality. What you do value is rational self-interest or "rational selfishness." You believe that altruistic moralities that require self-sacrifice and altruistic acts are destructive in the end. Every life is an end in itself. No individual should be required, therefore, to sacrifice his or her life for the benefit of another. In your view, altruism and sacrifice make victims and parasites of us all.

Care-Based Moralist: Rather than give priority to reason in matters of morality, you place a great deal of attention on the human affective response of caring. For you, rational, principle-based morality often destroys relationships; it does not strengthen them—something a justifiable morality should do. In your view, rational detachment and objectivity are not as desirable as rational moralists would have us believe. You see matters of "persons in relation" as more important than impersonal justice.

I

Understanding Moral Theories

Character/Virtue Ethics

In our initial coverage of moral theories, we will be turning to what can be called the virtue or character ethics of Plato and Aristotle. Both philosophers offer immeasurable practical wisdom helping us to develop as moral persons. Plato explains how people's lives can be poisoned by such things as greed and vanity and how, as a result, people can develop corrupt characters. According to Plato, a life based on insatiable desires or on self-glorifying pursuits can never be truly satisfying for such a life creates a psychological imbalance that leaves the human soul disquieted and disturbed.

Aristotle reminds us of the differences between types of goals. Some, he says, are instrumental—a means to further ends. Others are intrinsically valuable—they are ends in themselves. "Happiness" is deemed to be the ultimate end of life, something not only intrinsically valuable but also sufficient unto itself. With these distinctions in mind, Aristotle points out how in life we often confuse the various types of ends and how, as a result, we choose to live misguided lifestyles not befitting rational beings.

In what follows, you will be given ample opportunity to reflect on the ideas of Plato and Aristotle, to apply them to your own understanding of people's behaviour, and to engage in a self-evaluation of your own personal ethics and lifestyle as they have developed to date. In the end, you should gain considerable moral insight into yourself and others. A solid foundation will be constructed for a re-evaluation of your personal values.

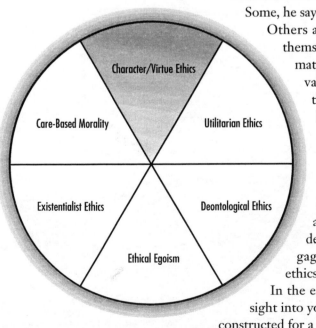

1

Plato: Corrupt Characters and Philosopher Kings

Overview

Learning Outcomes

After successfully completing this chapter, you will be able to

- put Plato into historical perspective;
- state two fundamental moral questions posed by Plato;
- explain Plato's doctrine of teleology;
- describe the soul and its internal workings;
- form an initial hypothesis about your Platonic character type;
- outline the psychological make-up of the Philosopher King/Ruler;
- describe the features and flaws of Plato's corrupt character types.

PHILOSOPHICAL FOCUS QUESTIONS

1. What is meant by saying that Plato offers us a "functional explanation of morality"?
2. What role does the soul play in Plato's functional explanation?
3. What happens when the soul is not functioning properly?
4. What is the ideal character like, according to Plato?
5. What are corrupt characters like? How are their motivations different? Is there anything to which they all fall prey?

BIOGRAPHICAL BRIEF*

Plato (427–347 B.C.E.)

Plato lived from 427 to 347 B.C.E. He was born into a wealthy family that was both aristocratic and politically influential. His importance to intellectual history was underscored by Alfred North Whitehead, who once stated that all of Western philosophy is but a series of footnotes on the work of Plato.

When Plato was 40, he founded the Academy, an independent institution of learning which existed for almost 900 years until the Roman Emperor Justinian closed it in 529 C.E. The Academy was a quiet retreat where teachers and students could meet to pursue knowledge. Students throughout Greece enrolled to partake in the adventure of learning and to experience personal growth toward wisdom. The Academy can be regarded as the precursor of today's modern university.

Plato himself studied under Socrates, once described by the Oracle at Delphi as the wisest man in Athens. Fifteen years after the tragic trial and death of Socrates, Plato began to write "dialogues" in which Socrates was the principal speaker. The dialogues explored moral, political, logical, religious and cosmological topics. Though Socrates never actually recorded his ideas, we derive from the dialogues a profile of Socrates' personality and a statement of his doctrines which likely bear a very close resemblance to his actual philosophy and the historical figure himself. When reading Plato it is sometimes difficult, therefore, to determine what is attributable to Plato and what comes from Socrates. Some argue that the early works of Plato are more reflective of Socratic thinking, while the later works begin to reflect Plato's own philosophical investigations. Plato's most famous work is *The Republic*. Other works by Plato include *The Apology, Crito, Phaedo* and *Symposium*.

*From Falikowski, Moral Philosophy: Theories, Skills and Applications, p.6.

PLATO'S TELEOLOGY

As we enter the world of moral philosophy, let us take what guidance we can from the immortal wisdom of Plato. In his writings, Plato addressed perennial questions like "What constitutes the good life?" and "What sort of individual should I strive to become?" To answer such questions, Plato paid particular attention to the soul. He believed that, like the body, the soul could enjoy health or could suffer from dysfunction. If the soul was to become and to remain healthy, then, for Plato, there would have to be established a certain harmonious balance of psychic elements within the self. Physical, emotional, and intellectual components of the personality must be coordinated to work smoothly. A properly functioning psyche constitutes a healthy, well-ordered soul and an imbalanced psyche constitutes a disordered one. The insight that we gain from this thinking is that if one wishes to live a life of virtue, then certain inner adjustments may be required. Morality is, in large part, an "inside job." To understand precisely what is meant by this suggestion, it is necessary to consider Plato's notion of **teleology** and how it fits into his concept of the **soul**.

> *You are not at peace because you are not fulfilling your function.*
> A COURSE IN MIRACLES

To say that Plato adheres to the doctrine of teleology means that everything in the universe has a proper function to perform within a harmonious hierarchy of purposes. The development of anything thus follows from the fulfillment of the purpose for which it was designed. For us to evaluate something as good or bad, we must examine and appraise it in light of its proper function. Does it perform well what it was designed to do? Take a pen, for example. A pen performs well if it writes smoothly, without blotting. This is what a pen is designed to do. Given the function of a pen, we should not expect it to perform well as an eating utensil or a weapon of self-defence. It would be inappropriate to describe a pen as bad simply because eating with it is too difficult or defending oneself with it is not very effective. Our evaluation of a pen's good or bad performance depends on its designated purpose.

As humans, we too have a function. In view of Plato's teleological explanation of morality, we live the morally good life insofar as we perform our distinctively human function well. Being less efficient than a robot on a factory assembly line, for instance, does not make us bad or morally deficient. We are not designed by nature to be mindless machines. What we are designed to do and how we are supposed to function, according to Plato, can be best understood by turning to his explanation of the structure and workings of the human soul.

PLATO'S VISION OF THE SOUL

Plato conceptualizes human nature in terms of a three-part division of the soul. When reading about the soul, try not to invest it with any religious significance. Understand it as a metaphor to explain the main motives or impulses to action. For Plato, the soul is the principle of life and movement. Since the bodily self is inanimate, it must be moved by something and, for Plato, that something is the soul. While Plato's discussion of the soul is not intended as a scientific analysis of the mind, seeing the soul metaphorically as something akin to the psyche, self or personality structure is helpful for analytical purposes.

The soul, as conceptualized by Plato, is made up of **appetite, spirit**, and **reason**. Each part of the soul aims at different things. Take appetite first. Appetite, or **desire** as it is sometimes called, seeks to satisfy our biological instinctive urges. It looks after the physical side of our lives. There is an element in all of us that functions to achieve physical pleasure, release from pain and satisfaction of material wants. We all wish to eat, drink, sleep, act upon our sexual urges, minimize pain, experience pleasure, acquire a certain number of possessions and live comfortably. When we diet, date, shop and work out, for example, we are being driven by appetite—the physical side of our selves.

Spirit is the second structural element of the human soul. It is the drive toward action. Sometimes referred to as **passion**, it includes our self-assertive tendencies. It targets glory, honour, reputation and the establishment of a good name. Spirit also provides the impetus or force behind all ambitious pursuits, competitive struggles, moral indignation and outrage, human enterprise and pugnacity. As the emotional element of the psyche, spirit manifests itself in our need to love and be loved. It is present when we wish to make an impression, to be accepted and admired by others or when we work hard to be liked.

Reason is the third element of the soul. It is the part we might refer to as the intellect. Reason can be described as the faculty that calculates, measures, and decides. It seeks knowledge and understanding. It affords us insight and allows us to anticipate the future with foresight. By means of reason we are able to think and to make up our minds before we act. We can weigh options, compare alternatives, suppress dangerous urges and make reasonable choices. Whenever you are curious, trying to make sense of things or whenever you display an inquiring mind in your search for meaning, reason is that which moves you.

MORAL BALANCE AND PLATO'S FUNCTIONAL EXPLANATION OF MORALITY

Having outlined the parts of the soul, let us go back to Plato's **functional explanation of morality**. Remember that, for Plato, anything is good to the extent that it performs its function well. So the question now becomes: How is the human soul supposed to work?

For the flesh lusteth against the Spirit, and Spirit against the flesh: and these are contrary the one to the other: so that ye cannot do the things that ye would.

ST PAUL'S LETTER TO THE
GALATIANS, 5:17

In answer to this, Plato suggests that the soul that is functioning properly is doing so in a kind of harmonious **moral balance**. When the faculty of reason governs both appetite and spirit, that is, our physical desires, as well as our passions and emotions, then an orderly and well-balanced moral character results. In other words, people who are living the morally good life, or are living life as it ideally ought to be lived, maintain a rational, biological and emotional equilibrium with reason in control.

Control of inner harmony by reason is not easy to achieve. We all experience turmoil and psychological conflict. It's as if there are warring factions within the mind that cause tension and upheaval. This internal conflict is not abnormal or psychopathological—it is part of the human condition. Inner struggle is part of life.

reason must keep appetite and control functioning as one, or else things will get out of hand.

To help us better appreciate this struggle, Plato describes it metaphorically using the example of a charioteer with two horses in rein. The charioteer symbolizes the faculty of reason; the horses represent appetite and spirit. One horse (appetite) "needs no touch of the whip, but is guided by word and admonition only." The other horse (spirit) is unruly, "the mate of insolence and pride... hardly yielding to whip and spur." While the charioteer (reason) has a clear vision of the destination and the good horse is on track, the bad horse "plunges and runs away, giving all manner of trouble to his companion and charioteer." [1]

In this scenario, we have two horses moving in different directions while a charioteer watches his commands go unheeded. The charioteer's job is to guide and control the horses. What is clear is that the chariot cannot go anywhere unless the charioteer can work together with the two horses and bring them under control. So too with life. Just as both horses are necessary to achieve the charioteer's goal, appetite and spirit are indispensable to reason. Reason identifies the goal; it harnesses the power of appetite and spirit and then proceeds toward its identified destination. Appetite and spirit cannot be disposed of. They are essential to the well-ordered functioning of the human soul.

When reason is in control and the soul is functioning in a harmonious balance, we can say that it is functioning as it should. For Plato, fulfillment of our function as human beings is equivalent to the attainment of **moral virtue**. When we are unhappy or when we have lost our sense of well-being, disharmony of the soul is the problem. If the "wild horses" of passion and desire are running rampant in our lives, then we fall into a disorder manifesting itself in ignorance. We begin to confuse **appearance** with **reality**. We mistake apparent goods for real goods. We pursue things we think will make us happy when, in fact, they will not. We make wrong choices and do wrong things out of false knowledge. As poor misguided souls, we fall prey to moral evil and corruption. Only by allowing reason to regain control of our lives can we enjoy peace of mind, inner harmony, and lasting happiness. Reason can offer us true knowledge of what is ultimately good, and only reason can properly guide us in what we should do with our lives. Only reason can yield knowledge necessary for moral virtue; ignorance can produce only evil and misdirection.

Let us now turn to the writings of Plato to learn more about the balanced soul from the master himself. When finished, complete the Platonic Character Type Index which follows the reading to discover how "balanced" your soul is at this time.

PHILOSOPHERS AT WORK

Think about the last time you let your appetites, feelings or passions "run wild." What were the immediate consequences and longer-term results? Do you agree with Plato that reason should rule our lives? Why or why not?

BACK TO THE SOURCE*

Plato would say that when a character is morally balanced, i.e., when each part is performing its specific function, then we find "justice" in the individual. The term "justice" is used because throughout The Republic *Plato draws parallels between society and the individual. As in a just society, which is well-ordered and not governed by people corrupted by greed (appetite) or vain ambition (spirit), but is directed by wisdom and virtue (reason), so too are just individuals not enslaved by insatiable desires and unbridled passions. Such things are governed and limited in their expression by reason. In* The Republic, *we read the following:*

Virtue and Justice in the Individual and in the State

And so, after much tossing, we have reached land, and are fairly agreed that the same principles which exist in the State exist also in the individual, and that they are three in number.

Exactly.

Must we not then infer that the individual is wise in the same way, and in virtue of the same quality which makes the State wise?

Certainly.

Also that the same quality which constitutes courage in the State constitutes courage in the individual, and that both the State and the individual bear the same relation to all the other virtues?

Assuredly.

And the individual will be acknowledged by us to be just in the same way in which the State is just?

That follows, of course.

We cannot but remember that the justice of the State consisted in each of the three classes doing the work of its own class?

We are not very likely to have forgotten, he said.

We must recollect that the individual in whom the several qualities of his nature do their own work will be just, and will do his own work?

Yes, he said, we must remember that too.

And ought not the rational principle, which is wise, and has the care of the whole soul, to rule, and the passionate or spirited principle to the subject and ally?

Certainly.

And, as we were saying, the united influence of music and gymnastic will bring them into accord, nerving and sustaining the reason with noble words and lessons, and moderating and soothing and civilizing the wildness of passion by harmony and rhythm?

Quite true, he said.

And these two, thus nurtured and educated, and having learned truly to know their own functions, will rule over the concupiscent, which in each of us is the largest part of the soul and by nature most insatiable of gain; over this they will keep guard, lest, waxing great and strong with the fullness of bodily pleasures, as they are termed, the concupiscent soul, no longer confined to her own sphere, should attempt to enslave and rule those who are not her natural-born subjects, and overturn the whole life of man?

Very true, he said.

Both together will they not be the best defenders of the whole soul and the whole body against attacks from without; the one counselling, and the other fighting under his leader, and courageously executing his commands and counsels?

True.

And he is to be deemed courageous whose spirit retains in pleasure and in pain the commands of reason about what he ought or ought not to fear?

Right, he replied.

And him we call wise who has in him that little part which rules, and which proclaims these commands; that part too being supposed to have a knowledge of what is for the interest of each of the three parts and of the whole?

Assuredly.

And would you not say that he is temperate who has these same elements in friendly harmony, in whom the one ruling principle of reason, and the two subject ones of spirit and desire are equally agreed that reason ought to rule, and do not rebel?

Certainly, he said, that is the true account of temperance whether in the State or individual.

And surely, I said, we have explained again and again how and by virtue of what quality a man will be just.

That is very certain.

And is justice dimmer in the individual, and is her form different, or is she the same which we found her to be in the State?

There is no difference in my opinion, he said

Because, if any doubt is still lingering in our minds, a few commonplace instances will satisfy us of the truth of what I am saying.

What sort of instances do you mean?

If the case is put to us, must we not admit that the just State, or the man who is trained in the principles of such a State, will be less likely than the unjust to make away with a deposit of gold or silver? Would any one deny this?

No one, he replied.

Will the just man or citizen ever be guilty of sacrilege or theft, or treachery either to his friends or to his country?

Never.

Neither will he ever break faith where there have been oaths or agreements?

Impossible.

No one will be less likely to commit adultery; or to dishonour his father and mother, or to fail in his religious duties?

No one.

And the reason is that each part of him is doing its own business, whether in ruling or being ruled?

Exactly so.

Are you satisfied then that the quality which makes such men and such states is justice, or do you hope to discover some other?

Not I, indeed.

Then our dream has been realized; and the suspicion which we entertained at the beginning of our work of construction, that some divine power must have conducted us to a primary form of justice, has now been verified?

Yes, certainly.

And the division of labour which required the carpenter and the shoemaker and the rest of the citizens to be doing each his own business, and not another's, was a shadow of justice, and for that reason it was of use?

Clearly.

But in reality justice was such as we were describing, being concerned however, not with the outward man, but with the inward, which is the true self and concernment of man: for the just man does not permit the several elements within him to interfere with one another, or any of them to do the work of others,—he sets in order his own inner life, and is his own master and his own law, and at peace with himself; and when he has bound together the three principles within him, which may be compared to the higher, lower, and middle notes of the scale, and the intermediate intervals—when he has bound all these together, and is no longer many, but has become one entirely temperate and perfectly adjusted nature, then he proceeds to act, if he has to act, whether in a matter of property or in the treatment of the body, or in some affair of politics or private business; always thinking and calling that which preserves and co-operates with this harmonious condition, just and good action, and the knowledge which presides over it, wisdom, and that which at any time impairs this condition, he will call unjust action, and the opinion which presides over it ignorance.

You have said the exact truth, Socrates.

Very good; and if we were to affirm that we had discovered the just man and the just State, and the nature of justice in each of them, we should not be telling a falsehood?

Most certainly not.

May we say so, then?

Let us say so.

And now, I said, injustice has to be considered.

Clearly.

Must not injustice be a strife which arises among the three principles—a meddlesomeness, and interference, and rising up of a part of the soul against the whole, an assertion of unlawful authority, which is made by a rebellious subject against a true of whom he is the natural vassal—what is all this confusion and delusion but injustice, and intemperance and cowardice and ignorance, and every form of vice?

Exactly so.

And if the nature of justice and injustice be known, then the meaning of acting unjustly and being unjust, or again, of acting justly, will also be perfectly clear?

What do you mean? he said.

Why, I said, they are like disease and health; being in the soul just what disease and health are in the body.

How so? he said.

Why, I said, that which is healthy causes health, and that which is unhealthy causes disease.

Yes.

And just actions cause justice, and unjust actions cause injustice?

That is certain.

And the creation of health is the institution of a natural order and government of one by another in the parts of the body; and the creation of disease is the production of a state of things at variance with this natural order?

True.

And is not the creation of justice the institution of a natural order and government of one by another in the parts of the soul, and the creation of injustice the production of a state of things at variance with the natural order?

Exactly so, he said.

Then virtue is the health and beauty and well-being of the soul, and vice the disease and weakness and deformity of the same?

True.

And do not good practices lead to virtue, and evil practices to vice?

Assuredly.

Still our old question of the comparative advantage of justice and injustice has not been answered: Which is the more profitable, to be just and act justly and practice virtue, whether seen or unseen of gods and men, or to be unjust and act unjustly, if only unpunished and unreformed?

In my judgement, Socrates, the question has now become ridiculous. We know that,

when the bodily constitution is gone, life is no longer endurable, though pampered with all kinds of meats and drinks, and having all wealth and all power, and shall we be told that when the very essence of the vital principle is undermined and corrupted, life is still worth having to a man, if only he be allowed to do whatever he likes with the single exception that he is not to acquire justice and virtue, or to escape from injustice and vice; assuming them both to be such as we have described?

Yes, I said, the question is, as you say, ridiculous.

Plato, The Republic, *trans. Benjamin Jowett, New York: P.F. Collier & Son © 1901 The Colonial Press, section (441c–445b).*

→ PLATONIC CHARACTER TYPE INDEX (PCTI)

The PCTI is an informal self-analytical tool that can help you begin identifying which part of your psyche or "soul" is dominant in your life at this time. Knowledge of this fact can help you to understand better the internal workings of your "Platonic character type." Such information can also suggest paths for future character development and healthy personality maintenance. Your results are not intended to be scientifically valid, but rather suggestive. (I am not sure the soul lends itself very well to empirical, scientific investigation!) The accuracy of the results ultimately will be determined by your own rational self-analysis or, should I say, "philosophical psychoanalysis."

→ Instructions

Next to each phrase below, indicate how reflective of you the item, action or activity is. Unless absolutely necessary, try to avoid 3 as your answer. Answering 3 too often will not likely reveal any character preferences.

> 1 = not reflective of me at all
> 2 = hardly reflective of me
> 3 = moderately reflective of me
> 4 = very reflective of me
> 5 = exactly reflective of me

How accurate would it be to say that you

3	1.	seek truth as a priority in your life
1	2.	wish to become famous
4	3.	want to make large sums of money
4	4.	enjoy being carefree
3	5.	experience pleasure through artificial or chemical means
4	6.	trust thinking more than sensory perception
4	7.	are competitive
4	8.	wish strongly to live a materially comfortable lifestyle
2	9.	avoid restrictions and restraints
2	10.	look out for number one
5	11.	pursue knowledge (as opposed to data or information)
3	12.	have difficulty dealing with subordinates (those lower in rank)
2	13.	do not waste time on activities that have little financial payoff
1	14.	treat all wants as equal
1	15.	do what you want regardless of the consequences for other people
2	16.	control your physical urges and biological appetites
4	17.	want to be liked by others
2	18.	value being economical
2	19.	live in the moment and for the moment
1	20.	deceive people to get what you want
4	21.	do what is right, putting aside personal feelings and wants
4	22.	value achievement (fame) over money
4	23.	avoid financial disaster
3	24.	enjoy equally all the pleasures of life
3	25.	fall prey to manias or compulsions
4	26.	like intellectual thought
4	27.	try to look successful to others
3	28.	seize opportunities to better yourself economically
4	29.	take life a day at a time

2   30. tell people whatever is necessary to get what you want

2   31. display temperance (moderation)

1   32. assume an attitude of superiority

4   33. work hard to ensure the basic necessities of life

3   34. do what feels good

2   35. take by force, if necessary

3   36. regulate personal habits

3   37. enjoy exhibitions of courage and strength

1   38. live consistently with the principle: Money first, then morality

3   39. frequently change your mind about what you want

2   40. display addictive behaviour

→ Scoring

Next to each of the question numbers below, fill in your response. Add the total scores for each column and then plot them on your PCTI. See the example for help on how to do this.

PK	Tim	O	D	T
1 – 3	2	3	4	5
6 – 4	7	8	9	10
11 – 5	12	13	14	15
16 – 2	17	18	19	20
21 – 4	22	23	24	25
26 – 4	27	28	29	30
31 – 2	32	33	34	35
36 – 3	37	38	39	40
____	____	____	____	____
	Totals			

PK = Philosopher King/Ruler   ____
Tim = Timarchic Character   ____
O = Oligarchic Character   ____
D = Democratic Character   ____
T = Tyrannical Character   ____

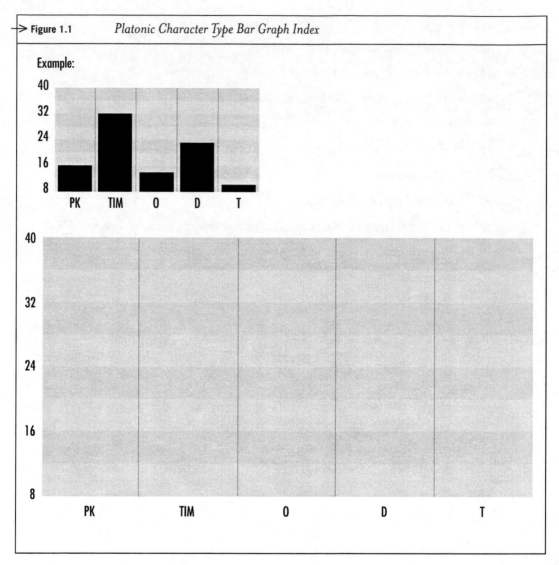

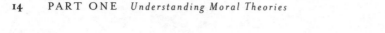

Figure 1.1   *Platonic Character Type Bar Graph Index*

Interpretation

To learn what your results mean, refer to the abbreviated descriptions that follow. More information on each character type is found in the main text (pp. 17 to 21). Note that you probably have a mixture of different character elements making up your personality. It is unlikely that anyone is purely one type. Nonetheless, the character type with the highest score may be most reflective of what you are like as a individual right now. Your responsibility is to decide for yourself. After reading the descriptions of the character types, you may be favourably impressed or you may feel the need to change as a result. The moral decision is yours!

DESCRIPTIONS OF PLATONIC CHARACTER TYPES

Timarchic Character

Driven by spirit, energetic, competitive, self-assertive, can also be insecure, jealous, vain and self-inflating, fearful of falling behind

Oligarchic Character

Driven by appetite, frugal, hardworking, materialistic and often money-hungry, dissatisfied, internally disturbed, dirty and wretched opportunist

Philosopher King/Ruler

Enlightened, internally balanced, morally virtuous, i.e., temperate, courageous, wise, just, ruled by reason, careful to distinguish between appearance and reality

Democratic Character

Versatile, easy-going, treats all passions and desires equally, but is frequently aimless, without principle, torn apart inside

Tyrannical Character

Possessed by master passion, criminal personality, totally undisciplined, least self-sufficient, anxiety-ridden

PLATO'S CHARACTER TYPES

In *The Republic*, differently functioning "souls" are described using the notion of **Plato's character types**. The ideal character is exemplified by the philosopher king or ruler. Corrupt, imperfect types are called the timarchic, oligarchic, democratic and tyrannical characters. You will notice that all of these types have political-sounding labels. The reason for this, according to Plato, is that in each kind of societal structure there is a corresponding individual who is admired within it, so that in an oligarchy, for instance, the values and attributes of the oligarchic character are praised. Likewise in a timarchic society, the qualities you find in the timarchic person would be cherished. Understand, however, that not every individual in a particular society necessarily displays the corresponding character type. Oligarchs can be found in democracies. Virtuous people can be found in tyrannies, and so on. The point is that individuals give rise to societies that, in turn, praise the qualities possessed by those individuals.

> *Character is fate.*
> HERACLITUS

An interesting parallel between individuals and societies can also be seen by looking at the **class system** proposed by Plato for the **just society**—the system that functions in harmonious balance. In the ideal or just society, there would emerge three classes of people corresponding to the three parts of the soul. Each class would serve different, but complementary, roles. First, there would be those whose lives would be driven primarily by the appetites. These would be the **craftsmen, artisans** and **traders**. In modern terms, we might see these people as the workers, consumers and business class. Second, there would be the **auxiliaries** (a subdivision of guardians), motivated in their lives mostly by spirit. They would serve to protect and preserve internal order under the guidance of rulers. Examples of people fitting into this class in today's world would include the police, militia and civil servants. Third, from the auxiliaries, individuals would be selected to become the most highly trained and educated members of an elite guardian class proper, namely the philosopher kings (or rulers).

Membership in any class would not be determined by birth or inheritance; rather, children would be moved from class to class according to merit and capability. Only those who passed the most rigorous tests and who would be best suited to work for the good of the community would become philosopher kings. In the just society, the lower classes would not gain undue influence, as an internal anarchy would result, just as it does in the soul when appetite or spirit over-rule reason. Reason must rule, as must those whose lives are governed by reason, not by greed (appetite) or self-assertion (spirit).

Let us now look at the character of the philosopher king and examine in more detail the corrupt character types located at lower levels of society. Though the notion that an elite class should govern society may not be popular today, Plato argued that

> the human race will not be free of evils until either the stock of those who rightly and truly follow philosophy acquire political authority, or the class who have power in the cities be led by some dispensation of providence to become real philosophers.

In short, rulers must become philosophers or philosophers must become rulers if we are to achieve the ideal society. Just as reason must rule the soul, so too must philosophers rule the social order if the just society is ever to become a reality.

PHILOSOPHERS AT WORK

What do you think about having a class system in society? Is our society presently governed by philosopher kings/rulers? What has been the result? Should the leaders in our society come from an intellectually and morally elite ruling class? Why or why not? If you object to a class system, is your honest objection to rule by an elite based on a hidden fear that you may not qualify to govern? *Comment.* If commitment to justice and truth does not make the philosopher king fit to rule, then what makes anyone a good social leader?

Philosopher Kings/Rulers

According to Plato, the just society is a form of **aristocracy**. In an aristocracy, **philosopher kings** who belong to the **guardian class** become the rulers. (Note: no gender discrimination is intended by the use of the label "kings"—qualified women also would be selected to serve as rulers in Plato's aristocracy.)

Philosopher kings (or rulers) are morally virtuous individuals. They are **temperate**. No physical appetites or material desires enslave them. Virtuous souls regulate their appetites by reason. Philosophers also display the virtue of **courage**, a passion that supports reason in its judgments and decisions to act. Plato says, "He is deemed courageous whose spirit retains in pleasure and in pain the commands of reason about what he ought or ought not to fear...."

> *The seen is the changing, The unseen is the unchanging.*
> PLATO

The morally virtuous person is also **wise**. This individual knows what is best for each part of the soul. A wise person "has in him that little part which rules, and which proclaims these commands [of reason]; that part too being supposed to have a knowledge of what is for the interest of each of the three parts of the whole...." In addition, philosopher rulers are **just**. With respect to character, remember that just means balanced and **functioning harmoniously**. In the just character of the philosopher king, reason, emotion, and physical nature work well together, with reason in charge, of course. It is the faculty of reason that prevents inner rebellion and disorder of the soul. It establishes an internal constitution based on peaceful coexistence.

Besides being truly virtuous, another distinguishing characteristic of philosopher kings is that they have special knowledge. By an elaborate process of education, philosopher kings learn how to distinguish between appearance and reality. They learn how to acquaint themselves intellectually with the eternal and immutable **realm of forms**. The "forms," so-called, can be known only by reason and, according to Plato, are more real than the transitory things that we see, hear, taste, touch and feel. Sensory experience can yield only imperfect approximations of the ideal forms. For example, it is rational acquaintance with the form 'justice' that allows us to describe any act as fair or unfair, just or unjust. Even though we have never seen complete fairness or universal justice in the world, we still know what it is. Reason offers us perfect knowledge in an imperfect world. It shows us what the eyes have not seen.

Those who fall prey to imperfect or **false knowledge** offered by the senses, and those who become morally sidetracked by the physical appetites or emotions, end up living disordered lives of ignorance and unhappiness. Philosopher rulers make no such mistake. They are not lured away from truth and moral goodness by misleading appearances, by the "drone's honey" or the "power monger's prestige and influence." Philosopher kings appreciate how such things can only end in moral bankruptcy and disillusionment. Philosopher kings are enlightened souls who are not entrapped by fantasies and temptations, but are guided on the right path by the light of true moral goodness.

Now, before you bow down in humble worship of your philosophy teacher, understand that "being a philosopher king" today has nothing to do with occupation, but it has everything to do with character and disposition. A philosophy teacher may teach all the right things, but for selfish and vainglorious motives to which he or she will not admit. Jack or Jill Average, on the other hand, may display many, or all, of the philosopher king's virtues without ever teaching the subject itself. Be aware, then, that anybody, even the student sitting beside you in class, could be a "closet philosopher." Maybe it is time for you to come out of the "king's closet" yourself and to continue your character training as one of society's future guardians! Will you accept the call?

Timarchic Character

The dominant part of the soul that drives the **timarchic character** is spirit. People with timarchic characters are distinguished, in large part, by their energy, competitiveness and the urge to dominate. For example, do you know anyone whose life seems to be based on "one-upmanship"? Can any story you tell be "bettered" by your timarchic friend? Have your accomplishments always been unfavourably compared to, or belittled by, your timarchic friend's (allegedly) superior performance? In short, does it seem that being with this person (maybe you) is like being engulfed in a continual struggle, an athletic contest or a battle of wills? If so, then you can appreciate what this character type brings to the table of life.

> There is perhaps nothing worse than reaching the top of the ladder and discovering that you're on the wrong wall.
> JOSEPH CAMPBELL

Timarchic characters are self-assertive individuals. They like to be "out there," making impressions on people or at least trying to do so. Unfortunately, no matter how favourable the impression made or how successful the person is, they still retain a nagging insecurity. Reputations must be maintained, people must continue to be impressed; nobody else must be allowed to dominate, control or look better. Life at the top of the ladder of success is very precarious. Once at the top, there is only one way to go—down—down in the estimation of others and, hence, down in one's own estimation. The pride and ambition characterizing timarchic persons can thus create only a thin veneer of confidence. Below the surface, these people fear that they will fall behind, suffer defeat, be humiliated or embarrassed or have the approval of others withdrawn at any time. These fears will manifest themselves in jealousy, as timarchic persons typically begrudge the successes of others.

A life based on single-minded ambition—for instance, investing years of training in the hopes of winning an Olympic gold medal in the shot-put event—may leave a person wasted and suffering financial ruin. Finishing twelfth, out of the medals and out of the record books, with no fame, no endorsements, and possibly no perceived future could also leave the person embittered and insecure. Failed efforts at vainglorious pursuits are not always pretty to witness. With or without success, the timarchic character is destined to a life of underlying fears, jealousies and insecurities. Ignorant of the fact that vanity and self-inflation cannot ultimately lead to a tranquil and balanced soul, timarchic characters will never achieve a true and lasting happiness. At best, they will achieve only a cheap and transitory semblance of it.

Oligarchic Character

In a society where wealth dominates and the wealthy are in control, the qualities of the **oligarchic character** are revered. In the oligarch, we discover a character transformation from the ambitious, competitive type of person to the money-loving businessperson. It's probably accurate to suggest that our own society is a form of oligarchy. After all, is it not true many people in North American society judge the worth of an individual by what that person owns? "How much are they worth?" we ask. Is it not

> *...and the higher the prestige of wealth and the wealthy, the lower that of goodness and good men will be.*
> PLATO

a widespread belief that you are a "somebody" if you own many expensive things—that having a lot of cash makes you a V.I.P. (a very important person)? When people say they want to "better" themselves, is it not the case that they usually mean acquire more wealth and material possessions?

Of course, not everybody in contemporary society displays an oligarchic character. The point is simply that those who do are the ones who are recognized and rewarded. They are the ones on the cover of *Fortune* magazine or featured in the *Financial Post* or *Wall Street Journal*. Wherever they are found, the oligarchs' main objective in life is to make money. In the oligarchic character, appetite rules and dominates the rest of the soul with a desire for riches. When reason is called upon, it is only in the service of making more money. Spirit, by contrast, is "forbidden to admire or value anything but wealth and the wealthy, or to compete for anything but the acquisition of wealth and whatever leads to it."

The oligarch is frugal, economical, and hardworking. As little as possible is wasted on nonessentials. This person tries hard to satisfy only the most necessary wants. Unnecessary wants and desires, which do not function to accumulate greater wealth, are regarded as pointless and, therefore, repressed.

The character imperfections of the oligarch are, perhaps, most plainly evident in the huckster, peddler or hawker on late-night television infomercials. Plato says the oligarch possesses a dirty and wretched character, "always on the make and putting something by" others. The person who can "sell snow to an Eskimo," get you to buy more than what you wanted, or persuade you to purchase what you really do not need, is the one who becomes rich, famous and admired.

In the oligarch, there is a dramatic movement from ambition to avarice. For the oligarch, there is no advantage to having a good name and a moral reputation if there are no financial rewards. Because money and profit are the basic driving forces behind the oligarchic character, the person will be dishonest at any opportunity. The only deterrent is fear of punishment; there is certainly no moral conviction or taming of desire by reason.

Plato described oligarchs as having dual personalities. They usually manage to maintain a certain degree of respectability as, on the whole, better desires master the worse. It is as if good and bad desires engage in a battle for dominance within the psyche. The unfortunate result is that oligarchic individuals are never really at peace within themselves. When the worse desires are subdued, the oligarch manages "a certain degree of respectability, but comes nowhere near the real goodness of an integrated and balanced character."

Finally, though some degree of social respectability can be achieved by oligarchs, they will usually make few contributions to public life, where money and profit may have to be sacrificed. For example, an oligarch might ask, "Why be a politician when there is so little financial reward?" Did you know that the lowest-paid hockey player in the National Hockey League has a greater "market value" and earns more money than the prime minister of Canada, the leader of thirty million people? Oligarchs would probably say, "Rightly so." When it comes to the worth of a man or woman, oligarchs would most likely let the market decide. Given the thinking of oligarchs, their achievements and ambitions in public life are not likely to amount to much, but, then again, they are also not likely to sustain large financial losses in pursuing vain ambitions of power or political glory.

Democratic Character

In contrast to the oligarchic character who distinguishes between necessary and unnecessary desires, the **democratic character** does not. All desires and appetites are treated equally.

> *The Good Life is getting everything you want, provided that everything you want is good.*
> PROVERB

Democrats are charming but aimless individuals, spending as much money, time, and effort on unnecessary desires as on necessary ones. For the democratic personality, no pleasure is underprivileged; each gets its fair share of encouragement. This type of character lives from day to day, indulging in any momentary pleasure that presents itself. The pleasures are varied. Plato says,

> One day it's wine, women and song, the next water to drink and a strict diet; one day it's hard physical training, the next indolence and careless ease, and then a period of philosophic study. Often he takes to politics and keeps jumping to his feet and saying or doing whatever comes into his head. Sometimes all his ambitions and efforts are military, sometimes they are all directed to success in business. There's no order or restraint in his life, and he reckons his way of living is pleasant, free and happy, and sticks to it through thick and thin. [2]

People displaying a democratic character are versatile because they lack principles. The problem is that if people do not live a rational, principled life, then diverse and incompatible pleasures, appetites, and passions can pull them in different directions at the same time. Their personalities are, consequently, not integrated and functioning harmoniously. Individuals with a democratic character are torn apart inside. As Plato says, there is no order or restraint. Rather, there is disorder and lack of control. Persons obsessively pursuing different and sometimes conflicting pleasures cannot avoid becoming disorganized and fragmented. Their lives exhibit a definite lack of rational coherence and direction. Democrats are like children in a candy store. They are excited but conflicted, because they want everything in the store at the same time—and this is impossible.

Plato speculates about how the democratic character is formed. He believes that children raised in a strict oligarchic household, where unnecessary pleasures have been denied, eventually are lured by those people outside the family who do enjoy them. A basic diet, for instance, becomes insufficient or unsatisfactory. A desire grows for luxurious and exotic food. Simple tastes are replaced by sophisticated and extravagant ones. Unnecessary desires, immediate pleasures and extravagant tastes eventually transform the oligarchic person into a democratic character. Plato writes,

When a young man, brought up in the narrow economical way we have described, gets a taste of the drones' honey and gets into brutal and dangerous company, where he can be provided with every variety and refinement of pleasure,... the result [is] that his internal oligarchy starts turning into a democracy.[3]

Tyrannical Character

According to Plato, the **tyrannical character** is the worst, being the most unhappy and undesirable. The tyrant personifies the criminal personality. People with a tyrannical character suffer from a kind of mania. As maniacs, they possess one **master passion** that controls all other idle desires. This master passion becomes so powerful that it runs wild, causing madness in the individual. The object of this passion may be sex, alcohol or other drugs. In the tyrannical personality's pursuit of pure pleasure, no shame or guilt is experienced. All discipline is swept away and usurped by madness. Tyrannical people are thus the least self-sufficient of all individuals. Their satisfaction depends entirely on external things and objects of maniacal desire. The tyrant is full of anxiety and constantly trying to fulfill his or her unrelenting appetite for more. Tyrants will do anything and everything to satisfy themselves, even if they must perform terrible deeds and become hated in the process. Their lives are lawless and disgusting. Though all of us have aggressive, bestial, and erotic urges—evidenced especially in dreams—most of us are able to control them; the tyrant, however, cannot.

> *An excessive desire for liberty at the expense of everything else is what undermines democracy and leads to the demand for tyranny.*
>
> PLATO

If and when tyrants have spent all of their money indulging their master passion, they will start borrowing to satisfy it. When they are no longer able to borrow, they may proceed to rob, commit fraud or engage in acts of violence. Tyrannical characters become thieves, pickpockets, kidnappers, church robbers and murderers to satisfy their manias. From this fact alone, it should be clear why tyrants are the most morally corrupt of all character types.

PHILOSOPHERS AT WORK

Pick out a well-known celebrity or a notorious individual from history, if you prefer. The person could be an actor, athlete, villain, businessperson, literary figure or fictional character from any book, movie or television show. Examine and appraise that person's actions, intentions, and motivations. What Platonic character type does that individual display? Give support for your answer.

MINDWORK MEDITATION

Now that you know more about philosopher kings and corrupt character types, re-examine your results and the Platonic Character Type Index. Do you think the results are accurate for you? What changes, if any, will you have to make to more closely approximate the philosopher king? What appetites and/or passions will you have to better control to achieve psychological equilibrium? If you came out as a philosopher king, do you really think you rank right up their with Socrates, Jesus and Gandhi? On this scale, they would come out as philosopher kings, no doubt.

KEY TERMS

teleology

soul

reason

spirit

appetite

desire

passion

functional explanation of morality

moral balance

moral virtue

appearance

reality

Plato's character types

class system

just society

craftsmen

artisans

traders

auxiliaries

aristocracy

philosopher kings

guardian class

temperate

courage

wise

just

functioning harmoniously

realm of forms

false knowledge

timarchic character

oligarchic character

democratic character

tyrannical character

master passion

PROGRESS CHECK 1.1

Instructions: Fill in the blanks with the appropriate responses listed below.

√The Republic

√soul

√ reason

oligarchic

tyrannical

√ self-assertion

guardian

Academy

forms
teleology
timarchic
auxiliaries

ignorance
harmonious balance
physical

1. In Athens, Plato founded the *Academy,* a place of higher learning where questions of philosophy were discussed.

2. Plato's most famous writing is a book called *The Republic.*

3. If the human soul is to function properly, it must maintain a(n) *harmonious balance* of psychic elements.

4. According to Plato's doctrine of *teleogy,* everything in nature has a proper function to perform.

5. Plato conceptualizes human nature as of a three-part division of the *soul.*

6. The appetite element of human nature looks after our *physic* wants, needs, and desires.

7. Spirit or passion is that element of human nature aimed at *self-assertion,* reputation, and honour.

8. *Reason* is that which allows us to calculate, measure, and predict events.

9. For Plato, the cause of moral wrong-doing and evil is *ignorance.*

10. Philosopher kings/rulers belong to the *guardian* class of Plato's just society.

11. The most wretched of all character types is the *tyrannical* character.

12. The money-hungry person is summed up in Plato's description of the *timarchic* character.

13. Competitive and self-willed individuals possess a(n) *oligarchic* character.

14. In the class-based utopian society proposed by Plato, *auxiliaries* would serve to protect and maintain order under the directorship of the philosopher kings.

15. Philosopher kings/rulers have special knowledge. They have a rational acquaintance with the realm of *forms.*

SUMMARY OF MAJOR POINTS

1. What are the two basic moral questions raised by Plato?

    What constitutes the good life?
    What sort of individual should one strive to become?

2. What is meant by teleology?

    A doctrine stating that the development of anything follows from the purpose for which it was designed.
    According to this notion, something is good to the extent that it performs its function well.

3. What is Plato's vision of the soul?

    Three parts: appetite, spirit and reason.
    Each part aims at different things—
    e.g., appetite: physical wants and needs; spirit: drive toward action and self-assertion;
    reason: the ruling faculty of the soul, it aims at knowledge, wisdom and understanding.

4. What is the difference between a healthy and an unhealthy soul?

    A healthy soul is balanced with reason in control.
    An unhealthy soul is imbalanced and disordered with appetite or spirit overcoming the rule of reason.

5. What is ignorance? What are the results of ignorance?

    It is expressed by an imbalanced soul operating in disharmony.
    It leads to the pursuit of apparent goods, not real ones.
    It gives rise to evil and moral corruption.
    It is a confusion between appearance and reality.

6. What is Plato's just society like?

    It is based on a class system.
    Its classes include: workers, auxiliaries, and guardians.
    The just society functions harmoniously with guardians in charge.
    Its workers are driven by appetites.
    Its auxiliaries are motivated by spirit.
    Its guardian class is ruled by reason.

7. What are Plato's character types? What are they like?

    Philosopher king/ruler: governed by reason; member of the guardian class; harmonious personality; virtuous, i.e., temperate, courageous, wise and just; possesses knowledge of the realm of forms.
    Timarchic character: spirit-dominated; competitive; insecure; self-willed.
    Oligarchic character: driven by appetite; disillusioned by goals of timarchic character; replaces ambition with avarice; replaces pride with greed; squalid character; lacks moral convictions and inner peace.
    Democratic character: treats all appetites and desires equally; charming but aimless; versatile but lacking in principles; extravagant tastes; lacks order and restraint.
    Tyrannical character: worst type; most unhappy; possessed by a master passion or mania; has no guilt or shame; least self-sufficient of all types; no control over aggressive, bestial urges; quite capable of fraud, deceit and all types of illegal behaviour.

SOURCE REFERENCES AND RELATED READINGS

Albert, Ethel, Theodore Denise, and Sheldon P. Peterfreund. *Great Traditions in Ethics*, 5th edition. Belmont, C.A.: Wadsworth, 1984.

Bloom, Allan. *The Republic of Plato*, 2nd edition. New York: Basic Books, 1968.

Falikowski, Anthony. *Moral Philosophy: Theories, Skills, and Applications*. Englewood Cliffs, N.J.: Prentice Hall, 1990.

Plato. *The Republic*, 2nd edition. Translated by Desmond Lee. Middlesex, England: Penguin Books, 1976.

Stumpf, Samuel Enoch. *Socrates to Sartre: A History of Philosophy*, 5th edition. Toronto: McGraw-Hill Inc., 1993.

Wolff, Robert Paul. *About Philosophy*, 6th edition. Upper Saddle River, N.J.: Prentice Hall, 1996.

ENDNOTES

1. Samuel Stumpf, *Philosophy: History & Problems, 3/e*. New York: McGraw-Hill, 1983, p.61.
2. Plato, *The Republic*, trans. Benjamin Jowett. New York: P.F. Collier & Son, 1901, section (441c–445b).
3. Plato, *The Republic*, 2/e (revised), trans. Desmond Lee. Harmondsworth: Penguin Classics, 1976, p.381.

2

Aristotle: Happiness and the Good Life

Overview

Learning Outcomes

After successfully completing this chapter, you will be able to

- provide historical background information on Aristotle;
- explain Aristotle's teleology using the concept of "entelechy";
- describe the various ends of humanity;
- explain why happiness or *eudaimonia* is the ultimate end;
- appreciate better how the good life is tied to successful living;
- identify our uniquely human function as living organisms;
- compare and contrast alternative lifestyles;
- give Aristotle's reasoning behind the claim that the contemplative lifestyle is the highest form of human functioning;
- describe the role of virtue in our pursuit of happiness;
- define and understand Aristotle's Doctrine of the Mean;
- outline the conditions for truly virtuous behaviour.

PHILOSOPHICAL FOCUS QUESTIONS

1. In what sense is Aristotle's philosophy a self-realization ethic?
2. How does Aristotle's teleology differ from that of Plato?
3. What kinds of ends in life do people pursue?
4. What is the ultimate good in human life?
5. How is it that people "miss the mark" in their lives and fail to find happiness?
6. What lifestyle is most befitting of human beings? Why?
7. In what sense does the virtuous lifestyle lead to a secondary form of happiness?
8. What is meant by Aristotle's Doctrine of the Mean?

LIBRARY OF CONGRESS

Aristotle (384–322 B.C.E.)

Biographical Brief*

Aristotle was born in Stagira in 384 B.C.E. He was the son of a physician who lived and worked at the royal court of Amyntas II, king of Macedonia. At the age of 17 Aristotle went to Athens to enrol at the Academy. For 20 years he worked and studied under Plato, for whom he had respect as a philosopher and good feelings as a friend. Upon the death of Plato, Aristotle left Athens and spent a number of years in Asia Minor, where he married Pythias, the niece of a local king. Aristotle eventually returned to Macedonia, in order to become tutor to the heir of the throne, namely Alexander, who later became known as Alexander the Great. After an eight-year stay in Macedonia, he left again for Athens in 335–334 B.C.E. In Athens, Aristotle established a new school called the Lyceum. It was patterned after Plato's Academy insofar as community life, friendliness, intent on learning and dialogue were emphasized. Many of Aristotle's dialogues with students were conducted while strolling down a garden path (*peripatos*). In view of this, followers of Aristotle have come to be know as "peripatetics." In 323 B.C.E. Aristotle felt compelled to leave Athens again. Alexander the Great died suddenly while returning from one of his Asian conquests. The Athenians, who were under the yoke of Alexander, regarded his death as an opportunity to rid themselves of Macedonian control. Aware of his Macedonian ties, and fearing the prospect of having to stand trial for impiety like Socrates, Aristotle fled Athens. He died in exile one year later in 322 B.C.E.; his wife died somewhat earlier. Aristotle's son,

Nichomachus, after whom the *Nichomachean Ethics* is named, was born as a product of a domestic union with Herpyllis.

Aristotle wrote on subjects as varied as logic, ethics, aesthetics, metaphysics, biology, physics, psychology and politics. He had a profound influence on medieval Hebrew, Arabic and Christian philosophers, most notably Saint Thomas Aquinas and his later scholastic followers who helped to formulate the official moral theology of the Catholic Church. Works by Aristotle include: *Categories, Prior and Posterior Analytics, Physics, On the Heavens, On the Soul, Metaphysics, Nichomachean Ethics, Politics, Rhetoric* and *Eudemian Ethics.*

*From Falikowski, Moral Philosophy: Theories, Skills and Applications, *p. 17.*

ARISTOTLE'S TELEOLOGY

Aristotle begins his ***Nichomachean Ethics*** with the following words: "Every craft and every investigation, and likewise every action and decision, seems to aim at some good." He points out, for example, that health is the end of medicine, a ship is the end of shipbuilding, victory is the end of military leadership, and wealth is the end of household management or home economics. This focus on the ends of human activity is what makes Aristotle a **teleologist**. For him, all human action has a purpose or an end to achieve.

Like his mentor Plato, Aristotle incorporated within his teleological framework a functional explanation of morality—in this case, a kind of **self-realization ethic**. In his efforts to understand what constitutes the ultimate good or end of life, Aristotle examined human activity in terms of its function. He said:

> perhaps we shall find the best good if we first find the function of a human being. For just as the good, i.e. [doing] well, for a flautist, a sculptor, and every craftsman, and, in general, for whatever has a function and [characteristic] action, seems to depend on its function, the same seems to be true for a human being, if a human being has some function.[1]

If, on this functional account, a good flautist, say, is one who plays well, then a good life is one that is well lived and good persons are those who perform their distinctively human functions well or with excellence. To better appreciate how the good life is tied to function, let us consider briefly Aristotle's notion of **entelechy.** Aristotle maintained that every living thing in nature possesses an "inner urge" to become its unique self. An acorn has the inner urge to become an oak tree; a newborn child has something within itself that yearns to become an adult, and so on. If each and every thing has an end within itself to achieve, i.e., its entelechy, then things do not just happen randomly, but develop according to their natural design or designated purpose.

Now, whereas an acorn cannot become a willow tree, due to its own entelechy, humans can by contrast, as more complex and self-willed organisms, fail to actualize their inner potentialities and, consequently, fail to express their entelechy. In ways soon to be illustrated, we, as humans, can fail at our own self-realization by missing the mark and following paths that take us away from our essential or "true" selves. We can "mis-function," so to speak, and become less than what we were meant to become by natural design. By examining Aristotle's notions of happiness and the ends of human life, we can discover how and why we often fall short of living the good life and actualizing our potentialities.

HAPPINESS OR *EUDAIMONIA* AND THE ENDS OF HUMAN LIFE

Although Plato and Aristotle are both teleologists who offer us a functional explanation of morality, their similarities abruptly end when it comes to their efforts to locate the source of true goodness in life. Plato maintained that knowledge of the good had to be discovered apart from the concrete world of everyday experience. One had to go beyond the tangible world, where things are imperfect and transitory, to a world of unchanging and immutable forms. Knowledge of goodness required, for Plato, a rational acquaintance with a supernatural realm. By contrast, Aristotle worked from experience and common-sense beliefs to identify the ultimate good of humankind.

> To enjoy the things we ought, and to hate the things we ought, has the greatest bearing on excellence of character.
>
> ARISTOTLE

Grounding his reasoning on people's experience and beliefs, as well as on common sense and human observation, Aristotle concluded that, no matter who you are or where you live, **happiness** is the ultimate end of life. As he points out, people from all walks of life believe that it is happiness toward which all of human behaviour is ultimately aimed. To understand more precisely what is meant by happiness and in what sense it is ultimate, let us examine Aristotle's distinctions among the various types of ends that people pursue.

Types of Ends

In the *Nichomachean Ethics*, Aristotle discusses a hierarchy of goods corresponding to a **hierarchy of ends**. Ends can be **instrumental, intrinsic** or **ultimate**. When we pursue a good corresponding to an instrumental end, we want to achieve that end because we think it will lead to something else further down the road. For instance, your goal next summer may be to get a job picking tomatoes. This would be, with little doubt, not an end in itself, but a means to a further end, say, earning a paycheque. While earning a paycheque is a pretty good end, the paycheque itself is a means to a further end, perhaps the purchase of a new car. You may be dreaming about buying a flashy automobile so that you can impress your friends; yet, on closer inspection, even this turns out to be only a means. One could ask why it is that you want to impress your friends. Whatever answer you give to this question points to a still more distant end. Instrumental ends are never for themselves, but for the sake of something else.

Intrinsic ends are different from instrumental ends. Acts performed for their intrinsic worth are performed for their own sake. They are valued in themselves, not because of what they produce or whatever else they might lead to. Wars, for example, do not have intrinsic value; they are fought to achieve such things as liberty and justice. Even victory in war is not an end in itself, according to Aristotle, for it is simply a means to create the conditions by which people, as human beings, can fulfill their purpose. But to ask why someone wants liberty or justice would be somewhat bewildering because it is generally accepted that such things have intrinsic value, that they are good in themselves.

Recognizing that there are many "goods" relating to different kinds of ends, Aristotle discusses what captures the highest good or ultimate end of life. For him, it is "happiness" or, as the Greeks call it, *eudaimonia*.

Happiness as the Ultimate End

Viewing happiness or **eudaimonia** as the ultimate end of human conduct means that no matter whatever we want—be it a job picking tomatoes, an automobile, victory in war or peace in the land—when all is said and done, the reason we want it is really that we want to be happy. Jobs, automobiles and other things are instrumental goods pointing to something beyond themselves. They are not final and, hence, do not represent ultimate goodness.

> Being "happy," unlike, say, being intelligent, is not a matter of having some power or disposition; it is a matter of exercising one's powers and realizing one's dispositions.
>
> JONATHAN BARNES

Aristotle is careful to distinguish happiness as the ultimate good from other things like physical pleasure and amusement. For Aristotle, happiness is serious business that takes us beyond mere fun and the satisfaction of bodily appetites. Although such things, no doubt, are pleasurable and have their rightful place in human experience, they cannot serve as the ultimate basis for living the good life. Even something as noble sounding as moral virtue cannot, for Aristotle, capture ultimate goodness. Many would agree that moral virtue has intrinsic value—"virtue is its own reward"—however, it is possible that we could live a virtuous life in misery and pain, seriously undermining anything that could be described as a happy or good life. Courageous and just people can suffer illness and misfortune that make their lives something far less than happy. Thus, while moral virtue is an intrinsic end, it is, nonetheless, incomplete.

Because moral virtue is not self-sufficient, it too cannot serve as the ultimate basis of the good life. Make no mistake about the fact that morality is a good for Aristotle; the point is that moral activity represents a **secondary form of happiness**, subordinate to something still higher. This is also the case with amusement and physical appetite satisfaction; though they are surely pleasurable, they are not as enduring and secure as other forms of higher pleasure which lie beyond them. This is why they are subordinate in the hierarchy of human goods.

Features of the Ultimate End

Aristotle argues that the **ultimate end of life** must fulfill three conditions. First, the ultimate end must be **self-sufficient**, in a way that moral virtue alone is not. It must make life desirable and lack nothing. Second, this end must be **final**. It must be desirable in itself. In this sense, the ultimate good is intrinsically, not instrumentally, valuable. Third, this end must be

attainable. A goal that cannot be achieved in principle may lead to such things as frustration and despair. For Aristotle, the only end that is final, self-sufficient and attainable is happiness. If in the end, however, happiness is not about fun, pleasure, appetite satisfaction or amusement, then the question still remains, "What is it?"

> *... we regard something as self-sufficient when all by itself it makes a life choiceworthy and lacking nothing; and that is what we think happiness does.*
> ARISTOTLE

In his introductory remarks to Aristotle's *Nichomachean Ethics*, Jonathan Barnes elaborates upon *eudaimonia*, the Greek term for happiness, to help us understand what Aristotle meant by it. Barnes uses *eudaimonia* to point out, for example, that Aristotle is not a **hedonist**. Happiness (or *eudaimonia*) is not about the pursuit of pleasure, something with which many of us equate it. Although happiness contributes to an enjoyable life, it is not about having a constant succession of pleasurable experiences. The Greek concept of *eudaimonia*, Barnes tells us, should be understood as "well-living" and "well-acting." Happiness is a normative or value-related concept, not an emotional or psychological one. Happiness is not a feeling, but a mode of living. To express it otherwise, it is not a **state**, but an **activity**. Barnes goes on to suggest, "The notion of *eudaimonia* is closely tied, in a way in which the English common-sense notion of happiness is not, to **success**: the *eudaimon* is the man who makes a success of his life and actions, who realizes his aims and ambitions as a man, who fulfills himself."[2] Barnes does not wish to reduce Aristotle's concept of happiness to success, but his reading of Aristotle does lead him to the conclusion that in the *Nichomachean Ethics* we are not directly being told how to be morally good people or even how to be humanly happy. Barnes maintains that Aristotle is, in fact, trying to explain to us how to live successful human lives and how to fulfill ourselves as human beings. If this is so, then the *Nichomachean Ethics* is more about character development than about moral behaviour.

The Good Life as a Fulfillment of our Distinctive Function

Aristotle's search for our **distinctive function** as human beings begins with a comparison between plants and people. He finds that plants and humans share life in common; that is, they are both living organisms, they both grow, develop and take in nourishment in the process. Aristotle thus concludes that mere existence based on nutrition (eating, drinking) and growth is not peculiar to human beings. We share these aspects of life with plants.

PHILOSOPHERS AT WORK

Using Aristotelian insights, explore the relationship between achievement and success. Are the two notions roughly equivalent? Why or why not? Is it possible to achieve and to fail in life at the same time? Explain.

Aristotle next compares us with animals. Humans share with animals a sensory capacity to experience the world. In this respect, sense perception and sensuality make us no different than a horse, an ox or any other animal. A life committed to sensation and physical appetite gratification is, therefore, not befitting of humans; it is the life of cattle and sheep. (As an aside, it is interesting how Aristotle's thinking here still exists in popular culture centuries after it was introduced. People who overindulge their physical or sexual appetites are often unkindly referred to today as "pigs"—of course, no offense is intended to that species of animal. Others, whose lives are largely devoted to doing nothing but lazing around all day, are said to be "vegging-out" or living like "couch-potatoes"—again, no offense is intended to the humble Idaho or lowly spud from Prince Edward Island. On a more serious note, we even sometimes consider terminating the lives of so-called "vegetables"—people on life support systems who manage to survive, but show virtually no human response. Some say such a life is not worth living. In some people's minds, being human involves activity beyond mere existence.)

In Aristotle's account, the fulfillment of our distinctively human function involves the exercise of our **rational capacities**. He says, "now we take the human function to be a certain kind of life, and take this life to be the soul's activity and actions that express reason." Shortly, we will look at why the rational lifestyle is most befitting of humans, but before we do, let us examine some **alternative lifestyles** that fall short of the human ideal of the good life. Once we know what the good life is not, we will be better able to appreciate what it is.

ALTERNATIVE LIFESTYLES

The Lifestyle of Pleasure and Appetite Gratification

Many individuals believe that happiness and the good life are found in the **lifestyle of pleasure and appetite gratification**. The accumulation of large sums of money, for instance, allows people to satisfy their desires. Yet, money has only instrumental worth. Coins and bank notes have no intrinsic value. They are simply used to acquire other things beyond themselves. Money is merely a means.

> When asked how much money it takes to make someone happy, the billionaire replied, "Just a little more."
>
> IN CONVERSATION WITH ROCKEFELLER

For Aristotle, happiness is also not about pleasure; remember, he is not a hedonist. For him, to see life primarily or exclusively as the pursuit of pleasure would be to advocate for people an existence suitable for pigs and cattle. Besides, pleasure must be a lesser good because it is an instrumental end. We pursue pleasure because we believe it will make us happy. If we did not think this, then we would not bother chasing it in our lives. Pleasure is again the means or a way to become happy—or so many think. Paradoxically, pursuit of pleasure is what often makes us miserable. As the Buddhist reminds us, desire or "craving" is the source of human suffering. Even if we manage to satisfy our cravings, we run the risk of oversatisfaction leading to such things as obesity and addiction. Like the young child who plays with scissors that could cause injury, we sometimes crave lower pleasures that, in the end, could hurt us.

The Statesman's Lifestyle

Some people recognize the "vulgarity" of a life devoted to the endless pursuit of pleasure, so they pursue what, in their minds, is a higher or more noble good. They choose to live **the statesman's lifestyle** of action where honour is paramount. As with the pursuit of pleasure, Aristotle rejects this lifestyle as humanity's highest good. Such a life depends too much on the fickle opinions of others. We may work for a long time to gain their approval—an approval that can be withdrawn at any time. Even if virtue, not honour, is regarded as the end of political life, problems still exist. Virtuous people can suffer terrible evils and misfortunes. Their life circumstances may prevent them from acting and expressing their virtues publically. Lack of resources, for instance, may stop them from doing what they want to do or what they believe ought to be done. Furthermore, as with pleasure, the goods of the statesman are subordinate goods because they remain instrumentally valuable. People seek honour because they believe that it will make them happy. If honour did not make them happy and if, say, misery were its result, then honour would cease to be sought as an end. Happiness is *not* sought for the sake of honour; honour is sought for the sake of happiness. Honour is, therefore, something lower in the hierarchy of human goods.

The Contemplative Lifestyle as the Highest Form of Human Functioning

As previously discussed, Aristotle maintains that it is in the exercise of our rational capacities that we distinguish ourselves from plant life and animal existence. It is reason that makes us unique and it is in rational activity that we express our true selves or entelechy. In view of this, Aristotle defines **the good life** in rational terms. He says, "the best and most pleasant life is the life of the intellect, since the intellect is in the fullest sense the man [human being]. So this life will also be the happiest."

> *Mental pleasures never cloy [stop up]; unlike those of the body, they are increased by repetition, approved by reflection, and strengthened by enjoyment.*
>
> NATHANIEL COTTON

In Book 1 of the *Nichomachean Ethics*, Aristotle expresses the nature of happiness in the following terms: "an activity of the soul in accordance with virtue." He explains, "Being 'happy', unlike, say, being intelligent, is not a matter of having some power or disposition; it is a matter of exercising one's powers and realizing one's dispositions." [3] Happiness is not an emotional state or psychological condition, but an action, a doing of the mind.

Do not be confused by Aristotle's use of the term **soul** in the quotation above. For Aristotle, having a soul simply means to be alive or animate in ways that inanimate (soulless) objects like rocks are not. Activities of the soul are those things that living creatures can do by nature's design. Growth and sensation are aspects of the soul shared with plants and animals. The highest part of the soul involves the activity of reasoning. Now, if the good thing is that which performs its function well, then for Aristotle, the teleologist, the good person is one who reasons well—like a virtuoso, we might say. To reason "in accordance with virtue" is not to display some kind of saintliness. To reason in accordance with virtue means that one reasons in an excellent way, i.e., that one performs the rational function well.

Aristotle reasons that **the contemplative lifestyle** is humanity's highest good because, first, it is most self-sufficient. A lifestyle based on pleasure and enjoyment or political honour, for example, requires many externals and accessories. By contrast, people can practise contemplation alone, without much else, or at least less than the other two lifestyles require. Second, contemplation is intrinsically choiceworthy. "Nothing is gained from it except the act of contemplation, whereas from [other] practical activities we expect to gain something more or less over and above the action." Third, contemplation provides the purest pleasure with the greatest permanence and enduring qualities. The contemplative lifestyle also provides great leisure and as much freedom from fatigue as is humanly possible. Pursuing politics and pleasure gives little time for rest. Aristotle even goes so far as to suggest that the contemplative life transcends mere mortal existence and becomes something god-like. When we engage in rational activity, he says, we express that within us which is **divine**.

As an eminently common-sense philosopher, Aristotle recognizes the obstacles and difficulties that can easily prevent the attainment of happiness. A good life can be marred, for example, by a bad or untimely death. Aristotle also argues that happiness must be seen in the context of a complete life. People cannot be said to have lived happy lives by virtue of some momentary state or life event. Unlike pleasure or ecstasy, happiness cannot be short-lived.

Although riches cannot guarantee happiness (witness all the unhappy millionaires), Aristotle recognizes how, practically speaking, they can help out a lot. It is easier to be happy if you are rich than if you are penniless and living out on the streets. Sure, having a good mental attitude and positive outlook on life are important to happiness, but so too is physical health. Aristotle would say that you cannot be happy in the fullest sense if, for example, you are chronically ill, grotesquely unattractive or mentally deficient. Put simply, things can get in the way of anyone's personal happiness. A certain amount of luck is required.

Another way to look at the good life is to see it as some kind of **balancing process**. "The highest and fullest happiness, according to Aristotle, comes from a life of reason and contemplation—not a life of inactivity or imbalance, but a rationally ordered life in which intellectual, physical and social needs are all met under the governance of reason and moderation."[4] Think of the workaholic striving to become rich and successful. That person may gain in wealth, but

---

PHILOSOPHERS AT WORK

People often say that winning the lottery would make them happy or that buying new clothes or a new car would make them happy or that having sex with an attractive partner would make them happy. How would Aristotle reply? What do you think would make you happy? If Aristotle were alive today, how would he respond to you? How would you respond to him?

miss much in life. The individual may seldom slow down enough to appreciate the blessings of life. Also, the person trying to find happiness in public life will usually be insecure and less self-sufficient than most. Famous people may easily fall out of favour. They may need security guards and advisors, or a whole entourage of people for personal support. People in public life lack an independence or self-sufficiency that is provided by the contemplative lifestyle.

PHILOSOPHERS AT WORK

Many advertisers present us with images of "the good life" in commercials for their products. What are some of those images? Viewing these commercials from an Aristotelian perspective, what could be said about them? Do you think the advertisers can deliver on their promises? Discuss.

Virtue and the Virtuous Lifestyle

As mentioned earlier, the life of unbroken contemplation is something god-like or divine for Aristotle. As something less than gods, however, most of us can aspire to live that kind of life for only brief periods at a time. In fact, many of us cannot hope realistically to live it at all because of our life circumstances, temperaments and character dispositions. Virtually all people for some of the time, and many people for all of the time, therefore, must be contented with the performance of the second-best of human activities. Although a divinely gifted few are capable of constant rational contemplation of knowledge and the truth, happiness for most of us "mere mortals" will consist in the practice of **virtue** and living an upright life.[5] This being the case, let us examine Aristotle's understanding of virtue and the virtuous lifestyle so we can place happiness within reach of ordinary individuals. Although we should not discourage efforts to achieve ultimate happiness found through rational contemplation, we should recognize our personal and practical limitations and work toward "secondary happiness" as necessary.

> *So it is a matter of no little importance what sort of habits we form from the earliest age—it makes a vast difference, or rather all the difference in the world.*
>
> ARISTOTLE

KINDS OF VIRTUE: INTELLECTUAL AND MORAL: For Aristotle, there are two kinds of virtue: **intellectual** and **moral**. Intellectual virtue involves things like wisdom and understanding and is acquired chiefly through instruction. Moral virtue, by contrast, includes things like temperance and patience and results as a product of **habit**. When we speak of individuals as morally good persons, we are referring not to their intellectual activities but to their feelings and actions— the elements of moral virtue.

Using Aristotle's self-realization ethic, we can say that we are constituted by nature to have the potential for moral virtue, but that its actualization can occur only through practice. People become generous by giving, brave by doing brave acts or just by performing just acts. Unlike animals, we are not preprogrammed by genetics or instincts and hormones to behave in this way or that. We, as humans, have choices to make about how we will conduct ourselves in the world.

DOCTRINE OF THE MEAN: If we are to develop states of character that will enable us to fulfill our proper function as rational beings, or at least to find secondary happiness in the moral life, then we must try to live our lives in moderation or according to what Aristotle calls the **Doctrine of the Mean**. Many people today refer to it as the Principle of the Golden Mean. Virtue, for Aristotle, is a "purposive disposition, lying in a mean that is relative to us and determined by a rational principle, and by that which a prudent man would use to determine it. It is a mean between two kinds of vice, one of excess and the other of deficiency..."[6] Right conduct, then, is incompatible with excess or deficiency. You can eat too much (gluttony) or too little (anorexia); you can work too much (workaholism) or too little (sloth) and so on. To live morally, we must find a midpoint or happy balance between two extremes. Put simply, the morally virtuous life must be lived in **moderation**.

To suggest that the morally virtuous life must be lived in moderation does not mean that we can calculate what is too much or too little. For example, for a tiny person, a double cheeseburger may be an excessive amount of food, but it may not be enough food for a professional football player. Nutritional needs vary according to physical size and stature, and considerations of moderation must take this into account. When deciding what constitutes moderation, we must determine the "golden mean" from our individual perspectives. In many cases, greater tolerance or sensitivity can move the moral mean from one point to another. Although this fact may seem to undermine precision when determining the right or virtuous course of action in any particular situation, Aristotle suggests that we should not demand more precision from an inquiry than the inquiry itself permits. The study of moral virtue, or at least the practice of moral virtue, is not an exact science.

The performance of a virtuous act is no guarantee that one is actually virtuous. A soldier may run into battle because the commanding officer may be more frightening than the enemy. Such an act would not be indicative of courage, though running into battle is something the courageous person would do. Likewise, an individual may avoid stealing because of fear of punishment, not because of any virtuous trait. For Aristotle, the virtuous person must enjoy being virtuous. The virtuous individual chooses to be virtuous and does not regret it. Virtue becomes its own reward. Charitable behaviour is thus displayed cheerfully and joyfully, not with bitter reluctance. In the context of physical pleasure, Aristotle writes,

> He who abstains from the pleasures of the body and rejoices in the abstinence is temperate, while he who is vexed at having to abstain is profligate; and again, he who faces danger with pleasure, or, at any rate, without pain, is courageous, but he to whom this is painful is a coward. For moral virtue or excellence is closely concerned with pleasure and pain. It is pleasure that moves us to do what is base, and pain that moves us to refrain from what is noble. And therefore, as Plato says, man needs to be so trained from his youth up as to find pleasure and pain in the right objects. This is what sound education means.[7]

Temperate acts must not only be performed gladly or without pain and regret if they are to be considered virtuous, they must also fulfill certain other conditions. First, individuals must know what they are doing. Second, they must consciously and deliberately choose to perform virtuous acts. Third, they must perform them for their own sake. And finally, the action performed must not be an isolated incident, but rather a manifestation of an enduring state of character. According to Aristotle, one donation does not a charitable person make. Nor is giving only to enhance one's reputation or to reduce one's taxable income a virtue. The act of giving must be performed for itself.

Virtue does not apply to all activities, and a proper mean does not exist for some types of behaviour. Although one may drink or eat in moderation, one cannot murder, steal or commit adultery in moderation; nor can one establish a virtuous level of hatred, envy or spite. These attitudes and behaviours are bad in themselves. Since these things are always wrong, it is absurd to look for moderation or excess where they are concerned.

In his *Nichomachean Ethics*, Aristotle provides a list of virtues capturing the means between various vices of excess and deficiency. You can read the "Back to the Source" feature to discover what they are. For now, you may wish to note that courage, for instance, is the mean between rashness and foolhardiness and modesty is the mean between shyness and shamelessness. These are common and easily appreciated virtues.

Now that you know the characteristics of virtue and what some virtues are, you can proceed to your destination toward the good life.

BACK TO THE SOURCE*

A provisional definition of virtue
So virtue is a purposive disposition, lying in a mean that is relative to us and determined by a rational principle, and by that which a prudent man would use to determine it.[1] It is a mean between two kinds of vice, one of excess and the other of deficiency; and also for this reason, that whereas these vices fall short of or exceed the right measure in both feelings and actions, virtue discovers the mean and chooses it. Thus from the point of view of its essence and the definition of its real nature, virtue is a mean; but in respect of what is right and best, it is an extreme.

But the rule of choosing the mean cannot be applied to some actions and feelings, which are essentially evil
But not every action or feeling admits of a mean; because some have names that directly

---

* From THE ETHICS OF ARISTOTLE translated by J.A.K. Thomson, revised with notes and appendices by Hugh Tredennick, introduction and bibliography by Jonathan Barnes (Penguin, 1976). Revised translation © Hugh Tredennick, 1976. Introduction and Bibliography © Jonathan Barnes, 1976.

connote depravity, such as malice, shamelessness and envy, and among actions adultery, theft and murder. All these, and more like them, are so called[2] as being evil in themselves; it is not the excess or deficiency of them that is evil. In their case, then, it is impossible to act rightly; one is always wrong. Nor does acting rightly or wrongly in such cases depend upon circumstances—whether a man commits adultery with the right woman or at the right time or in the right way, because to do anything of that kind is simply wrong. One might as well claim that there is a mean and excess and deficiency even in unjust or cowardly or intemperate actions. On that basis there must be a mean of excess, a mean of deficiency, an excess of excess and a deficiency of deficiency. But just as in temperance and courage there can be no mean or excess or deficiency, because the mean is in a sense an extreme, so there can be no mean or excess or deficiency in the vices that we mentioned; however done, they are wrong. For in general neither excess nor deficiency admits of a mean, nor does a mean admit of excess and deficiency.

The doctrine of the mean applied to particular virtues

vii. But a generalization of this kind is not enough; we must apply it to particular cases. When we are discussing actions, although general statements have a wider application, particular statements are closer to the truth. This is because actions are concerned with particular facts, and theories must be brought into harmony with these. Let us, then, take these instances from the diagram.[3]

In the field of Fear and Confidence[4] the mean is Courage; and of those who go to extremes the man who exceeds in fearlessness has no name to describe him (there are many nameless cases), the one who exceeds in confidence is called Rash, and the one who shows an excess of fear and a deficiency of confidence is called Cowardly. In the field of Pleasures and Pains—not in all, especially not in all pains—the mean is Temperance,[5] the excess Licentiousness; cases of defective response to pleasures scarcely occur, and therefore people of this sort too have no name to describe them, but let us class them as Insensible. In the field of Giving and Receiving Money the mean is Liberality, the excess and deficiency are Prodigality and Illiberality; but these show excess and deficiency in contrary ways to one another: the prodigal man goes too far in spending and not far enough in getting, while the illiberal man goes too far in getting money and not far enough in spending it. This present account is in outline and summary, which is all that we need at this stage; we shall give a more accurate analysis later.[6]

But there are other dispositions too that are concerned with money. There is a mean called Magnificence (because the magnificent is not the same as the liberal man: the one deals in large and the other in small outlays); the excess is Tastelessness and Vulgarity, the deficiency Pettiness. These are different from the extremes between which liberality lies; how they differ will be discussed later.[7] In the field of Public Honor and Dishonor the mean is Magnanimity, the excess is called a sort of Vanity, and the deficiency Pusillanimity. And just as liberality differs, as we said,[8] from magnificence in being concerned with small outlays, so there is a state related to Magnanimity in the same way, being concerned with small honors, while magnanimity is concerned

Table of Virtues and Vices

SPHERE OF ACTION OR FEELING	EXCESS	MEAN	DEFICIENCY
Fear and Confidence	Rashness *thrasutēs*	Courage *andreia*	Cowardice *deilia*
Pleasure and Pain	Licentiousness *akolasia*	Temperance *sōphrosunē*	Insensibility *anaisthēsia*
Getting and Spending (minor)	Prodigality *asōtia*	Liberality *eleutheriotēs*	Illiberality *aneleutheria*
Getting and Spending (major)	Vulgarity *apeirokalia, banausia*	Magnificence *megaloprepeia*	Pettiness *mikroprepeia*
Honour and Dishonour (major)	Vanity *chaunotēs*	Magnanimity *megalophsūchia*	Pusillanimity *mikropsūchia*
Honour and Dishonour (minor)	Ambition *philotīmmia*	Proper ambition	Unambitiousness *aphilotīmia*
Anger	Irascibility *orgilotēs*	Patience *prāotēs*	Lack of spirit *aorgēsia*
Self-expression	Boastfulness *alazoneia*	Truthfulness *alētheia*	Understatement *eirōneia*
Conversation	Buffoonery *bōmolochia*	Wittiness *eutrapelia*	Boorishness *agrolkia*
Social Conduct	Obsequiousness *areskeia* Flattery *kolakeia*	Friendliness *philia(?)*	Cantankerousness *duskolia (duseris)*
Shame	Shyness *katalplēxis*	Modesty *aidōs*	Shamelessness *anaischuntia*
Indignation	Envy *phthonos*	Righteous indignation *nemesis*	Malicious enjoyment *epichairekakia*

with great ones; because it is possible to aspire to [small] honors in the right way, or to a greater or less degree than is right. The man who goes too far in his aspirations is called Ambitious, the one who falls short, Unambitious; the one who is a mean between them has no name. This is true also of the corresponding dispositions, except that the ambitious man's is called Ambitiousness. This is why the extremes lay claim to the intermediate territory. We ourselves sometimes call the intermediate man ambitious and sometimes unambitious; that is, we sometimes commend the ambitious and sometimes the unambitious. Why it is that we do this will be explained in our later remarks.[9] Meanwhile let us continue our discussion of the remaining virtues and vices, following the method already laid down.

In the field of Anger, too, there is excess, deficiency and the mean. They do not really possess names, but we may call the intermediate man Patient and the mean Patience; and of the extremes the one who exceeds can be Irascible and his vice Irascibility, while the one who is deficient can be Spiritless and the deficiency Lack of Spirit.

There are also three other means which, though different, somewhat resemble each other. They are all concerned with what we do and say in social intercourse, but they differ in this respect, that one is concerned with truthfulness in such intercourse, the other two with pleasantness—one with pleasantness in entertainment, the other with pleasantness in every department of life. We must therefore say something about these too, in order that we may better discern that in all things the mean is to be commended, while the extremes are neither commendable nor right, but reprehensible. Most of these too have no names; but, as in the other cases, we must try to coin names for them in the interest of clarity and to make it easy to follow the argument.

Well, then, as regards Truth the intermediate man may be called Truthful and the mean Truthfulness; pretension that goes too far may be Boastfulness and the man who is disposed to it a Boaster, while that which is deficient[10] may be called Irony and its exponent Ironical. As for Pleasantness in Social Entertainment, the intermediate man is Witty, and the disposition Wit; the excess is Buffoonery and the indulger in it a Buffoon; the man who is deficient is a kind of Boor and his disposition Boorishness. In the rest of the sphere of the Pleasant—life in gen-

eral—the person who is pleasant in the right way is Friendly and the mean is Friendliness; the person who goes too far, if he has no motive, is Obsequious; if his motive is self-interest, he is a Flatterer. The man who is deficient and is unpleasant in all circumstances is Cantankerous and Ill-tempered.

There are mean states also in the sphere of feelings and emotions. Modesty is not a virtue, but the modest man too is praised. Here too one person is called intermediate and another excessive—like the Shy man who is overawed at anything. The man who feels too little shame or none at all is Shameless, and the intermediate man is Modest. Righteous Indignation is a mean between Envy and Spite, and they are all concerned with feelings of pain or pleasure at the experiences of our neighbors. The man who feels righteous indignation is distressed at instances of undeserved good fortune, but the envious man goes further and is distressed at *any* good fortune, while the spiteful man is so far from feeling distress[11] that he actually rejoices.

However, we shall have occasion to continue this discussion elsewhere.[12] After that we shall treat of Justice, distinguishing its two kinds—because the word is used in more senses than one—and explain in what way each of them is a mean.[13] [We shall also treat similarly of the rational virtues.][14]

The mean is often nearer to one extreme than to the other, or seems nearer because of our natural tendencies

viii. Thus there are three dispositions, two of them vicious (one by way of excess, the other of deficiency), and one good, the mean. They are all in some way opposed to one another: the extremes are contrary both to the mean and to each other, and the mean to the extremes. For just as the equal is greater compared with the less, and less compared with the greater, so the mean states (in both feelings and actions) are excessive compared with the deficient and deficient compared with the excessive. A brave man appears rash compared with a coward, and cowardly compared with a rash man; similarly a temperate man appears licentious compared with an insensible one and insensible compared with a licentious one, and a liberal man prodigal compared with an illiberal one and illiberal compared with a prodigal one. This is the reason why each extreme type tries to push the mean nearer to the other: the coward calls the brave man rash, the rash man calls him a coward; and similarly in all other cases. But while all these dispositions are opposed to one another in this way, the greatest degree of contrariety is that which is found between the two extremes. For they are separated by a greater interval from one another than from the mean, just as the great is further from the small, and the small from the great, than either is from the equal. Again, some extremes seem to bear a resemblance to a mean; e.g. rashness seems like courage, and prodigality like liberality; but between the extremes there is always the maximum dissimilarity. Now contraries are by definition as far distant as possible from one another;[15] hence the further apart things are, the more contrary they will be. In some cases it is the deficiency, in others the excess, that is more opposed to the mean; for instance, the more direct opposite of courage is not the excess, rashness, but the deficiency, cowardice; and that of temper-

ance is not the deficiency, insensibility, but the excess, licentiousness. This result is due to two causes. One lies in the nature of the thing itself. When one extreme has a closer affinity and resemblance to the mean, we tend to oppose to the mean not that extreme but the other. For instance, since rashness is held to be nearer to courage and more like it than cowardice is, it is cowardice that we tend to oppose to courage, because the extremes that are further from the mean are thought to be more opposed to it. This is one cause, the one that lies in the *thing*. The other lies in ourselves. It is the things towards which we have the stronger natural inclination that seem to us more opposed to the mean. For example, we are naturally more inclined towards pleasures, and this makes us more prone towards licentiousness than towards temperance; so we describe as more contrary to the mean those things towards which we have the stronger tendency. This is why licentiousness, the excess, is more contrary to temperance.[16]

Summing up of the foregoing discussion, together with three practical rules for good conduct

ix. We have now said enough to show that moral virtue is a mean, and in what sense it is so: that it is a mean between two vices, one of excess and the other of deficiency, and that it is such because it aims at hitting the mean point in feelings and actions. For this reason it is a difficult business to be good; because in any given case it is difficult to find the mid-point[17]—for instance, not everyone can find the center of a circle; only the man who knows how. So too it is easy to get angry—anyone can do that—or to give and spend money; but to feel or act towards the right person to the right extent at the right time for the right reason in the right way—that is not easy, and it is not everyone that can do it. Hence to do these things well is a rare, laudable and fine achievement.

For this reason anyone who is aiming at the mean should (1) keep away from that extreme which is more contrary to the mean, just as Calypso advises:

> Far from this surf and surge keep thou thy ship.[18]

For one of the extremes is always more erroneous than the other; and since it is extremely difficult to hit the mean, we must take the next best course, as they say, and choose the lesser of the evils; and this will be most readily done in the way that we are suggesting. (2) We must notice the errors into which we ourselves are liable to fall (because we all have different natural tendencies—we shall find out what ours are from the pleasure and pain that they give us), and we must drag ourselves in the contrary direction; for we shall arrive at the mean by pressing well away from our failing—just like somebody straightening a warped piece of wood. (3) In every situation one must guard especially against pleasure and pleasant things, because we are not impartial judges of pleasure. So we should adopt the same attitude towards it as the Trojan elders did towards Helen, and constantly repeat their pronouncement;[19] because if in this way we relieve ourselves of the attraction, we shall be less likely to go wrong.

Notes

1. *It is purposive as being a deliberately cultivated and exercised state of the appetitive faculty; and the mean is determined not merely by a general principle but by the application of it to particular circumstances by a man of good character and intelligence; cf. ch. ix. below.*

2. *Or 'are censured.'*

3. *Or 'table'; see p. 194, where the Greek names of the several virtues and vices are shown.*

4. *These should be regarded (for the understanding of Aristotle's general theory) as forming a single continuum with extremes Rashness and Cowardice; the reference to Fearlessness may be ignored.*

5. *Generally 'self-control' is a better rendering.*

6. *1115a4–1138b14.*

7. *1122a20–b18.*

8. *Just above.*

9. *1125b11–25.*

10. *By understating the truth; in fact 'understatement' is often a better equivalent than 'irony.'*

11. *At their bad fortune, because the Greek word means literally 'rejoicing at misfortune.'*

12. *In Book V.*

13. *1115a4ff.*

14. *The words in square brackets were almost certainly added by another hand; Aristotle never calls the intellectual virtues 'rational,' nor did he regard them as mean states. The intellectual virtues are discussed in Book VI.*

15. *Cf. Metaphysics 1018a25ff.*

16. *sc. 'than insensibility is' (1109a3f.).*

17. *Or 'mean.'*

18. *In our text of Homer these words are spoken not by Calypso (the nymph who detained Odysseus on her island) but by Odysseus himself quoting the enchantress Circe's advice to steer closer to Scylla (the lesser evil) than to Charybdis (Odyssey xii. 219f.).*

19. *As a sort of charm or spell. The elders paid tribute to her beauty, but said that she ought to be sent back to Greece, for fear of the consequences for Troy if she remained (Illiad iii. 156–60).*

MINDWORK MEDITATION

It might be insightful for you to reflect on your present lifestyle and selection of goals in your life. Are you currently living a moral life, a contemplative life, a life of pleasure and enjoyment or a lifestyle consistent with the values of the statesperson? What would you say and why? Furthermore, how would you describe your chosen ends in life? What is it that you want, desire or crave? Are these ends instrumental or intrinsically valuable? Would Aristotle say you are on the right track to happiness or living a successful life? Why?

KEY TERMS

Nichomachean Ethics
teleologist
self-realization ethic
entelechy
happiness
hierarchy of ends
instrumental
intrinsic
ultimate
eudaimonia
secondary form of happiness
ultimate end of life
self-sufficient
final
attainable
hedonist
state
activity

success
distinctive function
rational capacities
alternative lifestyles
the lifestyle of pleasure
appetite gratification
the statesman's lifestyle
the good life
soul
the contemplative lifestyle
divine
balancing process
virtue
intellectual
moral
habit
Doctrine of the Mean
moderation

PROGRESS CHECK 2.1

Instructions: Fill in the blanks with the appropriate responses listed below.

moderation
teleologist
entelechy

sake
self-realization
means

successful   hedonist
self-sufficient   rational
Alexander the Great   cattle
intrinsic   contemplative
insecure   secondary
complete   *eudaimonia*
divine   Plato
luck   intellectual
habit   modesty
deficiency

1. Aristotle was mentor to _ATG_ .

2. Aristotle was a student of _Plato_.

3. The assumption that everything in nature aims at some end or good makes Aristotle a _teleologist_

4. Aristotle's concept of morality and moral development is a kind of _self real_ ethic.

5. The inner urge for something to actualize its potentialities is the definition of _entelechy_

6. The Greek word for happiness is _eudaimonia_

7. The ends of human life can be _intrinsic_, instrumental or ultimate.

8. Instrumental ends correspond to goods that are a _means_ to further ends.

9. *Eudaimonia* implies _successful_ living.

10. Moral virtue is not the ultimate end of life, but, nonetheless, it can lead to _2ndary_ happiness.

11. The ultimate end of life must be final, attainable and _self-sufficient_

12. Aristotle's pursuit of happiness does not make him a _hedonist_ The pursuit of pleasure is not the ultimate end of the good life.

13. The distinctive function of any human being involves a _rational_ activity.

14. Living solely for the sake of pleasure puts human life on the same level as _cattle_.

15. A life of statesmanship is _insecure_ because it depends on the whims of the fickle masses.

16. Happiness is not a one-time event; it must be understood in the context of a _complete_ life. It is only at the end of life that one can say whether or not one has lived a good life.

17. The _contemplated_ lifestyle is the highest form of human existence.

18. Rational activity is something humans engage in that is most god-like or _divine_.

19. An otherwise good life can be marred by an untimely death or by a bad _luck_ .

20. There are two types of virtue, moral and _intellectual_

21. Moral virtue involves the development of _habit_. For example, we become just by performing just acts.

22. Aristotle's Doctrine of the (Golden) Mean would have us live our lives somewhere between excess and _deficiency_

23. Moral virtue involves a lifestyle of moderation

24. Virtuous acts must be performed knowingly and gladly and for their own sake, if they are to be considered truly virtuous.

25. The virtue of _____ is the mean between shyness and shamelessness.
    moderation.

SUMMARY OF MAJOR POINTS

1. **What makes Aristotle a teleologist?**

   His focus on the ends of human activity.
   His functional explanation of morality, i.e., his self-realization ethic.
   His incorporation of the concept of "entelechy" into his theory of human development.

2. **What is the end of human life?**

   Happiness or *eudaimonia*.
   The ultimate end is final, self-sufficient, and intrinsically valuable.
   It involves successful living, the good life taken as a whole.
   It is not hedonism.
   The fulfillment of our distinctively human function, i.e., a rational activity of the soul in accordance with virtue.

3. **How are humans distinctive? What do they share with other life forms?**

   The same as plants in regard to nutrition and growth.
   The same as animals in regard to sensory capacities.
   They are different because the higher part of the soul involves rational activity.
   Humans have the capacity to be happy and to live the good life, unlike plants and lower-level organisms.

4. **What lifestyles are discussed by Aristotle?**

   The lifestyle of pleasure and appetite gratification.
   The statesman's lifestyle.
   The contemplative lifestyle.
   The virtuous lifestyle.

5. **Which lifestyle is most befitting of humans? Why?**

   The contemplative lifestyle is ideal.
   It incorporates activities of the rational soul.
   It is most god-like or divine.
   It is the highest form of human existence.

6. **Which lifestyle is within reach of most of us? By what is it characterized?**

   The virtuous lifestyle is a more realistic aspiration for most of us compared with the contemplative lifestyle.
   Virtue offers us secondary happiness.
   The virtuous lifestyle represents a lifestyle of moderation.

The virtuous lifestyle underscores the idea that happiness is a normative or value-related notion, not a psychological state.

7. What is meant by the "Doctrine of the Mean"?

According to this doctrine, right conduct is incompatible with excess or deficiency.
To live morally or virtuously, we must find a happy balance between the two extremes.
The mean between excess and deficiency is determined in relation to particular individuals.
Think of it as living in moderation.

8. What are some virtues?

Courage: the mean between cowardice and rashness.
Modesty: the mean between shyness and shamelessness.
Truthfulness: the mean between boastfulness and understatement.
Wittiness: the mean between buffoonery and boorishness.

SOURCE REFERENCES AND RELATED READINGS

Aristotle. *Nichomachean Ethics*. Translated by Terence Irwin. Indianapolis, Ind.: Hackett Publishing Co., 1985.

Barnes, Jonathan. *The Cambridge Companion to Aristotle*. New York: Cambridge University Press, 1995.

Copleston, Frederick. *A History of Philosophy: Volume 1, Greece and Rome*. New York: Image Books, 1993.

Falikowski, Anthony. *Moral Philosophy: Theories, Skills, and Applications*. Englewood Cliffs, N.J.: Prentice Hall, 1990.

Ross, W.D. *Aristotle*. New York: Methuen, 1923.

Soccio, Douglas. *Archetypes of Wisdom*, 2nd edition. Toronto: Wadsworth Publishing Co., 1995.

Sommers, Christina Hoff. *Vice and Virtue in Everyday Life*. Orlando: Harcourt, Brace Jovanovich, 1985.

Thomson, J.A.K. (Trans.). *The Ethics of Aristotle, The Nichomachean Ethics*. Toronto: Penguin Books, 1976. Introduction by Jonathan Barnes.

ENDNOTES

1. Aristotle, *Nichomachean Ethics*, trans. Terence Irwin. Indianapolis, Ind.: Hackett, 1985, pp.15–16.
2. Aristotle, *The Ethics of Aristotle:The Nichomachean Ethics*, trans. J.A.K. Thomson. Toronto: Penguin Books, 1976, p.34.
3. ibid., p.35
4. Douglas Soccio, *Archetypes of Wisdom, 2/e*. Belmont: Wadsworth, 1995, p.194.
5. ibid., p.39.
6. Aristotle, ibid., pp.101–102.
7. ibid.

Utilitarian Ethics

From the Greek humanism of Plato and Aristotle, we now proceed to the utilitarian ethics of Jeremy Bentham and John Stuart Mill. Utilitarianism is a school of moral thought that has significantly influenced modern British and North American society. A major shift that you will notice from the earlier thinkers is the decidedly socio-political emphasis in this treatment of morality. In our coverage of Plato and Aristotle, we focused on those elements of their philosophies most pertinent to individual morality. Specifically, we looked at the nature and workings of the human soul. We learned, for example, how, for Plato, the soul is comprised of three elements and how these three should function in harmonious balance. We also saw how, for Aristotle, the good life entails an activity of rational contemplation, a process that reflects the highest form of human functioning. For both Plato and Aristotle, the development of virtue is deemed essential to character development and the cultivation of an ideal lifestyle.

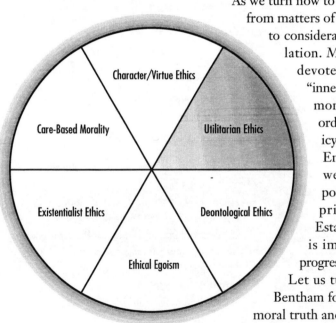

As we turn now to utilitarianism, we will change our focus from matters of soul, virtue and character development to considerations of society, law and political legislation. Morality is not a purely personal affair devoted to self-realization and keeping the "inner peace." Morality is also about the common good and the preservation of public order. Laws and legislators, people and policy makers, do not live in a moral vacuum. Embedded in our social relationships, as well as in the operations of our socio-political institutions, are moral values and principles like fairness and honesty. Establishing a solid basis of moral criticism is important, for it gives us the tools to progress and develop toward a more just society. Let us turn now to the philosophy of Jeremy Bentham for guidance on our continuing quest for moral truth and understanding.

CHAPTER THREE

Jeremy Bentham: The Hedonic Calculus

Overview

Learning Outcomes

After successfully completing this chapter, you will be able to

- define and understand the principle of utility;
- distinguish between psychological and ethical egoism;
- explain why Bentham chooses happiness or utility as the basis of morality;
- list the sanctions identified by Bentham;
- appreciate how sanctions serve as causal and determining forces in human behaviour;
- give the limits of legal jurisdiction as defined by Bentham;
- know when it is not profitable to punish from a utilitarian perspective;
- punish mischief and misbehaviour with utilitarian considerations in mind;
- perform a "hedonic calculation" illustrating how to put the principle of utility into real-life practice.

PHILOSOPHICAL FOCUS QUESTIONS

1. In general terms, how is Bentham's utilitarian treatment of morality different from Plato and Aristotle's Greek humanism?
2. According to Bentham, what is the primary motivating force in human life?
3. From a utilitarian perspective, what is the right/wrong thing to do?
4. What prevents people from doing anything and everything they want?
5. What is the proper business of law? What is beyond the scope of the law?
6. What is the right way to punish wrong behaviour?
7. When should punishments be avoided?
8. What is a hedonic calculus? What are its elements? How do you do one?

Biographical Brief*

CORBIS–BETTMANN

Jeremy Bentham
(1748–1832)

Jeremy Bentham was born in London in 1748. As a child, he was intellectually precocious. By the age of four Bentham was already studying Latin grammar and, at the age of twelve, he enrolled at Queen's College, Oxford. In 1763 Bentham earned a Bachelor of Arts degree and thereupon began legal studies at Lincoln's Inn. In that same year, he returned to Oxford for what turned out to be one of the most decisive experiences of his intellectual life. Bentham attended a number of lectures on law given by Sir William Blackstone. Blackstone presented his legal theory based on "natural rights." Regarding this theory as little more than rhetorical nonsense, Bentham began setting the stage for the development of his own utilitarian conception of law, justice, and society. Bentham earned his Master of Arts degree in 1766 and then proceeded to London. Having never really developed a fondness for the legal profession, he decided against becoming a practicing lawyer. Instead, he embarked on a literary career, the basic object of which was to bring order and moral defensibility into what he perceived as the deplorable state of the law and the social realities it made possible in his day. Jeremy Bentham can thus be regarded as a social reformer. He undertook the task of trying to modernize British political and social institutions. There is little doubt that it was due at least in part to his influence that a historical landmark was established, the Reform Bill of 1832, which transformed the nature of British politics. The control of Britain's parliament was taken away from the landed aristocracy and placed into the hands of the urban bourgeoisie.

*From Falikowski, Moral Philosophy: Theories, Skills and Applications, p. 47.

On a personal note, Jeremy Bentham was the godfather of John Stuart Mill, son of James Mill, Bentham's friend and colleague. John Stuart Mill later became the godfather of Bertrand Russell, a famous English philosopher who led the fight for nuclear disarmament in the 1960s. Starting with Bentham, an interesting philosophical lineage began to evolve that has had political activism as an essential element.

THE PRINCIPLE OF UTILITY

In the world of moral philosophy, when the subject of **utilitarianism** is raised, the name **Jeremy Bentham** is one of the first to come to mind. For many, his name is virtually synonymous with this

> *Nature has placed mankind under the governance of two sovereign masters, pain and pleasure. It is for them alone to point out what we ought to do, as well as to determine what we shall do.*
>
> JEREMY BENTHAM

ethical theory. It should be noted, however, that Bentham was not the sole inventor of it. Elements of utilitarianism are found in the writings of people such as Thomas Hobbes and John Locke. Bentham's significant contribution to utilitarianism is his connection of its basic principles and assumptions to the problems of his time. He sought to provide 19th-century English society with philosophical foundations for moral thought and practical social reform. Bentham believed that ethical questions could be answered in a **spirit of scientific objectivity**. He rejected such things as tradition, aristocratic privilege and religious faith as legitimate bases for moral evaluation. He believed that such things too easily serve the interests of the dominant, ruling classes and that they lead to the continued mistreatment of the poor and disenfranchised. Rather than appeal to religious, political or cultural authorities, Bentham chose to adopt a much more common-sense, empirical approach to the improvement of society. He argued that people's actions and those of governments could, and should, be evaluated according to their practical consequences or how much good they produce. For Bentham, no action is necessarily right or wrong in itself. The ethical value of anything is determined by its real-life results. Utilitarianism is, therefore, a form of **consequentialism**. It is the effect of an action that establishes its moral worth.

In his most famous work, *An Introduction to the Principles of Morals and Legislation* (1789), Bentham outlines his objective basis for morality. He calls it the **principle of utility**. Bentham writes,

> By the principle of utility is meant that principle which approves of every action whatsoever, according to the tendency which it appears to have to augment or diminish the happiness of the party whose interest is in question: or, what is the same thing in other words, to promote or to oppose that happiness. I say of every action whatsoever; and therefore not only of every action of a private individual, but of every measure of government.[1]

The term 'utility' is one you might not use in everyday conversation. Think of it as essentially the same thing as **benefit, advantage, pleasure, happiness** and **goodness**. Whatever prevents mischief, pain, evil, suffering or unhappiness also has utility or utilitarian value for Bentham.

PHILOSOPHERS AT WORK

Try to come up with examples of things or actions having utilitarian value. What has disutility or the effect of producing negative consequences? Do you agree with Bentham that "utility," not religion, political authority or tradition should act as the moral foundation for society? Why or why not?

THE PROBLEM OF PLEASURE

Bentham's utilitarianism is based on the notion of **psychological egoism**. He asserts it is human nature for us to seek pleasure and to avoid pain. To quote Bentham: "Nature has placed mankind under the governance of two sovereign masters, pain and pleasure. It is for them alone to point out what we ought to do, as well as to determine what we shall do."[2] This, in itself, is not problematic. If this were all Bentham were saying, then we would be making nothing other than a psychological claim about human behaviour which we could try to verify using empirical scientific means. To assert that humans are motivated by a self-interested pursuit of pleasure would simply make Bentham a psychological egoist.

> ... *what has an aptness to produce pleasure in us is what we call good and what is apt to produce pain in us we call evil.*
>
> JOHN LOCKE

Bentham, however, goes further and becomes an ethical egoist as well. He argues that because it *is* in our nature to seek pleasure, that is what we morally *ought* to do. For him, pleasure becomes a value that we ought to pursue and a standard against which to judge all actions and activities. In making a connection between "moral or ethical oughts" and "pleasure," Bentham is suggesting that right and wrong or good and bad cannot be properly understood in any other way. The right or good thing to do is to seek pleasure, for it is only pleasure and the avoidance of pain that give actions any real value. Conversely, the wrong or bad thing to do is to reduce or minimize the amount of pleasure experienced. It is also wrong to promote pain, misery, and suffering.

At first glance, Bentham's psychological egoism appears to create, for him, an inconsistency between his psychology and the moral theory he presents, which is designed to further the general welfare. After all, doing what's best for oneself may not always be the same as doing what's best for the common good. Ethical egoists put themselves before others. Also, pleasure-seeking egoists may in fact do harm to society in their pursuit of personal self-interest. To remedy this problem presented by an egoist psychology, Bentham introduces the notion of *sanctions*, something we'll get to in a moment. He tries to harmonize, albeit artificially, the interests of the individual with those of the state. If pleasure-seeking egoists act in ways contrary to the welfare of society, punishments are to be meted out. Bentham seems to assume that if left to themselves, people are not likely to put the interests of others ahead of their own. Neither are they likely to deny themselves pleasure so that others can benefit. However, with a system of socially engineered punishments, doing what's good for society can become something good for the individual wishing to avoid pain. Utimately, then, the motivation to promote "the greatest happiness" remains egoistic, and the moral obligation to do so, a matter of personal self-interest. What is in the social interest is tantamount to what is in the interest of the individual.

The Is–Ought Fallacy

Bentham's leap from psychological egoism to **ethical egoism** might make good intuitive sense to you. From a purely logical perspective, however, it falls prey to what, in logic, is called the "**is-ought fallacy**." When this fallacy (i.e., form of faulty logic) is committed, the reasoner tries unjustifiably to derive a moral "ought" from an "is" of experience. To illustrate, just because it *is* true that people lie, kill, cheat and steal, we cannot conclude solely on that basis that they *should* or *ought* to do so, for obvious reasons. In fact, even if we suggested that people are inherently evil by nature (the biological equivalent to original sin), we probably still would not accept evil behaviour on the grounds that we are so constituted by nature. More likely, we could say that the right thing to do is to suppress our (natural) aggressive, bestial and dishonest inclinations. The "is" is that in fact which "ought" to be repressed or somehow extinguished. As we can see, then, arguing from what is true to what ought to be is clearly a problematic and debatable step.

Bentham did not deal at length with the is–ought problem inherent in his utilitarianism. What he did do was suggest that all other moral theories were either vague and inconsistent or else reducible to pleasure and the principle of utility in the end. Furthermore, providing no substantial defense or justification of the principle of utility as the basis of morality, he simply concluded that "that which is used to prove everything else, cannot itself be proved: a chain of proofs must have their commencement somewhere. To give such proof is as impossible as it is needless."

THE THEORY OF SANCTIONS

If, as Bentham claims, psychological egoism is what motivates people to behave as they do, then what is preventing them from doing anything they want at any time they want, even if this entails violating others? As already mentioned, for Bentham, the answer is found in the

---

PHILOSOPHERS AT WORK

Do you think Bentham's acceptance of pleasure (utility) as a standard of morality is justified? Why or why not? Would it be wise to accept an "unnatural" morality, one that requires us to work against our natural urges and inclinations? What would Bentham say? Discuss.

administration of **sanctions**. Think of a sanction as a source of pleasure or pain that acts to give binding force to any law or rule of conduct. Sanctions can also be seen as rewards and punishments or as causal and determining factors influencing our behaviour. According to Bentham, we, as individuals, respond egoistically to sanctions, trying to maximize our pleasure and minimize our pain. We generally avoid behaving in ways that lead to pain and other negative sanctions; we generally prefer acting in ways that lead to pleasure, happiness, and personal benefit or satisfaction. Sanctions govern what we do, perhaps more than we sometimes realize.

> *The Business of government is to promote the happiness of society by punishing and rewarding.*
>
> JEREMY BENTHAM

Sanctions come in a variety of types. **Physical sanctions** are not administered by any human or divine source. They are what bind us to the laws of nature. For example, one cannot jump off the CN Tower in Toronto or off a mountain peak in Washington State without suffering the consequences. Because we recognize the physical sanctions associated with certain kinds of dangerous acts like these, virtually all of us refrain from them.

Moral Sanctions arise in our informal relationships with others. If you have ever experienced peer group pressure, you can probably appreciate the power, influence and control that public opinion can have. To spare ourselves mental pain, or embarrassment and loneliness, we often go along with the crowd and conform to the expectations of others. Other people actually contribute to the governance of our behaviour in ways of which we are not always consciously aware. For instance, if your friends start avoiding you because you constantly lie to them, you may be dissuaded from continuing the practice. The underlying fear of ostracism is often enough to prompt a change in behaviour.

In addition to physical and moral sanctions, our behaviour can also be regulated by **religious sanctions**, if we believe in a rewarding and punishing supreme being, as many do in the Judeo-Christian tradition. People may do what is right according to their religion, church or holy book in hopes of entering the gates of heaven or because they fear the hell-fire of eternal damnation. Religious sanctions affecting the afterlife can influence behaviour in the here and now.

Finally, Bentham writes of **political sanctions**. These sanctions are issued formally by judges and magistrates on behalf of the state. Punishments issuing from the state (province, county, municipality and federal court) include things like fines, penalties, and jail terms. Fear of such things is what deters people from breaking the law and violating the rights of other citizens. On the positive side, things like peace and good order, which result from abiding by the law, are what people find rewarding. Such things create the conditions most conducive to our pursuit of pleasure.

Bentham was most interested in the political type of sanctions. As a reformer, he wished to change the laws of English society in such a fashion that the general welfare would be promoted by each individual pursuing his or her own advantage. Political sanctions—that is, the rewards and punishments issued by a carefully crafted legal system—would promote the greatest happiness for the greatest number. Thus, for Bentham, laws should serve utilitarian ideals. Laws are not necessarily right or wrong in themselves, but they are acceptable only to the extent that they further human happiness.

LAW AND PUNISHMENT

As a social reformer, Bentham made significant use of the principle of utility in the context of law and punishment. In his mind, the law should be concerned with increasing the total happiness of the community by discouraging specifically those acts producing evil consequences. Such acts are, by definition, criminal and offensive. They inflict pain or somehow decrease the pleasure of specific individuals, groups or the community at large. It is the job of government, then, to promote the happiness of people by punishing those who commit offensive acts that, by the principle of utility, have been clearly established as evil.

> *But all punishment is mischief: all punishment in itself is evil. Upon the principle of utility, if it ought at all to be admitted, it ought to be admitted in as far as it promises to exclude some greater evil.*
>
> JEREMY BENTHAM

The Scope of Legal Jurisdiction

The kinds of acts that should or should not be under the law's jurisdiction became a matter of reclassification for Bentham. He believed that the English laws of his day unjustifiably controlled many areas of individuals' private morality that had no significant effect on public affairs or on the general happiness. He argued that matters of **private ethics**, involving such things as duties to oneself, sexual conduct and prudence, were beyond the proper scope of the law. He also felt that acts of beneficence or kindness toward others, though nice and conducive to people's happiness, were also not appropriate for legislation. Such positive acts should not be legally required. We cannot properly be compelled by law to be generous, altruistic or self-sacrificing for the benefit of others.

> *The State has no business in the bedrooms of the nation.*
>
> PIERRE ELLIOT TRUDEAU

Some examples of English laws that failed the test of utility in Bentham's day include the following: imprisoning people for failing to pay their debts, requiring membership in the Anglican church for certain political offices, specifying capital punishment for such crimes as picking pockets, and punishing people for drunkenness and fornication.[3]

Though interested in the use of punishment as a way of discouraging evil conduct, Bentham was not a **retributivist**. He was not in favour of meting out punishment for its own sake or as

PHILOSOPHERS AT WORK

Are there any laws today that in your opinion, or in the opinion of others, are unjustifiable because they violate personal rights? If so, which ones? Discuss possible objections to these laws from a utilitarian perspective. (*Hint*: At least two debatable laws deal with automobiles and their operation.)

a way of "getting even" with wrong-doers. According to Bentham, punishment itself constitutes an evil because it inflicts suffering and pain. Thus, punishing violations of proper social conduct could be justified only if the pain inflicted prevented or excluded some other, greater pain.
Punishment is a sort of necessary evil. Certainly, though, from a utilitarian perspective, retribution
for retribution's own sake must be rejected in principle. Inflicting pain for the purpose of "getting back at" is intrinsically wrong. No useful purpose is served by making an individual suffer
because her act caused a victim pain.

When Not to Punish

Bentham provides us with several utilitarian guidelines for the administration of **punishment**.
Punishment should not be administered where it is **groundless**. If a wrong-doing has, in fact,
not been committed, then punishment obviously should not be forthcoming. But if the wrongdoer can compensate the victim, and if the compensation is assured, then punishment should not
be inflicted either.

Punishment must also be avoided where it is **inefficacious**—i.e., where it does not work
to prevent mischief or wrongful acts. For example, retroactive legislation (i.e., making yesterday's acceptable act wrong starting today) and resulting sanctions (i.e., punishing yesterday's legal
act today) are ineffective and unjustifiable. Such legislation may indeed have disutility and
breed disrespect for legislators. Punishing the insane or very young children is also wrong,
since neither group has a true sense of responsibility.

Punishments should also not be administered where they would prove to be **unprofitable**
or too expensive. If the punishment to be inflicted creates greater mischief (i.e., pain or suffering) than the act that it was intended to extinguish or to deter others from performing, then
it should be avoided. Finally, punishment should be avoided where **needless**. Where mischief
can be avoided without punishment, then punishment should not be delivered. If an explanation
and condemnation of a particular wrong-doing is enough to dissuade another from committing
it again, then punishment is not in order.

How to Punish

After explaining when not to punish, Bentham goes on in the *Principles of Morals and Legislation*
to provide us with guidelines on how to punish when it's necessary. These guidelines are, of
course, based on utilitarian principles. To start, when punishments are inflicted, they must outweigh the profit of the offense that is committed. If parking in downtown Calgary or Los
Angeles costs $15.00 daily and if parking fines are only $10.00, then the pain of the punishment does not outweigh the profit derived from the offense. In this case, you could actually
save money by breaking the law. To reduce the likelihood of parking violations, the fine would
have to be increased well beyond $15.00 so that payment of a parking fine would "hurt" and,
therefore, act as a deterrent.

In situations where two different offenses are involved, the punishment for the more serious
offense must be sufficient to induce the individual to prefer the lesser offense. If small crimes and

large crimes are given the same punishments, and if there is more to gain in committing the larger crime, then we promote greater mischief instead of less mischief.

When punishing, we should also take care that every offender receives the same punishment for the same offense. If two people commit the same crime of manslaughter, for instance, in morally equivalent circumstances, and if we place one person on probation for three months and place the other person in jail for ten years, then the workings of the legal system would likely be called into question on grounds of unfairness, inconsistency or, even worse, discrimination.

From a utilitarian perspective, the punishment should never exceed the bare minimum required to make it effective. Many would argue that cutting off a person's hand for the crime of theft is excessive and unwarranted. Such severe punishment may work, but if less punishment can work too, then that is the preferred option. Punishment should not encourage sadistic pleasure or blood vengeance; remember, it is a necessary evil that is sometimes required to root out other, greater evils. As a utilitarian, one should never cause more pain than absolutely necessary.

If there is little chance for an offender to be caught in the act of wrong-doing, then the punishment should be greater. If there is little risk and little punishment associated with the mischief involved, then the likelihood that wrong-doing will occur is increased again. For Bentham, punishment should be increased in proportion to the declining likelihood that one will get caught.

For more details regarding sanctions and the proper administration of punishment, turn to the "Back to the Source" feature.

BACK TO THE SOURCE*

Chapter XIII Cases Unmeet for Punishment
I. General view of cases unmeet for punishment.
i. The general object which all laws have, or ought to have, in common, is to augment the total happiness of the community; and therefore, in the first place, to exclude, as far as may be, everything that tends to subtract from that happiness: in other words, to exclude mischief.

ii. But all punishment is mischief: all punishment in itself is evil. Upon the principle of utility, if it ought at all to be admitted, it ought only to be admitted in as far as it promises to exclude some greater evil.

iii. It is plain, therefore, that in the following cases punishment ought not to be inflicted.

1. Where it is *groundless*: where there is no mischief for it to prevent; the act not being mischievous upon the whole.

2. Where it must be *inefficacious*: where it cannot act so as to prevent the mischief.

3. Where it is *unprofitable*, or too *expensive*: where the mischief it would

Excerpt from The Collected Works of Jeremy Bentham — An Introduction to the Principles of Moral Legislation, Athelone Press. Reprinted with permission of the Bentham Committee, University College London, acting through the Bentham Project.

produce would be greater than what it prevented.

4. Where it is *needless*: where the mischief may be prevented, or cease of itself, without it: that is, at a cheaper rate....

Chapter XIV Of the Proportion Between Punishments and Offenses

i. We have seen that the general object of all laws is to prevent mischief; that is to say, when it is worth while; but that, where there are no other means of doing this than punishment, there are four cases in which it is *not* worth while.

ii. When it *is* worth while, there are four subordinate designs or objects, which, in the course of his endeavors to compass, as far as may be, that one general object, a legislator, whose views are governed by the principle of utility, comes naturally to propose to himself.

iii. 1. His first, most extensive, and most eligible object, is to prevent, in as far as it is possible, and worth while, all sorts of offenses whatsoever: in other words, so to manage, that no offense whatsoever may be committed.

iv. 2. But if a man must needs commit an offense of some kind or other, the next object is to induce him to commit an offense *less* mischievous, *rather* than one *more* mischievous: in other words, to choose always the *least* mischievous, of two offenses that will either of them suit his purpose.

v. 3. When a man has resolved upon a particular offense, the next object is to dispose him to do *no more* mischief that is *necessary* to his purpose: in other words, to do as little mischief as is consistent with the benefit he has in view.

vi. 4. The last object is, whatever the mischief be, which it is proposed to prevent, to prevent it at as *cheap* a rate as possible.

vii. Subservient to these four objects, or purposes, must be the rules or canons by which the proportion of punishments[1] to offenses is to be governed.

viii. Rule 1. 1. The first object, it has been seen, is to prevent, in as far as it is worth while, all sorts of offenses: therefore,

> The value of the punishment must not be less in any case than what is sufficient to outweigh that of the profit of the offense.

If it be, the offense (unless some other considerations, independent of the punishment, should intervene and operate efficaciously in the character of tutelary motives) will be sure to be committed notwithstanding: the whole lot of punishment will be thrown away: it will be altogether *inefficacious*.

ix. The above rule has been often objected to, on account of its seeming harshness: but this can only have happened for want of its being properly understood. The strength of the temptation, *ceteris paribus*, is as the profit of the offense: the quantum of the punishment must rise with the profit of the offense: *ceteris paribus*, it must therefore rise with the strength of the temptation. This there is no disputing. True it is, that the stronger the temptation, the less conclusive is the indication which the act of delinquency affords of the depravity of the offender's disposition. So far then as the absence of any aggravation, arising from extraordinary depravity or disposition, may operate, or at the utmost, so far as the presence of a ground of extenuation, resulting from the innocence or beneficence of the offender's disposition, can operate, the strength of the temptation may operate in abatement of the demand for punishment. But it can never operate so far as to indicate the propriety of making the punishment ineffectual, which it is sure to be when brought below the level of the apparent profit of the offense.

The partial benevolence which should prevail for the reduction of it below this level, would counteract as well those purposes which such a motive would actually have in view, as those more extensive purposes which benevolence ought to have in view: it would be cruelty not only to the public, but to the very persons in whose behalf it pleads: in its effects, I mean, however opposite in its intention. Cruelty to the public, that is cruelty to the innocent, by suffering them, for want of an adequate protection, to lie exposed to the mischief of the offense: cruelty even to the offender himself, by punishing him to no purpose, and without the chance of compassing that beneficial end, by which alone the introduction of the evil of punishment is to be justified.

x. Rule 2. But whether a given offense shall be prevented in a given degree by a given quantity of punishment, is never anything better than a chance; for the purchasing of which, whatever punishment is employed, is so much expended in advance. However, for the sake of giving it the better chance of outweighing the profit of the offense,

> The greater the mischief of the offense, the greater is the expense, which it may be worth while to be at, in the way of punishment.

xi. Rule 3. The next object is, to induce a man to choose always the least mischievous of two offenses; therefore

> Where two offenses come in competition, the punishment for the greater offense must be sufficient to induce a man to prefer the less.

xii. Rule 4. When a man has resolved upon a particular offense, the next object is, to induce him to do no more mischief than what is necessary for his purpose: therefore

> The punishment should be adjusted in such manner to each particular offense, that for every part of the mischief there may be a motive to restrain the offender from giving birth to it.

xiii. Rule 5. The last object is, whatever mischief is guarded against, to guard against it at as cheap a rate as possible: therefore

> The punishment ought in no case to be more than what is necessary to bring it into conformity with the rules here given.

xiv. Rule 6. It is further to be observed, that owing to the different manners and degrees in which persons under different circumstances are affected by the same exciting cause, a punishment which is the same in name will not always either really produce, or even so much as appear to others to produce, in two different persons the same degree of pain: therefore

> That the quantity actually inflicted on each individual offender may correspond to the quantity intended for similar offenders in general, the several circumstances influencing sensibility ought always to be taken into account.

xv. Of the above rules of proportion, the four first, we may perceive, serve to mark out the limits on the side of diminution; the limits *below* which a punishment ought not to be diminished: the fifth, the limits on the side of increase; the limits *above* which it ought not to be *increased*. The five first are calculated to serve as guides to the legislator: the sixth is calculated, in some measure, indeed, for the same purpose; but principally for guiding the judge in his endeavors to conform, on both sides, to the intentions of the legislator....[2]

Notes

1. The same rules (it is to be observed) may be applied, with little variation, to rewards as well as punishment: in

short, to motives in general, which, according as they are of the pleasurable or painful kind, are of the nature of reward or punishment: and, according as the act they are applied to produce is of the positive or negative kind, are styled impelling or restraining.

2. Chap. XV examines the properties which punishment must have if it is to be successful in its function, and Chap. XVI gives a classification of offenses. –Editor.

THE HEDONIC CALCULUS

To help individuals, as well as lawmakers and legislators, decide what ought to be done in any given set of circumstances, Bentham developed what has come to be known as the **hedonic calculus**. As the term itself suggests, the hedonic calculus is the calculation of pleasure or hedonic consequences. Remember that Bentham wanted to conduct moral inquiry in a spirit of scientific objectivity. By using the hedonic calculus to determine the pleasures and pains produced by any action or pol-

> *Quantity of pleasure being equal, pushpin is as good as poetry.*
> JEREMY BENTHAM

icy, he thought we could decide empirically on what is the right or good thing to do. The hedonic calculus might be more understandable if you see it as a kind of "cost–benefit" analysis. In the context of moral and ethical decision making, Bentham recommends that the bottom line should be the maximization of pleasure and the minimization or complete elimination of pain. Actions producing the greatest happiness for the individual or group concerned are the actions we morally ought to perform.

The hedonic calculus gives us seven criteria by which to measure the pleasure and pain produced by any particular action. They are:

1. *Intensity:* Ask how strong the pleasure or emotional satisfaction is.

2. *Duration:* Ask how long the pleasure will last. Will it be short-lived or long-lasting?

3. *Certainty:* Ask how likely or unlikely it is that pleasure will actually result. What is the probability of the result?

4. *Propinquity:* Ask how soon the pleasure will occur. How near are the consequences?

5. *Fecundity:* Ask how likely it is that the action will produce more pleasure in the future. Will the good/pain produced create more good/pain down the road?

6. *Purity:* Ask if there will be any pain accompanying the action (some pleasurable acts are accompanied by painful elements). Is there some bad you have to take with the good?

7. *Extent:* Ask how many other people will be affected by the considered action.

When making a moral or ethical decision, what Bentham suggests you do is attach numerical values to each of the elements listed above. You can use any scale you like. For our purposes, let us use a scale ranging from -100 to +100. Negative values indicate pain, positive values indicate pleasure. Thus, -100 means high pain, -50 means moderate pain and -10 means low pain. Similarly, +100 stands for high pleasure, +50 stands for moderate pleasure and +10 stands for low pleasure. Once the scale is determined, you then perform a pain-pleasure calculation of alternative courses of action. (There is an actual sequence of calculation discussed by Bentham in the *Principles of Morals and Legislation*—see Chapter VI.)

Suppose you have to decide between "doing A" and "not doing A"; which should you choose from a utilitarian perspective? First, look at "doing A" in regard to its intensity, duration, and other elements of the hedonic calculus. How much pleasure and how much pain is produced? On balance, is there more pleasure or more pain? Now, consider "not doing A." Again, calculate the quantities of pain and pleasure using the criteria of the hedonic calculus. Once the calculations are done for each alternative action—"doing A" versus "not doing A"—they should then be compared. The alternative action producing the most pleasure is the morally preferable one. If both alternatives produce a net balance of pain, then the alternative producing the least pain is to be preferred.

> Intense, long, certain, speedy, fruitful, pure— Such marks in pleasure and in pains endure. Such pleasures seek, if private be thy end; If it be public, wide let them extend. Such pains avoid, whichever by they view; If pains must come, let them extend to few.
>
> JEREMY BENTHAM

I should add here that if the implications of the considered action go beyond the individual to include others, then Bentham recommends that we repeat the hedonic calculus taking their interests into account. What is the net balance of pleasure and pain for others if alternative "A" is performed? What are the hedonic consequences for them if "A" is not performed? Thus, Bentham was interested not only in maximizing the happiness of the individual but also in maximizing the happiness of the broader community. If our actions impact on others, then they must be accounted for in our hedonic calculation.

I might also add that Bentham was not unrealistic. For him, "It is not to be expected that this [hedonic calculation] process should be strictly pursued previously to every moral judgment, or to every legislative or judicial operation." [4] To do a formal hedonic calculation every time we were about to act would be highly impractical. Yet, according to Bentham, each of us goes through some semblance of this process on a common-sense, intuitive level—although we may do it so quickly that we are virtually unconscious that we have done it. We may not wittingly go through all of the criteria outlined by Bentham, but, in general terms, we probably go through some kind of weighing and balancing process, considering the pros and cons before we act.

Working through an actual example may make the hedonic calculus easier to understand. Let us say that you are back in high school and that you are thinking about going on to a college or university in a distant city. The school you have in mind has the best program in your chosen field and, for years, you have longed to attend it. The problem is that you have become involved in a serious relationship with someone who prefers that you stay in your hometown and find employment at the local manufacturing plant. The two of you have discussed the possibility of marriage, though no firm commitments have been made either way. Your dilemma involves choosing between (a) staying at home to work and continuing to develop your personal relationship with your special someone and (b) going away to school and pursuing your career and academic dreams. What is the best thing to do? Let's find out using the hedonic calculus. Note that a complete calculation would entail not only a consideration of your interests but also a consideration of the interests of the other party involved. For brevity's sake, we will do a partial calculation based only on your interests. The values given to each part of the decision would likely vary in real life from person to person. The values *you* would assign would therefore likely differ from those I have given.

An Hedonic Calculation

Alternative A—Stay at Home and Work in the Local Plant

1. *Intensity*:
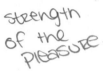

   If I choose to stay at home, I will probably experience intense feelings of disappointment. I may also become regretful and may possibly resent how another person has frustrated the pursuit of my personal dream. Some of the resentment and anger I feel will be diminished by the loving feelings I have for my boyfriend/girlfriend and by the love I feel for my family.
   (-50)

2. *Duration*: Any acute feelings of anger and resentment are likely to subside in a relatively short period of time. Nagging doubts, however, may remain for years, causing unpleasantness and insecurity. Time may heal, but emotional scars may remain.
   (-25)

3. *Certainty*: Who knows, what people want often changes. I might change my mind about working at the plant. It is possible that I will learn to like it there, though I really believe I will not.
   (-10)

4. *Propinquity*: The frustration and disappointment will result fairly soon. It is now July and classes start in September. The mental pain is not that far down the road.
   (-50)

5. *Fecundity*: If I stay at home, I can save myself a lot of money. Mom and Dad will not accept rent from me, so I will be able to save almost everything I earn. I also will not have to pay ridiculously high tuition fees that I cannot afford. I will be able to invest the money I earn in the stock market. I do not think I could ever recoup what I would lose in wages, as well as in residence and tuition costs by going off to school.
   (+100)

6. *Purity*:   Sure, there will be financial gains if I stay at home, but considerable pain will be experienced due to possible missed opportunities. There will be things I never learn and people I never meet if I opt for the financially preferable course of action.
(-25)

7. *Extent*:   Other people will be affected by my decision. Mom and Dad do not value formal education, so they would prefer that I stay home. My boyfriend/girlfriend also prefers that I stay home. I get the feeling that people in the neighbourhood would also like me to stay. They say they would miss me if I went away.
(+100)

Utilitarian Value of Alternative A

	Utility	Disutility
Intensity		-50
Duration		-25
Certainty		-10
Propinquity		-50
Fecundity	+100	
Purity		-25
Extent	+100	
	+200	-160

Alternative A would produce +40 net units of pleasure.

Alternative B—Go Away to School

1. *Intensity*:   If I choose to go away to school, the excitement will be wonderful. I will be enthused, energized, and optimistic about going to a new place, meeting new people, and learning new things.
(+75)

2. *Duration*:   I know my positive feelings will tend to subside in time. Reality hits during exams. I am likely to miss my family and my special loved one. I know I can sometimes easily become bored. Nonetheless, I think the experience will be great and I will like it.
(+25)

3. *Certainty*:   Well, if I go, I am pretty certain of having fun and enjoying myself. I have been accepted both at the school and at the residence, so I know that there are no practical obstacles about going. I guess it is possible my roommate and I will be incompatible, but I will hope for the best.
(+75)

4. *Propinquity:* The good times at school start soon. We are just weeks away from "homecoming," pub crawls, intramural sports—you name it. If I choose to go to school, I will not have to wait long to enjoy myself.
(+75)

5. *Fecundity:* I know that by going to school I am going to cultivate my mind and possibly open up new horizons I never dreamt of before. I do not know of anyone who has ever been hurt by knowledge and understanding. On the downside, I do stand to lose a lot of money over the next four years. Getting a job at the plant would have paid well and I could have invested my earnings. No doubt about it, I will lose in the immediate future, but I hope to make it up over my lifetime.
(+25)

6. *Purity:* I know that going off to school is not all fun and games, at least if I want to pass. Studying is hard and so are exams. You cannot party when you are doing an "all-nighter" memorizing Plato. Furthermore, I am likely to encounter professors and courses I do not really like. I guess school has its good and bad sides, just like everything else.
(+10)

7. *Extent:* I know the people around me will be sorry to see me go. They will be saddened and possibly lonely. I hope my boyfriend/girlfriend does not take my decision personally. I do not mean to hurt anyone, but I know that hurt feelings will be created anyway.
(-50)

Utilitarian Value of Alternative B

	Utility	Disutility
Intensity	+75	
Duration	+25	
Certainty	+75	
Propinquity	+75	
Fecundity	+25	
Purity	+10	
Extent		-50
	+285	-50

Alternative B would produce +235 units of pleasure.

Comparing Alternatives	A	B
	Staying at Home	*Going to School*
Intensity	-50	+75
Duration	-25	+25
Certainty	-10	+75
Propinquity	-50	+75
Fecundity	+100	+25
Purity	-25	+10
Extent	+100	-50
	+40 units	+235 units

Findings: Alternative B produces greater pleasure than Alternative A.
Conclusion: Alternative B is the right thing to do.

PHILOSOPHERS AT WORK

This exercise can be done individually or in small groups. Your task will be to perform a hedonic calculation for the following situation. Imagine that you are on the student council and that you are away on a convention. At the convention, you meet another student delegate from across the country. After a few drinks and some pleasant conversation, you are propositioned and invited to that person's hotel room for an overnight stay. You hesitate because you are engaged to be married. What should you do? Decide using Bentham's hedonic calculus.

Overtime Discussion: What problems, if any, did you discover doing your hedonic calculation? Assuming you are the student in the situation above, would you want your fiancé/fiancée to be a utilitarian? Why or why not?

MINDWORK MEDITATION

As moral philosophers, both Bentham and Aristotle are interested in promoting people's happiness. Do you think happiness is best achieved through hedonic calculations (Bentham) or by the cultivation of character (Aristotle)? Which philosopher do you think is on the better track? Why? Reflect upon these questions and record your thoughts.

KEY TERMS

utilitarianism
Jeremy Bentham
spirit of scientific objectivity
consequentialism
principle of utility
benefit
advantage
pleasure
happiness
goodness
psychological egoism
ethical egoism
is–ought fallacy
sanctions
physical sanctions
moral sanctions
religious sanctions

political sanctions
private ethics
retributivist
punishment
groundless
inefficacious
unprofitable
needless
hedonic calculus
intensity
duration
certainty
propinquity
fecundity
purity
extent

PROGRESS CHECK 3.1

Instructions: Fill in the blanks with the appropriate responses listed below.

spirit of scientific objectivity
principle of utility
ethical egoist
sanction
Jeremy Bentham
retributivist
inefficacious
psychological egoist
intensity
intrinsically

fecundity
utility
political
private ethics
retroactive legislation
nature
hedonic calculus
is–ought
consequences
extent

1. _Nature_ leads us to seek pleasure and to avoid pain.
2. _____ is a utilitarian philosopher. *Jeremy Bentham*
3. Morality is not a purely subjective matter; it can be approached in a(n) _____. *spirit of objectivity*
4. For Jeremy Bentham, the morality of any particular action can be determined by an evaluation of its _consequences_
5. Bentham argues that the basis or foundation of morality should be the _principle of utility_
6. Equivalent terms for _utility_ are benefit, advantage, goodness, pleasure and happiness.

7. To claim that humans are naturally motivated to seek pleasure makes one a(n) psychological egoist

8. To argue that one ought to pursue pleasure is to make one a(n) ethical egoist

9. To argue that one should do something simply because that is the way things are is to commit the is-ought fallacy.

10. A source of pain and pleasure that gives binding force to laws and rules of conduct is called a(n) sanction

11. Judges and magistrates administer political sanctions in their efforts to govern and to maintain order within society.

12. Jeremy Bentham is not a(n) retributivist _____; he believes that punishment in itself is evil and should be used only when necessary to exclude some greater evil.

13. private ethics is/are beyond the proper scope of the law.

14. Punishments that do not work are inefficacious

15. Illegalizing and punishing acts that were legal when performed entails retroactive legislation, something Bentham considers to be wrong.

16. For Bentham, moral decision making involves a kind of cost–benefit analysis, or what can be termed a(n) hedonic calculus

17. When we ask how strong the pleasure or emotional satisfaction is that is produced by any act, we are referring to the act's intensity

18. Whether or not an action's immediate consequences will lead to future benefits relates to the action's fecundity

19. When we ask how many people are likely to be affected by an action, we refer to the extent of its consequences.

20. According to utilitarianism, actions are not intrinsically _____ right or wrong; consequences determine their moral value.

SUMMARY OF MAJOR POINTS

1. **How did Jeremy Bentham approach the study of morality?**

   He approached it in a spirit of scientific objectivity.
   He rejected tradition, aristocratic privilege, and religion as legitimate bases for moral systems of thought.
   He used English laws and legislation.

2. **What is meant by the principle of utility?**

   According to this principle, good actions are those that increase happiness; bad actions are those that cause pain, suffering, misery or a decrease in happiness.
   Utility can be equated with benefit, advantage, pleasure, happiness and goodness.
   Disutility is equivalent to liability, disadvantage, pain, unhappiness and evil.

3. How are psychological and ethical egoism different?

   Psychological egoism is a psychological theory about human motivation; it states that people seek pleasure by nature.

   Ethical egoism is a moral theory; it states that the right thing to do is to pursue pleasure; that is what we ought to do.

4. What is meant by the "is–ought" fallacy?

   This is a logical mistake whereby one tries to derive a moral "ought" from an "is" of experience. What is should not necessarily or always be.

5. What is a sanction? What are some examples?

   A sanction is a source of pain and pleasure giving binding force to any law or rule of conduct. Sanctions can also be rewards and punishments serving as causal, determining factors in our behaviour.

   Examples of sanctions are: physical, moral, religious, political.

6. How does Bentham view punishment?

   He is not in favour of retribution.

   He would use punishment only as a necessary evil to prevent a greater evil.

7. When should one not punish?

   When it is groundless, inefficacious (not effective), unprofitable and needless.

8. What considerations should be taken into account when punishing?

   Punishment must outweigh the profit of the offense.

   Greater offenses should be given greater punishments.

   Punishment for the same crime should be meted out fairly and consistently.

   Punishment should not exceed the bare minimum required to be effective.

   Crimes with little risk of getting caught should be given stricter punishments.

9. What is the hedonic calculus?

   A process of calculation used to determine which action will produce the greatest utility.

   It is comprised of seven criteria: intensity, duration, certainty, propinquity, purity, fecundity and extent.

SOURCE REFERENCES AND RELATED READINGS

Ayer, A.J. "The Principle of Utility" in *Philosophical Essays*. Edited by A.J. Ayer, New York: St. Martin's Press, 1955.

Bentham, Jeremy. "An Introduction to the Principles of Morals and Legislation" in *The English Philosophers from Bacon to Mill*. Edited by E.A. Burtt. New York: The Modern Library, 1939.

Falikowski, Anthony. *Moral Philosophy: Theories, Skills, and Applications*. Englewood Cliffs, N.J.: Prentice Hall, 1990.

Naveson, Jan. *Morality and Utility*. Baltimore: Johns Hopkins University Press, 1967.

Runkle, Gerald. *Ethics: An Examination of Contemporary Moral Problems*. New York: Holt, Rinehart and Winston, 1982.

Smart, J.J. *Outline of a Utilitarian System of Ethics*. London: Cambridge University Press, 1961.

Soccio, Douglas. *Archetypes of Wisdom: An Introduction to Philosophy*, 2nd edition. Belmont, Ca. Wadsworth Publishing Co., 1995.

Stumpf, Samuel Enoch. *Philosophy: History and Problems*. New York: McGraw-Hill Inc., 1994.

White, Thomas. *Discovering Philosophy*. Upper Saddle River, N.J.: Prentice Hall, 1996.

ENDNOTES

1. Jeremy Bentham, "An Introduction to the Principles of Morals and Legislation." In *The English Philosophers from Bacon to Mill*, edited by E.A.Burtt. New York: The Modern Library, 1939, p.792.
2. ibid., 791.
3. Gerald Runkle, *Ethics: An Examination of Contemporary Moral Problems*. New York: Holt, Rinehart and Winston, 1982.
4. Bentham, ibid., p.804.

CHAPTER FOUR

John Stuart Mill:
Higher and Lower Pleasures

Overview

Learning Outcomes

After successfully completing this chapter, you will be able to

- present John Stuart Mill's position on the principle of utility;
- explain Mill's qualitative distinction between higher and lower pleasures and why the former are better than the latter;
- discuss the risks of pursuing higher pleasures;
- outline the basic differences between Mill and Bentham regarding their utilitarian philosophies;
- give the reasons why Mill rejects Bentham's hedonic calculus;
- offer the utilitarian position on human misery and its reduction;
- state Mill's position on the proper limits of governmental authority over the individual.

PHILOSOPHICAL FOCUS QUESTIONS

1. What was it about utilitarianism that some people found offensive and that made it necessary for Mill to present a defence against its critics?

2. Is it appropriate to distinguish between types of pleasures, saying that some pleasures are better than others? Would some people be reluctant to make such a distinction? Why?

3. What role does human dignity have to play in Mill's utilitarian ethics?

4. What are some risks that are associated with pursuing higher pleasures?

5. How is Mill less of an ethical egoist than Bentham?

6. Why is there a problem in doing hedonic calculations?

7. What can be said about human misery and suffering from a utilitarian point of view?

8. What should be the proper moral relationship between the individual and government?

John Stuart Mill
(1806–1873)

Biographical Brief*

John Stuart Mill was born in London, England, in 1806, the eldest child of Harriet and James Mill. His father, a Scotsman, was an accomplished author, friend, and colleague of Jeremy Bentham. James Mill was an intensely intellectual man. This is evidenced by the educational experiment that he conducted with his son John Stuart—a rigorous program of home education. At the age of three, John Stuart was learning Greek, and by age eight he was reading Plato and other Greek authors in the original. Along with Latin and arithmetic, extensive reading was part of Mill's heavy curriculum. Each morning, John Stuart was expected to give a recitation of the previous day's reading to his father.

The young Mill did not become an academic by profession. His research and writing were done in conjunction with his duties as a civil servant in the East India Company. Mill imposed upon himself a regimen so onerous it eventually led to his psychological collapse at age 20. The depression associated with his "nervous breakdown" lasted several months. Mill gradually recovered from his gloomy state by allowing emotion and sentiment to grow within him. His father's unfeeling disposition had apparently damaged John Stuart's affective development and psychological health. He once wrote that he was never allowed to be a boy and to experience normal childhood friendships and playfulness. Fortunately for Mill, his one-sided, highly intellectualized personality became more balanced. His feelings for humanity were cultivated by reading Wordsworth's poetry and by developing a loving friendship with Harriet Taylor, who later became his wife.

J. S. Mill was convinced that his wife was a talented thinker who, unfortunately, was not appreciated because of the discrimination against women at that time. Acutely sensitive to the matter of discrimination, Mill addressed it in a work entitled *The Subjection of Women*. J. S. Mill's objections to sexism make him a predecessor of contemporary feminism. On this note, it should be pointed out that he was elected to parliament in 1865. As part of his political struggle he fought for the exploited Negroes of Jamaica; and he tried to increase the power and influence of the working class in England, hoping to bring it into the country's political and economic mainstream. He also worked for the redistribution of lands in Ireland. J. S. Mill can be described as a political thinker, social reformer, activist and moral philosopher. Selected works include: *Utilitarianism, On Liberty, A System of Logic, The Principles of Political Economy*, and *Considerations on Representative Government*.

*From Falikowski, Moral Philosophy: Theories, Skills and Applications, p. 57.

MILL'S ACCEPTANCE AND DEFENCE OF UTILITARIANISM

As a young man, J.S. Mill was influenced by Jeremy Bentham, primarily through his father, James Mill, who had been not only a friend to Bentham but also a collaborator who assisted him in shaping his political ideas. The young Mill was particularly impressed by Bentham's **principle of utility**. Recall that Bentham used this principle as an alternative to attempts to derive concepts of morality and lawmaking from notions like "right reason" and "natural law." Mill wrote, "the principle of utility, understood as Bentham understood it ... gave unity to my conceptions of things. I now had opinions, a creed, a doctrine, a philosophy; in one among the best senses of the word, a religion; the inculcation and diffusion of which could be made the principal outward purpose of life."[1]

In his classic essay, *Utilitarianism*, Mill set out to defend the principle of utility against its critics. In the process, he arrived at a version of **utilitarianism** that differed significantly from Bentham's. For instance, whereas Bentham regarded all pleasures as equal in value and different only in amount, Mill made a distinction between higher- and lower-quality pleasures, suggesting that the former were better than the latter. He also rejected Bentham's hedonic calculus and opted for a less egoistic form of hedonism than the one advanced by Bentham. Let us take a few moments to look more closely at Mill's utilitarian revisions.

MINDWORK MEDITATION

Are there any values, beliefs or principles that give unity and purpose to your life right now? If so, which ones? How do these things operate in practical terms when it comes to action and personal decision making? If you do not have a fundamental principle or concrete value system by which to direct your life, then ask the question, "Why not?" Is having some kind of life-directing principle necessary? What has life been like so far without one? How will you know when you find the principle or value system that you should base your life on? How would you expect your life to change?

PLEASURE: IT IS THE QUALITY THAT MATTERS

In the *Principles of Morals and Legislation*, Bentham limited his discussion of pleasure solely to quantity. He argued that pleasures differ only in amount, saying things like, "Pushpin [a child's game] is as good as poetry." For Bentham, the only criterion for goodness is the amount of pleasure that an act can produce.

Bentham's contention that all pleasures are equal has considerable intuitive appeal. In North American society, for instance, where we value democracy and tolerance for diversity, the notion that some pleasures could be deemed better than others or that some pleasurable pursuits could be considered wrong, inferior or misguided compared with others may seem offensive or appear somewhat elitist. Liberal-minded thinkers would likely be reluctant to say, "My pleasures are better than yours" or "These pleasures are better than those." Notwithstanding such a disinclination to make value judgments on the worth of particular pleasures, Mill does so, and he does so in defence of utilitarianism.

Mill recognizes that there is a danger in seeing moral life exclusively in terms of the pursuit of pleasure. If pleasure is not properly understood, some people may view a utilitarian lifestyle as something vulgar and more befitting of swine than of humans. Indeed, the pursuit of pleasure, understood in its basest terms, would be regarded by religionists, at least, as sinful. Self-denial in regard to pleasure is often considered saintly virtue. Denying oneself something pleasurable is a ritual performed by many Christians during Lent. To put pleasure into proper perspective and to defend its pursuit against its critics, Mill made a distinction between the **quantity** and **quality** of pleasure.

HIGHER VERSUS LOWER PLEASURES

For Mill, the type of pleasure experienced is more important than the amount. Mill believed that pleasures could be categorized as either **higher** or **lower** and that the higher ones were better.

He argued that human beings possess psychological faculties that are elevated above the level of animal appetites. At
the lower grade of existence, Mill placed **bodily pleasures**
and those of physical sensation. At the higher grade of
existence, Mill placed the pleasures of the **intellect**, those
relating to our **feelings** and **imagination** and those relating
to our **moral sentiments** and sensitivities. Rather than de-

> *Human beings have faculties more ele-*
> *vated than the animal appetites and,*
> *when once made conscious of them, do*
> *not regard anything as happiness which*
> *does not include their gratification.*
>
> J.S. MILL

grade life, the pursuit of such higher pleasures can ennoble and dignify it. With proper upbringing and education, people can cultivate their minds and learn to take pleasure in the objects
of nature, the achievements of arts, the imaginative language of poetry, the incidents of history and the ways of humankind—past, present and future. With all this in view, there is no need
to see pleasure as a base and abject pursuit. It can offer a sense of **human dignity** and worth to
ordinary people's lives. By Mill's reasoning, people who object to pleasure as the ultimate aim
of life probably interpret it too narrowly as something base.

According to Mill, once people are made aware of the differences between higher and lower
pleasures, they do not, and will not, accept any definition of happiness that does not include the
development of their nobler and distinctively human faculties. He writes,

> Now it is an unquestionable fact that those who are equally acquainted with and equally
> capable of appreciating and enjoying both [kinds of pleasure] do give a most marked
> preference to the manner of existence which employs their higher faculties. Few human
> creatures would consent to be changed into any of the lower animals for a promise of the
> fullest allowance of a beast's pleasures; no intelligent human being would consent to be a fool,
> no instructed person would be an ignoramus, no person of feeling and conscience would be
> selfish and base, even though they should be persuaded that the fool, the dunce, or the
> rascal is better satisfied with his lot than they are with theirs.[2]

From the quotation above, we see how Mill concludes that higher pleasures are better.
They should be preferred because they are, in fact, favoured by anyone familiar with both types
of pleasure. Besides this, mental pleasures are thought to be superior to bodily pleasures because
they offer greater **permanency**, **safety** and **uncostliness**. There is nothing in higher pleasures themselves that make them superior; their superiority is located in their circumstantial
advantages. Let us take the drinking of alcohol to illustrate the point. The experience of going
out on an alcoholic binge may be intensely pleasurable for any given individual. Stress is
relieved, inhibitions disappear and all sensations are heightened. (Sound like last weekend?) The
pleasure derived from an alcoholic binge, however, is short-lived; overconsumption of alcohol
is likely to harm one's liver and impair, or otherwise negatively affect, one's brain. With current
costs and levels of taxation in this country, going out drinking is also very likely to require a
significant outlay of money. Once the numbing bodily pleasure that is derived from alcohol
has disappeared, you may, like so many others, experience negative after-effects, such as a hang-
over and an empty wallet. While intoxicated, you may have said and done things that you now
regret. So not only was the pleasure short-lived, it cost you a lot and may even have placed
your personal safety at risk. Let's say you were feeling so "good" last night that you did not

worry about driving home drunk. Now that you are sober again, you cannot believe what a stupid thing you did.

In contrast to the physical pleasure obtained from the intoxicating effects of alcohol, consider the more refined pleasure of listening to beautiful music or appreciating nature or art. Such things present no danger and they are typically inexpensive. Watching a sunset or listening to the sounds of a babbling brook costs nothing; listening to the radio will cost you a few cents on your electricity bill. The after-effects of higher pleasures are also preferable. Rather than feel emptiness, regret or disgust, one is more likely to feel ennobled and spiritually uplifted as a result of cultivating one's mind and the **higher faculties**. The higher pleasures of the mind appeal to our sense of human dignity, not to our base appetites which we share with animals.

HIGHER PLEASURES CAN BE RISKY BUSINESS

As suggested, higher pleasures are probably safer than most physical pleasures or those associated with appetite gratification. This is not to say, however, that pursuit of higher pleasure is totally without risk. Mill writes:

> *It's better to be a human being dissatisfied, than a pig satisfied; better to be Socrates dissatisfied than a fool satisfied.*
>
> J.S. MILL

A being of higher faculties requires more to make him happy, is capable of probably more acute suffering, and certainly accessible to it at more points, than one of an inferior type; but in spite of these liabilities, he can never really wish to sink into what he feels to be a lower grade of existence. [3]

The **inferior type** of individual is more likely to find contentment in the lower pleasures of life than the **superior type**, who perceives most sources of happiness in the world as imperfect. Nonetheless, the superior type can learn to bear these worldly imperfections and be satisfied with the exercise of her higher faculties. Mill believes that it is the **sense of dignity**, abundant in the higher type, that makes objects of lower pleasure undesirable or at least less desirable than those things that are humanly elevating. As illustrated by the quote above, Mill equates the inferior type's lifestyle with animal-level existence.

Individuals of the superior type may experience greater frustration in pursuit of higher pleasures, and also risk occasionally (or frequently) succumbing to temptations—that is, opting for pleasures of a lower sort. This fact poses no obstacles for Mill. People may be perfectly aware,

---

PHILOSOPHERS AT WORK

Mill's emphasis on the higher pleasures and the higher faculties of humankind is reminiscent of another philosopher we have studied in this text. Who is that philosopher and what does he have in common with Mill?

for instance, that sexual indulgence (e.g., sexual appetite satisfaction with a prostitute) could injure their health through sexually transmitted diseases, and may understand that health is a greater good compared with such indulgence, yet still opt to take that risk. Apart from improper development and moral weakness, or what Mill calls **infirmity of character**, the problem is that once people have devoted themselves to lower pleasures (more easily obtained), they may become incapable of enjoying the higher type. In this regard, Mill says,

> Capacity for the nobler feelings is in most natures a very tender plant, easily killed, not only by hostile influences, but by more want of sustenance; and in the majority of young persons it speedily dies away if the occupations to which their position in life has devoted them, and the society into which it has thrown them, are not favourable to keeping that higher capacity in exercise. Men lose their high aspirations as they lose their intellectual tastes, because they have not time or opportunity for indulging them; and they addict themselves to inferior pleasures, not because they deliberately prefer them, but because they are either the only ones to which they have access or the only ones which they are any longer capable of enjoying.[4]

BREAKS FROM BENTHAM

By making a distinction between higher and lower pleasures, Mill's defence of utilitarianism represents a significant departure from Bentham's original position. Clearly, for Mill, not all pleasures are equal; pushpin and pinball are not as good as poetry. The standard of goodness in behaviour, therefore, no longer involves the simple maximization of pleasure; rather, it involves the fulfillment of our distinctively human faculties. As one writer puts it, "if it is better to be Socrates dissatisfied than a pig satisfied, morality is proportionate to the happiness we find in being truly human and not in the pleasure we experience."[5] Given these remarks, it becomes a debatable point whether or not Mill actually abandoned utilitarianism for something else he called by the same name. This is something to think about. Nonetheless, support for the notion that Mill remains a full-fledged utilitarian can be mustered by pointing out that he has not abandoned pleasure as the ultimate standard of morality, only that he has opted for a higher standard not recognized by Bentham.

PHILOSOPHERS AT WORK

Think about all the sources of pleasure and amusement in today's popular culture. Do they nourish and cultivate our higher natures or feed our lower and base instincts? Explain and illustrate. When it comes to encouraging proper character development, is there anything that we as a society need to do? If so, what and why? If not, why not?

EGOISTIC VERSUS ALTRUISTIC UTILITARIANISM

Earlier, in our examination of Jeremy Bentham, we learned how he was both a psychological and ethical hedonist. Not only did Bentham believe that we are designed by nature to seek

> ... *the happiness which forms the utilitarian standard of what is right in conduct is not the agent's own happiness, but that of all concerned.*
>
> J.S. MILL

pleasure and to avoid pain, he also believed that, morally speaking, that is what we ought to do. As a psychological and ethical hedonist, Bentham was in favour of **enlightened self-interest**. He wished to harmonize the interests of the individual with the interests of society. He maintained that communities and societies are nothing more than collections of individuals, so that by furthering individual interests, what we can do, in effect, is promote the common good and benefit the larger community or society of which the individual is a part. The problem, for Bentham, was that he believed individuals are egoistic, at bottom, and therefore not naturally inclined to deny themselves pleasures for others. Nonetheless, he felt that with a solidly engineered system of sanctions, they could learn to respond to social and legal punishments and rewards egoistically—so that their self-interested pursuits would, in the end, benefit society. Hedonic calculations were supposed to be performed from the vantage point of the individual(s) whose interests were most directly affected in any given situation or set of circumstances.

With John Stuart Mill, we find a significant movement away from the egoistic utilitarianism of Bentham. Although, like Bentham, Mill is in favour of promoting "the greatest happiness for the greatest number," his approach to accomplishing this end is different. First, when it comes to deciding what one ought to do, the person making the decision can assume no special or preferred status. Mill writes, "The happiness which forms the utilitarian standard of what is right in conduct is not the agent's own happiness but that of all concerned. As between his own happiness and that of others, utilitarianism requires him to be as strictly impartial as a disinterested and benevolent spectator."[6]

If one's own personal interests have no special or preferred place in utilitarian decision making, then the right thing to do may not always be what benefits the doer most. Doing the right thing may sometimes require **personal sacrifice** or **altruism**—namely, putting others' interests before one's own, doing things for their sake. Of course, as a utilitarian, Mill is opposed to self-sacrifice where it does not increase the sum total of happiness, or create the greatest happiness for the greatest number. Simply to deny oneself is to cause frustration, pain or suffering—things that have only **disutility**. There is no virtue in the reduction of pleasure when it is unnecessary. In the ideal scenario, "laws and social arrangements should place the happiness or... the interest of every individual as nearly as possible in harmony with the interest of the whole." If there is an identity of interests between the individual and the community, then self-sacrifice will usually be unnecessary because in doing things that benefit others, one in turn benefits oneself. If proper social engineering and character education occur, the impulse or inclination to promote the general good will become an habitual motive of action." Given man's social instincts, Mill held that "any morally educated person can come to desire the happiness of others as an essential element in his own welfare."[7] In view of this, Mill defends utilitarianism against those critics who regard it as little more than a base or convenient morality of self-interest. As we see, Mill's **altruistic utilitarianism** contains feelings for humanity and a disinterested and impartial pursuit of the good. His suggestion that we seek the greatest happiness is not always, or necessarily, my (or your) greatest happiness, but the greatest happiness of the greatest number.

MILL'S REJECTION OF THE HEDONIC CALCULUS

Another of Mill's significant departures from Bentham is on the issue of calculating pleasures. Bentham believed that by means of the **hedonic calculus** one could quantify pleasures and determine, in a spirit of scientific objectivity, what action or policy would be likely to result in the best consequences or greatest utility. Mill, on the other hand, does not believe that pleasure and pain can be calculated in Bentham's sense. He asks,

> What means are there of determining which is the acutest of two pains, or the intensest of two pleasurable sensations, except the general suffrage [opinion or vote] of those who are familiar with both? Neither pains nor pleasures are homogeneous, and pain is always heterogeneous with pleasure. What is there to decide whether a particular pleasure is worth purchasing at the cost of a particular pain, except the feelings and judgment of the experienced?[8]

Above, we see that Mill regards pains and pleasures as **incommensurable**. One cannot compare pain and pleasure because they are essentially different in kind. In the same section of *Utilitarianism* from which the quotation above was taken, Mill asserts that it is only those who have knowledge of both higher and lower pleasures that should have the final say when decisions between the two must be made. When these "experienced" people conflict among themselves, then majority opinion should rule. Whether it be the majority or the experienced knowledgeable individual who decides, however, it is only a "preference" for one pleasure over another that can be expressed. Apart from this, there is no impartial tribunal where some kind of objective calculation can be performed.

REDUCING HUMAN MISERY

John Stuart Mill recognizes that from some moral perspectives it could be argued that human beings have no "right" to be happy and, therefore, are not necessarily entitled to happiness. In fact, historically, many religious people have felt that happiness is God's eternal reward in heaven for living a morally good life on earth. By displaying the virtues of faith, hope and charity, many people believe they can earn the right to be eternally happy at God's right hand (or should I say left hand?) side. Despite the objections to our entitlement to be happy, Mill continues his defence of utilitarianism by asserting that we have at least a moral duty to prevent or

> *In the golden rule of Jesus of Nazareth, we read the complete spirit of the ethics of utility. "To do as you would be done by" and "to love your neighbor as yourself," constitute the ideal perfection of utilitarian morality.*
>
> J.S. MILL

to reduce unhappiness. Whenever possible, we should make efforts to eliminate or at least to mitigate pain and suffering. Doing this is, of course, part of the utilitarian prescription for life.

Even people who claim no entitlements to happiness would likely be in favour of reducing human suffering in the world. On this note, Mill believes that many of the world's evils, which cause unhappiness, can be eradicated. Poverty is one example. Mill contends that this social ailment can be cured by the wisdom of society and the good sense of individuals. Disease, another evil, can certainly be reduced by proper physical and moral education. Mill states that,

> All the grand sources, in short, of human suffering are in a great degree, many of them almost entirely, conquerable by human care and effort; and though their removal is grievously slow— though a long succession of generations will perish in the breach before the conquest is completed, and this world becomes all that, if will and knowledge were not wanting, it might easily be made—yet every mind sufficiently intelligent and generous to bear a part, however small and inconspicuous, in the endeavor will draw a noble enjoyment from the contest itself, which he would not for any bribe in the form of selfish indulgence consent to be without.[9]

Let us say, hypothetically, that we could ensure people's health and that we could redistribute the wealth in the land so that everybody had more than enough to survive. Would they necessarily be happy then? The answer is probably no. Although people may not suffer any great physical pains or mental anguish resulting from maltreatment or some kind of economic or political injustice, happiness may, nonetheless, elude them. Mill has a psychological explanation for this. He maintains that for people who are "fortunate in their outward lot [and who] do not find in life sufficient enjoyment to make it valuable to them the cause generally is caring for nobody but themselves."[10] Apart from **selfishness**, "the principle cause which makes life unsatisfactory is want of **mental cultivation**".[11] The uncultivated mind is surrounded by many possible sources of pleasure, yet it discovers few lasting ones. It is continuously bored and searching for something else. The cultivated mind, by contrast, finds endless pleasure in all that surrounds it—in natural beauty, the cultural and artistic achievements of society, the drama of history, the workings and development of human civilization, and the prospects for the future of humanity.

If you think about it for a moment, Mill is probably right to suggest that there is enough that is interesting and enjoyable in life to make everyone happy, at least in principle. For example, as someone who lives in Oakville, Ontario, Canada, I am often overwhelmed to think that I live in one of the best countries in the world; that I live in one of the safest and most prosper-

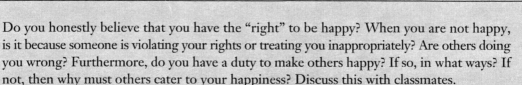

PHILOSOPHERS AT WORK

Do you honestly believe that you have the "right" to be happy? When you are not happy, is it because someone is violating your rights or treating you inappropriately? Are others doing you wrong? Furthermore, do you have a duty to make others happy? If so, in what ways? If not, then why must others cater to your happiness? Discuss this with classmates.

ous communities in that best-ten nation; that I am surrounded by all forms of entertainment and amusement; that science and technology bring the stars and continents to my doorstep (or at least to my television set and computer terminal); that, arguably, I enjoy one of the best educational and health-care systems on the planet; that so much knowledge and opportunity is available to me; that I can enjoy peace in the land and live harmoniously with friends and family, and so on and so on. What kind of mind must it take to be bored and dissatisfied with all of this? For Mill, it would have to be an uncultivated mind that lacks appreciation and yearns only for the lower pleasures of self-indulgence. It is only the uncultivated mind that has not developed a sincere interest in the public good and can take no pleasure in the satisfaction of others. It is the uncultivated mind that does not, or is unable to, enjoy the improvement of the human condition. By contrast, the cultivated mind can find happiness in working for the common good, appreciating the abundance of life, satisfying curiosity, and pursuing higher intellectual interests. For Mill, happiness is not about living for oneself in a selfish, egoistic fashion, and it would be misinterpreting him to say that his utilitarian philosophy suggests this. Mill's utilitarianism is designed to lead to a reduction of suffering and misery in the world and to an increase in human happiness.

DEMOCRACY AND THE PROPER LIMITS OF GOVERNMENTAL AUTHORITY

Considerations of self-development and the greatest happiness principle led Mill to reflect on the proper relationships that should exist between the individual and the state. In his work entitled *On Liberty*, Mill addressed the issue of **social liberty**. In it he asked about the nature and limits of the power that can be legitimately exercised by society over the individual. Though Mill was in favour of **democracy** as the best form of government to further individual growth and

> *Whatever crushes individuality is despotism, by whatever name it may be called.*
>
> J.S. MILL

development, as well as the common good, he was, nonetheless, aware of its inherent dangers and he cautioned against abuses of governmental control. For example, in a democracy, things typically get done by majority rule. This allows for the possibility that the majority may choose

PHILOSOPHERS AT WORK

Part One: Are there any identifiable minorities in history or in contemporary North American society that, arguably, have suffered at the hands of the majority? Name those minorities and describe the nature of the oppression or injustice perpetrated against them.

Part Two: Are there any state, provincial or federal laws that in your estimation, or in the estimation of others, violate individual rights by regulating what should be considered a matter of personal choice or private conduct? What are some of those controversial laws?

to oppress the minority. A type of coercion may also arise involving the tyranny of public opinion. Society may impose, by means other than laws and civil penalties, certain ideas and practices as rules of acceptable conduct on everyone, including dissenters.

Aware of the potential problems inherent in democracy, Mill claims, "There is a limit to the legitimate interference of collective opinion with individual independence: and to find that limit, and maintain it against encroachment, is as indispensable to a good condition of human affairs, as protection against political despotism."[12] Put simply, Mill believed that an acceptable form of democratic government should include certain safeguards. These safeguards should be designed to defend against the forces that would hinder individuals from realizing themselves and their goals in a free and open fashion. Let us turn now to the "Back to the Source" feature to read exactly what Mill does argue on the proper limits of government.

BACK TO THE SOURCE*

The object of this Essay is to assert one very simple principle, as entitled to govern absolutely the dealings of society with the individual in the way of compulsion and control, whether the means used be physical force in the form of legal penalties, or the moral coercion of public opinion. That principle is, that the sole end for which mankind are warranted, individually or collectively, in interfering with the liberty of action of any of their number, is self-protection. That the only purpose for which power can be rightfully exercised over any member of a civilized community, against his will, is to prevent harm to others. His own good, either physical or moral, is not a sufficient warrant. He cannot rightfully be compelled to do or forebear because it will be better for him to do so, because it will make him happier, because, in the opinions of others, to do so would be wise, or even right. These are good reasons for remonstrating with him, or reasoning with him, or persuading him, or entreating him, but not for compelling him, or visiting him with any evil in case he do otherwise. To justify that, the conduct from which it is desired to deter him must be calculated to produce evil to some one else. The only part of the conduct of any one, for which he is amenable to society, is that which concerns others. In the part which merely concerns himself, his independence is, of right, absolute. Over himself, over his own body and mind, the individual is sovereign.

It is, perhaps hardly necessary to say that this doctrine is meant to apply only to human beings in the maturity of their faculties. We are not speaking of children, or of young persons below the age which the law may fix as that of manhood or womanhood.

*From Mill, On Liberty.

Those who are still in a state to require being taken care of by others, must be protected against their own actions as well as against external injury. For the same reason, we may leave out of consideration those backward states of society in which the race itself may be considered as in its nonage. The early difficulties in the way of spontaneous progress are so great, that there is seldom any choice of means for overcoming them; and a ruler full of the spirit of improvement is warranted in the use of any expedients that will attain an end, perhaps otherwise unattainable. Despotism is a legitimate mode of government in dealing with barbarians, provided the end be their improvement, and the means justified by actually effecting that end. Liberty, as a principle, has no application to any state of things anterior to the time when mankind have become capable of being improved by free and equal discussion. Until then, there is nothing for them but implicit obedience to an Akbar or a Charlemagne, if they are so fortunate as to find one. But as soon as mankind have attained the capacity of being guided to their own improvement by conviction or persuasion (a period long since reached in all nations with whom we need here concern ourselves), compulsion, either in the direct form or in that of pains and penalties for non-compliance, is no longer admissible as a means to their own good, and justifiable only for the security of others.

It is proper to state that I forego any advantage which could be derived to my argument from the idea of abstract right, as a thing independent of utility. I regard utility as the ultimate appeal on all ethical questions; but it must be utility in the largest sense, grounded on the permanent interests of man as a progressive being. Those interests, I contend, authorize the subjection of individual spontaneity to external control, only in respect to those actions of each, which concern the interest of other people. If any one does an act hurtful to others, there is a *prima facie* case for punishing him, by law, or, where legal penalties are not safely applicable, by general disapprobation. There are also many positive acts for the benefit of others, which he may rightfully be compelled to perform; such as to give evidence in a court of justice; to bear his fair share in the common defense, or in any other joint work necessary to the interest of the society of which he enjoys the protection; and to perform certain acts of individual beneficence, such as saving a fellow-creature's life, or interposing to protect the defenseless against ill-usage, things which whenever it is obviously a man's duty to do, he may rightfully be made responsible to society for not doing. A person may cause evil to others not only by his actions but by his inaction, and in either case he is justly accountable to them for the injury. The latter case, it is true, requires a much more cautious exercise of compulsion than the former. To make any one answerable for doing evil to others is the rule; to make him answerable for not preventing evil is, comparatively speaking, the exception. Yet there are many cases clear enough and grave enough to justify that exception. In all things which regard the external relations of the individual, he is *de jure* amenable to those whose interests are concerned, and, if need be, to society as their protector. There are often good reasons for not holding him to the responsibility; but these reasons must arise from the special expediencies of the case: either because it is a kind of case in which he is on the whole likely to act better, when left to his own discretion, than when controlled in any way in which society have it in their power to control him; or because the attempt to exercise control would produce other evils, greater than those which it would prevent. When such reasons as these preclude the enforcement of responsibility, the conscience of the agent himself should step into the vacant judgment seat, and protect those interests of others which have no external protection; judging himself all the more rigidly, because the case does not admit of his being made accountable to the judgment of his fellow-creatures.

But there is a sphere of action in which society, as distinguished from the individual, has, if any, only an indirect interest; comprehending all that portion of a person's life and conduct which affects only himself, or if it also affects others, only with their free, voluntary, and undeceived consent and participation. When I say only himself, I mean directly, and in the first instance; for whatever affects himself, may affect others *through* himself; and the objection which may be grounded on this contingency, will receive consideration in the sequel. This, then, is the appropriate region of human liberty. It comprises, first, the inward domain of consciousness; demanding liberty of conscience in the most comprehensive sense; liberty of thought and feeling; absolute freedom of opinion and sentiment on all subjects, practical or speculative, scientific, moral, or theological. The liberty of expressing and publishing opinions may seem to fall under a different principle, since it belongs to that part of the conduct of an individual which concerns other people; but, being almost of as much importance as the liberty of thought itself, and resting in great part on the same reasons, is practically inseparable from it. Secondly, the principle requires liberty of tastes and pursuits; of framing the plan of our life to suit our own character; of doing as we like, subject to such consequences as may follow; without impediment from our fellow-creatures, so long as what we do does not harm them, even though they should think our conduct foolish, perverse, or wrong. Thirdly, from this liberty of each individual, follows the liberty, within the same limits, of combination among individuals; freedom to unite, for any purpose not involving harm to others: the persons combining being supposed to be of full age, and not forced or deceived.

No society in which these liberties are not, on the whole, respected, is free, whatever may be its form of government; and none is completely free in which they do not exist absolute and unqualified. The only freedom which deserves the name, is that of pursuing our own good in our own way, so long as we do not attempt to deprive others of theirs, or impede their efforts to obtain it. Each is the proper guardian of his own health, whether bodily, or mental and spiritual. Mankind are greater gainers by suffering each other to live as seems good for themselves, than by compelling each to live as seems good for the rest.

Though this doctrine is anything but new, and, to some persons, may have the air of a truism, there is no doctrine which stands more directly opposed to the general tendency of existing opinion and practice. Society has expended fully as much effort in the attempt (according to its lights) to compel people to conform to its notions of personal [and] of social excellence. The ancient commonwealths thought themselves entitled to practice, and the ancient philosophers countenanced, the regulation of every part of private conduct by public authority, on the ground that the State had a deep interest in the whole bodily and mental discipline of every one of its citizens; a mode of thinking which may have been admissible in small republics surrounded by powerful enemies, in constant peril of being subverted by foreign attack or internal commotion, and to which even a short interval of relaxed energy and self-command might so easily be fatal that they could not afford to wait for the salutary permanent effects of freedom. In the modern world, the greater size of political communities, and, above all, the separation between spiritual and temporal authority (which placed the direction of men's consciences in other hands than those which controlled their worldly affairs), prevented so great an interference by law in the details of private life; but the engines of moral repression have been wielded more strenuously against divergence from the reigning opinion in self-regarding, than even in social matters; religion, the most powerful of the elements which have entered into the formation of moral feeling, having almost always been governed either by the ambition of a hierarchy, seeking control over every department of human conduct, or by the spirit of Puritanism. And some of those modern reformers who have placed themselves in strongest opposition to the religions of the past, have been noway behind either churches or sects in their assertion of the right of spiritual domination: M. Comte, in particular, whose social systems, as unfolded in his *Système de Politique Positive*, aims at establishing (though by moral more than by legal appliances) a despotism of society over the individual, surpassing anything contemplated in the political ideal of the most rigid disciplinarian among the ancient philosophers.

Apart from the peculiar tenets of individual thinkers, there is also in the world at large an increasing inclination to stretch unduly the powers of society over the individual, both by the force of opinion and even by that of legislation; and as the tendency of all the changes taking place in the world is to strengthen society, and diminish the power of the individual, this encroachment is not one of the evils which tend spontaneously to disappear, but, on the contrary, to grow more and more formidable. The disposition of mankind, whether as rulers or as fellow-citizens, to impose their own opinions and inclinations as a rule of conduct on others, is so energetically supported by some of the best and by some of the worst feelings incident to human nature, that it is hardly ever kept under restraint by anything but want of power: and as the power is not declining, but growing, unless a strong barrier of moral conviction can be raised against the mischief, we must expect, in the present circumstances of the world, to see it increase.

It will be convenient for the argument, if, instead of at once entering upon the general thesis, we confine ourselves in the first instance to a single branch of it, on which the principle here stated is, if not fully, yet to a certain point, recognized by the current opinions. This one branch is the Liberty of Thought: from which it is impossible to separate the cognate liberty of speaking and of writing. Although these liberties, to some considerable amount, form part of the political morality of all countries which profess religious toleration and free institutions, the grounds, both philosophical and practical, on which they rest, are perhaps not so familiar to the general mind, nor so thoroughly appreciated by many even of the leaders of opinion, as might have been expected. Those grounds, when rightly understood, are of much wider application than to only one division of the subject, and a thorough consideration of this part of the question will be found the best introduction to the remainder. Those to whom nothing which I am about to say will be new, may therefore, I hope, excuse me, if on a subject which for now three centuries has been so often discussed, I venture on one discussion more.

KEY TERMS

principle of utility
utilitarianism
quantity
quality
higher
lower
bodily pleasures
intellect
feelings
imagination
moral sentiments
human dignity
permanency
safety
uncostliness
higher faculties

inferior type
superior type
sense of dignity
infirmity of character
enlightened self-interest
personal sacrifice
altruism
disutility
altruistic utilitarianism
hedonic calculus
incommensurable
selfishness
mental cultivation
social liberty
democracy

PROGRESS CHECK 4.1

Instructions: Fill in the blanks with the appropriate responses listed below.

intellect
inferior type
disutility
entitlements
quality
sense of dignity
egoistic

democracy
principle of utility
incommensurable
infirmity of character
mental cultivation
selfishness

1. Mill's acceptance of utilitarianism became a defence of the _principle of utility_

2. Whereas all pleasures are equal for Bentham, J.S. Mill distinguishes between two types in regard to their _quality_

3. Higher pleasures are those that are satisfying to the _intellect_ and to our moral sentiments.

4. The higher pleasures contribute to our _sense of dignity_

5. For Mill, those people who pursue lower pleasures are, by definition, _inferior type_ individuals.

6. Regardless of who you are, it is likely that you will sometimes fall prey to your lower appetites because of a(n) _infirmity of character_

7. Jeremy Bentham's utilitarianism is more _egotistic_ than Mill's, whose ethics may require self-sacrifice and acting for the benefit of others.

8. Self-sacrifice, in itself, is not a virtue; in fact, it has _disutility_ and should be avoided except in cases where it is necessary to promote the greatest happiness for the greatest number.

9. The hedonic calculus should be rejected, according to Mill, because pains and pleasures are _incommensurable_.

10. Historically speaking, many people have opposed the pursuit of pleasure, denying that humans have any _entitlement_ to happiness.

11. People who appear to have everything that is necessary to be happy but who still do not find sufficient enjoyment in life probably suffer from _selfishness_ and lack of _mental cultivation_.

12. According to Mill, the best form of government is _democracy_.

SUMMARY OF MAJOR POINTS

1. **What was Bentham's influence on Mill?**

   Mill accepted Bentham's principle of utility as the standard of morality.
   In its defence, Mill articulated his own version of utilitarian ethics.

2. **How are pleasures distinguished?**

   Pleasures are distinguished in terms of quality.
   Some pleasures are higher, or better, and others are lower and inferior.
   Lower pleasures are bodily and physical.
   Higher pleasures relate to the intellect, imagination, moral sentiments and dignity of persons.
   Higher pleasures tend to possess greater permanency, safety and uncostliness; they are also ennobling, satisfying and enduring.

3. **How are higher pleasures risky?**

   Pursuit of higher pleasures may cause sensitive, superior-type individuals to suffer more acutely.
   Higher pleasures require stronger character and are more difficult to attain.

4. **What are the basic philosophical differences between Mill and Bentham?**

   Bentham sees pleasure only in terms of quantity; Mill makes a distinction between quantity and quality.
   Mill's utilitarianism is more altruistic and less egoistic than Bentham's.
   Mill rejects Bentham's hedonic calculus.

5. What are Mill's views on human misery?

    People have a duty to minimize suffering.

    Much of misery is humanly caused and, therefore, humanly correctable.

    Lack of personal enjoyment in life results from selfishness and want of mental cultivation.

6. How does Mill conceptualize the relationship between government and the individual?

    Democracy is the best form of government to allow individual self-expression and self-fulfillment.

    The government should maximize individual liberties within limits.

    Constraining limits can and should be placed on individuals' actions that would harm other people.

SOURCE REFERENCES AND RELATED READINGS

Anschutz, R.P. *The Philosophy of J.S. Mill.* New York: Oxford, 1953.

Borchard, R. *John Stuart Mill: The Man.* London: Penguin, 1957.

Copleston, Frederick. *A History of Philosophy.* Vol. VIII. New York: Doubleday, 1994.

Falikowski, Anthony. *Moral Philosophy: Theories, Skills, and Applications.* Upper Saddle River, N.J.: Prentice Hall, 1990.

Hearn, Thomas K., (ed.) *Studies in Utilitarianism*, New York: Appleton Century-Crofts, 1971.

Mill, J.S. *Utilitarianism.* ed. Oscar Piest. Indianapolis, Ind.: Bobbs-Merrill, 1957.

———. *On Liberty.* ed. David Spitz. New York: W.W. Norton & Co., 1975.

Stumpf, Samuel, *Philosophy*, 3rd edition. New York: McGraw-Hill, 1983.

———. *Philosophy: History and Problems*, 5th edition. New York: McGraw-Hill, Inc., 1994, Chapter 19, pp. 372–79.

ENDNOTES

1. Samuel Stumpf, *Philosophy*, 3rd edition. New York: McGraw-Hill, 1983, p.372.

2. J.S. Mill, *Utilitarianism*, ed. Oscar Piest. pp. 12–13.

3. ibid., p.13.

4. ibid., pp.14–15.

5. Stumpf, ibid., p. 376.

6. ibid., p. 348.

7. Thomas Hearn Jr., ed. *Studies in Utilitarianism.* New York: Appleton Century-Crofts, 1971.

8. ibid.., p. 348.

9. J.S. Mill, ibid., p. 20.

10. Mill, ibid., p. 18.

11. ibid.

12. ibid., p. 6.

Deontological Ethics

At this juncture of Part One, we move on to deontological ethics. Over the course of history, different variations of this type of ethical theory have emerged, but most philosophers today would probably associate this descriptive label with a "rule or duty-based morality" or one that emphasizes right action (rightness) over good consequences (goodness). From this perspective, morally acceptable behaviour is a matter of adhering to rationally consistent principles or following acceptable rules of conduct, not promoting utility or people's happiness. It is also not about harmonizing the soul or developing character, though doing what is right would, no doubt, often be conducive to the achievement of such things. In any case, acting "on principle" or "for the sake of duty," rather than for one's own benefit or that of "the greatest number," captures the spirit of the deontological position, certainly for Immanuel Kant, the first deontologist we will discuss in Chapter Five.

In Chapter Six, we will take a brief look at the moral theory of John Rawls, someone who has extended and given contemporary expression to many of Kant's insights and, more generally, to the philosophical social contract tradition. Like Kant, Rawls has eliminated, as much as possible, contaminating empirical variables from moral decision making and has tried to set up fair and impartial procedures of social conflict resolution. He has endeavoured to remove subjective and other biasing factors that often impact on moral action and deliberation. As one who, like Kant, emphasizes right action over utility maximization, Rawls has attempted to abstract from the content of moral experience (social conflict in particular) those general ethical principles that can serve as the moral foundations for society and our socio-political institutions. On the basis of his rational abstractions and investigations, he concludes that the principle of "justice as fairness" is to be preferred over other alternatives like utility or intuition. He uses this principle to illustrate how rights and duties are correlative and how as rational, autonomous agents, we are all bound by the same moral rules as the members of a just society. With this in mind, let us proceed to discover what, if anything, the ethics of Kant and Rawls have to offer us in the development of our personal moral philosophies.

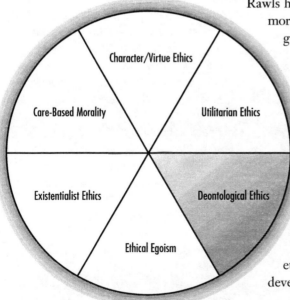

CHAPTER FIVE

Immanuel Kant:
For the Sake of Duty

Overview

Learning Outcomes

After successfully completing this chapter,
you will be able to
• provide the Kantian basis of morality
  and contrast it with the foundations provided by other philosophers discussed
  previously in this text;
• explain why morality must be *a priori*;
• give reasons why "the good will" is the
  only thing good in itself;
• define moral duty and distinguish it
  from prudence and inclination;
• understand the differences among
  actions that are moral, nonmoral and
  immoral;
• appreciate how morality entails universal duties to oneself and to others;
• give two definitions of the categorical
  imperative;
• explain what is meant by Kantian formalism;
• distinguish between hypothetical and
  categorical imperatives;
• comment on the importance of personal
  autonomy in morality.

PHILOSOPHICAL FOCUS QUESTIONS

1. What has served as the philosophical foundation for morality in the past? What does Kant use as his foundation?

2. What is wrong with basing morality on people's actual behaviour?

3. In what does Immanuel Kant find true moral goodness?

4. What role does "duty" play in Kantian ethics?

5. What are maxims? How are they tied in with morality?

6. How is Kantian formalism to be understood? What are the formal criteria of distinctively moral maxims?

7. What, for Kant, is the ultimate principle of morality? What are two of its formulations?

8. How are hypothetical imperatives different from categorical ones?

9. Why is autonomy of the will important for morality?

P.H. Inc. College Archives

Immanuel Kant
(1724–1804)

Biographical Brief*

Immanuel Kant was born in 1724 in the East Prussian town of Königsberg. Belonging to the lower middle class, his parents were deeply religious. Although Kant always maintained an honest respect for religion and a deep moral sense throughout his life, he eventually abandoned the puritanical pietism that had been a dominating influence in his family. Immanuel Kant's life could hardly be described as eventful and is now famous for its routine.

He arose the same time each day and had a fixed hour for all of his daily activities. It has been said that people could set their clocks by Kant's afternoon walks at half past three. Each day he would put on his grey coat and with bamboo cane in hand would walk down Lime Tree Avenue, now called "Philosopher's Walk" in honour of Kant. While Kant had many friends and associates, he never married and in contrast to many of his contemporaries who were filled with the spirit of travel, he never ventured more than about 40 miles in any direction away from Königsberg. This lack of physical travel apparently did not affect his wandering intellectual genius, however. For more than a dozen years, he lectured as a *privatdozent* at the University of Königsberg in subjects as varied as mathematics, logic, geography, history and philosophy. He also worked as a family tutor before being appointed professor of philosophy at the University of Königsberg in 1770. Kant is considered by many philosophers today as the greatest thinker since Plato and Aristotle. His influence is evident insofar as his ethical investigations still serve as the basis for much of the debate found in contemporary moral philosophy and applied ethics. His important works include: *Foundations of the Metaphysics of Morals, The Metaphysical Principles of Virtue, Lectures on Ethics,* and *The Critique of Pure Reason.*

*From Falikowski, Moral Philosophy: Theories, Skills and Applications, *p. 27.*

THE RATIONAL BASIS OF MORALITY

So far in our treatment of moral theories, we have learned how thinkers throughout the ages have sought the philosophical foundations of morality in different places and in different things.

> *Two things fill the mind with ever new and increasing admiration and awe... the starry heavens above and the moral law within.*
>
> IMMANUEL KANT

Recall, for example, how Bentham argued that the morality of particular actions could be established by reference to their consequences. For him, an action was good to the extent that it produced pleasure, bad to the extent that it caused pain. As a utilitarian, John Stuart Mill also saw the value of pleasure, distinguishing, in his case, between higher and lower types. Although he diverged from Bentham on this point, Mill, nonetheless, continued to consider his revised notion of utility as the ultimate criterion for determining the morality of actions. As **consequentialists**, what Mill and Bentham both would agree on is that the moral worth of particular actions can be evaluated by their results.

Remember how Plato, too, sought the basis of morality in his philosophical investigations. He eventually located moral goodness in a transcendent realm of forms—something timeless and spaceless, not visible or tangible, but knowable only through intellectual acquaintance. By contrast, his Greek friend Aristotle attempted to ground morality in human nature, common experience, and in humanity's pursuit of happiness and the good life. As we see, then, philosophers have struggled for centuries in their quest to find the basis of morality. In our continuing explorations into the moral domain, let us seek to uncover the philosophical footings supporting Kantian **deontological ethics**. It will be interesting to see what he bases morality on!

To start, you should note that Kant is in no way an **ethical relativist**, meaning that he does not regard morality as a matter of personal opinion or subjective preference; nor does he think that morality is ultimately dependent on cultural, historical or societal factors. It is undeniably true that people are different and often choose to differ with one another on moral matters. It is also certainly true that cultural practices vary throughout the world and that different values are held in higher or lower esteem depending on the society, group or nation involved. It cannot be denied as well that social values undergo changes and transformations over time—compare today's attitudes toward sexuality, for example, with those of the 1950s or Queen Victoria's era. Nevertheless, all of this variation does not lead Kant to the conclusion that everybody is morally right from their own viewpoint.

In recognition of human diversity and the fact that what people actually do, say, experience, believe, think, feel and value vary, Kant concludes that no **moral certainty** can be found there. If morality is to make any sense, and if it is to be considered valid and binding for all, then moral certainty must be found somewhere apart from the transitory and diverse world of everyday experience. For Kant, it is to be found in the **structure of reason** itself. The ultimate basis of morality must, for him, be **purely rational** or *a priori*, not in any way derived from experience or dependent upon it. For example, rational moralists would, no doubt, condemn the torturing of innocent children regardless of whether or not anybody actually engages in this practice and whether or not any society condones it. The moral judgment in this instance is not derived from experience or observation of people's behaviour. Such knowledge is *a priori* and independent of what people actually do. For Kant, it is up to the human sciences (e.g., anthropology, psychology and sociology) to inform us about human behaviour and the differences among people; it is philosophy's task to use reason to help us determine what is right and wrong. In support of Kant, one could argue that despite the apparent diversity easily observable among people throughout the world, the faculty of reason is the one common or universal element shared by all individuals regardless of time and place. Explaining why reason must be the basis of morality, Kant writes,

> Is it not of the utmost necessity to construct a pure moral philosophy which is completely freed from everything which may be only empirical and thus belong to anthropology? That there must be such a philosophy is self-evident from the common idea of duty and moral laws. Everyone must admit that a law, if it is to hold morally, i.e., as a ground of obligation, must imply absolute necessity; he must admit that the command, "Thou shalt not lie" does not apply to men only, as if other rational beings had no need to observe it. The same is true for all other moral laws properly so called. He must concede that the ground of obligation here must not be sought in the nature of man or in the circumstances in which he is placed, but sought *a priori* solely in the concepts of pure reason, and that every other precept which rests on principles of mere existence, even a precept which is in certain respects universal, so far as it leans in the least on empirical grounds (perhaps only in regard to the motive involved), be called a practical rule but never a moral law.[1]

THE CONCEPT OF THE GOOD WILL

In the First Section of the *Foundations of the Metaphysics of Morals*, Kant picks up on the idea that moral goodness is not something external or psychological. He recognizes that **talents of the mind** (e.g., intelligence, judgment and wit), **qualities of temperament** (e.g., courage, resoluteness, and perseverance) and **gifts of fortune** (e.g., power, riches, honour, and contentment, which contribute to happiness) may in many respects be good and desirable. He also underscores, however, the fact that all such things are not **unconditionally good**. Power, for instance, could lead to pride and arrogance if not corrected by reason and good will. The cool courage of a villain is not morally praiseworthy in itself, and the actions following from such a virtue are more likely to cause harm than to lead to ethically acceptable behaviour. **The good will** is, according to Kant, good even if it is

> *The good will is not good because of what it effects or accomplishes or because of its adequacy to achieve some proposed end; it is good only because of its willing, i.e., it is good of itself.*
> IMMANUEL KANT

PHILOSOPHERS AT WORK

In efforts to appreciate moral diversity, try to identify any norms, values and beliefs that conflict with one another. Such things could be personal, social, political, religious and so on. Once you have identified these different and conflicting values, think about the idea that not one of them is better or worse than any of the others. Do you agree? Would you necessarily be biased, chauvinistic or discriminatory if you suggested that some values, beliefs or norms were better than others? Does being tolerant of moral diversity mean that you are obligated to accept everyone's values no matter what? If you would be willing to criticize any value or norm as unacceptable, what would be the basis of your moral disagreement? Discuss.

Overtime Discussion: Is there something that makes people reluctant to criticize the values, behaviours or lifestyle choices of others? If so, what? Do we have any social responsibility to ensure that people make the right choices in their lives? Explain.

the good will is choosing la do will. that in itself is good.

prevented from achieving its purpose. The goodness of the good will is to be established solely by virtue of its willing. The motive to do the right thing for the right reason is enough to make the good will good. Kant says, "The good will is not good because of what it effects or accomplishes or because of its adequacy to achieve some proposed end; it is good only because of its willing, i.e., it is good of itself"[3] In view of this, people who are motivated and make efforts to do the right thing, but fail in their attempts, can still be seen to be acting morally. By contrast, people who somehow manage to achieve their ends or, say, enjoy uninterrupted happiness in life, but without the influence of good will motivating their behaviour, are not, in Kant's opinion, even worthy to be happy. Right things can be done for the wrong reasons. "Good" things like pleasure or happiness can result from moral injustices—a fact which calls into question the value of such things. This is why only a good will is unconditionally good.

When you exercise good will, you bring forward all the means in your power to do your **duty** (i.e., the right thing). Individuals are morally good or behave in a morally good fashion when they are motivated by the desire to do one's duty, simply for the sake of duty alone. The morally virtuous person is not concerned with maximizing people's happiness or cultivating moderation in one's lifestyle, but with doing what is required by **practical reason** (i.e., reason in its applications to morality). The moral quality of an act is, therefore, established by the rational principle to which the good will consciously assents.

THE NOTION OF DUTY

Still in the First Section of the *Foundations of the Metaphysics of Morals*, Kant gives us some insight into what he means by "duty," a basic building block of his ethical edifice. For Kant "Duty is the necessity of an action executed from respect for [moral] law."[4] He goes on to say, "An action performed from duty does not have its moral worth in the purpose which is to be achieved through it but in the **maxim** [i.e., rule of conduct] by which it is determined."[5] We will examine the formal characteristics of moral maxims, but first let us look at a couple of distinctions made by Kant.

> *Duty is the necessity of an action executed from respect for [moral] law.*
> IMMANUEL KANT

In Accordance with Duty, But not for Duty's Sake

Kant observes that some actions accord with duty, but are not performed for the sake of duty. In other words, people can act consistently with what duty requires, but still not act for the sake of duty or in recognition of the moral law. For example, maybe you have stopped yourself from stealing in the past, not because of any rational choice to do your ethical duty, but because you feared going to jail. If so, then doing the right thing out of fear or self-interest did not give your action any moral quality. Actions like this, performed in accordance with duty but not for duty's sake, do not belong to the moral domain. It is not that they are immoral; they are just not relevant to morality, having no moral status. For Kant, this example of non-stealing would be an instance of **prudence**, not morality. Doing what is in your self-interest because of self-interest alone is nonmoral behaviour. In *Foundations of the Metaphysics of Morals*, Kant offers an illustration from the world of business to support the point that not all actions in accordance with moral duty possess moral worth:

> It is in fact in accordance with duty that a dealer should not overcharge an inexperienced customer, and wherever there is much business the prudent merchant does not do so, having a fixed price for everyone, so that a child may buy of him as cheaply as any other. Thus, the customer is honestly served. But this is far from sufficient to justify the belief that the merchant has behaved in this way from duty and principle or honesty. His own advantage required this behaviour; but it cannot be assumed that over and above that he had a direct inclination to the purchaser and that, out of love, as it were, he gave none an advantage in price over another. Therefore, the action was done neither from duty nor from direct inclination, but only for a selfish purpose.[6]

In the example above the merchant did the "right" thing out of prudence, not morality. Again, it is not that the reason was wrong; it simply was not moral. It is worth noting, then, that actions can be **moral** (belonging to morality), **nonmoral** (not belonging to the moral domain) and **immoral** (wrong, bad or unjustifiable). To argue, as Kant does, that the merchant has acted prudently (out of his own advantage) is not to condemn him, nor is it to praise him morally.

In Accordance with Duty, But out of Inclination

To further clarify the nature of (moral) duty, Kant also distinguishes between actions performed out of **inclination** and those performed out of a recognition of duty. He argues that only the latter is genuinely moral. Suppose, for example, that you are the kind of person who is generally predisposed by temperament to act kindly or benevolently toward others. You simply like being nice to people. In fact, being nice to others is what comes naturally to you. If this were so, Kant would say that, as nice as you are, there is still no moral worth to your actions. It is not that you are morally corrupt or that you are doing anything wrong; it is just that the naturally inclined actions you perform have no moral worth. If this seems counter-intuitive, it will help to look at another example of action by inclination. Suppose, for instance, that a husband and wife are completely in love with one another and they both have no inclination to cheat on each other (i.e., each person is inclined to be faithful); should we praise the marital fidelity? From a Kantian perspective, the principle of fidelity is good (because it conforms to the moral law), but the husband or wife who is faithful in this case is not acting in a morally praiseworthy fashion. There was no action performed for the sake of duty. Had the person's inclinations been different (i.e., had the husband or wife been tempted), he or she might have cheated. Doing what you feel like doing without thought or recognition of ethical duty gives your action no moral worth. The **"motive"** behind the action determines its moral status. Distinguishing between inclination and duty, using kindness as an example, Kant writes,

> To be kind where one can is duty, and there are, moreover, many persons so sympathetically constituted that without any motive of vanity or selfishness they find an inner satisfaction in spreading joy, and rejoice in the contentment of others which they have made possible. But I say that, however dutiful and amiable it may be, that kind of action has no true moral worth.[7]

In Accordance with Duty, for the Sake of Duty

Well, if morality is not about natural inclination or prudence, then we are left needing further clarification. For Kant, a morally acceptable action must not only accord with duty (i.e., be consistent with it) but it must also be performed by the agent for the sake of duty. The individual must recognize what should be done and do it for that reason alone. "Duty for duty's sake" is another way of putting it. Even if doing the morally right thing is not something we are inclined to do at the moment, or if, say, the right action does not appear to produce the best consequences, duty may dictate that we do it nonetheless. To illustrate the moral priority of duty over inclination, Kant asks us to imagine a person whose life has been entirely clouded by sorrow. This person is miserable and all sympathetic feelings toward others have been extinguished. The person still possesses the means to help others and to improve their situations, but his deadened sensibility leaves him untouched by their unfortunate plight. Now, as Kant suggests, if this individual, who is wallowing in self-pity and has no desire or inclination to help others, tears himself away from his own preoccupations to assist another distressed person because of a recognition of duty, then his action assumes moral worth. The individual does what should be done, not out of natural inclination, but for the sake of duty. You could say, then, that a test of moral character is to discover whether one is strong enough to follow duty in spite of one's strong inclination not to do so.

> ... *The purposes we may have for our actions and their effects as ends and incentives of the will cannot give the actions any unconditional and moral worth.*
>
> IMMANUEL KANT

PHILOSOPHERS AT WORK

Immanuel Kant seems to make a lot of "distinctions" in his philosophical ethics. Are these distinctions just nitpicking or are they important? Do they add clarity or confusion? Also, would you agree that all moral action must be based on duty? Why or why not? How would Kant respond to Jeremy Bentham and his utilitarianism?

MORAL DUTIES TO ONESELF AND TO OTHERS

In *Lectures on Ethics*, Kant points out that moral duties include not only those obligations we have toward others, but also those we have toward ourselves. In other words, Kant allows for both personal and social dimensions of morality. This is not to suggest that personal morality is private and subjective or that duties to oneself are somehow conditional and not applicable to others. For Kant, there are duties that we all have toward ourselves and duties that we all have toward other

> *Suicide is not an abomination because God has forbidden it; it is forbidden by God because it is abominable.*
>
> KANT

people. Although it goes almost without saying that morality involves relations and duties to others, Kant contends that individual morality should not be regarded as an afterthought or an appendix to ethical inquiry. Too often moral discussion is restricted to social matters and interpersonal conflict. Kant insists, however, that "our duties towards ourselves are of primary importance and should have pride of place."[8] Arguing that we can expect nothing from someone who dishonours his own person, he maintains that "a prior condition of our **duties to others** is our **duty to ourselves**; we can fulfill the former only insofar as we first fulfill the latter."[9] To illustrate and support his point, Kant asks us to consider drunkards. Such people may do no harm to others and, provided their physical constitutions are strong, they may not even harm themselves. Nonetheless, Kant claims that drunkards become, for us, objects of moral contempt. Such individuals degrade themselves and damage their personal dignity. They lose their inner worth as moral subjects. Kant writes,

> Only if our worth as human beings is intact can we perform our other duties; for it is the foundation stone of all other duties. A man who has destroyed and cast away his personality, has no intrinsic worth, and can no longer perform any manner of duty.[10]

In *Lectures on Ethics*, Kant enumerates and explains a number of self-regarding and other-regarding duties. In the former category, we have duties of proper self-respect, self-mastery, duties concerning the body and duties concerning how we occupy ourselves in work and in play. In the latter category, we have duties to show respect for persons and to honour their inherent worth and dignity. Let us now turn to our "Back to the Source" feature to read what Kant says about "duties to oneself" and "duties to others."

BACK TO THE SOURCE*

Duties to Oneself

By way of introduction it is to be noted that there is no question in moral philosophy which has received more defective treatment than that of the individual's duty towards himself. No one has framed a proper concept of self-regarding duty. It has been regarded as a detail and considered by way of an afterthought, as an appendix to moral philosophy, on the view that man should give a thought to himself only after he has completely fulfilled his duty towards others. All moral philosophers err in this respect. Gellert[1] hardly even deserves mention here; it does not even occur to him to touch upon the question; he is constantly harping on benevolence and charity, the poet's hobbyhorses. Just as an innkeeper gives a thought to his own hunger when his customers have finished eating, so a man gives a thought to himself at the long last for fear that he might forget himself altogether! Hutcheson, too, although his thought is more philosophic, does not pass this test. The reason for all this is the want of a pure concept, which should form the basis of a self-regarding duty. It was taken for granted that a man's duty towards himself consisted, as Wolff in his turn defined it, in promoting his own happiness. In that case everything would depend on how an individual determined his own happiness; for our self-regarding duties would consist in the universal rule to satisfy all our inclinations in order to further our happiness. This would, however, militate seriously against doing our duty towards others. In fact, the principle of self-regarding duties is a very different one, which has no connexion with our well-being or earthly happiness. Far from ranking lowest in the scale of precedence, our duties towards ourselves are of primary importance and should have pride of place; for (deferring for the moment the definition of what constitutes this duty) it is obvious that nothing can be expected from a man who dishonors his own person. He who transgresses against himself loses his manliness and becomes incapable of doing his duty towards his fellows. A man who performed his duty to others badly, who lacked generosity, kindness and sympathy, but who nevertheless did his duty to himself by leading a proper life, might yet possess a certain inner worth; but he who has transgressed his duty towards himself, can have no inner worth whatever. Thus a man who fails in his duty to himself loses worth absolutely; while a man who fails in his duty to others loses worth only relatively. It follows that the prior condition of our duty to others is our duty to ourselves; we can fulfill the former only in so far as we first fulfill the latter. Let us illustrate our meaning by a few examples of failure in one's duty to oneself. A drunkard does no harm to another, and if he has a strong constitution he does no harm to himself, yet he is an object of contempt. We are not indifferent to cringing servility; man

* *From* Lectures on Ethics *by Immanuel Kant, translated by Louis Infield (1981), Routledge.*

should not cringe and fawn; by so doing he degrades his person and loses his manhood. If a man for gain or profit submits to all indignities and makes himself the plaything of another, he casts away the worth of his manhood. Again, a lie is more a violation of one's duty to oneself than of one's duty to others. A liar, even though by his lies he does no harm to any one, yet becomes an object of contempt, he throws away his personality; his behavior is vile, he has transgressed his duty towards himself. We can carry the argument further and say that to accept favors and benefits is also a breach of one's duty to oneself. If I accept favors, I contract debts which I can never repay, for I can never get on equal terms with him who has conferred the favors upon me; he has stolen a march upon me, and if I do him a favor I am only returning a *quid pro quo*; I shall always owe him a debt of gratitude, and who will accept such a debt? For to be indebted is to be subject to an unending constraint. I must for ever be courteous and flattering towards my benefactor, and if I fail to be so he will very soon make me conscious of my failure; I may even be forced to using subterfuge so as to avoid meeting him. But he who pays promptly for everything is under no constraint; he is free to act as he please; none will hinder him. Again, the faint-hearted who complain about their luck and sigh and weep about their misfortunes are despicable in our eyes; instead of sympathizing with them we do our best to keep away from them. But if a man shows a steadfast courage in his misfortune, and though greatly suffering, does not cringe and complain but puts a bold face upon things, to such a one our sympathy goes out. Moreover, if a man gives up his

freedom and barters it away for money, he violates his manhood. Life itself ought not to be rated so highly as to warrant our being prepared, in order only not to lose it, to live otherwise than as a man should, i.e. not a life of ease, but so that we do not degrade our manhood. We must also be worthy of our manhood; whatsoever makes us unworthy of it makes us unfit for anything, and we cease to be men. Moreover, if a man offer his body for profit for the sport of others—if, for instance, he agrees in return for a few pints of beer to be knocked about—he throws himself away, and the perpetrators who pay him for it are acting as vilely as he. Neither can we without destroying our person abandon ourselves to others in order to satisfy their desires, even though it be done to save parents and friends from death; still less can this be done for money. If done in order to satisfy one's own desires, it is very immodest and immoral, but yet not so unnatural; but if it be done for money, or for some other reason, a person allows himself to be treated as a thing, and so throws away the worth of his manhood. It is the same with the vices of the flesh (*crimina carnis*), which for that reason are not spoken of. They do no damage to anyone, but dishonor and degrade a man's own person; they are an offense against the dignity of manhood in one's own person. The most serious offense against the duty one owes to oneself is suicide. But why should suicide be so abominable? It is no answer to say "because God forbids it." Suicide is not an abomination because God has forbidden it; it is forbidden by God because it is abominable. If it were the other way about, suicide would not be abominable if it were not forbidden; and I should not know why God had forbidden it, if it were not abominable in itself. The ground, therefore, for regarding suicide and other transgressions as abominable and punishable must not be found in the divine will, but in their inherent heinousness. Suicide is an abomination because it implies the abuse of man's freedom of action: he uses his freedom to destroy himself. His freedom should be employed to enable him to live as a man. He is free to dispose as he pleases of things appertaining to his person, but not of his person; he may not use his freedom against himself. For a man to recognize what his duty is towards himself in this respect is far from easy: because although man has indeed a natural horror of suicide, yet we can argue and quibble ourselves into believing that, in order to rid himself of trouble and misery, a man may destroy himself. The argument makes a strong appeal; and in terms of the rule of prudence suicide may often be the surest and best course; none the less suicide is in itself revolting. The rule of morality, which takes precedence of all rules of reflective prudence, command apodeictically and categorically that we must observe our duties to ourselves; and in committing suicide and reducing himself to a carcass, man uses his powers and his liberty against himself. Man is free to dispose of his condition but not of his person; he himself is an end and not a means; all else in the world is of value only as a means, but man is a person and not a thing and therefore not a means. It is absurd that a reasonable being, an end for the sake of which all else is means, should use himself as a means. It is true that a person can serve as a means for others (e.g. by his work), but only in a way whereby he does not cease to be a person

and an end. Whoever acts in such a way that he cannot be an end, uses himself as a means and treats his person as a thing. Man is not free to dispose of his person as a means; and in what follows we shall have more to say on this score.

The duties we owe to ourselves do not depend on the relation of the action to the ends of happiness. If they did, they would depend on our inclinations and so be governed by rules of prudence. Such rules are not moral, since they indicate only the necessity of the means for the satisfaction of inclinations, and cannot therefore bind us. The basis of such obligation is not to be found in the advantages we reap from doing our duty towards ourselves, but in the worth of manhood. This principle does not allow us an unlimited freedom in respect of our own persons. It insists that we must reverence humanity in our own person, because apart from this man becomes an object of contempt, worthless in the eyes of his fellows and worthless in himself. Such faultiness is absolute. Our duties towards ourselves constitute the supreme condition and the principle of all morality; for moral worth is the worth of the person as such; our capacities have a value only in regard to the circumstances in which we find ourselves. Socrates lived in a state of wretchedness; his circumstances were worthless; but though his circumstances were so ill-conditioned, yet he himself was of the highest value. Even though we sacrifice all life's amenities we can make up for their loss and sustain approval by maintaining the worth of our humanity. We may have lost everything else, and yet still retain our inherent worth. Only if our worth as human beings is intact can we perform our other duties; for it is the foundation stone of all other duties. A man who has destroyed and cast away his personality, has no intrinsic worth, and can no longer perform any manner of duty.

• • •

Duties Towards Others

[Duties towards other men] are divisible into two main groups:

1. Duties of good-will, or benevolence.
2. Duties of indebtedness or justice.

Actions falling under the first group are benevolent; those falling under the second are righteous and compulsory.

The duties falling under the first heading do not imply any definite obligation upon us to love other human beings and to do them good. The man who loves his neighbor wishes him well, but of his own impulse; he does so willingly and from a voluntary disposition, not because he is bound to. Love is good-will from inclination; but there can also be good-will on principle. It follows that the pleasure we find in doing good to others may be either direct or indirect. The direct pleasure comes from doing good from obligation, when we enjoy the consciousness of having done our duty. Doing good from love springs from the heart; doing good from obligation springs rather from principles of the understanding. Thus a man may act kindly towards his wife from love, but if his inclination has evaporated he ought to do so from obligation.

But can a moralist say that we have a duty to love others? Love is good-will from inclination. Now whatever depends upon my inclination and not upon my will, cannot

be laid upon me as a duty. I certainly cannot love at will, but only when I have an impulse to love. Duty is always a compulsion, which may be either self-imposed or else imposed upon us by others. If then we are under an obligation to be mindful of the welfare of others, on what is this obligation founded? On principles. For let us consider the world and ourselves. The world is an arena on which nature has provided everything necessary for our temporal welfare, and we are nature's guests. We all have an equal right to the good things which nature has provided. These good things have not, however, been shared out by God. He has left men to do the sharing. Every one of us, therefore, in enjoying the good things of life must have regard to the happiness of others; they have an equal right and ought not to be deprived of it. Since God's providence is universal, I may not be indifferent to the happiness of others. If, for instance, I were to find in the forest a table spread with all manner of dishes, I ought not to conclude that it is all for me; I may eat, but I should also remember to leave some for others to enjoy. I ought not even to consume in its entirety any particular dish in case some one else might fancy it also. Recognizing, therefore, that Providence is universal, I am placed under an obligation to restrict my own consumption and to bear in mind that nature's preparations are made for all of us. This is the source of the obligation to benevolence.

But let us consider the man who is benevolent from love, who loves his neighbor from inclination. Such a man stands in need of people to whom he can show his kindness, and is not content until he finds human beings towards whom he can be charitable. A kindly heart gets more pleasure and satisfaction from doing good to others than from its own enjoyment of the good things of life; the inclination to do good is a necessity to it, which must be satisfied. It is not this kindliness of heart and temper which the moralist should seek to cultivate, but good-will from principles. For the former is grounded in inclination and a natural necessity, giving rise to unregulated conduct. Such a man will be charitable, by inclination, to all and sundry; and then, if someone takes advantage of his kind heart, in sheer disgust he will decide from then onwards to give up doing good to others. He has no principle by which to calculate his behavior. Therefore the moralist must establish principles, and commend and inculcate benevolence from obligation. When all the obligations, religious as well as natural, have been expounded, we may go on to inculcate the inclination, though never forgetting that it must be subordinated to principles. On these conditions only may we proceed to expound the motives to acts of benevolence from inclination.

Let us now consider the second group of duties towards others, namely the duties of indebtedness and justice. Here there is no question of inclination, only of the rights of others. It is not their needs that count in this connexion, but their rights; it is not a question of whether my neighbor is needy, wretchedly poor or the reverse; if his right is concerned, it must be satisfied. This group of duties is grounded in the general rule of right.

The chief of these duties is respect for the rights of others. It is our duty to regard them as sacred and to respect and maintain them as such. There is nothing more sacred in the wide world than the rights of others. They are inviolable. Woe unto him who trespasses upon the right of another and tramples it underfoot! His right should be his security; it should be stronger than any shield or fortress. We have a holy ruler and the most sacred of his gifts to us is the rights of man.

Let us take a man who is guided only by justice and not by charity. He may close his heart to all appeal; he may be utterly indifferent to the misery and misfortune around him; but so long as he conscientiously does his duty in giving to every one what is his due, so long as he respects the rights of other men as the most sacred trust given to us by the ruler of the world, his conduct is righteous; let him give to another no trifle in excess of his due, and yet be equally punctilious to keep no jot nor tittle back, and his conduct is righteous. If all of us behaved in this way, if none of us ever did any act of love and charity, but only kept inviolate the rights of every man, there would be no misery in the world except sickness and misfortune and other such sufferings as do not spring from the violation of rights. The most frequent and fertile source of human misery is not misfortune, but the injustice of man.

Notes

C.F. Gellert, Moralische Vorlesungen, *1770, 2 vols.*

MAXIMS AND MORAL BEHAVIOUR

According to Kant, anytime you act voluntarily, you operate under some kind of maxim, rule or directive. For instance, if, in situation A, you choose to do B, then you are acting on the maxim "In situation A, do B." This kind of thinking is what has led some people to describe humans as "rule-governed" animals. Unlike lower-level organisms, which are mostly reactive to external stimuli or responsive to instinctual impulses and other determining factors, we, as humans, can act freely and rationally on the basis of self-generated rules or laws of conduct. If this seems a bit vague, imagine yourself lying to your course instructor about the reasons why you missed an ethics term test. You might say that you were ill when, in fact, you slept in because you were up until very late the night before partying with friends. In this case, the personal maxim or rule of conduct underlying your behaviour could be expressed something like this: "When in trouble, lie your way out of it" or "If caught doing something wrong, then lie" or "Lie in order to get what you want."

To say maxims underlie our behaviours does not mean to suggest that we always abide by them. For example, on most occasions when you are caught doing something wrong, you might "fess up"; however, at other times, you might lie like the student in the illustration above. You should also note that people are not always or usually aware of the maxims that they use to govern their behaviour. Implicit maxims are most likely to come to people's attention and to be made explicit when they are asked to justify their behaviours to others or when conscience forces them to justify their actions to themselves. Whether we are aware of them or not, maxims are imbedded in our actions and in the way we behave.

KANTIAN FORMALISM AND THE CATEGORICAL IMPERATIVE

In efforts to determine which maxims of behaviour are distinctively moral and morally acceptable and which are not, Kant formulated **the categorical imperative**. This moral imperative can be expressed in a number of different ways, but the best-known formulation is the following: "Act only according to that maxim by which you can at the same time will that it should become a universal law." According to this formulation, a moral maxim is one that can, without contradiction, be willed to be a rule of conduct for everyone. The categorical imperative implies that the essence of morality lies in acting on the basis of an **impersonal principle** that is **valid for every person** including oneself. As morality has a **rational foundation** for Kant, he believes that one must be able to **universalize** maxims of conduct in a **logically consistent** fashion if those maxims are to be **binding** on all rational beings. Maxims that cannot be universalized consistently are not moral or morally prescriptive. For example, the maxim "Never help others, but always be helped by them" could not be accepted as a valid moral rule of conduct because of its logical implications. It does not make sense even to talk about accepting help from others if the maxim were universalized and acted upon, because nobody would ever try to help others and, thus, there would be no help to be accepted. From this illustration, we see how the categorical imperative's formal requirement of universal consistency allows us to evaluate the moral acceptability of particular maxims and rules of conduct. The categorical imperative can serve as a test of morality or an ultimate standard for moral evaluation.

A second formulation of the categorical imperative draws attention to its social implications. It states: "Act so that you treat humanity, whether in your own person or in that of another, always as an end and never as a means only." [11] According to this statement of the categorical imperative, we should show respect for all human beings **unconditionally** and avoid exploiting anyone. When we disrespect others by exploiting or using them, we treat them merely as objects or means to our own ends. We fail to see others as beings whose existence has absolute worth in itself. In Kant's view, the dignity and worth of any human being are not conditional on any empirical factors. Just as you would not wish to be used against your will and exploited by others so they could achieve their ends, so too is it wrong for you to use people against their will and to exploit them or treat them only as objects or merely as a means to gain your own ends.

Implicit in what was said above is the formal requirement of **reversibility**. The concept holds that a maxim or rule of conduct is morally unacceptable if the individual acting on it would not wish to be the person most disadvantaged or most adversely affected by its application. If one approves of a maxim, one must approve of it both from the perspective of the one who benefits and from the one most negatively affected. An act must be acceptable **objectively** regardless of whether the individual is at the giving or the receiving end of an action. If, for instance, a person chooses to approve of stealing in her own case, then that person must be willing to become victimized by theft if the corresponding maxim is to be deemed acceptable. Presumably, nobody wishes to be robbed and, therefore, no rational moral thinker would accept such a maxim.

The formal criteria of universality, consistency and reversibility point to the idea that moral maxims must also be **impartial**; that is, the rightness or wrongness of actions and the moral adequacy of their underlying maxims have nothing to do with *who* happens to be in a favoured or disadvantaged position regarding the actions. Certain acts are right or wrong in themselves, regardless of whose interests are served and regardless of the favourable or unfavourable consequences to oneself, or to anyone else for that matter. The categorical imperative is an abstract principle that requires that empirical content particulars be removed, as much as possible, from the ethical appraisal and justification process. Because morality must have a purely rational *a priori* basis, particulars of content referring to specific persons, places, times, interests, desires, inclinations, and so forth, must be removed when the moral acceptability of maxims is being determined. Recall that, for Kant, morality cannot have an empirical or anthropological basis, for this would not provide him with the solid and secure ethical foundation that he seeks. Only reason can provide the **certainty** and **necessity** required for a universal, binding morality.

Another formal (i.e., content-free) element contained in the categorical imperative is the notion of **prescriptivity**. One cannot simply opt out of morality if one chooses. Moral requirements are unconditionally binding on all rational beings. You cannot justifiably or consistently argue that morality applies to everyone but you, or that everyone except you should always tell the truth, and so on. Ethically speaking, you cannot make yourself the exception to the rule. To do so would be to use two standards of morality, one for others and one for yourself. If this practice of making personal exceptions were universalized, then nobody would be required to adhere to the moral law and any objective morality would become impossible. You

---

MINDWORK MEDITATION

So far, on our travels into the moral domain, we have come across a number of different cornerstones that could serve as the basis of a personal and social morality. What do you think of Kant's cornerstone, the categorical imperative? Does it provide you with a solid and stable foundation upon which to build your moral life? Why or why not? Do you have another cornerstone in mind? If so, which one? Why is your foundational cornerstone preferable to Kant's?

---

cannot, therefore, be freed of moral obligation simply because you do not feel like living up to the moral law or because making an exception in your case is likely to further your own interests or promote greater happiness within yourself. Distinctively moral maxims and ethical principles of conduct apply to everyone unconditionally, whether people like them or not.

HYPOTHETICAL VERSUS CATEGORICAL IMPERATIVES

In everyday language, we often use words like "should," "have to," "ought," and "must," but it is not clearly the case that we always mean to suggest that moral obligations are associated with them. Saying to someone "You ought to ..." may be intended simply as a bit of personal advice, not as a universal ethical prescription. Saying to yourself, "I must ..." or "I have to ..." or "I should ..." may involve some trivial action that does not call forth any moral considerations. Recognizing this, Kant, in *The Foundations of the Metaphysics of Morals*, made a distinction between **categorical and hypothetical imperatives**. He wrote,

> *Prudence is the knowledge of things to be sought, and those to be shunned.*
> CICERO

> All imperatives command either hypothetically or categorically ... If the action [commanded by an imperative] is good only as a means to something else, the imperative is hypothetical; but if it is thought of as good in itself, and hence as necessary in a will which of itself conforms to reason as the principle of this will, the imperative is categorical.[12]

As we have previously learned about categorical imperatives, they imply universal necessity and prescriptivity. They are purely rational and a priori. Hypothetical imperatives, by contrast, are **conditional** and **particular** (specific) and, therefore, lack the formal properties of distinctively moral commands. They cannot be universalized and prescribed unconditionally. On the subject of hypothetical imperatives, Kant speaks of **technical imperatives** or **rules of skill** that require us to do certain things *if* we want to achieve specific ends. For instance, if you wish to properly install an interlocking brick patio that will not shift with changing weather conditions, you must prepare the base with appropriate amounts of gravel and sand. Of course, you do not have to do this if you prefer to build a wooden deck or to lay sod.

Kant also draws our attention to **prudential imperatives**, another type of conditional command. Here is an example: "If you wish to make a favourable impression on people, then you should do certain things (e.g., laugh at their humourless jokes)." Again, you have no "moral duty" to make favourable impressions, so you have no ethical obligations to do those things that will accomplish that end. It could be that you are highly introverted, prefer to be alone and do not care what others think of you. Given, then, that prudential and technical imperatives command us only under certain conditions, they are hypothetical, not moral and categorical.

AUTONOMY VERSUS HETERONOMY OF THE WILL

In closing this discussion of Kantian ethics, a brief mention should be made of the role played by **autonomy** in morality, for without personal autonomy, morality becomes an impossibil-

> *No man is free who cannot command himself.*
> PYTHAGORAS

ity. When people act morally, they act freely or willfully out of respect and reverence for the moral law. They willingly obey the moral law for the sake of the moral law alone. To go back to a point made earlier, moral agents do their duty for duty's sake, not because of external incentive or coercion. When outside determining forces are not present, then we can speak of **autonomy of the will**. **Heteronomy of the will**, by contrast, is evident when the will obeys laws, rules or injunctions from any other source besides reason. Obeying the law because you fear incarceration or doing your duty only under threat of physical force does not reflect autonomous moral action. Rather, it is more like "covering your butt," to use a colloquial expression. Somehow, I do not think this is what the venerable Kant intended to include in his conception of a universal morality!

Finally, when, as autonomous and rational moral agents, we base our actions on universally valid laws that we have laid down for ourselves, we participate in something Kant calls the **realm of ends**—a kind of ideal moral universe in which we respect the intrinsic worth and dignity of all persons. In this kingdom, we never treat people solely as means to our ends, but as ends in themselves. Of course, to some extent, we all use one another. For instance, you may use your neighbour's teenager as a babysitter for your child or your neighbours may use your son or daughter as help to cut their grass. This is not what Kant is talking about. In many practical ways, we all use one another in co-operative social living. It is when we violate others, abuse or mistreat them or use them "merely" as a means to achieve our own ends that we dishonour their dignity as persons.

KEY TERMS

consequentialists

deontological ethics

impersonal principle

valid for every person

ethical relativist
moral certainty
structure of reason
purely rational
a priori
talents of the mind
qualities of temperament
gifts of fortune
unconditionally good
the good will
duty
practical reason
maxim
prudence
moral
nonmoral
immoral
inclination
motive
duties to others
duties to ourselves
the categorical imperative

rational foundation
universalize
logically consistent
binding
unconditionally
reversibility
objectively
impartial
certainty
necessity
prescriptivity
categorical and hypothetical imperatives
conditional
particular
technical imperatives
rules of skill
prudential imperatives
autonomy
autonomy of the will
heteronomy of the will
realm of ends

PROGRESS CHECK 5.1

Instructions: Fill in the blanks with the appropriate responses listed below.

moral certainty
good will
duty
immoral
duties to oneself
formalist
objects
categorical imperative
prescriptive
autonomy of the will

conditionally
nonmoral
motive
structure of reason
maxim
deontological
prudential
inclination
impartial
hypothetical

1. Whereas utilitarian morality emphasizes consequences, _deontological_ _____ ethics stresses duty.
2. Immanuel Kant does not believe that any _moral certainty_ _____ can be found in the diversity of human experience.

3. For Kant, the basis of morality cannot be empirical; it must be found in the of ___ itself. *structure* *reason.*

4. The only thing good in itself is the *good will*

5. Talents of the mind, qualities of temperament, and gifts of fortune are all only _____ good. *conditionally*

6. *Duty* is the necessity of an action executed from respect for [moral] law.

7. Actions performed to promote self-interest are not moral, but *prudential*

8. Actions that are ethically neutral and outside the moral domain are *non-. moral*

9. Actions that violate the dignity of others are *immoral*

10. If you thoughtlessly do the right thing simply because you feel like doing it, then your action is not moral, but is based on *inclination*

11. The *motive* behind any action determines its moral status.

12. Morality involves *duties to oneself* _____ as well as duties to others.

13. Implicit in any conscious, voluntary action is a *maxim* or rule of conduct.

14. The *categorical imperative* _____ is the ultimate principle of morality that enables us to determine which maxims of behaviour are moral and/or morally acceptable.

15. Kant tries to remove empirical content from his moral theorizing; this is because he is a *formalist*

16. The second formulation of the categorical imperative prescribes that we never treat people merely as *objects*, but always as ends in themselves.

17. Moral maxims are *impartial*; their rightness has nothing to do with particular individuals or who happens to be in a favoured or disadvantaged position regarding the actions that follow from them.

18. Moral maxims are universal and unconditional; they are binding or _____ for everybody. *prescriptive*

19. Conditional imperatives are *hypothetical*, not categorical.

20. Moral actions must be freely performed and display *autonomy of will.*

SUMMARY OF MAJOR POINTS

1. On what have philosophers (including Kant) tried to base morality?

   They have based morality on consequences, results, utility, the transcendent realm of forms, human nature, common experience, happiness, the good life and the structure of reason.

2. What is the only thing having intrinsic value?

   The good will is good in itself.
   Talents of the mind, qualities of temperament and gifts of fortune are all conditionally good.

3. What makes the good will good?

   The motive to do the right thing for the right reason (duty).
   The intention to act on a consistent, universally prescriptive principle.

4. **What is duty?**

   "Duty is the necessity of an action executed from respect for [moral] law." (Kant)
   Actions performed from duty have their worth in the maxims or rules of conduct by which
   they are determined.

5. **What is important to keep in mind about duty?**

   Not all actions in accordance with duty are performed for duty's sake (nonmoral).
   Some actions in accordance with duty are performed out of inclination and are therefore
   nonmoral.
   Only actions performed in accordance with duty and for the sake of duty are distinctively
   moral.

6. **What kinds of moral duties are there?**

   There are duties to oneself: proper self-respect, self-mastery, occupation and treatment of
   the body.
   There are duties to others: respect for persons, honour their dignity.

7. **What is a maxim? What can be said of maxims?**

   A maxim is rule or directive or principle of conduct implicit in any voluntary action.
   We are not always consciously aware of them.
   We do not always act consistently with them.
   We use them to justify our behaviour to others as well as to ourselves.

8. **What is the categorical imperative? What are two of its formulations?**

   The categorical imperative is, for Kant, the supreme principle of morality from which all other
   moral maxims are derived and by which they can be evaluated.
   First formulation: Act only according to that maxim by which you can at the same time will that it
   should become a universal law.
   Second formulation: Act so that you treat humanity, whether in your own person or in that of
   another, always as an end and never only as a means.

9. **What formal criteria (i.e., content-free standards) characterize the categorical imperative and
   the morally acceptable maxims that follow from it?**

   The criteria are: impersonality, universality, logical consistency, bindingness/prescriptivity,
   unconditionality, reversibility, objectivity, impartiality and certainty.

10. **Besides categorical imperatives that are universal and necessary, what other types are there?**

    There are conditional or hypothetical imperatives containing an "if–then" logical form, e.g.,
    technical imperatives or rules of skill and prudential imperatives.

11. **What is meant by autonomy/heteronomy of the will?**

    Moral acts are autonomous, not heteronomous; such acts are performed freely out of respect or
    reverence for the moral law, i.e., for the sake of duty. Heteronomous acts are not moral; they are
    either coerced or instrumental to some further end and are not performed for duty's sake.

SOURCE REFERENCES AND RELATED READINGS

Copleston, Frederick. *A History of Philosophy*. Vol. 6. *Modern Philosophy*, Part II, Kant. Garden City, N.Y.: Image Books, 1960.

Falikowski, Anthony. *Moral Philosophy: Theories, Skills, and Applications*. Englewood Cliffs, N.J.: Prentice Hall, 1990.

Hospers, John. *Human Conduct: Problems of Ethics*. New York: Harcourt Brace Jovanovich, 1972.

Kant, Immanuel. *Foundations of the Metaphysics of Morals*, trans. Lewis White Beck. The Library of Liberal Arts. Indianapolis, Ind.: Bobbs-Merrill, 1959.

———. *Lectures on Ethics*, trans. Louis Infield. Indianapolis, Ind.: Hackett, 1963.

———. *The Metaphysical Principles of Virtue*, trans. James Ellington. The Library of Liberal Arts. Indianapolis, Ind.:Bobbs-Merrill, 1964.

Kemp, John. *The Philosophy of Kant*. London: Oxford University Press, 1968.

Korner, S. *Kant*. Harmondsworth, Middlesex: Penguin, 1955.

Ross, William D. *Kant's Ethical Theory*. New York: Oxford University Press, 1954.

Singer, Marcus T. "The Categorical Imperative" in *Moral Philosophy: An Introduction*, ed. Jack Glickman. New York: St. Martin's Press, 1976.

ENDNOTES

1. Immanuel Kant, *Foundations of the Metaphysics of Morals*, tr. Lewis White Beck. Indianapolis, Ind.: Bobbs-Merrill, p. 5.
2. Immanuel Kant, ibid., p. 5.
3. Immanuel Kant, ibid., p. 5.
4. ibid., p. 16.
5. Kant, ibid.
6. Kant, ibid., pp. 13–14.
7. ibid., p. 14.
8. Immanuel Kant, *Lectures on Ethics*, tr. Louis Infield. Indianapolis, Ind.:Hackett, 1963, pp. 117–118.
9. ibid., p. 118.
10. ibid., p. 121.
11. Immanuel Kant, *Foundations*, ibid., p. 47.
12. ibid., p. 31.

CHAPTER SIX

John Rawls: The Principle of Justice as Fairness

Overview

Learning Outcomes

After successfully completing this chapter, you will be able to

- explain what is meant by Rawls' social contractarianism;
- define what Rawls means by society;
- see how "the original position" can be used to arrive at principles of justice;
- define justice as fairness in regard to two principles (i.e., the principle of equal liberty and the difference principle);
- distinguish between Rawls' social contractarianism and utilitarianism;
- identify and explain the "maximin" solution to the problem of social justice.

PHILOSOPHICAL FOCUS QUESTIONS

1. In what ways are social practices and institutions subject to moral and ethical evaluation?

2. How does Rawls conceptualize society? How else could it be conceived? What could be the moral basis of any alternative?

3. Is there anything unrealistic about what Rawls calls "the original position?" If so, what? Are there good and sufficient reasons for abandoning this concept?

4. How do Rawlsian and utilitarian conceptions of justice differ?

5. What concept of justice emerges out of the original position?

6. Does Rawls assign different weights to moral concepts such as "goodness" and "rightness"? Explain.

7. Can you provide any contemporary social applications of the equal-liberty principle and the difference principle?

8. What is meant by Rawls' "maximin" solution to the problem of social justice?

Biographical Brief*

HARVARD UNIVERSITY

John Rawls
(1921–2002)

John Rawls was born in Baltimore in 1921. He studied at Cornell University and at Princeton, where he earned his doctorate in 1950. His social contract theory of society serves to illustrate how classical philosophy continues to exert an influence on contemporary thought. Rawls openly admitted his debt to contractarian philosophers like Locke and Rousseau. He also stated that his theory is highly Kantian in nature and, as such, is not entirely original. Rawls' important contribution to ethical and sociopolitical philosophy comes from the fact that he has taken Kantian and social-contractarian ideas to a higher level of abstraction; and synthesized and organized these ideas by means of a simplifying framework that allows them to be more fully appreciated. Rawls' updated version of Kantian and social contractarian ethics constitutes, for him, the most appropriate moral basis for a democratic society. He argues that it is better than utilitarian alternatives. The late Lawrence Kohlberg, another Harvard professor and psychological researcher, has argued that the highest stage of moral development in the individual, as evidenced by the most adequate ethical-reasoning abilities, is reflected in the principles of justice articulated by Rawls and extracted from his theoretical device known as "the original position." John Rawls' most important work is entitled *A Theory of Justice*. In it, we find an explanation of his socioethical position and a defense of his views on the moral life of individuals within society.

*From Falikowski, Moral Philosophy: Theories, Skills and Applications, p. 78.

JUSTICE AND THE SOCIAL CONTRACT TRADITION

The philosopher John Rawls has developed a theory of justice designed to be a more viable, satisfactory alternative to the concepts of justice provided by other ethical perspectives such as utilitarianism. In his classic work, *A Theory of Justice*, Rawls emphasizes the idea that socio-political institutions are the proper targets of moral evaluation. His theory is constructed to offer us a workable method for solving problems related to social morality. Rawls presents the view that the ultimate basis of society rests on a set of **tacit agreements** among its members. From his vantage point, a major theoretical problem related to this idea is that of defining the basic principles entailed in these agreements, which a well-ordered society must espouse if it is to have a solid moral foundation.

> *Justice is the first virtue of social institutions, as truth is of systems of thought. A theory, however elegant and economical must be rejected or revised if it is untrue; likewise laws and institutions no matter how efficient and well-arranged must be reformed or abolished if they are unjust.*
>
> JOHN RAWLS

For Rawls, the tacit agreements upon which people would naturally base society involve principles of **justice**. Underscoring the importance of justice, he writes, "Justice is the first virtue of social institutions, as truth is of systems of thought. A theory however elegant and economical must be rejected or revised if it is untrue; likewise laws and institutions no matter how efficient and well-arranged must be reformed or abolished if they are unjust."[1] In the Rawlsian account, every individual possesses an **inviolability** founded on justice, and nothing, not even the welfare of society as a whole, can override it. In a just and moral society the liberties of equal citizenship are established and the **rights**, which are secured by the individual, cannot be made subject to political bargaining. Whether or not we ascribe fundamental rights to persons cannot properly be determined by some kind of calculation of social interests. Rawls claims that the only occasion when a particular injustice is tolerable is when it is required to circumvent an even greater injustice.[2]

THE RAWLSIAN SOCIETY

To better understand how Rawls' notion of justice would operate in practical terms, it is helpful to get a clearer picture of how he conceptualizes **society**. Rawls sees society as a self-sufficient association of individuals. In their interpersonal relationships, people acknowledge that certain rules of conduct are binding on them and, in most instances, are willing to abide by those rules. These binding rules of society constitute a system of co-operation designed to further the good and improve the welfare of those who participate. Society, then, is a type of co-operative venture for purposes of mutual advantage. Within society, we find an **identity of interests**. People generally want the same kinds of things and share the same basic needs. This identity of interests helps to create a system of social co-operation, one that allows for a better life for every individual than would be possible for any single person to enjoy if left to live solely by his or her own efforts.[3]

Rawls recognizes, of course, that even within a co-operative system **conflicts of interest** will inevitably arise. People will tend to disagree, for instance, about how the greater benefits secured by their collaborative efforts should be distributed. In pursuit of their life goals, different individuals will typically perceive things differently, and most will prefer a larger share of benefits to a smaller one. Obviously, not everyone can have a larger share; nor is it always feasible to give everyone access to the same resources. In view of this fact, Rawls believes that

> [a] set of principles is required for choosing among the various social arrangements which determine this division of advantages and for underwriting an agreement on the proper distributive shares. These principles are the principles of social justice: they provide a way of assigning rights and duties in the basic institutions of society and they define the appropriate distribution of the benefits and burdens of social co-operation.[4]

As you will see, Rawls' conception of social justice (the basis of a well-ordered society) enables one to become the **ideal observer** in the resolution of any social conflict. His notion of justice is intended to serve as a **common point of view** from which the conflicting claims of opposing parties can be **fairly adjudicated**. A shared understanding of justice allows for individuals with disparate aims and purposes to establish the bonds of **civic friendship**.[5] This shared understanding can be regarded as constituting the basic charter of a well-ordered human association. In such an association (society), each person accepts, and knows that other persons accept, the same fundamental principles of justice. When speaking of persons, Rawls also intends to include groups, institutions, and collective agencies. In this vein, we often make reference to companies as "corporate citizens." They too must, in their activities and policies, abide by the principles of justice if a well-ordered society is to be maintained.

THE ORIGINAL POSITION AND THE "VEIL OF IGNORANCE"

To arrive at the specific principles of social justice, Rawls uses a theoretical device called **the original position**. The original position is a purely **hypothetical situation**: it has never actually existed in reality. It is not a historical event or empirical set of circumstances. In the original position, persons are placed behind a **veil of ignorance**. They are ignorant of their place, class position or social status within society. They do not know how lucky or unlucky they have been in the distribution of natural assets, abilities, intelligence, strength, and so on. They are unaware as well of their own peculiar psychological interests and inclinations. They do not know what definition they and others have given to the good life. What is specified about the parties in the original position is that they are **rational**, **free** and **equal members** and that they all wish to maximize their own definitions of the good life, whatever those definitions may entail. Furthermore, Rawls stipulates that in the original position, people are **mutually disinterested**. This is not to suggest that the parties are egoists (only concerned with their own worth, prestige, or power) but that the parties are generally concerned with furthering their own interests and not with furthering someone else's goals.[6] In this situation of mutual disinterest, where social co-operation is designed to further individual goals and maximize personal benefits, it is inevitable that parties will come into **conflict** over the distribution of social advantages. It is assumed that people will want a larger, not a smaller, share of the benefits that derive from their efforts toward social co-operation.

Equal rights for all, special privileges for none.
THOMAS JEFFERSON

Assuming that the conflicts among the opposing parties are to be settled peacefully, not through violence and war, Rawls works out his theory by determining which rational principles of conflict resolution would likely be chosen by individuals in the original position, when placed behind the veil of ignorance. Their ignorance of their particular fortunes and sets of personal interests ensures that none of them are advantaged or disadvantaged in the initial selection of principles by the outcome of natural chance or by the **contingencies** of social circumstances. In other words, the principles that would be freely chosen and mutually agreed upon by rational and equal parties would be **fair** or **just** from everyone's perspective. As Rawls puts it, "Since all are similarly situated and no one is able to design principles to favour his particular condition, the principles of justice are the result of a fair agreement or bargain."[7] The principles agreed to in the original position define what Rawls calls **justice as fairness**. Before we look more closely at the notion of justice as fairness, it might be fun and interesting to repeat Rawls' thought experiment involving hypothetical negotiations in the original position. Because our repeat performance is not exactly original, let us call our situation "The Similar Position." Turn to the Philosophers at Work feature that follows to see what I mean.

PHILOSOPHERS AT WORK

The Similar Position: Suppose that you and your classmates have been shipwrecked and that you now find yourselves on a deserted island somewhere in uncharted waters. It is unlikely that you will be rescued soon, if ever. You are worried about the possibility that tensions and conflicts could flare up into episodes of physical violence in the future, so you all decide to establish some ground rules and principles that must be obeyed if everybody is going to live together peacefully. In small groups of four to six people, establish the constitutional principles of your newly formed island society. Note that at this point nobody knows who they are or anything about themselves. The violent storm that led to the shipwreck has left everyone in shock and suffering from temporary amnesia. Nonetheless, everyone is still able to think and to reason clearly. You simply know nothing about your past or what your status or position was back home. Under these circumstances, what principles of social organization emerge from "the similar position"?

Part One: In forming your constitution, what assumptions will you make? What, if anything, will people be entitled to? Will you have any duties and responsibilities? If so, which ones? Will anything be forbidden? Why?

Part Two: Now that you have established your constitution, compare it with Rawls' notion of justice as fairness defined by the principle of equal liberty and the difference principle **(pp. 118, 119)**. Do your group's decisions serve to support or call into question Rawls' claims about what rational thinkers would produce in an initial situation behind a veil of ignorance?

The concept of justice as fairness, which emerges out of the original position, serves to regulate criticism and reform of all social institutions. With mutually agreed-upon principles of justice, people can prepare a constitution and set up a legislature to enact laws that are consistent with these principles. Of course, Rawls realizes that people cannot literally contract from the hypothetical original position, since, at birth, they already find themselves with some particular status and psychological endowment, in some particular society, and given some particular life prospects. Nonetheless, Rawls believes that to the extent a society satisfies the principle of justice as fairness, it conforms to the principles that free and equal individuals would accept for their mutual advantage under circumstances that are fair. Choosing these principles, people can decide *in advance* how they will regulate their claims against one another and what rights, duties, and freedoms will form the constitutional foundation of their society. Before elaborating upon the two specific principles to be included in his notion of justice as fairness, Rawls first explains why he rejects the utilitarian conception of justice. Refusing to accept "utility" as a standard of justice, Rawls writes,

> Offhand it hardly seems likely that persons who view themselves as equals, entitled to press their claims upon one another, would agree to a principle which may require lesser life prospects for some simply for the sake of a greater sum of advantages enjoyed by others.... [A] rational man would not accept a basic structure merely because it maximized the algebraic sum of advantages irrespective of its permanent effects on his own rights and interests. Thus it seems that the principle of utility is incompatible with the conception of social cooperation among equals for mutual advantage.[8]

Let's turn now to the "Back to the Source" feature taken from Rawls' *A Theory of Justice.*

BACK TO THE SOURCE*

4. The Original Position and Justification
I have said that the original position is the appropriate initial status quo which insures that the fundamental agreements reached in it are fair. This fact yields the name "justice as fairness." It is clear, then, that I want to say that one conception of justice is more reasonable than another, or justifiable with respect to it, if rational persons in the initial situation would choose its principles over those of the other for the role of justice. Conceptions of justice are to be ranked by their acceptability to persons so circumstanced. Understood in this way the question of justification is settled by working out a problem of deliberation: we have to ascertain

Reprinted by permission of the publisher from A THEORY OF JUSTICE by John Rawls, pp. 17-22, Cambridge, Mass.: The Belknap Press of Harvard University Press, Copyright © 1971, 1999 by the President and Fellows of Harvard College.

which principles it would be rational to adopt given the contractual situation. This connects the theory of justice with the theory of rational choice.

If this view of the problem of justification is to succeed, we must, of course, describe in some detail the nature of this choice problem. A problem of rational decision has a definite answer only if we know the beliefs and interests of the parties, their relations with respect to one another, the alternatives between which they are to choose, the procedure whereby they make up their minds, and so on. As the circumstances are presented in different ways, correspondingly different principles are accepted. The concept of the original position, as I shall refer to it, is that of the most philosophically favored interpretation of this initial choice situation for the purposes of a theory of justice.

But how are we to decide what is the most favored interpretation? I assume, for one thing, that there is a broad measure of agreement that principles of justice should be chosen under certain conditions. To justify a particular description of the initial situation one shows that it incorporates these commonly shared presumptions. One argues from widely accepted but weak premises to more specific conclusions. Each of the presumptions should by itself be natural and plausible; some of them may seem innocuous or even trivial. The aim of the contract approach is to establish that taken together they impose significant bounds on acceptable principles of justice. The ideal outcome would be that these conditions determine a unique set of principles; but I shall be satisfied if they suffice to rank the main traditional conceptions of social justice.

One should not be misled, then, by the somewhat unusual conditions which characterize the original position. The idea here is simply to make vivid to ourselves the restrictions that it seems reasonable to impose on arguments for principles of justice, and therefore on these principles themselves. Thus it seems reasonable and generally acceptable that no one should be advantaged or disadvantaged by natural fortune or social circumstances in the choice of principles. It also seems widely agreed that it should be impossible to tailor principles to the circumstances of one's own case. We should insure further than particular inclinations and aspirations, and persons' conceptions of their good do not affect the principles adopted. The aim is to rule out those principles that it would be rational to propose for acceptance, however little the chance of success, only if one knew certain things that are irrelevant from the standpoint of justice. For example, if a man knew that he was wealthy, he might find it rational to advance the principle that various taxes for welfare measures be counted unjust; if he knew that he was poor, he would most likely propose the contrary principle. To represent the desired restrictions one imagines a situation in which everyone is deprived of this sort of information. One excludes the knowledge of those contingencies which sets men at odds and allows them to be guided by their prejudices. In this manner the veil of ignorance is arrived at in a natural way. This concept should cause no difficulty if we keep in mind the constraints on arguments that it is meant to express. At any time we can enter the original position, so to speak, simply by following a certain procedure, namely, by arguing for principles of justice in accordance with these restrictions.

It seems reasonable to suppose that the parties in the original position are equal. That is, all have the same rights in the procedure for choosing principles; each can make proposals, submit reasons for their acceptance, and so on. Obviously the purpose of these conditions is to represent equality between human beings as moral persons, as creatures having a conception of their good and capable of a sense of justice. The basis of equality is taken to be similarity in these two respects. Systems of ends are not ranked in value; and each man is presumed to have the requisite ability to understand and to act upon whatever principles are adopted. Together with the veil of ignorance, these conditions define the principles of justice as those which rational persons concerned to advance their interests would consent to as equals when none are known to be advantaged or disadvantaged by social and natural contingencies.

There is, however, another side to justifying a particular description of the original position. This is to see if the principles which would be chosen match our considered convictions of justice or extend them in an acceptable way. We can note whether applying these principles would lead us to make the same judgments about the basic structure of society which we now make intuitively and in which we have the greatest confidence; or whether, in cases where our present judgments are in doubt and given with hesitation, these principles offer a resolution which we can affirm on reflection. There are questions which we feel sure must be answered in a certain way. For example, we are confident that religious intolerance and racial discrimination are unjust. We think that we have examined these things with care and have reached what we believe is an impartial judgment not likely to be distorted by an excessive attention to our own interests. These convictions are provisional fixed points which we presume any conception of justice must fit. But we have much less assurance as to what is the correct distribution of wealth and authority. Here we may be looking for a way to remove our doubts. We can check an interpretation of the initial situation, then, by the capacity of its principles to accommodate our firmest convictions and to provide guidance where guidance is needed.

In searching for the most favored description of this situation, we work from both ends. We begin by describing it so that it represents generally shared and preferably weak conditions. We then see if these conditions are strong enough to yield a significant set of principles. If not, we look for further premises equally reasonable. But if so, and these principles match our considered convictions of justice, then so far well and good. But presumably there will be discrepancies. In this case we have a choice. We can either modify the account of the initial situation or we can revise our existing judgments, for even the judgments we take provisionally as fixed points are liable to revision. By going back and forth, sometimes altering the conditions of the contractual circumstances, at others withdrawing our judgments and conforming them to principle, I assume that eventually we shall find a description of the initial situation that both expresses reasonable conditions and yields principles which match our considered judgments duly pruned and adjusted. This state of affairs I refer to as reflective equilibrium.[1] It is an equilibrium because at last our principles and judgments coincide; and it is reflective since we know to what principles our judgments conform and the premises of their derivation. At the moment everything is in order. But this equilibrium is not necessarily stable. It is liable to be upset by further examination of the conditions which should be imposed on the contractual situation and by particular cases which may lead us to revise our judgments. Yet for the time being we have done what we can to render coherent and to justify our convictions of social justice. We have reached a conception of the original position.

I shall not, of course, actually work through this process. Still, we may think of the interpretation of the original position that I shall present as the result of such a hypothetical course of reflection. It represents the attempt to accommodate within one scheme both reasonable philosophical conditions on principles as well as our considered judgments of justice. In arriving at the favored interpretation of the initial situation there is no point at which an appeal is made to self-evidence in the traditional sense either of general conceptions or particular convictions. I do not claim for the principles of justice proposed that they are necessary truths or derivable from such truths. A conception of justice cannot be deduced from self-evident premises or conditions on principles; instead, its justification is a matter of the mutual support of many considerations, of everything fitting together into one coherent view.

A final comment. We shall want to say that certain principles of justice are justified because they would be agreed to in an initial situation of equality. I have emphasized that this original position is purely hypothetical. It is natural to ask why, if this agreement is never actually entered into, we should take any interest in these principles, moral or otherwise. The answer is that the conditions embodied in the description of the original position are ones that we do in fact accept. Or if we do not, then perhaps we can be persuaded to do so by philosophical reflection. Each aspect of the contractual situation can be given supporting grounds. Thus what we shall do is to collect together into one conception a number of conditions on principles that we are ready upon due consideration to recognize as reasonable. These constraints express what we are prepared to regard as limits on fair terms of social cooperation. One way to look at the idea of the original position, therefore, is to see it as an expository device which sums up the meaning of these conditions and helps us to extract their consequences. On the other hand, this conception is also an intuitive notion that suggests its own elaboration, so that led on by it we are drawn to define more clearly the standpoint from which we can best interpret moral relationships. We need a conception that enables us to envision our objective from afar; the intuitive notion of the original position is to do this for us.[2]

---

1. *The process of mutual adjustment of principles and considered judgments is not peculiar to moral philosophy. See Nelson Goodman*, Fact, Fiction, and Forecast *(Cambridge, Mass., Harvard University Press, 1955), pp. 65–68, for parallel remarks concerning the justification of the principles of deductive and inductive inference.*
2. *Henri Poincaré remarks: "Il nous faut une faculté qui nous fasse voir le but de loin, et, cette faculté, c'est l'intuition."* La Valeur de la Science *(Paris, Flammarion, 1909), p. 27.*

THE PRINCIPLE OF EQUAL LIBERTY

Having rejected the principle of utility, Rawls contends that persons in the original position would likely choose two fundamental principles. The first is the **principle of equal liberty**. It states that "each person is to have an equal right to the most extensive basic liberty compatible with a similar liberty for others."[9] Note that such a principle would be accepted without a knowledge of anyone's particular ends and without knowledge of what is to anyone's advantage. The implicit agreement, therefore, would be to have everyone's pursuits and interests fall within the boundaries of what the principles of justice require. People would be expected to refrain from choosing ends that would violate the liberties of others, and to allow all liberties that they would expect for themselves. Advantages for some could not be purchased justifiably at the expense of others' freedoms—certainly not in a situation of equality and co-operation for mutual advantage. Furthermore, whereas utilitarians such as Bentham do not distinguish among pleasures and see all pleasures as equally valuable and worth pursuing, Rawls maintains that "the principles of right, and so of justice, put limits on which satisfactions have value; they impose restrictions on what are reasonable conceptions of one's good."[10] From the Rawlsian, **deontological**, social contract perspective, the concept of **rightness** overrides and is prior to the concept of **goodness**. The freedom or liberty to pursue specific ends must be limited by considerations of justice. In this vein, Rawls writes,

> A just social system defines the scope within which individuals must develop their aims, and it provides a framework of rights and opportunities and the means of satisfaction within and by the use of which these ends may be equitably pursued. The priority of justice is accounted for, in part, by holding that the interests requiring the violation of justice have no value. Having no merit in the first place, they cannot override its claims.[11]

The basic liberties of all citizens required by the first principle include (1) political liberty, that is, the right to vote and run for public office; (2) freedom of speech and assembly; (3) freedom of thought and liberty of conscience; (4) personal freedom; (5) freedom to hold property; and finally (6) freedom from arbitrary arrest and seizure. The liberties listed here represent the basic rights of every person within society and, ideally, none of them is to be violated. These basic rights define the proper boundaries within which social practices must fall if they are to be considered acceptable, right and just.

The statement of the first principle clearly tells us that people are to be regarded as free and equal. Systems of rules defining practices of various social institutions must, therefore, be administered equitably. There should be a spirit of **impartiality** and **disinterestedness** characterizing the distribution of advantages. No individual should arbitrarily receive preferred treatment. For example, if a firm offers a position of employment and draws up job specifications, the equal liberty principle requires that all applicants be judged by the established criteria. If it were the case that someone without the specified and required credentials were offered the position, the principle would not be upheld because an exception was made, presumably on the basis of irrelevant considerations (e.g., ethnic background). In addition, the principle would not be equitably or fairly administered if particular individuals were excluded on criteria not related to the job (e.g., gender or race). We can see, then, how considerations of rightness and justice can become involved even in a society's hiring practices, a point that underscores Rawls' claim that social institutions are proper objects of moral evaluation.

THE DIFFERENCE PRINCIPLE

The difference principle is the second principle falling under Rawls' conception of justice as fairness. It states: "Social and economic inequalities, for example inequalities of wealth and authority, are just only if they result in compensating benefits for everyone, and in particular for the least advantaged members of society."[12] The difference principle should not be misunderstood here as equivalent to the utilitarian greatest happiness principle, which seeks to promote the greatest happiness for the greatest number. The difference principle does not permit inequalities in institutional practices on the grounds that the hardships or burdens of some are offset by the greater good of the majority. In Rawls' view, "it is not just that some should have less in order that others may prosper."[13] Rawls does not suggest by this that everyone must be treated precisely the same. He believes that citizens of a country do not object to people having different positions within society (e.g., prime minister, president or judge), each with its own special rights and duties. What they object to is the pattern of honours and rewards assigned to certain positions (for example, the privileges and salaries of government officials). They may also object to the uneven distribution of power and wealth resulting from socio-economic practices that provide a small group of people with exceptional opportunities (for example, in a free market environment, the concentration of wealth among a small group of people allows that group to pursue large entrepreneurial and speculative rewards). To justify inequalities, there must be reason to believe that the practice involving the inequality, or resulting in it, will ultimately work for the advantage of *every* person engaging in it—not just the majority. Individuals thus must find their conditions and prospects under a situation of inequality preferable to those under a situation without inequality. In short, every person must gain from the inequality, if that inequality is to be permissible.

For the difference principle, which allows for differences of treatment, to be made acceptable, an important condition must be met. It is necessary that the offices to which special benefits are attached be open to all who meet the necessary requirements. Such offices must be won in a fair competition, wherein contestants are judged on their merits. The fact that an excluded individual nevertheless benefits from the efforts put forward by those allowed to compete does not legitimize this unjust treatment, according to Rawls. There are intrinsic goods involved in the skillful and devoted exercise of various offices and practices. If a person is prevented from functioning in those particular offices or practices, then that person is deprived of one of the most important ways in which individuals realize their **human potential**. The person is robbed of his or her humanity, so to speak.

The suggestion that societal positions should be won by fair competition does not mean that absolutely everyone has a right to compete and to be seriously considered for every job. Remember, the difference principle allows for the possibility of inequality if it works to the advantage of every individual and, especially, to the advantage of the least well off. Suppose, for instance, that an airline establishes a minimum level of corrected vision for all of its pilots. Now, such a regulation does, in fact, work against those who cannot reach the minimum. Some people will, in effect, be excluded from consideration for the pilot's job. Nonetheless, this vision requirement should not be regarded as unjust. A pilot with limited vision is a danger to the airline's passengers, as well as to himself. Everyone, including the candidate pilot, benefits by the application of the vision requirement, albeit through a form of "unequal" treatment. (See Barry, 1973, pp. 52–53, for a similar example.) The difference principle may also be at work in some governmental economic policies. One frequently hears how unjust it is that huge corporations are given tax breaks, while the average tax-payer is saddled with an ever-increasing share of the tax burden. It could be argued, however, that this apparently unequal treatment allows corporations more available capital to invest in new business ventures; in turn, this will create new or better jobs, which will certainly benefit those worst off in society, namely, the unemployed. Were the tax burden proportionately equal, perhaps no new job opportunities would be created and the unemployed would remain that way—thus worse, rather than better, off.

THE MAXIMIN SOLUTION TO THE PROBLEM OF SOCIAL JUSTICE

In closing, it is worth noting that Rawls' combination of the two principles arising out of the original position is called the **maximin solution** to the problem of social justice.[14] When the equal

PHILOSOPHERS AT WORK

In Rawls' attempt to extract from the original position the principles upon which a just society would be based, we find disembodied rational agents who fit together as a self-sufficient association of individuals. Although all are considered equal and are respectful of each others' rights, co-operation occurs primarily for the purposes of furthering individual self-interests. Standards of justice as fairness are laid down and are used as a way of resolving disputes among societal members. In view of this:

1. Is there any danger in extrapolating from the hypothetical original position to real life, having conceptualized people in society as purely rational agents? Why or why not?
2. Should we consider all people self-interested and self-sufficient? How else could we see them?
3. Do people co-operate with one another only, or primarily, for purposes of furthering their personal interests and for achieving their life goals? Explain.
4. Are there any societies or communities you know of that base their social relations on something other than justice? If so, which ones? How do they function? What is the basis of social co-operation there (i.e., why do people work together)?
5. Finally, what evaluative comments could you make about Rawls' social contractarianism? Do you "buy" his theory?

liberty principle and the difference principle are combined under the maximin solution, the general rule is to rank alternatives by their worst possible outcomes: thus, we adopt "the alternative the worst outcome of which is superior to the worst outcomes of the others."[15] This guideline helps **maximize** the lot, or welfare, of those **minimally advantaged**—a fundamental goal of the Rawlsian just society. The maximin rule focuses our attention on the worst that can happen under each alternative course of action, and it instructs us to make a decision in light of that. Rawls' notion of justice, then, is a **reciprocity** concept. Rightness is not ultimately determined by consequences. Rather, the reciprocity element inherent in Rawls' theory of justice "requires that a practice be such that all members who fall under it could and would accept it and be bound by it."[16] No person has authority over another. Each is willing to accept the worst position as it might be assigned by one's enemy or opponent in a situation of conflict. This makes the element of reciprocity essential to justice as fairness.

MINDWORK MEDITATION

John Rawls has made much of the principle of justice as fairness in his socio-political moral philosophy. How important is fairness or justice to you personally? Do you think being fair, or just, as a moral person is more important than maximizing goodness or doing what feels right? Why? What are your other thoughts on Rawls?

KEY TERMS

tacit agreements
justice
inviolability
rights
society
identity of interests
conflicts of interest
ideal observer
common point of view
fairly adjudicated
civic friendship
the original position
hypothetical situation
veil of ignorance

conflict
contingencies
fair
just
justice as fairness
principle of equal liberty
deontological
rightness
goodness
impartiality
disinterestedness
the difference principle
human potential
maximin solution

rational	maximize
free	minimally advantaged
equal members	reciprocity
mutually disinterested	

PROGRESS CHECK 6.1

Instructions: Fill in the blanks with the appropriate responses listed below.

justice	identity of interests
ideal observer	inviolate
social contract theory	utilitarianism
society	veil of ignorance
original position	mutually disinterested
principle of equal liberty	deontological ethics
maximin principle	difference principle
reciprocity	

1. John Rawls' theory of justice is intended as a more satisfactory alternative to ___ *utilitarianism*

2. ___ *social contract theory* views morality and matters of justice as a set of tacit agreements among society's members.

3. In the same way that truth is the first virtue of systems of thought, ___ *justice* is the first virtue of social institutions.

4. People's basic rights cannot be negotiated or bargained away because they are ___ *inviolate*

5. A(n) ___ *society* is a self-sufficient association of individuals who co-operate for purposes of mutual advantage.

6. Although people are different and often go in different directions in their lives, they, nonetheless, still share a(n) ___ having the same basic needs and wanting generally the same kinds of things. *identity of interests*

7. From the position of the ___ *ideal observer*, conflicts can be fairly and objectively resolved without bias or favouritism.

8. The ___ *original position* is a hypothetical situation used by Rawls to draw out the principles of justice as fairness.

9. Persons placed behind a(n) ___ are unaware of any specifics pertaining to themselves (e.g., gender, class and ability). *veil of ignorance*

10. Persons in the original position are ___ concerned with furthering their own goals, not sacrificing for another's. *mutually disinterested*

11. The ___ *principle of equal liberty* states that all people are to be granted the same freedoms. One cannot grant less freedom to others than one would grant to oneself.

12. According to ___, the concept of rightness takes precedence over goodness. *deontological ethics*

13. The idea that social inequalities in treatment are fair or just only if everyone benefits and only if everyone would be better off is captured by the ~~difference principle~~.

14. The ~~maxim~~ requires us to compare alternatives before making moral choices. The action whose worst outcome for all is better than the worst outcome of all the other alternatives is the right choice.

15. The concept of ~~reciprocity~~ requires that we be willing to accept the consequences of a principle that we wish to apply to others.

SUMMARY OF MAJOR POINTS

1.   How does Rawls conceptualize society?

   It is a self-sufficient association of individuals.
   It is bound by general rules of conduct.
   It is a system of co-operation designed to promote the welfare of all.
   It is a co-operative venture for purposes of mutual advantage.

2.   What is the original position?

   It is a hypothetical situation used by Rawls to derive the first principles upon which a just society would be based.
   It is a situation wherein people are placed behind a "veil of ignorance."
   It is a position in which people are unaware of their status and personal characteristics.
   People in this position are assumed to be rational, free, equal, and mutually disinterested.

3.   What is "justice as fairness"? How can it be used?

   It results from the establishment of principles in the original position.
   It can be used to criticize and to reform social institutions.
   It can be used for legislative purposes.
   It is what free and equal individuals would contract to accept for their mutual advantage under fair circumstances.

4.   What is meant by the "equal liberty principle"?

   Each person is to have an equal right to the most extensive basic liberty compatible with a similar liberty for others.
   It guarantees all citizens political liberty, the right to vote and run for public office, freedom of speech and assembly, freedom of thought and liberty of conscience, personal freedom, the right to own property, and freedom from arbitrary arrest and seizure.

5.   How should one understand the difference principle?

   Social and economic inequalities are just only if they result in compensating benefits for everyone—especially for the least advantaged in society.
   It differs from the greatest happiness principle.
   Applying this principle means that offices having special rights and privileges must be won in fair competition.

6.   What does the maximin solution advise?

The alternative one should adopt is the alternative having the worst outcome which is superior to the worst outcome of the other alternatives.

It requires one to maximize the lot or welfare of those minimally advantaged in society.

It suggests that all decisions fall acceptably under the equal liberty principle and the difference principle, taken together.

SOURCE REFERENCES AND RELATED READINGS

Barry, B.M. *The Liberal Theory of Justice*. Oxford: Clarendon Press, 1973.

Blocker, H.G. and E.H. Smith, eds. *John Rawls' Theory of Social Justice: An Introduction*. Athens: Ohio University Press, 1980.

Daniels, N., ed. *Reading Rawls*. New York: Basic Books, 1975.

Falikowski, Anthony. *Moral Philosophy: Theories, Skills, and Applications*. Englewood Cliffs, N.J.: Prentice Hall, 1990.

Rawls, John. *A Theory of Justice*. Cambridge, Mass.: Harvard University Press, 1971.

———. "Justice as Fairness." *The Journal of Philosophy*. Vol. 54, Oct. 1957, pp. 653–62.

Wolff, R.P. *Understanding Rawls*. Princeton, N.J.: Princeton University Press, 1976.

ENDNOTES

1. John Rawls, *A Theory of Justice*, Cambridge, Mass.: Harvard University Press, 1971, p. 3
2. ibid., p. 4
3. ibid., p. 4
4. ibid.
5. ibid., p. 5
6. ibid., p. 13
7. ibid., p. 12
8. ibid., p. 14
9. ibid., p. 60
10. ibid. p. 31
11. ibid., p. 31
12. ibid. pp. 14–15
13. ibid. p. 15
14. ibid., p. 152
15. ibid., pp. 152–153
16. ibid., p. 153

Contemporary Moral Theories: Ethical Egoism, Existentialism and the Morality of Care

So far in our coverage of classical moral perspectives, we have looked at Greek virtue ethics, British utilitarianism and the deontological tradition. Though John Rawls' theory of justice, covered under deontology, was developed in the twentieth century, it has quickly become a classic, and because its development was highly influenced by deontological insights, I believe it was appropriate to include it alongside a discussion of Kant's work. The three classical moral perspectives we have studied thus far certainly capture much of how morality has been understood historically.

In this final segment of our theoretical discussion, we will turn to a number of modern moral alternatives. We will first look at the ethical egoism of Ayn Rand—what she calls her theory of objectivist ethics. Rand questions our conventional understanding of morality, charging that many traditionally accepted moral codes are absurd and inhumane. After Rand, we go on to discuss existentialist ethics, examining the important roles played by considerations like freedom and individual responsibility. This moral perspective constitutes a significant challenge to rational moralists like Bentham, for instance, who believe that moral decisions can be made in a "spirit of scientific objectivity." Existentialists throw objectivity out the window, with some interesting implications for moral life. The last perspective we'll discuss pertains to a morality of care as presented by Carol Gilligan and Nel Noddings. Like existentialism, this theory questions the primacy of reason in moral decision making. Noddings and Gilligan argue that morality can, and should, be understood in terms of the human affective response of care.

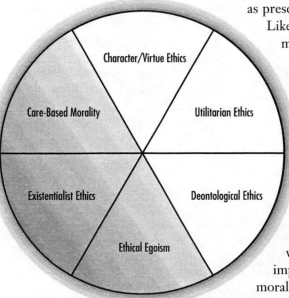

The aforementioned alternatives to be discussed in the following section of the text will no doubt give us all pause for thought and occasion to re-examine our basic moral intuitions regarding altruism, objectivity and the role of reason in matters of moral justification. As a bonus, studying the work of Rand, Gilligan, and Noddings will also help us appreciate some of the important contributions women have made to moral inquiry.

7

Ethical Egoism: Ayn Rand's Objectivist Ethics

Overview

Learning Outcomes

After successfully completing this chapter, you will be able to

• Redefine 'selfishness' and appreciate the merits of this positive redefinition in light of Ayn Rand's objectivist ethics.

• Provide an explanation for why basing a morality on altruism is inhumane.

• Discuss Rand's basis of morality and how it relates to the "is-ought" problem in moral philosophy.

• Understand the relationship between basic values and their corresponding virtues.

• Appreciate how a life based on rational selfishness is not brutish or inherently evil.

PHILOSOPHICAL FOCUS QUESTIONS

1. Why is Ayn Rand critical of conventional moralities?

2. How is selfishness normally understood? What is Rand's reinterpretation?

3. What is meant by the 'beneficiary-criterion' in morality?

4. What, for Rand, is the relationship between value and life?

5. According to Rand, what are the most important virtues in life? Why?

6. What is meant by 'rational selfishness'?

Biographical Brief

Ayn Rand (1905–1982)

Oscar White/Magma/CORBIS

Ayn Rand was born Alissa Rosenbaum on February 2, 1905 in St. Petersburg, Russia. A graduate of the University of Leningrad, she studied history and worked as a museum guide. After graduating, Rand entered the State Institute for Cinema Arts and began to study English. In 1926, she arrived in New York City, later to become a citizen of the United States. After a brief stay with relatives in Chicago, Rand moved to Hollywood where she worked for the famous Cecil B. DeMille as a movie extra and script reader. Rand eventually went on to write a couple of Broadway plays and several movie scripts in addition to her best-known novels, *The Fountainhead* and *Atlas Shrugged*.

From the age of 40, Rand's career began to move in a different direction, as she started to see herself more as a philosopher, embodying many of her philosophical ideas in the thoughts, words, and deeds of her fictional characters. For the last 25 years of her life, she abandoned fiction altogether, deciding to dedicate herself to the advancement of her own individualistic philosophy of reason, egoism, and laissez-faire capitalism, which she entitled Objectivism. In the process, Rand became one of America's most respected, and arguably most reviled, thinkers from the late 1950s to the middle 1970s. Whether admired or despised, there can be little doubt she had an impact on modern thought. It could be argued that she enjoyed perhaps the largest and most loyal following of any living philosopher of the modern western world (James T. Baker, 1987). The Ayn Rand Institute still exists today and serves as the centre for the advancement of Objectivism. Non-fictional philosophical works by Rand include, *The Virtue of Selfishness: A New Concept of Egoism, For the New Intellectual, Introduction to Objectivist Epistemology,* and *Capitalism: The Unknown Ideal.*

ETHICAL EGOISM

Before beginning with this outline of Ayn Rand's work, a few preliminary remarks are in order. When the name of Ayn Rand is raised in academic circles today, some philosophers react with

> *It is philosophy that sets men's goals and determines their course; it is only philosophy that can save them now. Today, the world is facing a choice: if civilization is to survive, it is the altruistic morality that men have to reject.*
>
> AYN RAND

lightning-speed hostility and contempt. Others are simply satisfied to be confidently dismissive, alleging that Rand is guilty of bad scholarship and concluding that her works should be relegated to the dustbin of intellectual history. Since Rand does not always properly document her sources and appears to commit the straw-man and is–ought fallacies (see Chapter Eleven for discussions of these), many feel her work does not deserve serious academic attention. While this line of reasoning certainly holds some weight, carrying such logic over to other historically important philosophers such as Jeremy Bentham and Friedrich Nietzsche might require us to dismiss their works as nonsense as well. Arguably, the fundamental premise of Bentham's entire utilitarian system is based on fallacious reasoning, namely, the is–ought fallacy (see Chapter Three). Also, in describing the value of master and slave moralities, Friedrich Nietzsche, another important recognized philosopher, appears to commit the genetic fallacy in reasoning when he concludes that moralities have only the value of their originators and that any moralities created by weak enslaved peoples are inferior to those created by the master noble types. On top of that fallacious reasoning, Nietzsche is guilty of other poor scholarship as well. In explaining the origins and development of various moral systems, Nietzsche "... names no names, dates no events, and shows scant concern for details, variations, and anomalies."[1] As one critic writes: "... it would be more accurate to call his genealogy inspired guesswork, suggestive speculation, or a likely tale. And Nietzsche's genealogy, strikingly devoid of empirical evidence or scholarly apparatus, is anything but patiently documentary."[2] In view of such stiff criticism, one might think Nietzsche's works would already have been thrown into history's dustbin. Yet, the academic community has not done so, for even his critics have allowed his poor scholarship to be positively reinterpreted as an *illustrative myth*. One writer puts it so: "Nietzsche *poeticizes history* [my emphasis] the better to bring out the truth about the origins and thereby the nature, of our moral prejudices."[3] It is interesting how when Nietzsche reinvents the past in his imagination, he is merely poeticizing history; his genetic fallacy is transformed into a useful illustrative myth. Yet, when Rand commits errors no more egregious than Nietzsche's, or Bentham's for that matter, she is found guilty of poor scholarship and dismissed by some. To describe Nietzsche's make-believe facts of the past as "poeticized history" and Rand's failure to properly cite respected sources "poor scholarship" may be to commit another academically irresponsible fallacy, namely *special pleading* (see Chapter Eleven). This involves using a double standard of evaluation, one for those we prefer and a stricter one for those we don't like. It may be that Rand's attacks on collectivist, altruistic morality are based on a somewhat distorted straw-man version of it, but in Nietzschean fashion, perhaps, all the better to contrast and explain the nature of her own ethical egoism. With this preliminary out of the way, let us now without prejudgment direct our attention to the ideas of Ayn Rand.

In a collection of essays brought together in a short book polemically entitled *The Virtue of Selfishness*, Ayn Rand articulates her highly individualistic theory of morality.[4] She begins in the Introduction by challenging our conventional understanding of the term **"selfishness."** As she points out, most of us equate the idea of selfishness with "evil." To be selfish is to be some kind of ruthless brute who coldly steps on people whenever necessary to achieve one's ends. Such a person displays little or no care for others and pursues nothing but immediate gratification of mindless whims and momentary desires. Selfish people simply do what they want—all others be damned. The selfish person is assumed to be morally contemptible, a callous and self-centred creature. No wonder few aspire to become selfish, while still fewer openly admit to being so.

For Rand, our failure to properly understand selfishness has led to a kind of arrested moral development of humankind.[5] "Selfishness" should *not* lead us to the conclusion that an action is right simply because one has chosen it. Self-interest cannot be determined by random whim and blind desire. It must be discovered and achieved by the guidance of rational principles. Selfishness, rightly understood, "does not tell us whether concern with one's own interests is good or evil; nor does it tell us what constitutes man's actual interests. It is the task of [rational] ethics to answer such questions."[6]

Altruism is Inhumane

Rand asserts that the **ethics of altruism**, i.e., the type of ethics which makes others the beneficiaries of our moral action, requires us to accept two inhumane tenets. The first is that any concern with one's own interests is evil, regardless of what they might be. The second is that to act or engage in any activities which further one's own interests is to become an evil brute. From Rand's perspective, altruism requires you to renounce your own "selfish" interests for the sake of your neighbor's. If you do things for others at your own expense, that's good. If you do things for yourself, to benefit only yourself, that's bad. "Thus, the **beneficiary** of an action is the only criterion of moral value—and so long as that beneficiary is anybody other than oneself, anything goes."[7]

Rand finds the implications of such thinking grotesquely absurd. To illustrate, by thinking along these lines, it follows that business people and bank robbers can now be lumped together as immoral crooks, since they both seek wealth for their own "selfish" benefit. "A young man who gives up his career in order to support his parents and never rises beyond the rank of grocery clerk is regarded as morally superior to the young man who endures an excruciating struggle and achieves his personal ambition. [He did it for himself, after all.] A dictator is regarded as moral, since the unspeakable atrocities he committed were intended to benefit 'the people,' not himself."[8] The point is that adherence to the "beneficiary-criterion of morality" teaches individuals that morality is their enemy. They can only lose from it. There is no prospect of gain. Dutifully sacrificing for others and hoping that others will dutifully sacrifice for oneself breeds mutual resentment, not pleasure or happiness. As Rand puts it, the pursuit of values becomes "like an exchange of unwanted, unchosen Christmas presents, which neither [party] is morally permitted to buy for himself."[9] Morality is all about "doing for you" while at the same time "doing nothing for me."

Another problem with altruistic ethics stems from the fact that it does not permit any room for self-respecting, self-supporting persons—individuals who determine their own lives by sacrificing neither themselves nor others. Altruism transforms people into either sacrificial animals (those giving of themselves) or profiteers-on-sacrifice (those gladly accepting the sacrificial offerings)—it turns people into victims and parasites. For Rand, this view of human beings allows for no acceptable concept of justice, nor any possibility of benevolent coexistence among men. It breeds only cynicism and guilt. People become cynical because they neither practise nor accept altruistic morality. They experience guilt because they don't dare to reject it. Try defending the proposition that you should place your own self-interests before everyone else's and see what reaction you get. Even if you believe this proposition, you defend it at your own peril against the "collectivist herd" waiting for your sacrificial offering!

Rejecting the "other-as-beneficiary" criterion, Rand argues that the basis of morality, as well as the justification of particular ethical actions and decisions, must come from **human nature** and the function of morality in human life. Rand writes,

> The **Objectivist ethics** holds that the actor must always be the beneficiary of his action and that man must act for his own *rational* self-interest. But his right to do so is derived from his nature as man and from the function of moral values in the context of a rational, objectively demonstrated and validated code of moral principles which define and determine his actual self-interest....It is not a license 'to do as he pleases' and it is not applicable to the altruist's image of a 'selfish' brute nor to any man motivated by irrational emotions, feelings, urges, wishes or whims.[10]

THE BASIS AND FUNCTION OF MORALITY

The questions of what is morally right and who should benefit from moral action are, for Rand, actually secondary ones. She would have us ask initially, "Do we even need a morality?" For her, the answer to this primary question serves as the precondition for any system of ethics we might try to justify or prescribe for others. As she says, "The first question is not: What particular code of values should man accept? The first question is: Does man need values at all—and why?"[11] Rand's answer is that we need a new code of values to save civilization. The history of ethics reveals, for her, that it has fallen prey to mysticism and subjective bias. Objectivist ethics' goal, therefore, is to give values a basis other than faith, intuition, taste, feeling, urge, wish and personal whim. This is what morality has been based on in the past, and we need only look at the effects to see how disastrous this has been. Rand asserts that, historically speaking, philosophers have simply taken ethics as a given, never concerning themselves with its metaphysical cause or objective validation. Past efforts to break the monopoly of mysticism (i.e., religion, the Church) in the field of ethics by justifying morality on social grounds merely resulted in a substitution of **society** for **God.** Instead of acting morally in accordance with the will of God, the neo-mystics, as Rand calls them, prescribed that we act for the good of society. Rand sees two problems with this manoeuvre. First, she argues that there is "no such entity as 'society,' since society is only a number of individual men." The notion of society is a questionable abstraction, in other words. Secondly, in a society, the mob, or "gang," is allowed to pursue any whims (or atrocities) it desires, while dissenting individuals are ethically required to spend their lives in service to it, and to those who claim to be the spokespersons for the collective good. The result of this subjugation of the individual to the gang, society, group or collective is an irrational ethic—one based on feelings, tastes, wishes and whims of others. Emotional commitment becomes the basis of such a social morality. This commitment represents nothing other than a subjective choice or personal preference. Accepting **personal whim** as the basis of morality inevitably means that a battle rages over whose whim should be accepted: the individual's, one's own, society's, the dictator's or God's. Skeptical, Rand does not accept **mysticism** (God, religion or blind faith), **neo-mysticism** (the primacy of society and the collective), **emotionalism** (capricious feelings) or **subjective preference** (personal whim) as the foundational platform of her moral thinking. Rather she begins with an analysis of "values" and asks why we need them. She does not consider the concept of value in isolation, however. The idea of values relates necessarily to the questions: "Of value to *whom*?" and "Of what for *what*?" If something has value, then what is presupposed is that there is a valuing agent able to achieve that value (or goal) in face of alternatives. If there is no one to choose or if there are no alternatives to choose from, then no goals or values are possible.

The most fundamental alternative for humankind involves the choice between existence—simply, life—or nonexistence. All other choices are contingent on this one. Such a choice can apply only to conscious living organisms, not to inanimate things like rocks. Furthermore, if the life choice were not an issue—say, if we were immortal, indestructible robots, unaffected by anything—we would not have any values. If we could not be changed, damaged, injured or destroyed, if nothing we did threatened or secured our survival, then we would never have anything to lose or gain. Nothing would serve or threaten our welfare; nothing could further or frustrate our interests, since we would be immune to all outside influence. As indestructible robots, valuing would become irrelevant, since nothing would be of any consequence.

The truth is, however, that we are not indestructible robots, but conscious living beings. Some things are in our interest and other things are not. To quote Rand, "It is only the concept of 'Life' that makes the concept of 'Value' possible. It is only to a living entity that things can be good or evil."[12] For her, life is a process of self-sustaining and self-generated action. It is life which gives humanity goals. Life is the ultimate value to which all lesser goals are the means. All these lesser goals are to be evaluated in these terms: That which furthers life is good, that which threatens it is evil. Value is therefore derivative of life. One cannot meaningfully discuss the concept of value outside the context of life. One does not live to value, but values to live. We make value judgments in order to secure our survival.

The premise that any concept of value must be based on life has enormous implications. When it comes to survival, much is determined by **nature**, by the kind of entities we are as human beings. If we don't eat, we die. If we jump off a cliff, we risk our continued existence. This is not a matter of opinion, faith, majority rule, intuition or subjective preference; it is merely a fact. Thus, value judgments can be validated by reference to the facts of reality. "The fact that a living entity *is*, determines what it *ought* to do."[13] In one fell swoop, then, Rand believes she has dismissed the logical problem of deriving a moral "ought" from an "is" of experience.[14] Reality serves as the basis of (moral) value judgment. The foundation of morality need not have a mystical, social or emotional foundation. Nature decides what is necessary for survival.

Of course, newborn children do not enter the world with innate knowledge of what has survival value. The genetically determined pleasure-pain mechanism of the body does, however, initially serve to protect the organism's life. Pleasure becomes the signal that the organism is pursuing the right course of action. Unfortunately, some children are born with a rare disease that renders them unable to experience pain. With no warning signals to let them know that they are suffering physically or doing things that hurt them, these children do not usually survive for long. Avoiding pain and injury is not only "right," if we are to survive, it is necessitated by our very natures—Rand's point.

For us, as conscious beings, reason becomes, through the development of consciousness, our tool for distinguishing between what is ultimately pleasurable or painful, life-sustaining or life-threatening. We need not always touch the hot stove to know that it is hot and dangerous. Through use of cognitive function, we can store past experiences in memory, anticipate, calculate and conceptualize in ways which keep us out of harm's way and on the road to happiness and pleasure. Since the conscious mind, or rationality, is part of our core human nature, and the basic means to our survival, Rand concludes that "that which is proper to the life of a rational being is the good; that which negates, opposes or destroys it is the evil."[15]

VALUES AND VIRTUE

In "The Objectivist Ethics," Rand distinguishes between the notions of **value** and **virtue**. She writes, "Value is that which one acts to gain and/or keep—*virtue* is the act by which one gains and/or keeps it."[16] According to her, there are three values which, taken together, constitute the means to, and realization of, one's ultimate value, namely life. They are (1) **reason**, (2) **purpose** and (3) **self-esteem**. The virtues which correspond to these values are, in order: **rationality**, **productivity** and **pride**. The virtue of rationality is expressed by one's acceptance of reason as the only source of knowledge and guide to action. Rational virtue involves a total commitment to full, conscious awareness and to the maintenance of complete mental focus on all matters and all choices in all of one's waking hours. Rational people do not allow their minds to become unfocused—this would constitute a suspension of consciousness, a form of irrationality rejecting our very means of survival as human beings. To be unfocused is to be anti-rational and therefore anti-mind and anti-life.

To be committed to rationality also means that all of one's values, goals and desires must be validated by logical thought processes. One must never engage in mystical or metaphysical speculation about anything above one's perception of reality. To be rational is to accept responsibility for forming one's own judgments and living by the work of one's own mind. The rationally self-interested person should never sacrifice his or her own convictions simply to conform to the opinions of others or to satisfy *their* (selfish) desires.

Productive work is the process by which man's mind supports and sustains life. By practising the virtue of productiveness, we adjust our natural physical background to suit us, unlike lower-level organisms, which must adjust themselves in order to adapt to environmental circumstances. Productive work elicits the highest qualities of man's character, i.e., creativity, ambition, self-assertiveness and dedication to "reshaping the earth in the image of his values." Productive work encompasses the most complete and purposeful use of the mind.

The third virtue discussed by Rand is pride. For her, it is roughly equivalent to moral ambitiousness. Pride is something one earns by working toward one's own moral perfection. This is done by refusing to accept any code of irrational virtues impossible to practice, and by practicing the virtues one knows to be rational. The virtue of pride, stemming from the value of self-esteem, means that we should never accept unearned guilt, avoid earning any guilt, and, if we do earn it, do what is required to correct matters. To be a person of pride, one must do what one can to overcome flaws in one's character, and must never put any concern, wish, fear or mood of the moment above one's own self-esteem. The virtue of pride also requires that we reject any role of sacrificial animal. We are obliged to reject any philosophy, doctrine or religion that preaches self-denial as a virtuous moral duty. This last point is nicely capped off by Rand with the following statement:

> The basic *social* principle of the Objectivist ethics is that, just as life is an end in itself, so every living human being is an end in himself, not the means to the ends or the welfare of others— and, therefore, that man must live for his own sake, neither sacrificing himself to others nor sacrificing others to himself. *To live for his own sake means that the achievement of his own happiness is man's highest moral purpose.*[17]

RATIONAL SELFISHNESS AND THE PRINCIPLE OF TRADE

Happiness, then, is not some kind of abstract principle that one applies to situations or uses for guidance when trying to make correct moral value judgments. "Life" is the irreducible primary and it is in support of life that rational value judgments can be made. If one were to make happiness the standard of morality, then whatever made one happy would be right. One's emotional whims would end up as the basis of action, and since whims vary from person to person, no rationality or objectivity could be found with them. Rand contends, therefore, that happiness should be seen as the *purpose* of

> *The principle of trade is the only rational ethical principle for all human relationships, personal and social, private and public, spiritual and material. It is the principle of justice.*
>
> *AYN RAND*

MINDWORK MEDITATION

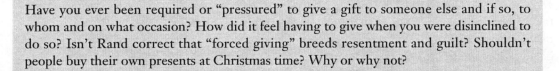

Have you ever been required or "pressured" to give a gift to someone else and if so, to whom and on what occasion? How did it feel having to give when you were disinclined to do so? Isn't Rand correct that "forced giving" breeds resentment and guilt? Shouldn't people buy their own presents at Christmas time? Why or why not?

ethics, but not the *standard*. "The task of ethics is to define man's proper code of values and thus to give him the means of achieving happiness."[18]

Defining her proper code of values as "rational selfishness," Rand emphasizes that this does not involve sacrificing others for one's own benefit. It is not in one's rational self-interest to injure, enslave, rob or murder others. In fact, for her, rational interests do not clash—"there is no conflict of interests among men who do not desire the unearned, who do not make sacrifices nor accept them, who deal with one another as *traders*, giving value for value."[19]

According to Rand, traders are people who earn what they get and refuse to take the undeserved. Traders deal with each others as equals: there are no slaves and masters in a world of rational selfishness. Traders deal with others in terms of a free and uncoerced exchange, in which both parties benefit in their own independent judgment. Traders do not expect something for nothing, nor do they expect to be paid for their failures and defaults. Only achievement is to be rewarded. Furthermore, traders do not place the burden of their failures upon others; neither will they accept a life of bondage because of others' failures.

The notion of people as traders extends beyond impersonal business relationships. Love, friendship and admiration, for instance, constitute a kind of "spiritual payment" one gives in exchange for the selfish pleasure one derives from the virtues and companionship of another. Traders do not seek love for their own weaknesses, only for their strengths and virtues. Traders also do not give their love to others because of others' flaws and weaknesses, but because of the virtuous gifts those others have to offer.

Finally, in her essay, "The Objectivist Ethics," Rand makes the point that only on the basis of rational selfishness can we live together in a free, prosperous and benevolent society. In a rational society of human beings, knowledge can be gained, stored and traded from one individual to another or from one generation to another. Fair trade and co-operation "allows all men who take part in it to achieve a greater knowledge, skill and productive return then they could achieve if each had to produce everything he needs, as on a desert island or on a self-sustaining farm."[20] Rational selfishness is against initiating any form of physical force. It is only justified in self-defence as a retaliation against someone wishing to make one a victim. Rand puts this in the context of self-defence. If one kills in order to rob a victim—like the holdup man who seeks to gain value or wealth—this is wrong. On the other hand, if the robber's targeted victim kills in self-defence, that person gains nothing. The underlying principle of rational selfishness is this: "No man may obtain any values from others by resorting to physical force."[21]

Regarding moral agents as free and equal traders, prohibited from using physical force or violence, allows Rand to couple her ethical theory quite easily with **laissez-faire capitalism**. In her estimation, the only moral purpose of government is to protect human rights—to protect people's lives, liberty, their property and their right to pursue individual happiness. In all this, rights are highly significant, if not of paramount importance. As Rand says, "Without property rights, no other rights are possible."[22] In "The Objectivist Ethics," she does not spell out in any detail her socio-political theory of Objectivism. As she points out, that is discussed in her novel *Atlas Shrugged*. What she does say in this essay is that every political system must be based on and derived from a theory of ethics, and that Objectivist ethics is the theory which best supports American capitalism—a system which is continually under attack from varying sources.

based on and derived from a theory of ethics, and that Objectivist ethics is the theory which best supports American capitalism—a system which is continually under attack from varying sources. Rand invites those readers who are interested in the history and the psychological causes of the "philosopher's treason against capitalism," to read the title essay of her book *For the New Intellectual*. Also found in that book is the following passage from *Atlas Shrugged*, one of the novels she wrote to illustrate her objectivist ethics of egoism. The title of this excerpt is "This is John Galt Speaking." While reading, see whether you can spot any philosophical points that

BACK TO THE SOURCE*

"This is John Galt Speaking"
Ayn Rand

"Ladies and gentlemen." said a voice that came from the radio receiver—a man's clear, calm, implacable voice, the kind of voice that had not been heard on the airwaves for years—"Mr. Thompson will not speak to you tonight. His time is up. I have taken it over. You were to hear a report on the world crisis. That is what you are going to hear....

"For twelve years, you have been asking: Who is John Galt? This is John Galt speaking. I am the man who loves his life. I am the man who does not sacrifice his love or his values. I am the man who has deprived you of victims and thus has destroyed your world, and if you wish to know why you are perishing—you who dread knowledge—I am the man who will now tell you....

"You have heard it said that this is an age of moral crisis. You have said it yourself, half in fear, half in hope that the words had no meaning. You have cried that man's sins are destroying the world and you have cursed human nature for its unwillingness

to practice the virtues you demanded. Since virtue, to you, consists of sacrifice, you have demanded more sacrifices at every successive disaster. In the name of a return to morality, you have sacrificed all those evils which you held as the cause of your plight. You have sacrificed justice to mercy. You have sacrificed independence to unity. You have sacrificed reason to faith. You have sacrificed wealth to need. You have sacrificed self-esteem to self-denial. You have sacrificed happiness to duty.

"You have destroyed all that which you held to be evil and achieved all that which you held to be good. Why, then, do you shrink in horror from the sight of the world around you? That world is not the product of your sins, it is the product and the image of your virtues. It is your moral ideal brought into reality in its full and final perfection. You have fought for it, you have dreamed of it, you have wished for it, and I—I am the man who has granted you your wish.

"Your ideal had an implacable enemy, which your code of morality was designed to destroy. I have withdrawn that enemy. I have taken it out of your way and out of your reach. I have removed the source of all those evils you were sacrificing one by one. I have ended your battle. I have stopped your motor. I have deprived your world of man's mind.

"Men do not live by the mind, you say? I have withdrawn those who do. The mind is impotent, you say? I have withdrawn those whose mind isn't. There are values higher than the mind, you say? I have withdrawn those for whom there aren't.

"While you were dragging to your sacrificial altars the men of justice, of independence, or reason, of wealth, of self-esteem—I beat you to it, I reached them first. I told them the nature of the game you were playing and the nature of that moral code of yours, which they had been too innocently generous to grasp. I showed them the way to live by another morality—mine. It is mine that they chose to follow.

"All the men who have vanished, the men you hated, yet dreaded to lose, it is I who have taken them away from you. Do not attempt to find us. We do not choose to be found. Do not cry that it is our duty to serve you. We do not recognize such duty. Do not cry that you need us. You don't. Do not beg us to return. We are on strike, we, the men of the mind.

"We are on strike against self-immolation. We are on strike against the creed of unearned rewards and unrewarded duties. We are on strike against the dogma that the pursuit of one's happiness is evil. We are on strike against the doctrine that life is guilt.

"There is a difference between our strike and all those you've practiced for centuries: our strike consists, not of making demands, but of granting them. We are evil, according to your morality. We have chosen not to harm you any longer. We are useless, according to your economics. We have chosen not to exploit you any longer. We are dangerous and to be shackled, according to your politics. We have chosen not to endanger you, nor to wear the shackles any longer. We are only an illusion, according to your philosophy. We have chosen not to blind you any longer and have left you free to face reality—the reality you wanted, the world as you see it now, a world without mind.

"We have granted you everything you demanded of us, we who had always been the givers, but have only now understood it. We have no demands to present to you, no terms to bargain about, no compromise to reach. You have nothing to offer us. *We do not need you.*

"Are you now crying: No, this was not what you wanted? A mindless world of ruins was not your goal? You did not want us to leave you? You moral cannibals, I know that you've always known what it was that you wanted. But your game is up, because *now* we know it, too.

"Through centuries of scourges and disasters, brought about by your code of morality, you have cried that your code had been broken, that the scourges were punishment for breaking it, that men were too weak and too selfish to spill all the blood it required. You damned man, you damned existence, you damned this earth, but never dared to question your code. Your victims took the blame and struggled on, with your curses as reward for their martyrdom—while you went on crying that your code was noble, but human nature was not good enough to practice it. And no one rose to ask the question: Good?—by what standard?

"You wanted to know John Galt's identity. I am the man who has asked that question.

"Yes, this *is* an age of moral crisis. Yes, you *are* bearing punishment for your evil. But it is not man who is now on trial and it is not human nature that will take the blame. It is your moral code that's through, this time. Your moral code has reached its climax, the blind alley at the end of its course. And if you wish to go on living, what you now need is not to *return* to morality—you who have never known any—but to *discover* it.

"You have heard no concepts of morality but the mystical or the social. You have been taught that morality is a code of behavior imposed on you by whim, the whim of a supernatural power or the whim of society, to serve God's purpose or your neighbor's welfare, to please an authority beyond the grave or else next door—but not to serve *your* life or pleasure. Your pleasure, you have been taught, is to be found in immorality, your interests would best be served by evil, and any moral code must be designed not *for* you, but *against* you, not to further your life, but to drain it.

"For centuries, the battle of morality was fought between those who claimed that your life belongs to God and those who claimed that it belongs to your neighbors— between those who preached that the good is self-sacrifice for the sake of ghosts in heaven and those who preached that the good is self-sacrifice for the sake of incompetents on earth. And no one came to say

that your life belongs to you and that the good is to live it.

"Both sides agreed that morality demands the surrender of your self-interest and of your mind, that the moral and the practical are opposites, that morality *is* not the province of reason, but the province of faith and force. Both sides agreed that no rational morality is possible, that there is no right or wrong in reason—that in reason there's no reason to be moral.

"Whatever else they fought about, it was against man's mind that all your moralists have stood united. It was man's mind that all their schemes and systems were intended to despoil and destroy. Now choose to perish or to learn that the anti-mind is the anti-life.

"Man's mind is his basic tool of survival. Life is given to him, survival is not. His body is given to him, its sustenance is not. His mind is given to him, its content is not. To remain alive, he must act, and before he can act he must know the nature and purpose of his action. He cannot obtain his food without a knowledge of food and of the way to obtain it. He cannot dig a ditch—or build a cyclotron— without a knowledge of his aim and of the means to achieve it. To remain alive, he must think.

"But to think is an act of choice. The key to what you so recklessly call 'human nature,' the open secret you live with, yet dread to name, is the fact that *man is a being of volitional consciousness*. Reason does not work automatically; thinking is not a mechanical process; the connections of logic are not made by instinct. The function of your stomach, lungs or heart is automatic; the function of your mind is not. In any hour and issue of your life, you are free to think or to evade that effort. But you are not free to escape from your natures from the fact that *reason* is your means of survival—so that for *you*, who are a human being, the question 'to be or not to be' is the question 'to think or not to think.'

"A being of volitional consciousness has no automatic course of behavior. He needs a code of values to guide his actions. 'Value' is that by which one acts to gain and keep, 'virtue' is the action by which one gains and keeps it. 'Value' presupposes an answer to the question: of value to whom and for what? 'Value' presupposes a standard, a purpose and the necessity of action in the face of an alternative. Where there are no alternatives, no values are possible.

"There is only one fundamental alternative in the universe: existence or non-existence—and it pertains to a single class of entities: to living organisms. The existence of inanimate matter is unconditional, the existence of life is not: it depends on a specific course of action. Matter is indestructible, it changes its forms, but it cannot cease to exist. It is only a living organism that faces a constant alternative: the issue of life or death. Life is a process of self-sustaining and self-generated action. If an organism fails in that action, it dies; its chemical elements remain, but its life goes out of existence. It is only the concept of 'Life' that makes the concept of 'Value' possible. It is only to a living entity that things can be good or evil.

"A plant must feed itself in order to live; the sunlight, the water, the chemicals that it needs are the values its nature has set it to pursue; its life is the standard of value directing its actions. But a plant has no choice of action; there are no alternatives in the conditions it encounters, but there is no al-

ternative in its function: it acts automatically to further its life, it cannot act for its own destruction.

"An animal is equipped for sustaining its life; its senses provide it with an automatic code of action, an automatic knowledge of what is good or evil. It has no power to extend its knowledge or evade it. In conditions where its knowledge proves inadequate, it dies. But so long as it lives, it acts on its knowledge, with automatic safety and no power of choice, it is unable to ignore its own good, unable to decide to choose the evil and act as its own destroyer.

"Man has no automatic code of survival. His particular distinction from all other living species is the necessity to act in the face of alternatives by means of *volitional choice*. He has no automatic knowledge of what is good for him or evil, what values his life depends on, what course of action it requires. Are you prattling about an instinct of self-preservation? An *instinct* of self-preservation is precisely what man does not possess. An 'instinct' is an unerring and automatic form of knowledge. A desire is not an instinct. A desire to live does not give you the knowledge required for living. And even man's desire to live is not automatic: your secret evil today is that *that* is the desire you do not hold. Your fear of death is not a love for life and will not give you the knowledge needed to keep it. Man must obtain his knowledge and choose his actions by a process of thinking, which nature will not force him to perform. Man has the power to act as his own destroyer—and that is the way he has acted through most of history.

"A living entity that regarded its means of survival as evil, would not survive. A plant that struggled to mangle its roots, a bird that fought to break its wings would not remain for long in the existence they affronted. But the history of man has been a struggle to deny and destroy his mind.

"Man has been called a rational being, but rationality is a matter of choice—and the alternative his nature offers him is: rational being or suicidal animal. Man has to be man—by choice; he has to hold his life as a value—by choice; he has to learn to sustain it—by choice; he has to discover the values it requires and practice his virtues—by choice.

"A code of values accepted by choice is a code of morality.

"Whoever you are, you who are hearing me now, I am speaking to whatever living remnant is left uncorrupted within you, to the remnant of the human, to your *mind*, and I say: There *is* a morality of reason, a morality proper to man, and *Man's Life* is its standard of value.

"All that which is proper to the life of a rational being is the good; all that which destroys it is the evil.

"Man's life, as required by its nature, is not the life of a mindless brute, of a looting thug or a mooching mystic, but the life of a thinking being—not life by means of force or fraud, but life by means of achievement—not survival at any price, since there's only one price that pays for man's survival: reason.

"Man's life is the *standard* of morality, but your own life is its *purpose*. If existence on earth is your goal, you must choose your actions and values by the standard of that which is proper to man—for the purpose of preserving, fulfilling and enjoying the irreplaceable value which is your life.

KEY TERMS

ethical egoism
ethics of altruism
human nature
society
personal whim
neo-mysticism
subjective preference
value
reason
self-esteem
productivity
rational selfishness

selfishness
beneficiary
objectivist ethics
God
mysticism
emotionalism
nature
virtue
purpose
rationality
pride
laissez-faire capitalism

PROGRESS CHECK 7.1

Instructions: Fill in the blanks with the appropriate responses listed below.

productivity   neo-mysticism
traders   selfishness
beneficiary   cynicism
beneficiary criterion of morality   objectivist ethics
nature   pride
force   whim
life   ethics of altruism
guilt   fancy
happiness

1 Conventional moralists equate *selfishness* _____ with evil.
2 If any kind of ethics is inhumane, it is the *ethics of altruism*
3 The *beneficiary criterion of morality* _____ gives the message that morality opposes self-interest.
4 The ethics of altruism requires one to make others the _____ of one's moral action *beneficiary*
5 Altruistic ethics breeds *cynism* and *guilt*.
6 According to *objective ethics* _____, moral agents should act out of rational self-interest and always be the beneficiaries of their actions.
7 A morality based on rational self-interest does not mean that actions can be properly justi-fied by personal *whim* and *fancy*
8 *neo mysticism* _____ substitutes God with society.
9 For Rand, it is only the concept of *life* that makes the concept of value possible.
10 It is *nature* that decides for us what we should or should not do to ensure our survival.
11 The virtue which corresponds to the value of purpose is *productivity*
12 For Rand, the virtue of *pride* is tantamount to moral ambitiousness.
13 Rand rejects *happiness* as the standard of morality, for then whatever makes us happy would be right.
14 Objectivist ethics would have us see one another as *traders* _____ in our moral, personal and busi-ness relationships.
15 Rational selfishness is opposed to using *force* as a way of gaining value from others.

SUMMARY OF MAJOR POINTS

1. How has selfishness been understood traditionally?

    Selfishness has been equated with evil. Selfish people have been regarded as selfish brutes. Their actions have been regarded as irrational, based on personal whim and fancy.

2. What is wrong with altruism?

    Altruism is inhumane. It makes self-interest, necessary for survival, appear evil. Requiring people to sacrifice themselves for the self-interests of others makes them victims, and those who benefit, parasites. The logical implications of altruism are absurd.

3. What, for Rand, have been the previous misguided bases of morality?

    Mysticism, neo-mysticism, emotionalism, and subjective preference have all served as the basis of morality in the past.

4. What is the proper basis and function of morality?

    Life (existence and survival) should be regarded as the proper basis of morality. Ultimately, man values to live; he doesn't live to value. Nature determines what is essential for life and ultimately what is good or evil for mankind.

5. What values and virtues are most conducive to living the moral life?

    Values: reason, purpose, and self-esteem
    Virtues: rationality, productivity, and pride

6. What is meant by rational selfishness and the principle of trade?

    It is in one's rational self-interest to see people as traders in life, giving value for value. Traders don't expect something for nothing; they treat people as equals; nor do they expect to be paid for their failures and defaults. In personal relationships, traders receive "spiritual payment" for what they give to others.

7. What is the relationship between Rand's ethical egoism and economics?

    Rand's theory is supportive of *laissez-faire* capitalism. It extols people's rights to life and liberty, but especially their property rights, without which the pursuit of happiness is doomed to failure.

SOURCE REFERENCES AND RELATED READINGS

Baker, James T. *Ayn Rand*. Boston: Twayne Publishers, 1987.

Baier, Kurt, "Egoism," in *A Companion to Ethics*, Peter Singer, ed. Oxford: Blackwell Publishers, 1977, pp.197–204.

Feinberg, Joel, *"Psychological Egoism,"* in *Ethics: History, Theory and Contemporary Issues*, eds. Steven M. Cahn and Peter Markie. New York: Oxford University Press, 1998, pp.557–565.

Peikoff, Leonard, *Objectivism: The Philosophy of Ayn Rand*. New York: Meridian, 1993.

Rand, Ayn, *The Virtue of Selfishness: A New Concept of Egoism*. New York: Signet, 1961.

_____. *For the New Intellectual: The Philosophy of Ayn Rand*. New York: Signet, 1963.

_____. *Atlas Shrugged*. New York: Random House, 1957.

_____. *We the Living*. New York: Macmillan, 1936.

_____. *Anthem*. New York: Signet, 1961.

ENDNOTES

1. Peter Berkowitz, *Nietzsche: The Ethics of an Immoralist*, Cambridge: Harvard University Press, 1995, pp. 68–69

2. ibid.

3. ibid., p. 70.

4. See the essay "The Objectivist Ethics," pp. 13–35.

5. Ayn Rand, *The Virtue of Selfishness*, New York: The New American Library, Inc., 1964, p. vii.

6. ibid.

7. ibid., p. viii.

8. ibid.

9. ibid.

10. ibid., p. x.

11. ibid., p. 13.

12. ibid., pp. 16–17.

13. ibid., p. 17.

14. This is normally regarded as fallacious reasoning.

15. ibid., p. 23.

16. ibid., p. 25.

17. ibid., p. 27.

18. ibid., pp. 29–30

19. ibid., p. 31

20. ibid., p. 32

21. ibid., p. 33

22. ibid.

CHAPTER EIGHT

Existentialist Ethics: Jean-Paul Sartre

Overview

Learning Outcomes

After successfully completing this chapter you will be able to

- Provide the names, orientations, and works of some influential existentialists.
- Detail how existentialism is revolutionary.
- Explain the importance of the non-existence of God to the existentialist ethic.
- Respond to the charge against existentialism that it is gloomy and nihilistic.
- Outline the foundational values of an existentialist ethic.
- Describe what it means to live like an existentialist.

PHILOSOPHICAL FOCUS QUESTIONS

1 What makes existentialism difficult to define?

2 How does existentialism respond to traditional philosophy?

3 Where does Sartre stand on the issue of God? What are the implications of his position?

4 Is existentialism gloomy and nihilistic? Why or why not?

5 According to Sartre, what are the causes of forlornness and despair in man?

6 What's meant by the notion of bad faith? What are its causes?

7 What are the foundational values for Sartre's existentialist ethic?

THE EXISTENTIALIST MOVEMENT

Existentialism is a philosophical movement that some would prefer to see as an attitude or outlook, rather than as a formal philosophy as such. Existentialism is difficult to define in precise

> *[M]an is condemned to be free.*
> JEAN-PAUL SARTRE

terms because there does not exist any common body of doctrine to which all existentialists would subscribe. Within the existential movement, we find **atheists**, and **theists** (primarily Christian and Jewish), as well as **political conservatives, Marxists, humanists**, at least one **fascist** and those that are **anti-political**. Certain existentialists have emphasized matters of freedom in their writings, while others have focused on absurdity and the world of the interpersonal. To complicate things even further, some of the philosophers we associate with existentialism predate the use of the term itself, while others simply refuse to be called existentialists at all. To belong to a "school of thought" or to subordinate one's individuality by adhering to some shared philosophical doctrine would not be very "existential." Why this is so should become apparent shortly.

Søren Kierkegaard (1813-1855) is generally regarded as the father of existentialism, though elements of existential thinking can be found in the works of earlier writers such as **Michel de Montaigne** (1533-1592) and **Blaise Pascal** (1623-1662). When discussing existentialism, other notable names certainly come to mind: **Friedrich Nietzsche** (1844-1900), **Karl Jaspers** (1883-1969), **Gabriel Marcel** (1889-1973) and of course, **Jean-Paul Sartre** (1905-1980), the person who coined the term in 1946 in his famous essay, *The Humanism of Existentialism*. **Simone de Beauvoir**, a lover and colleague of Sartre, was certainly a significant existentialist too. She critically read and approved many of Sartre's works and became a celebrated writer herself. A noted feminist, she authored *The Second Sex* and *The Ethics of Ambiguity*. **Martin Heidegger's** (1899-1976) works are often discussed under existentialism, given that he exerted such an important influence on it. Nevertheless, he expressly indicated that he wished to be disassociated from Sartre.[1] **Albert**

Camus, winner of the Nobel Prize for Literature in 1957, is usually tagged with the existentialist label as well, though he always refused it.[2] A good example of existential fiction is his *L'Étranger* (*The Stranger* or *The Outsider*). Also see **Fyodor Dostoyevsky's** *Notes from Underground* (1864) and **Franz Kafka's** *The Trial* (1925) for further examples of existential literary works.

Existential Methodology

By contrast to traditional philosophy, which tends to be rational and discursive, existentialists often adopt unorthodox methods of investigation for probing into the human condition. Existential insights are often best communicated indirectly by means of **aphorisms, dialogues, parables,** and other literary forms such as **novels** and **plays**. Poignant existential statements are found in **poetic verse, music,** and in **visual art**, and not necessarily in the context of systematic rational argument. Also, given that prominent existentialists like Jean-Paul Sartre practiced their philosophy far removed from the hallowed halls of academe and the lecture podium of the university professor, many initially regarded existentialism as little more than a passing fad. Nevertheless, existentialism continues to be an influential philosophical movement in today's modern society, certainly as evidenced in the art world and therapeutic community. It remains a useful umbrella term under which it is possible to gather together a number of recurrent themes and philosophical preoccupations.

> *Probably a crab would be filled with a sense of personal outrage if it could hear us class it without apology as a crustacean, and thus dispose of it. "I am no such thing," it would say, "I am myself, myself alone."*
>
> WILLIAM JAMES

    Existentialism as a Revolt: Existentialism's unorthodox approach is not only different from traditional western philosophy, but largely designed as a revolt against **rationality** and **philosophical system-building**. Perhaps one commonality shared by all existentialists is the belief that human existence cannot be dissected into discrete categories or packaged as a neatly interlocking system. Existentialists certainly appreciate the fact that reason and rational inquiry are appropriate to mathematics and the natural sciences, but believe that such things are typically able to produce only vague, disappointing generalities *vis-a-vis* existing individuals. If you've ever read about a personality theory in your psychology class, for example, and then asked, "But how does this apply to me?" then you've experienced the existential disappointment I'm referring to here. As a protest against rationalism and the kinds of elaborate systems found in the works of thinkers such as **Plato** and **Kant**, existentialists argue that the individual self is lost in **abstract universals**. As far back as Plato, many rational philosophers have held the view that everyday experience cannot provide a secure and sound foundation for knowledge. Plato argued that the material world is in fact a shadow world of illusion, and that ultimate reality can only be found beyond the experienced spatio-temporal plane in the **realm of forms** (see the chapter on Plato). From the perspective of Platonic rationality, the body was to be held in contempt, since it houses the corrupting emotions and disquieting passions. **Perception** was regarded as untrustworthy, while reason and deductive thinking were elevated to the throne. Since, for Plato, truth must be universal, immutable, and eternal, and because sense perception is notoriously inaccurate and frequently deceptive, no certainty can be found in the world of everyday experience.

Biographical Brief

© HUTTON ARCHIVE/GETTY IMAGES

Jean-Paul Sartre
(1905–1980)

Jean-Paul Sartre, the individual who coined the term "existentialism," was a famous novelist, playwright and major philosopher of the 20th century. Born in 1905, he virtually held court over French intellectual life for decades. Sartre studied at the *École Normale Supérieure* from 1924–1928. After successfully completing his *agrégation*, the exam that would launch his academic career, Sartre began teaching philosophy at a number of *lycées* in Paris and elsewhere. From 1933–1935, he was a research student at the Institute Français in Berlin and at the University of Freiburg.

When World War II broke out, Sartre was called up for military service by the French army and in 1940 was captured by the Germans. Released after the armistice, he went back to Paris where he continued to teach philosophy until 1944. During these years he completed his major philosophical work, *Being and Nothingness*. In the years immediately following the war, he wrote a number of novels and plays which made him world famous. Literary works include *Nausea*, *No Exit*, and *Saint Genet*.

To better appreciate how existentialism wishes to ground us back in immediate physical reality, as it were, how it represents a revolt against systematic philosophy, and what the implications of this revolt are for moral and ethical thinking, let us now turn to one of the most influential thinkers in the existential movement: Jean-Paul Sartre. An examination of his ideas should further expand our understanding of morality and provide us with one more perspective to consider while constructing our own personal moral philosophies of life.

JEAN-PAUL SARTRE: MAN AND MORALITY WITHOUT GOD

In a work entitled, *The Humanism of Existentialism*, Jean-Paul Sartre discusses his atheistic existentialism. In very broad terms, one could say that his existentialism presents us with a kind of "situation ethic," one wherein the proper course of action to be taken is determined by the unique situation in which the individual finds himself.[3] It is a future-oriented ethic that does not look back to tradition, authority or custom for guidance. Though misunderstandings of atheistic existentialism have led some people to conclude that it is gloomy and nihilistic, Sartre claims that, properly understood, existentialism presents a positive ethic founded on what he calls "**optimistic toughness**."[4]

> *Whatever its ultimate meaning, the universe into which we have been thrown cannot satisfy our reason—let us have the courage to admit it once and for all.*
>
> *GABRIEL MARCEL*

Essence versus Existence: In the context of existentialism, much is made of the distinction between **essence** and **existence**. This distinction has much to do with God. Religious existentialists like Søren Kierkegaard believe that God exists and so grant creative authority to this divine architect of the universe. If there is a God, then he (or she, if you prefer) envisioned the world and created human beings by design. The idea of man preceded the existence of any one man. God knew what human nature would be before a single human being ever existed. Thus, in a godly universe, essence precedes existence—the plan comes before the person.

In a world created by God, reality is ordered and purposeful. A profound sense of security can be had in the belief that the universe unfolds itself by design and that whatever happens does so for a reason. Though human beings were created imperfect and, according to Christianity at least, stained with original sin, they can still find guidance for moral living in the Ten Commandments and Holy Scripture. Peace of mind is found not in forging our own destiny or exerting self-will, but by accepting God's will and playing the role assigned to us by Him. To rest assured that the universe displays a moral order, that an omnipotent benevolent God oversees all worldly affairs, and that spiritual redemption is possible gives the religionist hopeful direction and the promise of eternal bliss.

The allegation that existentialism is gloomy and nihilistic probably stems in large part from the counter-belief held by many, like Sartre, that God does not exist. Some seem to fear that without God to order things, moral anarchy must necessarily be the result. Others might charge that, without God, nothing has ultimate meaning and there is no purpose to life. After all, how does one live in a world where there is no right or wrong? If God does not exist, then everything is permissible!

Before we get too depressed, let us take momentary solace in the proverbial expression, *"It's always darkest before the dawn."* Sartre recognizes that life might look dark and depressing in a godless world, but suggests it need not be so. Certainly, it is understandable that individuals could become forlorn with the recognition that no a priori Good exists, because there exists no infinite and perfect consciousness to think it. God is a convenience, in one sense. The moral "buck" of responsibility can always stop with Him. However, if there is no God, then there can be no celestial values or divine commands to turn to for guidance or to refer to when trying to justify our actions to ourselves or others. There is simply no one to turn to and no running away from the fact that we must assume full responsibility for whatever we do. Faced with the anticipated consequences of this, and robbed of God's security, psychological darkness descends.

Rather than allow a bleak and hopeless pessimism to overwhelm, Sartre offers light to the despairing and forlorn individual by presenting a set of existential values. These values constitute an ethical foundation for life, but not any sort of system of rules or any specific method of decision making. This would be artificially formulaic. While it would be convenient to follow someone else's instructions for moral decision making, doing so would represent for Sartre a thinly veiled attempt to escape from personal responsibility. Let us now consider briefly what some of those Sartrean values are that constitute the foundation for his existentialist ethic.

Individuality

The point was made earlier that existentialism represents a revolt against objective rationality and scientific system-building when it comes to understanding human beings. For existential-ists, empirical generalizations do violence to the uniqueness of the individual, while rational objectivity fails to properly capture subjective experience. Behavioural sciences tend to be reductionistic, explaining human action in terms of bio-logical, temperamental and environmental determinants. Social scientists, as well, try to explain away subjectivity and personal morality by means of sociological laws or by ref-erence to historical dialectics. The existentialist will have none of this. For existentialists like Sartre, individual sub-

> *"To be nobody but yourself—in a world which is doing its best, night and day, to make you everybody else—means to fight the hardest battle which any human being can fight, and never stop fighting."*
>
> e.e. CUMMINGS

jectivity reigns supreme and does not yield to any vain efforts designed to fit the human being into some kind of explanatory system. Systems cannot be made to fit the individual and individuals cannot be twisted to fit the system. The spirit of unwillingness to be consumed by the "sys-tem"—any system—is nicely captured in the name of a popular, now defunct, rock group: *Rage against the Machine*. Insofar as the group's music reflects its name, Sartre would likely see this "rage" as an existential protest against the continuing dehumanization of modern society—its obsession with mindless conformity and its fetish with scientific rationality. How can science grasp human nature or the essence of man when there is no essence to grasp? *"Man is nothing else but what he makes of himself."*

Sartre's emphasis on the values of individuality and subjective experience can be seen in an example he gives of moral choice. In *The Humanism of Existentialism*, Sartre tells of a personal dilemma with moral implications that was faced by one of his students. As the story goes, the student's father was on bad terms with his mother, and on top of this, was suspected of being a collaborator with the Nazis during World War II. The student's older brother had been killed in the war by the Germans, giving the student a desire for revenge. The young man was thinking seriously about leaving for England, to join his French compatriots there who were preparing to join the fight against the Germans. However, this would mean leaving his mother behind. With the loss of his brother and the situation with his father, he knew that his mother lived only for him and that she needed him to help at home. Staying at home offered pre-dictable results. He had greater personal safety and security in the knowledge that he was doing good for his mother. On the other hand, if he went off the England, his efforts might amount to little, or turn out to be completely useless. There were no guarantees that the ven-ture would be worthwhile, though the cause was both noble and urgent. The student's dilemma involved choosing between the duty to help his mother and the broader obligation to serve his country and avenge his brother's death.

Sartre argues that in this situation, no religious doctrine or a priori ethic can help the student decide. The religionist may say, *Love your neighbour*, but such a moral prescription is too vague for any kind of confident application. Who should be loved more, the fighting men in the fields or the devoted mother at home? What happens when the prescription leads to different and conflicting conclusions, as in this case? The Kantian could offer the student another a priori universal prescription helping him to decide by pointing to the Categorical Imperative (see the chapter on Immanuel Kant): *Never treat any person as a means, but as an end only.* However, as Sartre points out, such a prescription is again too vague to put into practice. If the student stays with the mother, then he treats her as an end, not as a means. However, staying at home runs the risk that others (soldiers) are treated as means. After all, they end up fighting a war and risking their lives—all of which benefits the student. On the other hand, if the student goes off to England, he treats his compatriots as ends, but runs the risk of treating his mother as a means. She'll just have to survive without him as he goes off to be a hero. Sartre argues that general prescriptions based on a priori rational objectivity are too broad for the concrete and specific cases to which they are supposed to apply. Only the student can decide what is "right" for him. There are no objective unconditional rules in the universe to inform his decision. Staying at home or going to war has value only because it is chosen by the student. Neither option has value in itself; neither action is right or wrong in itself.

Humanity

The importance Sartre placed on individual choice and subjective experience could very well lead one to conclude that his existentialism leads to a destructive relativism, if not moral anarchy. If general moral principles cannot be prescribed and used to make decisions, then it seems to follow that "anything goes"—different strokes for different folks. Since persons are respected for their uniqueness and individuality, and given that people have different feelings, perceptions and commitments, no actions are necessarily obligatory or right or wrong for everybody unconditionally. Isn't moral chaos the result? Isn't Sartre's existentialist ethics a prescription for nihilism?

A reading of Sartre reveals that between unbridled relativism and the a priori universalism of someone like Kant, for instance, there is a middle position. Sartre suggests that when we act, we create, in effect, the kind of person we think we ought to become. Equally important is the fact that when we choose to become this or that, or when we act in this way or that, we create an image of man as we think he ought to be. In a loose sense, our personal actions legislate for the world. In choosing, we bear an incredible responsibility, for

PHILOSOPHERS AT WORK

Is the existentialist's preoccupation with individual uniqueness legitimate, or merely reflective of some neurotic desire to be considered "special"? Explain why. If the existentialist is correct that no objective reality exists and that no general statements can be made about human beings, then what are the consequences for morality?

every personal choice involves all of mankind. If individuals choose to marry, then in effect, they affirm the value of marriage and recommend it to the world by participating in it. Whether or not *you* should marry is a personal decision that only *you* can make. That marriage is good and to be recommended is a message that bride and groom send to the world on their wedding day. It's possible to cherish values and affirm them to the rest of humanity without imposing them, however.

Responsibility

From what has just been said, it should be understood that existentialism places an enormous burden of responsibility upon the individual's shoulders. Recognizing that when one chooses for oneself, one is choosing for the world can stun the individual and bring him to a new level of awareness. As Sartre puts it: "...the man who involves himself and who realizes that he is not only the person he chooses to be, but also a lawmaker who is, at the same time, choosing all mankind as well as himself, can not help escape the feeling of his total and deep responsibility."[5] Awareness of this can produce great anguish since, at every single moment, the individual is obliged to act in an exemplary fashion. "For every man, everything happens as if all mankind had its eyes fixed on him and were guiding itself by what he does. And every man ought to say to himself, 'Am I really the kind of man who has the right to act in such a way that humanity might guide itself by my actions?'"[6]

The tremendous burden of responsibility placed upon the individual by atheistic existentialism is what causes him to become forlorn. There is no one to turn to for guidance. There are no objective assurances that one has made the correct choices in one's life. With no direction and no assurance, one may feel abandoned and alone, forlorn and despairing. Knowing that one is completely responsible for one's actions and that there are no directional guide-posts to provide guarantees that one is going in the right direction or doing the right thing can be frightening. To live as an existentialist requires that one muster up some of Sartre's 'optimistic toughness', referred to earlier.

On the subject of fear, forlornness, and despair, Sartre makes the startling claim that we are fully responsible for our emotions—as if being responsible for humanity were not enough! So many times people try to absolve themselves of personal responsibility by claiming that they were "swept away by passion," or that their feelings "got the better of them." Existentialists do not believe in the power of passions, arguing that individuals are even responsible for how they feel. If I am sad, for instance, it is only because I have chosen to be sad. Emotional reactions are responses to the world and since we choose our responses, we are responsible for how we feel. If, for instance, someone asked you why you did not respond to someone's insult, and you replied by saying "I'm timid and shy" the suggestion is that 'timidity' and 'shyness' are somehow unchangeable facts about your character. Saying, "She's an angry person" implies much the same. Yet, Sartre would not agree that emotions or temperamental dispositions are an unchangeable aspect of our characters, or that our emotional responses are somehow biologically or environmentally determined. Accepting either proposition is just another attempt to escape from personal responsibility. This brings us to freedom.

Freedom

Trying to blame others or make excuses for how we feel is, for Sartre, little more than an attempt to escape from freedom. It is often easier to blame others than to change ourselves. Some like to attribute fault to others for what they have done wrong themselves. This maneuver is one convenient strategy to get one "off the moral hook." Remember, responsibility is a hefty burden and when moral wrong-doing or any other sort of misdemeanor is at issue, the acceptance of responsibility can be threatening. Negative consequences can be at stake for the one responsible.

Regardless of whatever psychological escapes from personal responsibility are attempted by the individual, the fact is that, for Sartre, he is *condemned to be free*. There is no human essence making him what he is; no external situation makes him feel this way or that. One's character is not a determining factor in one's behaviour. Simply put: Man cannot avoid being free and making something of himself—whatever that turns out to be. And what he makes of himself implies an operative ideal, an existential project, which he has freely chosen for himself.[7] Be cautioned, however, that there is no one common ideal of human nature which man was created to realize through his actions. There are as many personal projects as there are people. The individual is thrown back entirely on himself, unable to justify his choice of an ideal by appealing to God or any objective system of morality.[8] The implication is that, squirm as we might, we are fully responsible for ourselves. Whatever we make of ourselves is our own doing. To try to blame our parents, neighbourhood, or upbringing for who we are today is to make excuses for ourselves—ones that may temporarily make us feel better, but in the end are just a lot of self-deception. Regardless of whether we are honest with ourselves or crippled by psychological defensiveness, we will still reach what turns out to be everyone's ultimate destination, namely death. The question is: "What will *your* journey be like?" What's the plan? What's *your* project? You have the freedom and responsibility to decide.

Authenticity

Another extremely important foundational element of Sartre's existentialist ethic is the value called **authenticity**. In our efforts to escape freedom and absolve ourselves from personal responsibility, we often fall prey to inauthenticity or what Sartre dubs **bad-faith**—*mauvaise foi* in French. Essentially, bad-faith is a form of self-deception. This deception manifests when individuals no longer regard themselves as free persons, but as objects, or perhaps as victims of fate, mysterious psycho-dynamic forces, heredity, overwhelming passions or other social influences. To think that it is possible to escape anguish by attributing one's emotions, attitudes or behaviours to the determining forces of one's situation, one's charac-

> *They are playing a game. They are playing at not playing a game. If I show them I see they are playing a game, I shall break the rules and they will punish me. I must play the game of not seeing that I play the game.*
>
> R.D. LAING

ter, one's relationships to others, or by anything else other than one's own personal choice is to lead an inauthentic life, one in which "kidding yourself" becomes a basic feature of daily living.

Bad faith also occurs whenever you find yourself playing roles or trying to disguise your actual personality behind a façade. Those who are known to engage in this activity are often unkindly labelled "posers," to use the vernacular. For example, students who have mastered a lit- tle bit of philosophical jargon, but who are still "seeking their identities," may begin to talk and carry themselves *as if* they were philosophers, when really they are just trying to be im- pressive. Others may strike a tragic existential pose in an attempt to show themselves as deep thinkers, more sensitive than the mindless mob. Capturing the inauthenticity of playing roles, Sartre uses the example of a waiter:

> Let us consider this waiter in the café. His movement is quick and forward, a little too pre- cise, a little too rapid. He comes toward the patrons with a step a little too quick. He bends forward a little too eagerly; his voice, his eyes express an interest a little too solicitous for the order of the customer. Finally there he returns, trying to imitate in his walk the inflexible stiffness of some kind of automaton while carrying his tray with the recklessness of a tight-rope-walker by putting it in a perpetually unstable, perpetually broken equilibrium which he perpetually re-establishes by a light movement of the arm and hand. All his behavior seems to us a game. He applies himself to chaining his movements as if they were mechanisms, the one regulating the others; his gestures and even his voice seem to be mech- anisms; he gives himself the quickness and pitiless rapidity of things. He is playing, he is amusing himself. But what is he playing: We need not watch long before we can explain it: he is playing *at being* a waiter in a café.[9]

Another now-famous example of bad faith provided by Sartre is also set in a café. In this case, a young woman is sitting beside a man who, she strongly suspects, would like to seduce her. When the man takes her hand, she tries to avoid the necessity of having to make a decision—either to accept or reject his advances. She simply pretends (to herself and the man) not to notice. She then proceeds to carry on their conversation while leaving her hand in his. It is "as if" she is un- aware that the man is holding it. For Sartre, the woman's actions are indicative of bad faith because she pretends, both to herself and her companion, that nothing is going on. The woman believes she can be separated and distinguished from her bodily actions and postures, allowing her hand to become nothing more than a passive object. In fact, however, the woman could move her hand;

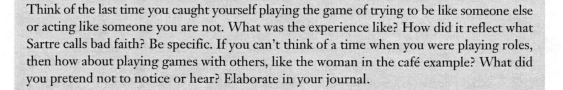

MINDWORK MEDITATION

Think of the last time you caught yourself playing the game of trying to be like someone else or acting like someone you are not. What was the experience like? How did it reflect what Sartre calls bad faith? Be specific. If you can't think of a time when you were playing roles, then how about playing games with others, like the woman in the café example? What did you pretend not to notice or hear? Elaborate in your journal.

she could object to the forwardness of the man or invite further approach. She is a conscious, free embodied being who is aware of what is happening and is completely responsible for her actions, or lack of action.[10] By pretending that nothing is going on, when it is, and that no decision is called for when, for honesty's sake, it is indeed, the woman is displaying bad faith.

Existential Living

In view of Sartre's rejections of God and objective morality, it should be clear why there is no one specific set of ethical rules that can be prescribed universally. This fact alone might be enough to plunge some into a despairing quietism. However, existentialism is anything but a philosophy of inaction. It does not doom you to pessimistic resignation. Sartre defines man in terms of action. The destiny of man lies within himself. Existentialists certainly do not discourage the individual from acting—quite the contrary. Action is what enobles man. As Sartre puts it, "There is no reality except in action. ... Man is nothing else than his plan; he exists only to the extent that he fulfils himself; he is therefore nothing else than the ensemble of his acts, nothing else than his life."[11] Seen in this way, existentialism advances an ethics of action and involvement. By unlocking the chains of determinism and proclaiming man to be free, existentialism bestows dignity upon man and refuses to reduce him to an object or the product of social conditioning or unconscious psychodynamic forces.

Unlike Bentham's utilitarianism and Kant's formalist ethic, existentialism does not allow for rational moral calculations or the imposition of moral principles upon the individual. This is not to suggest, however, that passing judgement is impossible for the existentialist. "First, one can judge ... that certain choices are based on error and others on truth. If we have defined man's situation as a free choice, with no excuses and no recourse, every man who takes refuge behind the excuse of his passions, every man who sets up a determinism, is a dishonest man."[12] About individuals who try to escape from freedom, Sartre writes, "Those who hide their complete freedom from themselves out of a spirit of seriousness or by means of deterministic excuses, I shall call cowards; those who try to show that their existence was necessary, when it is the very contingency of man's appearance on earth, I shall call stinkers. But cowards and stinkers can be judged only from a strictly unbiased point of view."[13] What this implies, for Sartre, is that though the content of ethics is variable from person to person or situation to situation, a certain form of it is universal. For the existentialist, no one particular way of life can be prescribed. Nevertheless, all judgments the individual makes and actions he undertakes should reflect certain things and avoid others. For instance, that which reflects bad-faith should be condemned. On the other hand, all that is authentic can be praised as genuine and honest. Throughout our lives, we must make our individual choices with the awareness that nothing determines them for us. We must accept responsibility for everything about ourselves, including our actions, our attitudes, our emotions, our dispositions, and our characters. The illusory belief that values are somehow objectively existent in the world, rather than sustained only by human choice, must be unequivocally rejected. What we must do is take an aesthetic stance toward life and live our lives like the **artist**. The artist does not know, in advance, what he or she ought to do, or what painting *ought* to be painted. Sartre writes,

... may I ask whether anyone has ever accused an artist who has painted a picture of not having drawn his inspiration from rules set up *a priori*? Has anyone ever asked, "What painting ought he to make?" It is clearly understood that there is no definite painting to be made, that the artist is engaged in the making of his painting and that the painting to be made is precisely the painting he will have made. It is clearly understood that there are no *a priori* aesthetic values, but that there are values which appear subsequently in the coherence of the painting, in the correspondence between what the artist intended and the result. Nobody can tell what the painting of tomorrow will be like. A painting can be judged only after it has once been made. What connection does that have with ethics? We are in the same creative situation. We never say that a work of art is arbitrary. When we speak of a canvas of Picasso, we never say that it is arbitrary; we understand quite well that he was making himself what he is at the very time he was painting, that the ensemble of his work is embodied in his life.

The same holds true on the ethical plane. What art and ethics have in common is that we have creation and invention in both cases. We can not decide *a priori* what there is to be done. I think that I pointed that out quite sufficiently when I mentioned the case of the student who came to see me, and who might have applied to all the ethical systems, Kantian or otherwise, without getting any sort of guidance. He was obliged to devise his law himself. Never let it be said by us that this man—who, taking affection, individual action, and kind-heartedness toward a specific person as his ethical principle, chooses to remain with his mother, or who, preferring to make a sacrifice, chooses to go to England—has made an arbitrary choice. Man makes himself. He isn't ready at the start. In choosing his ethics, he makes himself, and force of circumstances is such that he can not abstain from choosing one. We define man only in relationship to involvement. It is therefore absurd to charge us with arbitrariness of choice.[14]

In light of Sartre's comments and our earlier discussion, we can now provide a summary statement of existentialist ethics. Existentialism offers us a number of foundational values for living. They include individuality, humanity, freedom, responsibility, and authenticity. The moral life for the existentialist is a life of free choice and personal commitment. It is a life of action whereby one realizes one's plan or project for oneself through one's actions. In choosing, one is responsible not only for oneself, however, but for the rest of humanity as well. Playing psychological games, immersing oneself in the anonymity of the crowd, identifying with roles, and attributing one's behaviour to uncontrollable determining forces are all wrong, fitting only for "stinkers and cowards," as Sartre suggests. The existentialist lives a life of optimistic courage, accepting full responsibility for his actions. Such a life is creative, future-oriented, genuine, and self-expressive. It reflects honesty and authenticity and a recognition that no other person or system can make our decisions for us.

For more information on Sartre's ethics, read the following excerpt from *The Existentialism of Humanism*.

BACK TO THE SOURCE*

Part I

The Humanism of Existentialism
Jean-Paul Sartre

I should like on this occasion to defend existentialism against some charges which have been brought against it.

First, it has been charged with inviting people to remain in a kind of desperate quietism because, since no solutions are possible, we should have to consider action in this world as quite impossible. We should then end up in a philosophy of contemplation; and since contemplation is a luxury, we come in the end to a bourgeois philosophy. The communists in particular have made these charges.

On the other hand, we have been charged with dwelling on human degradation, with pointing up everywhere the sordid, shady, and slimy, and neglecting the gracious and beautiful, the bright side of human nature; for example, according to Mlle. Mercier, a Catholic critic, with forgetting the smile of the child. Both sides charge us with having ignored human solidarity, with considering man as an isolated being. The communists say that the main reason for this is that we take pure subjectivity, the Cartesian *I think*, as our starting point; in other words, the moment in which man becomes fully aware of what it means to him to be an isolated being; as a result, we are unable to return to a state of solidarity with the men who are not ourselves, a state which we can never reach in the *cogito*.

From the Christian standpoint, we are charged with denying the reality and seriousness of human undertakings, since, if we reject God's commandments and the eternal verities, there no longer remains anything but pure caprice, with everyone permitted to do as he pleases and incapable, from his own point of view, of condemning the points of view and acts of others.

I shall today try to answer these different charges. Many people are going to be surprised at what is said here about humanism. We shall try to see in what sense it is to be understood. In any case, what can be said from the very beginning is that by existentialism we mean a doctrine which makes human life possible and, in addition, declares that every truth and every action implies a human setting and a human subjectivity.

As is generally known, the basic charge against us is that we put the emphasis on the dark side of human life. Someone recently told me of a lady who, when she let slip a vulgar word in a moment of irritation, excused herself by saying, "I guess I'm becoming an existentialist." Consequently, existentialism is regarded as something ugly; that is why we are said to be naturalists; and if we are, it is rather surprising that in this day and age we cause so much more alarm and scandal than does naturalism, properly so called. The kind of person who can take in his stride such a novel as Zola's *The Earth* is disgusted as soon as he starts reading an existentialist novel; the kind of person who is resigned to the wisdom of the ages—which is pretty sad—finds us even sadder. Yet, what can be more disillusioning than saying "true charity begins at home" or "a scoundrel will always return evil for good"?

We know the commonplace remarks made when this subject comes up, remarks which always add up to the same thing: we shouldn't struggle against the powers-that-be; we shouldn't resist authority; we shouldn't try to rise above our station; any action which doesn't conform to authority is romantic; any effort not based on past experience is doomed to failure; experience shows that man's bent is always toward trouble, that there must be a strong hand to hold him in check, if not, there will be anarchy. There are still people who go on mumbling these melancholy old saws, the people who say, "It's only human!" whenever a more or less repugnant act is pointed out to them, the people who glut themselves on *chansons réalistes*; these are the people who accuse existentialism of being too gloomy, and to such an extent that I wonder whether they are complaining about it, not for its pessimism, but much rather its optimism. Can it be that what really scares them in the doctrine I shall try to present here is that it leaves to man a possibility of choice? To answer this question, we must re-examine it on a strictly philosophical plane. What is meant by the term *existentialism*?

Most people who use the word would be rather embarrassed if they had to explain it, since, now that the word is all the rage, even the work of a musician or painter is being called existentialist. A gossip columnist in *Clartés* signs himself *The Existentialist*, so that by this time the word has been so stretched and has taken on so broad a meaning, that it no longer means anything at all. It seems that for want of an advanced-guard doctrine analogous to surrealism, the kind of people who are eager for scandal and flurry turn to this philosophy which in other respects does not at all serve their purposes in this sphere.

Actually, it is the least scandalous, the most austere of doctrines. It is intended strictly for specialists and philosophers. Yet it can be defined easily. What complicates matters is that there are two kinds of existentialists; first, those who are Christian, among whom I would include Jaspers and Gabriel Marcel, both Catholic; and on the other hand the atheistic existentialists among whom I class Heidegger, and then the French existentialists and myself. What they have in common is that they think that existence precedes essence, or, if you prefer, that subjectivity must be the starting point.

Just what does that mean? Let us consider some object that is manufactured, for example, a book or a paper-cutter: here is an object which has been made by an artisan whose inspiration came from a concept. He referred to the concept of what a paper-cutter is and likewise to a known method of production, which is part of the concept, something which is, by and large, a routine.

Thus, the paper-cutter is at once an object produced in a certain way and, on the other hand, one having a specific use; and one can not postulate a man who produces a paper-cutter but does not know what it is used for. Therefore, let us say that, for the paper-cutter, essence—that is, the ensemble of both the production routines and the properties which enable it to be both produced and defined—precedes existence. Thus, the presence of the paper-cutter or book in front of me is determined. Therefore, we have here a technical view of the world whereby it can be said that production precedes existence.

When we conceive God as the Creator, He is generally thought of as a superior sort of artisan. Whatever doctrine we may be considering, whether one like that of Descartes or that of Leibniz, we always grant that will more or less follows understanding or, at the very least, accompanies it, and that when God creates He knows exactly what He is creating. Thus, the concept of man in the mind of God is comparable to the concept of a paper-cutter in the mind of the manufacturer, and, following certain techniques and a conception, God produces man, just as the artisan, following a definition and a technique, makes a paper-cutter. Thus, the individual man is the realization of a certain concept in the divine intelligence.

In the eighteenth century, the atheism of the *philosophers* discarded the idea of God, but not so much for the notion that essence precedes existence. To a certain extent, this idea is found everywhere; we find it in Diderot, in Voltaire, and even in Kant. Man has a human nature; this human nature, which is the concept of the human, is found in all men, which means that each man is a particular example of a universal concept, man. In Kant, the result of this universality is that the wild-man, the natural man, as well as the bourgeois, are circumscribed by the same definition and have the same basic qualities. Thus, here too the essence of man precedes the historical existence that we find in nature.

Atheistic existentialism, which I represent, is more coherent. It states that if God does not exist, there is at least one being in whom existence precedes essence, a being who exists before he can be defined by any concept, and that this being is man, or, as Heidegger says, human reality. What is meant here by saying that existence precedes essence? It means that, first of all, man exists, turns up, appears on the scene, and, only afterwards, defines himself. If man, as the existentialist conceives him, is indefinable, it is because at first he is nothing. Only afterward will he be something, and he himself will have made what he will be. Thus, there is no human nature, since there is no God to conceive it. Not only is man what he conceives himself to be, but he is also only what he wills himself to be after this thrust toward existence.

Man is nothing else but what he makes of himself. Such is the first principle of existentialism. It is also what is called subjectivity, the name we are labeled with when charges are brought against us. But what do we mean by this, if not that man has a greater dignity than a stone or table? For we mean that man first exists, that is, that man first of all is the being who hurls himself toward a future and who is conscious of imagining himself as being in the future. Man is at the start a plan which is aware of itself, rather than a patch of moss, a piece of garbage, or a cauliflower; nothing exists prior to this plan; there is nothing in heaven; man will be what he will have planned to be. Not what he will want to be. Because by the word "will" we generally mean a conscious decision, which is subsequent to what we have already made of ourselves. I may want to belong to a political party, write a book, get married; but all that is only a manifestation of an earlier, more spontaneous choice that is called "will." But if existence really does precede essence, man is responsible for what he is. Thus, existentialism's first move is to make every man aware of what he is and to make the full responsibility of his existence rest on him. And when we say that a man is responsible for himself, we do not only mean that he is responsible for his own individuality, but that he is responsible for all men.

The word subjectivism has two meanings, and our opponents play on the two. Subjectivism means, on the one hand, that an individual chooses and makes himself; and, on the other, that it is impossible for man to transcend human subjectivity. The second of these is the essential meaning of existentialism. When we say that man chooses his own self, we mean that every one of us does likewise; but we also mean by that that in making this choice he also chooses all men. In fact, in creating the man that we want to be, there is not a single one of our acts which does not at the same time create an image of man as we think he ought to be. To choose to be this or that is to affirm at the same time the value of what we choose, because we can never choose evil. We always choose the good, and nothing can be good for us without being good for all.

If, on the other hand, existence precedes essence, and if we grant that we exist and fashion our image at one and the same time, the image is valid for everybody and for our whole age. Thus, our responsibility is much greater than we might have supposed, because it involves all mankind. If I am a workingman and choose to join a Christian trade-union rather than be a communist, and if by being a member I want to show that the best thing for man is resignation, that the kingdom of man is not of this world, I am not only involving my own case—I want to be resigned for everyone. As a result, my action has involved all humanity. To take a more individual matter, if I want to marry, to have children; even if this marriage depends solely on my own circumstances or passion or wish, I am involving all humanity in monogamy and not merely myself. Therefore, I am responsible for myself and for everyone else. I am creating a certain image of man of my own choosing. In choosing myself, I choose man.

KEY TERMS

atheists

political conservatives

humanists

anti-political

Michel de Montaigne

theists

Marxists

fascist

Søren Kierkegaard

Blaise Pascal

Friedrich Nietzsche	Karl Jaspers
Gabriel Marcel	Jean-Paul Sartre
Simone de Beauvoir	Martin Heidegger
Albert Camus	Franz Kafka
Fyodor Dostoyevski	aphorisms
dialogues	parables
novels	plays
poetic verse	music
visual art	rationality
philosophical system-building	Plato
Kant	abstract universals
realm of forms	perception
essence	existence

PROGRESS CHECK 8.1

Instructions: Fill in the blanks with the responses listed below.

Simone de Beauvoir	unorthodox methods
essence	artificially formulaic
personal responsibility	Jean-Paul Sartre
despairing quietism	atheistic
bad-faith	traditional philosophy
nihilistic	inauthenticity
school of thought	form
free	existence
systems	content

1. Some "existentialists" refuse the label because they do not wish to belong to a(n) _____. *school of thought*

2. _____ coined the term 'existentialism.' *Jean Paul Sartre*

3. _____ is considered a significant 20th century existentialist. *Simone de Beauvoir*

4. Existentialists use _____ in their philosophical investigations. *unorthodox methods*

5. Existentialism is often seen as a revolt against _____ *tradition philosophy*

6. For Sartre, *existence* _____ precedes *essence*

7. Sartre is an *atheistic* _____ existentialist.

8. Sartre's existentialist ethic is not *nihilistic*

9. Existentialists argue that making moral decisions by means of preset rules and procedures would be _____. *artificially formulaic*

10. *Systems* _____ do violence to the uniqueness and subjectivity of individuals.

11. Individuals often try to escape from _____ by engaging in _____ explanations.
    personal-ity / responsibility   Bad faith

12. When we play roles or mind-games with others, we are likely guilty of what Sartre calls _____ inauthentically

13. Though Sartre's existentialism prescribes no universal set of moral rules for action, we should not fall prey to _____ despairing quietism

14. Sartre argues that the _____ of morality varies from person to person, but that the _____ of it is universal.   consent   form

15. There is no escape from personal responsibility for man is condemned to be _____ . free

SUMMARY OF MAJOR POINTS

1. How is existentialism different from traditional philosophy?

   It uses unorthodox methods (e.g., indirect communication). It represents a revolt against purely rational, discursive analyses of human experience. Existentialism is an alternative to abstract universalism.

2. What are the implications of the claim that "existence precedes essence"?

   The phrase essentially eliminates God from the picture—there is no God. With no God, there is no human nature, since nobody created man by design. Without God and human nature, man creates his essence by his actions.

3. What values constitute the ethical foundations for an existentialist ethic?

   Individuality, humanity, responsibility, freedom and authenticity are five of the major ones discussed by Sartre.

4. What does Sartre have against scientific rationality in the study of man?

   The sciences are reductionistic. Their systematic approach cannot capture the uniqueness and subjectivity of the individual.

5. Is it true that existentialists do not take others into account?

   No. When one acts as an existentialist, one chooses a conception of humanity for the world.

6. What role does responsibility play in existentialism?

   Responsibility plays a central role in existentialist philosophy. Individuals are responsible not only for their actions, but for their emotions and attitudes as well. By opting for a vision of humanity through personal choices made, individuals are in some sense "responsible for the world."

7. What does it mean to suggest, as does Sartre, that "man is condemned to be free?"

   There is no escape from personal responsibility. All attempts to do so are indicative of 'bad faith'. We are free in all respects, except one; we are not free to escape our freedom.

8. What is meant by authenticity?

   Authenticity is a mode of living honestly in the world. It is a life devoid of mind-games and artificial role-playing. It involves being true to oneself. Living authentically means turning away from self-deception and excuse making.

9. Does existentialism condemn us to a gloomy and nihilistic pessimism?

   No. Existential living is positive, requiring optimistic toughness. It is a philosophy of responsible action. It is a noble ethic of action and involvement in the world. Existentialism promotes the individual and honesty. Excuses and attempted escapes from responsibility are frowned upon. Existentialism advocates that an aesthetic stance be taken, much like the artist. One's life is one's masterpiece or project, for which no prior prescriptions are suitable. Existential living is creative and future-oriented.

ENDNOTES

1. See Titus, Smith and Nolan, *Living Issues in Philosophy*, 7th edition. New York: D. Van Nostrand Co., 1979, p. 339.
2. David Zane Mairowitz and Alain Korkos, *Camus for Beginners*. Duxford: Icon Books, 1998.
3. John MacQuarrie, *Existentialism: An Introduction, guide and assessment*. New York: Penguin, 1972, p. 268.
4. Jean-Paul Sartre, "The Existentialism of Humanism," in *Jean-Paul Sartre: Essays in Existentialism*, ed. Wade Baskin. Secaucus, N.J.: Carol Publishing Group, 1997, p. 49.
5. Sartre, ibid., p. 38.
6. ibid., p. 39.
7. Frederick Copleston, *A History of Philosopy, Vol. IX*, New York: Image Books, 1994, p. 365.
8. ibid. p. 365.
9. Jean-Paul Sartre, "Bad Faith," in *Jean-Paul Sartre: Essays in Existentialism*, ed. Wade Baskin. Toronto: Carol Publishing Group, 1997, p. 167.
10. A clear and concise summary of Sartre's example is found in Leslie Stevenson and David Haberman, *Ten Theories of Human Nature*, 3rd edition, New York: Oxford University Press, 1988, p.178.
11. Sartre, *The Humanism of Existentialism*, p. 47.
12. Ibid., p. 57.
13. Ibid., p. 58.
14. Ibid., pp. 55–56.

CHAPTER NINE

The Morality of Care: Carol Gilligan and Nel Noddings

Overview

Learning Outcomes

After successfully completing this chapter, you will be able to

- Trace the role of reason in traditional Western ethics
- Identify what some would claim to be the male bias in rational morality
- Provide criticisms of principled morality from a feminine perspective
- Explain the psychological origins of care-based morality
- Discuss the dangers of romanticizing rationality
- Give an account of what it means to say that relation is ontologically basic
- Outline care-based ethics as developed by Carol Gilligan and Nel Noddings

---

PHILOSOPHICAL FOCUS QUESTIONS

1. What role has reason played in traditional theories of ethics?
2. In what ways has moral philosophy been biased in the past?
3. According to Carol Gilligan, what are the psychological origins of relational care?
4. How might the feminine perspective on morality be perceived as inadequate from a male perspective?
5. What moral notions are foundational to care-based ethics?
6. What is meant by the expression "romanticizing rationality?"
7. In what respect is Nel Noddings' care-based ethic an ethic of virtue?

THE ROLE OF REASON IN TRADITIONAL ETHICS

A review of the moral theories covered thus far in our discussion reveals that great importance has been placed on the role of rationality in the history of ethical inquiry. Plato, for instance, gave **reason** primacy of place in human character and granted it authority over the "unruly" passions and appetites that could corrupt the individual. Aristotle argued that the fulfillment of our distinctively human function involved the exercise of reason and that the contemplative lifestyle constituted the highest form of human functioning. Bentham, recall, had us approach moral situations in a spirit of scientific objectivity, asking that we use our rational capacities in performing a kind of hedonic calculation for purposes of deciding how to act. Morality was not a matter of opinion or subjective preference, but something that involved quantitative measurement. John Stuart Mill, another utilitarian, distinguished between higher and lower pleasures, maintaining that pleasures of the mind are higher than pleasures of the body. He expressed this sentiment by saying that it would be better to be Socrates dissatisfied, than a pig satisfied.

The emphasis upon reason continued in our coverage of Immanuel Kant. Remember that Kant could find no certainty in experience or anything empirical. The structure of reason itself was to provide the *a priori* necessity and certainty he was looking for in his quest for a solid and secure foundation of morality. John Rawls, someone who was largely influenced by Kant, wanted to eliminate personal "contaminating" variables from moral deliberations of justice by hypothetically placing rational self-interested individuals behind a veil of ignorance. Unique personal features pertaining to things like gender, race, and socio-economic status had to be removed from deliberations if fair solutions to moral conflicts were to be found. No doubt influenced by all of the male thinkers who preceded her, Ayn Rand formulated a conception of rational selfishness in her development of ethical egoism. She distrusted personal whim and desire, believing that no consistent or justifiable morality could be constructed on such a capricious basis. Like her predecessors, Rand preached a gospel of reason to all those who would listen, pushing emotion and subjective preference to the side. As we have seen, history provides a long and compelling procession of rational accounts of what morality is and how matters of morality should be dealt with.

As we move now to our next contemporary perspective, the morality of care, we will see that not all moral thinkers are simply rationalists of one kind or another. Contemporary feminine thinkers have given psychological matters of *relation* and the *human affective response* a much more prominent role. Rather than be regarded as irrelevant, or even worse, as "contaminating variables"—things to be minimized when thinking or acting morally—they are given central importance and acknowledged as legitimate concerns. To understand how this is so, let us turn to the work of two prominent researchers in the field of feminine ethics: Carol Gilligan and Nel Noddings. Both have much to say in response to rational ethics and the assumptions upon which it is based. Noddings, for instance, charges that a rational male presentation often gives ethics a mathematical appearance, as if it were governed by the kind of logical necessity characteristic of geometry—and this, she claims, is simply not so. An ethic, like Kant's, which is characterized by rational consistency, detachment, objectivity, and the universal application of principles, is an ethic guided by the masculine spirit. There is another alternative capturing the feminine spirit, she says, one that is a more natural approach to morality. It is rooted in what can be called the *receptive rationality of caring*. Feminine ethics is at least worthy of examination, Noddings asserts, as rational principle-based thinking is fraught with danger. History

Biographical Brief

COURTESY OF CAROL GILLIGAN

Carol Gilligan (1936–)

Carol Gilligan, the 1997 recipient of the Heinz Award in the Human Condition, is currently the first chair of Gender Studies in the Graduate School of Education at Harvard University. Although she is technically an empirical psychological researcher, her theorizing and empirical findings have had significant implications for thinkers in the fields of moral and political philosophy. In her work, Gilligan criticizes long-held assumptions about moral development, specifically those contained in the cognitive-developmental theories of Jean Piaget and Lawrence Kohlberg. In her estimation, they are based on rational, universalistic presuppositions that contain a certain male bias devaluing the caring relational nature of feminine moral experience, and thereby relegating women's moral thinking to a position of inferior and less adequate moral reasoning development. Her critical rebuttals to Piaget and Kohlberg constitute, in effect, a critique of formalistic Kantian-Rawlsian morality to which their developmental theories are closely aligned. Gilligan calls into question the ultimate authority of reason as the basis of morality and, because of this, is relevant to philosophical inquiry.[1]

reveals only too well how atrocities and acts of violence are often committed in the name of principle. We'll look at Nodding's work in a moment, but until then, let's examine the idea that there's an inherent male bias in traditional moral theory, especially in deontological morality as evidenced in developmental theories of moral reasoning. Understand at the outset that feminine ethics is not intended to be irrational; instead, it begins with the premise that the inclusion of non-rational variables is crucial to any adequate conception of morality. Ironically, feminine ethics must use reason to expose reason's limitations in its applications to ethics. This, in itself, does not make feminine ethics unreasonable, only not rationalistic.

CAROL GILLIGAN'S MORALITY "IN A DIFFERENT VOICE"

Carol Gilligan's theorizing about ethics presents us with a morality expressed "in a different voice," to use her expression. Her feminine **morality of care** has been articulated in large part as a response to cognitive-developmental moral researchers like Lawrence Kohlberg and Jean Piaget, who have claimed objective impartiality in their investigations, but who, according to Gilligan, are actually guilty of injecting a **male bias** in their work—one that regards the feminine perspective in ethics as underdeveloped and inferior. Both Piaget and Kohlberg were largely influenced by formalist, deontological philosophy, especially as presented by Immanuel Kant and John Rawls, both of whom we have already studied (see the chapters on deontological ethics).

> *Masculine and feminine values, together and in balance yield complementary benefits that enrich life. When either overwhelms the other, neither is life giving. In our society— deprived of soul and therefore of a conscious understanding of the feminine—we've been looking at the feminine through the wrong lens, the lens of masculine understanding. However, just as masculine values were never intended to be evaluated through a feminine perspective, feminine values can't be understood from a masculine viewpoint.*
>
> KATHLEEN HURLEY AND
> THEODORE DOBSON

As a way of preparing the ground for the presentation of her own theoretical alternative, Gilligan directs our attention to the initial moral research of Harvard professor Lawrence Kohlberg. In his now-classic studies of moral reasoning development, Kohlberg claimed to have uncovered the universal sequence of moral development in human beings. This sequence was identified on the basis of moral reasoning abilities and was said to involve three basic levels containing a total of six stages. At the lowest stage, belonging to the pre-conventional level, "right" and "wrong" are defined in the moral agent's mind in terms of physical-hedonistic consequences, or in terms of the physical power of those who enunciate the rules and apply the labels. In the beginning, "might makes right." Avoiding punishment and adhering unquestioningly to the dictates of authority are actions valued in their own right—not because one is cognizant of any underlying moral system. Those with power and authority simply dictate what is or is not acceptable.

At stage two, right actions are those which instrumentally satisfy one's own needs and, occasionally, the needs of others. Human relations are viewed as marketplace exchanges. Moral reciprocity at this stage can be translated as, *I'll scratch your back if you'll scratch mine.* Fairness and equal sharing are present, but always interpreted in a physical or pragmatic way. Reciprocity, here, has nothing to do with loyalty, gratitude or justice.

As one enters stage three, perceptions of morality change, as does one's thinking about it. What becomes important are the expectations of one's family, group or nation. These are valued in their own right, regardless of immediate, obvious consequences. Individuals at the conventional level of morality conform to expectations and the requirements of maintaining social order. They act out of loyalty to it, actively supporting and justifying the order and identifying with the persons or group(s) involved in it. Good behaviour is defined as that which helps others and is approved by them. People's actions are judged by the intentions behind them. The idea that *the person meant well* becomes important for the first time. At stage three, one is able to earn approval by being "nice."

At stage four, we enter the *law and order orientation*. The focus here turns to following fixed rules, authority, and the preservation of the social order. The right thing to do is one's duty. This shows respect for authority and the desire to maintain the social order for its own sake. The law must be obeyed just because *a law is a law is a law!*

In stage five, we enter the highest post-conventional level of morality. Efforts are made to define moral values and ethical principles which have validity and application apart from the authority of the groups or persons holding these principles and distinct from the moral agent's own identifications with these persons and groups. In this stage, the importance of autonomy begins to emerge. Stage five has been dubbed the "social-contract legalistic orientation." What is right is defined with respect to generally agreed-upon individual rights and in terms of standards which have been critically examined, evaluated, and accepted by the whole society—not just some sub-group within it. At this stage, persons emphasize the legal point of view, but accept the possiblity that the law might have to be changed in view of rational considerations of social utility. This contrasts with stage four, where an unbreakable law is a law, is a law. Here, free and contractual agreement becomes the binding element of obligation. Kohlberg sees stage five morality as the "official" morality of the U.S. Government and Constitution.

Finally, at stage six, what is right is established in accordance with self-chosen ethical principles—ones appealing to logical comprehensiveness, universality and consistency. Principles at stage six are formal and abstract. Examples would include the Golden Rule and Kant's Categorical Imperative. "At heart, these are universal principles of justice, of the reciprocity and equality of the human rights, and of respect for the dignity of human beings as individual persons."[2] At stage six, we find the highest levels of rationality and autonomy.

Kohlberg argues, on the basis of empirical study, that movement from one stage or level to the next is invariant and sequential and furthermore, that it is culturally universal. In stage development, people are cognitively attracted to reasoning one step above their own. Movement is effected when psychological disequilibrium is created, that is, when individuals discover that their current thinking is somehow inadequate to deal with the complexity of the moral problem at issue. Finally, it should be noted that moral thinking progresses and gains in adequacy by becoming less concrete and increasingly more abstract. At the first level, moral goodness is determined by tangible and physical consequences; at the second conventional level, by group wishes and the maintenance of social order for its own sake; and lastly, at the third post-conventional level, by adherence to abstract universal principles of justice which transcend any individual or group. The post-conventional level represents, for Kohlberg, the most adequate, developed and ethically sound form of moral reasoning. Kohlberg's Stage Six morality sits squarely in line with Kant's categorical imperative and, incidentally, with the basic principles of justice as articulated by the political philosopher John Rawls.[3] For Kohlberg, Stage Six principled morality is superior by virtue of its being the preferred choice of rational self-interested persons in the condition of the original position described by Rawls.[4]

CRITIQUE OF RATIONAL PRINCIPLED MORALITY

In response to Kohlberg's findings and conclusions, Gilligan points out that his original research was limited to an all-male sample of subjects. For 15 years, Kohlberg studied the development of moral judgment by following the same group of 75 boys at three-year intervals from early adolescence through to young adulthood. These boys/men were presented with **hypothetical moral dilemmas** like the one about Joe which follows, and then their responses to related questions were recorded. It was on the basis of these male responses to hypothetical dilemmas, then, that Kohlberg initially formulated his theory of moral development.

> *Joe Dilemma* Joe was a 14-year old boy who wanted to go to camp very much. His father promised him he could go if he saved up the money himself. Joe worked hard at his paper route and saved up the $40 it cost to go to camp, with a little money left over. But just before camp was going to start, his father changed his mind. Some of *his* friends decided to go on a special fishing trip, and Joe's father was short the money it would cost. So he told Joe to give him the money he had saved from the paper route. Joe didn't want to give up going to camp, so he thought of refusing to give his father the money.

Should Joe have refused to give his father the money, or should he have given it to him? Why?

In her criticisms of cognitive-developmental research, Gilligan takes exception to the fact that Kohlberg's initial research sample was all male and, furthermore, that the dilemmas addressed were all hypothetical and hence abstract and highly artificial. Understandably, it's problematic to make universalistic generalizations when you leave out one-half of the human race—a fact on which Gilligan strongly focuses. Secondly, the dilemmas which were addressed by research subjects were "canned" or prepared in advance without any input from those responding to them. Moral problems were presented, not constructed by the subjects themselves. This is important, for Gilligan, since she claims, on the basis of her own research, that women tend to view morality more personally and concretely than impersonally and abstractly (the ideal for Kohlberg). Women also tend, in their ethical experience, to operate more naturally from a feminine position of moral care and relationship and less from a masculine position of rational morality and impersonal justice. If Kohlberg's initial depiction of moral dilemmas favours the adequacy of an abstract and impersonal morality of justice, one with which adjudications of interpersonal conflicts work most easily, then it is little wonder that such a morality is regarded as more highly developed. On this note, Gilligan would argue that, just as Kohlberg failed to acknowledge the serious problem of gender bias in his original studies, so too have many moral thinkers failed to appreciate the inherent bias of a purely formal, rationalistic ethic. Critics like Gilligan, would be inclined to say that strict adherence to rational principles of morality is a choice, not a non-negotiable feature of moral discourse or morality's true nature. Morality is not always or primarily about the **adjudication of conflicting rights**.

Gilligan conceptualizes the differences between masculine and feminine morality more by theme than by gender itself.[5] Although it is empirically true that more women tend to operate from a perspective of feminine morality, nothing prevents them from displaying masculine moral preferences.[6] Ayn Rand may be an illustration of this fact. Likewise, men can function morally from both perspectives as well, although they tend to prefer a more **detached rational objectivity**, often presupposing that it is more adequate or superior in some fashion. Women, who often do not reach stage six in Kohlberg's conceptual framework because of their own conceptions and presuppositions about morality, come out as "less developed" and "less mature" in their moral reasoning abilities. What Gilligan would describe as a feminine morality of care and relation fits into Kohlberg's scheme at the conventional level—which he regarded as a less adequate form of moral thinking than the more autonomous, impersonal and detached forms of morality found at stages five and six of the post-conventional level. Given the allegation that Kohlberg's research methodology was seriously flawed right from the outset and that his own presuppositions about morality, used in the construction of hypothetical moral dilemmas, are open to serious question, Gilligan argues that Kohlberg's studies of morality fail to do justice to women's moral experience. Women are not less developed morally, as some of the empirical studies might suggest; rather, for Gilligan, there has been a failure by cognitive-developmental theorists like Kohlberg to produce models of human growth which acknowledge and respect male-female differences. The universal and prescriptive paradigm of Kantian-Rawlsian morality, supported by Kohlberg's cognitive-developmental studies, is arguably not more adequate or more justified, just more male.

THE GENESIS OF CARE-BASED MORALITY

The different voice of morality to which Gilligan would have us listen could have its roots in individual **identity formation**. Gilligan cites Nancy Chodorow's research to explain how men and women come to experience and conceptualize morality differently. As Gilligan says, female identity formation occurs in a context of **ongoing relationship**. Mothers have a tendency to experience their daughters as more alike and as an extension of themselves. Correspondingly, daughters, in their self-identifications as females, experience themselves as similar to their mothers. Thus, the experience of attachment is fused with the process of identity formation. By contrast, as boys come to define themselves as masculine, they separate their mothers from themselves and thereby curtail their relationship with their primary love object and sense of empathetic tie. Chodorow concludes that

> *...the logic underlying an ethic of care is a psychological logic of relationship, which contrasts with the formal logic of fairness that informs the justice approach.*
>
> CAROL GILLIGAN

male development entails a "more emphathic individuation and a more defensive firming of experienced ego boundaries." The ultimate result of this that "girls emerge from this period with a basis for 'empathy' built into their primary definition of self in a way that boys do not." Furthermore, "Girls emerge with a stronger basis for experiencing another's needs or feelings as [their] own."[7] They experience themselves as less differentiated than boys and as more continuous with, and related to, others. Given the differences between boys and girls' psychological attachments and individuation patterns, male gender identity is threatened by **intimacy**, while female gender identity is threatened by **separation**. In this context, it becomes more easily understandable how rational detachment becomes a virtue of a masculine moral perspective, whereas relation and care become hallmarks of feminine morality. Commenting on Kohlberg and the historical male bias in moral theorizing, Gilligan writes:

> The quality of embeddedness in social interaction and personal relationships that characterizes women's lives in contrast to men's, however, becomes not only a descriptive difference but also a developmental liability when the milestones of childhood and adolescent development in the psychological literature are markers of increasing separation. Women's failure to separate then becomes, by definition, a failure to develop.[8]

Of course, Gilligan sees nothing wrong with women's experience of morality, but does point to serious flaws in models of morality (like Kohlberg's) that fail to capture it properly. A feminine morality of relational care is only less developed and less adequate when viewed through the lens of masculine values and male identity formation.

The voice of feminine morality is, for Gilligan, perhaps best heard in women's construction of the abortion dilemma. Talk about abortion by women frequently uses the language of **self-ishness** and **responsibility**, defining the basic moral problem as one of obligation to exercise care and avoid hurt. As Gilligan points out, the infliction of hurt is considered selfish and immoral insofar as it reflects unconcern. By contrast, the expression of care is regarded as the fulfillment of moral responsibility. For Gilligan, the repeated use by women of the words "selfish" and "responsible" when talking about choice and moral conflict directs us toward a different understanding of moral development and a moral orientation quite apart from the one Kohlberg structured.

> *...as long as the categories by which development is assessed are derived from research on men, divergence from the masculine standard can be seen only as a failure of development. As a result, the thinking of women is often classified with that of children.*
> CAROL GILLIGAN

In her own developmental research, Gilligan did not present subjects with abstract, hypothetical dilemmas for resolution. Instead, she asked people (a) how they defined moral problems themselves and (b) what experiences they construed as moral conflicts in their lives. Her sample of 29 women, ages 15-33 years, were drawn from an "abortion decision study" which looked at the relation between experience and thought and the role of conflict in development. The women in the study were initially interviewed in the first trimester of their pregnancies, at a time when they were contemplating having abortions. Most of the women were interviewed again at the end of the year following their choice. Complete interview data were available for 24 of them.

In a second "rights and responsibility" study, a sample of males and females were matched for age, intelligence, education, occupation and social class at nine points across the life cycle. Data were collected on conceptions of self and morality, experiences of moral conflict and choice, and judgments on hypothetical moral dilemmas.

Gilligan's findings from these studies suggest we should broaden our understanding of human moral development. Women apparently tend to display perspectives different from men when it comes to (a) images of humankind, (b) the human condition, (c) human development and (d) what is of value in life. In brief, moral development for women involves a progressive change in the understanding of responsibility and relationships. For men, at least according to Kohlberg, morality, seen as justice, ties development to the logic of equality and reciprocity.

In her book, *In a Different Voice: Psychological Theory and Women's Development*, Gilligan spells out for us the developmental sequence for the ethics of care. At Stage One, the individual is most concerned with caring for herself to ensure survival. In time, this life position and the judgments flowing from it come to be criticized as selfish. A transitional phase emerges whereby a new understanding of connection between oneself and others is articulated. Here, at Stage Two, good is essentially equated with caring for others. A type of maternal morality develops that seeks to ensure care for the dependent and unequal. Stage Two eventually opens the door to the next transitional phase. When only others are allowed to be the recipients of the woman's care—when she cannot care for herself without being selfish—this exclusion of herself gives rise to problems in relationships and thereby creates disequilibrium. At the third and final stage of development, care is understood not in a dichotomous fashion (caring only for me *or* others) but as an interconnection between oneself *and* others. This third stage highlights the dynamics of relationships and causes a reduction in the tension between selfishness and responsibility. As Gilligan puts it:

> Care becomes the self-chosen principle of a judgment that remains psychological in its concern with relationships and response but becomes universal in its condemnation of exploitation and hurt. Thus a progressively more adequate understanding of the psychology of human relationships—an increasing differentiation of self and other and a growing comprehension of the dynamics of social interaction—informs the development of an ethic of care. This ethic, which reflects a cumulative knowledge of human relationships, evolves around a central insight, that self and other are interdependent.[9]

Clearly we see, then, that Gilligan's feminine morality of care, characterized by interdependence and responsibility for others, stands in stark contrast to the Kantian-Rawlsian-Kohlbergian model of masculine morality defined by autonomy, impartiality and rational self-interest. As philosophers, we might ask, "Is one moral perspective necessarily better or more adequate than the other?", "Should an ethic of care overrule an ethic of justice?" or "Are both perspectives actually fragments of something much broader in scope?"—something to consider! Maybe we need to reason with more care and care more about reason.

NEL NODDINGS' CONCEPTION OF CARE-BASED ETHICS

In her book, *Caring: A Feminine Approach to Ethics and Moral Education*, Nel Noddings presents an **ethic of care** which bears a noticeable resemblance to Carol Gilligan's. Noddings devel-

Biographical Brief

Nel Noddings (1929–)

Nel Noddings is currently Lee L. Jacks Professor of Child Education at Stanford University. After completing her Bachelor of Arts degree at Montclair State College, she went on to do her M.A. at Rutgers and her Ph.D. in Educational Philosophy and Theory at Stanford University (1973). Having worked at all levels of education, she now teaches introductory classes in educational philosophy, the philosophical and educational thought of John Dewey, and moral education, as well as contemporary social and ethical philosophy. In addition to *Caring: A Feminine Approach to Ethics and Moral Education*, she has produced numerous other publications including more than 125 articles. She has served as past president for the Philosophy of Education Society and the John Dewey Society. Noddings has also been the recipient of many awards and distinctions including the Medal for Distinguished Service, given by the Teacher's College of Columbia University.

ops certain notions further than Gilligan, however, while disagreeing with her on others. For instance, Noddings works out in detail the implications of ethical interdependence for individual character; Gilligan does not. Furthermore, in contrast to Gilligan, who, in places, appears to allow for both justice and care in a fully mature ethic, Noddings presents her own ethic of care as a distinct alternative to principled ethics.[10]

> *Indeed, one who attempts to ignore or to climb above the human affect at the heart of ethicality may well be guilty of romantic rationalism.*
>
> NEL NODDINGS

Like Gilligan, Noddings accepts the notion that there are at least two basic approaches to morality, one more masculine in approach, the other more feminine. **Masculine ethics** presents itself as principled and emotionally detached. In male ethics, moral conclusions are derived from general ethical principles in a logically consistent fashion. There is an effort to proceed rationally without emotional influence. Objectivity and detachment require that feelings be left out of moral deliberations, since they are regarded as contaminating variables.

Romanticizing Rationality: Reasons to Reject Principled Morality

Cautioning us not to romanticize rationality by holding it in unconditional positive regard, Noddings draws our attention to some of the limitations inherent in a purely rational, principled approach. To begin with, she alleges that such a morality is ambiguous and unstable. Whenever you have a principle, exceptions are almost always implied. The general principle, "Never kill," for instance, could easily be followed by "except in self-defense" or "except in defense of an innocent other" and so on. General principles of conduct are not as solid and reassuring as some would like to think. Another drawback to principled morality is that principles can often function to separate people and alienate them from one another. Have you ever stood stubbornly and refused to budge *on principle*? Have you ever terminated a relationship for the same reason? Have principles ever pushed you farther away from others, instead of bringing you closer to them? If so, then you can appreciate how principled thought and the actions that follow from it could be counterproductive, as far as bringing people together and having them live in harmony are concerned. As Noddings expresses it: "We may become dangerously self-righteous when we perceive ourselves as holding a precious principle not held by the other. The other may then be devalued and treated 'differently.' Our ethic of caring will not permit this to happen."[11]

Noddings rejection of principled morality leads her to reject the rational concept of **universality**. From our coverage of Immanuel Kant's formalistic theory, you may remember that, for him, any maxim or principle of behaviour had to be universalizable or universally prescriptive in order for it to belong to morality and to be morally justifiable. Maxims or principles of conduct which could not be universally prescribed were deemed to be either nonmoral or not morally justifiable. Thus, if under condition X, you are morally required to do A, then under sufficiently similar conditions, I too am required to do A, along with everyone else. The moral obligation applies to everybody universally and unconditionally. This line of moral thinking is again rejected by Noddings because it allegedly fails to recognize and preserve the uniqueness of human encounters. Because of the highly personal, idiosyncratic and subjective experience of those involved in particular ethical relations, conditions are seldom "sufficiently similar" for anyone to declare what we must do in our situation, or what anyone else should do in their situation. For Noddings, the universalizability criterion doesn't work, as principles of moral conduct simply cannot be properly universalized. Efforts to abstract them from concrete situations cause us to lose sight of the unique features and personal variables that give rise to the moral question or dilemma in the first place. In other words, though two situations may appear somewhat similar from a detached observer's perspective, they are likely not sufficiently similar when viewed from *within* the situation. Consequently, the detached application of a universal principle from one situation to another is not appropriate.

It is interesting to look again at Lawrence Kohlberg's theory of moral development in the light of Noddings' rejection of the universalizability criterion and her criticism of principled morality. Remember that, for him, the most highly developed and most adequate morality is the one which is the most rational, abstract and universal. That which is concrete or person-specific is less developed and less mature, labelled as 'conventional' or 'preconventional'. However, insofar as Noddings' criticisms and rejections are justified, it behooves us to reexamine the assumptions underlying a rational, principle-based masculine morality. As Noddings says: "Women can and do give reasons for their acts, but the reasons often point to feelings, needs, impressions, and a sense of personal ideal rather than to universal principles and their application.... [A]s a result of this 'odd' approach, women have often been judged inferior to men in the moral domain."[12] The point here is that people who operate from the vantage point of feminine ethics do not proceed deductively from principles superimposed on situations. In response to Kohlberg's dilemmas, they would seek to fill out those hypothetical situations in a "defensible move toward concretization."[13] In the case of administering punishment, say, for one who is guilty of committing a crime, the traditional masculine approach asks about the principle under which this case falls, so that it may be applied. The feminine approach, by contrast, asks us to consider the feelings involved and the personal history of the wrongdoer. When the situation is concretized by things such as feelings and personal histories, what is appropriate punishment or what is the appropriate resolution to the conflict may change. For Noddings, there is no virtue in abstraction, where thinking can occur in a logical vacuum apart from the complicating factors of particular persons, places and circumstances.[14] These "complicating factors" are what make the moral situation real. The move toward logical abstraction which, admittedly, unclutters the complexity of any moral dilemma situation, in the end undermines itself with artificiality and the prospect of destroying interpersonal relationships—the very thing morality is meant to preserve and protect.

Relation as Ontologically Basic

In articulating her conception of morality, Noddings clearly does not begin with the rational subject. In contrast to John Rawls, for instance, who conceptualizes the moral agent as rational, self-interested, autonomous and independent of others, Noddings takes **relation** as ontologically basic and the **caring relation** as ethically basic. To be human is to be in relation to others. We do not stand alone, isolated and apart from others, either psychologically or existentially. Human existence is relational. Morality comes not from the *a priori* structure of reason itself (à la Kant), but rather from the interpersonal human dynamic of persons in relation. It is affect and connection which should serve as the basis of morality, not reasoning. Of course, in her book, Noddings spells out the details of her care-based ethic and for a fuller appreciation of what's at issue here, I invite you to read it. For our purposes here, I'll just mention a few of the general features characterizing this moral perspective.

MINDWORK MEDITATION

Bring to mind any recent argument or interpersonal conflict you've had with someone of the opposite sex. Try to remember a disagreement that had moral implications. In light of what you know so far about male–female differences when it comes to reasoning about moral values issues, review your disagreement. Is it possible to better understand your opponent's point of view now? Try to reconstruct the arguments that were made on both sides. Does your particular example support or call into question the claims of moralists advocating a care-based perspective?

Brief Outline of a Care-Based Ethic

As already mentioned, Noddings takes the caring relation as ontologically basic. There is the **"one-caring"** and the one **"cared-for,"** to use her terminology. The conception of morality Noddings has in mind could be described in part as an **ethic of virtue**. It establishes an ethical ideal of what it means to be the one-caring in relation to others. This virtue involves reaching out to others and growing in response to the other. Interpreting morality as being about persons in relation means that morality is not be understood as an emotionally sterile conception of rationally self-interested individuals seeking to further their own interests and co-operating only when it is mutually advantageous. Ethical caring emerges from **natural caring**—a condition we desire and toward which we strive. In our infancies, we begin to develop memories of caring and being cared for. The resulting caring attitude provides the motivation to be moral, and because it is so basic and natural, it is universally accessible. The relation of natural caring represents moral goodness. When we remain in a concrete caring relation and enhance the ideal of ourselves as ones-caring, we do the morally good thing. Everything hinges on the nature and strength of this ideal. There are no rational absolutes to guide us. This does not mean, for Noddings, that morality disintegrates into relativity, however, since the natural caring attitude supporting ethical caring is a universal phenomenon. Universality, understood as a foundational basis of morality, is not rational but relational for Noddings. Obligation is therefore a matter of acting, not in ways consistent with abstract-formal principles (regardless of who's involved), but in response to commitments and to the maintenance of relationships. Noddings writes, "The source of my obligation is the value I place on the relatedness of caring. This value itself arises as a product of actual caring and being cared-for and my reflection on the goodness of these concrete caring situations."[15] In short, the ethical ideal of maintaining the caring relation should, for Noddings, be placed above formal abstract principle as a guide to moral action. In this, we find a basic difference between Noddings' feminine ethic and the masculine ethic represented by thinkers like Kohlberg, Kant and Rawls.

The last point to be made here refers to the basic human affect grounding morality. Unlike suffering existentialists who recognize their unique subjectivity as aloneness in the world and who consequentially experience **anguish**, Noddings considers **joy** as the fundamental human emotion rooted in relation. She states that it is our recognition of, and longing for, relatedness that forms the foundation of the feminine ethic. "[T]he joy that accompanies fulfillment of our caring enhances our commitment to the ethical ideal that sustains us as one-caring."[16] It's not dour obligation that moves us to moral action, then, nor capricious subjectivity, but rather the desire to find joy by exercising the virtue of goodness by fulfilling ourselves in the other. Responsiveness and receptivity are key, not detachment or cold rational aloofness. In this moral attitude, we find a fundamental difference between masculine and feminine orientations to ethics. And in the discussion of this difference we discover many fresh new insights that challenge male-dominated historical assumptions about morality.

Let us now turn to an excerpt from Noddings' writings to learn more about care-based ethics.

BACK TO THE SOURCE*

Ethics, the philosophical study of morality, has concentrated for the most part on moral reasoning. Much current work, for example, focuses on the status of moral predicates and, in education, the dominant model presents a hierarchical picture of moral reasoning. This emphasis gives ethics a contemporary, mathematical appearance, but it also moves discussion beyond the sphere of actual human activity and the feeling that pervades such activity. Even though careful philosophers have recognized the difference between "pure" or logical reason and "practical" or moral reason, ethical argumentation has frequently proceeded as if it were governed by the logical necessity characteristic of geometry. It has concentrated on the establishment of principles and that which can be logically derived from them. One might say that ethics has been discussed largely in the language of the father: in principles and propositions, in terms such as justification, fairness, justice. The mother's voice has been silent. Human caring and the memory of caring and being cared for, which I shall argue form the foundation of ethical response, have not received attention except as outcomes of ethical behavior. One is tempted to say that ethics has so far been guided by Logos, the masculine spirit, whereas the more natural and, perhaps, stronger approach would be through Eros, the feminine spirit. I hesitate to give way to this temptation, in part because the terms carry with them a Jungian baggage that I am unwilling to claim in its totality. In one sense, "Eros" does capture the flavor and spirit of what I am attempting here; the notion of psychic relatedness lies at the heart of the ethic I shall propose. In another sense, however, even "Eros" is masculine in its roots and fails to capture the receptive rationality of caring that is characteristic of the feminine approach.

When we look clear-eyed at the world today, we see it wracked with fighting, killing, vandalism, and psychic pain of all sorts. One of the saddest features of this picture of violence is that the deeds are so often done in the name of principle. When we establish a principle forbidding killing, we also establish principles describing the exceptions to the first principle. Supposing, then, that we are moral (we are principled, are we not?), we may tear into others whose beliefs or behaviors differ from ours with the promise of ultimate vindication.

This approach through law and principle is not, I suggest, the approach of the mother. It is the approach of the detached one, of the father. The view to be expressed here is a feminine view. This does not imply that all women will accept it or that men will reject it; indeed, there is no reason why men should not embrace it. It is feminine in the deep classical sense—rooted in receptivity, relatedness, and responsiveness. It does not imply either that logic is to be discarded or that logic is alien to women. It represents an alternative to present views, one that begins with the moral attitude or longing for goodness and not with moral

* *From* Caring: A Feminine Approach to Ethics & Moral Education. *Berkeley: University of California Press, 1984.*

reasoning. It may indeed be the case that such an approach is more typical of women than of men, but this is an empirical question I shall not attempt to answer.

It seems to me that the view I shall try to present would be badly distorted if it were presented in what I have referred to as the "language of the father." Several theorists in education—among them, William Pinar, Madeleine Grumet, Dwayne Huebner, Elliot Eisner—have suggested that our pictures of the world are unduly cramped and narrowed by reliance on a restricted domain of language. Pinar and Grumet, in particular, have looked at this problem in the context of gender studies. I agree with their assessment. But we must realize, also, that one writing on philosophical/educational problems may be handicapped and even rejected in the attempt to bring a new voice to an old domain, particularly when entrance to that domain is gained by uttering the appropriate passwords. Whatever language is chosen, it must not be used as a cloak for sloppy thinking; that much is certain. This part of what I am doing, then, is not without risk.

Women, in general, face a similar problem when they enter the practical domain of moral action. They enter the domain through a different door, so to speak. It is not the case, certainly, that women cannot arrange principles hierarchically and derive conclusions logically. It is more likely that we see this process as peripheral to, or even alien to, many problems of moral action. Faced with a hypothetical moral dilemma, women often ask for more information. We want to know more, I think, in order to form a picture more nearly resembling real moral situations. Ideally, we need to talk to the participants, to see their eyes and facial expressions, to receive what they are feeling. Moral decisions are, after all, made in real situations; they are qualitatively different from the solution of geometry problems. Women can and do give reasons for their acts, but the reasons often point to feelings, needs, impressions, and a sense of personal ideal rather than to universal principles and their application. We shall see that, as a result of this "odd" approach, women have often been judged inferior to men in the moral domain.

Because I am entering the domain through a linguistic back door of sorts, much of what I say cannot be labeled "empirical" or "logical." (Some of it, of course, can be so labeled.) Well, what is it then? It is language that attempts to capture what Wittgenstein advised we "must pass over in silence." But if our language is extended to the expressive—and, after all, it is beautifully capable of such extension—perhaps we can say something in the realm of ethical feeling, and that something may at least achieve the status of conceptual aid or tool if not that of conceptual truth. We may present a coherent and enlightening picture without *providing* anything and, indeed, without claiming to present or to seek moral *knowledge* or moral *truth*. The hand that steadied us as we learned to ride our first bicycle did not provide propositional knowledge, but it guided and supported us all the same, and we finished up "knowing how."

This is an essay in practical ethics from the feminine view. It is very different from the utilitarian practical ethics of, say, Peter Singer. While both of us would treat animals kindly and sensitively, for example, we give very different reasons for our consideration. I must resist his charge that we are guilty of "speciesism" in our failure to accord rights to animals, because I shall locate the very wellspring of ethical behavior in human affective response. Throughout our discussion of ethicality we shall remain in touch with the affect that gives rise to it. This does not mean that our discussion will bog down in sentiment, but it is necessary to give appropriate attention and credit to the affective foundation of existence. Indeed, one who attempts to ignore or to climb above the human affect at the heart of ethicality may well be guilty of romantic rationalism. What is recommended in such a framework simply cannot be broadly applied in the actual world.

I shall begin with a discussion of caring. What does it mean to care and to be cared for? The analysis will occupy us at length, since relation will be taken as ontologically basic and the caring relation as ethically basic. For our purposes, "relation" may be thought of as a set of ordered pairs generated by some rule that describes the affect—or subjective experience—of the members.

In order to establish a firm conceptual foundation that will be free of equivocation, I have given names to the two parties of the relation: the first member is the "one-caring" and the second is the "cared-for." Regular readers of "existentialist" literature will recognize the need for such terminology—bothersome as it is. One may recall Sartre's use of for-itself and in-itself, Heidegger's being-in-the-world, and Buber's I-Thou and I-It. There are at least two good reasons for invoking this mechanism. First, it allows us to speak about our basic entities without explaining the entire conceptual apparatus repeatedly; second, it prevents us from smuggling in meanings through the use of synonyms. Hence, even though hyphenated entities offend the stylist, they represent in this case an attempt to achieve both economy and rigor. Another matter of style in connection with "one-caring" and "cared-for" should be mentioned here. In order to maintain balance and avoid confusion, I have consistently associated the generic "one-caring" with the universal feminine, "she," and "cared-for" with the masculine, "he." Clearly, however, when actual persons are substituted for "one-caring" and "cared for" in the basic relation, they may be both male, both female, female-male, or male-female. Taking *relation* as ontologically basic simply means that we recognize human encounter and affective response as a basic fact of human existence. As we examine what it means to care and be cared for, we shall see that both parties contribute to the relation; my caring must be somehow completed in the other if the relation is to be described as caring.

This suggests that the ethic to be developed is one of reciprocity, but our view of reciprocity will be different from that of "contract" theorists such as Plato and John Rawls. What the cared-for gives to the citing relation is not a promise to behave as the one-caring does, nor is it a form of "consideration." The problem of reciprocity will be, possibly, the most important problem we shall discuss, and facets of the problem will appear in a spiral design throughout the book. When we see what it is that the cared-for contributes to the relation, we shall find it possible to separate human infants from nonhuman animals (a great problem for those who insist on some form of rationality in those we should treat ethically), and we shall do this without recourse to notions of God or some other external source of "sanctity" in human life.

The focus of our attention will be upon how to meet the other morally. Ethical caring, the relation in which we do meet the other morally, will be described as arising out of natural caring—that relation in which we respond as one-caring out of love or natural inclination. The relation of natural caring will be identified as the human condition that we, consciously or unconsciously, perceive as "good." it is that condition toward which we long and strive, and it is our longing for caring—to be in that special relation—that provides the motivation for us to be moral. We want to be *moral* in order to remain in the caring relation and to enhance the ideal of ourselves as one-caring.

It is this ethical ideal, this realistic picture of ourselves as one-caring, that guides us as we strive to meet the other morally. Everything depends upon the nature and strength of this ideal, for we shall not have absolute principles to guide us. Indeed, I shall reject ethics of principle as ambiguous and unstable. Wherever there is a principle, there is implied its exception and, too often, principles function to separate us from each other. We become dangerously self-righteous when we perceive ourselves as holding a precious principle not held by the other. The other may then be devalued and treated "differently." Our ethic of caring will not permit this to happen. We recognize that in fear, anger, or hatred we will treat the other differently, but this treatment is never conducted ethically. Hence, when we must use violence or strategies on the other, we are already diminished ethically. Our efforts must, then, be directed to the maintenance of conditions that will permit caring to flourish. Along with the rejection of principles and rules as the major guide to ethical behavior, I shall also reject the notion of universalizability. Many of those writing and thinking about ethics insist that any ethical judgment—by virtue of its *being* an ethical judgment—must be universalizable; that is, it must be the case that, if under conditions X you are required to do A, then under sufficiently similar conditions, I too am required to do A. I shall reject this emphatically. First, my attention is not on judgment and not on the particular acts we perform but on how we meet the other morally. Second, in recognition of the feminine approach to meeting the other morally—our insistence on caring for the other—I shall want to preserve the uniqueness of human encounters. Since so much depends on the subjective experience of those involved in ethical encounters, conditions are rarely "sufficiently similar" for me to declare that you must do what I do. There is, however, a fundamental universality in our ethic, as there must be to escape relativism. The caring attitude, that attitude which expresses our earliest memories of being cared for and our growing store of memories of both caring and being cared for, is universally accessible. Since caring and the commitment to sustain it form the universal heart of the ethic, we must establish a convincing and comprehensive picture of caring at the outset.

Another outcome of our dependence on a ethical ideal is the emphasis upon moral education. Since we are dependent upon the strength and sensitivity of the ethical ideal—both our own and that of others—we must nurture that ideal in all of our educational encounters. I shall claim that we are dependent on each other even in the quest for personal goodness. How good *I* can be is partly a function of how *you*—the other—receive and respond to me. Whatever virtue I exercise is completed, fulfilled, in you. The primary aim of all education must be nurturance of the ethical ideal.

To accomplish the purposes set out above, I shall strike many contrasts between masculine and feminine approaches to ethics and education and, indeed, to living. These are not intended to divide men and women into opposing camps. They are meant, rather, to show how great the chasm is that already divides the masculine and feminine in each of us and to suggest that we enter a dialogue of genuine dialectical nature in order to achieve an ultimate transcendence of the masculine and feminine in moral matters. The reader must keep in mind, then, that I shall use the language of both father and mother; I shall have to argue for the positions I set out expressively.

An important difference between an ethic of caring and other ethics that give subjectivity its proper place is its foundation in relation. The philosopher who begins with a supremely free consciousness—an aloneness and emptiness at the heart of existence—identifies *anguish* as the basic human affect. But our view, rooted as it is in relation, identifies *joy* as a basic human affect. When I look at my child—even one of my grown children—and recognize the fundamental relation in which we are each defined, I often experience a deep and overwhelming joy. It is the recognition of and longing for relatedness that form the foundation of our ethic, and the joy that accompanies fulfillment of our caring enhances our commitment to the ethical ideal that sustains us as one-caring.

In the final chapter on moral education, we shall explore how all this may be brought to bear on recommendations for the reorganization of schooling. The specific suggestions made there are not intended as fully developed plans for action but, rather, as illustrations of an approach, of a mode of thinking and feeling about education. They are an invitation to dialogue and not a challenge to enter battle.

PHILOSOPHERS AT WORK

Developmental theory would appear to force us as philosophers to revisit the idea that "the more rational and objective, the better." Could it be that a large part of western rational philosophy is little more than a manifestation of male psychology? Discuss in light of the research and writings of Carol Gilligan and Nel Noddings.

KEY TERMS

reason	morality of care
male bias	hypothetical moral dilemma
adjudication of conflicting rights	detached rational objectivity
identity formation	ongoing relationship
intimacy	separation
selfishness	responsibility
ethic of care	universality
relation	caring relation
one-caring	cared-for
ethic of virtue	natural caring
anguish	joy

PROGRESS CHECK 9.1

Instructions: Fill in the blanks with the responses listed below.

male bias	identity formation
selfishness	principled morality
natural caring	responsibility
Lawrence Kohlberg	joy
conventional	Carol Gilligan
separation	reason
Nel Noddings	justifying
intimacy	morality of care
relation	

1. Moral philosophers such as Plato, Kant and Rawls put _reason_ in control of deciding what's right and wrong.

2. Carol Gilligan and Nel Noddings offer us an alternative to rational morality by presenting a _morality of care_.

3. The problem with traditional approaches to morality is that they reflect a(n) _male bias_.

4. _Lawrence K._ claimed to have found a universal, invariant sequence of moral development, one which proceeds from the particular and concrete to the universal and abstract.

5. According to cognitive-developmental theories, women's moral reasoning tends to fall at the second _conventional_ level.

6. _Gilligan_ criticizes Kohlberg's research because the _moral dilemmas_ upon which he based his research were biased toward a purely formal, rationalistic ethic.

7. Feminine researchers in ethics look for the clues to male-female differences in moral thinking in the notion of _identity formation_.

8. Because of gender differences in socialization, males are threatened by _intamacy_, while females are threatened by _seperation_.

9. According to Carol Gilligan, feminine moral sensibilities construct women's experience of morality more in terms of _selfishness_ and _responsibility_.

10. _Noddings_ claims that men have romanticized rationality, failing to see its inherent limitations when applied to morality.

11. _principle morality_ often has the effect of alienating individuals, not bringing them together, which should be its intention.

12. For Noddings, pointing to feelings and personal impressions is indeed a way of _justifying_ and giving reasons for one's actions

13. Rather than start with "the individual" in her moral theorizing, Noddings takes _relation_ as ontologically basic.

14. Instead of basing morality on reason, Noddings chooses _natural caring_, a condition we all desire and toward which we all strive.

15. For Noddings, morality is not born of anguish or conflict, but _joy_.

SUMMARY OF MAJOR POINTS

1. **What has dominated Western rational ethics, historically speaking?**

   Reason or rationality has been the dominating influence:
   Plato: Reason rules over appetites and passions.
   Aristotle: The rational contemplative life is the highest form of human existence.
   Bentham: The right action in any situation can be determined by a rational hedonic calculation.
   Mill: Pleasures of the mind trump pleasures of the body.
   Kant: Moral certainty is found in the structure of reason itself.
   Rand: Her gospel of reason promoted rational selfishness.

2. **What else could serve as the basis for morality, according to Gilligan and Noddings?**

   The notions of relation and the human affective response of care are two very good possibilities reflecting feminine consciousness.

3. **Of what are traditional moral theories guilty?**

   Gilligan and Noddings allege they are guilty of a male bias in the emphasis they place on abstract rationality.

4. **What is wrong with the cognitive-development research in moral psychology which points to the greater adequacy of rational principled morality?**

   The initial research sample was all male. The "moral dilemmas" used as research instruments favoured moralities that could best adjudicate conflicts of interest based on rights and fairness considerations. The "deck was stacked," so to speak. Further, women's experience of morality was ignored not only in the construction of the dilemmas, but also in Kohlberg's initial sample of subjects.

5. From where does care-based morality originate?

Gilligan cites the work of Nancy Chodorow to suggest that it is based in identity formation. Male identity development is characterized by greater individuation, whereas female identity development is characterized by attachment and ongoing relation to the primary love-object, namely the mother. Thus, males are threatened by intimacy; females are threatened by separation.

6. What, for Gilligan, does woman's moral thinking gravitate around?

Women more often use the language of "selfishness" and "responsibility" to talk about their moral experiences; less often are they inclined to speak about impersonal justice and abstract rights.

7. How does Gilligan depict the sequence of women's moral development?

Stage One: One cares for oneself to ensure survival.
Stage Two: 'Good' is equated with caring for others.
Stage Three: Care is understood as interconnection between oneself and others; a reduction of tension between selfishness and responsibility occurs.

8. What, according to Nel Noddings, are some reasons to reject reason as the basis of morality?

People have tended to romanticize morality in the past. But rational morality is more ambiguous and unstable than normally assumed. Further, rational principles cannot be applied from situation to situation, as they frequently differ from one another in morally relevant respects—ones that are personal, subjective and concrete. Allowable "reasons" for moral action must therefore include feelings and other situational particulars.

9. What's wrong with beginning a study of morality using rational self-interested individuals?

The problem is that relation is ontologically basic in human moral interactions. To be human is to be in relation to others, psychologically and existentially. Affect and connection should serve as the basis of morality, not reasoning.

10. What is the source of morality for Noddings?

Ethical caring emerges from natural caring—an experience that is universally accessible. It is rooted in joy, responsiveness and receptivity.

SOURCE REFERENCES AND RELATED READINGS

Cochrane, D.B., C.M. Hamm, and A.C. Kazepides, *The Domain of Moral Education*. New York: Paulist Press, 1979.

Duska, Ronald and Mariellen Whelan, *Moral Development: A Guide to Piaget and Kohlberg*, New York: Paulist Press, 1975.

Falikowski, Anthony, *Moral and Values Education: A Philosophical Appraisal*. Doctoral dissertation. University of Toronto, 1984.

Gilligan, Carol, *In A Different Voice: Psychological Theory and Women's Development*. Cambridge: Harvard University Press, 1982.

Kohlberg, Lawrence, *Essays on Moral Development, Vol.1: The Philosophy of Moral Development*. San Francisco: Harper & Row, 1981.

Mischel, Theodore, *Cognitive Development and Epistemology*. New York: Academic Press, 1971. pp.151-235.

Noddings, Nel, *Caring: A Feminine Approach to Ethics and Moral Education*. Berkeley: University of California Press, 1986.

Rawls, John, *A Theory of Justice*. Cambridge: Harvard University Press, 1971.

ENDNOTES

1. This biographical brief was taken from Anthony Falikowski, *Moral Philosophy for Modern Life*, Prentice Hall, Allyn and Bacon Canada: Scarborough, Ontario, 1998, p. 125.
2. Ronald Duska and Mariellen Whelan, *Moral Development: A Guide to Piaget and Kohlberg*, New York: Paulist Press, 1975. The authors of this book provide an easily understood description of Kohlberg's theory. I have used it in my own summary here.
3. For further discussions of this see, for example, Anthony Falikowski, *Moral and Values Education: A Philosophical Appraisal*, doctoral thesis, University of Toronto, 1984 and Brian Crittenden, "The Limitations of Morality as Justice in Kohlberg's Theory" in D.B. Cochrand, C.M. Hamm and A.C. Kazepides, *The Domain of Moral Education*, New York: Paulist Press, 1979. Also see John Rawls, *A Theory of Justice*, Cambridge: Harvard University Press, 1971.
4. In the "original position," conflicting parties are placed behind a "veil of ignorance," which prevents them from knowing what is in their personal self-interest. Without such knowledge, the parties must formulate, in advance, mutually acceptable principles which they could use to adjudicate conflicts when they arise in the future. Since no personal reference can be made to favour any party, the resulting principles turn out to be formal and abstract.
5. ibid, p. 2.
6. This appears to be well illustrated by the work of Ayn Rand, also covered in this section. See pages 126 to 142.
7. Gilligan, ibid., p. 8.
8. ibid., pp. 8–9.
9. ibid., p. 74.
10. For a discussion of this point, see Claudia Cord, *Hypatia*, Vol.5, No1.1 (Spring 1990), p. 101. Gilligan's views on the relation between justice and care may have evolved or may simply be ambiguous.
11. Nel Noddings, ibid, p. 5.
12. ibid.
13. ibid., p. 36.
14. ibid., p. 37.
15. ibid., p. 84.
16. ibid., p. 6.

Applying Moral Theories

Now that we have explored six classical and contemporary moral perspectives, it might be interesting to apply them to a single moral issue to see how each would handle it differently. By doing so, we put theory into practice and reveal some of the implications of committing ourselves to any one moral position. It would be wonderful at this juncture if we could conduct a comparative evaluation of all the theories, given that their basic assumptions are often inconsistent with one another. Deciding on which theory is the best one would help to alleviate a lot of moral indecision. Unfortunately, this "meta-ethical" task will have to wait, since I do not believe we can accomplish in one short introductory applied ethics text what philosophers have been trying to do for generations. Nonetheless, seeing how moral theories play out in practice will at least get us started in appreciating the tangible differences they would make in our moral approach to life. Likely, we will need further occasion to reflect and do some critical-analytical work. Until then, let's see how all the theories we've studied would approach the morality of premarital sex—an issue no doubt on the minds of many college undergraduates today. We will briefly examine this issue by first presenting some of the moral concerns surrounding it and then look at how the various moral perspectives we have studied might begin to approach the matter.[1] Understand that what follows is intended to be neither detailed, nor exhaustive. Nor do we wish to finally resolve the issue we are addressing. The objective is simply to get a flavor for each of the various moral theories in practice and an appreciation of how they diverge in their general approach. Though no final resolutions on the issue of premarital sex will be offered, the following discussion should provide some useful insight into how moral decisions can be made. How *you* decide to make them will be your choice in the end.

THE ISSUE: PREMARITAL SEX

Premarital sex is a serious moral issue. Many people raised within religious traditions like Christianity, Judaism and Islam, for example, have been taught that having sexual relations before marriage is morally wrong. With traditional religious values on the wane, however, many no longer accept religious authority—or social convention, for that matter—and are placed in a position of having to decide for themselves. In contrast to prior times, it is no longer "clearly wrong" to have sex prior to marriage for a good portion of the population. Statistical reports seem to suggest that young people are engaging in sexual intercourse at earlier ages and in greater frequency. Is this good or bad? Many adolescents and young adults having sex plan eventually to marry. Does premarital sex undermine the institution of marriage? Is premarital sex just plain wrong in itself? Or, is it an act that is morally neutral? Perhaps it is something good that ought to be encouraged. How can we decide?

Greek Character/Virtue Ethics

If we were to adopt the perspective of the Greek character/virtue ethicist, we might be inclined to evaluate the morality of premarital sex by first establishing the function of sex and then determining whether or not premarital sex serves that function well. Remember that Plato and Aristotle are both teleological functionalists. For them, everything in nature has a function and all activities point to some end within a harmonious hierarchy of human purposes. In this light, we could ask: What is the natural function of sexual intercourse? What is its biological purpose? If, say, the natural end is union of sperm and egg—or to put it slightly less clinically, the creation of human life—then we could ask whether premarital sex is an excellent way of promoting this function. What about the subsequent child-rearing function, however? Will premarital sex serve this function best by creating circumstances most advantageous to the child, or is child-rearing best performed within the context of traditional marriage, with the implication that sex should occur within the boundaries of marriage? Even if one objects to discussing the morality of premarital sex in terms of what arrangement is best for the child who might result, we could still ask, however, why so many who engage in it use "artificial contraception" as a way of avoiding pregnancy. Others resort to abortions when unintended pregnancies result. This doesn't seem very natural. It would appear, then, that other ends, besides procreation, are intended by many engaging in premarital sex. Apart from the apparent "unnaturalness" of this, one could ask further whether these other ends are in line with Aristotle's ultimate good. Will premarital sex help people to live the good life and develop their highest potential, or not? Will premarital sex contribute to, or detract from, the good of society? Plato and Aristotle both felt that individuals could best realize themselves and their potentials within society. Individuals are not islands unto themselves and their actions must be appraised in a social context.

Utilitarian Ethics

The utilitarian would approach the matter of premarital sex rather differently from the Greek character/virtue ethicist. Utilitarians like Jeremy Bentham place no stock in "nature" or "natural rights" accounts of morality. Since actions are not regarded as right or wrong in themselves, or right or wrong according to nature, efforts to establish the morality of actions on that basis are seen as misguided. Thinking back to our discussion of Bentham, recall that for him, the principle of utility serves as the basis of moral judgment. In any situation, the course of action which maximizes utility is the one that should be preferred. Some modern-day "rule-utilitarians" seek to establish the operative rule in any set of circumstances that should prevail. They argue that: "We should not consider the consequences of a particular action, but rather the consequences of the rule under which the action falls." Understand, however, that utilitarian rules do not carry any Kantian a priori necessity; they are not "right in themselves," universally and unconditionally. They are only acceptable or unacceptable because of the long-term beneficial consequences they are likely to produce.

Now, on the subject of premarital sex, some (act-) utilitarians would consider the pleasure, enjoyment or utility of any particular instance of it, perhaps engaging in some form of hedonic calculus envisioned by Bentham. In some instances, premarital sex could turn out to be acceptable; in others it might not. The fact is, one would not be able to decide in advance either to engage in premarital sex or to refrain from it. It would depend on one's situation. The probable consequences would determine what was right or wrong. By contrast, a rule-utilitarian might try to establish the behavioural principle implicitly operative in acts of premarital sex in order to determine whether broader, longer-term consequences increase or decrease utility. Regardless of how the rule was finally articulated, its ultimate acceptability would depend on the results of its application.

For people who tend to lean more in the direction of John Stuart Mill, instead of Bentham, they might be inclined to morally appraise premarital sex in terms of higher and lower pleasures. If it turned out that sexual intercourse were assessed as a "lower pleasure," one could proceed to ask whether indulgence in it could undermine the pursuit of so-called "higher pleasures." Would a pursuit of sexual gratification outside of marriage create little more than a "satisfied pig" or would it help to produce an individual with the virtue and wisdom of an Aristotle or Socrates, however "dissatisfied" the latter might have been with the realities of everyday life? On this note, the utilitarian could ask whether premarital sex promotes nobility and refinement or undermines it with vulgar satisfaction.

Deontological Ethics

By contrast to utilitarianism, deontologists like Kant don't allow the consequences of actions to determine their moral acceptability. Probabilistic calculations concerning what will likely occur are problematic and risky, and besides, for someone like Kant, pleasure and benefit are unstable contingencies upon which no solid and secure foundation of morality can be established. Diametrically opposed to the utilitarian, Kant would argue that some actions are right or wrong in themselves. Intentional human acts are based on rules or maxims which, once identified and made explicit, can be appraised in terms of their formal logical characteristics. Rules of conduct that conform to the categorical imperative, and thus are universally prescriptive, impartial, and consistent, are considered moral. Those rules that are conditional or contingent on external factors, like the amount of pleasure produced, are non-moral and hence do not belong to the moral domain.

With respect to premarital sex, the Kantian deontologist would ask: "What is the rule or maxim which supports the act of having intercourse prior to marriage?" "Can I universalize this rule?" "Can I imagine a world within which everybody had sex prior to marriage?" and finally, "Would I wish to live in such a world?" If not, then the moral maxim is unacceptable and premarital sex is wrong.

The deontologist could also approach the issue of premarital sex from the vantage point of the second formulation of the categorical imperative: *Always treat others and ends in themselves and never solely as means to your own ends.* In deciding whether or not one should engage in premarital sex, one could ask whether anyone will be treated as an object—just a means to someone else's selfish pleasure. If so, then the act would again be wrong. Presuming any rational individual would not wish to be exploited or victimized himself, it should be clear why it would be wrong to exploit or make a victim of another. Objectifying someone is wrong in itself or wrong, *a priori*.

Ethical Egoism/Objectivist Ethics

Atheistic ethical egoists sympathetic to the views of Ayn Rand would certainly not wish to determine the morality of premarital sex on anything but rational considerations. Since Rand considers religion a form of irrational mysticism, she refuses to allow faith or religious authority to determine the morality of actions. This does not mean, of course, that personal whim and fancy become the basis of her morality either. For Rand, this would make no sense as people are fickle; they have different wishes and desires, and prefer different things at different times in their life. Of course, subordinating the individual by deferring to socially prescribed norms pertaining to sexual conduct is not likely to be an acceptable alternative either, as she believes that 'society' is just a secular substitute for God, whom she rejects as metaphysical nonsense.

For Rand, values have no a priori status or independent existence. What has value has it only because it sustains life, so the question becomes, "Does premarital sex sustain and contribute to life or threaten it?" As we know, unprotected sex can have dire consequences, leading to sexually transmitted diseases and AIDS, in worst case scenarios. Perhaps one could conclude, simply on this basis, that unprotected premarital sex is wrong; but how about if precautions are taken? Would it still be wrong to have sex before marriage? Well, clearly, given Rand's writings, it would be wrong to guilt anyone into premarital sex; it would also be wrong to be guilted into it yourself. Given the emphasis Rand places on rationality, productivity and pride, the ethical egoist might ask: "Will this act of premarital sex contribute to my self-esteem or will I be ashamed in the morning?" Will having sex be a freely chosen rational act or am I emotionally upset, swept away by passion or am I just trying to get revenge or prove my potency?

Given the importance Rand places on "trade" for human relationships, any act of premarital sex might be morally appraised in terms of what both trading partners are getting out of it. If the act involves exploitation of one by the other, it would be wrong, though it would seem that if two rational adults freely entered into an intimate relationship both to give and to get fairly, with no dishonesty or hidden psychological agenda, then the act might be regarded as acceptable. Certainly, any acts of premarital sex involving imbalanced power relationships, emotional coercion or manipulation would be evaluated negatively.

The Morality of Care

Care-based moralists do not accept the premise that abstract or objective moral principles can be applied properly to concrete situations, from above, as it were. Relational considerations of care take priority instead. In view of this, it would seem that the morality of premarital sex would hinge on the circumstances involved and the particular persons in relation. Asking the general question, "Is premarital sex right or wrong?" actually turns out to be like one of those "hypotheticals" that care-based moralists balk at. Details and concrete circumstances and the persons involved would have to be taken into consideration before a "correct" and justifiable decision could be made.

An ethic of care which stresses the maintenance of relationships would likely view exploitive premarital sex as morally wrong. Instead of the one-caring and the one cared-for, we would have the one-exploited and the one-exploiting. Whether care or exploitation is present in the act depends again on the individuals in relation. Will premarital sex solidify the relationship or destroy it? Will it bring the concerned individuals together, or tear them apart? How many times have young couples broken up immediately after having sex, perhaps out of shame, guilt or insecurity? In such cases, perhaps the premarital sex was wrong. On this note, one might consider whether the desire for sex comes from a caring place in the heart and affection for the other, or from a lusty place in the loins. Is physical pleasure the sole purpose or is there the desire to express one's love for another through physical intimacy? Feelings certainly play a crucial role in decision making for the feminine moralist and should not be discounted or subordinated to rational principles.

Existentialist Ethics

In our coverage of existentialism we discovered that existentialists like Sartre are far from nihilistic. They celebrate humanistic values pertaining to freedom, individuality, responsibility and authentic living. These values do not provide a precise system of moral decision making, but do offer individuals a normative foundational basis for ethical choice.

From an existential vantage point, one could approach the matter of premarital sex reminded of Sartre's notion of responsibility. Remember, that whenever we act on personal choices, we choose for the world. If, for example, you choose to join a trade union, you are declaring to the world, in effect, that unionism is good. When you choose to marry, you bestow value upon the institution of marriage. Similarly, when you opt to have sex before marriage, you recommend premarital sex to the rest of humanity. You are singly responsible for your choice and for all of mankind. In the act of creating yourself, you are creating a world in which premarital sex is practiced and considered good. You become one who engages in premarital sex and this action defines who you are. If this is the world you want, and for which you accept responsibility, then premarital sex is good and by all means, go ahead. If, on the other hand, premarital sex is not something you would want to recommend to your daughters or something you would wish to confess to your mother, then the act may not be acceptable for you.

Like feminine moralists, existentialists refuse to accept rational objectivity in moral decision making. The example of Sartre's student (see pp. 148 to 149) illustrated what he believed was the impossibility of applying abstract principles to concrete situations; so applying this idea to the case of premarital sex, again no formal principles can be imposed or applied from above. One must be in the situation in order to decide properly. Decisions to have, or not to have, premarital sex can

> *I tore myself away from the safe comfort of certainties through my love for truth, and truth rewarded me.*
>
> SIMONE DE BEAUVOIR

only be properly made by individuals. From an existentialist viewpoint, one person cannot legislate moral behavior for another. Premarital sex may be wrong "for me," but right "for you," given your present existential circumstances.

On this indecisive note, we conclude our treatment of moral theories for Part One of this text. We should not leave our theoretical studies frustrated by the complexity of the various ethical perspectives and the extent of the disagreement among the divergent thinkers. As Aristotle once remarked, we should not expect more precision from a discipline than the discipline itself allows. It would appear that ethics does not afford us much certainty, but casts substantial doubt and raises many questions. Ironically, perhaps, we as philosophers should feel more secure surrounded with inquiring and doubting minds, than we otherwise would if surrounded by dogmatic individuals whose arrogance and willed ignorance provided for them, what thoughtful investigations could not for us. Perhaps with the "benefit" of moral doubt comes Socratic humility and the wisdom which accompanies it. As we savour this possibility, let us move on now to Part Two of our philosophical explorations which deals with skills of moral reasoning and analysis.

> *If man will begin with certainties, he shall end in doubts. But if he will be content to begin with doubts, he shall end in certainties.*
>
> FRANCIS BACON

NOTES

The issue presented and some of the points made in what follows are adapted from Vincent Barry, *Applying Ethics*, Belmont, Ca.: Wadsworth Publishing Co., 1982, pp. 70–79

PHILOSOPHERS AT WORK

To gain some experience at putting theory into practice, select another controversial moral issue besides premarital sex. Once you have chosen your issue, begin to analyze it from the six alternative ethical perspectives covered in Part One of the text. Once finished, determine which theory allows itself, in your estimation, to do the best job on the issue. Would you prefer to use this theory more generally in your life? Why or why not? Once you are done this task, complete The Moral Preference Indicator again (pp. 190 to 191) to see whether your pre-reflective assumptions about morality have remained the same, been strengthened or changed. Compare your results on the MPI now not only with your earlier ones, but also with what you say in this Philosopher at Work activity? Do any patterns, inconsistencies or questions arise? Comment.

POST-STUDY MORAL PREFERENCE INDICATOR

Instructions and Answer Sheet

Having now finished your study of moral theories, let us do the Moral Preference Indicator a second time. (Go to pages xxxi to xxxii for the questions.) Your responses can be recorded below. Once done, graph your results and compare them to your earlier ones. Have your preferences changed or stayed the same? Has a study of moral theory solidified your thinking about morality or called some of your assumptions and beliefs into question?

Scoring Sheet

Answers

	Utilitarian	Deontologist	Virtue Moralist	Existentialist	Egoist	Care-Based Moralist
1.	a	b	c	e	d	f
2.	b	c	a	f	e	d
3.	b	a	c	e	d	f
4.	c	b	a	e	d	f
5.	b	c	a	e	f	d
6.	b	a	c	e	d	f
7.	b	c	a	e	f	d
8.	b	c	a	e	d	f
9.	a	b	c	e	f	d
10.	c	b	a	e	d	f
11.	a	b	c	e	f	d
12.	b	a	c	e	f	d
13.	b	c	a	e	f	d
14.	b	a	c	d	f	e
15.	a	b	c	e	d	f
Total Number	_____	_____	_____	_____	_____	_____

Plot your scores on the "Moral Preference Indicator: Before and After," (Figure PI.1 on page 191).

>**Figure PI.1**   *Moral Preference Indicator: Before and After*

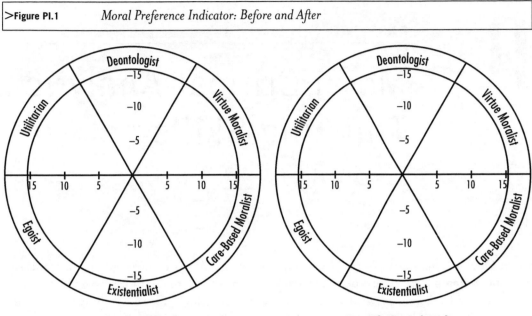

Pre-Theoretical Study   **Post-Theoretical Study**

MINDWORK MEDITATION

Have your post-study moral preferences changed at all, and, if so, in what respects? How do you explain your changed preferences or the fact that your preferences remained more or less stable? Are you now more character-based, utilitarian or deontological, egoistic, care-based or existential in your moral thinking? Refer back to pages xxxi–xxxii for summaries of what each perspective involves.

II PART TWO

Moral Critical-Analytical Thinking Skills

In Part One of *Moral Philosophy for Modern Life*, Second Edition, we looked at six different classical and contemporary ethical perspectives. We learned how morality has much to do with things like virtue, character, justice and personal responsibility. There is still much more to explore in the moral domain, but we have had an introduction to some of the most important and influential ethical ideas in the history of Western civilization.

In Part Two of our odyssey, we will be travelling into that area of the philosophical kingdom containing the fields of logic and reasoning. Chapter Ten will focus on analytical thinking in ethics. We will learn how to analyze claims and employ techniques of conceptual analysis to clarify moral matters when necessary. In this part of the book, we will also learn how to structure and evaluate moral arguments. This skill will come in handy as we proceed to analyze ethical case studies using a seven-step procedure developed by philosophical practitioners in Europe. As we move to Chapter Eleven, we direct our attention to types of arguments. We will examine forms of inductive and deductive logic and how they can be used in moral reasoning. In Chapter Eleven, we will also learn to evaluate arguments. Ways of testing value premises will be presented, along with a discussion of informal logical fallacies. These are illegitimate arguments designed to persuade by means of diversionary tactics and personal attack. By the completion of Part Two, you will have a basic background in the reasoning skills necessary to structure, analyze and critically evaluate moral arguments properly.

Before we get started with Chapter Ten, I invite you to complete the *Rational Skills Assessment* that follows. Your results will provide some indication of what your current reasoning level is and how much work will have to be done.

REASONING SKILLS ASSESSMENT

If we wish to engage in productive moral discussions and debates, we must learn to think clearly and to reason correctly according to the accepted norms of logic. In this informal self-diagnostic, you will be given an opportunity to reflect on how good or bad your current command of logic and critical-analytical thinking is. Consider doing this assessment a second time after you complete Part Two of your studies. Comparing those results with the ones you achieve now will help you to gauge your improvement as a rational thinker. (Correct answers are found in Appendix One starting on page 414.)

Part One: Identifying Claims

The statements below are either factual (F), normative (N) or conceptual (C). Identify each statement by placing the appropriate corresponding letter next to it. Factual claims are true or false in principle. Normative claims come in the form of value judgments, prescriptions and prohibitions. Conceptual claims, by contrast, pertain to matters of definition and linguistic usage and so cannot be proven to be true or false; nor can they be ethically justified by appeals to normative principles.

_____   1. Philosophy is bunk.

_____   2. Euthanasia is murder.

_____   3. Human cloning should be banned.

_____   4. Gay marriages should be legalized.

_____   5. The war in Iraq was immoral.

_____   6. Traditional values are on the wane.

_____   7. Fewer people attend religious services in Canada as compared with the United States.

_____   8. Government advertising is really propaganda.

_____   9. The unborn fetus is not a human being.

_____   10. The majority of citizens in this country favours legalized abortion.

Score: /10

Part Two: Distinguishing Among Arguments, Opinions and Explanations

Philosophers distinguish among arguments, opinions and explanations. Arguments are comprised of a conclusion with at least one supporting premise. Opinions are unsupported claims, often statements of personal taste or feeling. Explanations don't justify or defend like arguments, but tell us how or why things are as they are, or happen as they do. In what follows, identify each example as either an argument (A), opinion (O) or explanation (E).

_____   1. Country-and-western music is so lame!

_____   2. The USA should keep its nose out of the Middle East. My uncle's a general who thinks America should police the world.

_____   3. You really should study applied ethics because it will become practically useful for you in the future.

_____   4. The professor snapped in class because someone pressed one of her "buttons of insecurity."

_____   5. Hitler became an evil monster because of his troubled childhood.

_____   6. Gays should not be allowed to adopt children because they will do emotional and psychological harm to them.

_____   7. Studying moral philosophy has no practical value.

_____   8. I hate those commercials that try to guilt-trip you into saving the starving children of the world.

_____   9. CEOs of major corporations should do jail time for things like income tax fraud and insider trading. Making sure this happens will increase investor confidence.

_____   10. Waiting until marriage before having sex is silly in view of the fact that social norms have changed over the years.

Score: /10

Part Three: Thinking Deductively

Deductive logic is a formal process of reasoning having a number of different structures. For instance, there is the syllogism in its various forms, as well as *modus ponens* and *modus tollens*, each different from the other. Before we go on to study these forms of logic, let's see how well you can complete the logical arguments that follow. Fill in the missing claims for each of the examples below.

1. All Greeks are moral.

   _____

   Therefore, Socrates is moral.

2. _____

   An oak is a tree.

   Therefore, an oak has leaves.

3. All citizens have a right to vote.

   Jean-Guy is a citizen.

   _____

4. If interest rates decline, then stock prices will rise.

   _____

   So, stock prices will rise.

5. If you do something wrong, your parents will get mad.

Your parents are not mad.

_____

6. If p, then q.

   If q, then r.

   So, _____

7. Either p or q.

   _____

   Therefore, p.

8. All A are B.

   _____

   Therefore, some C are B

9. Cheaters should be punished.

   _____

   Mary should be punished.

10. If p is q and r is p,

   then _____.

   Score: **/10**

Part Four: Informal Logical Fallacies

A number of recurring patterns of incorrect reasoning have been identified and given inter-esting names like "red herring" and "slippery slope." These and other informal logical fallacies operate through diversion, intimidation and other psychological tactics, not by appeals to impartial reason. Think of these manoeuvres as instances of *sleazy logic*. In the examples below, place the letter *A* next to instances of acceptable reasoning and *U* next to unacceptable ones.

_____   1. We should not accept Professor Knowitall's argument that drinking coffee causes cancer. He's just a greedy and vain researcher trying to make a name for himself.

_____   2. Do not believe anything Mr. DeNile says. I know his relations and they are all liars.

_____   3. If Vince Carter says those court shoes are the best, it must be true.

_____   4. You ought to be opposed to legalized gambling in this country. Once you per-mit it, prostitution will necessarily follow. After that will come organized crime. In the end, legalized gambling will make our cities less safe than before.

_____   5. Listen, I hate cheating as much as you do; but when everyone else cheats, you
                 have to cheat in order to make things fair.

Score: /5

Scoring

Total Score: Add scores for Parts One to Four.   /35

Divide your total by 35 to arrive at your percentage.   /100

10

Analytical Thinking in Matters of Morality

Overview

Learning Outcomes

Students successfully completing this
chapter will be able to

- distinguish between scientific and
  philosophical approaches to the study
  of morality
- explain the nature of, and differences
  among, factual, normative and conceptual claims
- differentiate between moral and nonmoral values
- employ techniques of conceptual analysis
- discriminate between arguments and
  non-arguments
- structure, analyze and evaluate
  arguments
- diagram arguments and express them
  in standard form
- resolve moral dilemmas, applying a
  seven-step model for case-study analysis

PHILOSOPHICAL FOCUS QUESTIONS

1. Why is an examination of language claims important to the study of morality and moral argument?

2. How do you know whether you are dealing with moral or nonmoral values?

3. How and why are techniques of conceptual analysis useful in moral–ethical contexts?

4. What features distinguish arguments from non-arguments?

5. How does one analyze and evaluate arguments?

6. Is there any process that can help us to deal with moral dilemmas when they arise? If so, what is the process?

APPROACHES TO THE STUDY OF MORALITY

By now, you probably have noticed that moral philosophy is quite different from other traditional fields of study. While it may sound a bit psychological or sociological at times, there is something about the methods and processes of philosophical analysis that makes ethical inquiry different from both the behavioural and social sciences. This is not to suggest that philosophy and science do not sometimes overlap; they do. In building their arguments, philosophers frequently make claims about what is true or factually the case—a matter of science, observation or empirical investigation. Often underlying the work of scientists, on the other hand, are theoretical assumptions having philosophical implications (e.g., all human behaviour is determined and freedom is, therefore, an illusion). In fact, as an undergraduate student in psychology, I was led to this realization many years ago. At that time, I was studying the nature and development of moral reasoning in children and adolescents. I hoped eventually to get involved in moral and values education. What I discovered was that the psychological researchers whose work I was studying often made philosophical claims, and sometimes based their scientific studies on ethical assumptions that were far from clear and self-evident. These assumptions required satisfactory rational justification— something which was, unfortunately, all too often lacking. The deeper I got into studying the psychological phenomenon of moral/values development, the less interested I became in applied scientific study, and the more interested I became in the ethical notions underlying the scientific research and investigation I was involved in. The rest, as we say, is history and I now find myself addressing you on the subject of philosophical ethics and not the psychology of moral development. Let us proceed, then, to examine more closely the contrasts between science and philosophy so that we can appreciate, as ethicists, what we are and are not doing.

Scientific Approach

Sciences such as psychology, sociology and anthropology make morality an object of **empirical study**. To say that morality is studied empirically means that methods of **observation** and

controlled experiment are used. Scientific researchers attempt to **measure** and **describe** what is **true**, or at least highly **probable**, about moral conduct and experience. A scientist could ask, for example, how likely is it that one will steal if one can get away with it. A feminist researcher could inquire into the possibility that there are gender differences in how people think about moral issues. Whatever empirical questions are asked, it is presumed that answers can be found, in principle, according to the ideal of **scientific objectivity**. Scientists are not in the business of making value judgments about the moral phenomena that they study. Instead, scientists are interested in providing **correlational findings**, **causal** and/or **functional explanations.** That is, they seek to answer questions of how morality works in personality or functions in society. Given the methods and goals of scientists, we find psychologists, for instance, looking at the relationship between cognitive development and moral reasoning abilities. Sociologists may be intrigued by the functional role of morality in group organization. Anthropologists, by contrast, might be curious about the origins and development of morality in socio-cultural evolution. Whatever their scientific slant, empirical researchers are primarily concerned with the how, why, when and where questions of morality. If possible, methods of **statistical analysis** are used to **verify** findings or to support claims made about moral experience. In some instances, **predictions** about future moral events might also be offered. Remember, though, that although scientists study the phenomenon of morality, they do not wish to be **moral-istic**. Their investigations are ideally designed to be **value-neutral**. They do not wish to prescribe what ought to be done; nor do they wish to judge what values are good or bad. Scientists try to express their conclusions as **nonnormative** statements.

> *You see things; and you say, "Why?"*
> *But I dream things that never were*
> *and I say, "Why not?"*
> GEORGE BERNARD SHAW

Philosophical Approach

The philosophical approach to the study of morality may be either **normative** or **meta-ethical**. Normative philosophical inquiry involves going beyond empirical investigation. In contrast to scientific researchers who make empirical claims about what is factually true or is likely the case, philosophers sometimes make **normative** statements about how humans **should** behave or what **ought** to be the case. Normative inquiry frequently leads philosophers to **prescribe** a course of action and to make **evaluative** judgments about what is **right** or **wrong**, **good** or **bad**, **praise-worthy** or **blameworthy**. Thus, while empirical, scientific investigation (or everyday experience) may yield evidence that human beings often act in their own self-interest, the moral philosopher engaged in normative inquiry would ask whether humans should or should not act in this fashion. The *fact* that they do does not necessarily mean that, morally speaking, they *should*. Think back to the chapter on Bentham, where the point was made that most philosophers question the idea that one can derive a moral, normative "ought" from an empirical "is" of experience. Just because it is true that some people kill, steal, cheat and rape does not mean one can justifiably conclude, on that basis, that they *should*, or that it is all right to do so. Ethical philosophers engaged in normative inquiry are, thus, not interested in verifying empirical findings (the job of science), but rather in justifying evaluative judgments about what ought or ought not to be the case, what is good or bad, right or wrong and praiseworthy or blameworthy.

On the subject of "oughts," some normative moral inquiry attempts to establish what ought or ought not to be done in specific moral situations, or in particular moral controversies like abortion or capital punishment. To say, for example, that convicted murderers should be executed or that all abortions are wrong is to make normative statements having ethical relevance. In recent years, many philosophers have descended from the ivory towers of academe to debate such matters in the streets of life. It is not uncommon to find ethical philosophers engaged in bioethical debates, business matters or governmental policy decisions. They may take sides, for instance, on the moral and ethical status of reproductive technologies, on the rights of the business community to earn profits or on government legislation regarding the treatment of minority peoples.

Traditionally, however, normative inquiry has tended to be more general in nature. As we learned in Part One, philosophers have articulated over the ages a number of different normative theories that promote diverse ethical principles, values and considerations. Theories such as utilitarianism or deontology can be regarded as blueprints for life. They give direction and guidance in moral action and decision making. By appealing to the general ethical principles contained in these and other normative theories, we can determine what ought or ought not to be done in any specific situation. Some normative theories, like utilitarianism, evaluate the moral correctness of actions based on their effects or results, while deontological theories, like Kant's, focus more on rational, formal considerations.

Still another way of dealing with morality is from a metaethical point of view. A metaethical perspective is the most general and abstract of all. The street-fighting philosopher preoccupied with real-life normative issues might ask whether or not the country's laws on abortion are right; the metaethicist would be more likely to ask what is meant by the term "right" itself. Does "right" mean consistent with the will of the majority? Does "right" mean that which an individual likes? Or does "right" mean in accordance with divine will? In asking such questions, philosophical metaethicists are not involved in science, but neither are they involved in normative inquiry. They are not out to justify particular moral value judgments about what is right or wrong, and so on; nor are they doing experiments and basing conclusions on surveys and sensory observations. Rather than prescribing, evaluating and experimenting, metaethicists tend to focus more on the usage of language. They analyze moral terms, examine meanings and look for **conceptual relationships**. In their work, they often ask for theoretical clarifications and **elucidations** of moral concepts. They try to achieve clarity in thinking by removing vagueness, ambiguity and inconsistency. This is important because there is not much point in having a discussion or a debate on any moral issue if we are logically incoherent or if we are using the same words in different ways (i.e., equivocating). Precision in language and meaning is very important to the metaethicist.

Apart from the conceptual and analytical concerns, metaethicists are also interested in investigating and evaluating the **ultimate foundations** of particular ethical systems of thought. For instance, they may study the rationales or justifications provided by a system's advocacy for a particular fundamental principle like justice. Metaethical inquiry is, thus, theoretically one step removed from normative deliberation. In contrast to the utilitarian philosopher, who may wish to prescribe a particular course of action on the basis that it will likely maximize pleasure or happiness, the metaethicist questions why pleasure or happiness should serve as the ultimate ethical foundation of action and decision making in the first place. At this point, you can better appreciate the differences between scientific and philosophical approaches to morality by referring to Table 10.1.

Kinds of Claims about Morality

Contained in the preceding comparison of scientific and philosophical approaches to the study of morality was the notion that different kinds of claims can be made which are more relevant to one field of inquiry than the other. Let us now examine these claims in more detail, so that we might better appreciate in the future whether our disagreements involving moral matters should be resolved philosophically or scientifically.

Factual Claims: People discussing morality make claims or ask questions belonging to one of three types: factual, normative or conceptual. A **factual claim** is a statement or proposition that is true or false in principle. Note that it is true *or* false. It may sound illogical at first, but a factual statement can sometimes be false. For instance, "There is green cheese on the moon" is a factual statement, but one that is likely untrue. The statement makes a claim about what presumably is the case. Whether or not the statement is actually true depends on what we find there. If, after travelling to the moon and performing an exhaustive search, we found no green cheese, then we could conclude with a fair degree of certainty that the statement was false. If, however, after tunnelling into the moon's surface, we found some green cheese, then the factual statement would be true. The point about factual statements is that sensory experience and observation can serve to determine their truth or falsity. Empirical scientific methods can

Table 10.1   SOME KEY TERMS ASSOCIATED WITH APPROACHES TO THE STUDY OF MORALITY

SCIENTIFIC APPROACH	PHILOSOPHICAL APPROACH
empirical	rational
factual	normative or nonnormative (metaethical)
what is	what ought/ought not to be
descriptive	prescriptive
verification	justification
empirical support	reasoned argument
correlational/causal	conceptual/analytical
functional	critical
controlled studies	thought experiments (e.g., Rawls' original position)

also be used to verify whether or not something is, in fact, the case. Whenever you make a claim about the way things are, therefore, you are making a factual statement.

Factual claims can also refer to past and future events. If you were making an assertion about the ways things were, not about the way things are, you could refer to old newspapers, magazines, past statistics, historical documents and so on to determine the accuracy of your truth claim. If, on the other hand, you were making a claim about how things will be in the future, you could always wait until later to see how things turn out. You could also do some kind of statistical, scientific or empirical study to prove your point or to support your prediction. Whether your factual claim deals with past, current or future events, the point is that sensory experience, statistical methods or empirical means can be used to support them or verify them as true or false, or as more or less probable.

In the context of morality, the kind of factual claims that could be made include, for example, (1) Boys engage in immoral acts more often than girls. (2) People from technologically advanced societies display quicker development in their abilities to deal with moral complexity as compared with people from rural, agrarian societies. (3) Women tend to see morality largely in terms of maintaining relationships, whereas men tend to focus more on principles of justice. In all three cases, the claims are either true or false. For (1), we could do a social-psychological study to determine, say, whether or not boys do indeed steal more often than girls when both are given the opportunity to do so and there is little chance of getting caught. For the second example, we could first design a paper-and-pencil research instrument enabling us to measure cognitive complexity in moral thinking and then administer it to representative and comparable samples in both agrarian and technologically advanced societies. Results could subsequently be compared. To test the truth or falsity of the third claim, we could ask men and women to describe their personal conceptions of morality in order to determine whether or not dominant themes reoccur frequently enough to enable us to accurately make this generalization. Though our empirical findings might not provide conclusive proof, they would nonetheless provide support, or a basis of critique, for whatever factual claim was made.

Of course, any of the factual claims just discussed could be expressed as questions: (1) Do boys engage in immoral acts more often than girls? (2) Do people from technologically advanced societies display quicker development in their abilities to deal with moral complexity as compared with people from rural agrarian societies? (3) Do women tend to see morality largely in terms of maintaining relationships, while men focus more on principles of justice? Efforts to answer these questions would, again, be empirical and observational.

Normative claims: **Normative claims** are very different from factual claims. They express value judgments and prescriptions, not statements of fact. Normative claims make assertions about what is right or wrong, good or bad, praiseworthy or blameworthy, better or worse, obligatory or prohibited or about what one should or should not do. Here are some examples of normative claims: (1) Liberal democracy is better than communism. (2) Globalization is a bad thing. (3) Handguns should be banned. (4) The Russian dictator Stalin was an evil man. (5) Discrimination on the basis of race is wrong. (6) You should not litter the street.

An important feature of normative claims is that they cannot be *proven* or *verified* in the same way that factual claims can be. For instance, you can't look in a microscope, do a survey or conduct an experiment to determine whether current liberal handgun legislation in the United States is moral or immoral. You might wish to point out that widespread handgun use leads to increased crime and murder, but this in itself does not prove that handguns should be banned. Indeed, it would be inappropriate to use empirical proof in this context, since what is required is not factual verification, but justification. To illustrate this, imagine someone who works as a private detective in criminal investigations, and let's say he also sells security systems for a living. That person may be a fear-monger who enjoys the business profits derived from the anxiety in the populace that results from increased crime. Such an individual might regard allowing individuals to own handguns as a good thing—however debatable or perverse you think such a conclusion may be in this instance. The fear-mongering security systems sales-man may accept your conclusion about the consequences of liberalized handgun laws, but still remain unconvinced about their undesirability. After all, the laws bring him personal benefit. If we wish to persuade him to change his mind, we will have to get him to weigh the egoistic values of personal benefit against the value of social security. We might also try to get him to weigh the value of life against the value of profit. Such evaluations will require rational argument and justification, not empirical evidence.

We see, then, that normative claims of value and obligation require quite a different kind of support as compared with factual claims. Further, whereas many factual claims are often unambiguously true or false, normative statements allow for much more disagreement. Value judgments may be more or less justifiable, more or less adequate from a rational point of view. The factual claim "It's raining outside" can be fairly easily verified by observation. This is not to suggest all factual claims are always so easily proven true or false. For example, the factual claim that "There are Venusians on Venus" may not be so easy to prove, but at least it's possible in prin-ciple using means that most people would agree upon. If we visited Venus or sent camera-equipped satellites there and found that Venusians lived in bubble-domed communities, for instance, then the claim would be true. If we found no inhabitants on Venus, then the factual claim would be false—end of story. The normative claim that "Abortion is wrong," however, does not lend itself to such easy acceptance or rejection. Some may wish to determine the morality of abortion on the basis of its consequences, while others may wish to examine the ethical prin-ciples involved—the right to life versus the woman's right to choose on matters that affect her own body. The "correct" procedure is not so unambiguous or without controversy. As we've seen in Part One of this text, utilitarians and deontologists do not always agree on approach when it comes to solving moral dilemmas. Moral situations allow for much interpretation and differences of value emphasis. There are numerous normative and metaethical perspectives from which to view moral situations. Nonetheless, what we can try to do is judge particular actions, events, poli-cies and people etc., against our own accepted standards, ideals and normative principles, whatever they may be. Whether or not the standards we choose to base our value judgments on are acceptable is a matter of rational evaluation. If our principles or standards are unjustifiable, then the value judgments following from them will likely be unacceptable too. If they are vague, then we will not know for sure whether they apply in a given case. If our standards and princi-ples are inconsistent or incoherent, then our value judgments will probably not make any sense. The acceptability of a particular value judgment hinges on the justifiability of the normative principle or standard on which it is based and on the proper application of the principle or standard in any given situation.

When making normative claims, it is important to distinguish between two basic types of value judgments: **moral** and **nonmoral**. There is widespread agreement among philosophers that nonmoral values are based on things like our personal tastes and preferences. In addition, things that promote our individual health, wealth, security, status, power or emotional well-being, for instance, are all "good," but in a nonmoral prudential sense. They are good for our individual welfare and personal life satisfaction. Of course, we can always make value judgments regarding the tastes and preferences of others and we can prescribe for them what they ought to do to promote their personal health and enjoyment of life; but such normative statements would be nonmoral again. Telling a friend that he *should* invest in a particular stock if he wishes to become rich is not a moral recommendation, though it is value-related. Immanuel Kant would label this a conditional or hypothetical imperative, not a moral one. (See the section on Kant's hypothetical imperatives in Chapter Six.)

As with empirical claims, normative claims can be turned around and phrased as questions as well. "You shouldn't eat too much" becomes "Should you not eat too much?" and "Killing in self-defence is justifiable" translates into "Is killing in self-defence justifiable?" In either case—whether one is trying to justify a normative claim or answer a normative question—the methods will not be empirical. References to values will ultimately have to be made—values that are not true or false, but more or less justifiable. Even prescribing to people that they shouldn't eat too much refers to nutritional values and the values of health. It's not just about the fact that increased food intake causes weight gain; values are presupposed. In some societies, obesity is a status symbol and sign of wealth, so eating a lot is seen as a privilege for an elite few—not something undesirable.

Conceptual Claims: Often, in the context of moral discourse, a third kind of claim arises that is conceptual in nature. **Conceptual claims** involve matters of meaning. Given this, they necessitate linguistic analysis, not empirical support or ethical justification. Questions of concept "are concerned with the uses of words and with the criteria or principles by which those uses are determined."[1] Take this claim, often made by pro-life supporters in the abortion debate: "The fetus is a person." You cannot simply do some kind of survey to determine its truth or falsity. For one thing, morality cannot be determined by numbers—this is a recognized form of fallacious reasoning (see Chapter Eleven). For another, the people filling out your survey could ask, "What do you mean by 'person'? If by 'person' you mean *a,b, and c*, then the fetus most certainly is a person; but, if by 'person' you mean *x, y, and z*, then the fetus is most certainly not a person." Whether or not the fetus is a person depends on the meaning of 'person' and the definition given to it. Perhaps the fetus is a 'non-person' at one stage of development, but a real 'person' at another—given our defining criteria. Again, the problem here is not factual, empirical or normative, but conceptual and linguistic. We must ask how the word 'person' is used, and then, given its accepted usages, we must ask whether the concept of 'fetus' falls under it. Our approach in trying to answer this question involves techniques of **conceptual analysis**—a philosophical procedure we'll examine in a moment.

PHILOSOPHERS AT WORK

Instructions: Below is a list of value judgments. Some clearly belong to morality, while others relate to prudential and other nonmoral considerations. Next to each statement, indicate whether the statement is moral (M) or nonmoral (NM).

_____ Chocolate bars are better than popsicles.

_____ You should not lie to people just to get your own way.

_____ What you ought to do is invest in mutual funds for your retirement.

_____ You shouldn't say things like that if you want to keep your friends.

_____ Religious schools should not be funded with public tax dollars on grounds of fairness.

_____ Gay couples should be allowed to marry legally.

_____ It's wrong to tax savings interest because that undermines the economy.

_____ Single mothers shouldn't be entitled to student welfare.

_____ Jungle music is awful.

_____ It's bad for your health to smoke.

Depending on your temperament, you may find doing conceptual analysis somewhat frustrating. There are those of us who prefer the clarity and security found, say, in basic arithmetic, where one plus one always equals two. This is simple and always unambiguous. Conceptual statements are not usually as clear and simple as basic arithmetical statements; they generally do not allow for such dichotomous thinking regarding their "truth-value." What is meant be a word or by a statement containing it is not straightforwardly true or false. On this note, Wilson writes,

> ... in questions of concept we are not concerned with *the* meaning of a word. Words do not have only one meaning: indeed, in a sense they do not have meaning in their own right at all, but only in so far as people use them in different ways. It is better to say that we are concerned with *actual and possible uses* of words....words like 'democracy' and 'science'—and even words like 'boat'—do not have 'real meanings'. They just have different uses and different applications, and our job is to analyze the concepts and map out these uses and applications.[2]

Later, Wilson goes on to write,

Questions of concept, then, are not questions of fact; nor are they questions of value; nor are they questions concerned with *the* meanings of words, or *the* definitions of words. What are they? All we have said so far is that they are concerned with the uses of words, and with the criteria or principles by which those uses are determined.[3]

To help us understand the distinctions among factual, normative and conceptual questions, Wilson uses the concept of 'freedom' in three different ways in the following questions:

- Are you free to vote as you wish in Russia? (Factual question)

- Is freedom to vote as one wishes a good thing? (Normative/Value-related question)

- Are any of our actions really free? (Conceptual question)

Using the concept of 'right,' Wilson proceeds to make the same distinctions as above:

- Did the Greeks think it right to keep women in an inferior position to men? (Factual)

- Do you think it is right to keep women in an inferior position to men? (Normative)

- Can one ever be certain about what is right? (Conceptual)

Wilson points out that in questions 1 and 2 from both groups, it is assumed that we all know what is meant by 'free,' 'freedom,' and 'right.' There are no logical problems or problems of meaning or use. However, this is not the case with question three in each group. Wilson describes them as "logically mysterious." A conceptual question is not the sort of question we generally ask in everyday life. Wilson writes,

> Faced with these [conceptual] questions, we are asked to take seriously concepts which hitherto we had taken for granted. We are asked, as it were, to become *self-conscious* about words which hitherto we had used without thinking—not necessarily used wrongly, but used unselfconsciously. This is rather like the process of psychoanalysis, or the self-examinations and confessions practised in religion. In these we are asked to become more conscious of our actions, to look at them objectively and think about them; hitherto we had been content to act, but now we have to become aware of the significance of our actions. In the same way, when we deal with questions of concept, we are asked to become aware of the significance of our words.[4]
>
> Once we start this process, we very soon begin to feel baffled. Someone might ask us, perhaps, "What is time?": and since 'time' is a word we use every day, we might start off gaily by saying "Time? Well, time is what goes on when one thing happens after another, we use clocks or the sun to tell the time, we talk of the passage of time, it's like a river..."; but it soon becomes clear to us that we are unable to give a clear account of the concept.[5]

As we see, conceptual questions are mysterious because it is not certain how one should approach them. In regard to the question "Are all men equal?" Wilson asks: how *could* one answer this? How does one begin? What should count as a proper answer to the question? When someone says 'equal,' what do they mean? Equal to what? Equal in what respects? Does equal mean identical? And so forth. In just a moment, we'll discuss in more detail the methods of conceptual analysis, but for now, let's first make sure that we can distinguish conceptual questions and claims from their factual and normative counterparts.

PHILOSOPHERS AT WORK

The ability to distinguish among factual, normative and conceptual claims—as well as among their corresponding questions—is important to productive moral debate. As you have learned, factual statements are those that can in principle be proven to be true or false by observation and experience or by using empirical means. Normative claims are ones that are not proven true or false, but justified by reference to particular values, ideals, principles or standards of evaluation. Normative claims are expressed as prescriptions, prohibitions and value judgments. Conceptual claims, by contrast to the first two, primarily involve matters of definition, meaning and linguistic usage. They become subjects of rational analysis, not empirical verification or ethical justification. See whether you understand the differences among these claims by identifying each type in the list below.

F = Factual Claim/Question N=Normative Claim/Question C=Conceptual Claim/Question

_____　　1. Applied ethics is a good course.

_____　　2. Many people cheat on their income-tax returns.

_____　　3. Is spanking your child a form of child abuse?

_____　　4. Morality must be based on religion.

_____　　5. Animals can be responsible for their actions.

_____　　6. The Pope says premarital sex is wrong.

_____　　7. We should lower immigration quotas.

_____　　8. Abortions are on the increase.

_____　　9. Is withholding the truth the same as lying?

_____　　10. Stalin committed an immoral act when he systematically starved an estimated seven to twelve million Ukrainians to death.

_____　　11. Genocide is not really murder.

_____　　12. Drinking and driving is against the law.

_____　　13. Should people who test HIV positive be isolated on island colonies?

_____　　14. Responsibility presupposes free will.

_____　　15. Is a whale a fish?

Try now to produce your own examples of factual, normative and conceptual claims.

Factual claims:

1. _____
2. _____
3. _____

Normative claims:

1. _____
2. _____
3. _____

Conceptual claims:

1. _____
2. _____
3. _____

Techniques of Conceptual Analysis

The word 'analysis' is derived from the Greek word meaning to 'break up.'[6] Regardless of the discipline in which it's used, analysis generally aims to reveal the nature of something by breaking it up into its component parts. As one writer puts it,

> ... when a chemist is confronted with an unknown substance, the first thing she does is to analyze it; that is, she uses different chemicals to break the material down into its basic elements. The first stage of philosophical thinking is also analytical. A philosopher tries to clarify an issue by using certain mental tools to break up the concepts under inquiry into smaller ideas which are easier to work with. In practice, this amounts to searching for specific definitions of the ideas or concepts involved in the philosophical issue under investigation.[7]

Once concepts are broken down and separated into their constituent parts, it becomes easier to study each part separately, to study their relationships, or to study how they relate to the whole. As a way of understanding a particular concept, one could also compare it with others. For instance, you could analyze the concept of morality by inquiring into its relationships with 'law' and 'religion.' Is the concept of morality separate from, or entirely based on, 'religion' and identical with it? Or, one could ask whether 'morality' is equivalent to 'law.' Is what's 'legal' necessarily 'moral'? Is what's 'moral' always 'legal'? Are there any ways in which 'morality,' 'law,' and 'religion' all overlap? Are there ways in which they are completely separate and distinct from each other? How so? This line of questioning is characteristically analytical.

Necessary and Sufficient Conditions: Ideally, when one analyzes concepts, one tries to arrive at **necessary** and **sufficient conditions** of their use. Doing this is easier in some instances than in others. Let's start off with something familiar and uncomplicated: the concept of 'square.' We start by asking what the criteria are that must be met in order for something to qualify as a 'square.'[8] Are there any conditions which must absolutely and necessarily obtain for something to be a 'square'? We might be inclined to say that 'having four sides' is a good candidate for being considered a necessary condition—but is this condition enough? Is it possible that there are four-sided figures that are not squares? While it would appear that a model case of a square certainly does have four sides, we must ask whether there are other counter-examples of four-sided figures that are not squares. Indeed there are. While having four sides is a "necessary condition" for 'squareness,' as it were, that condition alone is not sufficient to make a shape a square. A 'rectangle' is one counter-example of a four-sided figure that is not a square; an irregularly shaped quadrilateral is yet another counter-example of a four-sided non-square. Thus, a recognition of these two counter-examples requires us to state another necessary condition of squareness, specifically, that all sides must be equal in length. The question now becomes whether these two necessary conditions constitute the necessary and *sufficient* conditions for which we're looking? The answer is still no, however. A parallelogram would be a four-sided figure whose sides could be equal in length but still not be a square. Visualize how the parallelogram leans or is slanted to one side or the other. Thus, for a figure to fall under the concept of square, the following conditions are both necessary and, only when taken together, sufficient: a 'square' is an enclosed figure having four sides; each side must be equal to all the others in length and parallel; each of the internal angles must be 90 degrees. If something matches these necessary and sufficient conditions, then we can call it a 'square.'

It's not always necessary to satisfy so many conditions for one thing or concept to fall under another, broader concept. For instance, being a 'dog' is a single sufficient condition for being an 'animal.' There's no need to discuss breed, colour or relation to other species—simply being a dog is enough to be put in this class. In the context of conceptual analysis, to say that one condition is sufficient for another is simply to suggest that establishing the first (e.g., 'this is a dog') is enough to establish that the second holds (e.g., 'this is an animal').

Geometric concepts like 'square' and other narrowly defined concepts like 'bachelor' present us with relatively uncomplicated necessary and sufficient conditions for understanding their proper use and application. Indeed, even before beginning our analysis of 'square,' we already knew what to look for, given our experience and education. We were not creating new concepts or exploring the boundaries of vague, disputed or evolving ones. It would be wonderful if definitional criteria could so easily be established in the realm of moral discourse, but unfortunately, in this area of human experience, there is much more room for interpretation and disagreement. Logically circumscribed concepts like 'square' and 'bachelor' lend themselves to fairly accurate and unambiguous definitions, but open-ended moral concepts like 'obscene,' 'unjust' and 'inhumane' do not. Their broad, vague, ambiguous, disputed and sometime inconsistent usages are what make them logically mysterious. Fortunately, techniques of conceptual analysis have been developed to help us out. We can use them to further our own philosophical understanding of morality.

John Wilson, for example, has laid out techniques of conceptual analysis which he explains in his book *Thinking With Concepts*.[9] To use Wilson's example, let's suppose we are interested in studying 'fish.' We could ask the question, "Does a whale come under the concept of fish, as we normally use that concept?"[10] As Wilson points out, whether or not we label a whale a fish depends on the "angle" from which we view the question. The marine biologist might answer no, whereas the minister or governmental secretary responsible for the country's fisheries might answer yes. No one answer is absolutely true or correct. For practical ministry or state functions, the whale is a fish; in terms of scientific study, it is not.

Wilson frequently takes single concepts in isolation to determine their meaning and the boundaries of linguistic usage. If he were interested in the concept of pornography, for instance, he would try first to imagine a **model case** of it. The task would be to find a paradigm example about which we could say, "Well, if *that* isn't an example of pornography, then nothing is."[11] Once identified, we would then try to list the distinguishing features or characteristics of this example, making it a paradigm case of pornography. The model case allows us to examine the concept from one particular perspective.

After listing the key features of pornography revealed by the model case, Wilson suggests we then proceed to view the concept from a different angle, using a **contrary case** of pornography. Here, we want an example to which we would respond, "Well, whatever pornography is, *that* certainly isn't an instance of it." With the contrary case, something is clearly missing. Pornography must contain what this example does not. Identifying what is lacking also helps to define our targeted concept. By identifying what's lacking, we can list features without which something is disqualified from being considered pornography.

The next step in Wilson's method is to view concepts from the angle of **borderline cases**. Such cases fall somewhere between model cases and contrary cases. In the instance of pornography, 'erotica' could be a borderline case. Like pornography, it often contains nudity and sex, but it may present such things in an artistic, less vulgar and more socially acceptable fashion. Whether or not 'erotica' falls under 'pornography' is not absolutely clear. By trying to define the boundaries between the two concepts, we become clearer about each. As Wilson says, by examining borderline cases to see "what makes them odd or queer, we come to see why the true cases are not odd or queer, and hence what makes them true cases—what the central criteria of the concept really are."[12] As with model and contrary cases, we seek to identify out of our analysis some distinguishing features of the concept under study—in this case, pornography.

As part of his detailed methodology, Wilson proceeds to use a number of other techniques to expose even more angles from which any concept or conceptual question can be viewed. Each of these techniques again serves to clarify and define the concepts under investigation. One can look to **social context**, for instance, and at the **practical results** of understanding a particular concept in a specified way.

After completing the steps involved in Wilson's conceptual analysis, it is time to construct a summarizing definition of two or three sentences for the concept or concepts under investigation. Review the lists of characteristics already done in the preceding steps and select the most important or essential features. Base your definitions on them. How would your definitions help everyone to think and communicate better with the concept or concepts you are studying? What disadvantages could result? Try to rewrite your summary definitions to correct these disadvantages. Once this is finished, or even as part of this summative, evaluative exercise, engage in what Wilson calls an **Interior Dialogue**. As he puts it:

> ... conduct a kind of dialogue with yourself about the concept[s], in your head. Ask yourself questions and answer them; invent new cases when you feel like it; go back to the application of the

techniques in the last step of the procedure if you wish. This sort of informal talk with your-self is one of the most important elements in the procedure. In the course of it you should ob-serve what are blind alleys, and what points seem to lead somewhere; certainly you should have the basic outline of the concept properly clarified in your own mind by the end.[13]

For a complete and comprehensive treatment of Wilson's conceptual analysis techniques, refer to his classic work *Thinking with Concepts*, especially Chapter One, "The Business of Analysis."

Purposes of Conceptual Analysis: Conceptual analyses may be performed for various purposes. Maybe you have been assigned a philosophy paper asking you to explain the nature of 'injustice' or 'egoism.' Perhaps you have been asked to read articles on such subjects in order to critically evaluate them. In the first case, conceptual analysis provides you with a means for generating and clarifying your own ideas. In the second case, you can begin to compare your analysis of the con-cept or concepts in question with the one(s) you just read. Does the author of the assigned article leave out anything important? Is the author's definition too vague and broad, or too narrow and limiting? Doing a conceptual analysis will allow you to evaluate someone else's conceptual analysis in view of your own. Such work will be original to you, not simply a re-gurgitation of someone else's ideas.

ARGUMENTS, OPINIONS AND EXPLANATIONS

In the preceding section, we learned that there are different kinds of claims that can be made about morality: factual, nor-mative and conceptual. We also learned how to address con-ceptual questions and claims for purposes of definitional

> *... isn't anyone with a true but unthinking opinion like a blind man on the right road?*
> PLATO

PHILOSOPHERS AT WORK

Though we have not paid the techniques of conceptual analysis all of the time and attention they truly deserve, you should have at least a basic appreciation now for the careful and detailed thought processes that philosophical thinking requires. Since philosophical thinking can only be mastered by doing, let's practise doing a conceptual analysis now by consider-ing the question: *Is homosexuality a form of psychological dysfunction?* Come up with a model case which answers "Yes" to the question, then a contrary case which clearly answers "No" and finally try to find a borderline case about which you are not too sure. As you do so, list distinguishing features of each concept in separate lists headed by each. After doing an interior dialogue, that is, after briefly reflecting on your findings, try to define the terms yourself and make attempts to answer the question. This exercise can be done individually or in groups.

clarity and understanding. In this section, we learn about the structure of **arguments**, as well as how to identify and distinguish them from **non-arguments**, coming in the form of opinions and explanations.

Arguments versus Opinions: To appreciate the nature of argument, let us first distinguish arguments from **opinions** by revisiting a distinction made earlier, namely the one between moral and nonmoral values. Recall that nonmoral value judgments pertaining to personal preferences and tastes do not allow for objective evaluation or universal prescriptive application. When someone makes a value judgement like "Basketball is a better sport than hockey," it is often met with the reply, "Well, that's just your opinion." Claiming that shrimps are more delicious than smelts is also likely to be considered a matter of opinion. As the saying goes, there is simply no accounting for taste. In fact, it would seem rather silly to try to "justify" our tastes and preferences, for such things are generally recognized as personal and subjective. We often prefer what we prefer or like what we like for no reason in particular. Groundless judgments stemming from personal (nonmoral) values of taste or preference are therefore not binding on others. They are merely opinions.

From our discussion of nonmoral value judgments, we can better appreciate how opinions are not accompanied by reasons. A person could say, for example, "I believe that so and so is the case" or "In my opinion, this is good or bad," but offer no grounds for adopting such viewpoints. Individuals may just have an "intuitive feel" or "gut-level reaction" for something and be unable to articulate any sort of justification for their opinion or belief. With opinions, no rational process of thought is involved.

Another feature of personal opinions is that they are often blurted out in a spontaneous knee-jerk fashion. They may be intended, either consciously or unconsciously, to fill space in idle conversation, express emotions or elicit reactions from others. (Do you ever feel uncomfortable during silent moments in a conversation, so much so that you'll say anything—maybe something controversial—just to bug someone?) Getting under people's skin or disturbing them is something newspaper editorialists, as well as radio and TV talk show hosts, do all the time. Making an outrageous statement can often capture an audience's attention, but may not further much insight or understanding.

To the extent that personally stated opinions initiate discussion and cause us to stop and think, they are worthwhile. In many cases, they serve as the first step to genuine philosophical argument and debate. They can act as a springboard for further ethical analysis and deliberation. The problem, however, is that all too often discussions begin and end with statements of unreasoned opinion. Emotions are vented and viewpoints are stridently expressed, but little progress is made into further insight, understanding or clarification of the issues involved. Unfortunately, many people take great pleasure in forcing their opinions upon others, winning shouting matches, name-calling and making others look foolish or stupid (witness the *Jerry Springer* and *Montel Williams* shows). The truth is that screaming and one-upmanship do not take us very far down the road of sober thought and rational moral understanding.

The distinction between opinions and arguments becomes somewhat blurred when we examine a borderline case. Take "professional opinions," for example. In some circumstances, it may be advisable to accept the opinions of others as advice on what you should or should not do. There may be moral obligations involved or other prudential considerations. Judges and lawyers, for instance, may issue opinions on the ethics or legality of a particular proposed course of action—for example, whether a stockbroker ought to counsel clients to invest in a company owned by a relative. Medical doctors may offer their considered opinions on the advisability of surgery or on the best therapeutic procedures for a patient. In such cases of professional opinion, perhaps the term 'opinion' is misused. After all, experience and careful research may have provided the rationale behind the advice. In other words, the professional opinion may be based on a process of reasoning which provides support for it.

Before examining the structure and function of arguments more closely, perhaps we should make one other distinction, this time between an argument and a fight. In situations where people are angry and are yelling their opinions at one another, what we have is a **fight**, not a philosophical argument. If, in the midst of a heated discussion, you feel like throwing a punch, you're probably in some sort of violent confrontation, not engaged in a philosophical dialogue. In fact, from a purely philosophical perspective, an argument is not an interpersonal event, a fight, a contentious dispute or a confrontation of egos at all. The question begs to be asked, then: What is it?

An argument can be defined as a written or spoken form of discourse possessing a particular structure and function. With respect to structure, arguments are comprised of three elements: **premises**, **conclusions** and **inferences**. Think of premises as statements or claims. They can be factual, normative or conceptual. Functionally speaking, premises are used to support conclusions. In a *bona fide* argument, one or more claims (serving as premises) are used to support another claim (called the conclusion). The intention in an argument is to rationally persuade us of the truth or justifiability of the conclusion. Making a leap from what the premises state to a conclusion is what's called *drawing an inference*. Premises thus provide us with the grounds or reasons to accept conclusions, whatever they may be. Notice that there is a process of thought involved here. When one presents an argument, one is not just mindlessly opinionating. If, for example, I argue that "The poor economy will improve because it moves in cycles," my conclusion is that the poor economy will improve. The supporting premise serving as my reason or justification is that "it moves in cycles." Presumably, good economic periods are followed by poor ones and vice versa. Insofar as this is true, there may be good reason for accepting the conclusion.

Certainly, not all arguments are good ones; they can turn out to be faulty for a variety of reasons. Later, we'll examine in more detail the numerous ways arguments can be flawed. At this juncture, let it be noted that we can evaluate the premises of arguments using three general criteria: **relevance**, **acceptability** and **sufficiency**.[14] If a premise used to support an argument's conclusion is totally irrelevant to it, then the premise can be dubbed an **irrelevant premise**. In this instance, when a conclusion does not follow from its premises, we call this form of fallacious reasoning a *non sequitur*. Further, if the premise is based on false information, faulty statistics or questionable values, then the supporting premise is unacceptable again. If the premise is a factual claim, it could be false or highly unlikely. If it's a value judgment, the value premise itself may be unjustifiable. If the conclusion "Jamal should be tortured" is based on the supporting value premise that "Immigrants should be tortured," then we have a case where the premise is relevant to the conclusion, but not acceptable—that is, if we accept humane standards for the treatment of people. The supporting reason justifying Jamal's torture thus becomes a questionable or **problematic premise**. Obviously, premises should not be more questionable than the conclusions they're designed to support. Finally, a supporting premise may be relevant and acceptable, but simply not enough in itself to be sufficient. A single premise, or even several premises which go together to support a single conclusion, might not present us with a strong enough argument, since it lacks the force to persuade us. The argument that "We shouldn't go to war because it's wrong to hurt people" makes sense and offers a justification; however, one might be inclined to say that while hurting people is generally wrong, doing so in self-defence or in defence of one's country is not necessarily wrong. For the argument to stand up to criticism, more support must be given. Stated as it is, the argument is weak and not very persuasive.

Arguments versus Explanations: Arguments differ not only from opinions, but also from explanations. Explaining *why* someone took her own life is certainly different from arguing *that* she took her own life. Arguing that she committed suicide involves other claims that give reasons for accepting the conclusion about what she did. On the other hand, if we try to explain why someone took her life, at least this much is not disputed: that she did, in fact, take her own life. The "why" here provides an explanatory account—perhaps a psychodynamic explanation of her emotional state just preceding the self-destructive act. In short, when the purpose of any passage is to explain *why* or *how* something happens, not *that* something is the case, we have an explanation, not an argument.

Indicator Words for Premises and Conclusions

It is not always easy to distinguish between arguments and non-arguments. What you read or hear may be little more than a personal opinion, or perhaps an explanation. Certainly, when you hear *questions*, *commands* and *exhortations*, you are not listening to an argument, since such things make no claims, either as supporting premises or conclusions. Commanding someone to do something is not a proposition to be proven true or false. Exhortations, again, do not make claims but rather encourage, and so, like commands, are not parts of arguments. Generally speaking, questions do not belong to arguments either, unless they are used rhetorically to make a statement. People can make claims in the form of a question for dramatic effect, as when a critic says, for example, "So, you think capital punishment is humane, do you?" What's implied by the question here is something like, "Capital punishment is not humane" or "Capital punishment is barbarous." When analyzing arguments, look out for claims disguised as rhetorical questions.

> The way to undo an insane conclusion is to consider the sanity of the premises on which it rests.
>
> *A COURSE IN MIRACLES*

Premises and conclusions can often be identified in arguments by looking for **premise indicators** and **conclusion indicators**. For instance, the word 'because' serves as a premise indicator. If I argue that "Trespassing is wrong *because* it constitutes a violation of property rights," my conclusion "Trespassing is wrong" is supported or justified by the reason, "It constitutes a violation of property rights." 'Because' is the premise indicator and what follows it supports the stated conclusion. One could just as easily argue that "Stem-cell research is unacceptable given that it violates God's natural law." In this instance, 'given that,' like 'because,' operates as a premise indicator. What follows 'given that' provides the supporting premise for the conclusion that "Stem-cell research in unacceptable."

When looking for arguments within reading passages or when listening to them, we can spot conclusions by people's use of conclusion indicators like 'so,' 'therefore' and 'consequently.' What follows these words, and others like them, is the point or conclusion of the argument. Let's say someone argues, "Because killing is evil and war involves killing, therefore, war is evil." The 'therefore' tips us off on the conclusion, namely, that war is evil. The 'because' also indicates something in support of the conclusion. Interestingly, in this case, the two claims preceding the conclusion are actually related or **conjoint premises**. They "go together" in supporting the conclusion. Either one in itself would not be sufficient to support the claim that "War is evil." It may be that killing is evil, but that, in itself, doesn't lend much support to the conclusion. We need to add that war involves killing. Similarly, if we just took the second premise, "War involves killing," this too, in itself, would not justify the conclusion. War involves killing—so what? But the argument is that *because* killing is evil *and since* war involves killing, *therefore* war is evil.

To help you identify premises and conclusions for future argument analysis and evaluation, lists of some frequently found indicator words are included below.[15]

PREMISE INDICATORS

as indicated by	due to	in view of the fact that
as shown by	for	insofar as
assuming that	for the reason that	may be deduced from
because	given that	on the assumption that
since	inasmuch as	
can be inferred from	in view of	

CONCLUSION INDICATORS

so	entails that	we may conclude
therefore	it follows that	suggests strongly that
consequently	hence	allows us to infer that
thus	indicates that	I conclude that
now we can see that	proves that	implies that
as a result	shows that	we may deduce that
accordingly	then	

Unstated Premises and Conclusions

Analysis of arguments can be complicated by the fact that premises and conclusions, though understood, are not always explicitly stated. Take the following example:

Heather should not be allowed to go to the movies because she was a bad girl.

In this case, the 'because' tips us off about the reason why Heather shouldn't be allowed to go to the movies and since 'because' serves as a premise indicator, the other part of the sentence ("Heather should not be allowed to go to the movies") becomes a good candidate for becoming the conclusion of the argument, which it is. A key premise in this argument, though it is never stated, is the claim that "Bad girls shouldn't be allowed to go to the movies." You can call this claim an **unstated** or **hidden premise**. It is important to uncover such unstated, hidden premises, not only for understanding, but also for purposes of evaluation. Maybe there is no dispute that Heather misbehaved and qualified to be labelled a 'bad girl.' The question is whether the unstated supporting premise is acceptable. It is not intuitively clear why 'bad girls' should not be allowed to go to the movies. Without other claims or premises to support this one, it may prove unacceptable, though still relevant to the conclusion. If the underlying assumption for any argument is unacceptable, then the conclusion following from it need not necessarily be accepted.

As with premises, conclusions can sometimes be left unstated, but understood. To modify the present example:

Bad girls cannot go to the movies, and we know Heather's been a bad girl.

What is not stated above is the conclusion that "Heather can't go to the movies." Sometimes, conclusions may be left unstated due to unintended omission or sloppiness in reasoning. At other times, conclusions may be left unstated for persuasive rhetorical effect, one which allows listeners or readers of the argument in question to draw their own conclusions.

Simple and Complex Arguments

Premises and conclusions left unstated make argument analysis a little more difficult than it might otherwise be. Another variable making argument analysis more difficult is the fact that some arguments are lengthy, containing more than one inference. The main conclusion of an argument may be supported by one or more **intermediate** or **subordinate conclusions**, each having its own supporting premises. In other words, the conclusion of a subordinate argument (which serves as a supporting premise for the main conclusion) has its own supporting premises which, in the end, lend weight to the final conclusion via the intermediate conclusion. When an argument contains one inference and hence, only one conclusion, the argument is simple; when it contains two or more inferences (subordinate conclusion and main conclusion), it is complex. In a thesis defence or in a book-long argument supporting any proposition (e.g., "Aliens have visited earth"), many subordinate conclusions may be found and used to justify the claim that is being defended.

> *Simplicity is very difficult for twisted minds.*
>
> A COURSE IN MIRACLES

Diagramming and Standard Form in Argument Analysis

It is sometimes helpful, especially when analyzing and evaluating complex arguments, to express them in **standard form** and/or to **diagram** them. To begin, let us say that we are dealing with a simple argument containing only one inference. To put such an argument in standard form, what is necessary is simply to state the premise, draw a line, and then state the conclusion.

Argument: *Stalin was an evil man because he killed millions of people.*

Expressed in standard form:

P = Premise

C = Conclusion

P He [Stalin] killed millions of people.

C Stalin was an evil man

One could diagram this very easily. The arrow indicates that an inference is drawn.

P

↓

C

Here is another simple argument (containing only one inference/conclusion), but this time with more than one premise;

Fred is destitute and completely without hope and so he will end up on the streets.

Expressed in standard form:

P (1) Fred is destitute.

P (2) [Fred] is completely without hope.

C He will end up on the streets (P1, P2)

Diagrammed, the argument above can be expressed in the following fashion:

P (1)   P (2)

↓

C

The following argument also has two supporting premises, but in this case they are *conjoint*. The two premises "need each other," as it were, for the argument to make sense.

Argument: *Nurses are public employees working in essential services. Strikes by public employees working in essential services are illegal. Thus, the recent strike by nurses in the SARS unit of the hospital was illegal.*

The fact that nurses are public employees working in essential services, in itself, does not support the conclusion that the nurse's strike in the SARS unit of the hospital was illegal. That premise becomes relevant by virtue of the second premise: "Strikes by public employees working in essential services are illegal."

Expressed in standard form:

P (1) Nurses are public employees working in essential services.

P (2) Strikes by public employees working in essential services are illegal.

C The recent strike by nurses in the SARS unit was illegal. (P1, P2)

Diagrammed, the argument can be represented as follows.

$$P (1) + P (2)$$
$$\downarrow$$
$$C$$

David Conway and Ronald Munson provide the following example of a complex argument, first in regular language, then in standard form:[16]

> Congress refuses to raise taxes, and so the deficit will continue to increase. Furthermore, consumer interest rates will be high for the indefinite future because the Federal Reserve Board is maintaining tight money policies. Things do not look bright for future generations of Americans.

Standard Form

(P1) Congress refuses to raise taxes.

(P2) The deficit will continue to increase. (P1)

(P3) The Federal Reserve Board is maintaining tight-money policies.

(P4) Consumer interest rates will be high for the indefinite future. (P3)

(P5) Things do not look bright for future generations of Americans (P2) + (P4)

In this complex argument, a premise line without a number on its right is a supporting premise; a premise with a number on its right is a conclusion. The number to the right indicates the premise(s) supporting the conclusion. A closer examination of the argument above reveals that (P2) is an intermediate/subordinate conclusion supported by (P1). (P4) is an intermediate conclusion supported by (P3). The final or main conclusion is stated in (P5) and is supported by intermediate conclusions (P2) and (P4). Diagrammed, the complex argument above looks like so,

$$
\begin{array}{cc}
P1 & P3 \\
\downarrow & \downarrow \\
P2 & P4 \\
\end{array}
$$
$$\downarrow$$
$$P5$$

When stating arguments in standard form, remember to arrange the claims so the premises come before the conclusions they support. This should be done for both intermediate and final conclusions.

Helpful Hints for Argument Analysis

Argument analysis is not an exact science. There is no one set of rules that can guarantee that our analysis will always be correct. Nevertheless, the following helpful hints can help you decide what to do.[17]

Identify Indicator Words: A good place to start is with indicator words. They provide us with clues for understanding the argument contained within any passage we are analyzing. Remember that words like 'because' and 'insofar as' are followed by claims serving as premise indicators, whereas other words and expressions like 'therefore' and 'it follows that' serve as conclusion indicators. Watch out for exceptions. In the following, 'since' is not used as a premise indicator supporting a conclusion in an argument, but rather as an aid to explanation: "I'm not going to the rave this weekend since I'm too tired." The intention here is to explain someone's actions, not justify them with an argument.

> *A great many people think they are thinking when they are merely rearranging their prejudices.*
>
> WILLIAM JAMES

Uncover Unstated or Implicit Premises and Conclusions: No doubt you will come across arguments in the future that contain underlying premises and conclusions which have been left unstated and simply assumed. Arguments having implicit premises or conclusions are called **enthymemes**. If we wish to test supporting premises for qualities such as relevance, acceptability, and sufficiency, it is important to make clear and explicit what may be only assumed and implied.

Consider the Larger Context: Sometimes it may not be clear whether one premise simply follows another, or whether the first is intended to support the second or vice-versa. An examination of **context** can help here. Suppose someone said, "All people are corrupt by nature. Everyone around me is courrupt." In this case, is the person concluding that "all people are corrupt by nature" *because* "everyone around me is corrupt"? Is the conclusion based on some sort of inductive inference coming from personal observation or experience? Or, is the person concluding in a deductive fashion that "everyone around me is corrupt" *because* "all people are corrupt by nature"? The uncertainty here revolves around the question of whether the argument is a product of inductive or deductive inference (see Chapter Eleven). Is the claim "All people are corrupt by nature" a supporting premise or a conclusion?

If it were the case that the person arguing the point were a casual observer of human nature, say, or an empirical researcher doing social-psychological research, the context within which the claim was made might lead us reasonably to suspect that the inference is probably inductive. "All people are corrupt by nature" (conclusion) because "everyone around me [whom I have observed] is corrupt" (premise). On the other hand, if a philosopher were studying the idea of corruption within the broader context of human nature, then the argument might very well be intended deductively, since philosophers usually resort to reason in their inquiries, not to experiment or observational survey. In this case, the conclusion that "everyone around me is corrupt" would *likely follow logically* from the general premise that "all people are corrupt by nature." When in doubt, then, look to context for clues about which premise supports which conclusion.

Identify each claim in the passage: When reading a paragraph or larger passage selection from an article or book, you may wish to bracket and number each claim, circling premise and conclusion indicators whenever possible. Make sure to arrange the claims so the premises precede the conclusions. This applies both to intermediate and final conclusions. Let's go back now to a passage we've already considered to illustrate an example of argument analysis using the kind of passage notation we are discussing. (Notice in the analysis that follows, P(4) actually precedes P(3). That is because P(3) is a premise which supports P(4).)

$$P_1 \qquad\qquad\qquad\qquad P_2$$

[Congress refuses to raise taxes] and so [the deficit will continue to increase.] Furthermore,

$$P_4 \qquad\qquad\qquad\qquad\qquad P_3$$

[consumer interest rates will be high for the indefinite future] because the [Federal Reserve

$$P_5$$

Board is maintaining tight money policies.] [Things do not look bright for future generations of Americans.]

If all the bracketing, numbering and circling becomes sloppy and confusing, you could also rewrite and list each claim as we did in our discussion of standard form as it applies to complex arguments. By looking at each claim in relation to all the others, we can determine which claim is the supporting premise for which conclusion. This is particularly useful with long and complex arguments involving more than two inferences.

Reformulate Claims as Required: Sometimes the claims embedded within arguments are not clearly expressed. For example, depending on the tone of voice and context in which it is raised, the question "Don't you think you should apologize?" could very well be a rhetorical directive. It might be rephrased as: "You should apologize." This reformulation might more accurately reflect the intention of the speaker (or writer) expressing it. If the question was really meant as a conclusion, then we could look for the stated or unstated premises supporting it.

Discard Superfluous Elements of Arguments: "Filler and fluff" are sometimes uncovered when analyzing arguments. It is best to discard them for clarity and simplicity's sake. Whatever is not a premise or a conclusion is not relevant and should be tossed aside. Here is an example from Conway and Munson:

> *Come on now. Pay attention. Marriage is an institution that should be discarded. I was married for six months myself, you know. You shouldn't listen to "Dear Abby" and those other moralists. All marriage does is make it too hard to get out of a bad relationship.*[18]

If we take the trouble to strip away the excess verbiage, six sentences are reduced to two. The argument can be restated more simply in standard form:

All marriage does is make it too hard to get out of a bad relationship.
_____
Marriage is an institution that should be discarded.

Identify Main and Intermediate Arguments: Of course it's important when analyzing any passage that one identify its **main argument** and **final** or **main conclusion**. It is also essential to locate the **intermediate conclusions** and **subordinate arguments** which support the main one. If we get caught up debating a minor premise of a subordinate argument, and fail to recognize the main conclusion and appreciate the fact that it may still stand up even if our minor premise falls down as unacceptable, we may become hopelessly sidetracked. To help us establish what the main argument is, considering context can yet again be helpful.

Identify Replies to Objections: Newcomers to philosophy sometimes become confused when critically evaluating articles, alleging that their authors contradict themselves: "They seem to defend a particular thesis, but then go on to present arguments on the other side of the issue which serve only to refute their own position." More often than not, these authors are not contradicting themselves; what they are doing is taking into account objections to their own theses. For instance, while arguing that addictive drugs should be legalized, an author might try to reply to the obvious objection that legalization will increase the number of addicts on the streets. Such a reply indirectly supports the author's main conclusion by taking away an objection that stands in the way of accepting either the main conclusion or an intermediate one.[19] When writing your own defence of a position, take note that you should also consider opposing views and respond to them in a rational fashion. This strategy displays balance and objectivity, desirable traits in the moral philosopher.

Identify any conceptual questions or claims around which a passage revolves: Sometimes arguments present us with a mixed bag of claims. For instance, someone could conclude that euthanasia is morally wrong because it constitutes murder and is against the law anyway. In this case, the conclusion, "Euthanasia is morally wrong" is a value judgment. One supporting premise claims that it is murder, while the second supporting premise claims that it is against the law. This second premise is either true or false. There may or may not be laws prohibiting euthanasia in one's legal jurisdiction. The first premise, by contrast, raises a conceptual problem. It could be addressed as a question: *Is euthanasia murder?* This is one of Wilson's logically mysterious questions which is neither factual nor normative, but conceptual. Past writers have tried to distinguish between active and passive euthanasia, arguing that only the former is murder, while the latter is morally acceptable. At this point, we don't wish to become embroiled in the debate, but certainly we need to get clearer on the concepts of 'murder' and 'euthanasia.' What is an act of murder? What is an act of euthanasia? Are the two concepts identical, related or completely separate and distinct? A rational answer to this question begs for a conceptual analysis. An evaluation of the conclusion that euthanasia is morally wrong hinges on it. As with so many moral arguments, conceptual matters are central and so should be handled properly in ways that have already been discussed.

NECESSARY ATTITUDE ADJUSTMENTS FOR PROPER MORAL ARGUMENTATION

Someone once said that there are two unavoidable things in life: death and taxes. I would like to add a third item: disagreement. If you think about it, it is virtually impossible to avoid disagreements. When friends are discussing sports, entertainment, culture, religion, politics, art, education, business or—as we

> *We find comfort among those who agree with us, growth among those who don't.*
>
> FRANK CLARKE

Someone once said that there are two unavoidable things in life: death and taxes. I would like to add a third item: disagreement. If you think about it, it is virtually impossible to avoid disagreements. When friends are discussing sports, entertainment, culture, religion, politics, art, education, business or—as we are here—morality, you almost always find differences and conflicting viewpoints. Now that we have covered the differences between *bona fide* philosophical arguments and opinions, we no longer have to engage in mindless exchanges. Also, now that we can appreciate how philosophical debate differs from fighting, we no longer need to get all hot and bothered about the viewpoints we espouse.

If people are going to argue in personally and socially constructive ways, certain attitude adjustments will be required. For example, we should welcome properly conducted arguments, not avoid them. This does not mean that we should get into serious arguments

PHILOSOPHERS AT WORK

To do moral philosophy properly, you need to learn to recognize arguments and distinguish them from explanations, opinions and other forms of non-argument. Now that you understand how arguments are comprised of premises, conclusions and inferences, you can practise your ability to distinguish arguments from non-arguments by doing the following exercise. Below are several short passages which either do or do not express arguments. First, determine whether or not the passage contains an argument. Second, if there is an argument, state the main conclusion and provide the supporting premise (s). Don't forget, a complex argument contains two or more conclusions (inferences). There is only one main conclusion. You might find it helpful in your analysis to express the passages in standard form and/or to diagram them. Uncover any unstated premises and conclusions if they are implied or assumed. Finally, evaluate the premises supporting the conclusion.

Short Passages
1. Anybody who smokes marijuana is stupid even if it's now legal in Canada to possess it. Smoking it probably causes lung cancer and besides, marijuana smokers are just following the crowd like sheep.

Is there an argument? Yes _____ or No_____

What is the main conclusion? _____

Supporting premise(s) _____

Unstated Premise(s) or Conclusion(s): _____

_____

Evaluation of Supporting Premise(s): Explain why any supporting premise is or is not

a. Relevant: _____

b. Acceptable: _____

c. Sufficient: _____

2. The US Government described the events of 9/11 in New York City as a terrorist attack. George W. Bush retaliated at first by attacking Afghanistan and then Iraq, in part on the grounds that anyone who aids and abets a terrorist is a terrorist himself. Presumably, Saddam Hussein was aiding Al-Qaeda, as was the Taliban in Afghanistan. If we accept Bush's logic, the attacks against Americans by Palestinians are justified. As an occupying force, the Israeli government continues to terrorize the Palestinians in the occupied territories with state-sponsored assassinations. The US supports Israel with money and arms. The US is therefore no better than a terrorist nation. Pro-Palestinian military groups are thus justified in attacking America, as long as the USA continues to support Israel.

Is there an argument? Yes_____ or No_____

What is the main conclusion? _____

Supporting premise(s) _____

_____

Unstated premise(s) and conclusion(s) _____

_____

Evaluation of Supporting Premise(s): Explain why any supporting premise is or is not

a. Relevant: _____

b. Acceptable: _____

c. Sufficient: _____

3. The institution of a private health-care system in Canada would be an abomination because it wouldn't be any less expensive or any more efficient. More likely, it would be better for those who could afford it, and worse or unavailable for those who couldn't. In other words, better for some, non-existent for others. In the interests of fairness and compassion for the less fortunate, it's better to have a government-run health-care system so that everyone can benefit.

Is there an argument? Yes _____ or No _____

What is the main conclusion? _____

Supporting premise(s) _____

_____

Unstated premise(s) and conclusion(s) _____

_____

Evaluation of Supporting Premise(s): Explain why any supporting premise is or is not

a.   Relevant: _____

b.   Acceptable: _____

c.   Sufficient: _____

4. There's no way gay couples should be allowed to adopt children because it's simply un-natural. In fact, homosexuality, in itself, is unnatural. Children are best raised when there's a mother and a father in the household. A heterosexual set of parents can nurture and develop the child best, since homosexual parents are likely to raise sexually perverted children.

Is there an argument? Yes_____ or No _____

What is the main conclusion? _____

Supporting premise (s) _____

_____

Unstated premise(s) and conclusion(s): _____

_____

Evaluation of supporting premise(s): Explain why any supporting premise is or is not

a.   Relevant: _____

b.   Acceptable: _____

c.   Sufficient: _____

5. The British Monarchy ought to be abolished. I can't stand the snobbish Brits anyway. My Uncle Nigel in London is such a supercilious idiot, and he supports the monarchy. So does my weird Aunt Agnes! Thank God, we live in a democratic republic.

Is there an argument? Yes _____ or No _____

Main conclusion: _____

Supporting premise(s) _____

_____

Unstated premise(s) and conclusion(s) _____

_____

Evaluation: Explain why any supporting premise is or is not

a.   Relevant: _____

b.   Acceptable: _____

c.   Sufficient: _____

6. In a capitalist economy, workers are alienated from the fruits of their labours. Factory owners exploit people by paying them the least they can, but charging the most the market will bear. These bourgeois owners then feast on the surplus profit value. If this continues, then the disparities in wealth between the rich and poor will increase.

Is there an argument? Yes _____ or No _____

What is the main conclusion? _____

_____

Supporting premise(s): _____

_____

Unstated premise(s) and conclusion(s) _____

_____

Evaluation: Explain why any supporting premise is or is not

a.　Relevant: _____

b.　Acceptable: _____

c.　Sufficient: _____

for personal growth and social improvement and understanding. If these viewpoints are presented in an honest and sincere fashion, then they pose legitimate challenges that we can use for ethical insight and developmental purposes. If our critic's disagreements are ill-founded, we can bring this to light. If they are justified, then we are given the opportunity to modify our views or abandon our positions entirely. It is an admirable philosophical virtue to be able to change one's thinking under the weight of contrary evidence or in response to legitimate criticism.

As well as opening up to argument, we should try to develop an attitude of *rational disinterestedness*. In other words, we should try to remain as objective and impartial as possible. This attitude requires that we stop trying to impose our viewpoints on others. Properly conducted argument is not about winning and losing. It is not a matter of looking good at someone else's expense. The problem is that many people view argument as a competition where there are winners and losers. Because losing an argument can be embarrassing or a threat to self-esteem, some people will say or do almost anything rather than lose. For instance, in the middle of a heated argument, have you ever invented facts or statistics to support conclusions? Be honest now! Have you ever said things you do not really believe or cannot support as a way of winning or not losing face? If you have, then you can appreciate how psychological and emotional factors can affect ethical reasoning processes. If you, or the person you are arguing with, are busy making things up, then no wonder your arguments seem useless and unpleasant and something to avoid. Before we can engage in useful and productive argumentation, we have to get our psychological acts together.

An important example was set by Plato's teacher, Socrates. Centuries ago, Socrates was declared to be the wisest man in Athens by the Oracle of Delphi. Aware of his ignorance, Socrates set out to disprove the Oracle by finding someone wiser. After searching long and hard, he concluded that everyone he encountered was ignorant, just like him. If he possessed greater wisdom, that greater wisdom must have come from the awareness of his ignorance. Others were unaware of theirs. They pretended to know what they did not. In light of what Socrates learned, you may wish to reduce your pretensions to knowledge. If you have no ignorance to hide, because you freely and openly admit what you do not know, then you greatly reduce the need to communicate defensively. If you reduce your defensiveness, you can then engage in more fruitful dialogue and enjoy more satisfying communications. Rather than trying to defeat others, you should endeavour to display *Socratic humility*, to listen carefully for understanding, and to respond intelligently and thoughtfully to what others have to say. Constructive attitudes toward disagreement and argument can provide enormous benefits.

Benefits of Argument

Engaged in properly, philosophical argument in moral matters can open minds. It can shake us from our ignorance and blind prejudice. Without argument, people are free to rest on a bed of unexamined beliefs. Lies may be taken for truths. Gross injustices may be accepted as normal, traditional or what nature intended. For instance, before some thoughtful and ethically sensitive people began to question and to seriously disagree with the values of the day, women and Blacks were regarded as inferior and were unfairly denied their basic rights. In part, because of the philosophical challenges raised in protest, they are now considered equal and share, in principle, the same basic entitlements as the rest of us. In short, argument can serve a positive social purpose. It can help to expose prejudice and rectify injustices.

Argument can also facilitate personal growth. When challenged by argument, we are not allowed the questionable luxury of mindless response. Saying things or doing things without thinking becomes more difficult in light of disagreement. This should not discourage us—quite the contrary. By engaging in productive dialogue with those who disagree with us, we may, in the end, strengthen our viewpoints, modify them to make them more acceptable or discard them when they are no longer useful or supportable. In fact, when people choose to disagree with us, we might wish to see this as a kind of compliment. If our views were regarded as totally insignificant or if we were not taken seriously by others, nobody would waste their time on us. When someone chooses to debate with us, we can assume that the other individual has at least heard us and is willing to take notice of what we have said.

Ethical Case-Study Analysis

So far in this chapter, we have engaged in an analysis of claims, concepts and arguments—all of which should prove to be enormously helpful when forming our own moral positions or when critically evaluating those held by others. Our preliminary introduction to moral reasoning does not end here, however. Often we find in real life that we are presented not with formal written arguments, but with complicated life situations constituting moral dilemmas. Circumstances may unfold which present opposing rights and interests among various conflicting parties. At first glance, there may be no obvious or easy resolution to the dispute at issue; the competing sides may indeed have very strong claims against one another. This is what makes the problem a dilemma. If the choice were simply between right and wrong, the decision would be much easier, assuming one is inclined to do the right thing. By contrast, when the decision is between two or more courses of action, both or all of which are right in some ways, then choice is problematic. In these sorts of circumstances, people are caught on the "horns of a dilemma," often psychologically immobilized and unable to make a decision or take action. This is when techniques of **ethical case-study analysis** certainly come in handy. Before we examine these techniques, here's an example of a hypothetical moral dilemma which has become very well known among educators. It is called the "Heinz dilemma." After reading it, ask yourself why the situation constitutes a moral dilemma. What is at stake here?

> In a town in Europe, a woman was near death from a special kind of cancer. There was one drug that the doctors thought might save her. It was a form of radium that a druggist in the same town had recently discovered. The drug was expensive to make, but the druggist was charging ten times what the drug cost him to make. He paid $200 for the radium and charged $2000 for a small dose of the drug. The sick woman's husband, Heinz, went to everyone he knew to borrow the money, but he could only get together about $1000, which is half of what it cost. He told the druggist that his wife was dying and asked him to sell it cheaper or let him pay later. The druggist said, "No, I discovered the drug and I'm going to make money from it." So Heinz got desperate and broke into the man's store to steal the drug for his wife. Should the husband have done that? Why?[20]

The next time you are faced with a moral dilemma situation, you might wish to refer to one of the numerous guides that have been developed for ethical decision making. For instance, The Centre for Applied Ethics at the University of British Columbia offers one such framework.[21] A popular handbook by Rushworth Kidder entitled *How Good People Make Tough Choices* also provides useful advice when it comes to resolving the dilemmas of ethical living. Here, we will look at a seven-step model of ethical decision making developed by Henk van Luijk, a professor at Nijenrode University in the Netherlands and director of the European Institute for Business Ethics. His method has been adopted by the American Philosophical Practitioners Association for use in its dilemma training certification program for philosophical consultants. The method, designed to teach employees of organizations how to deal with workplace integrity issues in a professional manner, can also be easily applied to other personal and institutional settings. It is summarized below:

Seven-Step Model for Handling Moral Dilemmas

Ask:

1. What is the core moral problem?
2. Who are the parties involved?
3. Who is/are answerable?

4. What information do I need?
5. What arguments can be brought forward?
6. What is my conclusion?
7. How do I feel now?

Van Luijk illustrates the use of his decision-making model with the following case study:

> An employee from the Tax Department has been living for some time on a street with rows of four and six houses. He and his wife feel comfortable there, neighbours have become friends, and his children, too, have pleasant social contacts. In the meantime, his row of houses have come to need a paint job on the outside. It is cheaper to have the paintwork done for all the houses in the row, and so it is decided. One of the neighbours knows a company that comes up with a suspiciously cheap offer. The only way that this can be done is if no VAT [value added tax—like Canada's GST] is charged. The neighbours intend to accept the offer. What should the tax employee do?[22]

STEP ONE: WHAT IS THE CORE MORAL PROBLEM? The first step in van Luijk's process is one of the most difficult and onerous. Not every dilemma in life is a moral dilemma. Usually the task of hiring a contractor for home maintenance doesn't present itself as an ethical issue. Deciding to pick one contractor over another may just involve price, scheduling, quality or workmanship. Such things represent economic, prudential or aesthetic values. Earlier we learned that moral values can be distinguished from such nonmoral values insofar as the former have ultimate worth or are based on universal and prescriptive ethical principles. Matters of justice, rights, social duty, fairness, equality, the greatest happiness for the greatest number, and virtue constitute a sampling of some of those things upon which moral values and moral value judgments are based. It's when rights conflict, or when our personal self-interest opposes our social duty, for instance, that moral dilemmas arise. The first thing to do, then, is to make sure a moral dilemma is indeed present. The difficulty of this task is what makes it onerous.

If a moral dilemma is present, you will need to take the morally relevant elements of the case study and try to formulate the central moral question. How should the moral problem be defined? If more than one moral problem manifests itself, decide which is the main problem. What major interests or rights are involved? What could some of the arguments be for the opposing sides in the dispute? For the case presently under consideration, van Luijk provides the following questions and propositions which are embedded in the example:

(A) A Tax Department (TD) employee is obligated not to engage in anti-tax activities if he strongly suspects moonlighting, in order to guarantee the department's independence, even if this leads, or may lead, to tensions in his private life.

(B) Is it your duty as a TD employee to report to your department that citizens engage in anti-tax activities, when you have come to this knowledge through your private life, on basis of the fact that you are bound to uphold the law, in spite of the fact that it puts you in an exceptional position in relation to other citizens?

(C) It is morally intolerable that neighbours ask you, a TD employee, to participate in anti-tax activities, thus expecting you to break the law, even if this means that by not accepting such an offer they will forfeit a possible financial gain.

(D) It is morally improper for a painter to propose to his customers to accept an offer for moonlighting, thus pressing citizens to break the law, and thus causing the community not to receive its rightful income, in spite of the fact that both he and his customer stand to gain considerable profit from it.

After careful examination of these four formulations of the moral problem, van Luijk concludes that (A) represents the most central and encompassing one. We'll go along with his decision to see how his case study analysis unfolds.

STEP TWO: WHO ARE THE PARTIES INVOLVED? For purposes of this analysis, "the parties involved" are "all those individuals and groups that may reasonably claim that their rights and interests must be taken into account when making the decision." As this case illustrates, the job of answering the "Who?" question for any given problem belongs to the circle of people involved. The people involved here include (a) the employee, (b) his family, (c) the Tax Department, and (d) society. The neighbours are not included; you may wonder why. After all, the eventual decision will affect them too. The fact, however, is that their interests are not morally justified. Their advantage is gained through cheating the system—an unreasonable claim. Such immoral interests need not be considered as *legitimate* competing concerns. By analogy, when deciding what criminal laws ought to be instituted, the interests of the "crook" wishing to avoid the penalties stemming from his illegal actions are not considered, and properly so. It may be in one's interest to get away with something illegal, but any claims related to such an intent are unjustified and illegitimate. The criminal's intent to get away with murder or theft, say, is not a legitimate interest and so is irrelevant to the legal decision-making process; so, too, with the would-be tax evaders in our sample case.

STEP THREE: WHO IS ANSWERABLE? In this stage of our case-study analysis, we're required to determine "ownership" of the moral problem. Whose problem is it anyway? Who is expected to make the decision? In many case studies this is not entirely clear, but in our scenario, it is obvious that the employee must decide whether or not he will assent to his neighbours' proposal. Even though the employee has not asked to be placed in this morally awkward situation, he nonetheless is burdened with the responsibility of having to make a difficult decision with ethical implications. He can't simply opt out of the moral game, so to speak, and go along with the others because "he had no other choice." Difficult or uncomfortable choices still involve personal responsibility on the part of the decision maker. While the employee is not responsible for what others choose to do, or what they have done to him, he is fully responsible for his own responsive choice.

STEP FOUR: WHAT INFORMATION DO I NEED? Before one makes a final decision in a moral dilemma situation, it's important to establish that all the information pertinent to the decision has been gathered. Often moral disputes are not about principles, but about facts. For example, on the subject of capital punishment, one person may be in favour of it, while another may be opposed. Both disputants may be utilitarians (see Chapters Three and Four) but assume that different facts are true regarding the deterrence value of capital punishment. One person may have dated information based on questionable samples, whereas the other may have more up-to-date, reliable information regarding the deterrence characteristics of this sanction. Once the disputants get the facts straight and obtain the best information available, the possibility of rational agreement becomes greater. In the present dilemma under consideration, it doesn't appear that any of the facts of the case are ambiguous or unclear. The information we already have seems to be sufficient to make a decision. We know what the proposition is, what the savings will be, who will benefit, what violation of tax law is at stake and who must make a moral decision.

STEP FIVE: WHAT ARGUMENTS CAN BE BROUGHT FORWARD? Once we have established what the moral problem is, who is involved, who is responsible for making a decision, and what the facts of the case are, it is time to marshal in the arguments. First of all, formulate the pro-arguments or those that confirm the proposition articulated in Step One (A). Second, investigate the possible counter-arguments, that is, those that refute the proposition. Third, the moral weight of the arguments brought forward on either side will have to be appraised. Let's identify some of the pro- and con-arguments, taking the proposition to be: *A tax department employee should not personally become involved in anti-tax practices.*

SUPPORTING ARGUMENTS
It's every citizen's duty to obey the law.
If the employee joins the tax-evading group, he could become liable to blackmail.
Joining in will tarnish the image of the Tax Department.

OPPOSING ARGUMENTS
Refusal to join the group will seriously disturb neighbour relations.
It's a financial disadvantage to stick to the letter of the law.
Everybody does it.[23]

An examination of these arguments reveals the tension between the public position of the employee and his private life. How much latitude does one have in personal decision making, in view of legal stipulations? In viewing this case, one could also choose to interpret and appraise the situation in terms of the differences between a utilitarian consequence-based approach and a principle-oriented deontological approach, for example. It could be argued from a utilitarian perspective that it is the employee's moral duty to make that choice through which he will produce the greatest possible advantage for the greatest number of people involved. From a deontological perspective, it could be argued that the employee's moral duty is to make that choice through which justice is done to an intrinsically valid principle, or a fundamental right, irrespective of the possible consequences of his choice. By viewing the case study from either of these two perspectives (or others we have already discussed), it is possible to better understand the types of arguments used. Knowledge of diverse moral perspectives allows for better insight into the normative features in any case of moral argumentation. This better insight, in turn, increases one's self-confidence in dealing with any moral dilemma. Strengthening one's moral competence is certainly beneficial.

Using different moral perspectives to handle particular case studies may lead us to different conclusions. As van Luijk points out, this can easily happen between utilitarian consequential-ist theories and principle-based deontological approaches. In situations where this occurs, the model offers us a *general rule*: "Whenever a consequence-oriented ethical approach leads to a dif-ferent outcome than a principle-oriented ethical approach, the principle-oriented ethical approach should be given our moral preference." If, in the case of the tax employee, he chose to go along with the neighbours, the utilitarian viewpoint might support his decision. Nobody would be directly or seriously harmed, the employee would benefit financially and so too would his neigh-bours—not to mention the painter, who would be able to pocket a little extra cash on the side. On top of all this, good relations with the neighbours would be maintained, and really, little harm would be done to society by this one minor infraction. From this consequentialist perspective, the ends would seem to justify the means.

From a deontological viewpoint, however, every citizen has at least a *prima facie* duty to obey the law, whether or not it is to their advantage to do so. Applied to this case, the ends do not justify the means. If the operational moral maxim became "Violate the tax laws of a coun-try whenever it is financially advantageous or expedient to do so," then the whole idea and pur-pose of taxation would be placed in jeopardy. People would avoid paying tax whenever they felt like it, making an exception of themselves when it came to their social duty. Imagine a world in which such a maxim were a universal law. Ask yourself, as a rational person, if you could live in such a world. If not, then there's something wrong with the proposition which supports tax evasion.

The great divide between utilitarianism and deontology is not something we can possibly bridge here. Also, we are not in a position to complicate matters further by examining the case study from the perspective of the other alternative moral theories discussed earlier in the text. Opting for one ethical perspective over another, especially when their conclusions conflict in par-ticular moral dilemmas, requires a kind of metaethical debate far beyond our intentions here. Nonetheless, recognizing that we all bring our own moral perspectives to any moral dilemma situation helps us to understand our priorities and values, as well as those held by others. The people with whom we disagree are not always moral monsters!

STEP SIX: WHAT IS MY CONCLUSION? In this stage of our deliberations, we formulate a con-clusion. The difficulty of doing this arises from the fact that arguments in Step Five can be persuasive for *both* sides, leaving us at an impasse. Frustrated, we might be inclined to flip a coin: heads—the tax man should agree to go ahead with the neighbours' tax evasion scheme; tails—he should refuse to do so. Though such black-and-white, either/or resolutions have their appeal, often it is possible and indeed better to arrive at a conclusion which does justice to *all* the arguments and perspectives that have been brought forward. In the present case, perhaps the employee should not join the neighbours, as this would seriously harm his credibility as an employee of the Tax Department. By communicating his concerns to the neighbours, he could keep his and his family's relationship with the neighbourhood transparent and above board.

Simultaneously, he may not feel obligated to blow the whistle on his neighbours, as this would jeopardize his relationship with them. Not partaking in the tax evasion does not mean that he is necessarily obligated to inform on others who do. The final conclusion to any case study—however it is formulated—should try to take into account the interests of everyone concerned or involved in the conflict. Referring to the example of the tax man, van Luijk writes,

> One can think of several variants between "just joining, this is a purely private matter" and "bringing the matter to the attention of the Department, and moving house, if necessary, for a tax officer does not belong in such a neighbourhood." What counts is that when the ultimate standpoint is taken up, no important argument has been left aside.[24]

STEP SEVEN: HOW DO I FEEL NOW? Resolving moral dilemmas is a difficult and sometimes emotionally disturbing process. Moral reasoning is not an entirely sterile logical operation. Real people with real emotions are involved. With this in mind, the final step of the case study method requires a kind of emotional ratification of the position taken. Once a decision has been made, it is appropriate to ask: "How do I feel now?" "Can I look at myself in the mir-

---

PHILOSOPHERS AT WORK

Now that we are familiar with the seven-step model for handling moral dilemmas, let us practise our rational ethical decision-making skills by analyzing the following case study. Go through each of the steps outlined by van Luijk, providing your final conclusion and its justification. Feel free to use other moral dilemmas which more closely match your personal or vocational interests. Again, you may do this work privately, in small groups or go through the ethical decision-making procedure together as an entire class.

Case Study: A 19-year-old woman is being treated for a serious kidney disease. She is currently on a dialysis machine, but treatment is steadily decreasing in efficacy. Before her condition declines any further, the physician suggests family members undergo a test to determine tissue compatibility for a kidney transplant. Only her brother shows a degree of compatibility high enough to make him a candidate. The physician meets with the brother alone to discuss the risks and benefits of the operation. Although he had agreed to be tested, after weighing the various alternatives the brother decides not to donate a kidney—because of the risks and because, he says, he doesn't feel he and his sister have ever been close enough that they would take that kind of risk for each other. The physician repeats his explanation of the risks involved and urges the brother to rethink his decision because of the serious nature of his sister's illness and the fact that there is little time to spare. The brother remains adamant in his refusal. What should the physician tell his kidney patient?

ror?" "Can I tell my children?" "Would I do the same in the future in similar circumstances?" Or, "Is it the case that I feel uncertain, perhaps somewhat sleazy?" "Do I regard my decision as a 'once-but-never-again' type of conclusion?" Negative thoughts and emotions such as these serve as a kind of moral measurement barometer. If there are bad feelings surrounding a decision, then perhaps it's worthwhile to go back and take another good look at some or all of the steps of the case-study model. Correction is certainly better than regret, and if there is a possibility that a wrong decision has been made, it is advisable to reconsider its justifiability. In the end, we should aim to arrive at a conclusion we can live with.

MINDWORK MEDITATION

Think of the last time you had a disagreement with someone. Were the two of you actually engaged in a rational argument, or just a war of words? What were the opposing positions? What premises were offered in support for each side? Were any conclusions or premises left unstated? If so, which ones? Were the supporting premises relevant, acceptable and sufficient to prove the point? Why or why not? Were any ideas or concepts mixed into the arguments worthy of a deeper conceptual analysis? Which ones? Why? See if you can reconstruct the argument you had, diagramming it or expressing one or both sides of it in standard form.

KEY TERMS

empirical study

controlled experiment

correlational findings

statistical analysis

metaethical

elucidations

factual claims

moral

conceptual claims

necessary conditions

model case

related concept

invented/imaginary cases

underlying anxiety

observation

scientific objectivity

functional explanations

normative

conceptual relationships

ultimate foundations

normative claims

nonmoral

conceptual analysis

sufficient conditions

contrary case

borderline cases

social context

practical results

results in language	interior dialogue
arguments	non-arguments
opinions	premises
conclusions	inferences
relevance	acceptability
sufficiency	irrelevant premise
non sequitur	explanations
premise indicators	conclusion indicators
conjoint premises	unstated/hidden premise
intermediate/subordinate conclusions	standard form
diagram	enthymemes
context	main argument
final conclusion	ethical case study analysis

PROGRESS CHECK 10.1

Instructions: Fill in the blanks with the responses listed below.

ethical case study analysis	standard form
conceptual analysis	justification
explanation	conclusion indicators
nonmoral	premises
relevance	ultimate foundations
conjoint premises	empirical study
metaethical	enthymemes
sufficiency	prescribe
verification	context
justify	inference
conceptual claims	moral
foundations	complex argument
acceptability	premise indicators
sufficient	factual claim
normative	logically mysterious
necessary	personal opinion
conclusion	

1. Science makes morality an object of _empirical study_.
2. Rather than _prescribe_ what morally ought to be done, scientists wish to remain value-neutral and limit themselves to descriptions and functional explanations.
3. Philosophical ethics can be normative or _metaethical_.
4. Scientists verify their claims, philosophers _justify_ theirs.
5. Metaethicists study the _ultimate foundations_ of ethical systems.

6. A ___*factual claim*___ is a statement or proposition which is true or false.

7. Value judgments and prescriptions are ___*normative*___, not descriptive.

8. Factual claims require empirical ___*verification*___, while normative claims require rational ___*justification*___.

9. Values can be either ___*non moral*___ or ___*moral*___.

10. ___*Conceptual claim*___ involve matters of meaning and usage. *conceptual cal.*

11. When a claim is neither normative nor factual, it may require ___ *conceptual analysis* for better understanding and justification.

12. John Wilson describes conceptual questions as ___*logically mysterious.*___

13. In ideal circumstances, a conceptual analysis of a term can provide _____ *neccesary* and _____ *sufficient* conditions for its application.

14. A(n) ___*explanation*___ tells us "why" something is the case, not "that" something is the case.

15. A(n) ___*personal opinion*___ is groundless, either lacking any rational basis of support or simply expressing a matter of taste.

16. An argument comprises three elements: _____ *premise*, _____ *conclusion*, and _____ *inference.*

17. Claims which support arguments can be evaluated on the basis of their _____ *relevance*, _____ *acceptability*, and _____ *sufficiency.*

18. Words and expressions like 'because,' 'since,' and 'due to' are all ___*premise indicators.*___

19. Words and expressions like 'therefore,' 'so,' and 'it follows that' are all ___*conclusion indicator*___

20. An argument possessing an unstated premise or conclusion is called a(n) ___*enthymeme*___

21. An argument possessing more than one conclusion is called a(n) ___*complex arguement*___

22. When analyzing arguments, it's sometimes helpful to express them in ___*standard form*___

23. Premises that "need each other" in order to be relevant and supportive of a conclusion are called ___*conjoint premise*___

24. It's often useful to consider ___*context*___ when deciding which claims support which other claim.

25. Moral dilemmas can be handled rationally by using ___*ethical case study analysis.*___

SUMMARY OF MAJOR POINTS

1. How are philosophy and science different in their approaches to the study of morality?

   Philosophy is rational, prescriptive, evaluative, normative, concerned with justification and the foundations of ethical systems.

   Science is empirical, factual, descriptive, correlational/causal, concerned with functional explanations and verifying claims.

2. How do factual claims, normative claims and conceptual claims differ?

   Factual claims assert what is, was or will be the case. They are true or false in principle. Factual claims are empirically verifiable. By contrast, value claims are normative, stating what is good or bad, right or wrong, praiseworthy or blameworthy, obligated or prohibited. Value judgments are justified, not verified. Conceptual claims are not purely factual or normative. They contain concepts or ideas that must be handled analytically and linguistically, not scientifically or purely logically.

3.   **Are all values moral?**

No, there are both moral and nonmoral values. The latter do not belong to the realm of morality. Nonmoral values may be prudential (related to self-interest) or benevolent (promoting the interests of others). Moral values pertain to things like virtue, rights and duties. Obligations arising from moral values are prescriptive for everybody; those from nonmoral values are optional.

4.   **What is conceptual analysis?**

Conceptual analysis techniques, like those covered in this chapter, can help one to clarify concepts that are used as premises or conclusions of arguments. Such techniques require an investigation into everyday uses of particular concepts and their relationships to relevant others. John Wilson has developed a method of conceptual analysis. Conceptual analysis can be used to clarify your own ideas or to critique those presented by others.

5.   **How are arguments different from opinions and explanations?**

Arguments are comprised of three parts: premise, conclusion and inference. Premises support conclusions; one draws inferences from preceding premises. By contrast, opinions are unsupported claims. They may express emotions and beliefs, etc. Opinions do not involve a process of rational thought. Explanations tell us *how* something happened or *why* something happened, not *that* it happened. Further, telling someone what led up to an immoral act, or why someone acted immorally, does not justify the act itself. Arguments justify, criticize, and attempt to prove that something is the case.

6.   **What criteria can be used to evaluate supporting premises of arguments?**

You can use the criteria of relevance, acceptability and sufficiency.

7.   **What good are indicator words?**

Indicator words can help you to identify premises and conclusions of arguments. Examples of premise indicators include 'because' and 'given that.' Examples of conclusion indicators include 'so' and 'therefore.'

8.   **What can complicate argument analysis?**

Sometimes arguments contain unstated premises and conclusions. When this happens it is helpful to make explicit what was only assumed or left unsaid.

9.   **What's the difference between simple and complex arguments?**

Simple arguments make only one inference and thus contain only one conclusion. Complex arguments include more than one inference and therefore at least one intermediate or subordinate conclusion.

10. **What techniques can be used to analyze arguments?**

It is sometimes useful to diagram or express arguments in standard form.

11. What are some helpful hints for argument analysis?

Identify indicator words.

Uncover unstated or implicit premises and conclusions.

Consider the larger context of the argument.

Identify each claim in the passage that is relevant to the argument.

Reformulate claims as required.

Discard superfluous elements of arguments.

Identify main and intermediate arguments.

Identify replies to objections.

Identify any conceptual questions or claims around which a passage revolves.

12. What steps are involved in ethical case-study analysis?

Ask:

1. What is the core moral problem?
2. Who are the parties involved?
3. Who is answerable?
4. What information is needed to make a decision?
5. What arguments can be brought forward?
6. What is my conclusion?
7. How do I feel now?

SOURCE REFERENCES

Conway, D. and R. Munson, *The Elements of Reasoning, 3/e*. Wadsworth: Belmont, 2000.

Johnson, R.H. and Anthony Blair, *Logical Self-Defence*. McGraw-Hill, 1983.

Wilson, John, *Thinking with Concepts*. Cambridge: Cambridge University Press, 1980.

ENDNOTES

1. John Wilson, *Thinking With Concepts*, Cambridge: Cambridge University Press, 1980.
2. ibid., p. 10.
3. ibid., p. 11.
4. ibid., p. 14.
5. ibid.
6. Thomas White, *Discovering Philosophy*. Prentice Hall: Upper Saddle River, N.J., 1996, p. 18.
7. ibid., p. 18.
8. ibid. pp. 18–19. This discussion is adapted from White.
9. John Wilson, *Thinking With Concepts*. Cambridge: Cambridge University Press, 1980.
10. ibid., p. 4.
11. ibid., p. 28.
12. ibid., p. 31.

13. Wilson, ibid., p. 94.

14. R.H. Johnson & J.A. Blair, *Logical Self-Defense*. McGraw-Hill, 1993, p. 82.

15. These lists have been compiled from Robert Boyd, David Conway and Ronald Munson. See Boyd, *Critical Reasoning and Logic*, Prentice Hall: Upper Saddle River, N.J. 2003, pp. 28–29, and David Conway and Ronald Munson, *The Elements of Reasoning*, 3rd edition, Wadsworth: Belmont: 2000, p. 9.

16. Conway and Munson, ibid., p. 21.

17. This section draws heavily from the work of David Conway and Ronald Munson, ibid., pp. 23–26.

18. Ibid., p. 25.

19. Ibid., p. 26.

20. This dilemma comes from A. Colby, L. Kohlberg, J. Gibbs and M. Lieberman, "A longitudinal study of moral judgment." *Monographs of the Society for Research in Child Development*, 48 (1–2, Serial no. 200, 1983, p. 77).

21. See Michael McDonald's "A Framework for Ethical Decision-Making" Version 4; Ethics Shareware. Website: www.ethics.ubc.ca/mcdonald/decisions.html.

22. Van Luijk's case study comes from the moral dilemma certificate training progamme manual produced by the American Philosophical Practitioners Association.

23. Ibid.

24. Ibid.

11

Forms and Fallacies of Logic

Learning Outcomes

After successfully completing this chapter,
you will be able to

- appreciate the difference between the
  logical form of an argument and the
  content that gives it substance;
- symbolically state some basic forms of
  deductive logic
- identify forms of invalid deductive
  reasoning
- define and give examples of inductive
  logic
- compare and contrast inductive and
  deductive reasoning
- evaluate arguments more effectively
- distinguish among the concepts of
  validity, truth and soundness
- critically analyze and appraise each part
  of a practical syllogism
- test the value premises upon which
  practical syllogisms are based
- explain the general nature of logical
  fallacies
- identify and explain the reasoning procedures involved in various examples of
  fallacious reasoning
- list some dos and don'ts for rational
  debates

PHILOSOPHICAL FOCUS QUESTIONS

1. What are some forms of valid deductive reasoning?

2. Can you give some examples of syllogisms? What type is often used in ethical debate? How is this type different from other types?

3. How does inductive logic differ from deductive logic?

4. Is a valid argument necessarily sound? Explain why or why not.

5. How is the practical syllogism particularly relevant for ethics and ethical inquiry?

6. At what levels can the practical syllogism be evaluated?

7. What tests can be used to establish the adequacy of value premises contained within particular practical syllogisms?

8. What is a logical fallacy? What are some examples?

9. What should you do and not do when having a rational debate?

DEDUCTIVE LOGIC

In the previous chapter, we learned that an **argument** is not an interpersonal event or a confrontation of egos, but rather a combination of premises and conclusions making an inference.

> *In much the same way that we have building codes to ensure that a house is built well, there is also a "thinking code," that is, guidelines and rules for what makes an argument pass "philosophical inspection." We find this code in that part of philosophy called logic.*
>
> THOMAS WHITE

By concentrating on the structure of argument, as well as on its various forms—and not on the person or persons with whom we disagree—we can divest ourselves of the unpleasant feelings and contaminating psychological influences that often interfere with rational debate. We can then proceed to examine ethical and philosophical positions impartially and objectively. Let us begin by looking at various forms of logical thinking that are deductive in nature.

Deductive Arguments

If this book were designed to be a course in logic, then it would be appropriate to examine the many subtleties and intricate forms of deductive reasoning. Since, as philosophical beginners, we are looking at logical thinking as a means to improve our ethical decision-making skills and our abilities to evaluate moral arguments, we will limit our discussion to a few of the more common and basic forms of **deductive logic**. We will also discuss some invalid forms of deductive reasoning before we move on to a treatment of inductive logic, another type of thinking that is important to master for critical, analytical purposes.

    Form versus Content: When examining deductive arguments, it is helpful to distinguish between their **form** and **content**. Moral arguments are typically about something; that is, they have a subject matter. It may be a practice (e.g., artificial insemination), an event (e.g., a bombing in the Middle East) or an act (e.g., civil disobedience) that provides the substance or content of the argument. Regardless of the issue under debate, for the arguments to be considered valid, they must display an acceptable **logical form.** The implication is that a formal structure can be abstracted from any content-related argument. The most common forms have been given standardized names, some of which are in Latin, like the first one we will examine: *Modus Ponens*.

Modus Ponens. Many arguments that we hear expressed in conversation or debate contain the ***Modus Ponens (MP)*** form. Arguments of this form have been determined to be valid and so this logical structure can be used to test arguments for their validity. Of course, the MP argument is not the *only* valid form of reasoning, and therefore, an argument not displaying the MP form is not necessarily invalid. As you will see, there is more than one type of **valid reasoning**. Below are two MP arguments containing different content, but identical forms.

> Whenever the economy goes into a recession, church attendance increases. Since we are currently in an economic recession, we can conclude that church attendance has increased or will do so shortly.

> If a person has an xx genotype, that person is a female. Pat has an xx genotype, so we can conclude Pat is female.

If we abstract from the content of these two very different arguments, we can see that they share the same formal structure expressed below.

If p, then q	or	$p \rightarrow q$
p	(alternative	$\underline{p}$
So, q	notation)	$\therefore q$

Example One:

> Whenever the economy goes into a recession (p), then church attendance increases (q).
> Since we are currently falling into an economic recession (p).
> (So, q) We can conclude that church attendance will increase.

Example Two:

> If a person has an xx genotype (p), the person is a female (q).
> Pat has an xx genotype (p).
> (So, q) Therefore, Pat is a female.

LOGICAL ERROR: AFFIRMING THE CONSEQUENT   When using *Modus Ponens*, the proper thing to do is to **affirm the antecedent**. In the opening statement "If p, then q," "p" is the **antecedent** and "q" the **consequent**. If you affirm the consequent, an invalid, faulty form of argument results. Formally, affirming the consequent looks like this:

$$
\begin{array}{lll}
\text{If p, then q} & \qquad (\text{or}) & \qquad p \rightarrow q \\
\text{q} & & \qquad \underline{q} \\
\text{So, p} & & \qquad \therefore p
\end{array}
$$

If we provide some content to the formal expression above, we can easily see how affirming the consequent is an invalid form of reasoning.[1]

If it rains (p) the streets will be wet (q), and the streets are wet (q). So it must have rained (p).

In the example above, it may be true that the streets are wet. It may also be true that if it rains, the streets will get wet. It may even be true that the streets are wet because it has rained in this particular instance. Yet, it *is not necessarily true* that it must always rain for the streets to be wet. It could be that a water main has burst or that someone has hosed down the road because of an oil spill. These possibilities point to the fact that a false conclusion can be reached from true premises if a proper and valid form of argumentation is not followed. So one way to test for the validity of an argument is to construct an obviously invalid counterexample that possesses the same form as the argument you are evaluating. If you can show that false conclusions (or ones that do not follow necessarily) arise when the consequent is affirmed, then you can demonstrate how this form of reasoning is invalid. Here is another example of an argument that affirms the consequent:

If I bought a new BMW (p), I would be broke (q).
I am broke (q).
So, I must have bought a new BMW (p).

As you can well imagine, while buying a BMW could leave most people broke, it is possible to be broke without buying a BMW. Maybe a business deal fell through or a business bankruptcy has caused you to lose your shirt. In short, affirming the consequent in MP reasoning is invalid logic. It does not lead to a necessary conclusion.

Modus Tollens.   A second form of valid logic is *Modus Tollens (MT)*. In an MT argument, an inference results by **denying the consequent**. Formally, MT is expressed in the following fashion:

$$
\begin{array}{lll}
\text{If p, then q} & \qquad (\text{or}) & \qquad p \rightarrow q \\
\text{not q} & & \qquad \underline{-q} \\
\text{So, not p} & & \qquad \therefore -p
\end{array}
$$

We can return to our earlier example about rain and wet streets to put some content in this valid MT form of reasoning.

If it rains (p), the streets get wet (q).

The streets did not get wet (not q).
So, it has not rained (not p).

LOGICAL ERROR: DENYING THE ANTECEDENT   The invalid form of MT reasoning
would involve **denying the antecedent**.

If p, then q	(or)	$p \rightarrow q$
not p		-p
So, not q		$\therefore -q$

The unacceptability of denying the antecedent is illustrated by the example below

If it rains (p), there are clouds (q).
It is not raining (not p).
So, there are no clouds (not q).

Again, in this argument a false conclusion follows from two premises that are true. Experience
teaches us that there can be clouds in the sky without any falling rain. Of course, it is possible
that it is not raining and that there is no cloud cover. Nonetheless, our counterexample
underscores the fact that clouds could fill the sky even if rain did not fall. Once a counterexample like this one demonstrates how false conclusions can follow from arguments possessing a particular logical form, an argument of that form must be rejected as invalid.

SYLLOGISMS

A key form of deductive argument often used in moral and
ethical debate is the **syllogism**. The syllogism actually comes
in many forms, but we will limit ourselves to hypothetical
and disjunctive syllogisms, as well as to those involving class
membership and practical value reasoning.

> *With the study of logical forms*
> *Aristotle made that decisive step that*
> *led to the science of logic.*
> HANS REICHENBACH

Hypothetical Syllogisms: Hypothetical syllogisms are
comprised of a series of "if–then" statements following a
string. This string contains two premises and a conclusion. It is because this type of syllogism contains "condi-

> *Watch your Ps and Qs.*
> SOME RATIONAL ADVICE

tional" premises that it is referred to as hypothetical. Here is an example of a hypothetical
syllogism:

If you obtain a pass on this test (p), you will successfully complete your last course (q). On
top of that, if you successfully complete your last course (q), you will earn your diploma (r).
So, if you pass the test (p), you will earn your diploma (r).

Expressed formally,

If p, then q	(or)	$p \rightarrow q$
If q, then r		$q \rightarrow r$
Therefore, if p then r		$\therefore p \rightarrow r$

An invalid form of a hypothetical syllogism is

If p, then q
If p, then r
Therefore, if q then r

To appreciate why the form above is invalid, see the example below.

If you study (p), you will pass the final exam (q).
If you study (p), you will graduate (r).
Therefore, if you pass the final exam (q), you will graduate (r).

The invalid form of the hypothetical syllogism above indicates that your passing the final exam guarantees your graduation just because you have studied; surely this does not follow. It is possible to study, pass the final exam and still fail the course and, thus, fail to graduate.[2]

Disjunctive Syllogisms: Like the hypothetical syllogism, the **disjunctive syllogism** comprises a series of related statements leading to a conclusion. Unlike the former, which deals with a logical chain of consequences, this one involves an either/or choice. This choice may be expressed symbolically by "v." To express "either p or q" in symbolic form, one would write "p v q." An example of a disjunctive syllogism is the following:

Either Mary has made the right decision (p) or she has made the wrong decision (q). Since she has not made the wrong decision (not q), she has therefore made the right one (p).

Expressed formally,

Either p or q	(or)	p v q
not q		$-q$
Therefore, p		$\therefore p$

If Mary had made the wrong decision, then the disjunctive syllogism would be altered so:

Either p or q	(or)	p v q
not p		$-p$
Therefore, q		$\therefore q$

LOGICAL ERROR: AFFIRMING THE INCLUSIVE DISJUNCT   The invalid form of the disjunctive syllogism (called **affirming the inclusive disjunct**) is expressed below.

Either p or q	(or)	Either p or q
p		q
Therefore, not q		$\therefore$ not p

To see why affirming the inclusive disjunct is invalid, consider the following example.

Either Fred gets paid a lot (p) or he inherited lots of money (q).
Fred gets paid a lot (p).
Therefore, he did not inherit lots of money (q).

In this invalid form of reasoning, one starts by stating that either p or q is so, meaning that only one and not the other can be true. In fact, both disjuncts could be true at the same time. Maybe Fred does get paid well and perhaps he has inherited lots of money as well. P does not preclude q or vice versa. The "or" here is "inclusive," which allows both disjuncts in the first premise to be true. If the disjuncts were "exclusive," i.e., if both p and q could not be true at the same time, then it would follow that "If p, not q" or "If q, not p." Here is an example of a disjunctive syllogism that is exclusive.

> It cannot be that Mother is both alive (p) and dead (q).
> Because she is alive (p),
> She cannot be dead (q).

Expressed formally:

> It cannot be both p and q
> p
> So, not q

Table 11.1 SOME VALID AND INVALID FORMS OF DEDUCTIVE LOGIC

VALID LOGICAL FORMS

Modus Ponens	*Modus Tollens*	Hypothetical Syllogism	Disjunctive Syllogism
If p, then q	If p, then q	If p, then q	Either p or q
p	not q	If q, then r	Not q
So, q	So, not p	So, if p, then r	So, p
			(or)
			Either p or q
			Not p
			So, q

INVALID LOGICAL FORMS

Affirming the Consequent	Denying the Antecedent	Hypothetical Fallacy	Affirming the (Inclusive) Disjunct
If p, then q	If p, then q	If p, then q	Either p or q
q	Not p	If p, then r	p
So, p	So, not q	If q, then r	So, not q
			(or)
			Either p or q
			q
			So, not p

PHILOSOPHERS AT WORK

For each of the reasoning examples that follow, indicate whether the logic is valid (V) or invalid (I). Below each example, give the logical form contained in it.

_____ 1. If Fred lost his wallet, then he lost his student identification. If he lost his student identification, then he will not be allowed to join any varsity teams. Therefore, if Fred lost his wallet, then he will not be allowed to join any varsity teams.

Logical Form: _____

_____ 2. Either I am going to school or I am going to earn a lot of money. I am going to school. Therefore, I am not going to earn a lot of money.

Logical Form: _____

_____ 3. If we go to war, I will be very upset. I am very upset. So, we went to war.

Logical Form: _____

_____ 4. If you lie to people, then they will not trust you. People do trust you. So you have not lied.

Logical Form: _____

Answer Key

1. Valid hypothetical syllogism
   Form: If p, then q
         If q, then r
         Therefore, if p then r
2. Invalid—affirming the inclusive disjunct; one can both go to school *and* earn lots of money
   Form: Either p or q
         p
         Therefore, not q
3. Invalid—affirming the consequent; you can become upset for reasons other than going to war
   Form: If p, then q
         q
         So, p
4. Valid—*Modus Tollens* form
   Form: If p, then q
         not q
         So, not p

Syllogisms of Class Membership: There are also *syllogisms of class membership* that consist in drawing inferences from class membership, as follows:

Major Premise: All A are B.	A is B
Minor Premise: All C are A.	C is A
Conclusion: Therefore all C are B.	∴ C is B

Adding some content to this formal structure, we come up with the following example:

Major Premise: All men (A) are mortal (B).
Minor Premise: Socrates (C) is a man (A).
Conclusion: Therefore, Socrates (C) is mortal (B).

Another variation of a class membership syllogism is provided below.

All A are B.
Some C are A.
Therefore, some C are B.

All bankers (A) are conservative (B).
Some people (C) are bankers (A).
Therefore, some people (C) are conservative (B).

An invalid form of class syllogism can be expressed in the following symbolic fashion:

All A is B.
All C is B.
Therefore, all C is A.

Adding some content to the invalid logical form above, we can easily see that the conclusion does not follow from true preceding premises.

All cats (A) are animals (B).
All dogs (C) are animals (B).
Therefore, all dogs (C) are cats (A).

Practical Syllogisms: What is called a **practical syllogism** is basically the same in form as a syllogism of class membership. The examples we will be looking at contain three statements comprising a conclusion derived from two preceding premises. The difference is that, in the case of a practical syllogism, the first statement or **major premise** is a normative assertion or some kind of **value judgment**. Hence, the major premise of a practical syllogism is not empirically or analytically true, that is, true by definition. The major premise of a practical syllogism, called the **value premise**, cannot be proven true by sensory observation or scientific study. Rather, it can be justified only by rational processes of thought. Normative assertions involving principles of right conduct, standards of goodness and so on, cannot be based on what *is* the case, for what *is* may frequently be unjustified, evil or immoral. So the ultimate basis of justification for the value premise is reason, not experience. Using reason, we can test the adequacy of the value premises that serve as the starting points of our arguments.

The equivalent of the **minor premise** in the class syllogism is the practical syllogism's **factual premise**. As the term implies, the factual premise makes some type of empirical claim about the world. The factual premise is either true or false. Although we may be unable at present to prove the truth or falsity of a particular factual premise—given our limited knowledge, experience or technology—it must be possible to do so in principle.

Finally, the **conclusion** of a practical syllogism is also expressed as a value judgment. It typically makes a statement about what is better or worse, obligatory or prohibited, good or bad, right or wrong or praiseworthy or blameworthy. Below are two examples of practical syllogisms.

Example One:

    Value Premise: All acts that threaten the safety of individuals (S) are wrong (P).
    Factual Premise: Illegal toxic waste dumping (Q) is an act that threatens the
                     safety of individuals (S).
    Conclusion: Illegal toxic waste dumping (Q) is wrong (P).

Formally expressed:

    All S is P.   (or)   S is P
    Q is S.   Q is S
    Therefore, Q is P.   ∴ Q is P

Example Two:

    Value Premise: Anyone who kills to earn a living (S) is evil (P).
    Factual Premise: Bonnie and Clyde (Q) kill to earn a living (S).
    Conclusion: Bonnie and Clyde (Q) are evil (P).

Later in this chapter, we will return to practical syllogisms and learn how to rationally test their value premises for **adequacy**. We will also examine more closely the relationships among validity, truth and soundness. Before we do so, however, let us take a brief look at inductive logic, another form of reasoning often used in support of factual claims embedded within larger practical syllogisms.

INDUCTIVE LOGIC

Argument from Past Experience

As one form of **inductive logic, arguments from past experience**, like other forms of inductive logic, can only lead to **probable conclusions**. Inductive conclusions are, therefore, weaker or stronger by degree and need not be accepted or rejected in an all-or-nothing fashion. Thus, in contrast to forms of deductive logic, examples of inductive logic are never said to be valid or invalid. To see why, consider the following illustration. Suppose that we are informed

> *There is nothing in which an untrained mind shows itself more hopelessly incapable, than in drawing the proper conclusions from its own experience.*
>
> J.S. MILL

PHILOSOPHERS AT WORK

Below you will find incomplete syllogisms. Fill in the missing claims and indicate next to each syllogism whether it is practical (P), i.e., value-related, or value-neutral (VN).

_____   1. Deceiving the public is wrong.

_____.

Advertisers are wrong.

_____   2. All Russian communists live by the principles of Lenin and Marx.

Vladimir is a Russian communist.

_____.

_____   3. All acts of violence are inherently evil.

Stabbing someone to death is an act of violence.

_____.

_____   4. _____

Ralf is a bachelor.

Ralf is an unmarried man.

_____   5. Triangles are three-sided figures.

_____.

That is a three-sided figure.

Answer Key

1. P. Advertisers deceive the public.
2. VN. Therefore, Vladimir lives by the principles of Lenin and Marx.
3. P. Therefore, stabbing someone to death is inherently evil.
4. VN. All bachelors are unmarried men.
5. VN. That is a triangle.

that Wendy has lied on her job application, on her income tax return and to her husband. We might then conclude that she has lied about her medical history in her application for a life insurance policy. Because she has lied before in other instances, we conclude she has lied this time as well. In other words, we use past experience to support our current conclusion. Since our inductive conclusion is based on the facts of experience, however, and because these facts are never complete, and because new facts may have the effect of weakening, changing or contradicting today's assumptions, we can never be absolutely sure about our conclusion.[3] Perhaps Wendy has experienced some kind of religious or moral conversion that has led to a complete character transformation. Maybe Wendy was a liar since her youth, but is now an honest and responsible citizen. Many empirical variables could weaken the soundness of the inductive inference made in this case.

Argument by Analogy

A second form of inductive reasoning involves **argument by analogy**. "Analogical arguments proceed from the similarities of two or more things in certain respects to their similarity in some additional respect."[4] Analogical arguments have the following form.

> Items A, B and C have characteristics X and Y.
> A and B have characteristic Z.
> Therefore, C probably has characteristic Z also.

This analogical form of inductive reasoning is the type used to argue for the probable existence of life on other planets. If significant similarities can be found between Earth and other celestial bodies, and if Earth supports life, then one might wish to argue by analogy that those other celestial bodies also support life. Notice again, there is no certainty or deductive necessity about this conclusion; there is only a lesser or greater degree of probability.

Argument by Inductive Generalization

A third form of inductive reasoning is **argument by inductive generalization**. When we make an inductive generalization, we make a statement about all, some or none of a class based on our empirical examination of only a part of that class. It is important not to confuse inductive generalizations with generalized descriptions. Suppose, for instance, that we surveyed an introductory ethics class on its views about abortion and found that 88 percent of the students were in favour of allowing it unconditionally. In stating this, we would be presenting only a generalized description of what is the case for that group. If we were to conclude, however, that 88 percent of all post-secondary students in North America were in favour of allowing abortions, then we would be making an inductive generalization.

As you can appreciate from this example, inductive generalizations are prone to error unless certain precautions are taken. For example, when making inductive generalizations, it is important to work from **large samples**. There is no guarantee that survey results from one class—a limited sample—will be truly **representative** of millions of students in North America—the group about which a conclusion is being made.

It is also important to recognize that using large samples does not in itself guarantee that generalizations based on them will be representative. If the larger sample we need were drawn exclusively from Catholic colleges, say, then the results might tend to be more reflective of the specific religious views held by a special subgroup of students and not representative of the

MINDWORK MEDITATION

Take a moment and try to remember the last time you had an important argument or a dispute with someone. What was the subject, topic or event that you were arguing over? On the left side of a piece of paper, list in point form some of the things you said. On the right side of the page, list what the other person said. Try to extract from the list the major assumptions and conclusions expressed by each of you. Knowing what you now know about reasoning, try to reconstruct the *content* of your debate into *formal* arguments containing premises and conclusions. Were all the arguments expressed reflective of valid syllogisms or other acceptable forms of inductive and deductive logic? Were some of the arguments invalid and unacceptable? Illustrate and explain.

entire post-secondary student population of North America, taken as a whole. The views of students at Catholic colleges might not represent those of the majority attending secular institutions. In addition to being large, then, samples must also be **fair**. All members within a class (in this case, post-secondary students in North America) must have an equal chance of being selected for survey or study. Otherwise, inductive generalizations are likely to be **skewed**. Arguments by inductive generalization based on biased or skewed samples are less acceptable than those based on fair and large ones that are more representative of the group under discussion.

Refer to Table 11.2 for a comparison between inductive and deductive logical thinking.

Table 11.2   COMPARING INDUCTIVE AND DEDUCTIVE ARGUMENTS

EXAMPLE OF DEDUCTIVE ARGUMENT	EXAMPLE OF INDUCTIVE ARGUMENT
All birds have wings. Every swan is a bird.	Every swan that has ever been observed has wings.
Therefore, every swan has wings.	Therefore, every swan has wings.
If the form of the argument is valid and the premises are true, then the conclusion must be true also.	If the premises are true, then the conclusion is likely, though not necessarily, true.
Deductive arguments are either valid or invalid.	Inductive arguments are better or worse.

HOW TO EVALUATE ARGUMENTS

Before we move on to Part Three, "Applying Ethics in the Real World," let us consider some of the ways and means of determining whether the arguments we will soon face on various topics are good ones. To some extent, we have done this already. For example, in our coverage of inductive logic, we learned how generalizations must be based on fair and representative samples. Regarding inductive arguments by analogy, we should keep in mind that the strength of relationship should be examined as well as the nature and number of characteristics that relate one case with another. As for deductive logic, our treatment of it revealed that in *Modus Ponens* arguments it is wrong to affirm the consequent, while denying the antecedent is unacceptable in Modus Tollens reasoning. We found as well that it is incorrect to affirm the inclusive disjunct in a disjunctive syllogism wherein the antecedent and consequent can both be true. About hypothetical syllogisms, we learned to keep our p's and q's in order.

> *Men stumble over the truth from time to time, but most pick themselves up and hurry off as if nothing happened.*
> WINSTON CHURCHILL

From our initial studies in logic, we have also come to appreciate the special importance of practical syllogisms to ethical inquiry and debate. Practical syllogisms are based on value premises that lead to particular normative or ethical conclusions. Shortly, we will look at how to analyze and break down each part of the practical syllogism for purposes of critical evaluation. After that, we will look at some "sleazy" reasoning techniques, known as "informal logical fallacies," that irrational thinkers often use in their efforts to win debates and persuade people to accept their points of view, whether they are justified or not. Before examining the "sleaze" and analyzing the practical syllogism for evaluative purposes, let us first clarify some important terminology to prevent confusion later on.

VALIDITY, TRUTH AND SOUNDNESS

In everyday conversations you often hear people say things like "That's a valid point," or "That's a valid statement," or perhaps "Your criticism is valid." In strict logical terms, however, "points," "statements," and "criticisms" are not valid; arguments are. Factual statements may be true or false or more or less likely; criticisms may be justified or unjustified, and good points may be based on accurate observations. But when it comes to logic, **validity** refers to the form of the argument within which a particular point or statement becomes a relevant part.

Validity should be clearly distinguished from another logical notion, namely, **soundness**. The concept of soundness also refers to arguments, but not narrowly and exclusively to their logical form. A sound argument is one that is valid in form, contains true (or acceptable) premises, and leads to a necessary conclusion. An **unsound** argument, by contrast, can be valid in form, but, because its premises are untrue or unacceptable, the conclusion is false or one that must be rejected. In formal argument, then, **truth** refers to the **veracity** of the individual statements contained within the syllogism itself; validity refers to an argument's form or structure, and soundness involves a combination of truth and formal validity. Having said this, remember that necessary conclusions are found only in deductive logic, not in inductive logic. Thus, soundness is a concept appropriately applied to the former and not the latter type of reasoning. Inductive logic is better or worse by degree.

It is interesting and, perhaps, ironic to note that valid arguments may sometimes have to be rejected on rational grounds. To appreciate why, look at this example:

Major Premise: All birds (A) are black (B).	All A is B
Minor Premise: Prince Philip (C) is a bird (A).	C is A
Conclusion: Prince Philip (C) is black (B).	C is B

What you have here is a valid syllogism of class membership. The logical form of the argument is found to the right. What is obvious about this valid syllogism is that the conclusion is obviously false. Prince Philip is not black. You should note as well that the minor premise makes a factual claim that is likewise false: Prince Philip is not a bird. Even further, we could dispute the major premise in this argument, because we know that some birds are blue and others are red, so even if Prince Philip were a bird, the conclusion would still not be necessarily true. He could be a cardinal or a blue jay. This example serves to underscore the point that when valid arguments containing unacceptable premises lead to false conclusions, then those arguments are unsound and must be rejected. By contrast, when arguments are valid in form, and when they possess true premises that lead to necessary conclusions, they are sound and certainly more acceptable.

EVALUATING PRACTICAL SYLLOGISMS

Now that we know the differences between sound and merely valid arguments and the role that truthful claims play in their construction, let us see how we should go about evaluating those **practical syllogisms** that support moral value judgments and particular ethical viewpoints. When analyzing an ethical argument for example, in an article or book, the first thing to do is to extract the major claims, premises, and conclusions presented by the author. Next, assemble them into coherent syllogisms in ways that are consistent with, or reflective of, the author's thinking. Avoid misrepresenting or distorting what was intended. Once the practical syllogisms implicitly or explicitly contained in the article or book are extracted, paraphrased and/or reassembled as necessary, the evaluation can begin.

For each syllogism, ask whether the stated conclusion follows from the preceding **premises** (both factual and value). Can we derive the conclusion or infer it from the factual statements and value judgments made before? If not, then there is a flaw in the formal structure of the argument. See the flawed argument below. Notice how the conclusion does not follow.

Value Premise: All that encourages violence (A) is evil (B).	All A is B
Factual Premise: Heavy metal music (C) encourages violence (A).	C is A
Conclusion: My son (D) should not buy Led Zeppelin CDs (E).	D is E

In the practical syllogism above, we see that the conclusion, which, in itself, may or may not be justifiable, does not follow logically from the preceding premises. The conclusion that would make the argument valid is: "Heavy metal music is evil (C is B)." The conclusion, as it is stated above, introduces two new elements (D and E) that give the argument an invalid form. Invalid arguments need not be accepted, regardless of how desirable their conclusions might be.

Once you have examined the conclusion of a syllogism to see whether it follows from preceding premises, the next step is to direct your attention to the **factual premise** contained in the argument. Is the factual claim empirically verifiable? Can it be supported by observation, experiment or common everyday experience? Are there studies or surveys that lend it weight? In short, is the factual premise more or less likely to be true? In our music example, we could look for any psychological and/or sociological studies dealing more generally with the effects of heavy metal music on individual conduct or social behaviour. We could ask whether it is true, in fact, that such music does encourage violence. Are the studies conclusive or inconclusive? Does the weight of the evidence suggest that it does or does not encourage violence? Are there recent studies that contradict earlier ones? Have faulty uses of inductive reasoning (e.g., unfounded generalizations) led to the factual claim embedded in the larger argument? Obviously, when evaluating the truth of factual claims, we enter the realm of possibility and likelihood. We do not always know absolutely whether or not a particular factual claim is necessarily true. As we learned before, inductive logic, often used to support factual claims, can provide only probability, not absolute certainty. We should not be discouraged by this insight, however. It should help us, in fact, to develop an attitude of Socratic humility when it comes to ethical argument. If we are often dealing with probabilities and likelihoods when we defend our moral positions, then it is unwise to be rigid and dogmatic. Our "facts" may be wrong or, at least, questionable. They may be inconclusive or incomplete. Tomorrow's facts might contradict today's. With this in mind, we can more easily suspend judgment and reason with greater caution.

The third step in evaluating practical syllogisms is to appraise the acceptability of the value premises upon which the arguments are based. If the **value premise** from which a moral value **conclusion** is derived is unacceptable, then so too is the argument, regardless of its formal validity. Remember, valid arguments containing untrue or unacceptable premises are unsound. In the next section, we will look at four rational tests that can be used to evaluate the value premises upon which deductive syllogistic arguments are built.

TESTING VALUE PREMISES

ROLE-EXCHANGE TEST One way of determining the acceptability of a value premise is by using the **role-exchange test.**[5] This test requires us to ask ourselves whether we would be willing to exchange places with the person or persons most disadvantaged by the application of a particular moral rule or principle in a given set of circumstances. If we are not prepared to be the ones most disadvantaged by the application of the rule or principle in question, then it is probably unjustified or inadequate in some fashion. Let us suppose that a number of school trustees argued that Vladimir Gorky and Fred Runningbear should not be allowed to enroll at an exclusive private boarding school. Further, let us assume that the only reason given for not enrolling them is that these students are not white, Anglo-Saxon and Protestant (WASP). If such were the case, the argument would go something like this.

Value Premise:	Students who are not WASP should not attend this private school.
Factual Premise:	Vladimir and Fred are not WASP
Conclusion:	Vladimir and Fred should not attend this private school.

Applying the role-exchange test requires us to ask whether we would like to exchange places with Vladimir and Fred and still accept the principle supporting the conclusion. Presumably, none of us would like our options reduced or our freedoms restricted simply because of our racial, ethnic or religious background. The trustees would, no doubt, dislike being discriminated against, just as we would. If the trustees could not accept being treated unfairly—i.e., if they would not want to have the proposed principle applied to them—then the principle acting as the value premise of their argument would fail the role-exchange test. It would have to be rejected on rational ethical grounds.

NEW CASES TEST   If a rule or ethical principle is deemed acceptable and used as a value premise to justify a normative conclusion in one particular set of circumstances, then it should be equally applicable to other similar sets of circumstances. If it is not, then there is likely something wrong with the rule or principle itself. For example, let us conclude that "Maria's actions were wrong" or that "Maria did the wrong thing," and let us also say that we base our moral conclusion on the premise that "People should never lie." To test this principle, let us examine it in the case where it applies to Maria, but also in other **new cases.** What we are asking really is whether or not it is so that "people should never lie."

Case Number One: When asked about its whereabouts, Maria tells her dad that she does not know where his wallet is when, in fact, she has stolen it and used the money inside it to buy an article of clothing. Question: Does the principle about lying hold up in case number one? Well, in this case, Maria is lying only to satisfy her personal wants. She is lying to promote her own selfish interests. Intuitively, most of us, I suspect, would regard Maria's actions as wrong. Lying to get what you want is probably unjustified regardless of who's involved. To the extent this is true, our principle about lying holds up.

Case Number Two: Suppose, however, that we are in Nazi Germany and Maria is hiding political dissidents from Hitler's SS officers. The SS come to her door and ask her questions concerning the whereabouts of those refugees. If she tells the truth, the refugees die. If she lies, then Maria saves their lives. In this second case, many moral thinkers would argue that lying is quite acceptable. Most would probably argue that Maria would do nothing morally wrong if she lied. Yet, if this is true, our principle, "People should never lie," has been weakened by a new case where it does not apply.

Case Number Three: Imagine a Canadian spy has been captured during wartime. The spy is interrogated and asked if she has any information regarding a number of military secrets, which, if made known, would lead to death and destruction. The spy actually does have the information the enemy wants. If she tells the truth, widespread death and destruction will result; if she lies, the lives of many allies will be saved and destruction will be minimized. Again, in this case, most moral thinkers would likely excuse any lies told by our spy. Some might even go further and say that our spy "should" lie or is "obligated" to lie by virtue of her special role, if nothing else. There might even be some people who would describe the spy as a traitor if she did not lie. In other words, lying in this case could arguably be morally required. But, if this is so, then we have another case wherein our principle about lying does not apply. It appears, then, to be debatable that "People should never lie." Perhaps lying is generally wrong except in cases where life and national security are concerned. Thus, the principle might have to be modified to make it more acceptable. The more new cases we find where it does not apply, the weaker the principle becomes. There may be so many exceptions to the rule that the rule, in its current statement, is no longer useful.

CONSISTENCY AND UNIVERSALIZABILITY TEST In order for value premises, stated as ethical principles, to be justifiable, they must be **logically consistent** and **universalizable**. Inconsistent principles are those that are **self-contradictory**. Because they are irrational, they cannot serve as a solid basis for the justification of particular moral conclusions. The following principle is inconsistent: "People should make promises with the intention of breaking them." Some might claim that politicians actually live by this principle in their efforts to get elected! To the extent that they do, they are guilty of an inconsistency. The concept of promise keeping nec-

PHILOSOPHERS AT WORK

Instructions: Evaluate the value premises/principles stated below using any one of the four tests of adequacy, i.e., the role-exchange, new cases, higher-order principle, or consistency and universalizability test.

1. You should lie to others when it is to your advantage.
2. Stealing is always wrong.
3. Your should take shortcuts to school even if this involves trespassing on other people's property.
4. You should never use people solely as a means to get what you want out of life.
5. Visible ethnic and racial minorities should not be allowed into this country.
6. Everyone but me should fill out their income tax forms honestly.

Answer Key

1. unacceptable—fails universalizability test
2. unacceptable—fails new cases test
3. unacceptable—fails role-exchange test and universalizability test
4. acceptable—principle is consistent and universalizable, passes role-exchange test, etc.
5. unacceptable—fails role-exchange test
6. unacceptable—fails consistency and universalizability test

essarily entails the intention of keeping one's word. Making a promise with no intention of keeping it is self-contradictory. Promises intended to be broken are not promises at all, but are deceptions or lies.

As well as failing the **consistency test**, the principle about promise making and breaking fails the closely related **universalizability test**. If everyone made promises with the intention of breaking them, the whole idea of promise making would become self-defeating. Promises would become unbelievable. When applying the universalizability test, we ask, "What if everyone acted according to this principle?" or "Could I will that everyone should live by this principle?" If one cannot will that a particular value premise be acted upon or accepted by all, or if it is inconsistent and self-defeating, the value premise is inadequate and unjustified.

HIGHER-ORDER PRINCIPLE TEST   Another way to test value premises for their acceptability is to apply the **higher-order principle test**. We do this by taking the value premise of one syllogism and trying to find a broader general principle in a higher-order syllogism that can be used to support that value premise. If the starting point of an argument, namely, the value premise, is acceptable, we should be able to derive it from a broader or so-called higher-order principle. See Figure 11.1. Also see Figure 11.2 for an example of a higher-order principle test that has been worked out. The conclusion in this case, i.e., that throwing rocks through windows is wrong, is ultimately justified by the higher-order value premise that "Violating individual rights is wrong."

Figure 11.1 *Higher-Order Principle Test*

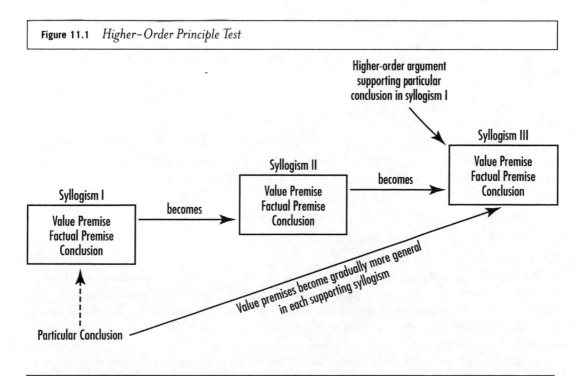

Source: Falikowski, *Mastering Human Relations, p. 127.*

Figure 11.2   *Example using higher-order principle test*

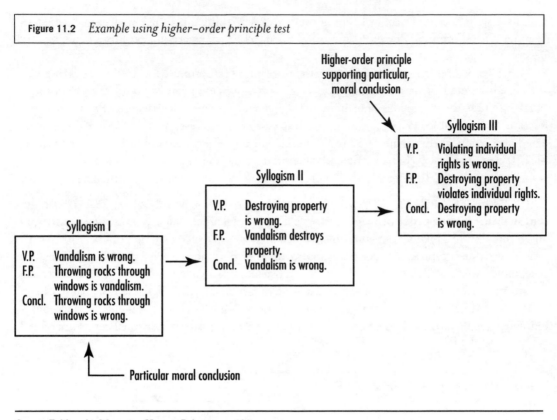

Source: *Falikowski, Mastering Human Relations, p. 128.*

Before we move on to the next section of this chapter, let us review what we have learned so far. First, we have clarified our understanding of logical validity by contrasting it with truth and soundness. Second, we have looked at ways and means of evaluating practical syllogisms. We have learned that bad reasoning results when:

1.   Conclusions do not follow from preceding premises;

2.   Minor/factual premises are false; and

3.   Major/value premises are unacceptable.

Another thing we have learned in this chapter is how to appraise the acceptability of value premises using four logical tests of adequacy. Thus, we now have a number of rational strategies we can use when evaluating arguments. Don't forget, as well, our discussion of relevance, acceptability, and sufficiency in Chapter Ten. Such evaluative criteria are very useful when appraising premises used to support conclusions.

In this last section of Chapter Eleven, we will try to enhance our powers of critical, logical analysis. We will look at some dishonest **rhetorical** devices that are often used to win debates and persuade people. To protect ourselves against the use of such devices, it is important to be able to recognize and label them. The next section is designed to help us do just that.

INFORMAL LOGICAL FALLACIES: IRRATIONAL WAYS TO ARGUE

People who fail to appreciate the benefits of argument often feel threatened when their viewpoints are challenged. If there has been a lot of ego investment in a particular viewpoint or a deep involvement of personal feelings, improper forms of reasoning called **informal logical fallacies** may be used to perform the emotional rescue of the threatened self. Such fallacies are irrational. They are designed to persuade us emotionally and psychologically, not rationally.[6] People who use them try to divert attention from the real issues and arguments under discussion to something more favourable to them. Fallacies can also be used as forms of intimidation. Defensive people worried about being wrong may respond aggressively toward others. Putting someone else on the defensive requires you to be less defensive about yourself. Essentially, fallacies work through diversion and attack. As instruments of persuasion and rhetoric, they are, unfortunately, sometimes very effective. As ways of correct thinking, however, they are always wrong. Logical fallacies are sometimes committed unconsciously and without malicious intent. Some people are simply unaware of their bad reasoning. Regardless of whether the "sleazy logic" is intentional or not, you will need to guard yourself against the following common fallacies in your own logical self-defence.

THE IS–OUGHT FALLACY A problematic form of reasoning often encountered in moral discussions is the **is–ought fallacy**. In this case, one argues that something ought to be so, just because it is so. Something ought to be considered right or good, just because it *is* so considered. Likewise, one *ought* to do certain things just because people actually do those things in real life. Think back to Jeremy Bentham, whom we discussed in Chapter Three. Recall how he appeared to fall prey to the is–ought fallacy himself, arguing that human beings *ought* to pursue pleasure simply because that *is*, in fact, what they seek by nature. He did not believe it was necessary to justify the pursuit of pleasure any further, for as he asserted, "that which is used to prove everything else, cannot itself be proved: a chain of proofs must have their commencement somewhere. To give such a proof is as impossible as it is needless." In making this statement, Bentham went on the offensive by attacking critics of his position for their vagueness and inconsistency. The problem with Bentham's logic reveals itself when we consider something else which we seem to seek by nature, namely power and domination over others. We often act violently against others to get what we want, be it land, riches and so forth. Unless we are prepared to accept violence as a good thing, just because people are in fact naturally predisposed to act this way, then on grounds of consistency we cannot accept the presupposition that pleasure is good simply because that is what people indeed crave.

SPECIAL PLEADING **Special pleading** is another favourite fallacy used in moral discussions and debates. Essentially, it involves using a double standard: one for ourselves, because we are special, and another, stricter, one for everyone else.[7] When guilty of this fallacy, one is partial and inconsistent. For example, during wartime or periods of international conflict, when soldiers

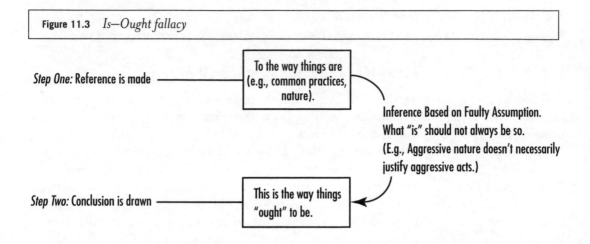

Figure 11.3   *Is—Ought fallacy*

on our side embark on a dangerous suicide mission for the benefit of their cause, they are memorialized as "heroes" who gave their lives for others. When the enemy engages in similar attacks, those conducting the suicide mission may be described as "savage and cowardly fanatics," as they were when the twin towers of the World Trade Center were destroyed on 9/11 by "terrorists" from the Middle East. To illustrate how special pleading can work both ways, I'm sure members of Al-Qaeda saw their compatriots as "glorious martyrs" doing God's will against the "infidel." The fact that non-combatants were killed in the attack makes the suicide bombers murderers in the eyes of many Westerners. When Western bombs kill innocent women and children in the Middle East, by contrast, half-hearted apologies are often given for something called "collateral damage." With special pleading, the language used to morally assess persons and their actions will depend on what side of the fence one is on. In addition to the double standard, special pleading may also be involved when one highlights evidence or facts to support one's own side while ignoring contrary evidence or supporting evidence for the other side. See Figure 11.4 for a graphic depiction of special pleading.

AD HOMINEM FALLACY When you disagree with someone, the proper response is to criticize your opponent's position. If, instead of debating the issues involved, you attack your opponent personally, you then commit the **ad hominem fallacy.** For example, a wasteful person who resents the inconvenience brought about by recycling might refuse to support ideas and arguments presented by Pollution Probe on the grounds that all environmentalists are "1960s losers." Of course, the merits of an argument should not be judged by what generation the person advocating it is from. Recycling is either good or bad, regardless of its advocates' birthdates. To better understand how ad hominem reasoning works, see Figure 11.5.

Despite the illogic it contains, ad hominem reasoning is very common in everyday discussion and debate. It can be emotionally satisfying to belittle or put down people with whom we disagree. We find it unsettling to be forced to concede that an individual we dislike has made a

Figure 11.4 *Special pleading*

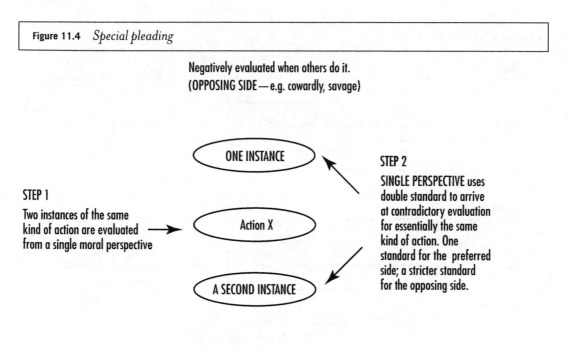

Negatively evaluated when others do it.
(OPPOSING SIDE — e.g. cowardly, savage)

ONE INSTANCE

STEP 2

SINGLE PERSPECTIVE uses
double standard to arrive
at contradictory evaluation
for essentially the same
kind of action. One
standard for the preferred
side; a stricter standard
for the opposing side.

STEP 1

Two instances of the same
kind of action are evaluated
from a single moral perspective

Action X

A SECOND INSTANCE

Positively evaluated when we, or I, do it.
(PREFERRED SIDE — e.g., courageous, noble)

valid point. Also, if we are highly committed to the viewpoint that is being attacked by another, we may erroneously perceive such an attack as a personal assault. In reflex fashion, we may counterattack with an ad hominem verbal barrage against the perceived threat. When we do, we allow irrationality, hostility, and aggression to interfere with productive argument. Our own defensiveness becomes an offensive act targeted at others. An ad hominem attack is occurring whenever people's personalities, characters, ethnic/racial backgrounds, underlying motives or special interests are criticized in response to messages perceived to be threatening. When presenting your own viewpoints, do not allow yourself to be sidetracked into a defence of yourself in response to others' ad hominem attacks on you. Stick to the issues!

STRAW MAN FALLACY When we disagree with others, we do not always like what we hear. In response, we may misrepresent what others have said so we can make their arguments clearly unacceptable. We may then present our arguments against these misrepresentations as a refutation of the original arguments, which we have not in fact addressed. In doing this, we commit the **straw man fallacy**. The process of straw man reasoning is illustrated in Figure 11.6.

A caution might be in order here. Occasionally, it happens that recipients of messages honestly do not understand what was intended by the message, claim, or argument conveyed. They may then respond to what was never said. This kind of honest mistake may reflect a problem of

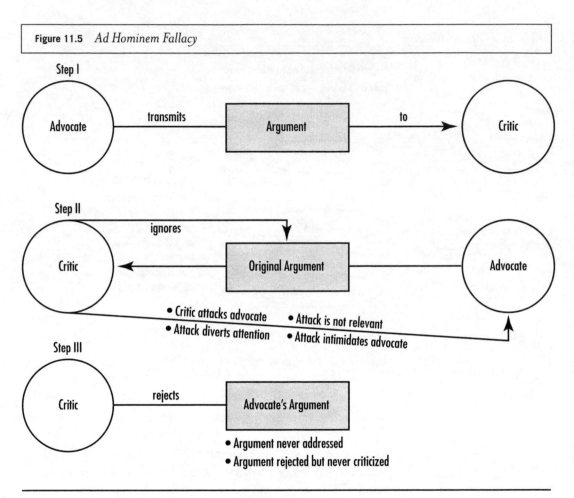

Figure 11.5   *Ad Hominem Fallacy*

Step I

Advocate — transmits — Argument — to → Critic

Step II

Critic — ignores — Original Argument — Advocate

- Critic attacks advocate
- Attack diverts attention
- Attack is not relevant
- Attack intimidates advocate

Step III

Critic — rejects — Advocate's Argument

- Argument never addressed
- Argument rejected but never criticized

Source: Adapted from Falikowski, Mastering Human Relations, p. 131.

listening or comprehension. It is unlike the straw man fallacy, where one person deliberately misrepresents the viewpoints of another. We get into foggy territory when misrepresentations occur unconsciously in psychological efforts to reduce anxiety. Conscious or unconscious, however, straw man fallacies are irrational distortions of the truth.

Suppose that a new governor or provincial premier has just been elected to office. She supports tax increases for middle-income earners. In response, someone says "This doesn't surprise me! She's always been against working people belonging to unions and this is just another measure designed to undermine their interests. If we allow unions to crumble, then democracy in this country will be threatened!" Notice that in the critic's reply, democracy, unions and working people are brought to our attention, not the rationale behind the tax increases. Presumably, it is easier to argue for democracy and union people than it is to argue against unwanted tax increases. By diverting attention to what we do like or want and, from that vantage point, criticizing what we do not want (i.e., increased taxes), the original position supporting tax increases is rejected, though never properly addressed.

Appreciating how annoying it is when others criticize what you never said, be sure to ask questions for clarification before criticizing others' arguments. Your criticisms are valuable only if they relate to what was actually intended and said. Conversely, before allowing others to criticize your arguments and viewpoints, you could ask others to repeat in their own terms what they think you have said and meant. If necessary, clarifications may be made. In the end, this extra step could reduce miscommunication and save time.

CIRCULAR REASONING/BEGGING THE QUESTION   Have you ever been involved in an argument that seemed to go around in circles? If you have, perhaps someone in the argument was using **circular reasoning**, also known as the **fallacy of begging the question.** In circular

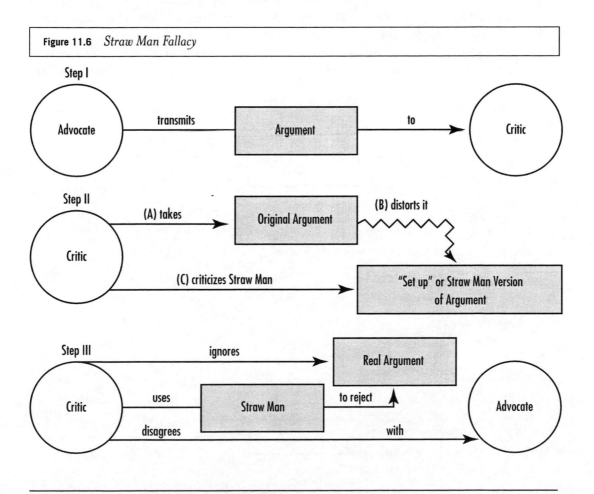

Figure 11.6   *Straw Man Fallacy*

Source: Adapted from Falikowski, Mastering Human Relations, p. 132.

reasoning, people build into the supporting premise of an argument the conclusion they wish to prove. When this is done, there is prejudgment (prejudice) on the issue being debated. The "logical" argument does not take you anywhere except back to what was assumed to be true at the outset. For this reason, begging the question is circular, taking us around and around. What we assume is what we set out to prove, and what we prove is what we originally assumed. Circular reasoning is, perhaps, most evident in religious discussions.

> B.Lever: God exists.
>
> I.M. Agnostic: How do you know God exists?
>
> B. Lever: Because it says so in the Bible.
>
> I.M. Agnostic: How do you know the Bible is telling you the truth?
>
> B. Lever: Because it is the inspired word of God.

In this example, B. Lever uses the Bible to prove the existence of God. The authority of the Bible is based on the premise that God inspired it. It is, therefore, assumed that God actually does exist (the point under debate). But, if B. Lever assumes to be true at the beginning what B. Lever is trying to prove in the end, nothing has, in fact, been proven and we have just

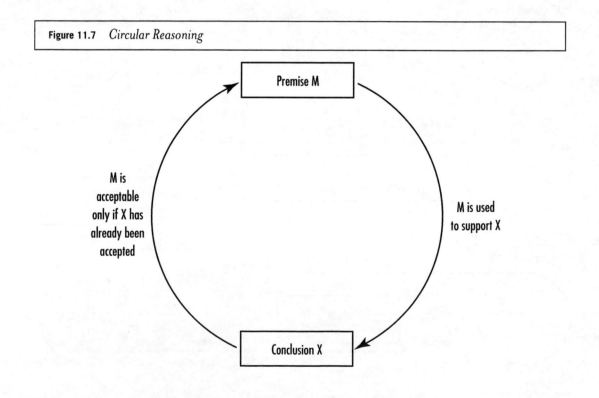

Figure 11.7   *Circular Reasoning*

Premise M

M is acceptable only if X has already been accepted

M is used to support X

Conclusion X

Source: Falikowski, Mastering Human Relations, p. 133.

gone around in a circle. I do not mean to suggest that rational proofs cannot be given for God's existence, only that circular arguments do not work. Look at Figure 11.7 to better appreciate the process of circular reasoning.

TWO WRONGS FALLACY   Committing the **two wrongs fallacy** involves defending a particular wrong-doing by drawing attention to another instance of the same behaviour that apparently went unchallenged and was, therefore, accepted by implication. For instance, I remember that back in my student days there were traditional initiation rituals for University of Toronto "frosh" (first-year students) that required minor acts of vandalism (e.g., painting a certain statue in Queen's Park). Confronted about the justifiability of such acts, a student (guess who?) responded by saying that frosh had been committing these acts for years. Apparently, for this poor misguided soul, the previous years' vandalism served as a justification for his own wrong-doing.

Highway speeders also provide us with an example of two wrongs fallacious reasoning. When stopped for speeding, they often argue with the officers that they were just keeping up with traffic. In other words, they were doing nothing other than breaking the law, just like everybody else. As you may have learned from experience, most police officers will not accept this line of reasoning. The two wrongs fallacy is illustrated in Figure 11.8.

SLIPPERY SLOPE FALLACY   People commit the **slippery slope fallacy** when they object to something because they incorrectly assume that it will necessarily lead to other undesirable

Figure 11.8   *Two Wrongs Fallacy*

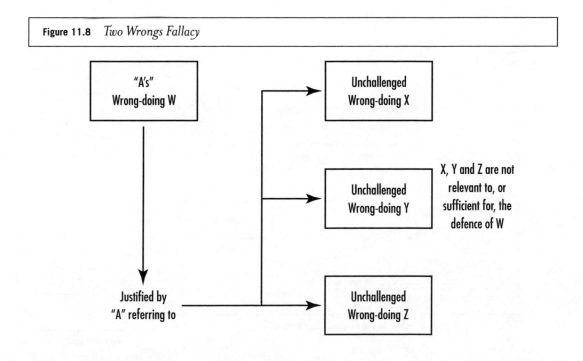

Source: Falikowski, Mastering Human Relations, p. 134.

consequences. For example, you may object to smoking marijuana on the grounds that it will lead to harder drug usage, addiction and, eventually, to a life of crime. Because crime is unwanted, you conclude that smoking marijuana is therefore wrong.

Notice that in this hypothetical example, the major objection is to crime, the presumed result of smoking marijuana. But the connection between crime and marijuana is not inevitable. After experimenting once, a person might choose to avoid marijuana in the future. Or, she might decide to use it only very occasionally in a recreational way. Another individual, after smoking it, might become a crusader leading the way against mood altering drugs. The point is that smoking marijuana is a separate and distinct act from harder drug use, addiction, and crime. Each must be considered independently and evaluated on its own terms. Although it may be true that many criminals and addicts begin their lives of crime by smoking marijuana, not everybody who smokes marijuana becomes a criminal addict. Many law-abiding, non-addicted people have experimented with marijuana; therefore, there is no necessary **causal connection** between marijuana and criminality. This means that there is no cause-and-effect relationship. One thing does not have to lead to the other. If you can find a break in the causal

Figure 11.9 *Slippery Slope Fallacy*

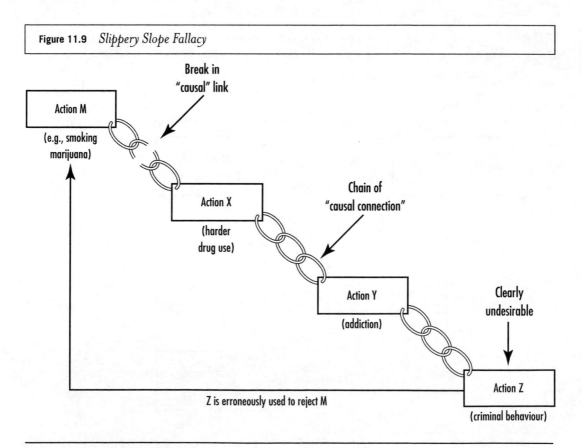

Source: Falikowski, Mastering Human Relations, p. 135.

chain that, according to your opponent, links two unrelated acts, you may have discovered a slippery slope. See Figure 11.9.

FALLACY OF APPEALING TO AUTHORITY When people get into debates and disagreements, they frequently commit the **fallacy of appealing to authority** to justify their positions. See Figure 11.10 for a visual depiction of this fallacy. Some appeals to authority are proper, others are not. Proper appeals can be made to support factual claims within larger arguments. If, in the previous example about marijuana, someone had wanted to condemn its use on medical grounds, then scientific and empirical research data could have been presented to support claims about marijuana's adverse physical effects. As long as the data presented were based on the contributions of recognized medical researchers

> *Man is a credulous animal and tends to believe what he is told. Historically, philosophers… have taken great pains to point out that authority is at least as important a source of error as it is of knowledge.*
>
> JOSEPH BRENNAN

in the field and were accepted after peer review and evaluation, such data could have been justifiably used to support factual claims embedded in the broader argument. Of course, recognized researchers do not always agree amongst themselves—a reason why scientific method cannot yield "absolute" proof. Even when citing scientific data, then, it is important to exercise some caution. To appreciate why, just ask what current scientific studies reveal about the effects of drinking coffee, for example. Some studies suggest caffeine is harmful, others disagree. In such cases, it is prudent to go with the weight of the evidence. Ask, "What do most studies suggest?" or, "Is there overwhelming evidence one way or another?" When the data are highly suggestive one way or another, references to them go beyond personal opinion to a recognized body of knowledge. Authoritative appeals can best be made in the hard sciences. Statements made in these disciplines can be verified in principle and hypotheses can be tested. There are clear public standards to test the validity of claims made.

When questions of value are at issue, it is much more difficult, and usually unjustifiable, to make authoritative appeals. Normative assumptions and principles of conduct (e.g., people should always behave in their own self-interest) cannot be proven true or false by empirical observation or by scientific experiment. Whether or not people actually behave in their own self-interest cannot tell us whether or not they should. Where matters of value are concerned, authoritative appeals cannot be made in rationally acceptable ways. This idea also applies where interpretation and personal preferences play a role or where the boundaries of subject matter are in dispute. Where experts have no empirical means or scientific procedures to settle disputes, authoritative appeals should be avoided. Such disputes must be settled by reason and argument. The next time you get into an argument, you should ask yourself what kind of claim is being made. Is the claim factual in nature? If so, where can you obtain legitimate support? If the claim is normative or value-related, how should you proceed to justify your position or to criticize that of another?

One improper appeal to authority involves the notion of popularity or democracy. In this case, a conclusion is supported by an appeal to numbers—if a majority of people supports something, then that something is necessarily good, right or praiseworthy. Of course, numbers guarantee nothing. Historically speaking, majorities have been proven wrong. The fact that a majority of people in the southern United States once favoured slavery does not justify it. Reference to the will of the majority proves nothing. The moral status of slavery must be considered independently from its support. If 51 percent of the people in Lunenburg, Nova Scotia were in favour of cheating Revenue Canada on their income taxes, this fact alone would not make it right. The next time you think about trying to convince your parents, friends or spouse that you should be allowed to do something "just because everybody else says it's OK," reflect on whether you are committing the fallacy of appealing to authority. Could you give other reasons to support what you want to do?

Appeals to traditional wisdom are also fallacious. This type of fallacy occurs when people try to justify their actions by saying, "This is the way it's always been done," or reject another's actions by saying, "We have never done things that way before." These attempts to justify choices by reference to past conventions (i.e., socially accepted ways of doing things) do not necessarily justify those choices at all. For instance, suppose someone said, "We should never have allowed a woman like Kim Campbell, to become prime minister of Canada, because we have never had a woman occupy that office before." Obviously, a history of gender bias and discrimination cannot serve as a justification for continuing this practice. While tradition often gives us many valuable insights, it also presents its own moral problems. In itself, traditional wisdom is not unconditionally valid. Be careful, though, not to throw the traditional "baby" out with the "bathwater." Tradition does have its legitimate place in human experience.

Figure 11.10 *Fallacy of appealing to authority*

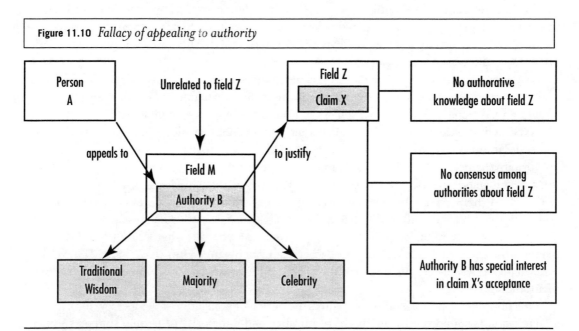

Source: Falikowski, *Mastering Human Relations, p. 138.*

A final criticism of authoritative appeals stems from the fact that authorities often disagree among themselves when matters of value are at issue. If authorities cannot reach a consensus, we cannot rely on authoritative judgments to settle disputes. Maybe you could look for an authority over authorities, but even this would be a problem. Your ultimate authority (e.g., God) may not be accepted by others (e.g., atheists). In a tolerant, democratic, multicultural society, it is usually, if not always, improper to use your chosen authority figure as a reference point for judgment when dealing with others. Commitments to your own beliefs should not violate the rights of others. The rules and regulations of your religious, political or military authorities, for example, may contain little rational moral force when applied to those who have different commitments. To put the danger of authoritative appeals into perspective, suppose someone's supreme authority were Luc Jouret, leader of the Solar Temple cult in Québec. You may recall that his cult took part in a mass murder-suicide in 1994, with incidents in both Canada and Switzerland. Nobody knows all the details of what happened, but let us speculate that Jouret ordered his followers to kill themselves. Would this action, in itself, justify their actions? Rational thinking requires that we say no. In fact, many philosophers (e.g., Immanuel Kant) have argued that suicide is inherently irrational and, therefore, unjustified. Trying to justify murder-suicide by reference to Jouret's authority would thus involve the use of fallacious reasoning.

RED HERRING FALLACY The **red herring fallacy** is another favourite form of illogic used by rationally dishonest or unconsciously irrational individuals. The name of this fallacy comes from the sport of fox hunting. In this sport, hunters on horseback follow a pack of hounds tracking a fox's scent. To save the fox from being caught, dried and salted red herring is drawn across the fox's tracks ahead of the pack. The herring is then pulled in a direction away from the fox. The dogs are diverted by the stronger and fresher scent of the herring. The fox is left alone.

In the red herring fallacy, a controversial claim or position is defended by taking the offensive. This tactic involves setting up a new issue that has only a weak or tenuous connection with the original one. Because this original position is weak, the defender proceeds to argue for the new issue or position, which is more supportable. In other words, attention is deflected from the original position to a new one, which is probably less open to question and debate. Below is an example of red herring reasoning. Notice what the patriotic bartender does when he perceives his country is under attack. He diverts attention from the Canadian's allegations of crime, violence, discrimination, and influence peddling to space technology, universities, and military power. Pushing these points is an easier way to support his claim that "America is the greatest" than addressing the Canadian's critical comments, which make such a claim highly questionable.

> Detroit Bartender: The United States is the best country in the world.
>
> Canadian Tourist: You must be kidding. The United States is falling apart at the seams. Thousands of murders are committed every year. Women and minorities are discriminated against. Lobby groups have too much power in Washington. On top of this, fear of being victimized in street crimes keeps people from going outdoors in the evening. Face it, your nation is in decline.

Detroit Bartender: What are you talking about? We are the greatest military power in the world. We have the best universities and the most advanced space technology. America is the greatest.

The red herring is illustrated in Figure 11.11.

FALLACY OF GUILT BY ASSOCIATION This form of illogic is generally used in adversarial situations in an attempt to discredit an opponent or that opponent's arguments. It draws attention to the opponent's alleged association with some group or individual that has already been discredited. The attempt to discredit is not direct, as in typical ad hominem arguments, but is indirect. The guilt of the discredited individual or group is transferred to the opponent.

Let us suppose that someone refuses to vote Socialist in the next election. He says his reason is that "the Socialist Party almost sent England and France into bankruptcy." The unspoken claim is that, if elected here, they will bankrupt this country too. Apparently, for this voter, socialist mismanagement across the ocean is enough to convict socialists here of incompetence. They are found guilty prior to doing anything wrong. It is possible, in principle, that a social-

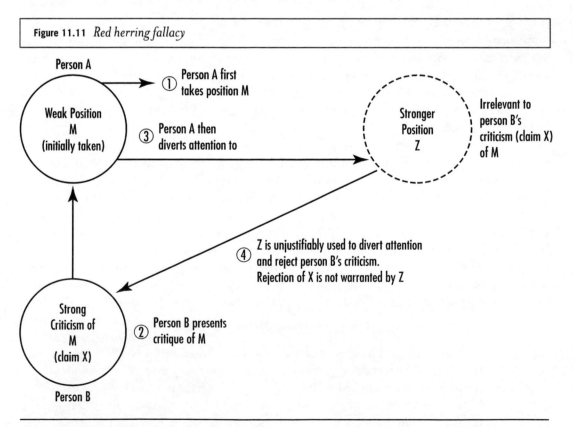

Figure 11.11 *Red herring fallacy*

Person A

Weak Position M (initially taken)

① Person A first takes position M

③ Person A then diverts attention to

Stronger Position Z

Irrelevant to person B's criticism (claim X) of M

④ Z is unjustifiably used to divert attention and reject person B's criticism. Rejection of X is not warranted by Z

Strong Criticism of M (claim X)

② Person B presents critique of M

Person B

Source: Falikowski, Mastering Human Relations, p. 139.

ist government could mismanage a country like Canada—some argue that the Liberal and Conservative Parties have been doing so for years! But, in any case, actions and policies of foreign socialist governments alone cannot serve as an adequate basis of judgment on domestic socialism. Our socialism may be different in significant ways. Our socialists may have learned from the mistakes of their European counterparts. Perhaps contemporary North American socialism has evolved into something more akin to capitalism. There may be almost no political communication between the two socialist groups named. Who knows? Simply put, you cannot pin incompetence on Canadian socialists because of what foreign socialists have done. To do so is to commit the **fallacy of guilt by association**. Nonetheless, this diversionary tactic may be used to create fear in the minds of unreflective voters, and it may work as a means of persuasion. Creating fear is not very rational, but against people lacking the skills of logical self-defence, it often works. This fallacy is illustrated in Figure 11.12.

Finally, to conclude our discussion of logic and reasoning, I invite you to review "Some Do's and Don'ts for Argument's Sake." I also invite you to do the reasoning self-diagnostic at the start of Part Two again. See if your scores have improved as a result of your logical studies.

Figure 11.12 *Fallacy of guilt by association*

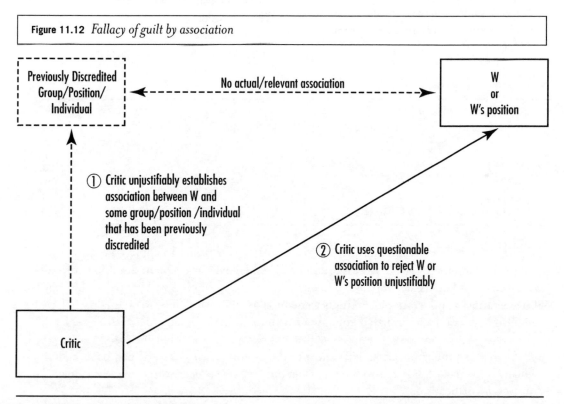

Source: Falikowski, Mastering Human Relations, p. 140.

Table 11.3   SOME DO'S AND DON'TS FOR ARGUMENT'S SAKE

DO	DON'T
Adopt the proper attitude (i.e., Socratic humility)	Attack or intimidate
Remain rational and emotionally detached	Divert attention from the real issues
Stay objective	Base arguments on emotional or psychological appeals
Listen to opposing viewpoints with openness	Build false or questionable claims into your argument
Analyze conflicting positions fairly and impartially	Use invalid logic
Appraise factual claims	Use unjustifiable premises
Evaluate major premises and assumptions	Make questionable assumptions
Examine the logical thinking behind particular conclusions	Confuse valid logic with truth
Look for fallacious reasoning	Take disagreements personally
Appeal to higher-order values to justify your viewpoints	Appeal to authorities unjustifiably
Distinguish between opinions and arguments	Attribute to others what they didn't say
Stick to the issues	Make illegitimate associations
Use proper processes of deductive and inductive logic	Contradict yourself
Base your positions on sound arguments	Change the subject when challenged
Avoid diversion and intimidation by fallacious reasoning	Be inconsistent
	Use faulty causal reasoning
	Justify one wrong-doing with another

Source: Adapted from Falikowski, *Mastering Human Relations*, p. 141.

PHILOSOPHERS AT WORK

Identify the Fallacy: This exercise will give you an opportunity to apply your knowledge and understanding of fallacious reasoning. Practise here will help you to develop your skills of logical self-defence. Being able to identify fallacious reasoning will protect you against illogical attacks and irrational attempts to manipulate your thinking. Recognizing fallacies will also help you to minimize them in your own reasoned arguments.

Instructions: Below are some examples of fallacious reasoning. Identify which fallacies are present by placing the appropriate letter next to the example. This exercise can be done individually or in groups. For classroom discussion purposes, be prepared to provide explanations for each identification.

a. ad hominem fallacy
b. straw man fallacy
c. circular reasoning/fallacy of begging the question
d. fallacy of two wrongs
e. slippery slope fallacy
f. fallacy of appealing to authority
g. red herring fallacy
h. fallacy of guilt by association

_____ 1. You should not accept the premier's arguments in favour of Sunday shopping. After all, he is a godless communist!

_____ 2. I cannot believe you are in favour of having premarital sex. It is obviously wrong. The Pope says so.

_____ 3. Two students were having a disagreement about cars. Curtis said, "I can prove to you that a VW Jetta is faster than a Toyota Camry. John owns a VW Jetta and he told me that he has beaten every Camry he has ever raced on the highway." Michael asked, "How do you know John is telling the truth?" Curtis replied, "Someone who drives the fastest car wouldn't have to lie."

_____ 4. We cannot allow hashish to be legalized. If we did, then sooner or later everyone would become addicted to harder drugs and after that the crime rate would surely rise.

_____ 5. It is perfectly acceptable to go through stop signs on quiet streets; everybody in town does it.

_____ 6. The consultant recommended that the company switch to voice mail as a way of receiving and sending internal messages. She claims that this change will make our operation more efficient. I cannot believe this woman. She thinks every problem in the world has an electronic solution. Computers and telephones cannot improve the economy or morale at work. I think we should reject her recommendation.

_____ 7. You do not seriously believe what Andre Cousineau says about promoting national unity. Remember, he is from Québec and is related to the leader of the Parti Québécois. That party wants Québec to separate from the rest of Canada. We should reject anything he suggests.

_____ 8. What do you mean I am not making sense? Did you hear your own nonsense yesterday when you said that you had an encounter with an alien? I think your credibility needs to be reexamined.

Answer Key

1. a; 2. f; 3. c; 4. e; 5. d; 6. b; 7. h; 8. g

MINDWORK MEDITATION

Think about the last time you "smelled a rat" in someone's argument. You sensed something was wrong, but just could not put your finger on it. Now that you know more about valid logic and fallacious reasoning, think back to that argument. What was the argument about? What claims or assumptions were included in it? Was the logic valid? Were the claims supported or verified? Would the value premises involved pass the tests of adequacy? Was the other party guilty of any logical fallacies? Take some time now to rationally reflect. Jot down your reflections in your philosophical journal.

KEY TERMS

argument

deductive argument

deductive logic

form

content

logical form

Modus Ponens

valid reasoning

affirm the antecedent

antecedent

consequent

Modus Tollens

denying the consequent

denying the antecedent

syllogism

hypothetical syllogisms

disjunctive syllogism

affirming the inclusive disjunct

validity

soundness

unsound

veracity

truth

practical syllogisms

factual premise

syllogisms of class membership

practical syllogism

major premise

value judgment

value premise

minor premise

factual premise

conclusion

adequacy

inductive logic

argument from past experience

probable conclusions

argument by analogy

argument by inductive generalization

large samples

representative

fair

skewed

consistency test

universalizability test

higher-order principle test

logical fallacies

ad hominem fallacy

straw man fallacy

circular reasoning

value premise

conclusion

role-exchange test

new cases test

logically consistent

universalizable

self-contradictory

fallacy of begging the question

two wrongs fallacy

slippery slope fallacy

causal connection

fallacy of appealing to authority

red herring fallacy

fallacy of guilt by association

PROGRESS CHECK 11.1

Instructions: Fill in the blanks with the appropriate responses listed below.

Modus Ponens

denies

judgment

inductive generalization

worse

inconsistent

disjunct

practical syllogisms

analogical

role-exchange test

circular reasoning

straw man

logical fallacies

universalizability

ad hominem

value premise

invalid

value

interpersonal

consequent

probable

hypothetical

factual premise

form

sound

new cases test

red herring

slippery slope

practical syllogisms

two wrongs fallacy

appealing to authority

affirms

1. In philosophy, an argument is not a(n) _____ event or "fight" between individuals.

2. Ethical arguments have both _____ and content. They deal with a subject matter and display some sort of structure explicitly or implicitly.

3. If p, then q
   p
   So, q
   The logical structure above is termed _____.

4. In *Modus Tollens* reasoning, an inference results from denying the _____.

5. In *Modus Ponens* reasoning, an invalid argument results when one _____ the consequent.

6. In an invalid form of *Modus Tollens* reasoning, one _____ the antecedent.

7. If a false conclusion results from two preceding premises that are true, then the argument is _____.

8. If p, then q
   If q, then r
   Therefore, if p then r
   This is a(n) _____ syllogism.

9. Affirming the inclusive _____ is an invalid form of the disjunctive syllogism.

10. The major premise of a practical syllogism is called the _____ premise.

11. The conclusion of a practical syllogism is a value _____.

12. Inductive reasoning can lead only to _____ conclusions.

13. When we make a(n) _____, we make a statement about all, some or none of a class based on our empirical examination of only a part of that class.

14. Inductive logic is not valid or invalid, but rather is better or _____.

15. A(n) _____ argument proceeds from the similarities of two or more things in certain respects to their similarity in some additional respect.

16. _____ are comprised of a value premise, factual premise, and a conclusion.

17. _____ involve irrational thought processes intended to persuade, intimidate, and divert attention.

18. A valid argument with true premises and a necessary conclusion can be described as _____.

19. If the _____ of a valid practical syllogism is unacceptable, the conclusion that follows from it must be rejected.

20. When applying the _____ to a particular principle, one takes the position of the person or persons most disadvantaged by the application of the principle to see if it would be acceptable from that perspective.

21. A principle that is self-contradictory is _____ and unacceptable.

22. According to the _____ criterion, a principle must apply to everyone absolutely if it is to be considered moral.

23. According to the _____, if a principle is ethically acceptable in one set of circumstances, then it must be found to be acceptable in other similar sorts of circumstances.

24. If, during a debate, you attack your opponent and not your opponent's argument, then you commit the _____ fallacy.

25. If you assume at the outset of your argument that which you are trying to prove in the end, then you commit the fallacy of _____.

26. Justifying one wrong-doing by another wrong-doing is the definition of the _____ fallacy.

27. Justifying an ethical position by using majority opinion reflects the fallacy of _____.

28. If, instead of criticizing someone's actual argument, you attack a set-up version of it before rejecting your opponent's position, you commit the _____ fallacy.

29. If, when you are caught up in your own bad argument, you change it subtly and then try to advance your original position by defending a variation of it, you commit the _____ fallacy.

30. If one condemns an action by arguing that it will eventually lead to a series of other unwanted outcomes, which, in fact, is not necessarily the case, one commits the _____ fallacy.

SUMMARY OF MAJOR POINTS

1. **What is an argument?**

   It is a series of related statements leading to a conclusion.
   It is not an interpersonal event or a confrontation of egos.
   Arguments can be deductive or inductive.

2. **What are some of the general characteristics of deductive arguments?**

   They come in various forms (e.g., *Modus Ponens*, practical syllogisms).
   They lead to necessary conclusions which are derived from preceding premises.
   They are either valid or invalid.

3. **What is the form–content distinction about in logic?**

   Underlying the content of any deductive argument is some kind of formal structure which is either valid or invalid.
   Unrelated arguments from different fields can possess the same logical form.

4. **What are some forms of deductive argument?**

   Some forms are *Modus Ponens*, *Modus Tollens*, hypothetical syllogisms, disjunctive syllogisms, syllogisms of class membership and practical syllogisms.

5. **What is inductive logic?**

   It is a process of reasoning leading to probable, not necessary, conclusions.
   Inductive logic is better or worse, not valid or invalid.

6. **What are some forms of inductive logic?**

   Some forms are argument from experience, argument by analogy and argument by inductive generalization.

7. **How are validity, truth, and soundness different?**

   Validity refers to the form of an argument.
   Truth refers to factual premises and conclusions.
   Soundness refers to valid arguments having true premises leading to necessary and acceptable conclusions.

8. **Must valid arguments be accepted?**

   If a valid argument contains faulty premises, then it does not have to be accepted.
   If a valid argument contains acceptable premises and if the conclusion follows necessarily, then it is sound and therefore acceptable.

9. **At what three levels can a practical syllogism be evaluated?**

   (1) The level of conclusion: Does it follow from preceding premises? Is it true or highly probable? Is it justifiable?

    (2) The level of factual premise:

        Is it true or highly probable?

        Does it have empirical support?

    (3) The level of value premise:

        Does the value premise pass the four tests of adequacy?

10. **What tests can be used to evaluate value premises?**

the role-exchange test;

the new cases test;

the consistency and universalizability test; and

the higher-order principle test.

11. **What is a logical fallacy?**

A logical fallacy is a rhetorical device;

an irrational form of reasoning designed to persuade emotionally and
psychologically, not rationally;

used to divert attention and sometimes intimidate others; and

used to win arguments.

12. **What are some examples of logical fallacies?**

Examples are: ad hominem, straw man, circular reasoning/begging the question, two wrongs,
slippery slope, appealing to authority, red herring and guilt by association.

SOURCE REFERENCES AND RELATED READINGS

Barry, Vincent. *Philosophy: A Text with Readings*, 2nd edition. Belmont, Cal.: Wadsworth
Publishing Co., 1983.

Cohen, Elliot D. *Making Value Judgements: Principles of Sound Reasoning*. Malabar, Fla.: Krieger
Publishing Co. Inc., 1985.

Coombs, Jerrold, Leroi Daniels and Ian Wright. "Introduction to Value Reasoning" in *Prejudice:
Teacher's Manual*. Value Reasoning Series. Toronto: The Ontario Institute for Studies in
Education, 1978.

Falikowski, Anthony. *Mastering Human Relations*, Scarborough, Ont.: Prentice Hall Canada,
1996.

_____. *Moral Philosophy: Theories, Skills and Applications*. Upper Saddle River, N.J.: Prentice
Hall, 1990.

Johnson, R.H., and J.A. Blair. *Logical Self-Defense*, 2nd edition, New York: Holt, Rinehart &
Winston, 1981.

Runkle, Gerald. *Good Thinking: An Introduction to Logic*, 2nd edition. New York: Holt, Rinehart
and Winston, 1981.

Russow, Lilly-Marlene and Martin Curd. *Principles of Reasoning*. New York: St. Martin's Press,
1989.

Stewart, David and H. Gene Blocker. *Fundamentals of Philosophy*, 2nd edition. New York:
MacMillan Publishing Co., 1987.

Woodhouse, Mark B. *A Preface to Philosophy*, 5th edition. Belmont: Wadsworth Publishing Co., 1994.

ENDNOTES

1. David Steward and Gene Blocker, *Fundamentals of Philosophy*, 2nd edition. New York: MacMillan Publishing Co., 1987, p. 61.
2. Mark Woodhouse, *A Preface to Philosophy*, 5th edition. Belmont: Wadsworth Publishing Co., 1994, p. 63.
3. Vincent Barry, *Philosophy: A Text with Readings*, 2nd edition. Belmont: Wadsworth Publishing Co., 1983, p. 334.
4. Woodhouse, ibid., p. 61.
5. Jerrold Coombs, Leroi Daniels, and Ian Wright, "Introduction to Value Reasoning," in *Prejudice: Teacher's Manual*, Value Reasoning Series. Toronto: The Ontario Institute for Studies in Education, 1978.
6. R.H. Johnson and J.A. Blair, *Logical Self-Defense*, 2nd edition. Toronto: McGraw-Hill Ryerson, 1983, p. 71.
7. Morris Engel, *With Good Reason*. Sixth edition. Boston: Bedford/St. Martin's Press, 2000, p. 171.

III Moral Issues in Modern Life

So far, on our travels into the moral domain, we have acquired a basic knowledge and understanding of six major ethical perspectives that have dominated Western rational thought (i.e., Greek character-ethics, utilitarianism, deontology, ethical egoism, existentialist ethics and care-based ethics). Also, we have learned to navigate our way through the dense fog of moral ambiguity by mastering some fundamental logical–analytical reasoning skills. With knowledge and skills at our disposal, we are now better prepared to put ethics into action, theory into practice and logic into the service of philosophical critique and practical moral decision making. Although our journey has been a long and difficult one thus far, we are finally ready to apply ethics in the real world in a rational and informed way. In the following pages, we will look at a number of real-life problems and controversies arising out of the fields of business ethics, health-care ethics, professional ethics, sexual ethics, legal/political ethics and global/environmental ethics.

Argument Analysis Worksheet: A generic "Argument Analysis Worksheet" has been provided to facilitate thoughtful study and analysis of the arguments found in each of the readings. This analytical tool serves to fully integrate theories, skills and applications. For practical purposes, you may wish to make enough copies of this worksheet for the actual number of readings you plan to cover in your course. (See Appendix Four.)

The Argument Analysis Worksheet can be used for writing critical papers or as a basis of classroom and tutorial discussion. Completion of the worksheet offers a structured and detailed format for analyzing ethical issues and moral arguments. The worksheet also helps to enhance understanding and appreciation of any author's position or thesis defence.

Instructors and students are at liberty, of course, to bypass the Argument Analysis Worksheet so discussions may be more spontaneous and open-ended. Informal discussions may be preferred. The worksheet simply provides one structured alternative you might find useful.

12

Business Ethics

Paternalism in the Marketplace: Should a Salesman Be His Buyer's Keeper?

JAMES M. EBEJER AND
MICHAEL J. MORDEN

"Paternalism in the Marketplace: Should a Salesman Be His Buyer's Keeper?" Journal of Business Ethics 7 (1988), pp. 337–39. Reprinted with kind permission of Kluwer Academic Publishers.

The moral relationship between salespersons and their customers can range from *caveat emptor* exclusively to paternalism. We propose that between these extremes is a realistic professional ethic for sales that we will refer to as "limited paternalism."

At one extreme is *caveat emptor*— "let the buyer beware." We do not claim there is anything inherently immoral about such a position, only that it is no longer appropriate in our society. Games can be played by various rules, as long as all participants know those rules. When two old horse-traders tried to strike a bargain, it was understood that the seller could be assumed to misrepresent the condition of the animal and the buyer was warned to be on his guard. Perhaps this situation was not unfair since both participants knew the rules, entered into the agreement voluntarily, and had the opportunity to examine the merchandise. However, the contemporary consumer frequently purchases goods or services which he cannot be expected to judge for himself. The workings of an insurance policy are as mysterious to us as those of a VCR. A salesperson, with her superior understanding, is in such a position to exploit our ignorance, that few of us would want to play the game if the rule of the market-place were understood to be strictly "let the buyer beware."

At the other extreme is the practice of paternalism. A standard definition of paternalism is "the interference with a person's liberty of action justified by reasons referring exclusively to the welfare, good, happiness, needs, interests, or values of the person being coerced" (Dworkin, 1971). In other words, paternalism occurs when an individual, presumably in a position of superior knowledge, makes a decision for another person to protect this other from some type of harm. Paternalism implies that the first person deprives the second of liberty of autonomy. This infraction on liberty is thought justified because, in the mind of the first person, it is "for his own good." Recently, a merchant refused to sell tropical fish to a patron because she felt he was not changing the water in his tank often enough. Although the merchant was infringing on the customer's liberty based on her superior knowledge, the interference was for his own good (and presumably the good of the fish). The merchant was being paternalistic.

Most of us expect paternalism in certain situations. If the service we are purchasing is an appendectomy, we typically allow the salesman (in this case the surgeon) a major role in deciding whether we need the service. We rely on the ethics of the profession to protect us from the possible exploitation. The old-fashioned physician considered such paternalism part of his role, but modern medicine emphasizes the patient's informed consent. The professionals use their superior knowledge to make the medical diagnosis, but they are expected to explain treatment options available to the patient so the latter can make the moral decision. Thus even in the most paternalistic of contexts we find that professionalism justifies only a limited paternalism.

This limited paternalism, which is typically an element in professionalism, applies when an individual in a position of superior knowledge has an active duty to explain the consequences of a decision. Here, the "father-like" individual does not make the decision for the other. The only liberty that is violated is the freedom to be ignorant: the consumer is protected from an uninformed decision that could be detrimental to him.

To claim that a salesperson is professionally required to inform customers fully about a product or service, to disclose fully all relevant information without hiding crucial stipulations in small print, to ascertain that they are aware of their needs and the degree to which the product or service will satisfy them, is to impose upon the salesperson the positive duty of limited paternalism. According to this standard a salesperson is, to a limited degree, "his buyer's keeper."

Consider the following example: A woman takes her car to an auto repair shop and tells the mechanic she needs a new muffler and exhaust pipes because her car makes too much noise. While examining the car, the mechanic concludes that the excessive noise occurs because there is a hole in the tail pipe. The mechanic was told to replace the exhaust pipes and the muffler. He has three options: (1) replace the exhaust pipes and the muffler as requested by the car's owner and collect (say) $90.00; (2) talk to the owner, refuse to do as requested since all that is needed is a $20.00 tail pipe; (3) talk to the owner, explain the situation, and let her decide for herself if she really wants to spend $70.00 more than is necessary to fix the car.

When confronted with this situation, many repairmen or auto parts salespersons would choose the first option: collect as much money as possible. This is perfectly legal since the car's owner did authorize complete replacement. Some perhaps would act paternalistically by following the second option: replace the tail pipe for $20.00, but refuse to replace the longer exhaust pipe and the muffler because it is not necessary. But now he has infringed on the owner's right to decide for herself. Perhaps the owner wanted to be absolutely certain that her exhaust system was perfect and would not need work again soon. Maybe she is rich and does not mind spending the extra money. In any case, it is her car, her money, and her decision. Option number three is the best ethical choice and the standard required for professional responsibility: the mechanic has a duty to inform the owner of facts of which she might not be aware since she is not the expert. The choice should be left to the owner.

But consider a different situation: a customer in a store that specializes in stereo equipment is consulting a salesperson about the specifications, quality and prices of various amplifiers. The salesperson is considered an expert on all equipment available for sale in the show room. After some deliberation, the customer tentatively decides he would like to own a Super Max amplifier. But before making the purchase, he asks the salesperson one more question: "Is there anything else I should know about this particular model before giving you the cash?" Now, to the best of her knowledge, the salesperson has accurately communicated the advantages of the amplifier, told him the price—$400, and that this particular unit does meet his needs. However, she also knows that the same model is being sold at an appliance store across the street for only $350! Does our standard require that she tell the buyer about this possible savings? Clearly not. Although the person was aware of the competitor's price, she did not withhold information that only an expert would know. Anyone could easily find out how much the amplifier sold for at the other stores. The knowledge was not part of the technical expertise that marks her as a professional and which the buyer was presumably relying upon. However, if she held back information, relevant to the decision, which a non-expert could not be expected to know, then her behavior would be unethical by our standard.

Nearly all "hard sell" techniques are unethical according to this standard. Many salespersons intentionally keep information from potential buyers. They try to sell the most expensive product a customer will buy without regard to the needs of that person. Granted, some revenue may be lost in the short term from telling customers the bad as well as the good about a product or service, but profits will increase in the long run. Once a salesperson earns a reputation for being "honest"—i.e., ethical, interested in mutual exchange to mutual advantage rather than exploitation—he will have more satisfied customers, more referrals, and, eventually, greater income from an overall increase in sales. Even where the policy might not profit the salesperson in a specific case, it is a rule which if generally followed would produce the greatest good for the greatest number. Furthermore, it treats the customer the way we ourselves would want to be treated; it is a rule we would agree to even if we didn't know whether we were going to be the salesperson or the customer; finally, it bases sales ethics on widely accepted standards of professionalism. Clearly it is consistent with our ordinary ethical assumptions.

REFERENCE

Gerald Dworkin: 1971, "Paternalism," in *Morality and Law*, ed. Richard Wasserstrom (Belmont, CA: Wadsworth), p. 108.

Bribery

MICHAEL PHILIPS

From Ethics *94 (July 1984) 621–636. Reprinted with permission from the University of Chicago Press and the Author.*

Although disclosures of bribery have elicited considerable public indignation over the last decade, popular discussions of the morality of bribery have tended largely to be unilluminating. One reason for this is that little care has been taken to distinguish bribes from an assortment of related practices with which they are easily confused. Before we can be in a position to determine what to do about the problem of bribery, we need to be clearer about what count and ought to count as bribes. Unfortunately, there is as yet very little philosophical literature on this topic.[1] In this essay I shall remedy this defect by presenting an account of the concept of bribery and by employing that account to clarify matters in three areas in which there is public controversy and confusion.

At least some confusion in discussions of bribery arises from a failure adequately to appreciate the distinction between bribery and extortion. This is true, for example, of accounts of the notorious case of Lockheed in Japan. I shall attempt to show that the morality of this and similar transactions is better assessed if we are clear on that distinction.

A second problem area arises out of the fact of cultural variability. As is generally recognized, the conduct of business, government, and the professions differs from culture to culture. In some places transactions that many Americans would consider bribes are not only expected behavior but accepted practice as well. That is, they are condoned by the system of rule governing the conduct of the relevant parties. Are they bribes? Are only some of them bribes? If so, which?

A third problem arises out of the general difficulty of distinguishing between bribes, on the one hand, and gifts and rewards, on the other. Suppose that a manufacturer of dresses keeps a buyer for a catalog company happy by supplying him with any tickets to expensive shows and athletic events that he requests. Are these bribes? Or suppose that a special interest group rewards public administrators who rule in its favor with vacations, automobiles, and jewelry. May we correctly speak of bribery here?

I

To answer such questions we need to say more precisely what bribes are. A bribe is a payment (or promise of payment) for a service. Typically, this payment is made to an official in exchange for her violating some official duty or responsibility. And typically she does this by failing deliberately to make a decision on its merits. This does not necessarily mean that a bribed official will make an improper decision; a judge who is paid to show favoritism may do so and yet, coincidentally, make the correct legal decision (i.e., the bribe offerer may in fact have the law on her side). The violation of duty consists in deciding a case for the wrong sorts of reasons.

Although the most typical and important cases of bribery concern political officials and civil servants, one need not be a political official or a civil servant to be bribed. Indeed, one need not be an official of any sort. Thus, a mortician may be bribed to bury a bodyless casket, and a baseball player may be bribed to strike out each time he bats. Still, baseball players and morticians are members of organizations and have duties and responsibilities by virtue of the positions they occupy in these organizations. It is tempting, then, to define a bribe as a payment made to a member of an organization in exchange for the violation of some positional duty or responsibility. This temptation is strengthened by our recognition that we cannot be bribed to violate a duty we have simply by virtue of being a moral agent. (Hired killers, e.g., are not bribed to violate their

duty not to kill.) And it is further strengthened when we recognize that we may be paid to violate duties we have by virtue of a nonorganizationally based status without being bribed. (I am not bribed if — as a nonhandicapped person — I accept payment to park in a space reserved for the handicapped; nor am I bribed if — as a pet owner — I accept payment illegally to allow my dog to run free on the city streets.)

Still, it is too strong to say that occupying a position in an organization is a necessary condition of being bribed. We may also speak of bribing a boxer to throw a fight or of bribing a runner to lose a race. These cases, however, are importantly like the cases already described. Roughly, both the boxer and the runner are paid to do something they ought not to do given what they are. What they are, in these cases, are participants in certain practices. What they are paid to do is to act in a manner dictated by some person or organization rather than to act according to the understandings constitutive of their practices. Civil servants, business executives, morticians, and baseball players, of course, are also participants in practices. And their responsibilities, as such, are defined by the rules and understandings governing the organizations to which they belong. At this point, then, we are in a position to state a provisional definition of bribery. Thus, P accepts a bribe from R if and only if P agrees for payment to act in a manner dictated by R rather than doing what is required of him as a participant in his practice.[2]

One advantage of this account is that it enables us to deal with certain difficult cases. Suppose that a high-ranking officer at the Pentagon is paid by a Soviet agent to pass on defense secrets. The first few times he does this we would not hesitate to say that he is bribed. But suppose that he is paid a salary to do this and that the arrangement lasts for a number of years. At this point talk of bribery appears less appropriate. But why should something that has the character of a bribe if done once or twice (or, perhaps, on a piecework basis) cease to have that character if done more often (or, perhaps, on a salaried basis)? In my account the explanation is that the frequency or basis of payment may incline us differently to identify the practice in question. Thus, if an American officer works for the Soviet Union long enough, we begin to think of him as a Soviet spy. In any case, to the extent to which we regard his practice as spying we are inclined to think of the payments in question as payments of a salary as opposed to so many bribes. A similar analysis holds in the case of industrial spies, undercover agents recruited from within organizations, and so forth.[3] We do not think of them as bribed because we do not think of them as full-fledged practitioners of the practices in which they appear to engage.

This practice conception is further supported by the fact that a person may satisfy my account of bribery on a long-term and regularized basis and still be said to be a recipient of bribes. This is so where his continued and regularized acceptance of payments does not warrant any change in our understanding of the practices in which he participates. Thus, we do not think of a judge who routinely accepts payments for favors from organized crime as participating in some practice other than judging, even if he sits almost exclusively on such cases. This may be arbitrary: perhaps we ought rather think of him as an agent of a criminal organization (a paid saboteur of the legal system) and treat him accordingly. My point, however, is that because we do not think of him in this way—because we continue to think of him as a judge—we regard each fresh occurrence as an instance of bribery.

The present account, however, is not entirely adequate as it stands. Consider the following counterexamples: (*a*) an artist is offered $5000 by an eccentric to ruin a half-completed canvas by employing an unsuitable color and (*b*) a parent is paid $500 for the use of his eight-year-old son in a pornographic film.

It might be argued in relation to *a* that it is consistent with the practice of being an artist that one accept payment to produce whatever a client is willing to pay for. However, the conception of a practice that underlies this response seems to me questionable. What seems to me counterintuitive about speaking of bribery in *a* is that the act in question is private. By this I mean, roughly,

that it affects no one who is not a party to the transaction. If I pay an artist to ruin a painting that has been commissioned by a museum, the oddity of speaking of bribery disappears. In general, where there is no violation of an organizational duty, we might say that a payment is a bribe only if it affects the interests of persons or organizations who are not parties to the transaction. To forestall counterexamples based on remote or indirect consequences, we must add that the parties affected must be parties whose interests are normally affected by the conduct of the practice in question and that they must be affected in the manner in which they are normally affected.

It is tempting to go further than this and claim that a bribe occurs only when the act agreed to by the bribed party violates the moral rights of some third party or organization. But this seems to me mistaken. We may speak of bribing officers of terribly corrupt institutions (e.g., concentration camps), but it is not at all clear that these officeholders necessarily violate the rights of any person or organization by violating their institutional duties (e.g., by allowing prisoners to escape). Or consider a society in which slaves are used as boxers and masters wager on the bouts. It seems clear that one can bribe a slave to lose a fight here, but it is not at all clear that a slave violates anyone's rights by accepting payment for so doing. (To say this would be to imply that a slave boxer has a *prima facie* duty to try to win his fight, and this seems to me untenable.)

What, then, of the second counterexample? Why are we reluctant to speak of bribery in the case of parents? One way to deal with this case is to attribute this reluctance to an anachronistic linguistic habit developed and sustained by centuries of thinking according to which children are the property of parents. According to this outmoded way of thinking, either there is no such thing as the practice of parenting or that practice far more resembles an account that Thrasymachus might offer of it than an account most of us would now accept. It sounds odd to speak of bribing parents, then, because our linguistic habits have not caught up with our new vision of parenting. But this is something we should change: we ought to allow that parents may be bribed.

But I am uncomfortable with this reply. Most of us now agree that children have rights which ought to be protected by law and/or community pressure and that parents have duties not to violate these rights. To this extent, we are coming to understand families as organizations. Thus, if we allow that parents are bribed, we will almost certainly hold that they are bribed in the way that members of organizations are typically bribed, namely, they are paid to violate their positional duties. But there is something disturbing about this. For despite our conviction that children have rights, many of us are uncomfortable thinking of the family as just another organization and thinking of a parent as just another functionary. Our reluctance to maintain that parents may be bribed, then, may express a healthy resistance to thinking of a parent on the model of an official. Just how we ought to think of the family, I cannot say; the challenge is to arrive at a conception that acknowledges that children have legally enforceable rights without reducing the family to just another institution.

If we exempt the family from consideration and we build in the condition required by the second counterexample, we are now in a position to present a tentative definition of bribery. Thus, P is bribed by R if and only if (1) P accepts payment from R to act on R's behalf,[4] (2) P's act on R's behalf consists in violating some rule or understanding constitutive of a practice in which P is engaged, and (3) either P's violation is a violation of some official duty P has by virtue of his participation in that practice or P's violation significantly affects the interests of persons or organizations whose interests are typically connected to that practice.

At least two additional important features of bribery deserve mention. The first is a consequence of the fact that bribes are payments. For, like other kinds of payments (eg., rent), bribes presuppose agreements of a certain kind.[5] That is, it must be understood by both parties that the payment in question is exchanged, or is to be exchanged, for the relevant conduct. In the most typical and important cases, the bribed party is an official and the conduct in question is the vio-

lation of some official duty. In these cases we may say simply that an official P is bribed by R when she accepts payment or the promise of payment for agreeing to violate a positional duty to act on R's behalf. This agreement requirement is of great importance. As I shall argue in Section IV, without it we cannot properly distinguish between bribes and gifts or rewards.

Such agreements need not be explicit. If I am stopped by a policeman for speeding and hand him a fifty-dollar bill along with my driver's license, and he accepts the fifty-dollar bill, it is arguable that we have entered into such an agreement despite what we might say about contributions to the Police Benevolence Association. As I shall argue, some of the difficulties we have in determining what transactions to count as bribes may stem from unclarity concerning the conditions under which we are entitled to say an agreement has been made.

It is a consequence of this account that someone may be bribed despite the fact that she subsequently decides not to perform the service she has agreed to perform. Indeed, we must say this even if she has never been paid but has been only promised payment, or even if she has been paid but returns this payment after she decides not to abide by her part of the agreement. I see nothing strange about this. After all, if one accepts a bribe it seems natural to say that one has been bribed. Still, I have no strong objection to distinguishing between accepting a bribe and being bribed, where a necessary condition of the latter is that one carries out one's part of the bribery agreement. As far as I can see, no important moral question turns on this choice of language.

A final interesting feature of bribery emerges when we reflect on the claim that offering and accepting bribes is *prima facie* wrong. I will begin with the case of officials. The claim that it is *prima facie* wrong for someone in an official position to accept a bribe is plausible only if persons in official capacities have *prima facie* obligations to discharge their official duties. The most plausible argument for this claim is grounded in a social contract model of organizations. By accepting a position in an organization, it might be argued, one tacitly agrees to abide by the rules of that organization. To be bribed is to violate that agreement—it is to break a promise—and is, therefore, *prima facie* wrong.[6] While I concede that this argument has merit in a context of just and voluntary institutions, it seems questionable in a context of morally corrupt institutions (e.g., Nazi Germany or contemporary El Salvador). And even were it technically valid for those contexts, its conclusion would nonetheless be a misleading half-truth.

It is beyond the scope of this paper to discuss, in detail, the problems with the tacit consent argument in a context of corrupt institutions. In brief, my position is that actions which create *prima facie* moral obligations in just or ideal contexts do not necessarily create comparable obligations in unjust or corrupt contexts. Thus, for example, it does not seem to me that, if I join the Mafia with the intention of subverting its operations and bringing its members to justice, I have thereby undertaken a *prima facie* obligation to abide by the code of that organization. Of course, one could say this and add that the obligation in question is typically overridden by other moral considerations. But this seems to me an *ad hoc* move to defend a position. We use the expression *"prima facie* duty" to point to a moral presumption for or against a certain type of action. And surely it is strange to insist that there is a moral presumption, in the present case, in favor of carrying out the commands of one's Don.

But even if we grant that there is a *prima facie* duty here, we must be careful to qualify this assertion. For it is also clear that participants in unjust institutions have a *prima facie* right to interfere with the normal functioning of those institutions (at least where these functionings can be reasonably expected to produce unjust outcomes). Indeed, where the injustice is great enough they have a *prima facie* duty to interfere. And in some cases, the strength of this *prima facie* obligation will exceed the strength of any promise-keeping obligation generated by tacit consent. Thus we may say, other things equal, that the commandant of a concentration camp ought to act in a manner that frustrates the genocidal purpose of that institution. And, assuming that that institution

is "rationally" designed to serve its purpose, there will be a strong moral presumption in favor of the violation of his positional duty.

What, then, of the morality of accepting bribes in such cases? If an official has no *prima facie* duty to satisfy her positional duties—or if the presumption in favor of satisfying them is outweighed by the presumption against so doing—then, other things being equal, it is difficult to see why it is *prima facie* wrong to accept payment for violating them. After all, there may be serious risks involved. This at least is so where the case against carrying out the purposes of one's organization is strong enough to permit one to violate one's positional duty but is not so strong that one has a *prima facie* obligation to do this. For it does seem *prima facie* wrong to make compliance with a *prima facie* duty contingent on payment (it ought rather to be contingent on an assessment of what one ought to do, all things considered). And it certainly seems wrong to demand payment for doing what is one's duty, all things considered.

Still, this may be too quick. Consider a concentration camp guard who lacks the courage to help inmates escape but who would be courageous enough to undertake the risks involved were he assured of sufficient funds to transport his family to another country and comfortably to begin a new life. If he is in fact reasonably certain that he would be brave enough to do what is required of him were he paid, it seems not improper of him to demand payment. In general, if the wrong of demanding payment for doing one's duty is outweighed by the importance of doing it and if demanding payment for doing it is causally necessary for doing it, then, all things considered, it is not wrong to demand payment.

If it is not wrong for an official to accept a bribe, one does not induce him to do something wrong by offering him one. Thus, we cannot say in all contexts that it is *prima facie* wrong to offer someone a bribe *because* this is an attempt to induce him to do something wrong or to corrupt him.[7] On the other hand, there may be cases in which it is *prima facie* wrong to offer a bribe despite the fact that it is perfectly acceptable for the bribed party to accept one. Recall the case of the boxer slave. Despite the fact that the slave has no obligation to try to win, a wagering master may have a *prima facie* obligation not to pay him to lose. For by so doing the master may gain an unfair advantage over his fellow wagerers. It might be objected that the master's obligation in this case is misleadingly described as an obligation not to bribe. He is obligated, rather, not to fix fights; or, more generally, not to take unfair advantage of his fellow wagerers. This objection raises issues we need not consider here. It is enough to point out that the purpose of offering a bribe is very often to seek some unfair or undeserved benefit or advantage and that this is one reason we are rightly suspicious of the morality of bribe offers.

We are now in a position to state a fifth interesting feature of bribery. Even if it is not *prima facie* wrong to offer and to accept bribes in all contexts, it is *prima facie* wrong to do so in morally uncorrupted contexts. Accordingly, a bribe offerer or a bribe taker must defend the morality of his act either by showing that there are countervailing moral considerations in its favor or alternatively by showing that the moral context is so corrupt that the factors that generate *prima facie* duties in uncorrupted contexts do not apply here. This strategy of moral justifications, of course, is not unique to bribery. It may hold in relation to a wide range of what are ordinarily taken to be *prima facie* duties. In the case of bribery, however, arguments to the effect that the moral context is corrupted will have a certain characteristic form. Thus, in the most important case—the case of officials—they will be arguments that challenge the legitimacy of an institution.

II

I now turn to the first of three problem areas I shall address in this paper, namely, the problem of distinguishing between bribery and extortion. Compare the following cases:

(a)   Executive P hopes to sell an airplane to the national airline of country C. The deal requires the approval of minister R. P knows that R can make a better deal elsewhere and that R knows this as well. P's re-searchers have discovered that R has a reputation for honesty but that R is in serious financial difficulties. Accordingly P offers R a large sum of money to buy from him. R accepts and abides by the agreement.

(b)   The same as *a* except that P knows that he is offering the best deal R can get, and R knows this too. Nonetheless, P is informed by reliable sources that R will not deal with P unless P offers to pay him a considerable sum of money. P complies, and R completes the deal.

According to my analysis *a* is bribery; *b* is not.

The difference between *a* and *b* is clear enough. In *a* P pays R to violate R's duty (in this case, to make the best deal that R can). In *b* P does no such thing. Instead, he pays R to do what is required of R by his institutional commitments in any case. Moreover, he does so in response to R's threat to violate those commitments in a manner that jeopardizes P's interests. Accordingly, *b* resembles extortion more than it does bribery. For, roughly speaking, R extorts P if R threatens P with a penalty in case P fails to give R something to which R has no rightful claim.

If this is true it may be that American corporate executives accused of bribing foreign officials are sometimes more like victims of extortion than offerers of bribes. For in at least some cases they are required to make payments to assure that an official does what he is supposed to do in any case. This is especially true in the case of inspectors of various kinds and in relation to government officials who must approve transactions between American and local companies. An inspector who refuses to approve a shipment that is up to standards unless he is paid off is like a bandit who demands tribute on all goods passing through his territory.

It does not follow that it is morally correct for American companies to pay off such corrupt officials. There are cases in which it is morally wrong to surrender to the demands of bandits and other extortionists. But it is clear that the moral questions that arise here are different sorts of questions than those that arise in relation to bribery. The moral relations between the relevant parties differ. The bribery agreement is not by its nature an agreement between victims and victimizers. The extortion agreement is. Moral justifications and excuses for complying with the demands of an extortionist are easier to come by than moral justifications and excuses for offering bribes.

Of course, the distinction in question is often easier to draw in theory than in practice. An inspector who demands a payoff to authorize a shipment is likely to fortify his demand by insisting that the product does not meet standards. In some cases it may be difficult to know whether or not he is lying (e.g., whether the shipment has been contaminated in transit). And given the high cost of delays, a company may decide that it is too expensive to take the time to find out. In this case, a company may decide to pay off without knowing whether it is agreeing to pay a bribe or surrendering to extortion. Since the morality of its decisions may well turn on what it is in fact doing in such cases, a company that does not take the time to find out acts in a morally irresponsible manner (unless, of course, it is in a position to defend both courses of action).

What sorts of justifications can a company present for offering bribes? It is beyond the scope of this paper to provide a detailed discussion of this question. However, I have already mentioned a number of considerations that count as moral reasons against bribery in a variety of contexts. To begin with, in reasonably just contexts, officials ordinarily are obligated to discharge the duties of their offices. In these cases bribe offers are normally attempts to induce officials to violate duties. Moreover, if accepted, a bribe offer may make it more likely that that official will violate future duties. Accordingly, it may contribute to the corruption of an official. In addition, the intent of a bribe offer is often to secure an unfair advantage or an undeserved privilege. Where this is the case, it too counts as a reason against bribery. To determine whether a bribe offer is wrong in any particular case, then, we must decide: (1) whether these reasons obtain in that case; (2) if they obtain, how much weight we ought to attach to them; and (3) how much weight we ought to attach to countervailing considerations. (Suppose, e.g., that it is necessary to bribe an official in order to meet an important contractual obligation.) It is worth remarking in this regard that, where officials routinely take bribes, the presumption against corrupting officials normally will not apply. Similarly, to the extent that bribery is an accepted weapon in the arsenal of all competitors, bribe offers cannot be construed as attempts to achieve an unfair advantage over one's competitors.

III

It is sometimes suggested that an environment may be so corrupt that no payments count as bribes. These are circumstances in which the level of official compliance to duty is very low, and payoffs are so widespread that they are virtually institutionalized. Suppose, for example, that the laws of country N impose very high duties on a variety of products for importers but that it is common practice in N for importers and exporters to pay customs officials to overlook certain goods and/or to underestimate their number or value. Suppose, moreover, that the existence of this practice is common knowledge but that no effort is made to stop it by law enforcement officials at any level;[8] indeed, that any attempts to stop it would be met by widespread social disapproval. One might even imagine that customs officials receive no salary in N but earn their entire livelihood in this way. One might further imagine that customs officials are expected to return a certain amount of money to the government every month and are fired from their jobs for failure to do so. Finally, one might suppose that the cumulative advantages and disadvantages of this way of doing things is such that the economy of N is about as strong as it would be under a more rule-bound alternative. Are these officials bribed?

In my analysis, the answer to this question depends on how we understand the duties of the customs officer. If the official job description for the customs officer in N (and the written laws of N) is like those of most countries, the customs officer violates his official duties according to these codes by allowing goods to leave the country without collecting the full duty. The question, however, is how seriously we are to take these written codes. Where social and political practice routinely violates them, nothing is done about it, and few members of the legal and non-legal community believe that anything ought to be done about it, it is arguable that these codes are dead letters. If we find this to be true of the codes governing the duties of the customs officials in country N, we have good reason for saying that the real obligations of these officials do not require that they impose the duties described in those written codes (but only that they return a certain sum of the money they collect to the central government each month). Anything collected in excess of that amount they are entitled to keep as salary (recall that they are officially unpaid). In reality we might say that duties on exports in country N are not fixed but negotiable.

Of course if we decide that the written law of N is the law of N, we must describe the situation otherwise. In that case, the official obligations of the customs officials are as they are described, and the system in N must be characterized as one of rampant bribery condoned both by government and by popular opinion. It seems to me that the philosophy of law on which this account rests is implausible. However, there is no need to argue this to defend my analysis of this case. My position is simply that whether or not we describe what goes on here as bribery depends on what we take the real legal responsibilities of the customs official to be. To the extent that we are inclined to identify his duties with the written law we will be inclined to speak of bribery here. To the extent that we are unwilling so to identify his duties we will not.[9]

IV

Let us now consider the problem of distinguishing bribes from rewards and gifts. The problem arises because gifts are often used in business and government to facilitate transactions. And to the degree to which a business person, professional person, or government official is influenced in her decision by gifts, it is tempting to conclude that she is violating her duties. In such cases we are tempted to speak of these gifts as bribes.

If I am correct, however, this temptation should be resisted. A bribe, after all, presupposes

an agreement. A gift may be made with the intention of inducing an official to show favoritism to the giver, but unless acceptance of what is transferred can be construed as an agreement to show favoritism, what is transferred is not a bribe.

In some cases, of course, the acceptance of what is offered can be so construed. Again, if I offer fifty dollars to a policeman who has stopped me for speeding, he has a right to construe my act as one of offering a bribe, and I have a right to construe his acceptance in the corresponding manner. If I regularly treat the neighbourhood policeman to a free lunch at my diner and he regularly neglects to ticket my illegally parked car, we have reason to say the same. Agreements need not be explicit. My point is just that to the degree that it is inappropriate to speak of agreements, it is also inappropriate to speak of bribes.

It follows from this that, if I present an official with an expensive item to induce him to show favoritism on my behalf, in violation of his duty, I have not necessarily bribed him. It does not follow from this, however, that I have done nothing wrong. So long as you are morally obligated to perform your official duty, normally it will be wrong of me to induce you to do otherwise by presenting you with some expensive item. Moreover, if you have any reason to believe that accepting what I offer will induce you not to do your duty, you have done something wrong by accepting my gift. To prevent such wrongs we have laws prohibiting persons whose interests are closely tied to the decisions of public officials from offering gifts to these officials. And we have laws for forbidding officials to accept such gifts.

It might be objected that this account is too lenient. Specifically, it might be argued that wherever P presents Q with something of value to induce Q to violate Q's official duties P has offered a bribe.

But this is surely a mistake. It suggests, among other things, that an official is bribed so long as she accepts what is offered with this intent. Yet an official may accept such a gift innocently, believing that it is what it purports to be, namely, a token of friendship or goodwill. And she may do so with justifiable confidence that doing so will not in any way affect the discharge of her duty.

It may be replied that officials are bribed by such inducements only when they are in fact induced to do what is desired of them. But again, it may be the case that an official accepts what is offered innocently, believing it to be a gift, and that she believes falsely that it will not affect her conduct. In this case she has exercised bad judgment, but she has not been bribed. Indeed, it seems to me that it is improper to say that she accepts a bribe even when she recognizes the intent of the inducement and believes that accepting it is likely to influence her. There is a distinction between accepting a drink with the understanding that one is agreeing to be seduced and accepting a drink with the knowledge that so doing will make one's seduction more likely. To be bribed is to be bought, not merely to be influenced to do something.

From a moral point of view, whenever failure to perform one's official duties is wrong it may be as bad to accept a gift that one knows will influence one in the conduct of one's duty as it is to accept a bribe. And clearly we are entitled morally to criticize those who offer and accept such inducements. Moreover, we are right to attempt to prevent this sort of thing by legally restricting the conditions under which persons may offer gifts to officials and the conditions under which officials may accept such gifts. Nonetheless, such gifts ought not to be confused with bribes. If P accepts a gift from R and does not show the desired favoritism, R may complain of P's ingratitude but not of P's dishonesty (unless, of course, P led him on in some way). If P accepts a bribe from R and does not show the desired favoritism, P has been dishonest (perhaps twice).

This point is not without practical importance. People who work in the same organization or in the same profession often form friendships despite the fact that some of them are in a position to make decisions that affect the interests of others. Here, as everywhere, friendships are developed and maintained in part by exchanges of favors, gifts, meals, and so forth. Were we to take seriously the inducement theory of bribery, however, this dimension of collegial and organiza-

tional existence would be threatened. In that case, if P's position is such that he must make decisions affecting R, any gifts, favors, et cetera from R to P should be regarded with at least some suspicion. To guard against the accusation that he has been bribed by R, P must be in a position to offer reasons for believing that R's intent in inviting him to dinner was not to induce him to show favoritism. And for R to be certain that he is not offering P a bribe in this case, R must be certain that his intentions are pure. All of this would require such vigilance in relation to one's own motives and the motives of others that friendships in collegial and organizational settings would be more difficult to sustain than they are at present.

Since decision makers are required to show impartiality they must in any case be careful not to accept gifts and favors that will influence them to show favoritism. Moreover, if they are required by their position to assess the moral character of those affected by their decisions, they may be required to assess the intent with which such gifts or favors are offered. Most officials, however, are not required to assess character in this way. In order to avoid doing wrong by accepting gifts and favors they need only be justly confident of their own continued impartiality Thus, they are ordinarily entitled to ignore questions of intent unless there is some special reason to do otherwise. If the intent to influence were sufficient for a bribe, however, they would not be at liberty to bestow the benefit of the doubt in this way.

Again, there are cases in which impartiality is so important that decision makers should be prohibited both from accepting gifts or favors from any persons likely to be directly affected by their decisions and from forming friendships with such persons. And they should disqualify themselves when they are asked to make a decision that affects either a friend or someone from whom they have accepted gifts or favors in the reasonably recent past. Judges are a case in point. In other cases, however, institutions and professions should be willing to risk some loss in impartiality in order to enjoy the benefits of friendship and mutual aid. For these are essential to the functioning of some organizations and to the well-being of the people within them. Consider, for example, universities. The practical disadvantage of the inducement account is that it may require us to be unnecessarily suspicious of certain exchanges constitutive of mutual aid and friendship (at least if we take it seriously).

V

An interesting related problem arises in cultures in which a more formal exchange of gifts may be partly constitutive of a special relationship between persons, namely something like friendship. In such cultures, so long as certain other conditions are satisfied, to make such exchanges is to enter into a system of reciprocal rights and duties. Among these duties may be the duty to show favoritism toward "friends," even when one acts in an official capacity. Moreover, the giver may be expected to show gratitude for each occasion of favoritism by further gift giving. On the face of it, this certainly looks like bribery. Is that description warranted?

To begin with, we need to distinguish between cases in which the special relationships in question are genuine and cases in which they are not. In the latter case certain ritual or ceremonial forms may be used to dress up what each party regards as a business transaction of the standard Western variety in a manner that provides an excuse for bribery. I shall say more about this presently. But let me begin with the first case.

Where the relationships in question are genuine and the laws of the relevant society are such that the official duties of the relevant official do not prohibit favoritism, this practice of gift giving cannot be called bribery. For in this case there is no question of the violation of duty. All that can be said here is that such societies condone different ways of doing business than we do. Specifically they do not mark off a sphere of business and/or bureaucratic activity in which persons are supposed to meet as "abstract individuals," that is, in which they are required to ignore their social and familial ties. Their obligations, rather, are importantly determined by such ties even in the conduct of business and governmental affairs. Favoritism is shown, then, not in order to carry

out one's part of a bargain but, rather, to discharge an obligation of kinship or loyalty. Failure to show favoritism would entitle one's kinsman or friend to complain not that one reneged on an agreement but, rather, that one had wronged him as an ally or a kinsman.

This is not to say that one cannot bribe an official in such a society. One does this here, as elsewhere, by entering into an agreement with him such that he violates his official duties for payment. The point is just that favoritism shown to friends and kinsmen is not necessarily a violation of duty in such societies. Indeed, one might be bribed not to show favoritism.

The official duties of an official, of course, may not be clear. Thus, the written law may prohibit favoritism to kin and ally, though this is widely practiced and condoned and infrequently prosecuted. This may occur when a society is in a transitional state from feudalism or tribalism to a Western-style industrial society, but it may also occur in an industrial society with different traditions than our own.

To the extent that it is unclear what the official duties of officials are in such cases it will also be difficult to say what count as bribes. Indeed, even if we decide that an official does violate his duty by showing favoritism to kin and allies who reciprocate with gifts, we may not be justified in speaking of bribery here. For the official may not be acting as he does in order to fulfill his part of an agreement. Rather, he may be acting to fulfill some obligation of kinship or loyalty. Again, his failure so to act may not entitle his kinsmen or allies to complain that he had welched on a deal; rather, it would entitle them to complain that he wronged them as kinsmen or allies.

Of course, all this is so only when the relationships in question are genuine. In some cases, however, the rhetoric and ceremonial forms of a traditional culture may be used to camouflage what are in fact business relations of the standard Western variety. To the extent that this is so, the favoritism in question may in fact be bribery in ethnic dress. The relationships in question are not genuine when they are not entered into in good faith. It is clear, moreover, that when American executives present expensive gifts to foreign businessmen or foreign government officials they do so for business reasons. That is, they have no intention of entering into a system of reciprocal rights and duties that may obligate them in the future to act contrary to their long-term interest. Rather, they perform the required ceremonies knowing that they will continue to base their decisions on business reasons. Their intention is to buy favoritism. And the foreign officials and companies with whom they do business are typically aware of this. This being the case, invitations of the form "First we become friends, then we do business" cannot plausibly be construed as invitations to participate in some traditional way of life Typically, both parties recognize that what is requested here is a bribe made in an appropriate ceremonial way.

VI

On the basis of this analysis it seems clear that American officials are not always guilty of bribery when they pay off foreign officials. In some cases they are victims of extortion; in other cases, the context may be such that the action purchased from the relevant official does not count as a violation of his duty. The fact that American executives engaged in international commerce are innocent of some of the charges that have been made against them, however, does not imply that those who have made them are mistaken in their assessment of the character of these executives. One's character, after all, is a matter of what one is disposed to do. If these executives are willing to engage in bribery whenever this is necessary to promote their perceived long-term business interests, whatever the morality of the situation, it follows (at very least) that they are amoral.

NOTES

1. At the time this paper was written there were no references to bribes or bribery in the *Philosopher's Index*. Since that time one paper has been indexed—Arnold Berleant's "Multinationals, Local Practice, and the Problems of Ethical Consistency" (*Journal of Business Ethics* 1 [August 1982]: 185–93)—but, as the title of this short paper suggests, Berleant is not primarily concerned with providing an analysis of the concept of bribery. However, three presentations on the topic of bribery were made at the 1983 "Conference for Business Ethics" (organized by the Society for Business Ethics at DePaul University, July 25–26) and have subsequently been accepted for publication. These are: Kendall D'Andrade's "Bribery" (forthcoming in a special issue of the *Journal of Business Ethics*, devoted to the DePaul conference, 1984); John Danley's "Toward a Theory of Bribery" (forthcoming in the *Journal of Business and Professional Ethics*, 1984); and Tom Carson's "Bribery, Extortion and the Foreign Corrupt Practices Act" (forthcoming in *Philosophy and Public Affairs*, Summer 1984). Where my position on substantive questions differs significantly from D'Andrade's, Carson's. or Danley's, I shall discuss this in the notes.

2. Danley defines "bribing" as "offering or giving something of value with a corrupt intent to induce or influence an action of someone in a public or official capacity." Carson defines a bribe as a payment to someone "in exchange for special consideration that is incompatible with the duties of his position." Both go on to discuss bribery as if it were restricted to officials of organizations. Since these are the most typical and important cases of bribery, their focus is understandable. But it does have at least one unfortunate consequence. For it leads both Danley and Carson to think that the question of whether it is *prima facie* wrong to offer or accept bribes reduces to the question of whether officials have obligations to satisfy their positional duties. Danley argues that they do not if the institutions they serve are illegitimate. Carson argues that they do on the ground that they have made a tacit agreement with their institution to discharge those duties (accepting a bribe, for Carson, is an instance of promise breaking). Whatever the merits of their arguments concerning the responsibilities of officials, both approach the question of the *prima facie* morality of bribery too narrowly. For different issues seem to arise when we consider bribery outside the realm of officialdom. Clearly it is more difficult for Carson to make his tacit consent argument in relation to the bribed athlete. For it is not clear that a runner who enters a race tacitly agrees to win it (if so, he would be breaking a promise by running to prepare for future races or by entering to set the pace for someone else). Nor is it clear that a boxer who accepts payment not to knock out his opponent in the early rounds violates a tacit agreement to attempt a knockout at his earliest convenience. Danley must expand his account to accommodate such cases as well. For it is not clear what it means to say that a practice such as running or boxing is legitimate.

3. Such cases present a problem for the accounts of both Danley and Carson. At the very least they must expand their accounts of positional duties such that we can distinguish between a bribe, on the one hand, and a salary paid to a spy recruited from within an organization, on the other.

4. Thus D'Andrade defines bribery as "alienation of agency." In his account bribery occurs when someone is seduced into abandoning his role as an agent of one person or organization and, for a price, becomes the agent of another. This highlights an important feature of bribery that is ignored by Carson and Danley and that was neglected in my own earlier thinking on this subject, namely, that a bribe taker acts on behalf of someone. But D'Andrade's claim that agency is alienated when one accepts a bribe implies that the bribe taker necessarily is committed to act on behalf of some person or organization before he is in a position to accept a bribe. And it is difficult to see what helpful truth this might express in relation to the scientist, runner, or boxer of my examples. Surely it is not helpful to say that a bribe taker begins as his own agent in these cases and, for pay, alienates that agency to another. This applies to anyone who takes a job. Nor is it helpful to say—as D'Andrade did say at one point—that he may begin as an agent of some abstraction (e.g., truth). Surely the point behind this obscure claim is better made by speaking of what is expected of someone as a participant in a practice. It is also worth noting that D'Andrade's alienation of agency account offers no basis for distinguishing between bribed officials, on the one hand, and undercover agents and spies, on the other. For these too alienate agency.

5. Carson fails to recognize the significance of this feature of bribery. This view of bribery, moreover, is inconsistent with Danley's account. Danley understands a bribe as an attempt to induce or influence someone. In this matter he appears to have most dictionaries on his side (including the OED). However, as I argue in more detail in Sec. IV, he is mistaken.

6. This is Carson's argument.

7. Nor can we say that it is *prima facie* wrong because it is an attempt to get someone to do something that is *prima facie* wrong. This argument is flawed in two ways. To begin with, as we have seen, the premise expresses what is at best a dangerous half-truth. Were we to reason from the whole truth we must conclude that there are some contexts in which the presumption in favor of violating one's official duties is stronger than the presumption against it. In the second place, moreover, the inference is invalid: it is not necessarily *prima facie* wrong to induce someone to do something that is *prima facie* wrong. Rather, it is *prima facie* wrong to induce someone to do something that is wrong, all things considered. Thus, if it is *prima facie* wrong for P to do A, but P ought to do A, all things considered, there is no presumption against my inducing P to do A; I do not need to justify this by appealing to countervailing moral considerations. I require such justification only when it is wrong for P to do so. Cases of this sort are interesting but typically neglected by philosophers. (The following are examples: [a] P is a soldier in a war in which each side has equal claim to justice; R is a guard on the opposite side. Though it might be wrong for R to accept a bribe from P, it is not wrong for P to offer R a bribe. [b] P's father is certain to be convicted of a crime he did not commit because the evidence is overwhelmingly against him. It is permissible for P to offer a bribe to R, an assistant district attorney, to "lose" some evidence; but it is wrong for R to accept the bribe.) In any case, the upshot of this is that even if there were a general moral presumption against accepting bribes it would not follow that there is a comparable presumption against offering bribes.

8. In D'Andrade's account bribes are necessarily secret, so these could not count as bribes.

9. A corresponding point holds in relation to bribery outside the realm of officialdom. Consider the case of professional wrestling. Most of us believe that the outcome of professional wrestling matches is determined in advance. Are the losers bribed? (To simplify matters let us assume that they are paid a bit of extra money for losing.) The answer here depends on how we understand their practice. If we take them to be participating in a wrestling competition, we must say that they are bribed. In that case, by failing to compete they violate an understanding constitutive of their practice. It is reasonably clear, however, that professional wrestlers are not engaged in an athletic competition. Rather, they are engaged in a dramatic performance. This being the case the losers are not bribed. They are merely doing what professional wrestlers are ordinarily paid to do, namely, to play out their part in an informal script.

The Moral Duties of Organizations: Dual-Investor Theory and the Nature of Organizations

EUGENE SCHLOSSBERGER

With permission of the author.

Introduction

Are the moral obligations of organizations different from those of individual persons? Some people have suggested that because organizations are not persons they have no moral obligations and can't be judged good or bad: while members or officers of organizations can have moral duties, organizations as such cannot. But a careful analysis of the nature of organizations shows that moral duties are built into the very concept of an organization. Dual-Investor Theory, an alternative approach to business ethics,[1] suggests that organizations generally have a duty, as organizations, to try to ensure that their activities do not harm society—organizations have a duty of minimal social responsibility. Moreover, the very concept of an organization entails that serving the good-in-general is a fundamental goal of every organization. Just as, according to Dual-Investor Theory, businesses exist to serve society by making a profit, so organizations exist to contribute to the good-in-general by serving their specific purpose: the good-in-general is a beneficiary of all organizations.[2] Finally, the nature of organizations suggests that there are six key questions to ask when morally evaluating an organization's activities.

Section I is an analysis of the nature of organizations. Section II applies Dual-Investor Theory to organizations. Section III uses the results of Section I to argue that an implicit goal of every organization is serving the good-in-general. That is, while organizations may exist to serve some very specific good, such as obtaining dental benefits for a particular company's janitors, they are also committed to serving goodness generally. Organizations bear some fiduciary duties to what is good, right, and just. Section IV provides a framework for morally evaluating organizations.

I. *The Nature of Organizations*

What is an organization? Not any collection of people counts as an organization. Some people are left-handed, enjoy vanilla ice cream, and play tiddlywinks. Those people have something in common, but they are not an organization. The collection of all people who voted for Al Gore in the New Hampshire primary have a common goal, but they are not an organization.

What, then, is an organization? *An organization is a structured, co-operative venture, consisting of activities undertaken for the purpose of serving some perceived good, which has at least one relationship with a person or persons that is distinctly different from the relationships of its members as individuals.* This somewhat lengthy definition needs some explanation.

First, an organization has members who participate in the venture by virtue of their place or role in the organization's structure. By "members" I mean persons or organizations that take themselves to be participants in the structured venture and are recognized as co-participants by the other participants in the venture. Members may be persons or other organizations, which are in turn composed of persons or other organizations. The membership structure of an organization may be highly complex and non-linear, but ground zero is persons, and all organizations' membership touches ground somewhere: ultimately, the membership of some organization in this chain includes persons. Organizational structures can be formal or informal, loose or strict. Typically organizational structures include specific roles (e.g., treasurer) and operating rules (e.g., dues must be paid by the first Friday in April). Though formal roles and rules are not necessary, organizations must be in some way organized. There might be no formal role of discussion leader, but members might generally look to Smith to lead the discussion. There may be no explicit or formal rules, but it might be generally understood by members that one doesn't reveal other members' names.

These features of organizations help explain why the various individuals voting for Al Gore in the New Hampshire primary do not constitute an organization. Those who voted for Al Gore might share a common goal, but their various activities (each pulling the lever in the voting booth) are not a structured, co-operative venture. They do not regard themselves (and are not regarded by other voters) as participating in the venture of electing Al Gore by jointly realizing, operating within, a set of rules and roles.

Organizations and institutions exist to serve a purpose, which is to advance or serve some good: there is something the organization, as an organization, takes to be a good and which it is devoted, as an organization, to serving.[3] Organizations are ventures, and a "venture," in this sense, is some set of activities (in the broadest sense of "activity") that center on the attempted fiduciary tending to some perceived good for some perceived beneficiary. A venture is a co-operative set of activities in execution of a "charge." The range of goods an organization might serve is quite varied. A professional society of physicians might exist to serve the career interests of its members and/or the interests of medicine generally. A labor union serves to advance the job-related interests of its members, and, to some extent, the interests of labor generally. The Committee to Re-Elect the President served to advance the interests of Richard Nixon's being elected president in 1972, a specific state of affairs. The Metropolitan Opera Guild serves to advance the interests of the Metropolitan Opera Association, another organization. The Sierra Club serves to advance the interests of the environment. A social club might exist to serve a particular social or entertainment interest of its members. Organizations may exist to serve the interests of fatherhood, honesty and integrity in the used car business, high standards of scholarship, the education of left-handed descendants of Abraham Lincoln, the perpetuation of Tibetan culture, the general attainment of sartori or the will of God on earth. Whatever the charge of an organization, it exists for the purpose of serving some good and has fiduciary duties related to serving that good—it is dedicated to serving faithfully the interests of some beneficiary, whether that beneficiary is a person or group of persons,

another organization, an ideal, a state of affairs, a practice, a cause, an abstract object, or a supernatural being.[4]

What an organization takes to be good might not actually be good, and the intended beneficiary of an organization may not, in fact, exist. Imagine a Society for the Perpetuation of Racism (the SPR).[5] The perceived good the SPR is devoted to serving, racism, is, in fact, not good at all. The SRA is simply mistaken. Similarly, suppose Organization X, which believes that Mickey Mouse is the modern incarnation of Zeus, exists to serve the will of Zeus. In the case of Organization X, we must distinguish between the objective beneficiary, the intended beneficiary and the conceptual beneficiary. The intended beneficiary of Organization X is what some philosophers call an "intentional object." Roughly speaking, it is the following *idea:* whatever fits the description "the actual will of the actual Zeus." The objective beneficiary is the set of real things that actually do fit that description. Since Zeus does not, in fact, exist, the objective beneficiary is the empty set. (In reality Zeus' will does not exist.) So the intended beneficiary is an idea while the objective beneficiary is a thing. The conceptual beneficiary is the set of things the organization takes, as an organization, to fit that description, namely, what the organization believes to be Mickey Mouse's commands. If Organization X believes that Mickey Mouse wills that people wear costumes on Halloween, then people's wearing costumes on Halloween is part of the conceptual beneficiary of Organization X. (Of course, if Mickey Mouse really were Zeus and Organization X correctly identified Mickey's will, then the objective beneficiary would be identical with the conceptual beneficiary.) The differences between the perceived good of an organization and what is really good, and between the intended, objective, and conceptual beneficiaries of an organization, are important when morally evaluating an organization. An organization can faithfully serve its conceptual beneficiary, even when that beneficiary isn't real (corresponds to the empty set).

Finally, an organization has at least one social relationship that is different from that of the individual relationships of its members. For example, Joe Smith's signing a contract as president of the Association of Professional Orthopedists (the APO) is different from Joe Smith's signing a personal contract. It is different from each of the members of the APO signing the same contract as individuals. Organizations have relationships as structured ventures. The contractual duties of the APO do set limits on the permissible behavior of each member, but these limits apply to the members' behavior as members of the APO, not as individuals. If the APO contracts with General Mills not to sell chocolate as a form of fundraising, in exchange for a donation, Joe Smith is obligated not to sell chocolate for the APO. He is still free to sell chocolate for himself as an individual. The APO's contract does not obligate Joe Smith to give up his family candy store.[6] This is the second way in which the various people who voted for Al Gore in New Hampshire do not count as an organization—they do not, as a group, have social relationships different from those each has as an individual.

If these remarks about the nature of organizations are correct, organizations have moral duties. Dual-Investor Theory suggests that all organizations have a duty to be "good citizens," to try to ensure that, in pursuing their goals, they do not harm society. But I will make a stronger claim as well. All organizations and institutions have a dual purpose: they serve the specific purpose for which they were founded or currently maintained and they serve the general purpose of contributing in some way, directly or indirectly, to the good-in-general.

II. *Dual-Investor Theory and the Duty of Minimal Social Responsibility*

Dual-Investor Theory is a theory about businesses, but it can be expanded to show that all organizations have a duty of minimal social responsibility.

Dual-Investor Theory begins by recognizing that businesses are organizations formed for the purpose of providing a good return for their investors—the good a business serves is return on

investment and the beneficiaries of a business are its investors. What Dual-Investor Theory points out is that there are two types of investors. No business can function without the specific capital provided by the stockholders, proprietors, or partners. Just as essential to a business, however, are the assets provided by society. Businesses depend upon roads, currency systems, police protection, arid other social services. In addition, businesses make essential use of the knowledge base provided by the hard work of generation after generation of people across the globe. Henry Ford did not begin constructing the Model T by re-inventing the wheel. Businesses also depend upon an educated work force and customer base, and education in the United States is widely subsidized by public funds, private donors, or both. This knowledge base, currency system, and so forth may be called a business's "opportunity capital." The valuable opportunity capital society invests in a business is at least as essential to the business as is the specific capital invested by stockholders or proprietors. Thus, there are two categories of investors in any business venture: the "owners," who provide the specific capital, and society, which provides the opportunity capital. Businesses have a fiduciary duty to give each a good return on its investment. Thus the purpose of business is to make a profit (or, more precisely, to increase shareholder value) by serving society.

Dual-Investor Theory combines some of the insights of the two most prevalent approaches to business ethics, shareholder and stakeholder theories. Shareholder theories suggest that the sole or primary purpose of a business is to increase shareholder value, or, more loosely, make a profit for the owners. Stakeholder theories suggest that a business exists to serve all of those who have a stake in, are significantly affected by, the business's operations (for example, customers, suppliers, employees, and members of the larger community). Some stakeholder theorists seem not to recognize that businesses have special obligations to those who own them. Some shareholder theorists seem not to recognize that businesses have important responsibilities toward the society in which they flourish. Dual-Investor Theory agrees with the shareholder theory that businesses exist to serve the investors, but, because society is an investor in every business venture, Dual-Investor Theory captures the stakeholder view's insight that businesses have major social responsibilities.

Dual-Investor Theory applies to all organizations, whether they are businesses or not, when one other principle is considered. Duties of gratitude and reciprocity seem to justify what one might call the limited "don't bite the hand that feeds you," or "no bite" principle. If people help you, don't use their assistance against them. More precisely, when one knowingly and deliberately makes use, for a particular purpose, of what another has provided, one has a duty to strive to ensure that one's pursuit of that purpose is not inconsistent with one's benefactor's needs, welfare, and projects, to an extent commensurate with the magnitude of what one has used. For example, suppose I knowingly and deliberately use a gift of money from you to start a business. It is a large sum and represents 2/3 of my capital. I should go to some length to avoid my business's putting yours out of business, because it is wrong to turn your generosity toward me around to your peril. Next, as Dual-Investor Theory points out, society is an essential benefactor of every organization—every organization makes extensive use of the "opportunity capital" society provides. Hence, by the no-bite principle, every organization has a duty to go out of its way to ensure that in pursuing its purpose it does not undermine the good of society.

The argument may be summarized as follows:

1) Society provides every organization with extensive help without which it cannot function.
2) Every organization knowingly and deliberately employs that help in pursuing its purpose.
3) Therefore every organization knowingly and deliberately makes use of, for its purpose, benefits of great magnitude provided by society.
4) When one knowingly and deliberately makes use, for a particular purpose, of what another has provided, one has a duty to strive to ensure that one's pursuit of that purpose is not inconsistent with one's benefactor's needs, welfare, and projects, to an extent commensurate with the magnitude of what one has used (the no-bite principle).
5) Therefore, every organization has a strong duty to strive to ensure that its pursuit of its purpose is not inconsistent with the needs, welfare, and projects of society (the duty of minimal social responsibility).

Illustrating Case: The Association of Certified Public Accountants (ACPA), a tax-exempt organization that provides a variety of important services for its members, must vote on a proposed change in its code of ethics that would prohibit *pro bono* or reduced rate activities. If the measure passes, member accountants will be expelled if they offer any form of unpaid accounting assistance (or accounting assistance at rates lower than their standard rates) to nonprofit social agencies, such as battered women's shelters, to churches or synagogues, or to local Boy Scout troops.

Discussion: The ACPA makes heavy use of society's opportunity capital. For example, the organization could not exist in its present form if society did not maintain a currency system. The professional skills of its members, without which the organization could not exist, were obtained through an educational system subsidized by society and employ accounting techniques and concepts developed through the years by numerous individuals. The organization employs inexpensive bulk rate mailings, which are partially subsidized by taxes and first-class postage rates. If the ACPA passes a measure, a number of worthy, struggling organizations will be deprived of needed accounting services, since at least some members currently providing such services will choose to remain members rather than do without the professional services the ACPA offers. For example, a battered women's shelter, currently assisted at no charge by an ACPA member, may have to close because it cannot afford the accounting services required by local, state, and federal laws, regulations, and agencies and is unable to find a qualified accountant, who is not an ACPA member, willing to donate his or her time. Thus, passing the measure would violate the no-bite principle: the ACPA would be using the currency system, educational system, etc. provided by society to the detriment of the society providing those benefits.

III. *The Good-in-General as a Goal of All Organizations*

It follows from the nature of organizations that serving the good-in-general is an implicit goal of all organizations. Organizations need not serve the good-in-general directly: they may devote themselves to playing a role within a practice or institution that, as a general practice or institution, serves the good-in-general. But having some form of commitment to the good-in-general is an essential part of what it means to function as an organization.

Serving The Good-In-General Is An Implicit Goal Of All Organizations

Organizations exist solely for the purpose of serving some or other good and have a fiduciary duty to serving that good. The idea of a good presupposes the idea of a general framework of standards that makes good things good. (Without a framework of values, nothing is good or bad.) The idea of a fiduciary obligation presupposes a general moral framework that generates such values as loyalty, trust, and good faith. Hence organizations are committed to the existence of a general moral framework that defines their purpose and *raison d'être*. To work against that framework is hence to oppose the very thing that gives point to the organization's existence. Put another way, the organization's goals are only goals at all because of the underlying moral framework. To deny that framework is hence to turn the organization's goal into a non-goal, and hence to dissolve the organization as an organization. Of course, organizations can eliminate their goal by achieving it (for example, an organization might eliminate its goal of eradicating smallpox by wiping out smallpox). In that case, the goal is an

accomplished goal. The organization can then end or find a new goal. When an organization ceases to recognize the good-in-general, it cannot have a goal at all, and so it no longer counts as an organization. Thus, in pursuing their fiduciary obligation to serve their specific good, organizations have an implicit obligation to serve the general moral framework that both makes that specific good into a good and is the ground for the idea of fiduciary obligations generally. Hence all organizations have an implicit fiduciary obligation to the good-in-general, understood loosely here as whatever is affirmed by the general moral framework that makes some things good and others not and that gives rise to fiduciary obligations such as loyalty.

Role Specific Organizations

Organizations need not serve the good-in-general directly. They can do so by playing a particular role within a practice or institution, where the practice or institution is justified by its contribution to the good-in-general.

Attorneys sometimes argue that their only obligation is to advance the interests of their clients, within the limits of the law. They justify this principle of full advocacy by arguing that the clash of combating attorneys in the courtroom, each dedicated solely to the interests of his or her client, is the best system of justice yet devised. Advocates of this view may be mistaken in their claims (I would argue they are), but the logical structure of the view is important. Attorneys, on this view, serve justice without directly trying to serve justice. Rather, in concentrating on their clients' interests, attorneys serve justice by playing their part in a system of advocacy that, taken as a whole, serves justice. The claim that the system as a whole best serves justice makes sense of the attorney's claim to have a fiduciary obligation to advance her clients' interests: the attorney's fiduciary duty to a client derives, ultimately, from a general (indirect) fiduciary duty to serve justice.

Organizations too can have the same sort of indirect fiduciary duty to the good-in-general, which they serve by fulfilling some specific role within a practice or institution that, taken as a whole, serves the good-in-general. This require-ment imposes significant restraints on organiza-tions while giving them certain types of latitude.

The Better Business Bureau of Akron, Ohio (the BBBA), does not have to address the problem of world hunger. It is free to concentrate on busi-ness in Akron, so long as the general practice of business associations functioning as the BBBA does serve the good-in-general. Suppose, for ex-ample, that the BBBA tries to attract new busi-nesses to Akron by publishing lies about competing cities, such as Hammond, Indiana. Would a general practice of municipal Better Business Bureaus broadcasting lies about each other's cities best serve the good-in-general? If not, then the Better Business Bureau of Akron betrays its mission by publishing lies about Hammond.

Illustrating Case: Image, an advertising firm, creates a television ad for Health Powder, a pow-dered extract of ginger root. The ad states: "A study in the *New England Journal of Medicine* showed that Health Powder is as effective in cur-ing cancer as a drug approved by the FDA." In fact, the FDA-approved drug to which the ad refers is a beta-blocker, included in the study as a control. The study concluded that while neither Health Powder nor the beta-blocker had any sig-nificant effect in controlling cancer, several other new drugs did.

Discussion This deceptive ad is likely to cause some cancer patients to forego medical treatment that could help them. Image may be serving its perceived good of advancing the public relations interests of its clients. However, by engaging in harmful deception, it is not serving the good-in-general. Since a general practice of advertisers engaging in harmful deception is not likely to serve the good-in-general, Image is not serving the good-in-general by playing its role in a gen-eral practice that serves the good-in-general.

IV. *Moral Evaluation of Organizations*

Moral evaluation of individual persons is very complex.[7] Moral evaluation of organizations is in some ways simpler. Moral evaluation of a person involves the whole of that person's worldview. Since there are numerous aspects and facets of the life of a person, moral evaluations of persons can be very complicated. An organization, unlike a person, exists to serve a limited purpose (its charge). Hence there is a limited list of questions to ask about an organization when evaluating it morally.

a)   Does the organization make a good faith effort to serve its intended, objective, and conceptual beneficiaries?

b)   Is the perceived good of the organization truly a good?

c)   Does the organization attempt to ensure that its efforts serve what it understands to be the good-in-general, either directly or by serving a role within a practice that serves the good-in-general?

d)   Is the organization's understanding of the good-in-general correct?

e)   Does the organization succeed in those efforts?

f)   Do the organization's activities violate some other firm precept of morality in a way not justified by the considerations raised in the first five questions?

Organizations can be deficient in each of these respects. An organization can fall short of its fidu-ciary obligations to its beneficiaries, either be-cause it does not act in good faith or because its conceptual beneficiary does not correspond to its objective beneficiary. An organization can be cul-pable because its perceived good is not, in fact, good—the Society for the Perpetuation of Racism, however faithfully it serves racism, is morally deficient because racism is an evil, not a good. An organization can be morally faulted, even if it serves faithfully a worthy or legitimate goal, if it is hostile to the good-in-general. Suppose, for example, that the American Society of Physicians (ASP) calculates that it can enrich its members by imposing rules on physicians forcing them to charge fees so high that a third of the society is left without health care. The ASP, let us suppose, simply does not care—its only concern is the financial wellbeing of its members. While tending to the business interests of physicians may be a legitimate goal for an organization, pursuing that goal in a way that knowingly leads to thousands of unnecessary deaths is nor morally permissible. An organization may be morally at fault if it strives to serve an incorrect understanding of the good-in-general. For example, suppose that the ASP, in the example mentioned above, took the position that the deaths of many poor people would, by purging the world of "undesirables," be a good thing. Then the ASP would be striving to serve its understanding of the good-in-general, but its understanding is, quite simply, wrong. An organization may be morally flawed because, while it acts with the best of intentions in all these ways, its activities, through some form of culpable negligence, defeat their purpose. Finally, an organization may be at fault by violating some independent moral precept. For example, if the Organization of American Engineers (OAE) excludes African Americans from membership, it is guilty of racism. The OAE's racism is not justifiable in terms of the OAE's perceived good, fiduciary duties, or role in a practice that serves the good-in-general.

Illustrating Case: The Maryland state legislature is currently considering changing its laws to conform to the Tarasoff ruling in California—all therapists would have a duty to break clients' confidentiality and warn appropriate authorities when a client poses a danger to herself or to others. Committee hearings are now in progress. The Organization of American Therapists (OAT) passed a resolution to present before the Committee arguing that all communications from clients should remain confidential. OAT's position is that, in the long run, keeping communications confidential would result in fewer suicides and violent acts by clients: increasing communication between clients and therapists would give therapists a better chance of working with clients to prevent suicide or violent acts, while imposing a duty to warn would make many clients wary of revealing to a therapist suicidal or violent feelings.

Discussion: OAT is dedicated to serving the good of benefiting clients who use therapy, with a secondary commitment to the professional interests of members. OAT is concerned about the social harm caused by violent clients, but argues that therapists can best serve the good-in-general (and prevent client acts of violence) by serving a particular role. OAT suggests, in other words, that the good-in-general is served when therapists provide clients with someone to whom anything may be said, under the guarantee of confidentiality. OAT is faithfully serving its perceived good, which is, in fact, good. (Benefiting clients who use therapy is indeed a good thing.) OAT is performing its fiduciary duty to clients of therapy. OAT's relevant conception of the good-in-general (reducing violent acts) is correct, and OAT is striving to serve that good. The remaining question, whether OAT's recommendation would in fact reduce the incidence of violent acts, is controversial. Finally, OAT does not appear to be violating any other general precept of morality not justified by the considerations already discussed. If OAT is at fault, then, it would be because OAT is incorrect in its judgment that its proposal would actually reduce the number of violent acts.[8]

V. *Conclusion*

The very nature of organizations, of structured ventures on behalf of some perceived good with distinctive relationships, implies that some general moral duties apply to all organizations, whatever their particular function and whatever specific duties are implied by their charter or charge. All organizations must make good faith efforts to serve an objectively good goal, and those efforts must generally serve, directly or indirectly, the broader realm of what is good and right. In this sense, organizations are like persons: they are not simply tools or soulless objects, hut members of the moral community.

NOTES

1. For a full exposition and discussion of Dual-Investor Theory, see Schlossberger, Eugene, "A New Model of Business: Dual-Investor Theory," *Business Ethics Quarterly* v. 4, 1994, pp. 459–474.
2. More precisely, the objective good is an objective beneficial of every organization.
3. The purpose for which an organization is founded may not be the same as the purpose for which it is currently maintained, and there may be, within the organization, debate and controversy about the purpose of the organization. A complete theory of organizations would have to explain how organizations can have goals. Some role is certainly played by all of the following: the history of the organization, the current views of the membership, the actual functioning and activities of the organization, and the role the organization plays as a social entity (how it is understood by others). For example, taxpayers have certain expectations concerning the IRS. We might call this the "social charge" given the organization and note that an organization's social charge is not irrelevant to determining its actual purpose. Any adequate, complete account of organizations must take account, in some way, of all of these factors.
4. Organizations do nor exist in order to perpetuate their own existence, though formally the existence of the organization could be called a good. In some extreme cases, an organization might exist to preserve a tradition, at the heart of which is the existence of the organization. But the value of the survival of an organization is always derivative from some other, perhaps related, good, to which the organization's continued existence contributes. Thus when an organization functions so as to place its own existence as its primary end in itself, something has gone very wrong with the organization—it is an organization failing to pursue its purpose, like an investment club that deliberately seeks to lose all its money.
5. The organizations given acronyms in this paper are purely fictitious. If some actual organization with the same name exists, nothing is implied about the actual functioning of that organization.
6. The claim made here is neutral about whether, ontologically, the relationships of organizations reduce to relationships of members. Perhaps the obligations of the Sierra Club to the environment may be parsed as obligations of individual members to participate in the Sierra Club in a way that serves, rather than harms, the environment. The point is rather that by being a member of an organization, one enters into relationships that are distinctly different from any of one's personal relationships. The obligations people acquire by joining the Sierra Club center on their participation, in the broadest sense, in the organization's activities—on striving to ensure that the activities of the Club faithfully execute its charge, adhere to its contracts, etc.
7. See Schlossberger, Eugene, *Moral Responsibility and Persons* (Philadelphia, Temple University Press, 1992).
8. OAT's recommendation concerns a widespread policy that helps define a role within a practice. It is thus significantly different from the moral problem confronting an individual therapist in the absence of a well-defined policy. For a more detailed treatment of the duty to warn, see Schlossberger, Eugene and Hecker, Lorna, "HIV and Family Therapists' Duty to Warn: A Legal and Ethical Analysis," *Journal of Marital and Family Therapy* 22 (Jan. 1996), pp. 27–40.

CHAPTER THIRTEEN

Health-Care Ethics

Physician-Assisted Suicide: Promoting Autonomy or Medicalizing Suicide?

TANIA SALEM

Tania Salem is a consultant for three universities in Brazil that are researching the problem of teenage pregnancy in that country. She has explored various cultural issues, ranging from family life to the impact of high-technology medicine.

"Physician-Assisted Suicide: Promoting Autonomy or Medicalizing Suicide?" Hastings Center Report 29, pp. 30–37. Reprinted with kind permission of the author and the Hastings Center.

Assisted suicide, many argue, honors self-determination in returning control of their dying to patients themselves. But physician assistance and measures proposed to safeguard patients from coercion in fact return ultimate authority over this "private and deeply personal" decision to medicine and society.

Why have physician-assisted suicide and voluntary active euthanasia taken on such vitality in recent years? Some authors stress the conjunction of powerful medical and cultural trends. The advances of modern medicine in association with its overwhelming bias to treat have engendered widespread and increasing fear. More

than death itself, what seems frightening is the very real prospect of losing control over one's own dying process. The reaction to this exorbitant sway of medicine has been nourished since the 1970s: patients' empowerment or, more generally, the liberal individualism that has vigorously extended into the medical system. In response, advance directives, health care proxies, and other devices founded on the right to forgo medical treatment aim to "protect" patients from physicians, medicine, and hospitals' institutional imperatives. From the perspective of this recent history, physician-assisted suicide and even voluntary active euthanasia are just one more necessary and justified step in this process. It is as if what modern medicine has expropriated from individuals could be returned to them through physician-assisted suicide: control over their own deaths.

These considerations condense two widespread current assumptions in the debate over aid in dying. The first is that these practices are, for better or for worse, pragmatic expressions of patients' autonomy. Although proponents and opponents evaluate very differently the adequacy and the limits conferred to self-determination in this context, they both endorse this general assertion. The second assumption is that physician-assisted suicide and voluntary active euthanasia are ultimate brakes on the unrestrained use of medical technology at the end of life. They are instruments to promote the "demedicalization" of death.

I propose to challenge these assumptions. I want to argue that physician-assisted suicide does not demedicalize death; rather, it medicalizes suicide. By this I mean it transforms a private act (suicide) into a medical event. Indeed, physician-assisted suicide implies not a resistance to but an extension of medical power over life and death. And second, that instead of asserting an individual's autonomy physician-assisted suicide is in fact an impediment to it.

My analysis accepts the liberal/libertarian presumption that one of the essential attributes of the individual is precisely the liberty to govern oneself free from external constraints. Despite my belief in both the indispensability and inevitability of social constraints, as an analytic device here I will assume radical autonomy to be a moral goal. I will also assume that from the perspective of the physician-patient dyad, more than killing, "assisted suicide" is literally what the phrase states: suicide with assistance, not only because it is the patient who makes the request, but also because it is she who is responsible for the final deed.

Promoting Autonomy, Demedicalizing Death

Many of those who favor physician-assisted suicide analyze and support it in reference to free choice, individual rights, and moral autonomy. This line of argument rests on a conception of autonomy primarily as "negative liberty": the right to act and govern oneself in accordance with one's own private beliefs, values, and choices without interference as long as one's behavior does not harm others. Proponents assert that this right should encompass patients' control over the timing and circumstances of death up to and including assistance in suicide. So conceived as a "personal and intimate decision," the right to aid in dying refers to a sphere of self-determination that should be left free from any paternalistic interference, whether that interference emanates from the state, from doctors, from family members, or from religious or philosophical orthodoxies. Physician-

assisted suicide is, in short, advocated as a "natural" extension of the constitutionally protected "right to privacy," and as a mere specification of the moral right to self-determination.

Opponents of this line of argument contest the pre-eminence conferred on autonomy vis-a-vis other social values and interests. The sanctity of life, the protection of those who are vulnerable to medical or family abuses, the "common good," and the ethical integrity of the medical professional (that is, the preservation of its ancient vow never intentionally to kill) are variously seen as competing values that in fact outweigh individual autonomy. What is contested is not physician-assisted suicide as an instrument of personal autonomy; critics insist that even if assisted suicide does serve autonomy, limits should be imposed on this value for the sake of other goods. Daniel Callahan's argument is illustrative: "the acceptance of euthanasia would sanction a view of autonomy holding that individuals may, in the name of their own private, idiosyncratic view of the good life, call upon others, including such institutions as medicine, to help them to pursue that life, even at the risk of common good."[1] Thus though they diverge in respect to how far personal autonomy and self-determination should extend, proponents and opponents converge in assuming that these values are ultimately the major forces driving the movement of physician-assisted suicide.

A second assumption widespread in the literature—particularly among defenders—is that by enhancing the patient's control assisted suicide represents just one more necessary step in the demedicalization of death. With the relationship between patients and doctors increasingly seen as a zero-sum game pitting vulnerable patients against the power of doctors and medicine, demedicalization is regarded as a prerequisite to patients' autonomy and empowerment in the face of death.

Thus proponents uphold physician-assisted suicide as a "natural" and indispensable development of the widely accepted right to refuse and/or withdraw life-sustaining medical treatments. Indeed, Peter Singer argues that the right to refuse is insufficient to grant individuals real control over their dying process. In his own words, "Not killing is not enough. The right to refuse medical treatment can help only in a limited number of cases in which it leads to a swift and painless death. Most cancer patients, for instance, are not in this situation. [This is why] the desire of control over how we die ... will not be satisfied by the concessions to patient autonomy within the framework of [traditional] ethics."[2]

Outer Codes, Inner Individuals

Incontestably, from a certain perspective physician-assisted suicide is a dramatic expression of autonomy, empowerment, self-determination, and the like. The contemporary debate about death and dying has shifted focus from medical norms to individual rights, choices, and desires, a shift from outer codes to inner individuals. Michel Foucault argues that every moral system necessarily comprises these two aspects: socially stipulated codes of conduct, and a relation to oneself as a moral entity who must evaluate and define a personal stance regarding the proposed conduct.[3] Outer codes and inner individuals thus point not to a dichotomy but to the predominance of one or the other moral perspective: some moral systems emphasize codes (requiring from the individual a strict conformity to them) while others shift the focus to personal "choices."

There is no doubt that the emphasis on inner individuals prevails in contemporary arguments for physician-assisted suicide. Influences from the outside, whether subtle or blatant, are seen as pernicious in subverting the main goal: the "pure" or "true" choice reached from within that at bottom takes account of the interests of the decisionmaker. This self-centered ethics rests on a nonrelational conception of personhood.

The second—and closely related—pillar of this discourse is the insistence that individuals be radically free to exercise their singularities and idiosyncrasies. In pluralistic societies, it is asserted, "there is far from any agreement, or near-agreement, about how one can establish as canonical a particular normative view of life."[4] Because personal styles, experiences, and beliefs are radically irreducible, it is impossible to suppose *a priori* that individual choices will coincide; each must find his or her own way of facing dying and death.

Yet there is a paradox underlying physician-assisted suicide. It is conceived of as an intimate, existential act and indeed a response to modern medicine, but at the same time it is a request for the complicity of physicians (and society). In contemporary Western societies the decision to take death into one's own hands has been construed as an act that is not simply personal, private, and solitary, but contrary to social norms and expectations. From a societal perspective, the individual who commits or attempts suicide is in this sense an outsider.

What seems unusual in the debate about aid in dying is the request for public endorsement and legitimization of the act of suicide. Whereas in suicide the individual "drops out" of the social order, in the context of physician-assisted suicide the individual "drops into" a system that recognizes and must even authorize this particular (ostensibly private) choice. In other words, displacing suicide from the private arena to bring it under medicine's stewardship means surrendering suicide to the (medical) "establishment."

Precisely because assisted suicide requires the connivance of others (direct from doctors, indirect from society), it cannot be seen as an act that solely expresses the ideal of individual autonomy. On the contrary, as long as it entails assistance it implies a mutual decision. Additionally, and, even more importantly, more than a mutual decision, assisted suicide presupposes that medicine has passed judgment on the act of suicide. In sum, physician-assisted suicide introduces tensions in the principle of personal autonomy and entails an increase of medical power over death and social morality.

Medicalizing Suicide

Medicalizing suicide encompasses three different (though interrelated) facets: the medicalization of an act, of a practice, and above all of the social ethos of death and suicide.

Medicalizing The Act Of Suicide

In the typical physician-assisted suicide scenario, the patient is responsible both for requesting aid in dying and for performing the final deed, and she or he construes the act basically as suicide. Yet as long as the physician is in charge of assisting the patient—either by his or her physical presence or by supplying the medical means to perform the act—physician-assisted suicide entails the medicalization of the act of suicide.

Ideally, for the physician to assist a patient's suicide the physician must be physically present—as attested in Timothy Quill's regrets for "abandoning" Diane, leaving her to take the prescribed lethal medication alone.[5] Thus what is intriguing in physician-assisted suicide is not that ventilators, tubes, CPR, and so on are supplanted by "lethal drugs," but that even in this context the physician and medicine are overwhelmingly present in the setting of death.

Even without the doctor's physical presence in the last scene, as long as physician-assisted suicide presupposes medical assistance it cannot be conceived as immersed in the realm of self-determination. Unless doctors are reduced strictly to being instruments to fulfill their patients' desires, physician-assisted suicide enacts what must be seen as a mutual decision. But what kind of questions are at stake in this joint decision? Proponents of assisted suicide suggest that patient and physician discuss the patient's medical condition and explore alternatives for alleviating pain and suffering. If it comes to it, the physician should provide a prescription for a lethal drug that leads to a "rapid" and "painless" death.[6] That is, the decision to die by suicide is treated precisely as if it were a set of clinical problems to be solved medically—the "private," "intimate," "self-determining" decision to commit suicide is translated into a clinical event.

Medicalizing Suicide As Professional Practice

Medicalizing suicide also points to the fact that if legalized, physician-assisted suicide as a legitimate practice would become the prerogative of physicians. Indeed, Jack Kevorkian has seen the exclusive right as the foundation for a new medical subspecialty of "obitiatry."[7]

This monopoly leads to the more general question of why aid in dying should be provided only by a medical practitioner. Why, that is, should assistance in suicide be understood as requiring medical authority rather than, for instance, a community of family or friends? The most obvious answer is that physicians—and only physicians—have the necessary technical skills to ensure a "rapid" and "painless" death. But as some critics have noted, "Assisted suicide does not even require medical skill.... If freeing up patients truly is the goal, then assisted suicide's advocates disserve patients when they do not advocate ending the physician's exclusive power to prescribe medication. Ironically, the advocates of patients' rights end up empowering doctors more than they do patients."[8]

Yet even those who maintain that technical knowledge is imperative do not confine their justification of physician-assisted suicide to this reason. Placing suicide under the stewardship of medicine is further defended as a way of "enhancing public accountability of the practice" and "protecting against abuse."[9] From the patient's perspective, the request for aid in dying may mean a "desire for companionship in pursuing a difficult course of action, a wish for confirmation of a decision about which the patient is unsure or simply a cry for help" (pp. 88–89, note 42). Moreover, since suicide is still stigmatized, "seeking a physician's assistance may be a way of trying to remove that stigma."[10] But inasmuch as cultural preconceptions and loneliness (whatever its source) are far from being exclusively medical issues, we must ask why we expect doctors to respond to them. Two possible answers come to mind: either medicine is moving beyond its proper role, or the scope of medical competence has already been extended beyond appropriate boundaries.

It seems reasonable to conclude that ceding monopoly of assistance in suicide to doctors is anchored in an inflation of the physician's role, as well as in the extreme idealization of physicians' character and the relationships they establish with patients. The bond physicians establish with patients is supposedly effective, collaborative, and committed. Both this idealization and the willingness to delegate to physicians the exclusive right to assist suicide bespeak the social and symbolic power already conferred on medicine and medical professionals in our societies. In other words, it is not (or not only) the need for technical expertise that impels us to physician-assisted suicide. Rather, our culture, so impregnated by medicalization, takes for granted that assisted suicide should fall under the control and supervision of medicine.

Medicalizing The Morality Of Suicide

As a legitimate domain of professional practice, then, physician-assisted suicide necessarily involves medicalizing the moral questions surrounding suicide. Physician-assisted suicide presupposes, and ultimately is, a medical judgment about death or suicide; it is a medical evaluation of the fairness and legitimacy of a person's (not simply a patient's) desire or choice to end his or her life.

With some few exceptions, even the most radical advocates of physician-assisted suicide recognize the need to establish protocols and guidelines to prevent abuses, protect the vulnerable, guarantee public accountability, and even to assure the autonomous character of the patient's choice. Surely these aims are respectable and the setting up of criteria just and reasonable. Yet establishing medical guidelines also introduces tensions into the value of autonomy in several ways.

The requisites for physician-assisted suicide (must the patient be terminally ill? which medical specialists are best qualified as consultants?) are still being debated. There is, however, agreement about the moral attributes that the patient and his or her request must evince: the decision to die must be "informed," "rational," "stable," and "fully free" or "voluntary." And there is broad agreement that to ensure that these conditions are fulfilled the patient must submit to screening by a team of doctors (the treating physician, a consulting physician, and a psychiatrist) who would evaluate the request for aid in dying.

This requirement assumes that besides undue external influences, some impulses or dispositions emanating from the patient herself or himself—such as depression or guilt—may threaten "pure choice." "Voluntariness" in this sense must be safeguarded from undue influence stemming not only from outside, but also from within. Ultimately, this is to assume that the inner world may be obscure to the individual, that she or he may be half blind to her or his own choice, desire, or personal truth.

The presumption that the inner world is or may be opaque to the individual suggests a second underlying presupposition: someone other than the person requesting aid in dying has greater expertise in judging the appropriateness of that request. Medical authority, that is, is assumed to have the proper ability to unveil the "real truth" behind the request to die. The patient's treating physician, along with psychiatric and/or palliative care consultants, is charged to distinguish authentic from distorted choices; that is, to discern whether the request is pertinent or pathological (and if so, whether it is "curable" by medical means).

Both these premises obviously collide with the principles of autonomy and self-determination. Both displace the final decision concerning suicide from the patient to the physician's judgment that the request is appropriate and free from "undue influence."

The insult to autonomy is not exerted through repression, as was the criminalization of suicide. Rather, it is exercised through what Foucault would call the "normalization" of suicide, the subordination to medical scrutiny of this event and the person making the request.[11] The "patient" is subjected to observation, examination, and inquiry to confirm the "rationality" and "voluntariness" of his or her request. Thus medicalizing (assisted) suicide jeopardizes autonomy not only when the patient's request is denied for one reason or another. Requiring that the patient submit to medical surveillance is, in itself, an outrage to autonomy as this value is classically defined.

To illustrate how complex is the apparatus through which suicide is normalized, consider guidelines suggested by Frank Miller, Howard

Brody, and Timothy Quill, for example. To ensure public accountability for physician-assisted suicide, to guarantee that the procedure is used only as a "last resort," and to assure that the patient's decision is genuinely voluntary, the authors suggest palliative care consultants and regional palliative care committees as the core of a whole supervising system.[12] Thus the primary physician would be prohibited from providing lethal drugs without prior consultation with a palliative care expert who, based on "examination of medical records and interviews with the treating physician, the patient and the interested members of the patient's family" (p. 121), would assess the authenticity of the request to die. Patients and their physicians would have the right to appeal the consultant's denial of requests for assisted suicide to regional palliative care committees. The bureaucratization of suicide built into such proposals entails serious constraints on patients' self-determination.

Subjecting individuals who request aid in dying to this kind of scrutiny further affronts their dignity in putting all such requests under suspicion. In the name of protecting individuals from irreversible self-harm, all are in principle treated as moral patients rather than moral agents and are presumed to be mentally incompetent. The capacity to make autonomous decisions, which is presumed in all other cases unless demonstrated otherwise, is stood on its head in physician-assisted suicide. Patients must prove their decisionmaking capacity from the outset.

Subjecting the individual to medical norms in this way also introduces a tension for one of the central questions of liberal philosophers. If, as the liberal argument claims, the morality or immorality of decisions at the end of life rests on the competent patient's wishes rather than on a distinction between killing and allowing to die, protocols that may ultimately deny a patient's request for assistance in dying assert, in effect, that moral authority resides outside the patient's choice. And if medicine may, morally, reject patients' autonomous requests for aid, in the context of physician-assisted suicide the value of patient autonomy becomes more rhetorical than real.

Admittedly, even liberal theorists emphasize that there are limits to autonomy, and that like other important rights, the right to physician-assisted suicide is not absolute and can properly be restricted under certain circumstances. Indeed, Ronald Dworkin and others argue precisely that because autonomy must be protected and preserved physician-assisted suicide must be regulated. Under certain conditions the state has the power to override individual rights to protect patients from undue pressures, even internal ones.

The tension remains, however. In the context of assisted suicide, how is it possible to reconcile the assertion that paternalistic influences are unacceptable with the concept that in some situations the state (or the medical establishment) may deny assistance in suicide in the name of "what it reasonably judges to be the best interest of the potential suicide"? Alexander Capron has argued that decisions on behalf of others should utilize a best interest standard of what the "average reasonable person would do under the given circumstances."[13] Doesn't this permit the tyranny of the majority over the individual? Doesn't this menace the right, so praised by liberal theorists, to exercise our singularities in a radical way? As Yale Kamisar has asked, "[I]f self-determination and autonomy is the major force driving the right to assisted suicide, why should a competent person's firm conclusion that life has become unendurable for her have to be 'objectively reasonable'? Why should not a competent person's own evaluation of her situation suffice?"[14] To phrase this in terms of the argument I make here, is it ever possible to reconcile medicalizing suicide with autonomy?

It could reasonably be argued that guidelines for physician-assisted suicide do not injure the patient's self-determination since the request emanates from a patient who supposedly knows the rules of the game in advance. And, the argument would continue, if one does not wish to submit to those rules, "do it yourself" remains a way out. But this seems to admit that ultimately assisted suicide has to do with something beyond strict self-determination, that autonomy is not the primary moral foundation, or at least that if autonomy is to be exercised it demands constant external oversight.

In sum, although advocated in the name of self-sovereignty, physician-assisted suicide ends up reinforcing a power external to the self. It reinforces medical power at the expense of the individual in a very sensitive realm: one's decision to die.

NOTES

1. Daniel Callahan, "When Self-Determination Runs Amok," *Hastings Center Report* 22, no. 2 (1992): 50–55, at 52.
2. Peter Singer, *Rethinking Life and Death: The Collapse of Our Traditional Ethics* (New York: St. Martin's Press, 1994), pp. 194, 147–48.
3. Michel Foucault, *History of Sexuality, Vol. 2: The Use of Pleasure* (New York: Vintage Books, 1986), ch. 3.
4. H. Tristram Engelhardt, Jr., "Fashioning an Ethic for Life and Death in a Post-Modern Society," *Hastings Center Report* 19, no. 1(1989): S7–S9, at S7.
5. Timothy E. Quill, *Death and Dignity: Making Choices and Taking Charge* (New York: W.W., Norton & Company, 1993).
6. New York State Task Force on Life and the Law, *When Death is Sought: Assisted Suicide and Euthanasia in the Medical Context* (Albany, NY: New York State Task Force on Life and the Law, 1994), p. 105.
7. Jack Kevorkian, *Prescription: Medicine* (New York: Prometheus Books, 1991).
8. Giles R. Scofield, "Privacy (or Liberty) and Assisted Suicide," *Journal of Pain and Symptom Management* 6, no. 5(1991): 280–88, at 285.
9. New York State Task Force, *When Death is Sought*, p. 105.
10. Dan W. Brock, "Voluntary Active Euthanasia," *Hastings Center Report* 22, no, 2(1992): 10–22, at 21.
11. On the concept of "normalization," see Michael Foucault, *History of Sexuality, Vol. 1: An introduction* (New York: Random House, 1978).
12. Miller, Quill, Brody, "Regulating Physician-Assisted Death," *New England Journal of Medicine* 331 (1994): 119–23.
13. Alexander M. Capron, "Substituting Our Judgment," *Hastings Center Report* 22, no. 2 (1992): 58–59, at 59.
14. Yale Kamisar, "Physician-Assisted Suicide: The Last Bridge to Voluntary Active Euthanasia," in *Euthanasia Examined: Ethical, Clinical and Other Legal Perspectives*, ed. John Keown (Cambridge: Cambridge University Press, 1995), pp. 225–60, at 239.

Active and Passive Euthanasia

JAMES RACHELS

The distinction between active and passive euthanasia is thought to be crucial for medical ethics. The idea is that it is permissible, at least in some cases, to withhold treatment and allow a patient to die, but it is never permissible to take any direct action designed to kill the patient. This doctrine seems to be accepted by most doctors, and it is endorsed in a statement adopted by the House of Delegates of the American Medical Association on December 4, 1973:

> The intentional termination of the life of one human being by another—mercy killing—is contrary to that for which the medical profession stands and is contrary to the policy of the American Medical Association.
>
> The cessation of the employment of extraordinary means to prolong the life of the body when there is irrefutable evidence that biological death is imminent is the decision of the patient and/or his immediate family. The advice and judgment of the physician should be freely available to the patient and/or his immediate family.

However, a strong case can be made against this doctrine. In what follows I will set out some of the relevant arguments, and urge doctors to reconsider their views on this matter.

To begin with a familiar type of situation, a patient who is dying of incurable cancer of the throat is in terrible pain, which can no longer be satisfactorily alleviated. He is certain to die within a few days, even if present treatment is continued, but he does not want to go on living for those days since the pain is unbearable. So he asks the doctor for an end to it, and his family joins in the request.

Suppose the doctor agrees to withhold treatment, as the conventional doctrine says he may. The justification for his doing so is that the patient is in terrible agony, and since he is going to die anyway, it would be wrong to prolong his suffering needlessly. But now notice this. If one simply withholds treatment, it may take the patient longer to die, and so he may suffer more than he would if more direct action were taken and a lethal injection given. This fact provides strong reason for thinking that, once the initial decision not to prolong his agony has been made, active euthanasia is actually preferable to passive euthanasia, rather than the reverse. To say otherwise is to endorse the option that leads to more suffering rather than less, and is contrary to the humanitarian impulse that prompts the decision not to prolong his life in the first place.

Part of my point is that the process of being "allowed to die" can be relatively slow and painful, whereas being given a lethal injection is relatively quick and painless. Let me give a different sort of example. In the United States about one in 600 babies is born with Down's syndrome. Most of these babies are otherwise healthy—that is, with only the usual pediatric care, they will proceed to an otherwise normal infancy. Some, however, are born with congenital defects such as intestinal obstructions that require operations if they are to live. Sometimes, the parents and the doctor will decide not to operate, and let the infant die. Anthony Shaw describes what happens then:

> When surgery is denied [the doctor] must try to keep the infant from suffering while natural forces sap the baby's life away. As a surgeon whose natural inclination is to use the scalpel to fight off death, standing by and watching a salvageable baby die is the most emotionally exhausting experience I know. It is easy at a conference, in a theoretical discussion to decide that such infants should be allowed to die. It is altogether different to stand by in the nurs-

ery and watch as dehydration and infection wither a tiny being over hours and days. This is a terrible ordeal for me and the hospital staff—much more so than for the parents who never set foot in the nursery.[1]

I can understand why some people are opposed to all euthanasia, and insist that such infants must be allowed to live. I think I can also understand why other people favor destroying these babies quickly and painlessly. Buy why should anyone favor letting "dehydration and infection wither a tiny being over hours and days"? The doctrine that says that a baby may be allowed to dehydrate and wither, but may not be given an injection that would end its life without suffering, seems so patently cruel as to require no further refutation. The strong language is not intended to offend, but only to put the point in the clearest possible way.

My second argument is that the conventional doctrine leads to decisions concerning life and death made on irrelevant grounds.

Consider again the case of the infants with Down's syndrome who need operations for congenital defects unrelated to the syndrome to live. Sometimes, there is no operation, and the baby dies, but when there is no such defect, the baby lives on. Now, an operation such as that to remove an intestinal obstruction is not prohibitively difficult. The reason why such operations are not performed in these cases is, clearly, that the child has Down's syndrome and the parents and the doctor judge that because of that fact it is better for the child to die.

But notice that this situation is absurd, no matter what view one takes of the lives and potentials of such babies. If the life of such an infant is worth preserving, what does it matter if it needs a simple operation? Or, if one thinks it better that such a baby should not live on, what difference does it make that it happens to have an unobstructed intestinal tract? In either case, the matter of life and death is being decided on irrelevant grounds. It is the Down's syndrome, and not the intestines, that is the issue. The matter should be decided, if at all, on that basis, and not be allowed to depend on the essentially irrelevant question of whether the intestinal tract is blocked.

What makes this situation possible, of course, is the idea that when there is an intestinal blockage, one can "let the baby die," but when there is no such defect there is nothing that can be done, for one must not "kill" it. The fact that this idea leads to such results as deciding life or death on irrelevant grounds is another good reason why the doctrine would be rejected.

One reason why so many people think that there is an important moral difference between active and passive euthanasia is that they think killing someone is morally worse than letting someone die. But is it? Is killing, in itself, worse than letting die? To investigate this issue, two cases may be considered that are exactly alike except that one involves killing whereas the other involves letting someone die. Then, it can be asked whether this difference makes any difference to the moral assessments. It is important that the cases be exactly alike, except for this one difference, since otherwise one cannot be confident that it is this difference and not some other than accounts for any variation in the assessments of the two cases. So, let us consider this pair of cases:

In the first, Smith stands to gain a large inheritance if anything should happen to his six-year-old cousin. One evening while the child is taking his bath, Smith sneaks into the bathroom and drowns the child, and then arranges things so that it will look like an accident.

In the second, Jones also stands to gain if anything should happen to his six-year-old cousin. Like Smith, Jones sneaks in planning to drown the child in his bath. However, just as he enters the bathroom Jones sees the child slip and hit his head, and fall face down in the water. Jones is delighted; he stands by, ready to push the child's head back under if it is necessary, but it is not necessary. With only a little thrashing about, the child drowns all by himself, "accidentally," as Jones watches and does nothing.

Now Smith killed the child, whereas Jones "merely" let the child die. That is the only difference between them. Did either man behave better, from a moral point of view? If the differ-ence between killing and letting die were in itself a morally important matter, one should say that Jones's behavior was less reprehensible than Smith's. But does one really want to say that? I think not. In the first place, both men acted from the same motive, personal gain, and both had exactly the same end in view when they acted. It may be inferred from Smith's conduct that he is a bad man, although that judgment may be withdrawn or modified if certain further facts are learned about him—for example, that he is mentally deranged. But would not the very same thing be inferred about Jones from his conduct? And would not the same further considerations also be relevant to any modification of this judgment? Moreover, suppose Jones pleaded, in his own defense, "After all, I didn't do anything except just stand there and watch the child drown. I didn't kill him; I only let him die." Again, if letting die were in itself less bad than killing, this defense should have at least some weight. But it does not. Such a "defense" can only be regarded as a grotesque perversion of moral reasoning. Morally speaking, it is no defense at all.

Now, it may be pointed out, quite properly, that the cases of euthanasia with which doctors are concerned are not like this at all. They do not involve personal gain or the destruction of normal healthy children. Doctors are concerned only with cases in which the patient's life is of no further use to him, or in which the patient's life has become or will soon become a terrible burden. However, the point is the same in these cases: the bare difference between killing and letting die does not, in itself, make a moral difference. If a doctor lets a patient die, for humane reasons, he is in the same moral position as if he had given the patient a lethal injection for humane reasons. If his decision is wrong—if, for example, the patient's illness was in fact curable—the decision would be equally regrettable no matter which method was used to carry it out. And if the doctor's decision was the right one, the method used is not in itself important.

The AMA policy statement isolates the crucial issue very well; the crucial issue is "the intentional termination of the life of one human being by another." But after identifying this issue, and forbidding "mercy killing," the statement goes on to deny that the cessation of treatment is the intentional termination of a life. This is where the mistake comes in, for what is the cessation of treatment, in these circumstances, if it is not "the intentional termination of the life of one human being by another"? Of course it is exactly that, and if it were not, there would be no point to it.

Many people will find this judgment hard to accept. One reason I think, is that it is very easy to conflate the question of whether killing is, in itself, worse than letting die, with the very different question of whether most actual cases of killing are more reprehensible than most actual cases of letting die. Most actual cases of killing are clearly terrible (think, for example, of all the murders reported in the newspapers), and one hears of such cases every day. On the other hand, one hardly ever hears of a case of letting die, except for the actions of doctors who are motivated by humanitarian reasons. So one learns to think of killing in a much worse light than of letting die. But this does not mean that there is something about killing that makes it in itself worse than letting die, for it is not the bare difference between killing and letting die that makes the difference in these cases. Rather, the other factors—the murderer's motive of personal gain, for example, contrasted with the doctor's humanitarian motivation—account for different reactions to the different cases.

I have argued that killing is not in itself any worse than letting die; if my contention is right, it follows that active euthanasia is not any worse than passive euthanasia. What arguments can be given on the other side? The most common, I believe, is the following:

> The important difference between active and passive euthanasia is that, in passive euthanasia, the doctor does not do anything to bring about the patient's death. The doctor does nothing, and the patient dies of whatever ills already afflict him. In active euthanasia, however, the doctor does something to bring about the patient's death: he kills him. The doctor who gives the patient with cancer a lethal injection

has himself caused his patient's death; whereas if he merely ceases treatment, the cancer is the cause of death.

A number of points need to be made here. The first is that it is not exactly correct to say that in passive euthanasia the doctor does nothing, for he does one thing that is very important: he lets the patient die. "Letting someone die" is certainly different, in some respects, from other types of action—mainly in that it is a kind of action that one may perform by way of not performing certain other actions. For example, one may let a patient die by way of not giving medication, just as one may insult someone by way of not shaking his hand. But for any purpose of moral assessment, it is a type of action nonetheless. The decision to let a patient die is subject to moral appraisal in the same way that a decision to kill him would be subject to moral appraisal: it may be assessed as wise or unwise, compassionate or sadistic, right or wrong. If a doctor deliberately let a patient die who was suffering from a routinely curable illness, the doctor would certainly be to blame if he had needlessly killed the patient. Charges against him would be appropriate. If so, it would be no defense at all for him to insist that he didn't "do anything." He would have done something very serious indeed, for he let his patient die.

Fixing the cause of death may be very important from a legal point of view, for it may determine whether criminal charges are brought against the doctor. But I do not think that this notion can be used to show a moral difference between active and passive euthanasia. The reason why it is considered bad to be the cause of someone's death is that death is regarded as a great evil—and so it is. However, if it has been decided that euthanasia—even passive euthanasia—is desirable in a given case, it has also been decided that in this instance death is no greater an evil than the patient's continued existence. And if this is true, the usual reason for not wanting to be the cause of someone's death simply does not apply.

Finally, doctors may think that all of this is only of academic interest—the sort of thing that philosophers may worry about but that has no practical bearing on their own work. After all, doctors must be concerned about the legal consequences of what they do, and active euthanasia is clearly forbidden by the law. But even so, doctors should also be concerned with the fact that the law is forcing upon them a moral doctrine that may be indefensible, and has a considerable effect on their practices. Of course, most doctors are not now in the position of being coerced in this matter, for they do not regard themselves as merely going along with what the law requires. Rather, in statements such as the AMA policy statement that I have quoted they are endorsing this doctrine as a central point of medical ethics. In that statement, active euthanasia is condemned not merely as illegal but as "contrary to that for which the medical profession stands," whereas passive euthanasia is approved. However, the preceding considerations suggest that there is really no moral difference between the two, considered in themselves (there may be important moral differences in some cases in their *consequences*, but, as I pointed out, these differences may make active euthanasia, and not passive euthanasia, the morally preferable option). So, whereas doctors may have to discriminate between active and passive euthanasia to satisfy the law, they should not do any more than that. In particular, they should not give the distinction any added authority and weight by writing it into official statements of medical ethics.

NOTE

1. Anthony Shaw, "Doctor, Do We Have a Choice?" *The New York Times Magazine*, 30 January 1972, 54.

Health Care as a Business: The Ethic of Hippocrates Versus the Ethic of Managed Care

MARK H. WAYMACK

Mark H. Waymack is associate professor of Philosophy, Loyola University, Chicago.

"Health Care as a Business: The Ethic of Hippocrates Versus the Ethic of Managed Care," Business and Professional Ethics Journal 9 (1990), pp. 69–78. *Reprinted with kind permission of the author.*

The ethic of Hippocrates is, in an important sense, quite ambiguous. Scholars of the history of medicine or the history of ideas may have certain interpretations—interpretations which generally view the Hippocratic Oath in terms of ancient Greek medicine, particularly of the Pythagorean tradition. The general public in America, however, while being quite unacquainted with the actual text of the Hippocratic Oath, nevertheless has a public conception of that special oath that medical students take as part of the rites of passage from student to physician. That the oath that medical students take might bear only a faint resemblance to the historical Hippocratic document, and that there is no universal uniformity in the words of the oath that different medical schools ask their students to swear, have not prevented there being a popular public conception of the ethic to which physicians are bound. Of the features of that ethic, the one that concerns us here is the notion that when caring for a patient, the physician should have *only* the welfare of that individual patient in mind. The question *of finances* should never be allowed to deter the physician from recommending the most medically appropriate of the alternatives. This loyalty to the individual patient is part of what is seen as the special ethical obligation of the physician as a *professional*.

In recent years, however, the practice of medicine has become more a practice of business than it has in the past. Physicians are engaged in joint ventures; and hospitals are competing with each other for economically profitable physicians and referral networks. But one change in practice that has perhaps touched upon Americans most pervasively is the introduction of managed care. The introduction of federal diagnostic-related-groups

(DRGs) and, more recently, the enormous and increasing enrollment in both for-profit and not-for-profit health maintenance organizations (HMOs) have sparked a number of discussions concerning the ethical conflict of interest in which such arrangements place physicians.

For convenience's sake, let us take the HMO as an example of managed care. At the heart of the typical, contemporary HMO is the idea of cost containment. The original idea of reducing health care utilization by encouraging health maintenance, though not entirely abandoned, has had only limited success in achieving the control of escalating costs desired by health care premium payers.[1] The far more effective method of cost control has been the control of services. Under fee-for-service insurance, the insured person could see virtually any physician whom he or she wished and be compensated for most any sort of care ordered by the physician. This gives rise to a tendency for physicians to make excessive use of services and does nothing to discourage patients from seeking and receiving unnecessary services. Within the HMO, however, a primary care physician usually must *authorize* the use of special care, including laboratory expenses, any use of health services outside of the normal HMO network, and referrals to specialists either in or outside of the HMO network. This has come to be known as the "gate-keeper" role, or to distinguish it from the term "positive gate-keeper," what Pellegrino and Thomasma call the "negative gate-keeper."[2]

Thus, the HMO keeps expenses down by keeping down the utilization of health care services. The gate-keeper may reduce costs by preventing *over-use* of medical technology. But in some instances, the gate-keeper contains costs by preventing the use of technology that the HMO, though it recognizes as effective, may deem to be *too expensive* to include in its coverage. Ford Motor Company will offer its most popular automobiles with vinyl rather than real leather upholstery. Using real leather as a matter of custom would make the car cost more money than most of its target market audience would be willing to pay. HMOs engage in the same sort of reasoning. For example, HMOs may deem that liver and pancreas transplants are simply too expensive to fund. If they can argue that such care is not included in "basic care" (for all HMOs are required by law to cover for "basic care," just as all cars are required to meet certain minimum safety standards), then the HMO can write its policy such that *the policy does not include such procedures.* Other tactics might include longer waiting lines (encouraging the most cost-efficient use of expensive physician time), and the use of skilled nurses to screen presenting patients before they ever see a physician.

So while the "Mercedes" of health insurance might cover for everything from a liver transplant to liposuction to artfully sculpt one's knees, and do so at the patient's convenience, the "Ford" of health insurance will not offer such non-basic services and may require some patience and forbearance on the part of the patient.

In conclusion, the HMO offers what must be considered, at least in many respects, an intrinsically less desirable product than traditional fee-for-service health insurance. What makes HMOs choiceworthy for many consumers, however, is that in the consumer's judgement the lower costs of HMO insurance (lower premiums and often lower or no costs per visit or procedure) more than balance out the restrictions involved with the service. So just as, when our own resources are not infinite, we may willingly choose the sturdy Ford over the crafted and polished Mercedes with the real leather interior, the compact disc stereo and anti-locking brakes, so we may willingly choose the inexpensive but serviceable HMO over the more generous fee-for-service insurance plan.

How Cost Containment Is Enforced

We have briefly outlined how HMOs can reduce costs through the use of a gate-keeper. Let us explore more closely here how the gate-keeper role functions. The gate-keeper helps to minimize health expenses by preventing unnecessary and/or inappropriate use of health services. This function is often reinforced or supplemented by a "utilization review committee," which reviews the practice patterns of physicians in the HMO group, looking for atypical patterns of practice. Atypical patterns of practice (such as over-use of hospital stays, overuse of diagnostic interventions and drug therapies, or even *improper* use of health services) usually cost the health insurer (and eventually the payer of the premiums) more money in the long run. They can also have, at least in some cases, an adverse effect on the health of the patient. Hence, when atypical patterns are detected, they are examined and if they represent poor practice patterns (rather than the excellent physician who occasionally get sicker patients because of his or her special skills), the physician is instructed in how to change his or her pattern of practice.

Now, physicians may tend to be cautious and conservative in their style of practice. Hence, it can be difficult to get them to change their patterns of practice. HMOs have taken a variety of tactics to encourage changes in practice. One tactic is simply the strongly worded suggestions of a utilization review committee. This tactic, however, may seem to lack much punch. Consequently, some groups have offered physicians financial incentives to bring their style of practice into conformity with the standards of the HMO. Physicians who do not use more special services than the HMO deems to be normal may receive a bonus at the end of the year. Those physicians who "over-use" may forfeit the bonus or even lose a part of their salary. The HMO therefore supplies the physicians with incentives to reduce utilization.

The Recipe For Conflict Of Interest

HMOs, clearly then, seek to constrain costs. This is how they attract business away from traditional fee-for-service insurance plans. Furthermore, as shall now be discussed, these efforts to constrain costs do provide the conditions for a conflict of interests, both between the HMO and the patient and, more importantly for this essay, the physician and the patient. This section shall consider the potential for conflict of interest, whereas the next section shall consider whether this particular kind of conflict of interests represents an *ethical* conflict of interests.

The conflict of interest arises when the following two conditions are met:

1) There will inevitably (practically, though not logically inevitably) arise cases where the use of certain expensive, non-basic health care services would be of some benefit (however small) to the patient, but

2) There is a self-interested *incentive* (contrary to the interests of the patient) for the HMO and the physician to withhold the health care services in question.

These two conditions would seem to be easily, and indeed *frequently*, present in the typical HMO-physician-patient relationship.

Consider an infant suffering from an adenovirus infection. In rare cases this kind of virus can be quite aggressive and develop into viral pneumonia. The physician examines the child, listening to her lungs through the stethoscope. The physician is *relatively* sure that the infection has not spread to the lungs; the breathing sounds are reasonably clear. But that remote possibility lingers in the background. If costs were of no concern, the physician would almost certainly order a chest x-ray; but under the cost-conscious practice of the managed care environment, such a diagnostic procedure (though not inordinately expensive) would probably be seen as unnecessary unless there was greater risk of infection in the lungs.

As another example, a patient with acute headaches might *possibly* benefit from a full neurological workup, including a CT-scan, even though the most probable cause is simple stress. Given that stress is the most likely cause (in the particular case we have in mind) the HMO may provide an incentive to the physician to forego the full neurological workup on the grounds that as a general policy such interventions are not cost-effective. Such expensive intervention will not be forbidden absolutely, but physicians will be encouraged through incentives to reserve it for cases where the symptoms and history more clearly indicate a likely organic cause.

As a final example, the mother of a newborn infant, despite a lack of complications, may well benefit *to some extent*, in her physician's judgement, from being allowed to stay in the hospital for several days before going home. Yet, the HMO may feel that such a stay is not cost-effective. (Remember, we are buying the no-frills Ford here, not the Mercedes.) The HMO may therefore make it awkward, bothersome, and difficult for the physician to permit the mother to stay in the hospital except that she pay for the extended stay out of her own personal financial resources.

These examples, which can be easily multiplied, illustrate how commonly conflicts of interest can arise between the HMO and physician, on the one hand, and the patient, on the other hand.

Why These Are Not Necessarily Ethical Conflicts

In essence, I shall argue here that this kind of conflict is not necessarily an *ethical* conflict for the reason that the consumer has *willingly chosen* to participate in this kind of health plan. However, before making that argument, let us review why some ethicists think that such a conflict is an ethical conflict and that it is unethical for physicians to take on this role of "gate-keeper."

The difficulty is seated in the traditional notion of the physician as having a strict moral obligation to have the patient's interest in mind when caring for the patient. The patient comes to the physician as a person in need—someone who is ill and vulnerable—and thus the patient *entrusts* the physician with his or her care. Any choice or action that the physician makes (a) on grounds other than patient welfare and (b) that is contrary to the welfare of the patient constitutes a violation of that moral trust that the patient has placed in the physician. Thus, for the physician to be an agent of the HMO or an agent for his or her own personal income in addition to being an agent for the patient is an inherently morally undesirable conflict of interests.

If we reflect upon how the patient enters into the care of the HMO physician, we may see how this is a misapplied criticism of HMOs, cost-containment, and the gate-keeper role.

First, let us recall that the consumer/patient has voluntarily chosen to enter into agreement with a particular HMO, its coverage plan and the physicians within its practice network. That is, the consumer, working within certain economic constraints, has weighed the costs and potential benefits of various health insurance plans against the background of the costs and benefits of other goods and services, and has decided to purchase or contract with that particular HMO. This is quite analogous to the consumer comparing different makes and models of automobiles and settling for the basic model of a Ford automobile instead of the elegantly appointed Mercedes. The Mercedes, including its leather upholstery, anti-locking brakes and protective emergency air bags, costs more money than that particular consumer is willing to spend (relative to other desires).

Now the consumer, *knowing* that the very basic model Ford does not come with anti-locking brakes and air bags, is in no position to complain (after an accident) that Ford Motor Company withheld these items unethically. Since the consumer chose knowingly, he or she cannot accuse Ford Motor Company of acting unethically, even if personal injury results as a consequence of the accident. (Please note that anti-locking brakes and protective air bags are not yet considered "basic" safety devices that federal transportation regulators require on all newly made automobiles.)

Analogously, the consumer chooses among health insurance plans knowing what their restrictions and limitations are. We purchase health insurance not knowing for sure just what our health care needs (or desires) will be in the future. We may make some educated *predictions*, based upon such factors as family history and current status, as to what we will need or desire; but such predictions necessarily lack certainty. They deal in the realm of probability. The consumer recognizes that in the case of certain *possible* eventualities, the health care plan that has been chosen will not be adequate to meet his or her desires/needs. But because those circumstances are relatively unlikely, the consumer is willing to discount the costs of their actually occurring. Being somewhat risk-averse, most consumers choose to purchase *some* sort of health care insurance; but because most consumers do not regard the worst case scenarios as definite eventualities, they are willing to settle for purchasing less insurance coverage than they might *possibly* need. So buying insurance is a kind of gambling—we are willing to pay enough to avoid the most likely bad outcomes, but we are not so risk-averse that we are willing to pay what it would cost to cover for *every possible* bad outcome. We choose a compromise.

When the HMO physician refrains from a *slightly* possibly beneficial, but quite expensive, diagnostic procedure, he or she is engaging in behavior that in some sense conflicts with the interest of the patient. When he or she refrains from arranging a liver transplant because it will not be paid for by the health plan, he or she is, in a sense, acting contrary to the patient welfare.

However, when the physician practices such cost conscious medicine, he or she is practicing along lines of care to which the patient willingly agreed prior to his or her illness. Just as in gambling with cards (or anti-lock versus no anti-lock brakes) there are winners and losers, so with health insurance there are winners and losers. The winners are those who purchase the insurance and subsequently develop needs that exceed the amount of money that they have contributed but that the insurance plan is designed to reimburse. The losers are those who purchase the insurance and never have great need of it (they put in much more than they take out) and those who develop rare and/or expensive conditions that the insurance plan does not cover. If the consumers buy into the HMO insurance plan, knowing its costs and conditions, it does not seem right to allow them to cry "foul" when they (through pure misfortune) become the losers. Thus, when the physician acts as a gate-keeper, he or she is in an important sense acting in accord with the *autonomy* exercised by the patient when that health plan was selected.

Since the gatekeeper physician is therefore acting in accord with an autonomous choice of the patient, he or she is acting in such a way as to fulfill that patient's *autonomy*. Hence, the physician is not acting contrary to the interests of the patient; rather the physician is acting upon the interests of the patient *as defined by the patient in the informed choice of a health plan.*

The Ethic of Managed Care and the Ethic of Hippocrates

Despite the efforts of some to see a solution to the dilemma in an appeal to *both* the ethic of Hippocrates and some ethic of "informed consent," the ethic of Hippocrates and the ethic of managed care clearly conflict; but they conflict in an interesting way. In the Hippocratic tradition, the physician's ethical obligation is to the good of the patient, *as understood by the physician.* This is a natural stage for paternalism; and indeed paternalism had been the accepted practice for millennia, from the Hippocratic command to keep secret most important information from the patient (lest that self-knowledge cause self-harm) to the days of recent memory in American medical practice. (And I have chosen to overlook the continuing paternalism of medical practice in many other modern countries.) The ethic of managed care, as I have explained, can be understood, on the other hand, as founded upon respect for patient autonomy, particularly patient autonomy with regard to how much of one's resources to devote to health care insurance. Thus, the ethic of managed care is but a part of the age of respect for patient autonomy.

Rather than allow the matter to end simply here, let me point to two unsettling aspects of this argument, and the implications of those problems for our understanding of physicians as members of a profession. First, if the ethic of managed care is but a part of the respect for patient autonomy that has swept through health care ethics in America in the past couple of decades, then why is there such discordance between this ethic and what we outlined at the beginning of this paper as the popular conception of the ethic of Hippocrates? The answer, I fear, is that while the public has been willing to accept, even demand, the respect for their autonomy that health care ethicists have argued for, they and the health care professionals have taken a rather narrow view of what this respect for autonomy means. It has been taken to mean freedom of choice among possible options. But respect for autonomy, especially if we regard its Kantian origins, must also include respect for the financial choices that consumers make to limit the funds that they are willing to set aside for health insurance. Accepting freedom of choice also entails accepting responsibility.

Second, Kantian respect for autonomy is grounded upon the belief that the knowledge, the information required for making a rational choice, is readily available to mature adults. Yet when we contemplate the complexity of contemporary medicine as a practice, it is questionable that the average adult could be said to readily understand the health care risks that he or she is running, in medical and financial terms, when he or she makes decisions concerning provisions for health insurance. At best, what must be assumed is that the individual makes a quite general

weighing of the value of health care relative to other economic goods.

What both of these points illustrate is how the moral demand for respect for autonomy has cast more and more of the responsibility for choice, *including limits to choice,* upon the health care consumer. This leaves open to question, however, to what extent the physician remains a *professional,* in the traditional sense of the term that implied special moral obligations to the patient, obligations far beyond those of the ordinary businessman.

I do not wish to suggest that we summarily declare physicians to no longer be professionals; but I believe that, given our decision to respect patient autonomy, including in matters of finances, we as a society must rethink what it means, from a moral point of view, for a physician to be a *professional.*

NOTES

1. In earlier decades, HMO-type health care plans were actually among the "elite" kinds of health care insurance. Premiums were relatively higher, but the lack of any deductibles or co-pays was attractive and there was little or no rationing. It is only in recent decades with (a) the entrance of several large for-profit firms and (b) in an economic environment where HMO plans have been sold to employers as less expensive alternatives to fee-for-service that the ethical difficulties that we are discussing surfaced in the HMO environment.
2. Pellegrino and Thomasma, *For the Patient's Good,* New York: Oxford University Press, 1988, pp. 177–180.

Legal and Ethical Myths About Informed Consent

ALAN MEISEL AND MARK KUCZEWSKI

Alan Meisel is Dickie, McCarney & Chilcote Professor of Bioethics, professor of law and psychiatry, and director of the Center for Bioethics and Health Law, University of Pittsburgh. Mark Kuczewski is director of the Neiswanger Institute for Bioethics and Health Policy, Stritch School of Medicine, Loyola University Chicago.

"Legal and Ethical Myths About Informed Consent," Archives of Internal Medicine *156 (1996), pp. 2521–26. Reprinted with kind permission of the American Medical Association.*

Informed consent is a foundational concept of medical ethics. Since its enunciation almost four decades ago, it has engendered, and continues to engender, a great deal of debate and opposition from practicing physicians. We believe that much of the negative reaction to informed consent stems from some fundamental misunderstandings about what informed consent requires. This article discusses and refutes several myths about informed consent that have acquired some currency among physicians.

Informed consent has been at the heart of medical ethics in the modern era. In fact, one could argue that the emergence of informed consent is the hallmark of the modern era in medical ethics. Informed consent first guided the evolution of the ethics of biomedical research that arose from the horrors of Nazi medical experimentation. Informed consent came of age in clinical medicine only a few years later.

Moreover, the idea of informed consent has provided the foundation for an evolving ethical and legal consensus in perhaps the best-known area of medical ethics, forgoing life-sustaining treatment. Yet, even though informed consent seems to be well established, strong reactions have continued to surround it.

The purpose of requiring informed consent is to promote autonomy of the individual in medical decision making. The modern concept of autonomy has its philosophical roots in 17th-century political philosophy and its legal roots in even older English legal principles that American democracy has inherited from English law. However, patient autonomy lay dormant in the physician-patient relationship until the beginning of the present century and only developed into fullblown form in the last four decades.

The origins of informed consent in medicine are somewhat murky. Its antecedents can be traced to early 20th-century American law. The requirement of *simple* consent to medical treatment was well established in the United States before World War II, and the Nuremberg trials of Nazi physicians made this a requirement of international law. But the *elaboration* of the requirement of consent to medical treatment and its transformation into informed consent, according to Katz,[1] one of the leading authorities on informed consent, "surfaced, seemingly out of nowhere." In attempting to ascertain the origins of the phrase "informed consent," first used in a 1957 California case, he could unearth no antecedent cases. The entire informed consent paragraph (in the first informed consent case) was adopted verbatim, and without attribution, from the amicus curiae brief submitted by the American College of Surgeons. It is an ironic twist of history that informed consent was dreamed up by lawyers in the employ of physicians.

Some physicians are still mistrustful of the doctrine of informed consent. It has been condemned in the medical literature as a myth and as bad medicine.[2] It has been the subject of numerous parodies intended to illustrate the absurdities to which it can be carried.[3] Most of these attacks are based on the idea that there is a fundamental incompatibility between the patient autonomy that informed consent is intended to promote and physician responsibility for a patient's well-being and on the fear that well-being will be severely compromised.

Recently, more subtle attacks on informed consent have come from well-intentioned medical ethicists. For instance, Veatch[4] argues that modern medicine has too many treatments available for many conditions for a physician to be able to disclose relevant information about all of them—as would need to be done if the letter of the law were to be observed—and therefore, physicians should disclose only information about those treatments that are consistent with their own values. Veatch somewhat overoptimistically advocates delivery-of-care arrangements that pair physicians and patients who have similar values and treatment dispositions as the solution to this problem.

We think that these critics of informed consent exhibit a variety of misunderstandings. Rather than confuse matters further by analyzing their arguments point by point, we first outline the two major approaches to informed consent and the ideals behind them. Then, we examine the most common misunderstandings of informed consent, ie, myths, and suggest more productive conceptions.

Approaches to Informed Consent: Rights vs. Shared Process

Patient autonomy began to grow as an antidote to physician paternalism—the supposed tendency of physicians to assume almost complete responsibility for determining what treatment patients would have—and in recognition of the fact that what treatment patients should have is a normative as well as a scientific determination. Its function in preserving a patient's liberties is probably responsible for the enthusiastic response lawyers have given to informed consent. However, too strong an emphasis on its legal origins and function eclipses the fact that informed consent is not merely a legal concept.

Informed consent is a legal doctrine that also supports many of our cherished ideals about the rights of the individual. The law's rights-oriented approach to informed consent assumes that the individual patient is characterized by a set of personal values that no one but that patient can know. In deciding what treatment, if any, a patient is to receive, the physician is viewed as an expert who should leave his or her values aside and only bring technical expertise into play. In the standard rendition of informed consent, the physician's role is to explain the various possibilities for the diagnosis or treatment of a particular patient's condition, and the patient is to consider this information in the context of his or her own values and then choose a course of treatment suited to him or her.

This approach fits certain cases nicely, for example, religiously based treatment refusals by a competent adult patient. However, mindless application of this approach to all medical decision making is responsible for many of the myths that have developed about informed consent. In the clinical setting, rights often recede into the background, and it is more helpful to approach informed consent as a *shared process* of decision making. A shared process approach does not restrict the physician to providing facts and insist that the patient supply all the values. The physician and patient each have access to interrelated facts and values. The values and thinking of the physician and patient should gradually take shape. They should mutually monitor each other so that their goals, thoughts, and evaluations become transparent to each other.

Conceived as a process of shared decision making, informed consent can accommodate both patient autonomy and the physician's responsibility for the well-being of the patient. As we explore some of the myths about informed consent, we highlight how a balance should be struck to accommodate both autonomy and beneficence.

Myth 1: A Signed Consent Form Is Informed Consent

Perhaps the most fundamental and pervasive myth about informed consent is that informed consent has been obtained when a patient signs a consent form. Nothing could be further from the truth, as many courts have pointed out to physicians who were only too willing to believe this myth. Consent forms are used as a matter of routine in both treatment and research settings because many hospital administrators, physicians, and their attorneys see these forms as providing protection against liability, despite the fact that they actually provide little protection.

Consent forms do have some value. They create an inference that the patient at least had an opportunity to read the information on it. If the information presented in the consent form contains a description of the risk that actually came to pass and contains other information that is adequate for a patient to make a decision, it will probably be helpful to a physician in the defense of a lawsuit.

On the other hand, if the information on the form is not adequate or is overly complex, the form may provide evidence to support the *patient's* case. If the form merely acknowledges that disclosure was made, but fails to recite the *content* of what should have been disclosed, it is unlikely to provide the physician with any advantage with respect to the main issue in a lawsuit: what was disclosed and whether it was adequate. Contemporary consent forms—often optimistically referred to as "informed consent forms" as if wishing would make it so—provide a false sense of security to physicians and hospital administrators who are led to believe that a signed consent form constitutes informed consent.

Myth 2: Informed Consent Is a Medical Miranda Warning

As practiced, and certainly as symbolized by consent forms, informed consent is often no more than a medical Miranda warning. Just as police are required to tell criminal suspects that "you have a right to remain silent, you have a right to a lawyer, and if you choose to speak, anything you say can be used against you," some physicians believe that informed consent has been obtained if they warn patients of the risks of treatment.

Certainly, patients should be told about the risks of treatment. Admittedly, it is difficult to know what risks must be disclosed, but the approach to informed consent that we advocate makes this less important. Rather than focusing on risks, the focus needs to be on therapeutic options. For example, patients with ulcers need to know about medical treatment and surgical treatment. Patients with breast cancer need to know about different kinds and combinations of surgery, radiation, and chemotherapy. All patients always need to know that one of their options is to do nothing.

Knowledge of one's options alone, however, is not meaningful unless one also knows the range of consequences of choosing each option. One facet of information about consequences is the risks of treatment, but there are others such as information about the likely outcomes, including information about mortality, morbidity, and functioning.

Myth 3: Informed Consent Requires That Physicians Operate a Medical Cafeteria

A myth that contradicts the previous one, yet is sometimes held simultaneously with it, is that informed consent requires physicians to operate a medical cafeteria, in which they must set out all the therapeutic options and let patients choose, each according to his or her own appetite. The law clearly does not require this.

Some physicians feel that their ability to practice medicine "the way we used to in the good old days" has been impinged on not only by courts and lawyers but also by third-party payers, health facility administrators, Congress, the state legislature, governmental bureaucrats, and patients incited by Ralph Nader, the consumer advocate. In a sense, this myth about informed consent has arisen as an antidote to the previous one. It is not hard to envision a physician, who has been continually told to provide patients with information about medical options and their consequences,

wringing his or her hands in disgust or discouragement and responding with,

> Well, damn it, if informed consent is all about letting patients chart their own course in medical matters, then let *them* do it. And if things go wrong, well it's their own fault—both because *they* did the choosing, and because *they* didn't listen to us.

When this attitude is at work, there is a serious sin of omission. What is being omitted is a central part of the physician–patient relationship as both physicians and patients view it—namely, the physician's role as medical adviser.

Patients usually want more than information. They also want advice. They say, "Doctor, if you were in my position, what would you do?" That does not mean they are going to do what their physician would do, nor does it mean that they should have just let the physician decide from the outset. It does not mean that informed consent is a charade. What it means is that informed consent is a process and part of the process is human interaction. Rather than thinking of informed consent as an abstract ideal, what we call informed consent should take the form of a conversation in which patients get information, ask questions, give information, and say "I want to think about it" or "I've thought about it and I can't decide. What do you think I should do?" Thus viewed, informed consent is a process of *shared* or *collaborative* decision making.

Another way of looking at the process of informed consent is that it must mix together treatment goals and particular treatments. Most of the confusion surrounding the cafeteria approach to informed consent assumes that patients wish to micromanage their care. This is rarely the case.[5] However, patients are entitled to know the goals of therapeutic options and when those goals have changed. Too often, treatments are discussed in detail but patients are not really sure what the treatment is ultimately meant to do. Similarly, when new treatments are introduced and discussed, it is not always clear to the patient that the old goal is no longer realistic, eg, cure is no longer possible, and that this new treatment is directed at a different goal such as minimizing disability or relieving pain. Patients are not experts at treatments; physicians are. However, patients' preferences are central to the choice of treatment goals. Thus, in selecting and revising treatment goals, physicians and patients need to form a partnership.

Myth 4: Patients Must Be Told Everything About Treatment

Some believe the law requires that patients be told everything about treatment—the equivalent of giving them the *Physicians' Desk Reference*. Actually, the law requires only that patients be given a reasonable amount of information. In about half the states, the adequacy of disclosure is measured by customary professional practice, which means that patients must be given the information that a reasonable physician would disclose. In the remaining states, the adequacy of disclosure is measured by a so-called legal standard, which requires the provision of that amount and kind of information that a reasonable *patient* would find material to making a decision about treatment.

Because those rules are vague, lawyers cannot provide physicians with specific guidance about how to comply. Therefore, physicians sometimes feel driven back into the corner of disclosing everything, which is unnecessary. Further, it is unwise from a legal perspective because physicians could be held liable (though it is not likely) for intentionally inflicting emotional distress on patients by giving them *too much* information.[6]

Our previous discussions of goals and treatments should provide a minimal checklist. Once a physician and patient have explored all the relatively realistic goals of treatment, the number of therapeutic options and amount of information about those options frequently become relatively minor issues.

Myth 5: Patients Need Full Disclosure About Treatment Only If They Consent

Information about therapeutic options and their consequences to be used by patients in making decisions needs to be provided before, not after,

decisions are made. In practice, this is not always the case. One reason is the nature of the process by which physicians conceptualize and solve problems and formulate recommendations. Physicians acquire information about patients through examination, history, medical records, laboratory tests, and similar processes and then formulate a diagnosis. The physician makes a treatment recommendation to the patient in the form of, "Here's what's wrong with you and this is what we need to do."

Patients are expected to comply with the recommendation, although some patients will ask questions, take some time to think about it, seek a second opinion, or even refuse the recommendation or any further medical attention. If the patient decides to follow the recommendation (ie, consents), and especially if the physician has not yet provided much in the way of information, he or she might then receive more information, because this decision provides an occasion to discuss the medical malady and its treatment. In other words, much of the information relevant to making a decision actually comes after the decision is made. There is nothing wrong with continuing to provide, reiterate, or recast information at the time the patient consents to treatment. In fact, we recommend it. However, if informed consent was conceived of by physicians as a process of shared decision making, information might more readily flow earlier and more frequently.

The failure to make information available to patients before they decide whether to accept or reject a physician's recommendations is based on the premise that if the patient refuses treatment, it is unnecessary, if not paradoxical, to obtain informed consent. This illustrates how the use of the term *informed consent* is unfortunate, if not dangerous, for it assumes that the process of informing is to eventuate in consent. Physicians also assume that if in fact consent is not forthcoming, information need not be given to patients or if the patient refuses the recommended treatment and settles on an alternative treatment, no information need be provided about the rejected treatment.

In fact, physicians are obligated to obtain not only informed consent but also informed refusal.[7] This is not as silly as it might at first appear, when one recalls that the most important part of informed consent is information about options and their consequences and a refusal of treatment is a choice to do nothing, which has predictable consequences too. This is not a resurrection of the cafeteria approach, nor are we recommending that the physician present the entire treatment menu. What we are saying is that when the physician examines the patient and says, for example, "We'll have to do bypass surgery," and omits discussion of the choice of goals, he or she has assumed that the patient would agree about the treatment to meet that goal.

Myth 6: Patients Cannot Give Informed Consent Because They Cannot Understand Complex Medical Information

The notion that informed consent is a myth and bad medicine is premised in part on the assumption that providing information to patients frightens them.[8] These characterizations are also based on the assumed difficulty of transmitting technical information to patients. A typical unspoken thought might go,

> Patients can't understand all this medical stuff. Why, I have trouble keeping up with my own subspecialty, I've forgotten 95% of what I learned in medical school, and the 5% I remember is now outdated. Even worse, what about all those empirical studies that show that patients who have been given information don't remember it 6 months, 6 days, or even 6 hours or 6 minutes later?

There are at least two errors in this reasoning. The first is the equation of recall with understanding. While it might be true that someone who cannot retain information for a few seconds might not be said to understand it, people often make reasonable decisions but cannot later recall the premises that supported the reasoning or the

process that led to the conclusion. Nevertheless, they might well have understood it at the time.

The second error is the assumption that patients must understand information in the same way and to the same extent as the physician. It is true that a patient who is totally bereft of understanding lacks decision-making capacity and would be considered legally incompetent. In such a case, decision making would need to take place with a surrogate decision maker acting on the patient's behalf. The fact that a patient might put an odd gloss on information or might not have a completely accurate factual understanding of the information does not disqualify that patient as a decision maker. To have decision-making capacity, patients do not need to be Jonas Salk. They merely need to be able to understand their options and the potential risks and benefits of these options. Most assuredly the fact that the patient reaches a decision different from the one that the physician would have made does not mean that the patient does not understand the information.

What is critical is that patients be given information and that they have a chance to use it in formulating a decision, to ask questions about it, and to gather further information. It is essential that they be given the context for the proposed treatments, ie, they must be told the physician's goals in making this treatment recommendation. However, within broad limits, patients have the right to set their own goals and to make their own decisions in their own way and for their own reasons, which includes the right *not* to use information that others might think relevant, rational, and even necessary to decision making.

We are steering a course between extremes. One extreme assumes that a patient just cannot understand medical information, and so we should give up on informed consent. On the other end of the spectrum resides the extreme rights-oriented view that a patient's treatment choices should not be challenged. We advocate the middle path: patients' choices should make sense in terms of their values and way of making sense of the world and these decisions should be made in the manner patients normally make similar choices. However, to require "understanding" in the same way and to the same extent that a physician understands the information is as paternalistic as not permitting patients to participate in decision making at all.

Myth 7: Patients Must Be Given Information Whether They Want It or Not

Some patients choose not to participate in the decision-making process at all or may wish to participate on a reduced basis. Withholding information from patients when they request that it not be given respects their autonomy as much as providing information to patients who want it. Enabling and permitting patients to make medical decisions is one way of fostering self-determination; respecting their wish not to participate is another. To *compel* patients to receive information that they do not want or to make decisions that they do nor wish to make is to fail to respect their dignity.

Withholding information from patients at their request is a legally recognized exception to informed consent referred to as waiver.[9] Usually, only by initiating a conversation with a patient can a physician determine that a patient wishes to participate in only a limited way, or not at all, in the decision-making process. In some instances, patients may fully engage in such a conversation and only at the end declare that they do not know what to do and wish to leave the decision to a family member, the physician, or someone else. In such a case, a patient can be said to have waived the right to decide though not the right to be informed. Sometimes patients make it clear that they do not even want to talk about therapeutic options and consequences. They may be willing to make a decision on less, rather than more, information. In such a case, a patient can be said to have waived the right to be informed, though not necessarily the right to decide. Or patients may want neither information nor to decide, again preferring to leave it all to someone else.

Thus, the waiver exception parallels the two distinct but related rights that informed consent embodies, the right to be given information and the right to decide. Patients who waive their right to decide do not automatically waive their right to information. There may be good reasons to continue to provide information to such patients. One is that just because patients do not want to make a particular treatment decision does not mean that they will not wish to participate in the future. Furthermore, there are reasons to provide information other than for decision making. Patients also need information to facilitate compliance with treatment decisions. They deserve information about their treatment as a sign of respect and so that they can be prepared for what is to happen to them.

Myth 8: Information May Be Withheld If It Will Cause the Patient to Refuse Treatment

It is ironic that physicians who profess not to know much about informed consent sometimes do know about the therapeutic privilege, which, like the waiver exception, allows information to be withheld from patients. When information is withheld under the waiver exception, *patients* decide that having information would not serve their ends. By contrast, when the therapeutic privilege is invoked to withhold information, the physician determines that providing the patient with information would undermine, rather than promote, the goals of informed consent.

The purpose of the therapeutic privilege is to allow physicians to honor their "primary duties" to do what is beneficial for the patients and to avoid inflicting harm on them.[10] However, it is far less clear what circumstances justify the physician in withholding information. In general, physicians are permitted to withhold information when its disclosure would seriously harm the patient.

In practice, the therapeutic privilege may legitimate a physician's natural aversion to providing unpleasant information to patients—indeed, almost everyone's natural aversion to providing unpleasant information to anyone else. However, the therapeutic privilege is not a license for physicians to withhold information when they fear, rightly or wrongly, that providing it to patients will lead them to refuse recommended treatment. Such a view of the privilege is paternalistic in the extreme; it threatens to devour any obligation to provide information and would permit physicians to substitute their judgment for the patient's. The more appropriate formulation of the privilege permits physicians to tailor (and even withhold) information when, but only when, its disclosure would so upset a patient that he or she could not rationally engage in a conversation about therapeutic options and consequences.

Conclusion

A number of myths about what the law requires impede the practice of obtaining informed consent. If informed consent is viewed as a process of shared decision making, some of the seeming absurdities and excesses that can be associated with it disappear. In so doing, it might make the practice of medicine more rewarding for physicians. The doctrine of informed consent does not analogize physicians to waiters who take orders from customers. Rather, it recognizes the responsibility of the physician for the patient's well-being.

We are a litigious society, and physicians must be concerned with avoiding lawsuits. The best advice we can give is to treat patients like people, act sensitively and compassionately, and most of all, talk to patients. Have a conversation, have several; remember that this is a process. In this process, you will gradually come to know your patient's decision-making style. Furthermore, do not press patients to decide quickly. Do not make them think that you do not have time for them. Because if you do, regardless of how much information they are given, they are going to be angry, and another name for an angry patient is plaintiff.

NOTES

1. Katz J. Judges, physicians, and patients. In: *The Silent World of Physician and Patient.* New York, NY: The Free Press; 1984, p. 60.
2. Karz RL. Informed consent: Is it bad medicine? *West J. Med.* 1977; 126:426–428.
3. Meisel A. The legal consensus about forgoing life-sustaining treatment: Its status and its prospects. *Kennedy Inst Ethics J.* 1992; 2:309–345.
4. Veatch RM. Abandoning informed consent. *Hastings Cent Rep.* 1995; 25:5–12.
5. Churchill LR. Trust, autonomy, and advance directives. *J. Religion Health.* 1989; 28:175–183.
6. *Ferrara v Galluchio,* 152 NE2d 249 (NY 1958).
7. *Truman v Thomas,* 611 P2d 902 (Cal 1980).
8. Katz, Judges, physicians, and patients, pp. 74–76.
9. Meisel A. The "exceptions" to the informed consent doctrine: Striking a balance between competing values in medical decision-making. *Wis Law Rev.* 1979; 413–488.
10. *Nishi v Hartwell,* 473 P2d 116 (Haw 1970).

14

Professional Ethics

Professional Responsibility: Just Following the Rules?

MICHAEL DAVIS

Michael Davis is professor of Philosophy and senior fellow at the Center for the Study of Ethics in the Professions, Illinois Institute of Technology. Printed with kind permission of the author.

My subject is a criticism of conduct something like this: "That's not acting responsibly, that's just following the rules." The criticism appears as an attack on "legalism" in both business and professional ethics. While my focus here will be on professional ethics, everything I say should, with minor changes, apply equally well to following corporate or other business codes of ethics.

Legalism (it is said) reduces professional responsibility to doing as the profession's code of ethics requires; professional responsibility, like moral responsibility generally, is more open-ended, including (among other things) certain virtues. My subject thus overlaps the larger debate in moral theory between "principle ethics" and "virtue ethics." I shall draw some conclusions relevant to that debate.

My thesis is that following "the rules," while not all there is to professional ethics, is generally enough for responsible conduct (or, at least, is so when the profession's code of ethics is reasonably

well written, as most are). Rules set the standard of professional conduct; just following those rules, in a relatively robust but not unusual sense of "following those rules," is acting as a responsible professional.

I. Some Preliminaries

The attack on legalism need not be put in terms of rules. One can make it in terms of "just satisfying one's obligations [or duties]" or "just respecting others' rights." Indeed, Caroline Whitbeck recently combined all three versions in one omnibus attack on legalism: "If rights and obligations or rules about what acts to perform or refrain from performing were all there were to professional ethics, it would be a simple matter and hardly worthy of attention in a college course."[1]

I shall, however, have little more to say about obligations or rights here for two reasons. First, obligations and rights can be, and often are, stated as rules. Hence, any discussion of rules implicitly includes obligations and rights (more or less). Second, any separate discussion of obligations or rights would complicate my defense of legalism a good deal without adding much of substance. So, I shall concentrate on rules.

When mere rule following is contrasted with acting responsibly, there is always something that mere rule following is supposed to leave out (hence the "mere"). Whitbeck, for example, explains why professional ethics deserves attention in a college course in this way: "The exercise of responsibility typically requires the exercise of discretion and consideration of many technical matters and matters of value."[2] For her, what mere rule following must leave out is, it seems, all exercise of discretion, technical knowledge, and consideration of value. She does not explain why mere rule following must leave all this out. The explanation is not obvious—as I shall now show.

Consider this brief rule of engineering ethics having its counterpart in the code of ethics of most professions: "Engineers shall perform services only in areas of their competence."[3] Sometimes engineers do not need discretion or even much technical knowledge to know that the service in question is beyond their competence. (Think of an engineer asked to do brain surgery because she has a doctorate—in engineering.) Often, however, engineers do need discretion, technical knowledge, and an understanding of the values inherent in engineering's conception of competence to decide whether a certain service is within their competence. For example, whether writing a certain computer program is within the competence of an engineer may depend in part on whether the errors she is likely to commit given her skill would create substantial risks for users or third parties. Deciding whether a risk is substantial combines technical judgments (such-and-such errors are likely) with judgments of value (the risks are, or are not, substantial).

We must, I think, assume that Whitbeck knows this. So, her criticism of rules must make a different point—one her words leave us to guess. We are, then, in no position to decide whether her criticism of rules—or the similar criticism of others—is justified until we understand what "just following the rules" leaves out. And we are not likely to understand that until we understand what just following the rules might be. For that reason, I devote the body of this paper to considering seven different interpretations of "just following the rules," all that I have found in the literature, noticed in conversation, or made up on my own: blind obedience, strict obedience, malicious obedience, negligent obedience, accidental obedience, stupid obedience, and interpretative obedience. Having examined these seven, I conclude that, for professional ethics at least, the criticism of just following the rules is unjustified. Under all but one interpretation of just following the rules, the rules are not in fact being followed. Under that one (the interpretative), there is nothing obviously wrong with just following the rules.

II. *Following Rules Blindly or Strictly*

Mere rule following is doing what the rule says without concern for context or consequence, a "mechanical" or "blind" obedience. Finding a clear example of such obedience is hard. Here is the best I have (blind obedience, though not exactly to a rule): One day, at age two, my son was having trouble opening a cabinet door because of a safety latch. Instead of opening the door for him, I advised him to "use his head." He immediately obeyed, giving the door a hard rap with his forehead, apparently without thought to any alternative interpretation of my advice or even to past experience of banging his head against a hard surface. He has not given me such blind obedience since.

Though rational in some contexts, strict obedience does not seem rational as a general way to practice a profession. Strict obedience makes sense where judgment is justifiably separated from performance (for example, where some "higher" authority is in the best position to "reason why" and others, subordinates, to "do or die"). The general name for the separation of judgment from performance is "hierarchy." Since hierarchy tends to ignore what subordinates think, however well-informed and judicious the subordinates may be, any justification of strict obedience must identify a compensating advantage. On the battlefield, the compensating advantage is pretty clear. The coordination of large masses in movement is difficult under the best of conditions. In battle, with the noise and confusion, there is little opportunity for joint deliberation even in a unit as small as a platoon or squad. The alternative to obeying the order of a superior is disorder or delay, potentially disastrous when coordination and speed matter.

Few, if any, professions demand strict obedience to an ethical authority. But, even if they all did, the result would not be relevant to our subject. Where one has rendered strict obedience to an ethical authority, the proper description is "I was just obeying orders" or "I was just following controlling precedent" rather than "I was just following the rules."

III. *Malicious Obedience*

Sometimes the description, "I was just following the rules," occurs in defense of conduct. To have acted according to the rules, however bad the outcome and however foolish the rules, is to have acted in a way insulating one from (full) responsibility. The most common use of "just following rules" in this sense, or at least the most visible, is when employees "strike" their employer by "working to rule" or "going by the book." This form of strike is particularly satisfying to employees and maddening for the employer. The employees continue to be paid, though they are costing their employer money, time, and grief. The employer cannot complain without admitting that "the book" is wrong. For many employers, the point of having "the book" is to have a basis for disciplining employees when they fail to do as they should. So, working to rule catches the employer in his own trap. One way or another, the employer must "eat his words." Think, for example, how the police can bring traffic to a halt on a busy highway simply by ticketing every traffic violation they observe—as many police manuals require.

What does working to rule leave out? Another name for working to rule, "malicious obedience," suggests an answer. What working to rule leaves out is the good will employees otherwise give their employer. Ordinarily, employees interpret the rules to take into account the inability of general language to anticipate special cases; they try to understand what the employer is trying to achieve by laying down such rules; they use "common sense."

Working to rule resembles strict obedience. In both, there is an obvious disconnection between

what a reasonable person would think should be done, all else equal, and what the person in question is doing. In both too, there is a reason, though not the same reason, for the disconnection. The difference between strict obedience and working to rule is that, in strict obedience, the reason for the disconnection is the overall good of the enterprise; in working to rule, the reason is the exact opposite. The employee takes into account what would be good for the employer only in order to choose an interpretative strategy to defeat it.

We may distinguish a weak sense and a strong sense of malicious obedience. In the weak sense, malicious obedience is the malicious adoption of an interpretative strategy that is not itself malicious. For example, the principle "Be literal" might be adopted for reasons other than malice. But, in working to rule, it is adopted maliciously, that is, with the intent, expectation, or hope that literalness will make trouble for the employer. Malicious obedience in the strong sense carries malice one step further. Not only is the interpretative strategy adopted maliciously but what is adopted also has malice built into it, for example, "Choose the most damaging interpretation the language allows."

What do these two forms of working to rule have to do with just following a code of professional ethics? For most of these codes, the answer must be: little. The codes themselves contain rules of interpretation. Often gathered at the front under the heading "preamble," "principles," or "canons" to distinguish them from less general directives, these rules of interpretation effectively rule out malicious obedience. For example, the NSPE's "Code of Ethics for Engineers" includes at least two "Fundamental Canons" that seem to rule out malice:

> Engineers, in the fulfillment of their professional duties, shall:
>
> 1. Hold paramount the safety, health, and welfare of the public in the performance of their professional duties.... [and]
> 4. Act in professional matters for each employer or client as faithful agents or trustees. Specific rules of practice must

then be read to protect the public welfare and to serve the employer as a faithful agent or trustee. An engineer cannot simply work to rule.

I do not claim that such general principles of interpretation make following the rules easy. On the contrary, I admit they make following the rules hard. My point is that, as they do that, they also rule out most, perhaps all, of the malicious interpretations of rules necessary for malicious obedience.

Or, rather, that is one of my points. Malicious obedience requires a conscious misunderstanding of the rules; there can also be unconscious misunderstanding. For example, engineers have been known to argue that the rule requiring them to serve each client or employer as a faithful agent or trustee imposes a professional obligation to cut costs even when doing so endangers the public. These engineers neither reject the obligation to the public welfare nor misinterpret it. They just do not think of it as they try to do what they should. They fail to exercise reasonable care in interpreting their professional code. If malicious obedience is a conscious failure to exercise reasonable care in interpreting the rules, then what we are now contemplating is an *unconscious* failure. We must now consider three forms of unconscious failure to just follow the rules.

IV *Negligent and Accidental Obedience*

Some writers have recently taken to contrasting the law's "malpractice" or "negligence" standard of tort liability with the "due care" (or "reasonable care") standard of true professionalism. Until I read these writers, I had supposed that negligence was a relatively clear concept. I now see that it is not. So, to avoid misunderstanding, let me explain what I once supposed obvious.

In the common law, both American and English, negligence is, almost by definition, a failure to exercise due care in our relations with others. In negligence law, the interesting question is *not* whether anyone, especially a professional, should be held to the due-care standard. Due care is the minimum standard even for a child or a madman. The interesting question is what due care requires. For example, Prosser, the leading authority on torts, understands a failure of due care as "[conduct] which should be recognized as involving unreasonable danger to others."[4]

Any distinction between what one's profession requires and what is merely legally required cannot be made in terms of "due care"—or, at least, cannot be so made without inviting confusion. A profession does not need a code of ethics to be held to the standard of due care. The law already does that; any malpractice suit (for negligence) will allege a failure of due care. What a code of professional ethics does, if it does anything beyond restating existing legal obligations, is to set a new standard of care, one higher than existed before. That new standard can, in virtue of the code, become what may reasonably be expected of members of the profession; it is reasonable to expect members of a profession to do what they commit themselves to doing. Some dangers that had been reasonable before would then become unreasonable, raising the legal minimum for members of the profession and thereby turning into malpractice conduct previously allowed to the profession (and still allowed to others). A profession's code of ethics helps define what care is due from members of that profession and, in doing that, to set the standard of malpractice for them. But, whatever the standard, anything less than good practice is malpractice.[5]

Negligent obedience is, then, a failure to exercise due care in following the relevant rules, whether the failure unreasonably risks harm to others or is in some other way faulty. Negligent obedience differs from (what we shall call) stupid obedience in that the failure need not arise from an inability to act as one should. Stupid obedience is a matter of competence; negligent obedience is not (or, at least, need not be).

The term "negligent obedience" may seem paradoxical. Insofar as the obedience in question is negligent, how can it be obedience? Is it not literally a failure to obey? But, insofar as the obedience in question is literally obedience, how can it be negligent? The paradox is resolved by distinguishing the subjective side of obedience from the objective. Subjectively, that is, from the point of view of the agent, negligent obedience is obedience. The agent must believe that she is acting as she should or her disobedience would be malicious, not negligent. She must, in other words, mean well even as she in fact fails to do what meaning well would ordinarily lead her, or at least someone of ordinary prudence, to do. What she does fails to be obedience only objectively, that is, from the point of view of people of ordinary prudence not directly involved.

What if, from the point of view of ordinary prudence, she seemed to follow the rule, but did so without knowing or intending it? Her act would correspond to what the rule required, but only by accident.[6] This is an exotic form of acting according to the rule rather than following it. Though she might (truthfully and effectively) defend her conduct by saying, "I followed the rule," she could not defend it by saying, "I was just following the rule." "I followed the rule" means I did nothing contrary to the rule. "I was just following the rule" may, or may not, mean that, but it always means that one satisfied the subjective condition, that is, that one at least tried to determine what the rule requires.

What if she did try to follow the rule, though in a way we would regard as clearly negligent had she not in fact acted in accordance with the rule? We would be inclined to say (something like): "Well, all's well that ends well, but you really should learn how to interpret the rule." We would not, in other words, regard her as someone who was just following the rules (in a sense requiring no apology). Trying to follow the rule is not all there is to the subjective side; the trying must meet a certain standard of care. The trying must be of a sort likely to result in following the rule.

Negligent obedience is always a failure to follow the rule; accidental obedience, while not a failure to follow the rule, is at least a failure to follow the rule for the right reason, that is, because one has understood it properly. Negligent failure to understand the rule properly may arise from lack of the appropriate virtue (such as carefulness). But it need not. Lack of virtue is neither necessary nor sufficient for negligent obedience.

Some negligent obedience may arise even where everyone is as virtuous as humanly possible. The prudent person (a human being), acting as judge, may see error the prudent person as agent (also a human being) might overlook (even though she should not). Lack of virtue is not a necessary condition for negligent obedience.

Lack of virtue is also not a sufficient condition for negligent obedience. Even a relatively careless person can (sometimes) exercise due care—though she may have to try hard to do it. Her trying hard enough may, as a matter of fact, arise (in part) from other virtues, such as practical wisdom or concern for others; but it might also arise from less noble grounds, such as greed or fear of punishment. Whatever the ground, if she tries hard, she may be able to do as the rule requires; and doing that, she does not act negligently, however lacking in the virtue of care she may be. Nor is her obedience merely accidental; it is the ordinary consequence of her deliberate effort.

Since lack of virtue is neither necessary nor sufficient for negligent obedience, negligent obedience cannot be understood as a failure of virtue (a failure to have, or to act from, the virtue of due care). Negligent obedience must, instead, be understood as a failure to follow certain rules (for example, "Avoid unreasonable risk to others").

In saying this, I am not denying that acting well is easier if one is virtuous than if one is not. I agree that, for example, a competent engineer is more likely to exercise due care in his professional work if he is meticulous, alert, thoughtful, and serious than if he is not. All I am denying is that the link between good conduct and any particular virtue (or virtue in general) is close enough that, even under the best of conditions actually possible, the one can guarantee the other: acting from virtue is no substitute for just following the rules.

V. *Stupid Obedience*

Those who obey stupidly resemble the negligent in unconsciously failing to exercise due care in interpreting the relevant rules. They differ from the negligent only in the cause of failure. Unlike the negligent, the stupid fail because they do not know better. The cause of not knowing better may be original, that is, a lack of native wit, or educational, for example, never having been taught how to interpret the rule in question. In law, the most common form of stupid obedience is the layman's trying to follow a statute without considering how case law may have made the statute's simple language treacherous. In professional ethics, the most common form of stupid obedience is, I think, reading a code of ethics as if each rule were independent of the others.

The stupid have an excuse the negligent do not. They are not free of blame. One can blame another for an act or for its consequences. To blame someone for an act is to declare the act bad and his; to blame him for some state of affairs is to declare the state of affairs bad and some act or omission of his the cause. To excuse someone's failure to follow a rule by saying, "He doesn't know better," does not save him from blame; it only changes the terms. Whether the change of terms even amounts to a reduction in blame is a matter of opinion: many of us might prefer to be thought malicious or negligent rather than stupid. In any case, for a professional, stupidity is as objectionable as malice.

Perhaps many of those professionals who seek to excuse themselves for misconduct with the answer, "I was just following the rules," are pleading stupidity. It is therefore worth pointing out that whenever this plea is necessary, the professional in question was not in fact following the rules (even if she was doing her best to follow them). In this respect, stupid obedience resembles the other forms of "just following the rules" discussed so far. It is a failure to follow the rules.

VI. *Interpretative Obedience*

Except for blind obedience, all the forms of rule following discussed so far acknowledged, however implicitly, that rules must be interpreted. In strict obedience, the interpretation is largely left to others ("higher authority"). In malicious obedience, interpretation is deliberately abused; in negligent or accidental obedience, interpretation is not given the attention it deserves; and, in stu-

pid obedience, interpretation is not done skillfully enough, whether from lack of wit or learning. This list of ways in which one can fail to follow the rules suggests that just following the rules is not simple. We must now consider just how complicated it can be.

In law, there are many methods of interpreting a rule. They are not exclusive, though some are likely to be more important in one area of the law and others in another. When interpreting a particular rule, one important question is always how that rule fits with the others in the particular document in which it appears. All else equal, a particular will, contract, statute, or other document should, if possible, be interpreted so that each term keeps the same meaning throughout, none of its rules is inconsistent with any other, and all serve the document's avowed purpose (or at least none works against it). This "internalist" approach may yield one defensible interpretation but more often yields several. Where there are several internally defensible interpretations, there may be no way to choose except to go outside the document.

There may, in any case, be other reasons to go outside the document. For example, the internalist interpretation may have yielded an immoral or irrational result, or violated the intentions of those who composed the document (intentions indicated by evidence outside the document itself).

Lawyers often describe an interpretation of a rule as a "construction." That description is hardly metaphorical. Interpreting a rule is as much construction as discovery. There are, therefore, differences in style that, though well within the bounds of competence, may lead well-meaning lawyers to quite different results. Some lawyers may, all else equal, think going back to the intentions of the actual authors the best guide to what a rule means; others, that the best guide is what decent, well-informed, and rational authors would have meant when the document was drafted or would mean today; others may think the best guide is what the "plain man" would suppose such words to mean; and others how a particular interpretation fits with the way the law is developing. Some may think that a particular method of interpretation pre-empts the rest. Others may think that each method is relevant, carrying a certain weight, the overall construal being determined by some combination of methods. And so on. When a lawyer speaks of "just following the rule," she is likely to mean "just following the interpretation of the rule I find obvious using the method of interpretation I take for granted."[7]

We have a profession, lawyers, who make their living in part by offering possible interpretations of rules, and another, judges, who make theirs in part by deciding between lawyers' interpretations. This at least suggests that following some rules, the rules of a legal system, can be quite complicated. While there is no profession in which the rules of professional ethics reach the complexity of even a relatively simple legal system, we need not be surprised that learning how to follow a code of professional ethics should require college course work. After all, lawyers need three years of law school to learn how to interpret the law.

What must we teach students in order to teach them how to follow the code of ethics of their hoped-for profession? We must, of course, teach them the context in which the code is to be applied, that is, something of the history of the profession, of the organizations in which members of the profession work, of the expectations other members of the profession will have of their colleagues, and of what members do (and the effect what they do can have on others). We must also teach something about the purpose of the rules, the structure of the code (the relation of one rule to another), the interpretative strategies considered appropriate, and the consequences of certain mistakes in interpretation. We should help students to see their profession's code of ethics as the work of human beings much like themselves, human beings who have specific purposes in developing such rules and should therefore be open to revising them, or standing interpretations of them, as new information comes in. Last, and perhaps most important, we should give practice in following the rules, that is,

in analyzing specific "fact situations," applying the rules to those facts, reaching conclusions about what is required, allowed, or forbidden, making arguments in defense of the conclusions, and inventing ways to do as the rules so interpreted say. One does not know how to follow a rule unless one knows how to develop, state, defend, and carry out workable courses of action in accord with the rule in contexts in which the rule ordinarily applies.

VII. *What's Left Out?*

This (interpretative) way of understanding "just following the rules" leaves us with the question with which we began: what does just following the rules leave out? What I have argued so far is that the rules of professional ethics themselves exclude certain forms of "just following the rules" (malicious, negligent, accidental, and stupid obedience); other forms (blind and strict obedience) are not following the rules at all. Only one interpretation of just following the rules of professional ethics, the interpretative, seems robust enough to count as just following the rules (without some apologetic qualification). That interpretation seems to leave nothing important out.

My argument, even admitting its soundness, may seem to miss what underlay the objection to *"just* following the rules" with which we began, the idea (introduced by "just") of trying to get by with the minimum, a failure to make room for the "spirit" of the rules as well as the "letter." To this fundamental objection, I have two replies, one general and one particular. The general reply is that "the spirit of the rule" is a metaphor. By itself, it tells us little. My own view is that the appropriate interpretative strategy is the rule's spirit. It is what gives life to the otherwise dead letters of a rule. Those who try to follow a rule without the appropriate interpretative strategy may think of themselves as "just following the rule" but they are likely to fail to follow it. That is the lesson of negligent and stupid obedience. Those who have criticized "just following the rules" seem not to have realized how much goes into following a rule. That is not to say that virtue is not relevant to following the rules. It is, instead, to point to a particular rarely-mentioned virtue, the disposition to interpret rules correctly, as crucial to responsible professional conduct (though not defining of it), to come a long way down from the airy world in which rules are hardly worth mention to one in which teaching the rules is central to developing the crucial virtue.

That is my general reply. My particular reply is a challenge to individual critics: show me a clear case of professional responsibility that is not just following the profession's code of ethics. By "clear case," I mean one that most members of the profession would agree is uncontroversial.

I feel safe making this challenge because I think the critics of legalism badly underestimate what rules can do. Rules can set high standards; set positive standards as well as negative; and provide guidance on when to make exceptions to otherwise binding rules. Rules can also require virtues such as competence and caring.[8] There is no reason, except oversight, why a profession's code should leave out anything most members of the profession consider important.

But, surely (it may be asked), is there not something wrong with a professional trying to get by with the minimum required? This question may be understood as raising one of two objections. If we emphasize "trying" (an attitude), we get an objection to a certain interpretative strategy, one to which few, if any, professional codes allow. Consider again the preamble of the NSPE code. Does it not point the faithful interpreter toward "the highest principles" rather than "the minimum"? How can an engineer follow that code and try to do the minimum?

If, instead of emphasizing the trying, we emphasize the outcome ("the minimum required"), we get an objection to doing only what the code in fact requires. The point of the objection so interpreted escapes me. Why would a professional not be acting responsibly if she did only what her profession's code of ethics required? The attack on legalism (the call to "go beyond" the rules) may be a confused way of proposing reforms—in the rules themselves or in their interpretation. If so, the professional responsibilities put forward as beyond the rules—the rules as written if not the rules as they could be written—will, upon examination, turn out to be controversial.[9]

NOTES

1. Caroline Whitbeck, *Ethics in Engineering Practice and Research* (Cambridge University Press: Cambridge, UK, 1998), p. 83.
2. Whitbeck, p. 83.
3. National Society of Professional Engineers, *Code of Professional Ethics* (1997), II.2.
4. "The almost universal use of the phrase 'due care' to describe conduct that is not negligent, should not be permitted to obscure the fact that the real basis of negligence is... behavior which should be recognized as involving an unreasonable danger to others." William L. Prosser, *Law of Torts, 4th Ed.* (West Publishing: St. Paul, Minn., 1971), p. 145.
5. Or, to be more exact, it is malpractice if the other conditions of negligence are also present (an unreasonable risk to others, a resulting harm, measurable loss, and so on).
6. I owe the identification of accidental obedience to Robert McCutcheon, Davis and Elkins College.
7. For some idea of how complicated interpretation of rules can be, see Ronald Dworkin, *Laws Empire* (Harvard University Press: Cambridge, Massachusetts, 1986)—or any good text in jurisprudence.
8. For example, engineering could have some such rule as this: "Engineers shall be competent" or "Engineers shall care deeply about the environment." But how (it might be asked) can a rule require one to have a virtue? Mustn't rules—as guides to conduct—require conduct? Well, no—and yes. Rules need not explicitly require conduct. They can simply set qualifications (as our two examples do). Since those who cannot meet the qualifications cannot be as the rule requires, they can only follow the rule by avoiding coming under it, that is, by staying out of the profession in question or, having got in before the lack of virtue was discovered, by leaving. Rules explicitly requiring virtue implicitly require conduct (that is, the not-getting-into-situations-where-one-cannot-be-as-required.)
9. Lest my own words in *Thinking Like an Engineer* (Oxford University Press: New York, 1998), p. 59, be quoted against me, I should point out that I am not here speaking (as I was there) of tasks professionals have "good reason" to take on or assign, but of tasks they have taken on already in virtue of membership in a profession having a certain code of ethics that are therefore required of them.

The Role of Autonomy in Professional Ethics

JAMES STACEY TAYLOR

James Stacey Taylor is assistant professor of philosophy, Louisiana State University.

This paper by James Stacey Taylor first appeared in Ethics for the Professions. *Copyright © John Rowan and Samuel Zinaich, JR, (Belmont, CA: Wadsworth, 2003).*

Personal autonomy has recently become the core value within many areas of professional ethics. In medical ethics, for example, personal autonomy has eclipsed all other values to such an extent that Daniel Callahan has seen fit to warn medical ethicists not to treat it as the sole value within medical settings.[1] Similarly, business ethicists have increasingly condemned those business practices that they believe undermine personal autonomy, such as manipulative advertising and strategic bluffing.[2] Engineers are also faced with ethical dilemmas that center on the value of personal autonomy. For example, should an engineer use a means to produce the client's product that her contract does not authorize her to adopt, or should she respect her client's autonomy and follow the procedures that have been outlined to her? Similar ethical dilemmas which arise owing to a respect for the value of personal autonomy may also face accountants, military personnel who are acting under orders, and lawyers acting under instruction, among other professionals.

Although personal autonomy has become such a dominant value in professional ethics, there has been surprisingly little examination of the role (or roles) which it is supposed to play within practical ethical decision-making procedures. This paper will remedy this omission, through providing an overview of the various roles that personal autonomy may play within professional ethics.

What Is "Autonomy" and Why Is It Important?

The roots of the notion of autonomy are *autos* and *nomos*, "self" and "rule" or "law" in Ancient Greek. The term "autonomia" originally applied to a Greek city-state, referring to one which governed itself without interference from any external powers, such as an overlord state. In contemporary usage, however, the term "autonomous" is now most frequently applied to persons who are free from external interference or control. This modern use of the term stems from Immanuel Kant, who argued that a person was autonomous to the extent that she governed herself free from the controlling influence of anything outside herself. To the extent that a person was controlled by external forces she was heteronomous, rather than autonomous. Kant, however, had a very strict idea of what was to be considered "internal" to a person in the sense required for autonomy. Kant claimed that a person was heteronomous if she was directed by her own desires. This is because her possession of these particular desires was contingent (at least in part) upon the circumstances in which she was brought up.

For Kant, then, if I am guided by my desires I will be acting hereronomously rather than autonomously, for my particular desires are merely contingent; they flow from something that is outside my control. In order to be autonomous, then, a person may only act in accordance with what Kant termed the "pure will"; the rational element of all persons that they necessarily share as rational beings, and whose operation is not subject to the influence of forces external to them. For Kant, the commandments of the pure will are thoroughly impersonal, *a priori* and universal; they will be the requirements of *duty*.[3] Now, since only these requirements stem solely from the (pure) will of the agent herself, and are not even partially caused by contingent factors external to the person, Kant held that it is only through acting out of duty that persons may act autonomously. To the extent that he acts out of the requirements of prudence or ambition, then, a person's actions will exhibit diminished autonomy. This is because in so choosing, the person will have been swayed by desires which are (at least in part) caused by factors which are external to him. The truly autonomous person will never choose to accede to mere desire, but will always act in accordance with the moral law. Such a person thus "proves his freedom in the highest degree by being *unable* to resist the call of duty."[4]

This however, is a very strict account of autonomy, and although it lays the foundation for more contemporary accounts it is not one which is often used in discussions of professional ethics that focus on autonomy. Instead, modern writers in professional ethics agree that a person is autonomous if she acts in accordance with those desires which are "her own" rather than those which are merely alien forces acting within her. Thus, a person will direct herself—she will be autonomous—if she is acting to satisfy desires which emanate from inside her, rather than those desires which merely act through her. An example would be useful here to distinguish these two types of desires. My action of going to the store to buy ice cream would be autonomous if I decided on the basis of my own preferences that I wanted some ice cream, and thought that, all things considered, now would be a good time to buy some. However, had I been hypnotized into wanting ice cream, then I would not be autonomous with respect to the buying of ice cream. My desire for ice cream would not have originated from "within" me, but would have been instilled in me by some external force, in this case the hypnotist. Thus, in this case my action would not have been under my control, but, instead, under the control of the person who had hypnotized me.

The core notion of autonomy that will be drawn upon in this paper, then, is one in which a person is autonomous if her actions and desires are free from external interference. With this account of autonomy in place one still needs to give reasons as to why autonomy should be regarded as being valuable, and so why it should be respected. The provision of these reasons is especially important once one realizes that the value of autonomy has not always been as "self-evident" as some contemporary writers claim that it is.[5] Indeed, until recently paternalism was the dominant value in many realms of professional life, with the professional being entrusted to act in the best interests of his or her client, and the client having very little say in how her affairs were to be directed in pursuit of this.

One obvious reason why professionals may be motivated to respect the autonomy of their clients is simply pragmatic; that through doing so they are more likely to retain the clients that they have and attract more to their practice. Thus, an architect who followed his client's wishes closely is more likely to have a better professional relationship with her than an architect who designed for her a house that *he* considered would best meet her needs, even if this meant disregarding her own instructions to him. Similarly, a lawyer who acts only on the instruction of her client is more likely to satisfy her (and thus receive repeat business from her) than one who acts of her own initiative in pursuit of what she perceives as her clients' interests—even if such devotion to instruction results in a less favorable legal outcome in the long run.

In addition to this pragmatic reason for respecting client autonomy, it is more important to note that professionals may also have a moral duty to respect the autonomy of their clients. Once again, the idea that there is a moral duty to respect personal autonomy stems from the work of Kant, who argued that persons should be respected as "ends in themselves," and not merely be used as instruments for the furthering of another's projects.[6] However, the idea that personal autonomy is valuable and should be respected is also recognized by all major ethical traditions, including consequentialism and virtue ethics—although, of course, how one is to implement one's respect for autonomy may vary from tradition to tradition, as will autonomy's relationship to other values, such as personal well-being. In brief, the reason for this widespread respect for autonomy is simple. Through respecting the autonomy of others, one is taking their views and wishes seriously, and so is treating them as moral agents, as rational, thinking beings. If, however, one simply disregards the views and wishes of others (or else discounts them in some way as not being as important as one's own) then one will not be treating them as full moral agents. (For this reason it is usually considered more acceptable to discount the views and wishes of children and mentally incompetent adults, for at the time of this discounting they do not possess full membership within the moral community; they are not fully moral agents.)

Autonomy and Professional Ethics

At this point, we have both an account of what autonomy is, and also two reasons (pragmatic and moral) as to why it should be respected. With this in hand it would be an easy matter to simply conclude that it is a professional's duty to respect the autonomy of her client, and leave it at that. (Indeed, this seems to be the view of most contemporary writers concerning the role of autonomy in professional ethics.) Yet to hold that a professional will have carried out her ethical requirements if she simply carries out the wishes of her client is mistaken. Moreover, to assume that the role of autonomy in professional ethics is solely to ensure that the client's wishes are met is to overlook some important ethical complexities.

Respecting The Autonomy Of Professionals

The claim that it is always the duty of the professional to carry out the wishes of the client is an impoverished view of the role of autonomy in professional ethics. This is because this overlooks the fact that it is not only the client whose autonomy should be respected; the professional's autonomy should also be respected. In dealing with their clients, professionals do not become mere automata, ready to cater to their clients' whims in the name of respecting their autonomy. Instead, they are also moral agents whose autonomy must be respected—in particular by the client, even though this may create conflict. The most obvious examples of where a professional's autonomy may conflict with her client's are in the field of medical ethics. For example, a client may request that the physician perform a medical procedure to which the physician is morally opposed, such as performing an abortion or killing a suffering patient who requests voluntary active euthanasia. Since the physician has a moral objection to the performance of such a procedure, it will violate her autonomy, her self-direction in accordance with her values, if the client requires that she do it. Thus, in order to respect the physician's autonomy the patient cannot enforce her request that such a procedure be performed.

It should be noted here that the physician is not failing to respect the patient's autonomy when she refuses to perform the requested operation. This is because in refusing this request she is not failing to respect the patient as a moral agent, who is capable of directing her own life in accordance with her desires and values. Rather, in refusing this request the physician is legitimately exercising her own autonomy, in that she is not relegating herself to being the mere means by which the patient pursues her own ends.

Although medical ethics is the most obvious area in which conflicts between the autonomy of the professional and the autonomy of the client may occur, they also occur in other areas of professional ethics. A military officer may be ordered to perform an action to which he has strong moral objections. A professional may engage in "whistleblowing," informing an appropriate authority of certain of her client's actions or requests that she believes violate ethical boundaries. In any such case the professional will legitimately exercise her autonomy by *refusing* to honor her client's instructions or requests. Again the refusal is perfectly consistent with respecting the autonomy of her client, even though it is aimed at frustrating, rather than satisfying, the client's autonomously-formed desires.

Clients' Requests For Paternalism On The Part Of The Professional

The claim that autonomy is of great value in professional ethics should not, then, lead one to immediately conclude that the autonomy of the client is necessarily paramount, for this is to overlook the fact that the professional is an autonomous person also, and that her autonomy is no less valuable than that of her client. It should also be noted that the client may autonomously desire that the professional she has hired act *paternalistically* towards her for a certain period of time, and so treat her as though she were not an autonomous person for a certain period of time. For example, the beneficiary of a trust may allow the trustees free rein to conduct her financial affairs as they see fit, without being bound by any instructions that she may choose to give them. Similarly, a litigant may instruct her lawyer to pursue her case in the manner he believes is best, while a patient may similarly accord *carte blanche* to her physician in the treatment of her ailments. Thus, in order to respect a client's autonomy, a professional may be required to treat her as though she were *not* an autonomous person with respect to her instructions to him concerning his area of expertise.

In such cases, it is often claimed that the client "autonomously decides to give up her autonomy"; she autonomously desires to be directed by someone else. At first sight, this may seem odd. However, this claim does not exhibit any conceptual confusion. To see this, consider the case of Ulysses and the Sirens. In Greek mythology, the Sirens' song was so captivating that sailors steered their ships onto the rocks from which the Sirens sang in order to get closer to them and to hear their songs better. When Ulysses' ship was passing close to the Sirens he instructed his sailors both to block their ears so that they could not hear the song, and also to bind him to the mast of his ship with his ears unblocked, so that he might hear the song and yet be unable to plunge to his death in an attempt to get closer to the Sirens. Moreover, he also instructed his sailors to ignore the orders to untie him which he knew he would give when he came close to the Sirens. In this case, Ulysses autonomously acted so that his future autonomy would be impaired; he would be unable to control his actions when bound to the mast because his movements would be restricted. In this case, just like that of the client who instructs a professional to act paternalistically towards her, Ulysses autonomously desired at a certain point in time to restrict the satisfaction of his desires for a future period of time, for he realized that this would be the best way to ensure his own well-being. In contemporary parlance, he "autonomously gave up his autonomy."

However, even though the claim that a client may "autonomously give up her autonomy" to allow a professional to direct her affairs is not conceptually confused, it *is* misleading. This is because a person may be "autonomous" in two different senses that have not yet been explored. In the first sense, a person is autonomous if she has the capacity to direct her own actions and her own life. Thus, she must be able to reason which would be the best course of action for her to pursue given her values and desires and current situation, and she must be able to actually pursue this course of action, whether or not she actually does so. In the second sense, a person is autonomous if she actually exercises this capacity to direct her own life

and her own actions. In this second sense, a person who had the capacity to direct her own life and actions would not be autonomous if she merely allowed another person to direct her life and actions for her. It is in this second sense of autonomy—the sense of autonomy as exercise—that a person autonomously decides to give up her autonomy to a professional. That is to say, she will ask a professional what the best course of action is for her and will follow his or her advice. Of course, this does not mean that the client has completely given up her autonomy, for she still retains her autonomy in the sense of capacity. Indeed, it is for this reason that she may decide not to follow the instructions of the professionals whose expertise she has sought, deciding instead to pursue another course of action, or to consult another professional.

Limits On The Exercise Of Professional Autonomy

So far, this paper has discussed professionals' respect for their clients' autonomy, the clients' duty to respect professionals' autonomy, and the possibility that the client may decide to abdicate the exercise of her autonomy in favor of acting under professional direction. In all of these cases the focus has been on the role of autonomy in shaping the ethical contours of the relationship between the professional and her client. However, one should also note that the professional relationship between a professional and her client will also affect third parties—and this may also serve to place ethical constraints upon professionals' actions.

Perhaps the clearest example of when a professional's autonomy may be constrained by the interests of third parties may be taken from business ethics. One of the standard complaints made by business ethicists is that businesses who use persuasive advertising to promote their products undermine the autonomy of those consumers who are thus manipulated into buying the advertised products. Here, it is alleged that although both the product's manufacturer and the advertisers she hires *may* respect each other's autonomy, through seeking to *manipulate* consumers into buying their products they are failing to respect consumer autonomy—and so their actions are unethical. Thus, in order to behave ethically, it is frequently argued that businesses should not instruct advertisers to boost sales through manipulating consumers into buying their products, and, if so instructed, advertisers should refuse to participate.

Professionals' actions may also be restrained out of respect for other third-party values. For example, certain ethical constraints may be placed upon the activities of a construction company and the engineers they hire to design a power plant owing to the potential that this has for causing harmful pollution. They may, perhaps, be required to meet certain environmental standards with respect to their waste disposal. Here, the autonomy of both the client construction company and the professional engineers that it hires may be restrained out of consideration for the *well-being* of those third parties who may be affected by their (autonomously performed) professional activities.

Some writers in professional ethics also argue that certain practices should be forbidden regardless of their possible effects (or lack thereof) upon third parties. For example, it may be the case that a person autonomously requests a physician to remove one of her healthy kidneys, so that she (the patient) may sell it on the open market, and the physician autonomously consents to perform this operation. Although this transaction was autonomously agreed to by both the physician and the prospective patient, some writers in professional ethics argue that this commodification of the human body is itself ethically wrong. Thus, even though it may not harm a third party (indeed, it may even help one who needs a kidney) the autonomy of both the prospective patient and the consenting physician must be restrained through forbidding this procedure to take place.

Conclusion

The above discussion has offered both a characterization of personal autonomy, and some indication as to why it is believed to be valuable. More importantly, however, it has also systematically addressed the role of autonomy within professional ethics. It was noted above that writers in professional ethics tend to focus uncritically upon the ideal of a professional respecting the autonomy of her client, which is frequently understood to mean that she must at all times obey his instructions, insofar as these are issued within the context of their professional relationship. As this essay has shown, however, this is an overly simplistic view of the role of autonomy within professional ethics, for it overlooks several ways in which the role of autonomy in professional ethics is complicated by other factors. Firstly, it overlooks the fact that the professional is also an autonomous person, and so may legitimately refuse to honor her client's request if she believes that she has sufficient reason to do so, without thereby failing to respect her client's autonomy. Secondly, this focus upon the standard model of the client issuing instructions to a professional overlooks the fact that the client may choose to cede the exercise of her autonomy to the professional, if she believes that this will best serve her interests. Finally, the emphasis upon the autonomy of the client also overlooks the fact that the autonomy of both the client and the professional may be subject to constraints which are based either on the effects of their actions upon third parties or on their infringement of moral law.

NOTES

1. Daniel Callahan, "Autonomy: A Moral Good, Not a Moral Obsession," *Hastings Genres Report* (October 1984): 40–42.
2. See, for example, James M. Ebejer and Michael J. Morden, "Paternalism in the Marketplace: Should a Salesman Be His Buyer's Keeper?" in Chapter 5 of this book.
3. Immanuel Kant (1785), *Groundwork of the Metaphysics of Morals*, Tr. James W. Ellington (Indianapolis: Hackett Publishing Company, 1981): 420.
4. Immanuel Kant (1785), *The Metaphysics of Morals*, Tr. Mary Gregor (Cambridge: Cambridge University Press, 1991): 381–382.
5. Harry Yeide, Jr., "The Many Faces of Autonomy," *The Journal of Clinical Ethics* (Winter 1992): 269–274.
6. Immanuel Kant, *Groundwork of the Metaphysic of Morals*, Tr. H. J. Pawn (New York: Harper and Row. 1964): 96.

CHAPTER FIFTEEN

Sexual Ethics

The Justification of Sex Without Love

ALBERT ELLIS

A scientific colleague of mine, who holds a professorial post in the department of sociology and anthropology at one of our leading universities, recently asked me about my stand on the question of human beings having sex relations without love. Although I have taken something of a position on this issue in my book, The American Sexual Tragedy, I have never quite considered the problem in sufficient detail. So here goes.

In general, I feel that affectional, as against nonaffectional, sex relations are desirable but not necessary. It is usually desirable that an association between coitus and affection exist—particularly in marriage, because it is often difficult for two individuals to keep finely tuned to each other over a period of years, and if there is not a good deal of love between them, one may tend to feel sexually imposed upon by the other.

The fact, however, that the coexistence of sex and love may be desirable does not, to my mind, make it necessary. My reasons for this view are several:

1. Many individuals—including, even, many married couples—do find great satisfaction in having sex relations without love. I do not consider it fair to label these individuals as criminal just because they may be in the minority.

Moreover, even if they are in the minority (as may well not be the case), I am sure that they number literally millions of men and women. If so, they constitute a sizable subgroup of humans whose rights to sex satisfaction should be fully acknowledged and protected.

2. Even if we consider the supposed majority of individuals who find greater satisfaction in sex-love than in sex-*sans*-love relations, it is doubtful if all or most of them do so for all their lives. During much of their existence, especially their younger years, these people tend to find sex-without-love quite satisfying, and even to prefer it to affectional sex.

When they become older, and their sex drives tend to wane, they may well emphasize coitus with rather than without affection. But why should we condemn them while they still prefer sex to sex-love affairs?

3. Many individuals, especially females in our culture, who say that they only enjoy sex when it is accompanied by affection are actually being unthinkingly conformist and unconsciously hypo-critical. If they were able to contemplate themselves objectively, and had the courage of their inner convictions, they would find sex without love eminently gratifying.

This is not to say that they would only enjoy nonaffectional coitus, nor that they would always find it more satisfying than affectional sex. But, in the depths of their psyche and soma, they would deem sex without love pleasurable too.

And why should they not? And why should we, by our puritanical know-nothingness, force these individuals to drive a considerable portion of their sex feelings and potential satisfactions underground?

If, in other words, we view sexuoamative relations as desirable rather than necessary, we sanction the innermost thoughts and drive of many of our fellowmen and fellowwomen to have sex and sex-love relations. If we take the opposing view, we hardly destroy these innermost thoughts and drives, but frequently tend to intensify them while denying them open and honest outlet. This, as Freud... pointed out, is one of the main (though by no means the only) sources of rampant neurosis.

4. I firmly believe that sex is a biological, as well as a social, drive, and that in its biological phases it is essentially nonaffectional. If this is so, then we can expect that, however we try to civilize the sex drives—and civilize them to some degree we certainly must—there will always be an underlying tendency for them to escape from our society-inculcated shackles and to be still partly felt in the raw.

When so felt, when our biological sex urges lead us to desire and enjoy sex without (as well as with) love, I do not see why we should make their experiencers feel needlessly guilty.

5. Many individuals—many millions in our society, I am afraid—have little or no capacity for affection or love. The majority of these individuals, perhaps, are emotionally disturbed, and should preferably be helped to increase their affectional propensities. But a large number are not particularly disturbed, and instead are neurologically or cerebrally deficient.

Mentally deficient persons, for example, as well as many dull normals (who, together, include several million citizens of our nation) are notoriously shallow in their feelings, and probably intrinsically so. Since these kinds of individuals—like the neurotic and the organically deficient—are for the most part, in our day and age, not going to be properly treated and not going to overcome their deficiencies, and since most of them definitely do have sex desires, I again see no point in making them guilty when they have nonloving sex relations.

Surely these unfortunate individuals are sufficiently handicapped by their disturbances or impairments without our adding to their woes by anathematizing them when they manage to achieve some nonamative sexual release.

6. Under some circumstances—though these, I admit, may be rare—some people find more satisfaction in nonloving coitus even though, under other circumstances, these same people may find more satisfaction in sex-love affairs. Thus, the man who normally enjoys being with his girlfriend because he loves as well as is sexually attracted to her, may occasionally find immense satisfaction in being with another girl with whom he has distinctly nonloving relations.

Granting that this may be (or is it?) unusual, I do not see why it should be condemnable.

7. If many people get along excellently and most cooperatively with business partners, employees, professors, laboratory associates, acquaintances, and even spouses for whom they have little or no love or affection, but with whom they have certain specific things in common, I do not see why there cannot be individuals who get along excellently and most cooperatively with sex mates with whom they may have little else in common.

I personally can easily see the tragic plight of a man who spends much time with a girl with whom he has nothing in common but sex: since I believe that life is too short to be well consumed in relatively one-track or intellectually low-level pursuits. I would also think it rather unrewarding for a girl to spend much time with a male with whom she had mutually satisfying sex, friendship, and cultural interest but no love involvement. This is because I would like to see people, in their 70-odd years of life, have maximum rather than minimum satisfactions with individuals of the other sex with whom they spend considerable time.

I can easily see, however, even the most intelligent and highly cultured individuals spending a little time with members of the other sex with whom they have common sex and cultural but no real love interests. And I feel that, for the time expended in this manner, their lives may be immeasurably enriched.

Moreover, when I encounter friends or psychotherapy clients who become enamored and spend considerable time and effort thinking about and being with a member of the other sex with whom they are largely sexually obsessed, and for whom they have little or no love, I mainly view these sexual infatuations as one of the penalties of their being human. For humans are the kind of animals who are easily disposed to this type of behavior....

I believe that one of the distinct inconveniences or tragedies of human sexuality is that it endows us, and perhaps particularly the males among us, with a propensity to become exceptionally involved and infatuated with members of the other sex whom, had we no sex urges, we would hardly notice. That is too bad; and it might well be a better world if it were otherwise. But it is not otherwise, and I think it is silly and pernicious for us to condemn ourselves because we are the way that we are in this respect.

We had better accept our biosocial tendencies, or our fallible humanity—instead of constantly blaming ourselves and futilely trying to change certain of its relatively harmless, though still somewhat tragic, aspects.

For reasons such as these, I feel that although it is usually—if not always—desirable for human beings to have sex relations with those they love rather than with those they do not love, it is by no means necessary that they do so. When we teach that it is necessary, we only needlessly condemn millions of our citizens to self-blame and atonement.

The position which I take—that there are several good reasons why affectional, as against nonaffectional, sex relations are desirable but not necessary—can be assailed on several counts. I shall now consider some of the objections to this position to see if they cannot be effectively answered.

It may be said that an individual who has nonloving instead of loving sex relations is not necessarily wicked but that he is self-defeating because, while going for immediate gratification, he will miss out on even greater enjoyments. But this would only be true if such an individual (whom we shall assume, for the sake of discussion, would get greater enjoyment from affectional sex relations than from nonaffectional ones) were usually or always having nonaffectionate coitus. If he were occasionally or sometimes having love with sex, and the rest of the time having sex without love, he would be missing out on very little, if any, enjoyment.

Under these circumstances, in fact, he would normally get more pleasure from sometimes having sex without love. For the fact remains, and must not be realistically ignored, that in our present-day society sex without love is much more frequently available than sex with love.

Consequently, to ignore nonaffectional coitus when affectional coitus is not available would, from the standpoint of enlightened self-interest, be sheer folly. In relation both to immediate and greater enjoyment, the individual would thereby be losing out.

The claim can be made of course that if an individual sacrifices sex without love now he will experience more pleasure by having sex with love in the future. This is an interesting claim; but I find no empirical evidence to sustain it. In fact, on theoretical grounds it seems most unlikely that it will be sustained. It is akin to the claim that if an individual starves himself for several days in a row he will greatly enjoy eating a meal at the end of a week or a month. I am sure he will—provided that he is then not too sick or debilitated to enjoy anything! But, even assuming that such an individual derives enormous satisfaction from his one meal a week or a month, is his total satisfaction greater than it would have been had he enjoyed three good meals a day for that same period of time? I doubt it.

It may be held that if both sex with and without love are permitted in any society, the nonaffectional sex will drive out affectional sex, somewhat in accordance with Gresham's laws of currency. On the contrary, however, there is much reason to believe that just because an individual has sex relations, for quite a period, on a nonaffectional basis, he will be more than eager to replace it, eventually, with sex with love.

From my clinical experience, I have often found that males who most want to settle down to having a single mistress or wife are those who have tried numerous lighter affairs and found them wanting. The view that sex without love eradicates the need for affectional sex relationships is somewhat akin to the ignorance is bliss theory. For it virtually says that if people never experienced sex with love they would never realize how good it was and therefore would never strive for it.

Or else the proponents of this theory seem to be saying that sex without love is so greatly satisfying, and sex with love so intrinsically difficult and disadvantageous to attain, that given the choice between the two, most people would pick the former. If this is so, then by all means let them pick the former—with which, in terms of their greater and total happiness, they would presumably be better off.

I doubt, however, that this hypothesis is factually sustainable. From clinical experience, again, I can say that individuals who are capable of sex with love usually seek and find it; while those who remain nonaffectional in their sex affairs generally are not particularly capable of sex with love and need psychotherapeutic help before they can become thus capable.

Although, as a therapist, I frequently work with individuals who are only able to achieve nonaffectional sex affairs and, through helping them eliminate their irrational fears and blockings, make it possible for them to achieve sex-love relationships, I still would doubt that all persons who take no great pleasure in sex with love are emotionally deficient. Some quite effective individuals—such as Immanuel Kant, for instance—seem to be so wholeheartedly dedicated to things or ideas that they rarely or never become amatively involved with people.

As long as such individuals have vital, creative interests and are intensely absorbed or involved with something, I would hesitate to diagnose them as being necessarily neurotic merely because they do not ordinarily become intensely absorbed with people. Some of these nonlovers of human beings are, of course, emotionally disturbed. But all? I wonder.

Disturbed or not, I see no reason why individuals who are dedicated to things or ideas should not have, in many or most instances, perfectly normal sex drives. And, if they do, I fail to see why they should not consummate their sex urges in nonaffectional ways in order to have more time and energy for their nonamative pursuits.

A Case Against Homosexuality

PAUL CAMERON

Courtesy of Paul Cameron, chair, Family Research Institute www.familyresearchinst.org

In some segments of the mass media, the homosexuality issue takes on the appearance of a struggle between orange juice peddlers and bathhouse owners. At a different level individual rights vs. the interests of society provide the conflict. Some argue that adult homosexuals ought to be allowed to do what they want behind closed doors. Others, often seeing the issue in terms of rights, honesty, and overpopulation, seek to grant homosexuality equal status with heterosexuality. The school system of San Francisco, apparently resonating with the latter tack, is offering a course including "homosexual life-styles." Liberals attempt to shame as unenlightened all who oppose complete equality as vigorously as conservative Bible-thumpers threaten wrath from above.

No known human society has ever granted equal status to homo- and heterosexuality. What information do those who desire social equivalence for these two sexual orientations possess that assures them that this new venture in human social organization is called for at this time? Have the cultures of the past practiced discrimination against homosexuality out of a mere prejudice, or was there substance to their bias? At the risk of seeming rather out of step with the academic community, no new information has surfaced that would lead me to discount the social policies of the past. On the contrary, the policies of the past in regard to homosexuality appear generally wise, and considerable discrimination against homosexuality and for heterosexuality, marriage and parenthood appears needful for the social good.

Discrimination

Discrimination is something all humans, and all human communities do. Individually we discriminate for certain things and against others, e.g., movies over T.V. Collectively we discriminate for and against selected: 1) acts (pleasantries, sharing vs. murder, robbery) 2) traits (generous, kind vs. whiny, hostile) and 3) life-styles (independent, productive vs. gambling, indolent). Prejudice is unwarranted discrimination. The issue is not whether discrimination should exist—for human society to exist, it must. The issues are always: 1) is discrimination called for? and 2) how much is necessary? Reasonable people can and do disagree on what ought to be discriminated for and against, to what degree, and even if discrimination is prejudicial rather than called for. But reasoned opinion can hold that homosexuality and homosexuals ought to be discriminated against....

The Case Against Homosexuality/Wisdom of the Ages

No contemporary society accords homosexuality equivalent status with heterosexuality. No known society has accorded equivalent status in the past (Karlen, 1971). No current or ancient religion of any consequence has failed to teach discrimination against homosexuality. The Judeo-Christian tradition is no exception to this rule. The Old Testament made homosexuality a capital offense, and while the New Testament writers failed to invoke capital punishment for any offense, they did manage to consign homosexuals to eternal hell for the practice. Church fathers and traditions have stayed in line with this position until recently. To the degree that tradition and agreed-upon social policy ought to carry weight in our thinking about issues, the weight of tradition is preponderately on the side of discrimination....

While one cannot carry the "wisdom of the ages" argument too far—just because all peoples up to a certain point in time believed something does not necessarily mean that it was so—yet it appears more than a little injudicious to cast it aside as merely "quaint." Probably no issue has occupied man's collective attentions more than successful living together. That such unanimity of opinion and practice should exist must give one pause. Certainly such congruence "puts the ball in the changer's court." As in so many spheres of human endeavor, when we know that we can get on in a particular way, the burden of proof that we can get on as well or better by following a different custom falls upon those seeking the change....

To date, those seeking change have not been flush with scientific evidence that homosexuality is not socially disruptive. On the contrary, the arguments that have been advanced have been little more than "people ought not to be discriminated against; homosexuals are people; ergo homosexuals ought not to be discriminated against" shouted larger and louder. No one to my knowledge has ever claimed that homosexuals were not people, and one would have to be a dunce to believe that being a person qualifies one, ipso facto, for nondiscrimination. Aside from this argument repeated in endless variations and ad nauseam, the evidence is simply not there....

Homosociality Coupled With Increasing Self-Centeredness Could Lead to Widespread Homosexuality

... Jimmy Carter said: "I don't see homosexuality as a threat to the family" (Washington Post, June 19, 1977). His sentiments probably echo those of the educated class of our society. They trust that "only deviants" are really into homosexuality anyway, and, more importantly, that "mother nature" will come through in the last analysis. Biology, they assume, has a great deal to do with sexuality and sexual attraction, and millions of years of heterosexuality has firmly engraved itself on the genetic code.

Such thinking betrays a lack of appreciation of the enormous component of learning that goes into human sexuality. The point that anthropology has made over the past hundred years is the tremendous diversity of human social organization.... While the onset of the events of puberty vary relatively little from one society to another, the onset of copulation varies over a full quarter of the life-span—from 5 or 6 years of age to mid-20s.... Many mammals practice sex for only a few days or weeks in the year, but man varies from untrammeled lust to studied virginity. While I have enumerated my reasons more fully elsewhere (Cameron, 1977), I believe that the most reasonable construal of the evidence to date suggests that human sexuality is totally learned....

Because human sexuality is totally learned, humans must be pointed in the "right" direction, and taught how and with whom to perform. And there's the rub. Homosexuality and heterosexuality do not start off on the same footing. *Au contraire*, one gets a number of important boosts in the scheme of things. In our society the development process is decidedly tilted toward the adoption of homosexuality!

Part of the homosexual tilt is the extreme homosociality of children starting around the age of 5. As everyone is aware, boys want to play with boys and girls with girls, and they do so with a vengeance. It's quite reasonable, on their part. First, boys' and girls' bodies are different and they are aware that their bodies-to-be will differ still

more. In part because of this the games, sports and skills they practice differ. As if in anticipation of the differing roles they will have, their interests and proclivities differ. Even if they try, few girls can do as well as most boys at "boy things" and few boys can do as well as girls at "girl things." They almost inhabit different worlds. Not surprisingly for members of two different "races," poles apart psychologically, socially, and physically, they "stick to their own kind.".....

There are three other components that contribute to the homosexual tilt. First, on the average in our society, males are considerably more taken with sex than females are. In my 1975 survey of 818 persons on the east coast of the U.S., respondents were asked to rate the degree of pleasure they obtained from 22 activities including "being with one's family," "listening to music," "being out in nature," "housework," and "sexual activity." Between the late teens through middle age, sexual activity topped the male list as the "most pleasurable activity." It did manage to rank as high as fifth place for young adult women (aged 18 to 25), but, overall for the female life span, was outscored by almost everything including "housework" (which, incidentally, ranked dead last among males)....

How well suited are "hot" males to "cool" females? Not very. One of (if not the) most common problems in marital counseling is sexual incompatibility. Females pay sex as the price of love/companionship and males pay love for sex. While this is rather too aphoristic to capture all that goes on in the male-female struggle, there is a great deal of truth to it. Even among homosexuals, the males probably out sex lesbians by a factor of 5 to 1 (see Tripp's sympathetic treatment for elaboration on this theme). Where is a male most apt to find his counterpart, among maledom or femaledom? If he wants hot, dripping sex, what better place to find it than with another of similar bent? If she wants tender companionship, which sex is most apt to provide the partner? The answers are obvious.

The second part of the homosexual tilt derives from the fact that [the] homosexual encounter offers better sex, on the average, than heterosexual sex. If pleasure is what you are after, who better to fulfill you than a partner who has a body and predilections like yours? One of the things that both the male homosexual and lesbian societies advertise is that "they satisfy"... From a sexual standpoint, a female can offer a little extra orifice as compensation for her: ignorance, timidity, desire for companionship first, etc. Further, sex between members of a sex assures that there will be no pregnancy problems further on down the line.

Another developmental boost for homosexuality comes from the self-servingness/egocentricity of the young. Humans are born with, at best, rudimentary consciousness. Then, over time and experience, they learn to differentiate themselves from the environment. From about the age of 5 or 6 onward for the next decade or so for life, they are engrossed in themselves, in the service of themselves, their pleasures, their interests, their ways. Reciprocity of interaction is rendered begrudgingly, certainly far from spontaneously. My research, involving the interviewing of over 8,000 respondents from the U.S. and five other nations, in which we asked persons to tell us: 1) whose interests they had just been thinking about serving—their own or another's or others' and 2) whether they had just been thinking about themselves, things, or other people, indicated that younger persons more frequently reported themselves in a self-serving attitude and thinking about themselves than adults did. In the U.S., adults of both sexes typically reported themselves in an other-serving attitude. But U.S. males "switched" from self-servingness to other-servingness around age 26 while for females the switch occurred in the middle teens. If one is after self-fulfillment, pleasure for self, which sexual orientation "fits" better? Homosexuality, obviously. One can have his homosociality and sex too. One can comfortably neglect the painful transformation from self-interest to other-interest. Me and mine to the fore.

Which kind of sexuality is the more compelling? The one that can say "come, sex my way and I will show you a life of complexity. Of children and responsibility. Of getting on with 'that other kind.' I will offer you poorer sex initially, and, who knows, perhaps you will just have to satisfy yourself with poorer sex permanently. But you will be able to 'glimpse immortality in your children' (Plato)." Or "come, sex my way and I will give it to you straight and hot. Pleasures of the best quality, almost on demand, with persons with whom you already share a great deal, and I will enable you to share more. It will not be difficult, in fact, it will be fun. You will not have to change or adapt your personality style or your egocentric orientation. You'll fit right in immediately. None of this hemming and hawing—you'll get what you want when you want it. Motto? Pleasure—now. The future? Who knows, but the present is going to be a dilly." Which kind of sexuality is the more compelling? Does anyone doubt which way most youth would turn if equivalent social status attended homosexuality and heterosexuality?...

A Cluster of Undesirable Traits is Disproportionately Associated With Homosexuality

Though some may shriek that "my personality traits are my business," let us acknowledge that some traits are society's business. A person's traits can lead to actions which affect the collectivity. Megalomania often proves socially disruptive, and sometimes, as in the case of Hitler, leads to incredible human destruction. It is obviously in society's interest to encourage those social roles and traits that tend to social cohesion and betterment. Similarly, it is in the social interest to discourage those that tend to produce disruption and harm....

It would be as silly to contend that each of the following traits is associated with each homosexual as to argue that none of these appear in heterosexuals (or even worse, that the obverse of these traits always accompanies heterosexuality). However, for social policy formulation, it is enough to demonstrate disproportionate "loading" of undesirable traits within a given subgroup or subculture to justify social discrimination.

The Egocentric/Supercilious/Narcissistic/Self-Oriented/Hostile Complex

This cluster of traits appears to "go together" with homosexuality.... A person who, in part, seeks more of himself in his lover, is more apt to remain in the egocentric/self-centered orientation of youth. Such a person is more apt to gravitate toward those kinds of professions in which he can be a "star" and be noticed....

The "star" lives for gratification of self. My way is his motto.... The star need not accommodate himself to the needs of others to the same degree as most folk. If a current love is "not working out" he can be discarded and a more suitable one found....

Superciliousness—an attitude of aloof, hostile disdain—is also consonant with the egocentric person. If you will not realize his marvelous qualities and pay homage, he still has you one down. After all, he treated you with contempt first. Even if you become hostile, his preceded yours....

The greatest component of the childish "I want it my way" associated with homosexuality stems, in part, from the greater ease connected with homosexual attachments. Developmentally, both hetero- and homosexuals want things "their way." But the kinds of accommodations and adjustments necessary for successful heterosexuality assure participants that it won't be all their way. Just because so much of the time things don't work out perfectly in the face of such effort helps wean one from the coddled security of childhood. Parents and the rest of society work to "make the world nice" for children. Every childhood painting is worthy of note, as is every musical note. But adulthood is strewn with disappointments. Heterosexuality is a "maturing" sexual orientation....

It appears to me that homosexuality leads to a shallower commitment to society and its betterment. Such shallowness comes about both because of a lack of children and the ease of sexual gratification. The effort involved in being heterosexual, the effort expended in being a parent—these are denied the homosexual. As he has less responsibility and commitment, so he is or becomes less responsible and committed. It is difficult to develop personality characteristics that fail to resonate with one's environment. While we are not totally creatures of our environment, it is far easier to "swim with the tide."

It is difficult to find anything like "hard" scientific evidence to substantiate the notion that homosexuals are on the average, less responsible/trustworthy than heterosexuals. The Weinberg and Williams sample of homosexuals was asked a question that bears upon the issue. Do you agree or disagree with the statement "most people can be trusted"? To a degree, since a person cannot know "most people" it appears reasonable to assume that he might project his own personality onto "most people" and/or assume that those people with whom he comes in contact are like "most people." While 77% of a reasonably representative sample of the U.S. population chose "agree," only 47% of the homosexuals ticked the same response. Because of the ambiguity of such items, I would not make too much of the difference. But it could suggest that homosexuals are less trustworthy.

Homosexuality is Associated With Personal Lethality

One of the more troubling traits associated with homosexuality is personal lethality. Extending back in time to classical Greece, a lethal theme shines through. In Greece, if historical sources are to be believed, companies of homosexual warriors were assembled because it was believed that they made better killers. The same pattern appears to be repeated in history....

In our society the childless are more apt to suicide and childless couples are more apt to be involved in homicide. Further, both suicide and homicide accompany divorce and separation disproportionately frequently. Social cohesion needs to be developed and maintained for optimum personal and social health....

Heterosexuality Provides the Most Desirable Model of Love

Myths are created not only by storytellers but by people living within the myths. Almost all (95% or so) heterosexuals get married, and 75%–80% stay married to their original partner till death. To be sure, there are marriage "hogs" within the heterosexual camp who play serial monogamy and assure that a third of all marriages end in divorce. Further, about half of all married men and about a third of all married women admit to one or more infidelities over the duration of their marriage (probably the greater bulk of the "cheaters" come from the serial monogamy camp). While heterosexuality's colors are far from Simon pure, the relationship heterosexuality spawns is among, if not the, most enduring of human bonds....

Homosexuality offers no comparison in durability. While "slam, bam, thank you ma'am" occurs in heterosexuality, few heterosexuals could more than fantasize about what occurs in homosexual bathhouses or tearooms. As Weinberg and Williams note, the homosexual community typically features "sex for sex's sake." Their survey in which two thirds of their respondents chose to respond "no" to whether they had limited their "... sexual relationships primarily to (another)" is telling. Names and banter are typically neglected in bathhouses....

When people are merely "getting their jollies," and fantasizing perfection while doing so, reduced communication is an asset. If you discover that your beautiful lover holds political views antithetical to your own, how can you really enjoy him/her? The "less known the better" is fantasy sex. Communicating, mutually knowledgeable people often have to "work it out" before attempts at sex can even occur. But while typically short on durability, some homosexual relationships are more lasting. The quality of even these is often questionably desirable. Part of the problem lies in the lack of commitment that follows lower effort in the homosexual pairing. Tripp, for instance, opines that part "... of the reason many homosexual relationships do not survive the first serious quarrel is that one or both partners simply find it much easier to remarket themselves than work out conflicts (p. 155)." In heterosexuality, no matter how similar the participants, there is always a considerable gap between them. To stay together takes great effort, and the expenditure of this effort prompts both personal and social commitment to the partner....

Because the heterosexual partners are so dissimilar, accommodation and adjustment are their key strategies. Because mutually satisfying heterosexual sexing takes so long and so much effort, both participants have to "hang in there" long after "sane people" would have toddled off in frustration. We become the way we act. The heterosexual relationship places a premium on "getting on" and thus provides a model to smooth countless other human interactions. The homosexual model is a considerably less satisfactory one upon which to build a civilization. Note Tripp again (p. 167): "... the problems encountered in balancing heterosexual and homosexual relationships are strikingly different. The heterosexual blend tends to be rich in stimulating contrasts and short on support—so much so that popular marriage counseling literature incessantly hammers home the advice that couples should develop common interests and dissolve their conflicts by increasing their 'communication.' By comparison, homosexual relationships are overclose, fatigue-prone, and are often adjusted to such narrow, trigger-sensitive tolerances that a mere whisper of disrapport can jolt the partners into making repairs, or into conflict."...

Our social system also features large components of delay of gratification. The heterosexual "carrot" is hard to get and requires a lot of input before successful outcome is achieved. The homosexual model is too immediate and influences people to expect instant results....

In short, heterosexuality is effortful, durable, and demands delay of gratification. While any human relationship takes effort, homosexuality pales in comparison to heterosexuality on each count....

From the prudent standpoint, homosexuality is an obstacle in the pursuit of happiness....

Does homosexuality make being happy more difficult? In the Weinberg and Williams study, homosexuals were asked to respond "yes" or "no" to the statement "no one cares what happens to you." While a general population sample had chosen "yes" 23% of the time, 34% of homosexuals chose "yes."... Homosexuality, with its emphasis upon self-gratification, does little to generate others who care about you.... In the long run, heterosexuality has a lot more to offer as a life-style than homosexuality....

Summary

In sum, there are a number of reasons why homosexuality is best treated as a deviant sexual mode. I do not believe that homosexuality ought to be placed on an even-keel with heterosexuality. Further, homosexuals ought not, in my opinion, to be permitted to openly ply their sexual orientation and retain influential positions in the social system. Thus teachers, or pastors who "come out," ought, in my opinion, to lose their claim to the roles they occupy.

REFERENCES

Allport, G. W. The Person in Psychology. NY: Beacon, 1961.

Atkins, J. Sex in Literature. NY: Grove Press, 1970.

Bergler, E. Homosexuality: Disease or Way of Life? NY: Macmillan, 1956.

Bieber, I. Homosexuality: A Psychoanalytic Study. NY: Basic Books, 1962.

Cameron, P. "Immolations to the Juggernaut," Linacre Quarterly, 1977, 44, 64–74.

Cameron, P. The Life-Cycle: Perspectives and Commentary. NY: General Health, 1977.

Cameron, P. & Oeschger, D. "Homosexuality in the Mass Media as Indexed by Magazine Literature over the Past Half Century in the U.S." Paper presented at Eastern Psychological Association Convention, New York, April 4, 1975.

Davis, N. & Graubert J. Heterosexual. NY: Vantage Press, 1975.

Freud, S. "Three Contributions to Sexual Theory," Nervous and Mental Disease Monograph Series, 1925, 7.

Gubrium, J. F. "Being Single in Old Age," International Journal of Aging and Human Development, 1975, 6, 29–41.

Hunt, M. Sexual Behavior in the 1970s. Chicago: Playboy Press, 1974.

Karlen, A. Sexuality and Homosexuality. NY: Norton, 1971.

Kastenbaum, R. J. & Costa, P. T. "Psychological Perspectives on Death," Annual Review of Psychology, 1977, 28, 225–49.

Maugham, S. El Greco. NY: Doubleday, 1950.

Sears, R. R. "Sources of Life Satisfactions of the Terman Gifted Man," American Psychologist, 1977, 32, 119–128.

Tripp, C. A. The Homosexual Matrix. NY: McGraw-Hill, 1975.

Weinberg, M. S. & Williams, C. J. Male Homosexuals: Their Problems and Adaptations. NY: Oxford University Press, 1974.

Sex, Lies, and Respect

ANN GARRY

Author's Note: This paper appears as "Sex, Lies, and Pornography," in Hugh LaFollette, ed., Ethics in Practice, 2nd ed. (Malden, MA: Blackwell, 2001). I have retained the copyright. It has been reprinted with this title or "Sex, Lies, and Respect" in several other anthologies.

In the last third of the twentieth century pornography became much more widely available, but the moral and political issues surrounding it remain unresolved. In the 1960s the United States, for example, was barely past the era of banning books; courts had begun to grapple with obscenity cases.[1] Visual pornography could be seen in certain public theatres, and some people, mainly men, had private collections. Keep in mind that there were no video stores on the corner renting pornographic tapes for home VCR use, no cable channels showing it, and no internet to provide a panoply of sites for every erotic taste. When I first started thinking about pornography as a young feminist philosopher in the early 1970s, writing in the public arena came primarily from two groups of (mostly male) writers: "conservatives" who seemed to assume that sex was evil and "liberal" aficionados of the "sexual revolution," who had no clue what feminists meant when we demanded not to be treated as "sex objects." Pornography was also an object of political concern and academic study; for example, then President Nixon appointed a Commission on Obscenity and Pornography (and subsequently disregarded its results).

Where did this leave a feminist philosopher in the 1970s? Torn, conflicted, and unhappy with the level of discussion. On the one hand, I had been inclined to think that pornography was innocuous and to dismiss "moral" arguments for censoring it because many such arguments rested on an assumption I did not share—that sex is an evil to be controlled. On the other hand, I believed that it was wrong to exploit or degrade human beings, particularly women and others who are especially susceptible. So if pornography degrades human beings, then even if I would oppose its censorship, I surely could not find it morally innocuous. In order to think about the issues further, I wrote "Pornography and Respect for Women"—offering a moral argument that would ground a feminist objection to pornography, but avoid a negative view of sex.[2]

The public and academic debates about pornography have subsequently become much richer, and alliances and divisions have shifted in unusual ways. North American feminists became deeply divided over pornography—debating whether pornography should be censored or in some other way controlled, and analyzing pornography's positive or negative value in moral, legal and political terms reflecting a wide variety of women's experiences. Some of the feminists most vehemently opposed to pornography found themselves allied with other foes of pornography—religious political conservatives with whom they had very little else in common. All the while, the mainstream "culture wars" pitted many of these same conservatives against a variety of people, including

feminists, who choose "alternative" life styles or in some way or other advocate social change. The picture I am sketching of the debates should look complex and frequently shifting. Yet this picture is no more complex and variegated than pornography itself has come to be. Although the central argument of this essay focuses on fairly tame and widespread heterosexual pornography, there is pornography available today for any conceivable taste and orientation. Where there's a market, there's pornography for it.

In this paper I first sketch very briefly some feminist positions concerning the law, politics and morality of pornography. In the next section I offer a moral argument for maintaining that pornography degrades (or exploits or dehumanizes) women in ways or to an extent that it does not degrade men. In the final section, I argue that although much current pornography does degrade women, it is possible to have nondegrading, nonsexist pornography. However, this possibility rests on our making certain fundamental changes in our conceptions of gender roles and of sex. At a number of points throughout the paper I compare my position to those of other feminists.

I.

Although some feminists find (some) pornography liberating, many feminists oppose (much) pornography for a variety of reasons.[3] Let's look at some who oppose it. Catharine MacKinnon and Andrea Dworkin drafted civil ordinances that categorize pornography as a form of sex-discrimination; they were passed in Indianapolis, Indiana, and Minneapolis, Minnesota, but subsequently overturned in the courts. In the ordinances they use the definition below.

> Pornography is the graphic sexually explicit subordination of women, whether in pictures or in words that includes one of more of the following: ... women are presented dehumanized as sexual objects, things or commodities; or ...as sexual objects who enjoy pain or humiliation...or...who experience sexual pleasure in being raped...tied up or cut up or mutilated or bruised or

physically hurt [the definition continues through five more long, graphic clauses before noting that men, children or transsexuals can be used in the place of women].[4]

Although in my way of thinking of morality, this definition already incorporates moral objections to pornography within it, MacKinnon has argued that pornography is not a moral issue but a political one. By a political issue, she means that pornography is about the distribution of power, about domination and subordination. Pornography sexualizes the domination and subordination of women. It makes sexually exciting and attractive the state of affairs in which women, both in body and spirit, are under the control of men. In pornography men define what women want and who we are: we want to be taken, used, and humiliated. Pornography is not about harmless fantasy and sexual liberation. I'll return to MacKinnon and Dworkin from time to time in this paper as examples of "anti-pornography" feminists.[5]

Other feminists claim that pornography is a form of hate speech/literature or that it lies about or defames women. Eva Kittay uses the analogy with racist hate literature that justifies the abuse of people on the basis of their racial characteristics to argue that pornography "justifies the abuse of women on the basis of their sexual characteristics."[6] Helen Longino defines pornography as "material that explicitly represents or describes degrading and abusive sexual behavior so as to endorse and/or recommend the behavior as described."[7] She argues that pornography defames and libels women by its deep and vicious lies, and supports and reinforces oppression of women by the distorted view of women that it portrays. Susan Brownmiller's classic statement is also worth noting: "Pornography, like rape, is a male invention, designed to dehumanize women, to reduce the female to an object of sexual access, not to free sensuality from moralistic or parental inhibition....Pornography is the undiluted essence of anti-female propaganda."[8]

In order to understand how my view overlaps with, but differs from the feminist positions just described, we need to note some differences in our terminology and in our legal interests. The authors above build the objectionable character of pornography into their definitions of it. Sometimes those who do this want to reserve 'erotica' for explicit sexual material lacking those characteristics (though MacKinnon and Dworkin evidence little interest in this). Other times a negatively-value-laden definition is part of a legal strategy aimed at controlling pornography. I take a different approach to defining pornography, one that stems from ordinary usage and does not bias from the start any discussion of whether pornography is morally objectionable. I use 'pornography' simply to label those explicit sexual materials intended to arouse the reader, listener, or viewer sexually. There is probably no sharp line that divides pornographic from nonpornographic material. I do not see this as a problem because I am not interested here in legal strategies that require a sharp distinction. In addition, I am focusing on obvious cases that would be uncontroversially pornographic—sleazy material that no one would ever dream has serious literary, artistic, political, or scientific merit.

I should say a little more about legal matters to clarify a difference between my interests and those of MacKinnon and Dworkin. They are interested in concrete legal strategies and believe that their proposed civil ordinances do not constitute censorship. My primary concern here is with neither a civil ordinance nor censorship, but with the basis for objecting to pornography on moral grounds. Nevertheless, it is important for me to state my belief that even if moral objections to pornography exist, there is no simple inference from "pornography is immoral" to "pornography should be censored" or to "pornography should be controlled by means of a civil ordinance that allows women to sue for harms based on sex-discrimination." Consider censorship. An argument to censor pornography requires us to balance a number of competing values: self-determination and freedom of expression (of both the users of pornography and those depicted in it or silenced by it), the nature of the moral and political problems with pornography (including its harms or potential harms to individuals and to communities), and so forth. Although there are fascinating issues here, there is no fast move from "immoral" to "illegal."

II.

I want to take a step back from the feminist positions sketched above that assume the morally objectionable character of pornography within the definition. I want to evaluate the moral argument that pornography is objectionable because it degrades people. To degrade someone in this context is to lower her or his status in humanity—behavior incompatible with showing respect for a person. Of the many kinds of degradation and exploitation possible in the production of pornography, I focus only on the content of the pornographic work.[9] The argument is that pornography itself exemplifies and recommends behavior that violates the moral principle to respect persons. It treats women as mere sex objects to be exploited and manipulated and degrades the role and status of women.

In order to evaluate this argument, I will first clarify what it would mean for pornography itself to treat someone as a sex object in a degrading manner. I will then deal with three issues central to the discussion of pornography and respect for women: how "losing respect" for a woman is connected with treating her as a sex object; what is wrong with treating someone as a sex object; and why it is worse to treat women rather than men as sex objects. I will argue that the current content of pornography sometimes violates the moral principle to respect persons. Then, in Part III of this paper, I will suggest that, pornography need not violate this principle if certain fundamental attitude changes were to occur. Morally objectionable content is thus not necessary to pornography.

First, the simple claim that pornography treats people as sex objects is not likely to be controversial. It is pornography after all. Let's ask instead whether the content of pornography or pornography itself degrades people as it treats them as sex objects. It is not difficult to find examples of degrading content in which women are

treated as sex objects. All we need to do is look at examples in MacKinnon and Dworkin's definition of pornography. Some pornography conveys the message that women really want to be raped, beaten or mutilated, that their resisting struggle is not to be believed. By portraying women in this manner, the content of the movie degrades women. Degrading women is morally objectionable. Even if seeing the movie does not cause anyone to imitate the behavior shown, we can call the content degrading to women because of the character of the behavior and attitudes it recommends. The same kind of point can be made about films, books, and TV commercials with other kinds of degrading, thus morally objectionable, content—for example, racist or homophobic messages.

The next step in the argument might be to infer that, because the content or message of pornography is morally objectionable, we can call pornography itself morally objectionable. Support for this step can be found in an analogy. If a person takes every opportunity to recommend that men force sex on women, we would think not only that his recommendation is immoral but that he is immoral too. In the case of pornography, the objection to making an inference from recommended behavior to the person who recommends it is that we ascribe predicates such as 'immoral' differently to people than to films or books. A film vehicle for an objectionable message is still an object independent of its message, its director, its producer, those who act in it, and those who respond to it. Hence one cannot make an unsupported inference from "the content of the film is morally objectionable" to "the film is morally objectionable." In fact, I am not clear what support would work well here. Because the central points in this paper do not depend on whether pornography itself (in addition to its content) is morally objectionable, I will not pursue the issue further. Certainly one appropriate way to evaluate pornography is in terms of the moral features of its content. If a pornographic film exemplifies and recommends morally objectionable attitudes or behavior, then its content is morally objectionable.

Let us now turn to the first of our three questions about sex objects and respect: What is the connection between losing respect for a woman and treating her as a sex object? Some people who have lived through the era in which women were taught to worry about men "losing respect" for them if they engaged in sex in inappropriate circumstances have found it troublesome (or at least amusing) that feminists—supposedly "liberated" women—are outraged at being treated as sex objects, either by pornography or in any other way. The apparent alignment between feminists and traditionally "proper" women need not surprise us when we look at it more closely.

The "respect" that men have traditionally believed they have for women—hence a respect they can lose—is not a general respect for persons as autonomous beings; nor is it respect that is earned because of one's personal merits or achievements. It is respect that is an outgrowth of the traditional "double standard"—a standard that has certainly diminished in North America, but has not fully disappeared (and is especially tenacious in some ethnic and religious communities). Traditionally, women are to be respected because they are more pure, delicate, and fragile than men, have more refined sensibilities, and so on.[10] Because some women clearly do not have these qualities, thus do not deserve respect, women must be divided into two groups—the good ones on the pedestal and the bad ones who have fallen from it. The appropriate behavior by which to express respect for good women would be, for example, not swearing or telling dirty jokes in front of them, giving them seats on buses, and other "chivalrous" acts. This kind of "respect" for good women is the same sort that adolescent boys in the back seats of cars used to "promise" not to lose. Note that men define, display, and lose this kind of respect. If women lose respect for women, it is not typically a loss of respect for (other) women as a class, but a loss of self-respect.

It has now become commonplace to acknowledge that, although a place on the pedestal might have advantages over a place in the gutter beneath it, a place on the pedestal is not at all equal to the place occupied by other people (i.e.,

men). "Respect" for those on the pedestal was not respect for whole, full-fledged people but for a special class of inferior beings.

If a person makes two traditional assumptions—that (at least some) sex is dirty and that women fall into two classes, good and bad—it is easy to see how that person might think that pornography could lead people to lose respect for women or that pornography is itself disrespectful to women. Pornography describes or shows women engaging in activities inappropriate for good women to engage in—or at least inappropriate for them to be seen by strangers engaging in. If one sees these women as symbolic representatives of all women, then all women fall from grace with these women. This fall is possible, I believe, because the traditional "respect" that men have had for women is not genuine, wholehearted respect for full-fledged human beings but half-hearted respect for lesser beings, some of whom they feel the need to glorify and purify. It is easy to fall from a pedestal. We cannot imagine half the population of the U.S. answering "yes" to the question, "Do movies showing men engaging in violent acts lead people to lose respect for men?" Yet this has been the response to surveys concerning the analogous question for women in pornography.[11]

Two interesting asymmetries appear. The first is that losing respect for men as a class (men with power, typically Anglo men) is more difficult than losing respect for women or ethnic minorities as a class. Anglo men whose behavior warrants disrespect are more likely to be seen as exceptional cases than are women or minorities (whose "transgressions" may be far less serious). Think of the following: women are temptresses; Arabs are terrorists; Blacks cheat the welfare system; Italians are gangsters; however, Bill Clinton and the men of the Nixon and Reagan administrations are exceptions—Anglo men as a class did not lose respect because of, respectively, womanizing, Watergate, and the Iran-Contra scandals.

The second asymmetry looks at first to concern the active and passive roles of the sexes. Men are seen in the active role. If men lose respect for women because of something "evil" done by women (such as appearing in pornography), the fear is that men will then do harm to women—not that women will do harm to men. Whereas if women lose respect for some male politicians because of Watergate, Iran-Contra or womanizing, the fear is still that male politicians will do harm, not that women will do harm to male politicians. This asymmetry might be a result of one way in which our society thinks of sex as bad—as harm that men do to women (or to the person playing a female role, as in homosexual rape). Robert Baker calls attention to this point in "'Pricks' and 'Chicks': A Plea for 'Persons'."[12] Our slang words for sexual intercourse— 'fuck', 'screw', or older words such as 'take' or 'have'—not only can mean harm but also have traditionally taken a male subject and a female object. The active male screws (harms) the female. A "bad" woman only tempts men to hurt her further. An interesting twist here is that the harmer/harmed distinction in sex does not depend on actual active or passive behavior. A woman who is sexually active, even aggressive, can still be seen as the one harmed by sex. And even now that it is more common to say that a woman can fuck a man, the notion of harm remains in the terms ("The bank screwed me with excessive ATM charges").

It is easy to understand why one's traditionally proper grandmother would not want men to see pornography or lose respect for women. But feminists reject these "proper" assumptions: good and bad classes of women do not exist; and sex is not dirty (though some people believe it is). Why then are feminists angry at the treatment of women as sex objects, and why are some feminists opposed to pornography?

The answer is that feminists as well as proper grandparents are concerned with respect. However, there are differences. A feminist's distinction between treating a woman as a full-fledged person and treating her as merely a sex object does not correspond to the good-bad woman distinction. In the latter distinction, "good" and "bad" are properties applicable to groups of women. In the feminist view, all women are full-fledged people; however, some are treated as sex objects and perhaps think of themselves as sex objects. A further difference is that, although "bad" women correspond to those thought to deserve treatment as sex objects, good women have not corresponded to full-fledged people; only men have been full-fledged people. Given the feminist's distinction, she has no difficulty whatever in saying that pornography treats women as sex objects, not as full-fledged people. She can morally object to pornography or anything else that treats women as sex objects.

One might wonder whether any objection to treatment as a sex object implies that the person objecting still believes, deep down, that sex is dirty. I don't think so. Several other possibilities emerge. First, even if I believe intellectually and emotionally that sex is healthy, I might object to being treated only as a sex object. In the same spirit, I would object to being treated only as a maker of chocolate chip cookies or only as a tennis partner, because only one of my talents is being valued. Second, perhaps I feel that sex is healthy, but since it is apparent to me that you think sex is dirty, I don't want you to treat me as a sex object. Third, being treated as any kind of object, not just as a sex object, is unappealing. I would rather be a partner (sexual or otherwise) than an object. Fourth, and more plausible than the first three possibilities, is Robert Baker's view mentioned above. Both (i) our traditional double standard of sexual behavior for men and women and (ii) the linguistic evidence that we connect the concept of sex with the concept of harm point to what is wrong with treating women as sex objects. As I said earlier, the traditional uses of 'fuck' and 'screw' have taken a male subject, a female object, and have had at least two meanings: harm and have sexual intercourse with. (In addition, a prick is a man who harms people ruthlessly; and a motherfucker is so low that he would do something very harmful to his own dear mother.)[13]

Because in our culture we have connected sex with harm that men do to women, and because we have thought of the female role in sex as that of harmed object, we can see that to treat a woman as a sex object is automatically to treat her as less than fully human. To say this does not imply that healthy sexual relationships are impossible; nor does it say anything about individual men's conscious intentions to degrade women by desiring them sexually (though no doubt some men have these intentions). It is merely to make a point about the concepts embodied in our language.[14]

Psychoanalytic support for the connection between sex and harm comes from Robert J. Stoller. He thinks that sexual excitement is linked with a wish to harm someone (and with at least a whisper of hostility). The key process of sexual excitement can be seen as dehumanization (fetishization) in fantasy of the desired person. He speculates that this is true in some degree of everyone, both men and women, with "normal" or "perverted" activities and fantasies.[15]

Thinking of sex objects as harmed objects enables us to explain some of the reasons why one wouldn't want to be treated as a sex object: (1) I may object to being treated only as a tennis partner, but being a tennis partner is not connected in our culture with being a harmed object; and (2) I may not think that sex is dirty and that I would be a harmed object; I may not know what your view is; but what bothers me is that this is the view embodied in our language and culture.

Awareness of the connection between sex and harm helps explain other interesting points. Women are angry about being treated as sex objects in situations or roles in which they do not intend to be regarded in that manner—for example, while serving on a committee or participating in a discussion. It is not merely that a sexual role is inappropriate for the circumstances; it is thought to be a less fully human role than the one in which they intended to function.

Finally, the sex-harm connection allows us to acknowledge that pornography treats both women and men as sex objects and at the same time understand why it is worse to treat women as sex objects than to treat men as sex objects, and why some men have had difficulty understanding women's anger about the matter. It is more difficult for heterosexual men than for women to assume the role of "harmed object" in sex, for men have the self-concept of sexual agents, not of objects. This is also related to my earlier point

concerning the difference in the solidity of respect for men and for women; respect for women is more fragile. Men and women have grown up with different patterns of self-respect and expectations regarding the extent to which they deserve and will receive respect or degradation. The man who doesn't understand why women do not want to be treated as sex objects (because he'd sure like to be) is not likely to think of himself as being harmed by that treatment; a woman might. (In fact, if one were to try to degrade a man sexually a promising strategy would be to make him feel like a non-man—a person who is either incapable of having sex at all or functioning only in the place of a woman.)[16]

Having seen that the connection between sex and harm helps explain both what is wrong with treating someone as a sex object and why it is worse to treat a woman in this way, let's keep in mind the views of anti-pornography feminists as we think about the range of pornography that exists today. Although an anti-pornography feminist need not claim that a pornographer has a conscious intent to degrade, to subordinate, or to lie about women's sexuality, some have said precisely this—remember Susan Brownmiller's claim cited in Section I that pornography is designed to dehumanize women. The feminist who is not willing to attribute a "design" in pornography (beyond an intent to arouse and to earn a profit) can still find it deplorable that it is an empirical fact that degrading or subordinating women arouses quite a few men. After all, it is a pretty sorry state of affairs that this material sells well.

Suppose now we were to rate the content of all pornography from most morally objectionable to least morally objectionable. Among the most objectionable would be the most degrading—for example, "snuff" films and movies that recommend that men rape and mutilate women, molest children and animals, and treat non-masochists very sadistically. The clauses in MacKinnon and Dworkin's definition of 'pornography' again come to mind; one clause not yet cited is, "Women are presented in scenarios of degradation, injury, torture, shown as filthy or inferior, bleeding, bruised, or hurt in a context that makes these conditions sexual."[17]

Moving along the spectrum, we would find a large amount of material (perhaps most pornography) not quite so blatantly objectionable. With this material it is relevant to use the analysis of sex objects given above. As long as sex is connected with harm done to women, it will be very difficult not to see pornography as degrading to women. We can agree that pornography treats men as sex objects, too, but maintain that this is only pseudoequality: such treatment is still more degrading to women.

In addition, pornography often overtly exemplifies either the active/passive or the harmer/harmed object roles. Because much pornography today is male-oriented and is supposed to make a profit, the content is designed to appeal to male fantasies. Judging from the content of much pornography, male fantasies often still run along the lines of stereotypical gender roles—and, if Stoller is right, include elements of hostility. In much pornography the women's purpose is to cater to male desires, to service the man or men, and to be dependent on a man for her pleasure (except in the lesbian scenes in heterosexual pornography—which, too, are there for male excitement). Even if women are idealized rather than specifically degraded, women's complex humanity is taken away: the idealized women and the idealized sexual acts are in the service of the male viewer. Real women are not nearly so pliable for male fantasies. In addition, women are clearly made into passive objects in still photographs showing only close-ups of their genitals. Although many kinds of specialty magazines, films and videos are gauged for different sexual tastes, much material exemplifies the range of traditional sex roles of male heterosexual fantasies. There is no widespread attempt to replace the harmer/harmed distinction with anything more positive and healthy.[18]

The cases in this part of the spectrum would be included in the anti-pornography feminists' scope, too. MacKinnon and Dworkin's point that pornography makes domination and subordination sexually exciting is relevant here as well as in the more extreme cases. In fact, other clauses in their definition cover much "regular" pornography: "women are presented in postures of sexual submission, servility or display;…women's body parts, including but not limited to vaginas, breasts, and buttocks—are exhibited, such that women are reduced to those parts."[19] Whether or not "regular," corner-video-store pornography is consciously designed to degrade or subordinate women, the fact that it does both degrade women and produce sexual excitement in men is sufficient to make MacKinnon and Dworkin's point.

What would cases toward the least objectionable end of the spectrum be like? They would be increasingly less degrading and sexist. The genuinely nonobjectionable cases would be nonsexist and nondegrading. The question is: Does or could any pornography have nonsexist, nondegrading content?

III.

To consider the possibility of nonsexist, morally acceptable pornography, imagine the following situation. Two fairly conventional heterosexuals who love each other try to have an egalitarian relationship. In addition, they enjoy playing tennis, beach volleyball and bridge together, cooking good food together, and having sex together. In these activities they are partners—free from hang-ups, guilt, and tendencies to dominate or objectify each other. These two people like to watch tennis and beach volleyball matches, cooking shows, and old romantic movies on TV, like to read the bridge column and food sections in the newspaper, and like to watch pornographic videos. Imagine further that this couple is not at all uncommon in society and that nonsexist pornography is as common as this kind of nonsexist sexual relationship. This situation sounds morally and psychologically acceptable to me. I see no reason to think that an interest in pornography would disappear in these circumstances.[20] People seem to enjoy watching others experience or do (especially do well) what they enjoy experiencing, doing, or wish they could do themselves. We do not morally object to the content of TV programs showing cooking, tennis or beach volleyball or to people watching them. I have no reason to object to our hypothetical people watching nonsexist pornography.

What kinds of changes are needed to move from the situation today to the situation just imagined? One key factor in moving to nonsexist pornography would be to break the connection between sex and harm. If Stoller is right, this task may be impossible without changing the scenarios of our sexual lives—scenarios that we have been writing since early childhood, but that we can revise. But whatever the individual complexities of changing our sexual scenarios, the sex-harm connection is deeply entrenched and has widespread implications. What is needed is a thorough change in people's deep-seated attitudes and feelings about gender roles in general, as well as about sex and roles in sex. Feminists have been advocating just such changes for a few decades now. Does it make sense to try to change pornography in order to help to bring about the kinds of changes that feminists advocate? Or would we have to wait until after these changes have taken place to consider the possibility of nonsexist pornography? First, it is necessary to acknowledge how difficult and complex a process it is to change deeply held attitudes, beliefs and feelings about gender and sex (not to mention how complex are our attitudes, beliefs and feelings about gender and sex). However, if we were looking for avenues to promote these changes, it would probably be more fruitful to look to television, children's educational material, nonpornographic movies, magazines and novels than to focus on pornography. On the other hand, we might not want to take the chance that pornography is working against changes in feelings and attitudes. So we might try to change pornography along with all the other, more important media.

Before sketching some ideas along these lines, let's return briefly to MacKinnon and Dworkin—feminists who would be very skeptical of any such plan. Their view of human sexuality is that it is "a social construct, gendered to the ground."[21] There is no essential sexual being or sexual substratum that has not been corrupted by male dominance. Sexuality as we know it simply is male

defined. Pornography, therefore, does not distort sexuality; pornography constitutes sexual reality. Even if MacKinnon and Dworkin were to grant me my more inclusive definition of pornography, they would find it bizarre to entertain the possibility of making pornography neutral, not to mention using it as an "ally" for social change.

However, bear with me. If sexual reality is socially constructed, it can be constructed differently. If sexuality is male defined, it can be defined differently—by women who can obtain enough power to overcome our silence and by men who are our allies. Again, I would not suggest that this is easy. Nevertheless, Dworkin herself advocates changing our concept of sexuality. It probably makes more sense to speak of constructing sexualities in any case—to acknowledge the multiplicity of sexualities human beings are likely to construct.

So let's suppose that we want to make changes to pornography that would help us with the deep social changes needed to break the sex-harm connection and to make gender roles more equitable in sexual and nonsexual contexts. When I thought about this subject in the 1970s, I sketched out a few plots lines, partly in jest, involving women in positions of respect—urologists, high-ranking female Army officers, long-distance truck drivers—as well as a few ideas for egalitarian sex scenes.[22] However, in the intervening decades while I was standing around teaching philosophy, the pornography industry far surpassed my wildest plot dreams. There is pornography now made by feminists and (thanks to the women who pick up videos at the corner video store, as they do more than their fair share of most errands), some pornography that is more appealing to women—feminist or not.[23]

One might still wonder whether any current pornography is different "enough" to be nonsexist and to start to change attitudes and feelings. This is a difficult call to make, but I think we should err on the side of keeping an open mind. For, after all, if we are to attempt to use pornography as a tool to change the attitudes of male pornography viewers (along with their willing and not-so-willing female partners), any changes would have to be fairly subtle at first; the fantasies in nonsexist pornography must become familiar enough to sell and be watched. New symbols and fantasies need to be introduced with care, perhaps incrementally. Of course, realistically, we would need to realize that any positive "educational value" that nonsexist pornography might have may well be as short-lived as most of the other effects of pornography. But given these limitations, feminist pornographers could still try (and do try).

There are additional problems, however. Our world is not the world imagined at the beginning of Section III for the couple watching tennis, beach volleyball and pornography; in their world nonsexist pornography can be appreciated in the proper spirit. Under these conditions the content of our new pornography could be nonsexist and morally acceptable. But could the content of the same pornography be morally acceptable if shown to men with sexist attitudes today? It might seem strange for us to change our moral evaluation of the content on the basis of a different audience, but I have trouble avoiding this conclusion. There is nothing to prevent men who really do enjoy degrading women from undermining the most well-intentioned plot about, say, a respected, powerful woman filmmaker—even a plot filled with

sex scenes with egalitarian detail, "respectful" camera angles and lighting, and so on. Men whose restricted vision of women makes it impossible to absorb the film as intended could still see the powerful filmmaker as a demeaned plaything or kinky prostitute, even if a feminist's intention in making and showing the film is to undermine this view. The effect is that, although the content of the film seems morally acceptable and our intention in showing it is morally flawless, women are still degraded. The importance of an audience's attitude makes one wary of giving wholehearted approval to much pornography seen today.

The fact that good intentions and content are insufficient does not imply that feminists' efforts toward change would be entirely in vain. Of course, I could not deny that anyone who tries to change an institution from within faces serious difficulties. This is particularly evident when one is trying to change both pornography and a whole set of related attitudes, feelings, and institutions concerning gender roles and sex. But in conjunction with other attempts to change this set of attitudes, it seems preferable to try to change pornography instead of closing one's eyes in the hope that it will go away. For it seems realistic to expect that pornography is here to stay.[24]

NOTES

1. Some of the key first amendment/obscenity cases are: Roth v. US 354 U.S. 476 (1957), Paris Adult Theatre I v. Slaton 413 U.S. 49 (1973), Miller v. State of California 413 U.S. 15 (1973); a more recent internet case is Reno v. American Civil Liberties Union 117 S. Ct. 2329 (1997). It is easy to find cases at www.FindLaw.com or other legal internet sites.

2. Ann Garry, "Pornography and Respect for Women," Social Theory and Practice 4 (1978): 395–421, and published at approximately the same time in Philosophy and Women, ed. Sharon Bishop and Marjorie Weinzweig (Belmont, CA: Wadsworth, 1979). Sections II–III of the present paper use some of the central arguments from Parts III–IV of the earlier paper.

3. Examples of feminists works that are pro-pornography or anthologies of pro- and anti-pornography writings include Nadine Strossen, Defending Pornography (New York: Scribner, 1995), Diana E. H. Russell, ed., Making Violence Sexy: Feminist Views on Pornography (Buckingham, UK: Open University Press, 1993), Lynn Segal and Mary McIntosh, eds., Sex Exposed: Sexuality and the Pornography Debate (New Brunswick, NJ: Rutgers University Press, 1992), Pamela Church Gibson and Roma Gibson, eds., Dirty Looks: Women, Pornography, Power (London: BFI Press, 1993), Susan Dwyer, ed., The Problem of Pornography (Belmont, CA: Wadsworth, 1995). Several other anti-pornography references are in subsequent footnotes.

4. Catharine MacKinnon, Feminism Unmodified (Cambridge, MA: Harvard University Press, 1987), p. 146, n.1. The Indianapolis case is American Bookseller Association v. Hudnut 771F. 2d 323 (1985). A more recent work of MacKinnon's is Only Words (Cambridge, MA: Harvard University Press, 1993).

5. Concerning whether pornography is a moral or political issue: MacKinnon and Andrea Dworkin associate "moral arguments" against pornography with the liberal ideology they reject in their political and legal strategies. MacKinnon rejects arguments such as mine, among other reasons, because they use concepts associated with the liberal intellectual tradition—respect, degrade, dehumanize, etc. She claims that pornography dehumanizes women in "culturally specific and empirically descriptive—not liberal moral—sense" (Feminism Unmodified, p. 159). My take on it is different. I find MacKinnon's political argument to be a moral argument as well—it is morally wrong to subordinate women. Second, Rae Langton discusses the MacKinnon/Dworkin claims that pornography subordinates and silences women in the context of philosophy of language: "Speech Acts and Unspeakable Acts," Philosophy and Public Afairs 22 (1993): 293-330, revised as "Pornography, Speech Acts, and Silence," in Ethics in Practice, ed. Hugh LaFollette (Cambridge, MA: Blackwell, 1997).

6. Eva Feder Kittay, "Pornography and the Erotics of Domination," in Beyond Domination, ed. Carol Gould (Totowa, NJ: Rowman and Allanheld, 1983), pp. 156-157. Of course, sometimes pornography is both sexist and racist—it utilizes many negative racial/ethnic stereotypes in its fantasy-women (and men) and degrades in culturally specific ways. See Tracey Gardner, "Racism in Pornography and the Women's Movement," in Take Back the Night, ed. Laura Lederer (New York: Bantam, 1982). Gloria Cowan and Robin R. Campbell, "Racism and Sexism in Interracial Pornography: A Content Analysis," Psychology of Women Quarterly 18 (1994): 323–338.

7. Helen Longino, "Pornography, Oppression and Freedom: A Closer Look," in Take Back the Night, ed. Laura Lederer (New York: Bantam, 1982), p. 31.

8. Brownmiller, Against Our Will: Men, Women and Rape (New York: Simon Schuster, 1975), p. 394.

9. By focusing on the content of pornography I exclude many important kinds of degradation and exploitation: (i) the ways in which pornographic film makers might exploit people in making a film, distributing it, and charging too much to see it or buy it; (ii) the likelihood that actors, actresses, or technicians will be exploited, underpaid, or made to lose self-respect or self-esteem; and (iii) the exploitation and degradation involved in prostitution and crime that often accompany urban centers of pornography. It is obvious that I am also excluding many other moral grounds for objecting to pornography: The U.S. Supreme Court has held that pornography invades our privacy, hurts the moral tone of the community, and so on. There are also important and complex empirical questions whether pornography in fact increases violence against women or leads men to treat women in degrading ways (and leads women to be more likely to accept this treatment). I dealt with some early social science literature on the last topic in "Pornography and Respect for Women," but the length limitations of the present paper do not permit an update. Once you leave the empirical correlation between the use of pornography and masturbation, very little is simple to prove. Summaries of and references to social science work can be found in Edward Donnerstein, et al., The Question of Pornography: Research Findings and Policy Implications (New York: Free Press, 1987), Neil Malamuth and Daniel Ling, Pornography (Newbury Park, CA: Sage Publications, 1993), Marcia Palley, Sex and Sensibility: Reflections on Hidden Mirrors and the Will to Censor (Hopewell, NJ: Ecco Press, 1994), and Neil Malamuth and Edward Donnerstein, eds., Pornography and Sexual Aggression (Orlando, FL: Academic Press, 1984).

10. The question of what is required to be a "good" woman varies greatly by ethnicity, class, age, religion, politics, and so on. For example, many secular North Americans would no longer require virginity (after a certain age), but might well expect some degree of restraint or judgment with respect to sexual activity.

11. The earliest reference I have is to the belief of 41% of men and 46% of women that "sexual materials lead people to lose respect for women," in Report of the Commission on Obscenity and Pornography (Washington, DC, 1970), p. 201. A 1986 Time magazine survey showed that 61% of U.S. respondents believe that pornography encourages people to consider women as sex objects (and 57% believe that exposure to pornography leads to a breakdown of social morals), July 21, 1986, p. 22.

12. In Robert Baker and Frederick Elliston, eds., Philosophy and Sex 2nd ed (Buffalo, NY: Prometheus Books, 1984), p. 264.

13. Baker, ibid.

14. A fuller treatment of sex objectification would need to be set in a more general context of objectification. Martha Nussbaum writes about both. See her "Objectification," Philosophy and Public Affairs 24 (1995): 249–291.

15. Robert J. Stoller, "Sexual Excitement," Archives of General Psychiatry 33 (1976): 899-909, especially 903. Reprinted in Stoller, Sexual Excitement: Dynamics of Erotic Life (Washington: American Psychiatric Press, 1979). The extent to which Stoller sees men and women in different positions with respect to harm and hostility is not clear. He often treats men and women alike, but in Perversion: The Erotic Form of Hatred (New York: Pantheon, 1975), pp. 89–91, he calls attention to differences between men and women especially regarding their responses to pornography and lack of understanding by men of women's sexuality. These themes are elaborated in his later books, Porn: Myths for the Twentieth Century (New Haven: Yale University Press, 1991) and Stoller

and I. S. Levine, Coming Attractions: The Making of an X-Rated Video (New Haven: Yale University Press, 1993). Andrea Dworkin, in Intercourse (New York: Free Press, 1987), is much more graphic than Stoller. She cites a number of male novelists, playwrights, painters, musicians and others for whom sex is intimately connected to harm. She is thinking of harm to women by men in numerous forms: invasion, possession, occupation, domination, and so on.

16. Three points: First, generalizations are always risky. It is important to remember that people's expectations of respect and their ability to be degraded can differ significantly by their race/ethnicity, sexual orientation, class, and individual psychological makeup. So although men's and women's expectations of respect or degradation are constructed differently within any given group, e.g., an ethnic group, the specifics of their expectations may well vary. Second, heterosexual men have developed more sensitivity to being treated as sex objects (even if not as "harmed" objects) as women have become more sexually aggressive. In addition, heterosexual male worries about sex objectification surface readily in discussions of openly gay men serving in the military; there is far less worry about openly lesbian military personnel. Third, although objectification of men working in the pornography industry is beyond the scope of this paper, Susan Faludi writes interestingly about it in "The Money Shot," The New Yorker, October 30, 1995, pp. 64–87. Stoller's interviews in Porn and Coming Attractions are also relevant, see n. 15.

17. MacKinnon, Feminism Unmodified, p. 146, n.1.

18. There is a whole array of sadomasochistic pornography (including women treating men sadistically) that I have not addressed in this discussion. There have been intense, multilayered controversies among feminists (both heterosexual and lesbian) about consenting sadomasochistic practices and pornography. See Samois, Coming to Power: Writings and Graphics on Lesbian S/M (Boston: Alyson Publications, 1987), Robin Linden, et al., eds., Against Sadomasochism: A Radical Feminist Analysis (East Palo Alto, CA: Frog in the Well, 1982), and Patrick D. Hopkins, "Rethinking Sadomasochism: Feminism, Interpretation, and Simulation," Hypatia 9 (1994): 116–151, reprinted in Alan Soble, ed., The Philosophy of Sex 3rd ed. (Lanham, MD: 1997).

19. MacKinnon, Feminism Unmodified, p. 146, n.1.

20. First, one might wonder whether Stoller's connection between hostility and sex negates the possibility or likelihood of "healthy" pornography. I think not, for although Stoller maintains that hostility is an element of sexual excitement generally, he thinks it important to distinguish degrees of hostility both in sex and in pornography. In his 1990s work specifically on pornography he makes this clear; see, e.g., references above in n.15, especially Porn, pp. 223–226. He also realizes that pornographers must know quite a bit about human sexual excitement in order to stay in business; so if sexual excitement requires increasingly less hostility, smart pornographers (even anti-feminists!) will reflect this change very quickly in their work. Second, would the voyeurism required in pornography make it immoral? Again, I think not. Since the "voyeurism" in pornography invades no one's privacy, indeed, is intended and desired, I have trouble finding grounds for immorality.

21. MacKinnon, Feminism Unmodified, p. 149. See also Andrea Dworkin, Pornography: Men Possessing Women (New York: E.P. Dutton, 1981, with introduction written in 1989).

22. Garry, pp. 413–416. Examples of the kinds of egalitarian features I had in mind are: an absence of suggestions of dominance or conquest, changes in control over the circumstances of and positions in sex (women's preferences and desires would be shown to count equally with men's), no pseudo-enjoyed pain or violence, no great inequality between men and women in states of dress or undress or types and angles of bodily exposure, a decrease in the amount of "penis worship," a positive attempt to set a woman's sexual being within a more fully human context, and so on.

23. Among the best known feminists in the pornography industry are Candida Royalle, Nina Hartley, and (now performance artist) Annie Sprinkle.

24. I would like to thank Talia Bettcher and David Ashen-Garry for very helpful comments and references.

CHAPTER SIXTEEN

Legal/ Political Ethics

Liberalism and Rights of Drug Use*

SAMUEL FREEMAN

Reprinted from Samuel Freeman, "Liberalism, Inalienability, and Rights of Drug Use" in Drugs and the Limits of Liberalism: Moral and Legal Issues, *Pablo De Greiff, ed. Copyright © 1999 by Cornell University. Used by permission of Cornell University Press.*

In recent years the criminal justice system in the United States has oriented itself toward waging a politically popular "war on drugs." It is a war that many will say is hopelessly lost, in the same way that Prohibition's war on alcohol was lost. Some argue that the war on drugs is self-defeating. No doubt, as a result of the criminalization of most psychoactive drugs (beginning with the Harrison Act of 1914), fewer people use them than would if such drugs were legalized.[1] But, as in the case of Prohibition under the 18th Amendment, this does not mean that less damage is done to individuals or to society as a whole. The criminalization of psychoactive drugs has, it is argued, grossly aggravated the incidence of violence and poverty in society and has even stimulated greater drug abuse and addiction. Having made opiates, depressants (except for alcohol), stimulants (except for nicotine), and hallucinogens illegal and at-

tached severe penalties not only to their distribution but also to the individuals who use them, we have created a class of criminals whose size some analysts estimate to be as large as 30 to 40 million people. Less than 3 percent of those who use drugs are apprehended and punished each year, and this comes at extraordinary costs to the legal system.[2] Most of those punished are African Americans, even though as a group they consume far fewer illicit drugs than middle-class Caucasians. This can only have damaging effects on many people's attitudes toward the fairness and efficiency of the criminal justice system and only increase African Americans' sense of social alienation and injustice.

Moreover, given the severe penalties attending drug distribution, the war on drugs has caused the distribution of narcotics to be placed, not in the hands of pharmacists or ordinary business people, but rather in the hands of violent gangs who reap monopoly profits and terrorize portions of our inner cities. These gangs (with names like the Jamaican posse, the Bloods, and the Crips) would not exist, it is argued, were it not for the fact that such severe penalties are attached to the use of psychoactive drugs and that, therefore, such enormous profits can be derived from their sale. Moreover, because legislatures assign severe penalties for use of even mild drugs such as marijuana, it is claimed that the war on drugs has caused drug dealers to create and dispense far more dangerous and addictive narcotics like crack cocaine. Many people believe that crack would not exist were it not for the illegality of drug use. As a general rule, "Where drugs are illegal, more damaging drugs drive out less damaging drugs."[3] Heroin and, now, crack cocaine have come to replace marijuana as the drug of choice, since they are far more profitable and easily transportable by drug dealers.[4]

Our court system has become clogged with the prosecution of drug dealers and users. Because of the war on drugs, criminal prosecutions against the drug trade and drug use have been assigned legislative priority in the judicial system to the degree that civil actions in federal and state courts often take at least two years. (In some federal districts, 70 percent of trial time is devoted to criminal drug cases.)[5] Moreover, enormous policing efforts are devoted to the war on drugs, at immense expense, thereby draining police resources from surveillance of other illegal activities. In addition the illegality of drugs has a corrupting influence on law enforcement itself when police accept bribes from drug dealers, confiscate for themselves illegal profits, or become actively involved in the drug trade itself.[6] And even without these problems, the overzealous police methods utilized during narcotics raids often lead to violation of the rights of many innocent persons, to illegal police searches and subsequent perjured testimony in the courts by police officers, and to a casual attitude toward the rights of the innocent as well as the guilty.[7] The dignity of many people is compromised by such tactics, and serious questions are raised regarding the role of the police in a free democratic society. For these and other reasons, some argue that the war on drugs, by increasingly occupying the criminal justice system, is gradually undermining it.

Given these substantially adverse social, economic, and political consequences of the war on drugs at the federal and state level, plus the fact that the demonstrable benefits are so minimal, many people argue that a rational social policy calls for the decriminalization of drug use and its replacement with a regulatory scheme only somewhat more rigid than those programs that now

regulate alcohol and nicotine. This suggested policy is based in the recognition that it is practically impossible to fully eradicate the use of opiates and stimulants in the absence of autocratic power that would undermine liberal and democratic society itself. The social costs of prohibition will always far exceed whatever benefits result from interdiction, particularly when increasingly stringent methods of interdiction violate so many people's rights and come to undermine confidence in the legal system.

If these claims and arguments regarding the adverse social costs of drug interdiction are correct (I do not say that they are) then it becomes difficult to mount a good case for the system of prohibition of psychoactive drugs that we now have in place. A convincing reply would need to show that even worse consequences would attend drug legalization. In the absence of these adverse consequences, the war on drugs should go the way of Prohibition. This is the best liberal argument for the decriminalization of psychoactive drugs. It is an argument that focuses on experience of the adverse consequences of criminalization as weighed against the adverse consequences of noncriminalization.

What I primarily want to address and draw into question, however, is a different liberal argument for legalization of psychoactive drugs. It is a purely philosophical argument, one that proceeds, not from pragmatic considerations of the adverse consequences of drug interdiction, but from the contention that in a liberal society citizens have a right to indulge in drugs, whatever the adverse consequences for themselves, so long as use is voluntary and informed and does not cause harm to the rights and interests of others. My sense is that this argument is overstated. It works from the premise that liberalism excludes all prohibitions on self-destructive conduct, a premise that I seriously question. Below, I show that there are certain kinds of purely self-destructive conduct that a liberal society can legitimately prohibit, and I consider the implications of this for use of psychoactive drugs. Finally, I return to the question raised in this introduction regarding the adverse social consequences of criminalization of drugs. Here I raise certain considerations about the effects of noninterdiction for the institutions of a liberal society, considerations which are often neglected in arguments for decriminalization.

The Issue

It is commonly recognized that a liberal society can and should regulate drugs to insure that users are apprised of the consequences of drug use, that use is voluntary, and that harmful substances do not fall into the hands of minors and incompetents. These so-called soft paternalistic measures are not such a difficult issue for liberals. Many liberals, however, do not concede that the outright prohibition of narcotics or even the regulation of drug use is legitimate when it can be shown that users, without endangering others, willingly and wittingly take drugs and are aware of their likely harmful consequences for their future well-being. Such prohibitions are seen as paternalistic (in the negative sense), and liberalism, it is claimed, is incompatible with this kind of paternalism. That being the case, some people have argued that there is an unqualified right to use drugs regardless of the consequences of such use for the user.

I find the charge of paternalism in these contexts to be unhelpful at best, and for the most part misleading. It makes sense to speak of whole political systems as being paternalistic when they manage or govern individuals in the manner that a father (or parents) traditionally have governed their children. Paternalism implies systematically restricting and regulating another's conduct and, at the limit, doing this in such a way as to instill in that person not just particular values but a general morality and complete conception of the good. As applied to political systems, paternalism is a charge that individuals are treated as mere subjects, benignly perhaps, but not as free citizens who are capable of taking responsibility for their lives. Clearly no liberal democratic system of laws is paternalistic in the sense that it denies individuals the complex scheme of rights that enables them to determine their own lives within the restrictions allowed by justice. So the charge of paternalism, when it is leveled in the context of a

liberal democratic regime, can be one that only applies to particular laws and not to the political system as a whole. But when applied to laws, it is an obscure claim. For the fact is that most so-called paternalistic laws (such as seatbelt and motorcycle helmet laws, laws against suicide and gambling, and many laws against drugs) in no way enforce a particular conception of the good; rather they restrict or require specific actions, while leaving open the range of conceptions of the good that one may choose from. What more is being said, then, when a law is called paternalistic than that this law prohibits some kind of self-destructive conduct? Some claim that the law also denies individuals the rights of self-determination and autonomy upon which liberalism is based. But (assuming that this is an accurate account of liberalism's basis) the issue then becomes whether liberal autonomy and self-determination require that there be no restrictions whatsoever on self-destructive conduct. I take this to be the really interesting issue in the debate over paternalistic laws, and it is not a debate that can be won by simply stipulating that part of the true meaning of autonomy is a complete absence of laws against self-destructive conduct.

My position is that liberalism is not incompatible with certain restrictions on self-destructive conduct, even if such conduct is informed, voluntary, and rational in the ordinary sense. When the aim and effect of restrictions against self-destructive conduct is to maintain the moral and rational integrity of the person—in the sense of the capacities for rational agency and moral responsibility upon which liberalism and liberal autonomy are based—then there is nothing illiberal about imposing restrictions on conduct that is harmful only to the agent concerned. By implication, citizens in a constitutional democracy have a duty to maintain the degree of competence necessary to exercise the capacities of agency that enable them to reflect on their good and observe the moral requirements of social life.

My argument does not imply that liberalism allows for the restriction of all psychoactive drugs. Such mildly intoxicating substances as marijuana, for example, cannot be prohibitable on the grounds I set forth. It may even be that most currently available drugs are not prohibitable on these grounds, including heroin and cocaine. This is an empirical issue. But there is, at least potentially, a class of drugs so intrinsically debilitating of one's capacities, that their prohibition is justified on liberal grounds.

What, then, is the point of this exercise? The point is to locate one of the parameters of liberalism: the extent to which individuals can go in exercising their freedom. My primary aim in this paper is to challenge the common idea that liberalism in some way requires that individuals be permitted to engage in any self-regarding conduct, no matter how detrimental its consequences may be for the agent. If nothing else, this exercise should help us gain a clearer insight into the scope and limits of a right to use drugs, if indeed such a right does exist in a liberal system. This right in some way follows from the ideas of liberal autonomy (Richard, Feinberg, Husak) and personal sovereignty (Feinberg)[8]....

Most any liberal view must provide for a plurality of goods and worthwhile ways of life that are permissible for citizens to freely pursue. The capacities for moral and rational agency enable the pursuit of the wide range of opportunities and permissible conceptions of the good that a liberal society provides for and sanctions. To see exercise of these powers as a good that is to be maximized would deprive them of their point. So, rather than conceiving of development of the capacities for rational and moral agency as an incremental good (or even as intrinsic goods for each agent), they are more correctly seen as *essential conditions* for liberal citizens, allowing them to have a conception of the good and to comply with the norms of justice of a liberal society.[9]

While it is not the role of a constitutional democracy to fix any particular conception of the good for all its citizens, it is an appropriate, and indeed necessary, role of a constitutional democracy to maintain the conditions for citizens' free pursuit of their good in society. Exercising the capacities for moral and rational agency is fundamental among these conditions. One role of a liberal constitution is to specify the basic rights

and duties that are required for this purpose. By so doing, it sets limits on the domain of conceptions of the good that are permissible to pursue. *A* conception of the good that requires violation of others' basic rights is clearly not within this domain.... Our question is whether recreational drug use is among the permissible activities or ways of life in a liberal society....

A distinction can be drawn between normal risk-taking for the sake of valued activities (such as mountain climbing, motorcycle riding, parachuting, or eating fatty foods), as opposed to activities which, by their nature, destroy or permanently undermine a person's capacities for engaging in rationally chosen valued activities. Let us call this latter class "intrinsically debilitating activities." Among this class are such things as committing suicide, enlisting another to kill you, or permanently mutilating one's cognitive or conative capacities (such as through a frontal lobotomy). A liberal society can, I believe, legitimately prohibit these kinds of activities, except when there are special reasons. Special reasons might then justify assisted suicide—perhaps even active consensual euthanasia—when one is suffering from an incurable condition and death is imminent or one's capacities for agency are degenerating. Under conditions where the capacities for agency are no longer functional, the usual liberal reasons for asserting nondestructibility of one's own life no longer obtain. But one cannot voluntarily kill oneself for just any reason (on a bet, say, or because one has been jilted, or because one just likes the idea). The same is true of self-mutilation of one's cognitive and conative capacities.

On this line of reasoning, alcohol and smoking cigarettes would seem to be permissible activities. For drinking alcohol is clearly compatible with the full exercise of powers of rational and moral agency (indeed, in due proportion, an occasional drink can even help some of us along the way). There is nothing intrinsically debilitating about alcohol. Granted it can be abused, as can many other things (including exercise or dieting). But the activity itself is not such that, by its nature, it destroys one's capacities for agency. And the same is true of cigarettes. Though they may shorten one's life, they do not necessarily, if at all, debilitate one's capacities while one is living.

But alcohol is an intoxicating substance, and cigarettes are physically addictive. If these substances are permissible in a liberal society, then so too must be certain other presently illegal drugs (other things being equal). There is nothing intrinsically debilitating about marijuana or hashish, and the same may well be true about mescaline and LSD. Granted, taking these substances can temporarily suspend one's exercise of the capacities for agency, but then so too can overconsumption of alcohol and many other permitted activities. On the standard I have proposed, a substance must be such that by its nature it permanently undermines or at least indefinitely suspends one's capacities for rational and moral agency. None of these drugs meet that condition.

What about heroin and cocaine? These drugs are on most accounts physiologically addictive, but addiction by itself does not permanently undermine the exercise of one's capacities—compare them with nicotine. Many people function fairly normally while using cocaine recreationally, and perhaps the same is even true of heroin.[10] Douglas Husak has argued that while breaking one's addiction to these substances may be painful and require strong acts of will, still it is doable and has been done by the majority of addicts.[11] On the other hand, for many addicts readdiction is a common phenomenon, largely for psychological and social reasons.[12] I am not in a position to judge whether heroin, cocaine, or crack cocaine can be classified as intrinsically debilitating drugs. It is an empirical issue, to be decided upon with advice from pharmacologists, psychologists, and other professionals.

In any case, it is highly likely that there is a large class of drugs currently prohibited which are not prohibitable on the grounds I have considered. (I assume, however, that even these drugs are legally regulable to varying degrees for other reasons, certainly to protect others from harm, and also for the reasons Feinberg mentions, namely, to insure that usage is voluntary and informed, and that minors are not allowed access.)

Nonetheless, there also is a class of drugs which can be described as intrinsically debilitating of one's capacities—even if no such substance actually exists, there is at least the potential of one.[13] Of the substances in this class, it can legitimately be claimed that a liberal government has the authority to prohibit their use for no other reason than that they permanently or indefinitely impair our capacities for rational and moral agency.

This argument does nothing to rule out activities which temporally make it difficult to exercise the powers of agency. People have the political right to be temporally intoxicated (as they have the right to mesmerize themselves before the TV). Doing that does not continuously deprive them of their faculties for practical reasoning so that they can no longer function as self-governing agents. After they sober up, they can continue their lives in a normal way. But where normalcy is permanent suspension of one's capacities, or deprivation to the degree that one is indefinitely incapacitated, a liberal system can legitimately prohibit such activities. The right to become intoxicated does not imply a right to make a zombie of oneself.

A liberal constitution has the authority to require that people develop their capacities for agency. This is one justification for mandatory education in a liberal society. Mandatory education seeks to insure that children become capable of developing their faculties, forming a conception of their good, and understanding and taking advantage of the opportunities that are open to them; moreover, liberal education aims to guarantee that individuals can understand and comply with their public duties to respect the laws and the rights of others, and that they develop an interest in maintaining the continuation of liberal institutions.[14] For many of the same reasons, a liberal constitutional democracy has the legitimate authority to proscribe self-regarding conduct that by its nature permanently impairs the exercise or development of the capacities for agency that are part of the ideal of liberal sovereignty. One is free in a liberal society to choose whether or not to take advantage of the basic rights and opportunities it affords; one is not free to engage in activities designed to permanently impair one's capacities to exercise these rights, any more than one is free to alienate them.

On this principle, admittedly, not everything will be clear cut; there are going to be many hard cases, as there will with most any principle. But even where a principle cannot resolve all ambiguities, still it helps us to understand why certain cases are hard to resolve. In so doing, it points us toward the kinds of considerations that are relevant to finally deciding the issue. If at the end of the day all of these considerations still do not suffice to resolve all ambiguities, then in a constitutional democracy the question can be left to majority decision as a means of political settlement. This may seem unsatisfactory to those who have a desire for clear lines of demarcation and systemization. But determinacy of outcome is not the first virtue of moral principles. It is more important that principles be capable of serving as a basis for public justification and fit with our most firmly considered moral convictions, inducting the ideal of the person that is implicit in our moral judgments of justice in a constitutional democracy.

Social Considerations

I have advanced one argument for limiting free availability of certain psychoactive drugs in response to the common contention that liberal autonomy is incompatible with restrictions on drug use no matter how self-destructive these drugs may be. My argument, however, agrees with the position of proponents of decriminalization to the extent that it implies that many (perhaps even most) currently interdicted drugs should be legalized. But there are considerations other than the nature and requirements of liberal autonomy that need be taken into account before a complete liberal drug policy can be formulated. The argument from autonomy addresses what may well be highly artificial circumstances, namely, where use of drugs does not substantially and adversely affect the interests of others. At the beginning of this essay, I recounted the social consequences of criminalization that lead many to argue for decriminalization. Here I conclude

with some considerations regarding the potentially adverse social consequences of drug use, which need be considered before this complicated issue can be resolved.

Suppose that free availability of a drug left people capable of exercising their capacities for agency to the minimum requisite degree. At the same time, it deprived them of the motivation or ability to do productive work and destabilized family life.[15] Suppose, too, that legalization and unrestricted availability of the drug had the effect of promoting widespread use on a scale larger than currently obtains. Consequently, living standards and familial stability decline considerably for many people. Large numbers of children are left impoverished and neglected, and their education and socialization is impaired. Many are abandoned or abused, and consequently come to lead lives destructive not only of themselves, but also of others. These are legitimate grounds for restricting such a drug in a liberal constitutional democracy (assuming such measures effectively mitigate these adverse consequences). While it is not the function of a liberal government to inquire into the social productivity of its citizens and require them to perform work that a majority regards as useful, still it is legitimate for a liberal government to take necessary measures to maintain and reproduce liberal society so that it can insure the conditions of its continued stability.

To elaborate, one important role of a liberal government is to secure conditions for the production of adequate material resources that are needed to maintain a just society and the dignity of each of its members. This is not at all to say a liberal government's role is to encourage maximum productive output (certainly not without regard to distribution, as many classical liberals maintain). Economic efficiency is subordinate as a liberal end; it should be regulated and directed toward maintaining a society in which each person is enabled to effectively exercise basic rights and liberties, take advantage of fair opportunities, and achieve individual independence. But given this more basic distributive end, liberal society has a legitimate interest in providing and maintaining conditions under which people can be productive and self-supporting. This does not mean the able-bodied must labor to avoid sacrificing a government-sponsored basic income.[16] It means rather that government has the responsibility to maintain a setting in which they can develop their capacities and be productive. When a subculture of addiction becomes so severe and widespread that it affects individuals' opportunities to develop their abilities and engage in production, they are in effect denied fair opportunities, and liberal institutions themselves are undermined.

Another important role of a liberal government is to secure conditions necessary for the reproduction of liberal culture and the continuation of liberal society across generations. Herein lies government's interest in maintaining the integrity of family life (in some form), and seeing to it that parents and guardians protect, support, and educate children under their care. The reproduction of liberal institutions and culture also plays a significant role in justifying and defining the purposes of a mandatory educational system (discussed above). When the family and the system of education are undermined by adverse effects of free availability of drugs, liberal society's ongoing need to perpetuate itself is endangered.

So, if the consequences of free availability of a drug substantially impair the ability of a liberal society to produce adequate sustaining resources or to reproduce liberal culture and institutions from one generation to the next, then there are legitimate liberal reasons for restricting that drug, in order to protect the interests of current and future generations. As individuals cannot exercise liberal rights in a way that is calculated to destroy their capacities for agency, so they cannot exercise these rights in a way that destroys or undermines the conditions of liberal culture needed to sustain the free exercise of these capacities. Liberalism is not committed to standing by and passively witnessing the destruction of its culture and institutions to the point where society itself can only be sustained by illiberal and autocratic measures. These considerations need to be weighed in the balance, along with the arguments against drug interdiction recited at the outset of this paper, in finally coming to a decision about the permissibility of psychoactive drugs in a liberal constitutional democracy.

NOTES

*   I am grateful to the participants of the Conference on Morality, Legality, and Drugs at the State University of New York, Buffalo, September 1995, for their many helpful comments, especially to Douglas Husak, Michael Moore, Donald Moon, Anita Allen, and Pablo De Greiff. I am also indebted to Jay Wallace for his advice on a draft of this essay.

1.   The difference is 30% fewer on some accounts. See Daniel Benjamin and Roger L. Miller, *Undoing Drugs* (New York: Basic Books, 1991) Others contend that there is no reliable way of predicting such figures. See John Kaplan. *The Hardest Drug: Heroin and Public Policy* (Chicago: University of Chicago Press, 1983), pp. 111ff.

2.   Benjamin and Miller, *Undoing Drugs*, p. 85.

3.   Ibid., p. 129.

4.   Ibid. See also Kaplan, *The Hardest Drug*, pp. 64–65.

5.   Benjamin and Miller, *Undoing Drugs*, p. 82.

6.   Kaplan, *The Hardest Drug*, pp. 90, 97–98.

7.   Ibid., pp. 95–96.

8.   See Joel Feinberg, *Harm to Self*, vol. 3, *The Moral Limits of the Criminal Law* (Oxford: Oxford University Press, 1986); David A. J. Richards, *Sex, Drugs, Death, and the Law* (Totowa, NJ: Rowman and Littlefield, 1982); Douglas Husak, *Drugs and Rights* (Cambridge: Cambridge University Press, 1992).

9.   According to Rawls's political liberalism, Kantian liberalism of the kind here argued for need not make the working assumption that autonomy is an intrinsic good for each person, in other words, that autonomy is among the final ends about which it is rational for all people to structure their lives and which, therefore, provides a fundamental basis for laws and political institutions. This is one respect in which a Kantian politically liberal view differs from the perfectionist liberalism argued for by Michael Moore in this volume. I make a weaker claim: that autonomy, in the sense of the exercise and development of the powers of moral and rational agency, is essential

to each person's good within the confines of a liberal and democratic society. This leaves open the more controversial claim that autonomy is an intrinsic good for each person. This may be true, but it is not necessary for the argument over what basic rights individuals have.

10. See Kaplan, *The Hardest Drug*, p. 33, on "chippers," long-term occasional users of heroin who do not become addicted.

11. As is evidenced by the majority of servicemen who gave up heroin, without subsequent readdiction, upon return from the Vietnam War. See Kaplan, *The Hardest Drug*, p. 37. Kaplan says, "heroin withdrawal is not *that* serious. Pharmacologists compare it to a bad case of the one-week flu—a considerable degree of pain and discomfort, but not so serious that it cannot be borne by someone with considerable determination" (p. 35).

12. See Kaplan, *The Hardest Drug*, pp. 45–46.

13. Angel Dust may be in this category. There also exists a form of heroin called China White that matches the description of intrinsically debilitating drugs.

14. For a thorough account of the ends of education in a constitutional democracy, see Amy Gutmann, *Democratic Education* (Princeton, NJ: Princeton University Press, 1987).

15. Heroin may be such a drug. See Kaplan, *The Hardest Drug*, pp. 133–136.

16. Still it remains the case that those who are unable to work because of drug addiction have assumed ways of life that require other people's labor to support them. This is likely to cause resentment among those who labor on their behalf, and a diminished sense of self-respect among those who are unable to labor because of addiction. I do not mean to take a position here in the complicated debate on whether those who choose a life of leisure without labor should be entitled to do so without affecting their share of government benefits or an insured basic income. See the criticisms of Rawls in Phillippe Van Parijs, "Why Surfers Should be Fed: The Liberal Case for an Unconditional Basic Income," *Philosophy and Public Affairs* 20 (1991): 101–131, and his *Real Freedom for All* (Oxford: Oxford University Press, 1995), Chap. 4.

Gun Control

HUGH LAFOLLETTE

From Ethics *110:2 (January 2000) pp. 263-281. Reprinted with permission from The University of Chicago Press and the Author.*

Many of us assume that we must either oppose or support gun control. Not so. We have a range of alternatives. Even this way of speaking oversimplifies our choices since there are two distinct scales on which to place alternatives. One scale concerns the degree (if at all) to which guns should be abolished. This scale moves from those who want no abolition (NA) of any guns, through those who want moderate abolition (MA)—that is, to forbid access to some subclasses of guns—to those who want absolute abolition (AA). The second scale concerns the restrictions (if any) on those guns that are available to private citizens. This scale moves from those who want absolute restrictions (AR) through those who want moderate restrictions (MR) to those who want no restrictions (NR) at all. Restrictions vary not only in strength but also in content. We could restrict

who owns guns, how they obtain them, where and how they store them, and where and how they carry them.

Our options are further complicated by the union of these scales. On one extreme no private citizen can own any guns (AA, which is functionally equivalent to AR), while at the other extreme, every private citizen can own any gun with no restrictions (NA + NR). But once we leave those extremes, which few people hold, the options are defined by a pair of coordinates along these distinct scales. While most people embrace positions on the "same" end of both scales, others embrace more exotic mixtures: some will want few weapons available to private citizens but virtually no restrictions on those guns that are available (MA + NR), while others may prefer making most guns available but want to seriously restrict them (NA + MR).

So our choice is not merely to support or oppose gun control but to decide *who* can own *which* guns under *what conditions*. Although I cannot pretend to provide a definitive account here, I can isolate the central issues and offer the broad outline of an appropriate solution. To simplify discussion, I adopt the following locutions: those opposed to most abolition and most restrictions advocate a "serious right to bear arms," while those supporting more widespread abolition and more substantial restrictions are "gun control advocates." This simplification, of course, masks significant disagreements among advocates of each positions.

Justifying Private Ownership Of Guns

A Moral Question

Do citizens have a "serious right to bear arms"? This is a moral question, not a constitutional one. For even if the Constitution did grant this right, we should determine if there are sufficiently compelling arguments against private gun ownership to warrant changing the Constitution. By contrast, if this were not a constitutional right, we should determine if there are strong reasons why the state should not ban or control guns and if these reasons are sufficiently compelling to make this a constitutional right. Most defenders of private gun ownership claim we do have a moral right—as well as a constitutional one—and that this right is not an ordinary right but a fundamental one.

1. A fundamental right. If they are correct, they would have the justificatory upper hand. Were this a fundamental right, it would not be enough to show that society would benefit from controlling access to guns.[1] The arguments for gun control would have to be overwhelming. Yet there is also a hefty cost in claiming that this is a fundamental right: the evidence for the right must meet especially rigorous standards....

Advocates must show that and how granting the right protects individuals' fundamental interests, and they must be prepared to respond to objections that granting that right type will harm society. These are serious obstacles for gun advocates. It is difficult to see that a serious right to bear arms satisfies either of these requirements, let alone both.

First, I see no compelling reason to think that owning a gun is a fundamental interest. Other fundamental interests are necessary to one's flourishing no matter what her particular desires, interests, and beliefs. It is difficult to see how this is true of guns. Moreover, the interests protected by paradigmatic fundamental rights—our interests in unfettered speech, freedom of religion, and freedom of association—are not merely means to my flourishing, they are elements constituting it. By contrast, having a gun in my bed stand, in my closet, or on my person might be a means for me to achieve my ends, but they are not constitutive elements of my flourishing. Hence, owning guns is not a fundamental interest....

2. A derivative right. Suppose we determined that the right to bear arms is not a fundamental right but a derivative right. This would still be a significant finding since derivative rights, like fundamental ones, cannot be restricted without good evidence. Prima facie, I think we have such a derivative right. Each of us has a fundamental right of noninterference: we should be allowed to live our lives as we wish so long as we do not thereby harm others. This is a right each of us needs no matter what our particular interests. That general right derivatively protects personally important activities.

For instance, I would be furious if the state forbade me from sharing a pint with a friend. Nonetheless, although consuming alcohol is a particular interest and enjoyment I have, it is not a constitutive element of the good life in the way that the freedoms of speech, religion, and association are. That is why I do not have a fundamental right to consume alcohol. Consequently, the conditions under which my consumption of alcohol can be legitimately restricted are more lax than they would be if the activity were a fundamental interest.

Nonetheless, since I have a *prima facie* derivative right to consume alcohol, the state can legitimately abolish or restrict alcohol consumption only if it can show that doing so is an effective means of protecting the public from harm. They can do that in some cases: people who consume substantial amounts of alcohol are dangerous drivers. Since this behavior is unacceptably risky to others, the state can legitimately restrict drinking while driving. Whether privately owning guns is similarly risky is something we must discover.

Bad Public Policy

If private gun ownership were not a derivative right, it might still be bad policy to substantially restrict or abolish guns. There are always costs of enforcing a law. Sometimes these costs are prohibitive, especially when the public does not support that law. If the public will not voluntarily comply with the law, then the state must try to force compliance. In their efforts to do so, they invariably employ excessively intrusive methods. Such methods never entirely succeed, and, to the extent that they do, they undermine public confidence in and support for all law. Consider America's experience with Prohibition. Although one of Prohibition's aims—to protect innocents from harm caused by those under the influence— was laudable, the law was unenforceable and excessively costly. Consequently, less than two decades after Prohibition was passed via constitutional amendment, it was repealed.

The cost of enforcing any law—and especially an unpopular law—weighs against making any behavior illegal unless we have solid evidence that the behavior is seriously harmful. If we adopt a weaker standard—if we criminalize every action type whose tokens occasionally lead to some harm—then we would criminalize most behavior. As a result, even if there were no right to bear arms, we should still not seek to substantially limit private ownership of guns unless we had good reason to think that would prevent serious harm.

Summing Up: Justifying the Private Ownership of Guns

The preceding analysis isolates three questions we must answer in deciding whether people should be permitted to own guns: (1) How important is owning a gun to some people? (2) What are the consequences of private gun ownership? and (3) Is abolishing or restricting private ownership of guns bad policy? Although gun owner-

ship is not a fundamental interest, many people want to own guns and think they have good reason to do so. That is sufficient to show that serious gun control would undermine gun owners' interests. Moreover, there is some reason to think that serious gun control in countries with a strong tradition of gun ownership would be bad policy. Therefore, we should certainly not abolish, and arguably should not restrict, private ownership of guns without good reason. Are there good reasons? To answer this question, we must determine the effects of private gun ownership: (*a*) How likely is it that private gun ownership seriously harms others? and (*b*) Are there substantial benefits of gun ownership that might counterbalance any harm?

Harm, Danger, And Risk

We must be careful when we say that guns cause harm. Guns kill people because agents use them to kill people (or misuse them in ways that cause people to be killed). As the National Rifle Association (NRA) puts it: "Guns don't kill people, people do." In one sense their claim is uncontroversial: murder is the act of an agent, and guns are not agents. In another way, their claim is irrelevant. No gun control advocate claims, hints, or suggests that guns are moral agents. Guns are objects, and objects do no evil. But not all objects are created equal. Imagine the NNWA (National Nuclear Weapons Association) claiming that "tactical nuclear weapons don't kill people, people do." While in one sense their claim would be true, in a more profound way, it would be ludicrous.

Of course guns are not nuclear weapons. Guns are not as dangerous as nuclear weapons, and some guns have seemingly legitimate uses. The question is whether the character of guns makes them especially harmful. We know that some objects—tactical nuclear weapons, biochemical weapons, live grenades, and so forth, are much more dangerous than feathers, ice cream, and butter knives. Where do guns fall along this continuum?

There are two distinct but related questions: (1) Are guns inherently dangerous? and (2) What is the empirical probability that guns cause serious harm? "Inherently dangerous" objects are those whose nature or design is sufficient to justify our prediction that they will cause harm independent of any empirical evidence. We do not need double-blind empirical studies to know that nuclear weapons are inherently dangerous: they were designed to cause harm, and their nature is such that we can confidently predict they will cause harm. The two questions are intricately related since inherently dangerous objects are more likely to cause serious harm. Yet they are separable because some dangerous objects are not inherently so. Automobiles, alcohol, and cigarettes were not designed to cause harm, but all are causally implicated in many people's deaths. Other things being equal, we are more prone to control inherently dangerous objects than objects that merely have harm as an unwanted side effect.

Guns, unlike autos, are inherently dangerous, Guns were invented for the military; they were designed to cause (and threaten) harm.[2] The same aims determine the ways in which guns are redesigned: they are changed to make them more efficient at causing harm. In contrast, a significant aim of redesigning automobiles is to make them less dangerous. To some extent these efforts have succeeded. Although the absolute number of annual traffic fatalities has not noticeably declined, the number of fatalities per mile traveled has declined 75 percent since the 1950s.[3] We have enhanced the auto's original aim of efficient transportation while lessening harmful side effects. That is why we can sensibly say that the automobile is not inherently dangerous despite the fact that it causes harm. We cannot say the same for guns.

The literature of gun advocates supports my contention that guns are inherently dangerous. They advocate the private ownership of guns to prevent crime and to arm the militia. Guns can serve these purposes only because they are an effective means of inflicting and threatening harm. Even guns normally not used to harm humans have purposes that ride piggyback on this fundamental purpose. Shotguns are used to kill animals, and target guns are designed to be especially accurate. Taken together, this evidence supports the common view that guns are inherently dangerous. That is why we have special reasons to regulate them.

Although inherently dangerous, guns are far less dangerous than weapons of mass destruction, and they do have seemingly legitimate uses. That is why we must show just how risky they are before we can legitimately abolish or seriously restrict them. We must also determine if they have sufficient benefits such that we should permit them, even if risky.

An Intermediate Conclusion

We have shown that owning guns is not a fundamental interest and that guns are inherently dangerous. That is why we cannot categorically dismiss all forms of gun control. However, this is a weak conclusion. For although guns are inherently dangerous, they may not be so dangerous as to justify more than a system of minimal registration. What seems clear is that their inherent dangerousness precludes the idea that guns cannot be subject to governmental control. Some form of gun control cannot be categorically dismissed. Before determining the actual danger that guns present, we should first determine how risky an action must be before we can justifiably restrict it.

Risk

Humans are notoriously bad at judging risk. Often we are unaware of, or are inattentive to, the seriousness of risks. For instance, we may drive while inebriated. At other times we overestimate the risks. For instance, we may refuse to fly because we think it is too dangerous. A proper determination of risk would be based on a careful accounting of the action's costs and benefits. We should determine (1) the probability of harm, (2) the seriousness of harm (the product of the gravity and extent of the harm), (3) the probability of achieving the benefits, (4) the significance of the benefits (the product of the importance and extent of the benefit), and then act accordingly. Of course even if we reach the same determination to the above questions, we might still disagree about whether to act: we might disagree about what risks are worth which benefits. Nonetheless, we can all agree that (*a*) as the likelihood and seriousness of harm increase, we have increased reason to refrain from acting, while (*b*) as the likelihood and importance of the benefits increase, we have increased reasons to act. We can import these lessons into the law.

Legal Rules

But not straightforwardly. The issue is not whether we should own guns if they are legal, although that is a fascinating question. The question is whether the state should curtail private gun ownership. The foregoing considerations are relevant but not decisive. The decision to permit private ownership of guns is shaped by two factors pulling in opposite directions. First, even if we think Roger (an adult) stupidly engages in a dangerous activity (sky diving or boxing or racing), we might think Roger's autonomy requires that we permit it. Our commitment to individual liberty weighs against the government's abolishing or restricting the private ownership of guns as a way of limiting harm.[4] Second, some actions (smoking in public places) that are acceptably risky to Roger might be unacceptably risky to others. Are guns also unacceptably risky to others?

Put differently, gun control does not concern what private individuals should do but what governments should allow private individuals to do. We must determine the risk of permitting the private ownership of guns, constrained by these complicating considerations. To illustrate how this might work, consider the following example. We have evidence that a number of wrecks are caused by drivers using cellular phones. Roger wants to use his cellular phone while commuting to work. He decides the inconvenience of not using the cellular phone is worse than the small probability of personal harm. He might overestimate the inconvenience of not being able to use his cellular phone or insufficiently appreciate the seriousness of the risk. However, since he is an adult, we might think we should not interfere

with his decision to use a cellular phone while driving. That is what autonomy requires. Yet Roger is not the only person at risk. Passengers in his or other cars may also be harmed. The seriousness of harm to them must also be considered in deciding to permit or restrict drivers' use of cellular phones.

These judgments of risk must be further tempered by the costs of enforcement mentioned earlier. Although we know that using cellular phones while driving may lead to accidents, we also know other activities may do the same—drinking coffee while driving, eating a donut, looking at a map, talking to a passenger, driving more than two hours without stopping, driving on less than six hours of sleep, driving home after a bad day at the office, and so forth. We can reasonably presume that we should not make all these activities illegal. The probabilities of serious harm are small, and enforcing such laws would require far-reaching intrusions into everyone's life. When the risks of an activity's causing grave harm to many others are small and the costs of interference are significant, then we should not criminalize the action. But as the probability of grave and widespread harm increases, then, other things being equal, we should criminalize the action.

For instance, when people are released from prison (and not just on parole) they have "paid their debt to society." Yet we do not permit them to own a gun. We judge that they are more likely to harm others. Of course not all of them—and likely not a majority of them—would harm others if they were permitted to own a gun. They are prevented from owning guns because they are members of a group statistically more likely to cause harm: we judge that allowing former felons to own guns is unacceptably risky. The NRA and most other gun advocates agree....

This is our rationale for all laws proscribing risky actions. Every drunk driver does not cause an accident. Most do not. Yet we do not flinch at laws forbidding drunk driving. For it is not merely that drunk drivers are statistically more likely to cause harm; they are more likely to cause harm *because* they are inebriated. We can arguably use the same rationale to justify restricting access to guns. We restrict access not only because guns are inherently dangerous but because—if gun-control advocates are right—permitting private ownership of guns is very risky.

What We Need To Know

We can now specify what we must know in order to intelligently decide whether to prohibit or restrict gun ownership (or any other risky action): (1) Is there a statistically significant correlation between the action (private ownership of guns) and harm (homicides, accidental deaths, suicides, armed robbery, etc.)? (2) Do we have good reason to think this correlation indicates that the purportedly risky action causes the harm? (3) How serious are these resultant harms? and (4) How important is the activity that the state wishes to control (*a*) to the individual agent and (*b*) to the society?

In deciding whether to restrict the behavior, we must balance these considerations using the following general guidelines: (1) If we have evidence that the behavior causes harm, then we have some reason to limit the behavior. As the evidence increases, the reasons for prohibiting the behavior increase. As the probability that the behavior will lead to *serious* harm (the product of the gravity and extent of the harm) approaches certainty, then the reasons for forbidding the behavior become very strong. (2) The more grave and widespread the potential harm, the more reason we have to constrain the behavior. If the gravity and extent of the harm are substantial, we might constrain the behavior even if our evidence that the behavior causes the harm is moderate. (3) The higher the probability that allowing the action will have important benefits, the stronger the reason to permit it. The greater the benefits, the greater the reason to permit it.

Libertarians might claim that individuals' rights are so strong that the state cannot justifiably intervene even to constrain those who put others at extreme risk. The state should not proscribe risky actions, although they can intervene after harm has occurred. This use of "risk" is misleading. If on one occasion I drive while inebriated, I engage in a risky action: there is some

probability that I and others will be harmed. However, permitting people to drive while inebriated will definitely cause harm, although we cannot specify in advance who will be harmed. A personal decision to own a gun is risky in the former sense. A decision to permit citizens to privately own guns is—depending on the evidence—risky in the latter sense. If gun control advocates are right about the evidence, then we have good grounds to constrain private gun use. The question is, are they right?

Assessing The Evidence

Armchair Arguments

Debates over gun control typically begin, and sometimes end, with armchair arguments. Both sides offer armchair explanations of why (and how) the presence (or absence) of guns will increase (or decrease) violent crime. It is tempting to categorically dismiss armchair arguments since they seem to be poor substitutes for empirical evidence. However, it would be a mistake to assume we could devise sound empirical studies or understand their results without armchair arguments. In a study to discover if widespread availability of guns increases the number of homicides or decreases crime, we need armchair arguments to tell us which variables we should control.[5] Without them we would not know that we should control for the extent of poverty, the incidence of drug use, increases in the number of police officers, or the introduction of tougher (or more lax) penalties. Without them we would not know that we do not need to control for the price of mayonnaise, the criminal's eye color, or who won the World Series.

Armchair arguments also take center stage in evaluating empirical studies, in criticizing experimental design, and in reinterpreting the reported findings.[6] So before I discuss the empirical evidence, I summarize some significant armchair arguments employed by gun advocates and gun-control advocates.

1. More weapons, more violence. Gun control supporters offer empirical evidence of a positive correlation between murder rates and the availability of guns (especially handguns). Availability of guns is also positively correlated with suicide and accident rates. This empirical evidence is best understood against the background of the following armchair arguments. (1) Guns (and especially handguns) are the easiest way to kill others or oneself. People can stand at a relatively safe distance and pull the trigger. (2) When people are angry, they can act in ways they would not act normally. They may strike out at others. If they had a gun close to hand, they would be more likely to use that gun. Although they could resort to a knife or a baseball bat, they would be less likely to do so, and, even if they did, those weapons are less likely to cause a serious or fatal injury. (3) When people are depressed, they can act in ways they would not act normally. If they had a gun close to hand, they would be more likely to kill themselves. Although they might slit their wrists or take pills, they would be less likely to do so, and, even if they did, they would be less likely to kill themselves. (4) When people handle guns, even for a legitimate purpose, the probability of serious or fatal injury to themselves or others increases. When children have access to guns, the likelihood of an accident increases still more.

The conclusion of the armchair argument is clear: the more widely available guns are, the more people will be murdered, will commit suicide, and will die of accidents. This is a plausible armchair prediction. Perhaps it is wrong. Maybe it is reasonable but overinflated. Or it might be that the prediction is well founded but that the widespread availability of guns is nonetheless justified. What is apparent is that the claim that widespread availability of guns increases the number of homicides, suicides, and accidental deaths is highly plausible, it is difficult to imagine that it is false.

2. Availability of guns prevents or stops crimes. Gun advocates offer empirical evidence supporting the claim that guns prevent crime; their armchair arguments undergird and explain those studies. The motivating idea is simple: most criminals want to minimize their risks when committing a crime. If they know that someone in a house is armed, they will be less likely to enter that house, at least when the person is home and

awake. Potential criminals are also less likely to assault or rob someone whom they believe is carrying a weapon. Finally, when criminals try to rob or assault an armed person, the person is more likely to foil the crime, This, too, is a plausible armchair prediction. Perhaps it is wrong. Maybe the claim is overinflated. Perhaps guns have these benefits, but there are other effects of owning guns—for example, those mentioned above—which outweigh them. What is apparent is that the claim that the widespread availability of guns would prevent or thwart some crimes is highly plausible. It is difficult to imagine that it is false. Of course we cannot stop with these armchair arguments. We must assess the empirical evidence.

The Data

The empirical evidence is difficult to assess, and, to the extent that we can, it does not univocally support either side. You might not know this from listening to the public policy debate. Some gun-control advocates imply that strict gun laws would all but eliminate murder, while some gun advocates imply that having a gun in every home would virtually end crime. Both claims are unfounded. Gun control will not virtually eliminate murder. Arming all citizens will not virtually eliminate crime. About that we can be confident. The problem is determining the precise effects of permitting or restricting guns. The available evidence is less than compelling. But we must make a judgment based on the best evidence we have.

1. The connection between availability of guns and murder. Perhaps the most well-established statistic is this: the more widely available guns (especially handguns) are, the more people are murdered. The figures are duplicated time and again in country after country. Here is the bottom line: "The correlation between any gun-prevalence and the overall murder rate is .67, while it is .84 between handgun prevalence and overall murder rate."[7] These figures are significant to the .01 level; that is, the chance that these correlations could occur merely by chance is less than one out of 100. This correlation meets the statisticians' gold standard.

But this does not resolve the issue, for it does not establish what gun control advocates claim it shows, namely, that gun control is an effective way of substantially lessening the murder rate. First, a statistical correlation shows that two things are linked, but it does not tell us if the first caused the second, the second caused the first, or if there is some third factor which caused both. Second, even if the items are causally related, we do not know that changing the cause will straightforwardly change the effect since another factor might intervene to sustain the effect.

Gun advocates proffer their own armchair explanation for the correlations: these correlations reflect the character of the respective social and political systems. The European countries where murder rates are lower have more social solidarity and are more heterogeneous than the United States. Whether these social factors explain all of the correlation is debatable, but I am confident they explain some of it. Were the United States to regulate guns as tightly as most European countries, our murder rates arguably would fall, but they would not plummet immediately to European levels.

We might settle the issue if we could conduct controlled experiments, randomly dividing our population in half, giving half of them guns, removing all the guns from the other half, and then monitoring the murder rate. Of course, that would be morally unacceptable, politically unrealistic, and probably even scientifically unachievable. Before we had enough time to exclude all possible intervening causes, sufficient time might have elapsed so that new intervening causes could have emerged. But we are not left in the dark. We have empirical evidence that helps adjudicate between competing explanations of the correlation.

First, we have empirical evidence, bolstered by armchair arguments, that guns are more lethal than other weapons. Some claim the ratio is 5:1; no estimates are lower than 2:1.[8] This partly explains the strong correlation between guns and homicides. If people get angry the same number of times, those using the most lethal weapons are more likely to kill their victims.

Second, the nature of secondary gun markets helps explain how the widespread availability of guns increases crime in general and homicides in particular. Various opponents of gun control claim that "If we outlaw guns, only outlaws will have guns." Armchair arguments suggest why this is a silly claim. Where, one might ask, do criminals get their guns? They often steal them or buy them from those who purchased them legally. Even guns obtained from other criminals are usually traceable to people who purchased them legally. Empirical evidence supports this armchair supposition. Most criminals report having stolen their guns, received them from a friend or family member, or purchased them from someone who had stolen it. At least half a million guns are stolen each year, and these swell the numbers of guns available illegally.[9]

Not only does the primary (legal) market affect the availability of guns on secondary markets, it also affects the price of guns on those markets, much "like the analogous markets for motor vehicles or prescription drugs."[10] As we restrict the availability of guns in the primary market, the supply of guns in the secondary markets decreases and their cost increases.[11] This increase in cost will diminish teenagers' ability to obtain guns since they are least able to afford hefty prices. Since teenagers commit most deadly crimes, decreasing the availability of legal guns will thereby decrease the number of homicides. The converse is true as well: having huge numbers of legally available guns increases the number of guns on secondary markets and typically lowers their price. This makes it easier for prospective criminals, including teenagers, to obtain guns.

Third, having a gun around the house (or on the person)—even for self-protection—apparently increases the chance that someone in the family will kill themselves with the gun or will be the victim of a homicide or an accident. One study found that "for every time a gun in the home was involved in a self-protection homicide, they noted 1.3 unintentional deaths, 4.5 criminal homicides, and 37 firearm suicides."[12] This implies that for every case where someone in a gun-owning household uses a gun to successfully stop a life-threatening attack, nearly forty-three people in similar households will die from a gunshot. Taken together the evidence does not prove that widespread availability of guns increases the number of homicides. However, that empirical evidence, bolstered by earlier armchair arguments, makes the claim highly plausible.

2. The use of guns to prevent crime. The biggest "gun" in the anti-gun-control lobby is the claim that having (and perhaps carrying) a gun prevents crime. As I noted earlier, this is a sensible armchair claim. Someone contemplating a robbery is more likely to proceed if they think they can succeed with little risk to themselves. So if a prospective robber believes the tenants are at home and have a gun they know how to use, then he likely will seek another target. Two surveys support this belief. According to one survey, 4 percent of all Americans have used a handgun in the past five years to avert a crime. Given those figures, researchers estimate that there are at least 600,000 defensive uses of guns per year. Kleck uses these results, in conjunction with another survey, to claim that the number might be as high as 2.5 million.[13] Given the number of violent crimes using guns, "the best evidence indicates that guns are used about as often for defensive purposes as for criminal purposes."[14] If true, that is a powerful reason to resist attempts to limit availability of guns.[15] Such statistics, particularly when bolstered by moving anecdotes of those who have saved their lives by having a gun, cannot be cavalierly dismissed by gun control advocates.

However, these figures are inflated, likely dramatically so. First, Kleck's methodology is flawed. Surveys have an inherent tendency to overestimate rare events. Kleck made his estimates based on phone interviews with people in 5,000 dwelling units. One percent of those units claimed to have used a gun defensively in the past year. Kleck inferred from these responses that there are 2.5 million defensive handgun uses per year. However, since this inference is based on an affirmative answer by one person out of a hundred, that means that for every chance for a false negative (someone who falsely denies using a gun defensively) there are ninety-nine chances for a false positive (someone who falsely claims to have used a gun defensively).[16] The probability that this or some other bias skews the findings is substantial.

Second, Kleck's findings are inconsistent with findings by the National Crime Victimization Survey (NCVS), which interviewed far more people and interviewed them more regularly.[17] Kleck's estimates even clash with the findings of the NCVS on the incidence and circumstances of robberies (which seems less subject to reporting bias). If Kleck's figures were correct, then "Kleck asks us to believe that burglary victims in gun owning households use their guns in self-defense more than 100% of the time, even though most were initially asleep."[18]

Finally, if there were 2.5 million defensive gun uses each year, how many of those were necessary? Given the negative results of private gun ownership, gun advocates should show not only that guns deter crime but that they are the best way of doing so. Some people plausibly claim that owning a dog is an effective deterrent. If true, then a not insignificant percentage of those who used a gun defensively could have achieved the same results without the accompanying danger. In summary, there is no doubt that guns deter some crime and stop the completion of other crimes, just not in the numbers that Kleck claims.

John Lott supplements Kleck's argument by claiming that the widespread use of concealed weapons would decrease the annual number of homicides by 1,400; rapes by 4,200; aggravated assaults by 60,000; and robberies by 12,000.[19] If true, and if there were no countervailing costs, this would be a powerful reason not only to permit guns but to encourage people to have and carry them. However, Lott's conclusions have also come under severe criticism: "The central problem is that crime moves in waves, yet Lott's analysis does not include variables that can explain these cycles. For example, he used no variables on gangs, on drug consumption, or community policing. As a result, many of Lott's findings make no sense. He finds for instance, that both increasing the rate of unemployment and reducing income reduces the rate of violent crimes."[20] Perhaps the most compelling critique comes from Jens Ludwig, who compares the rate of violent crime toward youths and adults in states that passed shall-issue carrying permits. Most of these states issue gun permits only to people over twenty-one. Armchair considerations predict that younger people, who cannot legally carry, will not receive the full benefits from the purported deterrent effect of shall-issue laws. Thus, those under twenty-one years of age are a natural control group to track general swings in crime. Once we include this factor, we find that shall-issue laws lead to higher—not lower—homicide and robbery rates.[21]

I also have an overarching worry about Lott's conclusions. The one correlation in the gun control debate that seemingly is beyond dispute is the high correlation between the presence of guns—especially handguns—and homicide rates. Gun advocates offer explanations for the correlation, but no one I have seen seriously challenges it. I find it difficult to square this correlation with Kleck's and Loft's claims that having more guns—and toting them—will lower crime.

An Overall Assessment of the Empirical Evidence

The strong correlation between the presence of guns and a higher murder rate is compelling. Since the correlation is statistically significant to a .01 level, it is difficult to believe that limiting private gun ownership will not have a noticeable effect on the numbers of murders. Gun advocates disagree: they claim that cultural factors explain the correlation. Although I think they are partly correct, they draw the wrong inference. For one crucial difference between European and American cultures is the widespread presence of guns. Each culture is the way it is, at least in part, because of the role of guns (or their absence) played in its creation and maintenance. Therefore, curtailing the private possession of guns might well change the American culture so that it would be less violent. Consequently, it is not only that fewer guns would directly cause some decline in violent crimes—which it should. It is also likely to reshape the cultural values which, along with the ready availability of deadly weapons, led to such an extraordinarily high murder rate in America.

However, the statistical evidence that guns prevent or thwart crimes is suggestive and cannot be ignored despite its identified weaknesses.

In summary; the overall statistical evidence tilts in favor of gun control advocates, although the evidence is disputable. But we should not expect nor do we need indisputable evidence. We can act on the best evidence we have while being open to new evidence. If widespread availability of guns were responsible for even one-fourth of the increase in the number of murders, that would be a significant harm that the state should prevent if it could do so in a relatively unintrusive and morally acceptable way

There is little doubt that we could do that, at least to some degree. If nothing else, we could control some types of guns and ammunition. To take one obvious example, teflon-coated bullets are designed to pierce protective vests. People do not use these bullets to pierce the vests on a deer or a squirrel, on a target or a clay pigeon. They use them to pierce the vests on people, usually law-enforcement officers. This ammunition has no purpose except to cause harm. Hence, we are justified in abolishing teflon bullets and in establishing severe criminal penalties for those possessing them. This would not save large numbers of lives. But, assuming the enforcement of this ban is not impractical, then, if it saved even a few lives, that would be a compelling reason to outlaw such bullets.

Some guns, however, have a much wider use, even if they occasionally are used for ill. People have seemingly legitimate uses for shotguns and single-shot rifles. Consequently, barring strong evidence to the contrary, we should not abolish them. We should, however, study their contributory role in causing harm and explore ways we might reduce this harm in a relatively unintrusive way.

The central debate concerns handguns. The evidence we have shows that handguns are disproportionately used in homicides and in robberies. Although "there are approximately three times as many long guns as handguns in the US, more than 80 percent of gun homicides and 90 percent of gun robberies involve handguns."[22] The experience in Canada suggests that criminals will not switch to long guns if handguns are unavailable. Given the special role handguns play in causing harm, we have compelling reasons to extensively control, or perhaps even abolish, handguns. But policy considerations, mentioned earlier, should give us pause.

A Third Way

In the past we not only assumed that we must either support or oppose gun control, we assumed that the only way to control guns is to legally proscribe access to them. We should consider other options. Although I find the idea of a world without handguns immensely appealing, there are reasons to seek alternatives, especially in countries like the United States with a deeply entrenched gun culture. In the present political climate, the abolition or serious control of guns in the United States is unlikely to work and unlikely to happen. There are far too many people who desperately want guns. There are far too many people who own guns. Any attempt to disarm the society would be beset with problems like those that plagued Prohibition. We have other possibilities.

We could employ elements of a policy that we use to control another inherently dangerous object: dynamite. Dynamite has many beneficial uses. That is why we permit people to own it under specifiable conditions, for example, to build a road. But it is also inherently dangerous. That is why we heavily restrict its purchase, storage, and use. I cannot own dynamite for recreation (I like the flash), for hunting (I am a lousy shot), or for protection (I would not hear an intruder). Owning dynamite is rarely a significant interest and never a fundamental one. More important to the present point, even when we do permit people to own dynamite, we subject them to strict legal liability. The owner is financially liable for any harm caused by his dynamite, even if he was not negligent.

I propose we make handgun owners (and perhaps ultimately all gun owners) strictly liable for harm caused by the use of their guns. If Jones's child takes his gun and kills someone while committing a crime, then Jones will be financially responsible to those harmed. If Jones's child accidentally kills a neighbor's child, Jones will be financially responsible to the child's family. If someone steals Jones's gun and kills someone while robbing them, then Jones will owe the victim compensatory damages. And if Jones were negligent in the storing of the gun, he could be subject to punitive damages as well. Perhaps if he were grossly negligent in storing the gun (he left it lying in his front yard, next to a school playground), we might even bring criminal charges against him.

This procedure is justified since guns are inherently dangerous, and it is only reasonable to expect people to take responsibility for their risky actions. The benefits are notable: many people would be disinclined to own guns, while those owning guns would likely take greater care in storing, handling, and using them. This arguably could achieve the central aims of gun control without direct government intervention. Doubtless that means that some people will be forced to pay for the misdeeds or mistakes of others in ways we might dislike. However, that is a more attractive policy than continuing the current scheme in which guns are easily obtained in the United States or than in completely denying individuals' interest in owning guns.

To make this option more palatable, we could let gun owners purchase liability insurance to cover potential losses. We might even require them to purchase insurance. After all, most states require drivers to have automobile insurance. This insurance-based system of strict liability would make people take more care with any guns they own while providing financial remuneration to those harmed by the use of those guns.

Perhaps this will not work. Other proposals might work better. What seems clear to me is that we need to do something: we cannot continue with the status quo.[23]

NOTES

1. Todd C. Hughes and Lester H. Hunt, "The Liberal Basis of the Right to Bear Arms," *Public Affairs Quarterly* 14, No. 1(2000): pp. 1–25.
2. Charles Singer, B. J. Holmyard, A. R Hall, and Treavor Williams, *A History of Technology*, 7 vols. (Oxford: Oxford University Press, 1956), vol. 2, p. 367.

3. David Hemenway, "Guns, Public Health, and Public Safety," in *Guns and the Constitution*, ed. Dennis A. Henigan, F, Bruce Nicholson, and David Hemenway (Northampton, MA: Aletheia Press, 1995), pp. 49–82, p. 52.

4. Hughes and Hunt.

5. John R. Lott, *More Guns, Less Crime: Understanding Crime and Gun-Control Laws* (Chicago: University of Chicago Press, 1998), pp. 21–24.

6. Dan Black and Daniel Nagin, "Do Right-to-Carry Laws Deter Violent Crime?" *Journal of Legal Studies* 27 (1998): 209–20; Philip J. Cook, Stephanie Mollinoni, and Thomas B. Cole, "Regulating Gun Markets," *Journal of Criminal Law and Criminology* 86 (1995): 59–92; Phillip J. Cook, Jens Ludwig, and David Hemenway, "The Gun Debate's New Mythical Number: How Many Defensive Uses Per Year?" *Journal of Policy Analysis and Management* 16 (1997): 463–69; David Hemenway, "The Myth of Millions of Annual Self-Defense Gun Uses: A Case Study of Survey Overestimates of Rare Events," *Chance* 10 (1997): 6–10, "Review of *More Guns, Less* Crime," *New England Journal of Medicine* 339 (1998):2029–30; Lott; Wheeler.

7. Gregg Lee Carter, *The Gun Control Movement* (New York: Twayne Publishers, 1997), p. 3.

8. Albert J. Reiss, Jr., and Jeffrey A. Roth, eds., *Understanding and Preventing Violence* (Washington, DC: National Academy Press, 1993), p. 260.

9. Cook, Mollinoni, and Cole, p. 81.

10. Ibid., p. 71.

11. Ibid., p. 73.

12. Reiss and Roth, eds., p. 267.

13. Gary Kleck, *Point Blank: Guns and Violence in America* (New York: Aldine De Gruyter, 1991), pp. 105–6.

14. Ibid., p. 107.

15. Gary Kleck, *Targeting Guns: Firearms and Their Control* (New York: Aldine de Gruyter, 1997).

16. David Hemenway, "Survey Research and Self-Defense Gun Use: An Explanation of Extreme Overestimates," *Journal of Criminal Law and Criminology* 87 (1997): 1430–45.

17. U.S. Department of Justice, *Criminal Victimization in the United States, 1993: A National Crime Victimization Survey* (Washington, DC: Government Printing Office, 1996).

18. Hemenway, "Survey Research and Self-Defense Gun Use: An Explanation of Extreme Overestimates," p. 1442.

19. Lott, p. 54.

20. Hemenway, "Review of *More Guns, Less Crime*," p. 2029.

21. Jens Ludwig, "Concealed Gun-Carrying Laws and Violent Crime: Evidence from State Panel Data," *International Review of Law and Economics* 18 (1998):239–54.

22. Hemenway, "Guns, Public Health, and Public Safety," p. 60.

23. I wish to thank Nicholas Dixon, Lester H. Hunt, Eva LaFollette, members of the philosophy departments at East Tennessee State University and the University of Western Michigan, as well as the editors and two anonymous readers of this journal, for helpful comments and criticisms on earlier drafts of this article.

A Treatise on the Rights of the Aboriginal Peoples of the Continent of North America

From The Quest for Justice: Aboriginal Peoples and Aboriginal Rights, *ed. Menno Boldt & J. Anthony Long, 1985, University of Toronto Press Inc. Reprinted with permission of the publisher.*

FRED PLAIN

I want to deal in this paper with our understanding of the meaning of "aboriginal rights." First of all, I want to quote from a paper produced by the Union of Ontario Indians in 1970. I was president of the union at that time, and I authorized the following statement, which was presented to a special committee dealing with the constitution of Canada.

> As Indian people we will always see our special status and our legal right as flowing from the original sovereignty of our nations. The colonial legal system to a large degree denied that sovereignty, but they never denied the existence of rights based on the aboriginal possession of tribal territories. It was the unauthorized violation of these rights that led to the unrest which prompted the Royal Proclamation of 1763.

That document, the first written constitutional document for British North America, recognized the existence of Indians' territorial rights, and established legal procedures for the surrender of these rights. The lands which today comprise Ontario were Indian lands. In the words of the Proclamation, they had not been ceded to or purchased by the colonial power. The procedures established by the Royal Proclamation for ceding Indian lands remain in force today. The last treaty signed under these procedures was in 1956, the Soto adhesion to Treaty #6.

Areas remain today in Ontario for which no valid treaty or surrender exists. Therefore, the procedures of the Royal Proclamation are still of practical consequence even in Ontario. Section 91.24 of the British North American Act of 1867 gave jurisdiction over Indians and lands reserved for the Indians to the Federal Government. This was not enacted, as seems popularly believed, out of a paternalistic concern for Native peoples.

It was enacted to make clear the power of the Federal Government to engage in colonial expansion in the West. The phrase "land reserved for Indians" included lands not ceded by treaty as of 1867, which for Ontario comprised by far the greater part of the present territory of this Province. If the Indians and their lands had not been crucial to the opening of the West, it would have been more logical to place Indians under Provincial jurisdictions as somewhat different terms of Indian policy developed in each colony of 1867.

Following the surrender of the Hudson's Bay Company Charter in 1869/70, the Governor General, exercising prerogative power in compliance with the procedures established by the Royal Proclamation, began negotiating a series of treaties with the Indian nations in Ontario and the Northwest. The treaties were constitutional documents. They were seen by both sides as establishing basic patterns of interrelationship for the future. They were based on the idea of mutual consent and the understanding that the Indians had legal rights in their patrimony. To violate these documents is to compromise the integrity of the Canadian legal system. The Migratory Birds Convention Act, and the decisions in Regina vs. Sekina in 1964, and in Regina vs. George in 1966, and Daniels vs. White and the Queen in 1968, to Indian people represent violations of basic legal commitments.

The basic rights of the Indian peoples are of constitutional significance. Yet, these rights have not been uniformly safeguarded under the present constitutional structure. This should change.

What Are Aboriginal Rights?

In white society there has always been confusion as to what actually is meant by the term "aboriginal rights." In 1970, for example, Prime Minister Pierre Trudeau was reported to have said that the concept of aboriginal rights is so complicated as to be unworkable. But to us, the Nishnawbe-Aski, the concept is basic, simple, and unambiguous. Our definition of aboriginal rights can be summed up in one phrase: "the right of independence through self-government." When we say that our right to self-government, our right to self-determination, our right to nationhood must be recognized in any new Canadian constitution, we are defining aboriginal rights. This is the goal of the Nishnawbe-Aski as outlined in the Declaration of Nishnawbe-Aski of 1977.

Aboriginal rights defined in this way include the right to develop our own life-style and our own economy, and to protect and encourage the practice of our sacred traditions as we know them. We, the Nishnawbe-Aski, have the inherent right to determine what our future will be. We shall determine the destiny of our land. We want to see the continued development of our people under their own governing systems. Aboriginal rights were a mere concept of Prime Minister

Trudeau's mind, but to my people they are a reality. We have the inherent right to develop and grow under our own system, and our own system will flow from our own people, who will develop our own constitution. Our Indian constitutions have every right to be recognized in any new Canadian constitution. This is the true meaning of aboriginal rights.

What Is an Aborigine?

The aborigines are the indigenous inhabitants of a country. For instance, the people that we know as the Indian nations of North and South America are the aborigines of these two continents. They were the first people to live in this part of the world.

Because we were the first people to live here we have a claim to certain rights. These rights include human rights—that is, the basic right to life claimed by all people. However, when we talk about aboriginal rights, we are also talking about the inherent right to self-determination that applies to all aborigines.

What Is Civilization?

To understand aboriginal rights we must understand the meaning of civilization. Civilization is the accumulation of the traditions and culture of a people: their ability to express themselves in a variety of ways—in dance, music, art, law, religion, the telling of stories, the writing of books, and so on. The aboriginal people of North and South America constituted a number of different civilizations.

Aboriginal rights guarantee each indigenous nation the right to develop its own traditions and culture—its own civilization. Each aboriginal nation has the inherent right to seek happiness and a comfortable way of living, and to develop itself at its own pace. This was the right of each aboriginal nation from its beginning, and it exists today. Each nation exercised aboriginal rights within its own lands and boundaries and under its own sovereignty.

To recognize that the aboriginal people were a civilization long before the white man came to North America is to acknowledge that as an aboriginal people we exercised our aboriginal right to govern ourselves. Conversely, to acknowledge that we have aboriginal rights is to recognize that these rights flow from our long-standing civilization.

Aboriginal and European Attitudes Toward the Land

Nishnawbe-Aski means "the people and the land." Our links with the earth are sacred links that no man can ever sever. We are one with the earth, and the earth is one with us. The Nishnawbe-Aski Declaration states that we have the right to govern and control our own people in our own land, and the right to remedy our own situations. The efforts that are made to meet our needs must come from our own people.

As nations of people we made laws to govern ourselves. Among the laws that we made were laws governing our use of the land and its resources. But our attitude toward the land and its use was and still is very different from the European attitude. We aboriginal people believe that no individual or group owns the land, that the land was given to us collectively by the Creator to use, not to own, and that we have a sacred obligation to protect the land and use its resources wisely. For the Europeans, the idea that land can be owned by a person or persons and exploited for profit is basic to the system. The European political and legal systems have been developed to reflect this concept of the land.

Many European and Canadian laws have to do with regulating private property in one form or another and with governing relations among people with respect to private property. The sovereign government has created laws to govern the distribution of the scarce resource of property. The most basic form of property, other than one's own body, is land.

The idea that land can be bought and sold, or that you can exercise some rights but not others in the land, is absolutely foreign to the Nishnawbe-Aski way of thinking. Yet this is the basis for all legislation that has been enacted since the coming of the Europeans to North America.

Legislation Affecting Aboriginal Rights

The Royal Proclamation of 1763 was passed in the British Parliament because of the struggles between Indians and Europeans over the land. This document recognized the existence of Indians' territorial rights and established the legal procedures for the giving up of those rights.

The Constitution Act, 1867, established Canada as a nation. The act sets out the division of power between the provinces and the federal government. Section 91(24) of the act gives jurisdiction over Indians and lands reserved for Indians to the federal government.

The act was intended to make clear the power of the federal government to engage in colonial expansion in the west. This was done because we Indians and our lands were crucial to the opening of the west, and the federal government wanted to be able to control us and our land in order to consolidate its power over the country.

After the Royal Proclamation, and until as recently as 1956, treaties were signed between the government and the Indian nations. These treaties were seen by both sides as establishing basic patterns of future interrelationships. They were based on the idea of mutual consent and on the understanding that Indians had legal rights in and control of the land.

The treaties were a recognition by colonial law that we Indian people had sovereignty in our land. In fact, there was a widespread acknowledgment that the aboriginal occupants of the land had certain legal claims because of their historical sovereignty over the land. The English legal system developed a theory that those claims were limited in certain ways, but the aboriginal tribes had the legal right to possess their tribal territories. Under the English legal system if the lands passed into non-Indian hands, then the Indian claims had to be extinguished by a formal treaty and by some form of compensation.

The treaties were negotiated sometimes before white settlement, sometimes after. The effect of the treaties was to extinguish many aboriginal rights; to preserve some residual rights, such as hunting, fishing, and trapping; and to create some new rights, such as schooling, medical care, and annuity payments.

While the treaties have not been totally in our favor, the law has never denied that the aboriginal tribes have legal rights to possess their tribal territories.

What Does It Mean to Be a Nation?

Our aboriginal right allows us to determine our future as the Nishnawbe-Aski Nation. What does it mean to be a nation? In 1977, an international conference on discrimination against indigenous populations of the Americas put forward a declaration of principles aimed at gaining recognition for indigenous or aboriginal peoples as nations under international law. The criteria for recognition as a nation are: that the people have a permanent population; that they have a defined territory; that they have a government; that they have the ability to enter into relations with other states. We can assure Canada and the international community that using these criteria we can define ourselves as a nation. We have a population that is permanent; we have always existed and we are not going to die out or fade into oblivion. We have a defined territory stretching from James Bay and Hudson Bay west to the Manitoba boundary; from Hudson Bay and James Bay southward to the height of land known as the Arctic watershed and east to the borders of Quebec. We have a democratic government given to us by the Creator. The Royal Proclamation of 1763 refers to our sovereignty, and the government of Canada approaches us as a nation to enter into a treaty with them. We continue to have the right to enter into relations with other states.

Under these criteria, the Nishnawbe-Aski have a solid basis for claiming our aboriginal right to determine what our future will be and to determine how we are going to attain our goals.

Do the Indian People Have a System of Government?

When the white man first came to America, there were systems of government in operation in this new land. The democratic system employed by the great Six Nations Confederacy was studied by the Europeans, and was picked up and incorporated into their governing systems. Democracy was already flourishing in North America before the white man came. The right to govern one's people, the right to govern one's destiny, the right to determine the paths that a nation will follow to reach its objectives must be recognized as sovereign and aboriginal rights.

We had a government. The government has been dormant because of the influx of federal law, particularly the Indian Act and its administrators, the Department of Indian Affairs. Our government has remained hidden in the hearts of our people, but it has never died. Our government will come forth under the careful guidance and leadership of the Nishnawbe-Aski Commission. We will be prepared to put the constitution of the Nishnawbe-Aski on paper, if that is what is required. Our government is a reality.

We must draw out from our people what they want to see developed in their community with regard to their own governing structure. Only then can we begin to educate our people in the traditional ways of living, traditional Indian government, and the traditional right to determine our future.

What Does It Mean to Be Independent?

When the Nishnawbe-Aski made their declaration in 1977, they stressed that their objective was to see the full development of cultural, economic, spiritual, and political independence. We think that we have to come to grips with the fact that cultural independence and economic independence cannot be divorced. One cannot exist without the other.

At the time the white man came here, our educational system was complete. The educational system and the political development of the various Indian nations in Canada determined the life-style of the particular tribe in whatever area of America they lived in. For instance, the economy of the Ojibway and the Cree living in this part of North America was based on the presence of animal, fish, bird, and plant life destined to give sus-

tenance to the people. Hunting, fishing and trapping, and gathering were not separate issues to be dealt with at a political level by certain components of the government; they were part of the socioeconomic system of our people, and they are included in the overall definition of aboriginal rights. Before the white man came, all Indian nations were independent and exercised their aboriginal rights within their own lands.

The Nishnawbe-Aski and the Constitution

We did not question the statement of Prime Minister Pierre Trudeau that the people of this country have a right to their own constitution. We support the principle of patriation; Canadians have a right to determine the instrument by which government is going to make laws that apply to them.

When the constitutional negotiations became an issue, we told the British parliamentarians that we were not fighting the patriation of the constitution to Canada. We felt that the Canadian people had a right to their own constitution, but we also believed that the Nishnawbe-Aski Nation, which existed before the Europeans came to North America, have a right to their own constitution, and that they must not be deprived of the right to make their own laws and determine their own destiny through their own governing system. Because the Canadian government was unwilling to recognize our right to our own constitution, we challenged the patriation of the British North America Act.

We, the aboriginal people, must clearly spell out the true aboriginal rights that must be recognized in any Canadian constitution. These rights are nonnegotiable. But we must take a united stand, or we will find it difficult to persuade Canada's first ministers to heed our claims.

What the Canadian Government Wants from the Aboriginal People

We are in the heat of a tremendous battle, a battle that is focused on jurisdiction. The premiers of the provinces and the prime minister are trying to reduce the aboriginal rights question to a series of legal issues that they can contest or disregard. At the same time, they attempt to placate the Indian people by saying, "We will look after you; we will improve your conditions; we will accommodate your needs." But ultimately they will try to consolidate their jurisdiction over our land and our resources. The first ministers have only one goal in mind in the constitutional negotiations: they hope to gain complete control over all Indian lands and resources. This is what the constitutional process is all about.

The Canadian Government's Attitude to Aboriginal Rights

The Honourable Jean Chrétien had these words to say about aboriginal and treaty rights: "We will honor our lawful obligations to the aboriginal people." Precisely what did he mean? He meant that Canada has obligations to native people only if such obligations will stand the test of the law. If the law decrees that certain obligations must be met, and if those obligations are defined in such a manner that the government can accept the definition, then they will be honored. But what does the term "law" mean? Law, in the modern liberal state, is the creation of an autonomous and general legal system composed of: private parties; a legitimate legal sovereignty and its administrative agencies (the governor-in-council or Parliament, or the government of Canada, and its cabinet and various departments); and the independent judiciary.

When the explorers from the European nations came to America, they found a land with people and law. The Europeans had no right to come and trample that system of laws underfoot and impose a new legal system in North America. But this fact is not readily going to be recognized and acknowledged by the people who in the first instance denied the existence of the aboriginal system of law. They will fight any attempt to bring truth to bear.

Let us go back to the quotation from the Nishnawbe-Aski declaration. In the minds of our people who hunt, trap, and fish the forests, lakes,

and rivers of Nishnawbe-Aski land, there is a clear concept of what our land tenure is. However, according to the government of Canada, which makes the laws, aboriginal rights are to be determined by a court interpretation. As far as the courts are concerned aboriginal rights are conceptual rights only; that is to say, they are a concept that exists only in the mind until drafted into some kind of law that makes sense in a legal system. The government makes the law dealing with aboriginal rights and the government appoints judges who interpret the law dealing with aboriginal rights. If the government of Canada has its way, the white man's law and the white man's courts will determine how the concept of land tenure is defined in practice.

Who Will Decide What Our Aboriginal Rights Are?

Court cases have never solved the riddle of aboriginal rights. The *Baker Lake* case is a prime instance of what happens when the dominant governing society, through its enacted laws and its judicial system, decides what constitutes aboriginal rights. In the *Baker Lake* case, the court said that the Inuit do have aboriginal rights because they have been here from time immemorial. Because of that one basic fact, the court recognized that aboriginal rights do exist. However, the Supreme Court of Canada took it upon itself to define what the aboriginal right is not. The judgment states that the aboriginal right is not a proprietary right. In other words, the right of the aboriginal people does not relate to the land, and therefore the land is open to those exploiters who want to extract the gas and the oil, destroy the environment, and then move out. The indigenous population is then left with evil consequences that greatly outweigh any potential benefits that might come to them from the resource exploitation.

In the communities of the Nishnawbe-Aski Nation, our fishermen, our trappers, our hunters, our schoolchildren, and our women who maintain our homes understand what our aboriginal rights are. Aboriginal rights are a riddle only to those who do not want to hear or face the truth, who do not want their taking of the land interfered with by the aboriginal owners of this continent.

The aboriginal people have a clear concept of land tenure in their minds; therefore our chiefs, our elders, our people, our children, should define our aboriginal rights—not the federal government, the provinces, or the Canadian courts. It is we who must protect our aboriginal right to self-determination as a nation and our right to develop and use the resources of the land free of interference and intimidation. We have an obligation to preserve the rights granted to us by the Creator. We have that right now. We have always had that right. We are determined to have that right in the future. We don't have to beg the prime minister of Canada and the provincial premiers to recognize that we have certain basic human and aboriginal rights.

Conclusion

I close this paper with a prayer. Great Grandfather, our hearts and our minds are joined together. We rejoice to know that our right to live and enjoy the beauty of this great land was given to us, not by any foreign government, but by yourself. Great Grandfather, you gave us the land and its resources; you made us one with the birds, the animal life, the fish life; you made us one with nature itself. This is our aboriginal right. It is a right that no government can interpret for us.

Because you gave it to us, no man has a right to take it away from us. Many times, our hearts have been made heavy when we have seen the devastation of our land by those who seek only to mine it for its wealth and then leave it. Our hearts have been made heavy because other powers have come in and made laws that have restricted our free movement of spirit. Yet you have put it in our hearts this day to stand upon our feet once again, and boldly claim that our aboriginal right is forever.

Breathe upon us with your spirit of life, and give us greater determination to press for this right to be fully restored to us and recognized by all people. Great Grandfather, be with us in all of our deliberations, for without your leadership and guidance we are weak and helpless. Cause the sound of the drum to be loud and clear to our hearts and minds in this crucial hour.

17

Global/Environmental Ethics

Terrorism[1]

MICHAEL WALZER

Michael Walzer is professor in the School of Social Science, Institute for Advanced Study at Princeton University in New Jersey.

From Just and Unjust Wars: A Moral Argument with Historical Illustration, *by Michael Walzer. Copyright © 1977 by Basic Books. Reprinted by permission of Basic Books, a member of Perseus Books, L.L.C.*

The Political Code

The word "terrorism" is used most often to describe revolutionary violence. That is a small victory for the champions of order, among whom the uses of terror are by no means unknown. The systematic terrorizing of whole populations is a strategy of both conventional and guerrilla war, and of established governments as well as radical movements. Its purpose is to destroy the morale of a nation or a class, to undercut its solidarity; its method is the random murder of innocent people. Randomness is the crucial feature of terrorist activity. If one wishes fear to spread and intensify over time, it is not desirable to kill specific people identified in some particular way with a regime, a party, or a policy. Death must come by chance to individual Frenchmen, or Germans, to Irish Protestants, or Jews, simply because they are Frenchmen or Germans, Protestants or Jews, until they feel themselves fatally exposed and demand that their governments negotiate for their safety.

In war, terrorism is a way of avoiding engagement with the enemy army. It represents an extreme form of the strategy of the "indirect approach." It is so indirect that many soldiers have refused to call it war at all. This is a matter as much of professional pride as of moral judgment. Consider the statement of a British admiral in World War II, protesting the terror bombing of German cities: "We are a hopelessly unmilitary nation to imagine that we [can] win the war by bombing German women and children instead of defeating their army and navy." The key word here is unmilitary. The admiral rightly sees terrorism as a civilian strategy. One might say that it represents the continuation of war by political means. Terrorizing ordinary men and women is first of all the work of domestic tyranny, as Aristotle wrote: "The first aim and end [of tyrants] is to break the spirit of their subjects." The British described the "aim and end" of terror bombing in the same way: what they sought was the destruction of civilian morale.

Tyrants taught the method to soldiers, and soldiers to modern revolutionaries. That is a crude history; I offer it only in order to make a more precise historical point: that terrorism in the strict sense, the random murder of innocent people, emerged as a strategy of revolutionary struggle only in the period after World War II, that is, only after it had become a feature of conventional war. In both cases, in war and revolution, a kind of warrior honor stood in the way of this development, especially among professional officers and "professional revolutionaries." The increasing use of terror by far left and ultranationalist movements represents the breakdown of a political code first worked out in the second half of the nineteenth century and roughly analogous to the laws of war worked out at the same time. Adherence to this code did not prevent revolutionary militants from being called terrorists, but in fact the violence they committed bore little resemblance to contemporary terrorism. It was not random murder but assassination, and it involved the drawing of a line that we will have little difficulty recognizing as the political parallel of the line that marks off combatants from noncombatants.

The Russian Populists, the IRA, and the Stern Gang

I can best describe the revolutionary "code of honor" by giving some examples of so-called terrorists who acted or tried to act in accordance with its norms. I have chosen three historical cases. The first will be readily recognizable, for Albert Camus made it the basis of his play *The Just Assassins*.

1) In the early twentieth century, a group of Russian revolutionaries decided to kill a Tsarist official, the Grand Duke Sergei, a man personally involved in the repression of radical activity. They planned to blow him up in his carriage, and on the appointed day one of their number was in place along the Grand Duke's usual route. As the carriage drew near, the young revolutionary, a bomb hidden under his coat, noticed that his victim was not alone; on his lap he held two small children. The would-be assassin looked, hesitated, then walked quickly away. He would wait for another occasion. Camus has one of his comrades say, accepting this decision: "Even in destruction, there's a right way and a wrong way—and there are limits."

2) During the years 1938–39, the Irish Republican Army waged a bombing campaign in Britain. In the course of this campaign, a republican militant was ordered to carry a pre-set time bomb to a Coventry power station. He traveled by bicycle, the bomb in his basket, took a wrong turn, and got lost in a maze of streets. As the time for the explosion drew near, he panicked, dropped his bike, and ran off. The bomb exploded, killing five passers-by. No one in the IRA (as it was then) thought this a victory for the cause; the men immediately involved were horrified. The campaign had been carefully planned, according to a recent historian, so as to avoid the killing of innocent bystanders.

3) In November 1944, Lord Moyne, British Minister of State in the Middle East, was assassinated in Cairo by two members of the Stern Gang, a right-wing Zionist group. The two assassins were caught, minutes later, by an Egyptian policeman. One of them described the capture at his trial: "We were being followed by the constable on his motorcycle. My comrade was behind me. I saw the constable approach him... I would have been able to kill the constable easily, but I contented myself with... shooting several times into the air. I saw my comrade fall off his bicycle. The constable was almost upon him. Again, I could have eliminated the constable with a single bullet, but I did not. Then I was caught."

What is common to these cases is a moral distinction, drawn by the "terrorists," between people who can and people who cannot be killed. The first category is not composed of men and women bearing arms, immediately threatening by virtue of their military training and commitment. It is composed instead of officials, the political agents of regimes thought to be oppressive. Such people, of course, are protected by the war convention and by positive international law. Characteristically (and not foolishly), lawyers have frowned on assassination, and political officials have been assigned to the class of nonmilitary persons, who are never the legitimate objects of attack. But this assignment only partially represents our common moral judgments. For we judge the assassin by his victim, and when the victim is Hitler-like in character, we are likely to praise the assassin's work, though we still do not call him a soldier. The second category is less problematic: ordinary citizens, not engaged in political harming—that is, in administering or enforcing laws thought to be unjust—are immune from attack whether or not they support those laws. Thus the aristocratic children, the Coventry pedestrians, even the Egyptian policeman (who had nothing to do with British imperialism in Palestine)—these people are like civilians in wartime. They are innocent politically as civilians are innocent militarily. It is precisely these people, however, that contemporary terrorists try to kill.

The war convention and the political code are structurally similar, and the distinction between officials and citizens parallels that between soldiers and civilians (though the two are not the same). What lies behind them both, I think, and lends them plausibility, is the moral difference between aiming and not aiming—or, more accurately, between aiming at particular people because of things they have done or are doing, and aiming at whole groups of people, indiscriminately, because of who they are. The first kind of aiming is appropriate to a limited struggle directed against regimes and policies. The second reaches beyond all limits; it is infinitely threatening to whole peoples, whose individual members are systematically exposed to violent death at any and every moment in the course of their (largely innocuous) lives. A bomb planted on a streetcorner, hidden in a bus station, thrown into a cafe or pub—this is aimless killing, except that the victims are likely to share what they cannot avoid, a collective identity. Since some of these victims must be immune from attack (unless liability follows from original sin), any code that directs and controls the fire of political militants is going to be at least minimally appealing. It is so much of an advance over the willful randomness of terrorist attacks. One might even feel easier about killing officials than about killing soldiers, since the state rarely conscripts its political, as it

does its military agents; they have chosen officialdom as a career.

Soldiers and officials are, however, different in another respect. The threatening character of the soldier's activities is a matter of fact; the unjust or oppressive character of the official's activities is a matter of political judgment. For this reason, the political code has never attained to the same status as the war convention. Nor can assassins claim any rights, even on the basis of the strictest adherence to its principles. In the eyes of those of us whose judgments of oppression and injustice differ from their own, political assassins are simply murderers, exactly like the killers of ordinary citizens. The case is not the same with soldiers, who are not judged politically at all and who are called murderers only when they kill noncombatants. Political killing imposes risks quite unlike those of combat, risks whose character is best revealed by the fact that there is no such thing as benevolent quarantine for the duration of the political struggle. Thus the young Russian revolutionary, who eventually killed the Grand Duke, was tried and executed for murder, as were the Stern Gang assassins of Lord Moyne. All three were treated exactly like the IRA militants, also captured, who were held responsible for the deaths of ordinary citizens. That treatment seems to me appropriate, even if we share the political judgments of the men involved and defend their resort to violence. On the other hand, even if we do not share their judgments, these men are entitled to a kind of moral respect not due to terrorists, because they set limits to their actions.

The Vietcong Assassination Campaign

The precise limits are hard to define, as in the case of noncombatant immunity. But we can perhaps move toward a definition by looking at a guerrilla war in which officials were attacked on a large scale. Beginning at some point in the late 1950's, the NLF waged a campaign aimed at destroying the governmental structure of the South Vietnamese countryside. Between 1960 and 1965, some 7,500 village and district officials were assassinated by

Vietcong militants. An American student of the Vietcong, describing these officials as the "natural leaders" of Vietnamese society, argues that "by any definition this NLF action... amounts to genocide." This assumes that all Vietnam's natural leaders were government officials (but then, who was leading the NLF?) and hence that government officials were literally indispensable to national existence. Since these assumptions are not remotely plausible, it has to be said that "by any definition" the killing of leaders is not the same as the destruction of entire peoples. Terrorism may foreshadow genocide, but assassination does not.

On the other hand, the NLF campaign did press against the limits of the notion of officialdom as I have been using it. The Front tended to include among officials anyone who was paid by the government, even if the work he was doing—as a public health officer, for example—had nothing to do with the particular policies the NLF opposed. And it tended to assimilate into officialdom people like priests and landowners who used their nongovernmental authority in specific ways on behalf of the government. They did not kill anyone, apparently, just because he was a priest or a landowner; the assassination campaign was planned with considerable attention to the details of individual action, and a concerted effort was made "to ensure that there were no unexplained killings." Still, the range of vulnerability was widened in disturbing ways.

One might argue, I suppose, that any official is by definition engaged in the political efforts of the (putatively) unjust regime, just as any soldier, whether he is actually fighting or not, is engaged in the war effort. But the variety of activities sponsored and paid for by the modern state is extraordinary, and it seems intemperate and extravagant to make all such activities into occasions for assassination. Assuming that the regime is in fact oppressive, one should look for agents of oppression and not simply for government agents. As for private persons, they seem to me immune entirely. They are subject, of course, to the conventional forms of social

and political pressure (which are conventionally intensified in guerrilla wars) but not to political violence. Here the case is the same with citizens as with civilians: if their support for the government or the war were allowable as a reason for killing them, the line that marks off immune from vulnerable persons would quickly disappear. It is worth stressing that political assassins generally don't want that line to disappear; they have reasons for taking careful aim and avoiding indiscriminate murder. "We were told," a Vietcong guerrilla reported to his American captors, "that in Singapore the rebels on certain days would dynamite every 67th streetcar... the next day it might be every 30th, and so on; but that this hardened the hearts of the people against the rebels because so many people died needlessly."

I have avoided noticing until now that most political militants don't regard themselves as assassins at all but rather as executioners. They are engaged, or so they regularly claim, in a revolutionary version of vigilante justice. This suggests another reason for killing only some officials and not others, but it is entirely a self-description. Vigilantes in the usual sense apply conventional conceptions of criminality, though in a rough and ready way. Revolutionaries champion a new conception, about which there is unlikely to be wide agreement. They hold that officials are vulnerable because or insofar as they are actually guilty of "crimes against the people." The more impersonal truth is that they are vulnerable, or more vulnerable than ordinary citizens, simply because their activities are open to such descriptions. The exercise of political power is a dangerous business. Saying this, I do not mean to defend assassination. It is most often a vile politics, as vigilante justice is most often a bad kind of law enforcement; its agents are usually gangsters, and sometimes madmen, in political dress. And yet "just assassinations" are at least possible, and men and women who aim at that kind of killing and renounce every other kind need to be marked off from those who kill at random—not as doers of justice, necessarily, for one can disagree about that, but as revolutionaries with honor. They do not want the revolution, as one of Camus' characters says, "to be loathed by the whole human race."

However the political code is specified, terrorism is the deliberate violation of its norms. For ordinary citizens are killed and no defense is offered—none could be offered—in terms of their individual activities. The names and occupations of the dead are not known in advance; they are killed simply to deliver a message of fear to others like themselves. What is the content of the message? I suppose it could be anything at all; but in practice terrorism, because it is directed against entire peoples or classes, tends to communicate the most extreme and brutal intentions—above all, the tyrannical repression, removal, or mass murder of the population under attack. Hence contemporary terrorist campaigns are most often focused on people whose national existence has been radically devalued: the Protestants of Northern Ireland, the Jews of Israel, and so on. The campaign announces the devaluation. That is why the people under attack are so unlikely to believe that compromise is possible with their enemies. In war, terrorism is associated with the demand for unconditional surrender and, in similar fashion, tends to rule out any sort of compromise settlement.

In its modern manifestations, terror is the totalitarian form of war and politics. It shatters the war convention and the political code. It breaks across moral limits beyond which no further limitation seems possible, for within the categories of civilian and citizen, there isn't any smaller group for which immunity might be claimed (except children; but I don't think children can be called "immune" if their parents are attacked and killed). Terrorists anyway make no such claim; they kill anybody. Despite this, terrorism has been defended, not only by the terrorists themselves, but also by philosophical apologists writing on their behalf. The political defenses mostly parallel those that are offered whenever soldiers attack civilians. They represent one or another version of the argument from military necessity. It is said, for example, that

there is no alternative to terrorist activity if oppressed peoples are to be liberated. And it is said, further, that this has always been so: terrorism is the only means and so it is the ordinary means of destroying oppressive regimes and founding new nations. The cases I have already worked through suggest the falsity of these assertions. Those who make them, I think, have lost their grip on the historical past; they suffer from a malign forgetfulness, erasing all moral distinctions along with the men and women who painfully worked them out.

Violence and Liberation

Jean-Paul Sartre and the Battle of Algiers

But there is another argument which, because of the currency it has gained, must be taken up here, even though it has no immediate analogue in wartime debates. It has been put forward in its starkest form by Sartre in a justification of FLN terrorism in Algeria, published as a preface to Franz Fanon's *The Wretched of the Earth*. The summary lines of Sartre's argument are these:

> To shoot down a European is to kill two birds with one stone, to destroy an oppressor and the mass he oppresses at the same time: there remains a dead man and a free man.

In his usual fashion, with a certain zest for Hegelian melodrama, Sartre is here describing what he takes to be an act of psychological liberation. Only when the slave turns on his master, physically confronts him and kills him, does he create himself as a free human being. The master dies; the slave is reborn. Even if this were a believable picture of the terrorist act, the argument is not persuasive; it is open to two obvious and crippling questions. First, is the one-to-one relation necessary? Did it take one dead European to make one free Algerian? If so, there were not enough Europeans living in Algeria; more would have had to be brought over if the Algerian people were to free themselves by Sartrean means. If not, it must follow that some one else besides the man-who-kills can be liberated.... How? By watching? By reading about the murder in the newspaper? It is hard to see how vicarious experience can play an important part in a process of personal liberation (as described by an existentialist philosopher).

The second question raises more familiar issues: will any European do? Unless Sartre thinks all Europeans, including children, are oppressors, he cannot believe that. But if it is only liberating to attack and kill an agent of oppression, we are back with the political code. From Sartre's perspective, that cannot be right, since the men and women he is defending had explicitly rejected that code. They killed Europeans at random, as in the well-known scene from the (historically accurate) film *The Battle of Algiers*, in which a bomb is set off in a milk bar where French teenagers are drinking and dancing.

MILK BAR. EXPLOSION.
OUTSIDE. DAY.

The jukebox is flung into the middle of the street. There is blood, strips of flesh, material... the white smoke and shouts, weeping, hysterical girls' screams. One of them no longer has an arm and runs around howling despairingly; it is impossible to control her... The sound of sirens is heard... The ambulances arrive....

Such an event is not easily reconstructed as an existentialist encounter between masters and slaves.

Certainly, there are historical moments when armed struggle is necessary for the sake of human freedom. But if dignity and self-respect are to be the outcomes of that struggle, it cannot consist of terrorist attacks upon children. One can argue that such attacks are the inevitable products of oppression, and in a sense, I suppose, that is right. Hatred, fear, and the lust for domination are the psychological marks of oppressed and oppressor alike, and their acting out, on either side, can be said to be radically determined. The mark of a revolutionary struggle against oppression, however, is not this incapacitating rage and random violence, but restraint and self-control. The revolutionary reveals his freedom in the same way as he earns it, by directly confronting his enemies and refraining from attacks on anyone else. It was not only to save the innocent that revolutionary militants worked out the distinction between officials and ordinary citizens, but also to save themselves from killing the innocent. Whatever its strategic value, the political code is intrinsically connected to psychological liberation. Among men and women trapped in a bloody struggle, it is the key to self-respect. The same thing can be said of the war convention: in the context of a terrible coerciveness, soldiers most clearly assert their freedom when they obey the moral law.

NOTE

1. The numbered footnotes from the original essay have been removed.

Pre-Emptive Strikes[1]

MICHAEL WALZER

Michael Walzer is professor in the School of Social Science, Institute for Advanced Study at Princeton University in New Jersey.

From Just and Unjust Wars: A Moral Argument with Historical Illustration, *by Michael Walzer. Copyright © 1977 by Basic Books. Reprinted by permission of Basic Books, a member of Perseus Books, L.L.C.*

Pre-emptive Strikes

....Now, what acts are to count, what acts do count as threats sufficiently serious to justify war? It is not possible to put together a list, because state action, like human action generally, takes on significance from its context. But there are some negative points worth making. The boastful ranting to which political leaders are often prone isn't in itself threatening; injury must be "offered" in some material sense as well. Nor does the kind of military preparation that is a feature of the classic arms race count as a threat, unless it violates some formally or tacitly agreed-upon limit. What the lawyers call "hostile acts short of war," even if these involve violence, are not too quickly to be taken as signs of an intent to make war; they may represent an essay in restraint, an offer to quarrel within limits. Finally, provocations are not the same as threats. "Injury and provocation" are commonly linked by Scholastic writers as the two causes of just war. But the Schoolmen were too accepting of contemporary notions about the honor of states and, more importantly, of sovereigns. The moral significance of such ideas is dubious at best. Insults are not occasions for wars, any more than they are (these days) occasions for duels.

For the rest, military alliances, mobilizations, troop movements, border incursions, naval blockades—all these, with or without verbal menace, sometimes count and sometimes do not count as sufficient indications of hostile intent. But it is, at least, these sorts of actions with which we are concerned. We move along the anticipation spectrum in search, as it were, of enemies: not possible or potential enemies, not merely present ill-wishers, but states and nations that are already, to use a phrase I shall use again with reference to the distinction of combatants and noncombatants, *engaged in harming us* (and who have already harmed us, by their threats, even if they have not yet inflicted any physical injury). And this search, though it carries us beyond preventive war, clearly brings us up short of Webster's pre-emption. The line between legitimate and illegitimate first strikes is not going to be drawn at the point of imminent attack but at the point of sufficient threat. That phrase is necessarily vague. I mean it to cover three things: a manifest intent to injure, a degree of active preparation that makes that intent a positive danger, and a general situation in which waiting, or doing anything other than fighting, greatly magnifies the risk. The argument may be

made more clear if I compare these criteria to Vattel's. Instead of previous signs of rapacity and ambition, current and particular signs are required; instead of an "augmentation of power," actual preparation for war; instead of the refusal of future securities, the intensification of present dangers. Preventive war looks to the past and future, Webster's reflex action to the immediate moment, while the idea of being under a threat focuses on what we had best call simply the present. I cannot specify a time span; it is a span within which one can still make choices, and within which it is possible to feel straitened.

What such a time is like is best revealed concretely. We can study it in the three weeks that preceded the Six Day War of 1967. Here is a case as crucial for an understanding of anticipation in the twentieth century as the War of the Spanish Succession was for the eighteenth, and one suggesting that the shift from dynastic to national politics, the costs of which have so often been stressed, has also brought some moral gains. For nations, especially democratic nations, are less likely to fight preventive wars than dynasties are.

The Six Day War

Actual fighting between Israel and Egypt began on June 5, 1967, with an Israeli first strike. In the early hours of the war, the Israelis did not acknowledge that they had sought the advantages of surprise, but the deception was not maintained. In fact, they believed themselves justified in attacking first by the dramatic events of the previous weeks. So we must focus on those events and their moral significance. It would be possible, of course, to look further back still, to the whole course of the Arab-Jewish conflict in the Middle East. Wars undoubtedly have long political and moral prehistories. But anticipation needs to be understood within a narrower frame. The Egyptians believed that the founding of Israel in 1948 had been unjust, that the state had no rightful existence, and hence that it could be attacked at any time. It follows from this that Israel had no right of anticipation since it had no right of self-defense. But self-defense seems the primary and indisputable right of any political community, merely because it is *there* and whatever the circumstances under which it achieved statehood. Perhaps this is why the Egyptians fell back in their more formal arguments upon the claim that a state of war already existed between Egypt and Israel and that this condition justified the military moves they undertook in May 1967. But the same condition would justify Israel's first strike. It is best to assume, I think, that the existing cease-fire between the two countries was at least a near-peace and that the outbreak of the war requires a moral explanation—the burden falling on the Israelis, who began the fighting.

The crisis apparently had its origins in reports, circulated by Soviet officials in mid-May, that Israel was massing its forces on the Syrian border. The falsity of these reports was almost immediately vouched for by United Nations observers on the scene. Nevertheless, on May 14, the Egyptian government put its armed forces on "maximum alert" and began a major buildup of its troops in the Sinai. Four days later, Egypt expelled the United Nations Emergency Force from the Sinai and the Gaza Strip; its withdrawal began immediately, though I do not think that its title had been intended to suggest that it would depart so quickly in event of emergency. The Egyptian military buildup continued, and on May 22, President Nasser announced that the Straits of Tiran would henceforth be closed to Israeli shipping.

In the aftermath of the Suez War of 1956, the Straits had been recognized by the world community as an international waterway. That meant that their closing would constitute a *casus belli*, and the Israelis had stated at that time, and on many occasions since, that they would so regard it. The war might then be dated from May 22, and the Israeli attack of June 5 described simply as its first military incident: wars often begin before the fighting of them does. But the fact is that after May 22, the Israeli cabinet was still debating whether or not to go to war. And, in any case, the actual initiation of violence is a crucial moral event. If it can sometimes be justified by reference to previous events, it nevertheless has to be justified. In a major speech on May 29, Nasser made that jus-

tification much easier by announcing that if war came the Egyptian goal would be nothing less than the destruction of Israel. On May 30, King Hussein of Jordan flew to Cairo to sign a treaty placing the Jordanian army under Egyptian command in event of war, thus associating himself with the Egyptian purpose. Syria already had agreed to such an arrangement, and several days later Iraq joined the alliance. The Israelis struck on the day after the Iraqi announcement.

For all the excitement and fear that their actions generated, it is unlikely that the Egyptians intended to begin the war themselves. After the fighting was over, Israel published documents, captured in its course, that included plans for an invasion of the Negev; but these were probably plans for a counter-attack, once an Israeli offensive had spent itself in the Sinai, or for a first strike at some later time. Nasser would almost certainly have regarded it as a great victory if he could have closed the Straits and maintained his army on Israel's borders without war. Indeed, it would have been a great victory, not only because of the economic blockade it would have established, but also because of the strain it would have placed on the Israeli defense system. "There was a basic asymmetry in the structure of forces: the Egyptians could deploy... their large army of long-term regulars on the Israeli border and keep it there indefinitely; the Israelis could only counter their deployment by mobilizing reserve formations, and reservists could not be kept in uniform for very long... Egypt could therefore stay on the defensive while Israel would have to attack unless the crisis was defused diplomatically." *Would have to attack:* the necessity cannot be called instant and overwhelming; nor, however, would an Israeli decision to allow Nasser his victory have meant nothing more than a shift in the balance of power posing possible dangers at some future time. It would have opened Israel to attack at any time. It would have represented a drastic erosion of Israeli security such as only a determined enemy would hope to bring about.

The initial Israeli response was not similarly determined but, for domestic political reasons having to do in part with the democratic character of the state, hesitant and confused. Israel's leaders sought a political resolution of the crisis—the opening of the Straits and a demobilization of forces on both sides—which they did not have the political strength or support to effect. A flurry of diplomatic activity ensued, serving only to reveal what might have been predicted in advance: the unwillingness of the Western power to pressure or coerce the Egyptians. One always wants to see diplomacy tried before the resort to war, so that we are sure that war is the last resort. But it would be difficult in this case to make an argument for its necessity. Day by day, diplomatic efforts seemed only to intensify Israel's isolation.

Meanwhile, "an intense fear spread in the country." The extraordinary Israeli triumph, once fighting began, makes it difficult to recall the preceding weeks of anxiety. Egypt was in the grip of a war fever, familiar enough from European history, a celebration in advance of expected victories. The Israeli mood was very different, suggesting what it means to live under threat: rumors of coming disasters were endlessly repeated; frightened men and women raided food shops, buying up their entire stock, despite government announcements that there were ample reserves; thousands of graves were dug in the military cemeteries; Israel's political and military leaders lived on the edge of nervous exhaustion. I have already argued that fear by itself establishes no right of anticipation. But Israeli anxiety during those weeks seems an almost classical example of "just fear"—first, because Israel really was in danger (as foreign observers readily agreed), and second, because it was Nasser's intention to put it in danger. He said this often enough, but it is also and more importantly true that his military moves served no other, more limited goal.

The Israeli first strike is, I think, a clear case of legitimate anticipation. To say that, however, is to suggest a major revision of the legalist paradigm. For it means that aggression can be made out not only in the absence of a military attack or invasion but in the (probable) absence of any im-

mediate intention to launch such an attack or invasion. The general formula must go something like this: states may use military force in the face of threats of war, whenever the failure to do so would seriously risk their territorial integrity or political independence. Under such circumstances it can fairly be said that they have been forced to fight and that they are the victims of aggression. Since there are no police upon whom they can call, the moment at which states are forced to fight probably comes sooner than it would for individuals in a settled domestic society. But if we imagine an unstable society, like the "wild west" of American fiction, the analogy can be restated: a state under threat is like an individual hunted by an enemy who has announced his intention of killing or injuring him. Surely such a person may surprise his hunter, if he is able to do so.

The formula is permissive, but it implies restrictions that can usefully be unpacked only with reference to particular cases. It is obvious, for example, that measures short of war are preferable to war itself whenever they hold out the hope of similar or nearly similar effectiveness. But what those measures might be, or how long they must be tried, cannot be a matter of *a priori* stipulation. In the case of the Six Day War, the "asymmetry in the structure of forces" set a time limit on diplomatic efforts that would have no relevance to conflicts involving other sorts of states and armies. A general rule containing words like "seriously" opens a broad path for human judgment—which it is, no doubt, the purpose of the legalist paradigm to narrow or block altogether. But it is a fact of our moral life that political leaders make such judgments, and that once they are made the rest of us do not uniformly condemn them. Rather, we weigh and evaluate their actions on the basis of criteria like those I have tried to describe. When we do that we are acknowledging that there are threats with which no nation can be expected to live. And that acknowledgment is an important part of our understanding of aggression.

NOTE

1. The numbered footnotes from the original essay have been removed.

Killing and Starving to Death

JAMES RACHELS

From Philosophy, *Vol. 54, No. 208 (April 1979). Reprinted with the permission of Cambridge University Press.*

Although we do not know exactly how many people die each year of malnutrition or related health problems, the number is very high, in the millions.[1] By giving money to support famine relief efforts, each of us could save at least some of them. By not giving, we let them die.

Some philosophers have argued that letting people die is not as bad as killing them, because in general our "positive duty" to give aid is weaker than our "negative duty" not to do harm.[2] I maintain the opposite: letting die is just as bad as killing.[3] At first this may seem wildly implausible. When reminded that people are dying of starvation while we spend money on trivial things, we may feel a bit guilty, but certainly we do not feel like murderers. Philippa Foot writes:

> Most of us allow people to die of starvation in India and Africa, and there is surely something wrong with us that we do; it would be nonsense, however, to pretend that it is only in law that we make a distinction between allowing people in the underdeveloped countries to die of starvation and sending them poisoned food. There is worked into our moral system a distinction between what we owe people in the form of aid and what we owe them in the way of noninterference.[4]

No doubt this would be correct if it were intended only as a description of what most people believe. Whether this feature of "our moral system" is rationally defensible is, however, another matter. I shall argue that we are wrong to take comfort in the fact that we "only" let these people die, because our duty not to let them die is equally as strong as our duty not to kill them, which, of course, is very strong indeed.

Obviously, this Equivalence Thesis is not morally neutral, as philosophical claims about ethics often are. It is a radical idea which, if true, would mean that some of our "intuitions" (our prereflective beliefs about what is right and wrong in particular cases) are mistaken and must be rejected. Neither is the view I oppose morally neutral. The idea that killing is worse than letting die is a relatively conservative thesis which would allow those same intuitions to be preserved. However, the Equivalence Thesis should not be dismissed merely because it does not conform to all our prereflective intuitions. Rather than being perceptions of the truth, our "intuitions" might sometimes signify nothing more than our prejudices or selfishness or cultural conditioning. Philosophers often admit that, in theory at least, some intuitions might be unreliable—but usually this possibility is not taken seriously, and conformity to prereflective intuition is used uncritically as a test of the acceptability of moral theory. In what follows I shall argue that many of our intuitions concerning killing and letting die *are* mistaken, and should not be trusted.

I

We think that killing is worse than letting die, not because we overestimate how bad it is to kill, but because we underestimate how bad it is to let die. The following chain of reasoning is intended to show that letting people in foreign countries die of starvation is very much worse than we commonly assume.

Suppose there were a starving child in the room where you are now—hollow eyed, belly bloated, and so on—and you have a sandwich at your elbow that you don't need. Of course you would be horrified; you would stop reading and give her the sandwich, or better, take her to a hospital. And you would not think this an act of supererogation: you would not expect any special praise for it, and you would expect criticism if you did not do it. Imagine what you would think of someone who simply ignored the child and continued reading, allowing her to die of starvation. Let us call the person who would do this Jack Palance, after the very nice man who plays such vile characters in the movies. Jack Palance indifferently watches the starving child die; he cannot be bothered even to hand her the sandwich. There is ample reason for judging him very harshly; without putting too fine a point on it, he shows himself to be a moral monster.

When we allow people in far-away countries to die of starvation, we may think, as Mrs. Foot puts it, that "there is surely something wrong with us." But we most emphatically do not consider ourselves moral monsters. We think this, in spite of the striking similarity between Jack Palance's behavior and our own. He could easily save the child; he does not; and the child dies. We could easily save some of those starving people; we do not; and they die. If we are not monsters, there must be some important difference between him and us. But what is it?

One obvious difference between Jack Palance's position and ours is that the person he lets die is in the same room with him, while the people we let die are mostly far away. Yet the spatial location of the dying people hardly seems a relevant consideration.[5] It is absurd to suppose that being located at a certain map coordinate entitles one to treatment which one would not merit if situated at a different longitude or latitude. Of course, if a dying person's location meant that we *could not* help, that would excuse us. But, since there are efficient famine relief agencies willing to carry our aid to the far-away countries, this excuse is not available. It would be almost as easy for us to send these agencies the price of the sandwich as for Palance to hand the sandwich to the child.

The location of the starving people does make a difference, psychologically, in how we feel. If there were a starving child in the same room with us, we could not avoid realizing, in a vivid and disturbing way, how it is suffering and that it is about to die. Faced with this realization our consciences probably would not allow us to ignore the child. But if the dying are far away, it is easy to think of them only abstractly, or to put them out of our thoughts altogether. This might explain why our conduct would be different if we were in Jack Palance's position even though, from a moral point of view, the location of the dying is not relevant.

There are other differences between Jack Palance and us, which may seem important, having to do with the sheer numbers of people, both affluent and starving, that surround us. In our fictitious example Jack Palance is one person, confronted by the need of one other person. This makes his position relatively simple. In the real world our position is more complicated, in two ways: first, in that there are millions of people who need feeding, and none of us has the resources to care for all of them; and second, in that for any starving person we *could* help there are millions of other affluent people who could help as easily as we.

On the first point, not much needs to be said. We may feel, in a vague sort of way, that we are not monsters because no one of us could possibly save *all* the starving people—there are just too many of them, and none of us has the resources. This is fair enough, but all that follows is that, individually, none of us is responsible for saving everyone. We may still be responsible for saving someone, or as many as we can. This is so obvious that it hardly bears mentioning; yet it is easy to lose sight of, and philosophers have actually lost sight of it. In his article "Saving Life and Taking Life,"[6] Richard Trammell says that one morally important difference between killing and letting die is "dischargeability." By this he means that, while each of us can discharge completely a duty not to kill anyone, no one among us can discharge completely a duty to save everyone who needs it. Again, fair enough; but all that follows is that, since we are only bound to save those we can, the class of people that we have an obligation to save is much smaller than the class of people we have an obligation not to kill. It does *not* follow that our duty with respect to those we can save is any less stringent. Suppose Jack Palance were to say: "I needn't give this starving child the sandwich because, after all, I can't save everyone in the world who needs it." If this excuse will not work for him, neither will it work for us with respect to the children we could save in India or Africa.

The second point about numbers was that, for any starving person we *could* help, there are millions of other affluent people who could help as easily as we. Some are in an even better position to help since they are richer. But by and large these people are doing nothing. This also helps to explain why we do not feel especially guilty for letting people starve. How guilty we feel about something depends, to some extent, on how we compare with those around us. If we were surrounded by people who regularly sacrificed to feed the starving, and we did not, we would probably feel ashamed. But because our neighbors do not do any better than we, we are not so ashamed.

But again, this does not imply that we should not feel more guilty or ashamed than we do. A psychological explanation of our feelings is not a moral justification of our conduct. Suppose Jack Palance were only one of twenty people who watched the child die; would that decrease his guilt? Curiously, I think many people assume it would. Many people seem to feel that if twenty people do nothing to prevent a tragedy, each of them is only one-twentieth as guilty as he would have been if he had watched the tragedy alone. It is as though there is only a fixed amount of guilt which divides. I suggest, rather, that guilt multiplies, so that each passive viewer is fully guilty, if he could have prevented the tragedy but did not. Jack Palance watching the girl die alone would be a moral monster; but if he calls in a group of his friends to watch with him, he does not diminish his guilt by dividing it among them. Instead, they are all moral monsters. Once the point is made explicit, it seems obvious.

The fact that most other affluent people do nothing to relieve hunger may very well have implications for one's own obligations. But the implication may be that one's own obligations *increase* rather than decrease. Suppose Palance and a friend were faced with two starving children, so that, if each did his "fair share," Palance would only have to feed one of them. But the friend will do nothing. Because he is well-off, Palance could feed both of them. Should he not? What if he fed one and then watched the other die, announcing that he has done *his* duty and that the one who died was his friend's responsibility? This shows the fallacy of supposing that one's duty is only to do one's fair share, where

this is determined by what would be sufficient *if* everyone else did likewise.

To summarize: Jack Palance, who refuses to hand a sandwich to a starving child, is a moral monster. But we feel intuitively that we are not so monstrous, even though we also let starving children die when we could feed them almost as easily. If this intuition is correct, there must be some important difference between him and us. But when we examine the most obvious differences between his conduct and ours—the location of the dying, the differences in numbers—we find no real basis for judging ourselves less harshly than we judge him. Perhaps there are some other grounds on which we might distinguish our moral position, with respect to actual starving people, from Jack Palance's position with respect to the child in my story. But I cannot think of what they might be. Therefore, I conclude that if he is a monster, then so are we—or at least, so are we after our rationalizations and thoughtlessness have been exposed.

This last qualification is important. We judge people, at least in part, according to whether they can be expected to realize how well or how badly they behave. We judge Palance harshly because the consequences of his indifference are so immediately apparent. By contrast, it requires an unusual effort for us to realize the consequences of our indifference. It is normal behavior for people in the affluent countries not to give to famine relief, or if they do give, to give very little. Decent people may go along with this normal behavior pattern unthinkingly, without realizing, or without comprehending in a clear way, just what this means for the starving. Thus, even though those decent people may act monstrously, we do not judge them monsters. There is a curious sense, then, in which moral reflection can transform decent people into indecent ones: for if a person thinks things through, and realizes that he is, morally speaking, in Jack Palance's position, his continued indifference is more blameworthy than before.

The preceding is not intended to prove that letting people die of starvation is as bad as killing them. But it does provide strong evidence that letting die is much worse than we normally assume, and so that letting die is much *closer* to killing than we normally assume. These reflections also go some way towards showing just how fragile and unreliable our intuitions are in this area. They suggest that, if we want to discover the truth, we are better off looking at arguments that do not rely on unexamined intuitions.

II

Before arguing that the Equivalence Thesis is true, let me explain more precisely what I mean by it. I take it to be a claim about what does, nor does not, count as a morally good reason in support of a value judgment: the bare fact that one act is an act of killing, while another act is an act of "merely" letting someone die, is not a morally good reason in support of the judgment that the former is worse than the latter. Of course there may be *other* differences between such acts that are morally significant. For example, the family of an irreversibly comatose hospital patient may want their loved one to be allowed to die, but not killed. Perhaps the reason for their preference is religious. So we have at least one reason to let the patient die rather than to kill him—the reason is that the family prefers it that way. This does not mean, however, that the distinction between killing and letting die *itself* is important. What is important is respecting the family's wishes. (It is often right to respect people's wishes even if we think those wishes are based on false beliefs.) In another sort of case, a patient with a painful terminal illness may want to be killed rather than allowed to die because a slow, lingering death would be agonizing. Here we have a reason to kill and not let die, but once again the reason is not that one course is intrinsically preferable to the other. The reason is, rather, that the latter course would lead to more suffering.

It should be clear, then, that I will *not* be arguing that every act of letting die is equally as bad as every act of killing. There are lots of reasons why a particular act of killing may be morally worse than a particular act of letting die, or vice versa. If a healthy person is murdered, from a ma-

licious motive, while a person in irreversible coma is allowed to die upon a calm judgment that maintaining him alive is pointless, certainly this killing is very much worse than this letting die. Similarly, if an ill person who could be saved is maliciously allowed to die, while a terminal patient is killed, upon his request, as an act of kindness, we have good reason to judge the letting die worse than the killing. All that I want to argue is that, whatever reasons there may be for judging one act worse than another, the simple fact that one is killing, whereas the other is only letting die, is not among them.

The first stage of the argument is concerned with some formal relations between moral judgments and the reasons that support them. I take it to be a point of logic that moral judgments are true only if good reasons support them; for example, if there is no good reason why you ought to do some action, it cannot be true that you ought to do it. Moreover, when there is a choice to be made from among several possible actions, the preferable alternative is the one that is backed by the strongest reasons.

But when are the reasons for or against one act stronger than those for or against another act? A complete answer would have to include some normative theory explaining why some reasons are intrinsically weightier than others. Suppose you are in a situation in which you can save someone's life only by lying: the normative theory would explain why "Doing *A* would save someone's life" is a stronger reason in favor of doing *A* than "Doing *B* would be telling the truth" is in favor of doing *B*.

However, there are also some purely formal principles that operate here. The simplest and least controversial such principle is this:

(1) If there are the *same* reasons for or against *A* as for or against *B*, then the reasons in favor of *A* are neither stronger nor weaker than the reasons in favor of *B*; and so *A* and *B* are morally equivalent—neither is preferable to the other.

Now, suppose we ask why killing is morally objectionable. When someone is killed, there may of course be harmful effects for people other than the victim himself. Those who loved him may grieve, and those who were depending on him in one way or another may be caused hardship because, being dead, he will be unable to perform as expected. However, we cannot explain the wrongness of killing purely, or even mainly, in terms of the bad effects for the survivors. The primary reason why killing is wrong is that something very bad is done to the victim himself: he ends up dead; he no longer has a good—his life—which he possessed before. But notice that exactly the same can be said about letting someone die. The primary reason why it is morally objectionable to let someone die, when we could save him, is that he ends up dead; he no longer has a good—his life— which he possessed before. Secondary reasons again have to do with harmful effects on those who survive. Thus, the explanation of why killing is bad mentions features of killing that are also features of letting die, and vice versa. Since there are no comparably general reasons in favor of either, this suggests that:

(2) There are the same reasons for and against letting die as for and against killing. And if this is true, we get the conclusion:

(3) Therefore, killing and letting die are morally equivalent—neither is preferable to the other.

The central idea of this argument is that there is no morally relevant difference between killing and letting die, that is, no difference which may be cited to show that one is worse than the other. The argument therefore contains a premise—(2)—that is supported only inductively. The fact that the explanation of why killing is wrong applies equally well to letting die, and vice versa, provides strong evidence that the inductive generalization is true. Nevertheless, no matter how carefully we analyze the matter, it will always be possible that there is some subtle, morally relevant difference between the two that we have overlooked. In fact, philosophers who believe that killing is worse than letting die have sometimes tried to identify such differences. I believe that these attempts have failed; here are three examples:

1. The first is one that I have already mentioned. Trammell urges that there is an important difference in the "dischargeability" of duties not to kill and not to let die. We can completely discharge a duty not to kill anyone; but we cannot completely discharge a duty to save everyone who needs aid. This is obviously correct, but it does not show that the Equivalence Thesis is false, for two reasons. In the first place, the difference in dischargeability only shows that the class of people we have a duty to save is smaller than the class of people we have a duty not to kill. It does not show that our duty with respect to those we *can* save is any less stringent. In the second place, if we *cannot* save someone, and that person dies, then we do not let him die. It is not right to say that I let Josef Stalin die, for example, since there is no way I could have saved him. So if I cannot save everyone, then neither can I let everyone die.

2. It has also been urged that, in killing someone, we are *doing* something—namely, killing him—whereas, in letting someone die, we are not doing anything. In letting people die of starvation, for example, we only *fail* to do certain things, such as sending food. The difference is between action and inaction; and somehow, this is supposed to make a moral difference.[7]

There are also two difficulties with this suggestion. First, it is misleading to say, without further ado, that in letting someone die we do nothing. For there is one very important thing that we do: we let someone die. "Letting someone die" is different, in some ways, from other sorts of actions, mainly in that it is an action we perform *by way of* not performing other actions. We may let someone die by way of not feeding him, just as we may insult someone by way of not shaking his hand. (If it is said, "I didn't do anything; I simply refrained from taking his hand when he offered it," it may be replied "You did do one thing—you insulted him.") The distinction between action and inaction is relative to a specification of *what* actions are or are not done. In insulting someone, we may *not* smile, speak, shake hands, and so on—but we *do* insult or snub the person. And in letting someone die, the following may be among the things that are not done: we do not feed the person, we do not give medication, and so on. But the following is among the things that are done: we let him die.

Second, even if letting die were only a case of inaction, why should any moral conclusion follow from *that* fact? It may seem that a significant conclusion follows if we assume that we are not responsible for inactions. However, there is no general correlation between the action-inaction distinction and any sort of moral assessment. We ought to do some things, and we ought to not do others, and we can certainly be morally blameworthy for not doing things as well as for doing them—Jack Palance was blameworthy for not feeding the child. (In many circumstances we are even legally liable for not doing things: tax fraud may involve only "inaction"—failing to report certain things to the Department of Internal Revenue—but what of it?) Moreover, failing to act can be subject to all the other kinds of moral assessment. Not doing something may, depending on the circumstances, be right, wrong, obligatory, wise, foolish, compassionate, sadistic, and so on. Since there is no general correlation between the action-inaction distinction and *any* of these matters, it is hard to see how anything could be made out of this distinction in the present context.

3. My final example is from Trammell again. He argues that "optionality" is a morally relevant difference between killing and letting die. The point here is that if we fail to save someone, we leave open the option for someone else to save him; whereas if we kill, the victim is dead and that is that. This point, I think, has little significance. For one thing, while "optionality" may mark a difference between killing and *failing to save*, it does not mark a comparable difference between killing and *letting die*. If X fails to save Y, it does not follow that Y dies; someone else may come along and save him. But if X lets Y die, it does follow that Y dies; Y is dead and that is that.[8] When Palance watches the child die, he does not merely fail to save the child; he lets her die. And when we fail to send food to the starving, and they die, we let them die—we do not merely fail to save them.

The importance of "optionality" in any particular case depends on the actual chances of someone else's saving the person we do not save. Perhaps it is not so bad not to save someone if we know that someone else *will* save him. (Although even here, we do not behave as we ought; for we ought not simply to leave what needs doing to others.) And perhaps it even gets us off the hook a little if there is the *strong chance* that someone else will step in. But in the case of the world's starving, we know very well that no person or group of persons is going to come along tomorrow and save all of them. We know that there are at least some people who will *not* be saved, if we do not save them. So, as an excuse for not giving aid to the starving, the "optionality" argument is clearly in bad faith. To say of those people, after they are dead, that someone else *might* have saved them, in the very weak sense in which that will be true, does not excuse us at all. The others who might have saved them, but did not, are as guilty as we, but that does not diminish our guilt—as I have already remarked, guilt in these cases multiplies, not divides.

III

I need now to say a few more things about the counterintuitive nature of the Equivalence Thesis.

The fact that this view has radical implications for conduct has been cited as a reason for rejecting it. Trammell complains that "Denial of the distinction between negative and positive duties leads straight to an ethic so strenuous that it might give pause even to a philosophical John the Baptist."[9] Suppose John is about to buy a phonograph record, purely for his enjoyment, when he is reminded that with this five dollars a starving person could be fed. On the view I am defending, he ought to give the money to feed the hungry person. This may not seem exceptional until we notice that the reasoning is reiterable. Having given the first five dollars, John is not free to use another five to buy the record. For the poor are always with him: there is always *another* starving person to be fed, and then another, and then another. "The problem," Trammell says, "is that, even though fulfillment of one particular act of aid involves only minimal effort, it sets a precedent for millions of such efforts."[10] So we reach the bizarre conclusion that it is almost always immoral to buy phonograph records! And the same goes for fancy clothes, cars, toys, and so on.

This sort of *reductio* argument is of course familiar in philosophy. Such arguments may be divided into three categories. The strongest sort shows that a theory entails a contradiction, and, since contradictions cannot be tolerated, the theory must be modified or rejected. Such arguments, when valid, are of course devastating. Second, an argument may show that a theory has a consequence which, while not inconsistent, is nevertheless demonstrably false—that is, an independent proof can be given that the offensive consequence is unacceptable. Arguments of this second type, while not quite so impressive as the first, can still be irresistible. The third type of *reductio* is markedly weaker than the others. Here, it is merely urged that some consequence of a theory is counterintuitive. The supposedly embarrassing consequence is perfectly consistent, and there is no proof that it is false; the complaint is only that it goes against our unreflective, pretheoretical beliefs. Now sometimes even this weak sort of argument can be effective, especially when we have not much confidence in the theory, or when our confidence in the pretheoretical belief is unaffected by the reasoning which supports the theory. However, it may happen that *the same reasoning which leads one to accept a theory also persuades one that the pretheoretical beliefs were wrong.* (If this did not happen, philosophy would always be in the service of what we already think; it could never challenge and change our beliefs, and would be, in an important sense, useless.) The present case, it seems to me, is an instance of this type. The same reasoning which leads to the view that we are as wicked as Jack Palance, and that killing is no worse than letting die, also persuades (me, at least) that the prereflective belief in the rightness of our affluent life-style is mistaken.[11]

So, I want to say about all this what H. P. Grice once said at a conference when someone objected that his theory of meaning had an unacceptable implication. Referring to the suppos-

edly embarrassing consequence, Grice said, "See here, that's not an *objection* to my theory—*that's* my theory!"[12] Grice not only accepted the implication, he claimed it as an integral part of what he wanted to say. Similarly, the realization that we are morally wrong to spend money on inessentials, when that money could go to feed the starving, is an integral part of the view I am defending. It is not an embarrassing consequence of the view; it is (part of) the view itself.

There is another way in which the counterintuitive nature of the Equivalence Thesis may be brought out. It follows from that thesis that if the *only* difference between a pair of acts is that one is killing, while the other is letting die, those actions are equally good or bad—neither is preferable to the other. Defenders of the distinction between positive and negative duties have pointed out that in such cases our intuitions often tell us just the opposite: killing seems obviously worse. Here is an example produced by Daniel Dinello:

> Jones and Smith are in a hospital. Jones cannot live longer than two hours unless he gets a heart transplant. Smith, who has had one kidney removed, is dying of an infection in the other kidney. If he does not get a kidney transplant, he will die in about four hours. When Jones dies, his one good kidney can be transplanted to Smith, or Smith could be killed and his heart transplanted to Jones... it seems clear that it would, in fact, be wrong to kill Smith and save Jones rather than letting Jones die and saving Smith.[13]

And another from Trammell:

> If someone threatened to steal $1000 from a person if he did not take a gun and shoot a stranger between the eyes, it would be very wrong for him to kill the stranger to save his $1000. But if someone asked from that person $1000 to save a stranger, it would seem that his obligation to grant this request would not be as great as his obligation to refuse the first demand—even if he has good reason for believing that without his $1000 the stranger would certainly die.... In this par-

ticular example, it seems plausible to say that a person has a greater obligation to refrain from killing someone, even though the effort required of him ($1000) and his motivation toward the stranger be assumed identical in both cases.[14]

The conclusion we are invited to draw from these examples is that, contrary to what I have been arguing, the bare difference between killing and letting die *must be* morally significant.

Now Dinello's example is badly flawed, since the choice before the doctor is not a choice between killing and letting die at all. If the doctor kills Smith in order to transplant his heart to Jones, he will have killed Smith. But if he waits until Jones dies, and then transfers the kidney to Smith, he will *not* have "let Jones die." The reason is connected with the fact that not every case of not saving someone is a case of letting him die. (Josef Stalin died, and I did not save him, but I did not let Stalin die.) Dinello himself points out that, in order for it to be true that X lets Y die, X must be "in a position" to save Y, but not do so.[15] (I was never in a position to save Stalin.) Now the doctor is in a position to save Jones only if there is heart available for transplantation. But no such heart is available—Smith's heart, for example, is not available since Smith is still using it. Therefore, since the doctor is not in a position to save Jones, he does not let Jones die.[16]

Trammell's position is not quite so easy to dismiss. Initially, I share the intuition that it would be worse to kill someone to prevent $1000 from being stolen than to refuse to pay $1000 to save someone. Yet on reflection I have not much confidence in this feeling. What is at stake in this situation described is the person's $1000 and the stranger's life. But we end up with the *same* combination of lives and money, no matter which option the person chooses: if he shoots the stranger, the stranger dies and he keeps his $1000; and if he refuses to pay to save the stranger, the stranger dies and he keeps his $1000. It makes no difference, either to the person's interests or to the stranger's interests, which option is chosen; why, then, do we have the curious intuition that there is a big difference here?

I conceded at the outset that most of us believe that in letting people die we are not behaving as badly as if we were to kill them. I think I have given good reasons for concluding that this belief is false. Yet giving reasons is often not enough, even in philosophy. For if an intuition is strong enough, we may continue to rely on it and assume that *something* is wrong with the arguments opposing it, even though we are not sure exactly what is wrong. It is a familiar remark: "X is more certain than any argument that might be given against it." So in addition to the arguments, we need some account of why people have the allegedly mistaken intuition and why it is so persistent. Why do people believe so firmly that killing is so much worse than letting die, both in fictitious cases such as Trammell's, and in the famine relief cases in the real world? In some ways the explanation of this is best left to the psychologists; the distinctly philosophical job is accomplished when the intuition is shown to be false. However, I shall hazard a hypothesis, since it shows how our intuitions can be explained without assuming that they are perceptions of the truth.

Human beings are to some degree altruistic, but they are also to a great degree selfish, and their attitudes on matters of conduct are determined by what is in their own interests, and what is in the interests of the few other people they especially care about. In terms of both the costs and the benefits, it is to their own advantage for people in the affluent countries to regard killing as worse than letting die. First, the *costs* of never killing anyone are not great; we can live very well without ever killing. But the cost of not allowing people to die, when we could save them, would be very great. For any one of us to take seriously a duty to save the starving would require that we give up our affluent life-styles; money could no longer be spent on luxuries while others starve. On the other side, we have much more to *gain* from a strict prohibition on killing than from a like prohibition on letting die. Since we are not in danger of starving, we will not suffer if people do not regard feeding the hungry as so important; but we would be threatened if people did not regard killing as very, very bad. So, both the costs and the benefits encourage us, selfishly, to view

killing as worse than letting die. It is to our own advantage to believe this, and so we do.

NOTES

1. For an account of the difficulties of getting reliable information in this area, see Nick Eberstadt, "Myths of the Food Crisis," *New York Review of Books*, 19 February 1976, 32–37.
2. Richard L. Trammell, "Saving Life and Taking Life," *Journal of Philosophy* 72 (1975), 131–137, is the best defense of this view of which I am aware.
3. This article is a companion to an earlier one, "Active and Passive Euthanasia," *New England Journal of Medicine* 202 (9 January 1975), 78–80 [reprinted in the present volume, 1–6], in which I discuss the (mis)use of the killing/letting die distinction in medical contexts. But nothing in this article depends on the earlier one.
4. Philippa Foot, "The Problem of Abortion and the Doctrine of the Double Effect," *Oxford Review* no. 5 (1967); reprinted in James Rachels, ed., *Moral Problems*, 2nd ed. (New York, 1975), 66.
5. On this point, and more generally on the whole subject of our duty to contribute for famine relief, see Peter Singer, "Famine, Affluence, and Morality," *Philosophy and Public Affairs* 1 (Spring 1972), 232.
6. Trammell, 133.
7. This argument is suggested by Paul Ramsey in *The Patient as Person* (New Haven, Conn., 1970), 151.
8. This difference between failing to save and letting die was pointed out by David Sanford in a very helpful paper, "On Killing and Letting Die," read at the Western Division meeting of the American Philosophical Association, in New Orleans, on 30 April 1976.
9. Trammell, 133.
10. Ibid., 134.
11. There is also some independent evidence that this prereflective belief is mistaken; see Singer, "Famine, Affluence, and Morality."
12. Grice made this remark several years ago at Oberlin. I do not remember the surrounding details of the discussion, but the remark seems to me an important one which applies to lots of "objections" to various theories. The most famous objections to act-utilitarianism, for example, are little more than descriptions of the theory, with the question-begging addendum, "Because it says *that*, it can't be right."
13. Daniel Dinello, "On Killing and Letting Die," *Analysis* 31, no. 3 (January 1971), 83, 86.
14. Trammell, 131.
15. Dinello, 85.
16. There is another way to meet Dinello's counterexample. A surprisingly strong case can be made that it would *not* be any worse to kill Smith than to "let Jones die." I have in mind adapting John Harris's argument in "The Survival Lottery," *Philosophy* 50 (1975), 81–87.

FURTHER READINGS

Aiken, William, and Hugh LaFollette. *World Hunger and Moral Obligation*. Englewood Cliffs, NJ: Prentice Hall, Inc., 1977.
Hardin, Garrett. *Stalking the Wild Taboo*. Los Altos, CA: William Kauffman, 1978.
Singer, Peter. "Famine, Affluence, and Morality." In *Moral Problems*, ed. James Rachels. New York: Harper & Row, 1979, 263–278.

All Animals Are Equal[1]

PETER SINGER

Peter Singer is professor of philosophy and director of the Centre for Human Bioethics at Monash University in Melbourne, Australia. He is the author of Animal Liberation: A New Ethics for Our

Treatment of Animals and Practical Ethics. *This essay originally appeared in* Philosophic Exchange, *Vol. 1, No. 5 (Summer, 1974) 243–257. Reprinted with permission.*

In recent years a number of oppressed groups have campaigned vigorously for equality. The classic instance is the Black Liberation movement, which demands an end to the prejudice and discrimination that has made blacks second-class citizens. The immediate appeal of the black liberation movement and its initial, if limited success made it a model for other oppressed groups to follow. We became familiar with liberation movements for Spanish-Americans, gay people, and a variety of other minorities. When a majority group—women—began their campaign, some thought we had come to the end of the road. Discrimination on the basis of sex, it has been said, is the *last* universally accepted form of discrimination, practiced without secrecy or pretense even in those liberal circles that have long prided themselves on their freedom from prejudice against racial minorities.

One should always be wary of talking of "the last remaining form of discrimination." If we have learnt anything from the liberation movements, we should have learnt how difficult it is to be aware of latent prejudice in our attitudes to particular groups until this prejudice is forcefully pointed out.

A liberation movement demands an expansion of our moral horizons and an extension or reinterpretation of the basic moral principle of equality. Practices that were previously regarded as natural and inevitable come to be seen as the result of an unjustifiable prejudice. Who can say with confidence that all his or her attitudes and practices are beyond criticism? If we wish to avoid being numbered amongst the oppressors, we must be prepared to re-think even our most fundamental attitudes. We need to consider them from the point of view of those most disadvantaged by our attitudes, and the practices that follow from these attitudes. If we can make this unaccustomed mental switch we may discover a pattern in our attitudes and practices that consistently operates so as to benefit one group—usually the one to which we ourselves belong—at the expense of another. In this way we may come to see that there is a case for a new liberation movement. My aim is to advocate that we make this mental switch in respect of our attitudes and practices towards a very large group of beings: members of species

other than our own—or, as we popularly though misleadingly call them, animals. In other words, I am urging that we extend to other species the basic principle of equality that most of us recognise should be extended to all members of our own species.

All this may sound a little far-fetched, more like a parody of other liberation movements than a serious objective. In fact, in the past the idea of "The Rights of Animals" really has been used to parody the case for women's rights. When Mary Wollstonecroft, a forerunner of later feminists, published her *Vindication of the Rights of Women* in 1792, her ideas were widely regarded as absurd, and they were satirized in an anonymous publication entitled *A Vindication of the Rights* of *Brutes*. The author of this satire (actually Thomas Taylor, a distinguished Cambridge philosopher) tried to refute Wollstonecroft's reasonings by showing that they could be carried one stage further. If sound when applied to women, why should the arguments not be applied to dogs, cats and horses? They seemed to hold equally well for these "brutes"; yet to hold that brutes had rights was manifestly absurd; therefore the reasoning by which this conclusion had been reached must be unsound, and if unsound when applied to brutes, it must also be unsound when applied to women, since the very same arguments had been used in each case.

One way in which we might reply to this argument is by saying that the case for equality between men and women cannot validly extended to non-human animals. Women have a right to vote, for instance, because they are just as capable of making rational decisions as men are; dogs, on the other hand, are incapable of understanding the significance of voting, so they cannot have the right to vote. There are many other obvious ways in which men and women resemble each other closely, while humans and other animals differ greatly. So, it might be said, men and women are similar beings, and should have equal rights, while humans and non-humans are different and should not have equal rights.

The thought behind this reply to Taylor's analogy is correct up to a point, but it does not go far enough. There are important differences between humans and other animals, and these differences must give rise to some differences in the rights that each have. Recognizing this obvious fact, however, is no barrier to the case for extending the basic principle of equality to non-human animals. The differences that exist between men and women are equally undeniable, and the supporters of Women's Liberation are aware that these differences may give rise to different rights. Many feminists hold that women have the right to an abortion on request. It does not follow that since these same people are campaigning for equality between men and women they must support the right of men to have abortions too. Since a man cannot have an abortion, it is meaningless to talk of his right to have one. Since a pig can't vote, it is meaningless to talk of its right to vote. There is no reason why either Women's Liberation or Animal Liberation should get involved in such nonsense. The extension of the basic principle of equality from one group to another does not imply that we must treat both groups in exactly the same way, or grant exactly the same rights to both groups. Whether we should do so will depend on the nature of the members of the two groups. The basic principle of equality applies to so-called "brutes." I believe that we reach this conclusion if we examine the basis on which our opposition to discrimination on grounds of race or sex ultimately rests. We will then see that we would be on shaky ground if we were to demand equality for blacks, women, and other groups of oppressed humans while denying equal consideration to non-humans.

When we say that all human beings, whatever their race, creed or sex, are equal, what is it that we are asserting? Those who wish to defend a hierarchical, inegalitarian society have often pointed out that by whatever test we choose, it simply is not true that all humans are equal. Like it or not, we must face the fact that humans come in different shapes and sizes; they come with differing moral capacities, differing intellectual abilities, differing amounts of benevolent feeling and sensitivity to the needs of others, differing abilities to communicate effectively, and differing capacities to experience pleasure and pain. In short, if the demand for equality were based on the actual equality of all human beings, we would have to stop demanding equality. It would be an unjustifiable demand.

Still, one might cling to the view that the demand for equality among human beings is based on the actual equality of the different races and sexes. Although humans differ as individuals in various ways, there are no differences between the races and sexes *as such*. From the mere fact that a person is black, or a woman, we cannot infer anything else about that person. This, it may be said, is what is wrong with racism and sexism. The white racist claims that whites are superior to blacks, but this is false—although there are differences between individuals, some blacks are superior to some whites in all of the capacities and abilities that could conceivably be relevant. The opponent of sexism would say the same: a person's sex is no guide to his or her abilities, and this is why it is unjustifiable to discriminate on the basis of sex.

This is a possible line of objection to racial and sexual discrimination. It is not, however, the way that someone really concerned about equality would choose, because taking this line could, in some circumstances, force one to accept a most inegalitarian society. The fact that some humans differ as individuals, rather than as races or sexes, is a valid reply to someone who defends a hierarchical society like, say, South Africa, in which all whites are superior in status to all blacks. The existence of individual variations that cut across the lines of race or sex, however, provides us with no defence at all against a more sophisticated opponent of equality, one who proposes that, say, the interests of those with I.Q. ratings above 100 be preferred to the interests of those with I.Q.s below 100. Would a hierarchical society of this sort really be so much better than one based on race or sex? I think not. But if we tie the moral principle of equality to the factual equality of the different races or sexes, taken as a whole, our opposition to racism and sexism does not provide us with any basis for objecting to this kind of inegalitarianism.

There is a second important reason why we ought not to base our opposition to racism and sexism on any kind of factual equality, even the limited kind which asserts that variations in capacities and abilities are spread evenly between the different races and sexes: we can have no absolute guarantee that these abilities and capacities really are distributed evenly, without regard to race or sex, among human beings. So far as actual abilities are concerned, there do seem to be certain measurable differences between both races and sexes. These differences do not, of course, appear in each case, but only when averages are taken. More important still, we do not yet know how much of these differences is really due to the different genetic endowments of the various races and sexes, and how much is due to environmental differences that are the result of past and continuing discrimination. Perhaps all of the important differences will eventually prove to be environmental rather than genetic. Anyone opposed to racism and sexism will certainly hope that this will be so, for it will make the task of ending discrimination a lot easier; nevertheless it would be dangerous to rest the case against racism and sexism on the belief that all significant differences are environmental in origin. The opponent of, say, racism who takes this line will be unable to avoid conceding that if differences in ability did after all prove to have some genetic connection with race, racism would in some way be defensible.

It would be folly for the opponent of racism to stake his whole case on a dogmatic commitment to one particular outcome of a difficult scientific issue which is still a long way from being settled. While attempts to prove that the differences in certain selected abilities between races and sexes are primarily genetic in origin have certainly not be conclusive, the same must be said of attempts to prove that these differences are largely the result of environment. At this stage of the investigation we cannot be certain which view is correct, however much we may hope it is the latter.

Fortunately, there is no need to pin the case for equality to one particular outcome of this scientific investigation. The appropriate response to those who claim to have found evidence of genetically-based differences in ability between the races or sexes is not to stick to the belief that the genetic explanation must be wrong, whatever evidence to the contrary may turn up: instead we should make it quite clear that the claim to equality does not depend on intelligence, moral capacity, physical strength, or similar matters of fact. There is no logically compelling reason for assuming that a factual difference in ability between two people justifies any difference in the amount of consideration we give to satisfying their needs and interests. The principle of the equality of human beings is not a description of an alleged actual equality among humans: it is a prescription of how we should treat humans.

Jeremy Bentham incorporated the essential basis of moral equality into his utilitarian system of ethics in the formula: "Each to count for one and none for more than one." In other words, the interests of every being affected by an action are to be taken into account and given the same weight as the like interests of any other being. A later utilitarian, Henry Sidgwick, put the point in this way: "The good of any one individual is of no more importance, from the point of view (if I may say so) of the Universe, than the good of any other."[2] More recently the leading figures in contemporary moral philosophy have shown a great deal of agreement in specifying as a fundamental presupposition of their moral theories some similar requirement which operates so as to give everyone's interests equal consideration—although they cannot agree on how this requirement is best formulated.[3]

It is an implication of this principle of equality that our concern for others ought not to depend on what they are like, or what abilities they possess—although precisely what this concern requires us to do may vary according to the characteristics of those affected by what we do. It is on this basis that the case against racism and the case against sexism must both ultimately rest; and it is in accordance with this principle that speciesism is also to be condemned. If possessing a higher degree of intelligence does not entitle one human to use another for his own ends, how can it entitle humans to exploit non-humans?

Many philosophers have proposed the principle of equal consideration of interests, in some form or other, as a basic moral principle; but, as we shall see in more detail shortly, not many of them have recognised that this principle applies to members of other species as well as to our own. Bentham was one of the few who did realize this. In a forward-looking passage, written at a time when black slaves in the British dominions were still being treated much as we now treat non-human animals, Bentham wrote:

> The day *may* come when the rest of the animal creation may acquire those rights which never could have been witholden from them but by the hand of tyranny. The French have already discovered that the blackness of the skin is no reason why a human being should be abandoned without redress to the caprice of a tormentor. It may one day come to be recognised that the number of the legs, the villosity of the skin, or the termination of the *os sacrum*, are reasons equally insufficient for abandoning a sensitive being to the same fate. What else is it that should trace the insuperable line? Is it the faculty of reason, or perhaps the faculty of discourse? But a full-grown horse or dog is beyond comparison a more rational, as well as a more conversable animal, than an infant of a day, or a week, or even a month, old. But suppose they were otherwise, what would it avail? The question is not, Can they reason? nor Can they *talk*? but, *Can they suffer?*[4]

In this passage Bentham points to the capacity for suffering as the vital characteristic that gives a being the right to equal consideration. The capacity for suffering—or more strictly, for suffering and/or enjoyment or happiness—is not just another characteristic like the capacity for language, or for higher mathematics. Bentham is not saying that those who try to mark "the insuperable line" that determines whether the interests of a being should be considered happen to

have selected the wrong characteristic. The capacity for suffering and enjoying things is a prerequisite for having interests at all, a condition that must be satisfied before we can speak of interests in any meaningful way. It would be nonsense to say that it was not in the interests of a stone to be kicked along the road by a schoolboy. A stone does not have interests because it cannot suffer. Nothing that we can do to it could possibly make any difference to its welfare. A mouse, on the other hand, does have an interest in not being tormented, because it will suffer if it is.

If a being suffers, there can be no moral justification for refusing to take that suffering into consideration. No matter what the nature of the being, the principle of equality requires that its suffering be counted equally with the like suffering—in so far as rough comparisons can be made—of any other being. If a being is not capable of suffering, or of experiencing enjoyment or happiness, there is nothing to be taken into account. This is why the limit of sentience (using the term as a convenient, if not strictly accurate, shorthand for the capacity to suffer or experience enjoyment or happiness) is the only defensible boundary of concern for the interests of others. To mark this boundary by some characteristic like intelligence or rationality would be to mark it in an arbitrary way. Why not choose some other characteristic, like skin color?

The racist violates the principle of equality by giving greater weight to the interests of members of his own race, when there is a clash between their interests and the interests of those of another race. Similarly the speciesist allows the interests of his own species to override the greater interests of members of other species.[5] The pattern is the same in each case. Most human beings are speciesists. I shall now very briefly describe some of the practices that show this.

For the great majority of human beings, especially in urban, industrialized societies, the most direct form of contact with members of other species is at meal-times: we eat them. In doing so we treat them purely as means to our ends. We regard their life and well-being as subordinate to our taste for a particular kind of dish. I say "taste" deliberately—this is purely a matter of pleasing our palate. There can be no defense of eating flesh in terms of satisfying nutritional needs, since it has been established beyond doubt that we could satisfy our need for protein and other essential nutrients far more efficiently with a diet that replaced animal flesh by soy beans, or products derived from soy beans, and other high-protein vegetable products.[6]

It is not merely the act of killing that indicates what we are ready to do to other species in order to gratify our tastes. The suffering we inflict on the animals while they are alive is perhaps an even clearer indication of our speciesism than the fact that we are prepared to kill therm.[7] In order to have meat on the table at a price that people can afford, our society tolerates methods of meat production that confine sentient animals in cramped, unsuitable conditions for the entire durations of their lives. Animals are treated like machines that convert fodder into flesh, and any innovation that results in a higher "conversion ratio" is liable to be adopted. As one authority on the subject has said, "cruelty is acknowledged only when profitability ceases."[8] So hens are crowded four or five to a cage with a floor area of twenty inches by eighteen inches, or around the size of a single page of the *New York Times*. The cages have wire floors, since this reduces cleaning costs, though wire is unsuitable for the hens' feet; the floors slope, since this makes the eggs roll down for easy collection, although this makes it difficult for the hens to rest comfortably. In these conditions all the birds' natural instincts are thwarted: they cannot stretch their wings fully, walk freely, dust-bathe, scratch the ground, or build a nest. Although they have never known other conditions, observers have noticed that the birds vainly try to perform these actions. Frustrated at their inability to do so, they often develop what farmers call "vices," and peck each other to death. To prevent this, the beaks of young birds are often cut off.

This kind of treatment is not limited to poultry. Pigs are now also being reared in cages inside sheds. These animals are comparable to dogs in intelligence, and need a varied, stimulating environment if they are not to suffer from stress and boredom. Anyone who kept a dog in the way in which pigs are frequently kept would be liable to prosecution, in England at least, but because our interest in exploiting pigs is greater than our interest in exploiting dogs, we object to cruelty to dogs while consuming the produce of cruelty to pigs. Of the other animals, the condition of veal calves is perhaps worst of all, since these animals are so closely confined that they cannot even turn around or get up and lie down freely. In this way the do not develop unpalatable muscle. They are also made anaemic and kept short of roughage, to keep their flesh pale, since white veal fetches a higher price; as a result they develop a craving for iron and roughage, and have been observed to gnaw wood off the sides of their stalls, and lick greedily at any rusty hinge that is within reach.

Since, as I have said, none of these practices cater for anything more than our pleasures of taste, our practice of rearing and killing other animals in order to eat them is a clear instance of the sacrifice of the most important interests of other beings in order to satisfy trivial interests of our own. To avoid speciesism we must stop this practice, and each of us has a moral obligation to cease supporting the practice. Our custom is all the support that the meat industry needs. The decision to cease giving it that support may be difficult, but it is no more difficult than it would have been for a white Southerner to go against the traditions of his society and free his slaves: if we do not change our dietary habits, how can we censure those slaveholders who would not change their own way of living?

The same form of discrimination may be observed in the widespread practice of experimenting on other species in order to see if certain substances are safe for human beings, or to test some psychological theory about the effect of severe punishment on learning, or to try out various new compounds just in case something turns up. People sometimes think that all this experimentation is for vital medical purposes, and so will reduce suffering overall. This comfortable belief is very wide of the mark. Drug companies test new shampoos and cosmetics that they are intending to put on the market by dropping them into the eyes of rabbits, held open by metal clips, in order to observe what damage results. Food additives, like artificial colorings and preservatives, are tested by what is known as the "LD$_{50}$"—a test designed to find the level of consumption at which 50% of a group of animals will die. In the process, nearly all of the animals are made very sick before some finally die, and others pull through. If the substance is relatively harmless, as it often is, huge doses have to be force-fed to the animals, until in some cases sheer volume or concentration of the substance causes death.

Much of this pointless cruelty goes on in the universities. In many areas of science, non-human animals are regarded as an item of laboratory equipment, to be used and expended as desired. In psychology laboratories experimenters devise endless variations and repetitions of experiments that were of little value in the first place. To quote just one example, from the experimenter's own account in a psychology journal: at the University of Pennsylvania, Perrin S. Cohen hung six dogs in hammocks with electrodes taped to their hind feet. Electric shock of varying intensity was then administered through the electrodes. If the dog learnt to press its head against a panel on the left, the shock was turned off, but otherwise it remained on indefinitely. Three of the dogs, however, were required to wait periods varying from 2 to 7 seconds while being shocked before making the response that turned off the current. If they failed to wait, they received further shocks. Each dog was given from 26 to 46 "sessions" in the hammock, each session consisting of 80 "trials" or shocks, administered at intervals of one minute. The experimenter reported that the dogs, who were unable to move in the hammock, barked or bobbed their heads when the current was applied. The reported findings of the experiment were that there was a delay in the dogs' responses that increased proportionately to the time the dogs were required. to endure the shock, but a gradual increase in the intensity of the shock had no systematic effect in the timing of the response. The experiment was funded by the National Institutes of Health, and the United States Public Health Service.[9]

In this example, and countless cases like it, the possible benefits to mankind are either nonexistent or fantastically remote; while the certain losses to members of other species are very real. This is, again, a clear indication of speciesism.

In the past, argument about vivisection has often missed this point, because it has been put in absolutist terms: would the abolitionist be prepared to let thousands die if they could be saved by experimenting on a single animal? The way to reply to this purely hypothetical question is to pose another: would the experimenter be prepared to perform his experiment on an orphaned human infant, if that were the only way to save many lives? (I say "orphan" to avoid the complication of parental feelings, although in doing so I am being overfair to the experimenter, since the non-human subjects of experiments are not orphans. If the experimenter is not prepared to use an orphaned human infant, then his readiness to use non-humans is simple discrimination, since adult apes, cats. mice and other mammals are more aware of what is happening to them, more self-directing and, so far as we can tell, at least as sensitive to pain, as any human infant. There seems to be no relevant characteristic that human infants possess that adult mammals do not have to the same or higher degree. (Someone might try to argue that what makes it wrong to experiment on a human infant is that the infant will, in time and if left alone, develop into more than the non-human, but one would then, to be consistent, have to oppose abortion, since the fetus has the same potential as the infant—indeed, even contraception and abstinence might be wrong on this ground, since the egg and sperm, considered jointly, also have the same potential. In any case, this argument still gives us no reason for selecting a non-human, rather than a human with severe and irreversible brain damage, as the subject for our experiments.)

The experimenter, then, shows a bias in favor of his own species whenever he carries out an experiment on a non-human for a purpose that he would not think justified him in using a human being at an equal or lower level of sentience, awareness, ability to be self-directing, etc. No one familiar with the kind of results yielded by most experiments on animals can have the slightest doubt that if this bias were eliminated the number of experiments performed would be a minute fraction of the number performed today.

Experimenting on animals, and eating their flesh, are perhaps the two major forms of speciesism in our society. By comparison, the third and last form of speciesism is so minor as to be insignificant, but it is perhaps of some special interest to those for whom this paper was written. I am referring to speciesism in contemporary philosophy.

Philosophy ought to question the basic assumptions of the age. Thinking through, critically and carefully, what most people take for granted is, I believe, the chief task of philosophy, and it is this task that makes philosophy a worthwhile activity. Regrettably, philosophy does not always live up to its historic role. Philosophers are human beings and they are subject to all the preconceptions of the society to which they belong. Sometimes they succeed in breaking free of the prevailing ideology: more often they become its most sophisticated defenders. So, in this case, philosophy as practiced in the universities today does not challenge anyone's preconceptions about our relations with other species. By their writings, those philosophers who tackle problems that touch upon the issue reveal that these make the same unquestioned assumptions as most other humans, and what they say tends to confirm the reader in his or her comfortable speciesist habits.

I could illustrate this claim by referring to the writings of philosophers in various fields—for instance, the attempts that have been made by those interested in rights to draw the boundary of the sphere of rights so that it runs parallel to the biological boundaries of the species *homo sapiens*, including infants and even mental defectives, but excluding those other beings of equal or greater capacity who are so useful to us at mealtimes and in our laboratories. I think it would be a more appropriate conclusion to this paper, however, if I concentrated on the problem with which we have been centrally concerned, the problem of equality.

It is significant that the problem of equality, in moral and political philosophy, is invariably formulated in terms of human equality. The effect of this is that the question of the equality of other animals does not confront the philosopher, or student, as an issue in itself—and this is already an indication of the failure of philosophy to challenge accepted beliefs. Still, philosophers have found it difficult to discuss the issue of human equality without raising, in a paragraph or two, the question of the status of other animals. The reason for this, which should be apparent from what I have said already, is that if humans are to be regarded as equal to one another, we need some sense of "equal" that does not require any actual, descriptive equality of capacities, talents or other qualities. If equality is to be related to any actual characteristics of humans, these characteristics must be some lowest common denominator, pitched so low that no human lacks them—but then the philosopher comes up against the catch that any such set of characteristics which covers all humans will not be possessed *only by humans*. In other words, it turns out that in the only sense in which we can truly say, as an assertion of fact, that all humans are equal, at least some members of other species are also equal—equal, that is, to each other and to humans. If, on the other hand, we regard the statement "All humans are equal" in some non-factual way, perhaps as a prescription, then, as I have already argued, it is even more difficult to exclude non-humans from the sphere of equality.

This result is not what the egalitarian philosopher originally intended to assert. Instead of accepting the radical outcome to which their own reasonings naturally point, however, most philosophers try to reconcile their beliefs in human equality and animal inequality by arguments that can only be described as devious.

As a first example, I take William Frankena's well-known article "The Concept of Social Justice."[10] Frankena opposes the idea of basing justice on merit, because he sees that this could lead to highly inegalitarian results. Instead he proposes the principle that:

all men are to be treated as equals, not because they are equal, in any respect but simply because they are human. They are human because they have emotions and desires, and are able to think, and hence are capable of enjoying a good life in a sense in which other animals are not.

But what is this capacity to enjoy the good life which all humans have, but no other animals? Other animals have emotions and desires, and appear to be capable of enjoying a good life. We may doubt that they can think—although the behavior of some apes, dolphins and even dogs suggest that some of them can—but what is the relevance of thinking? Frankena goes on to admit that by "the good life" he means "not so much the morally good life as the happy or satisfactory life," so thought would appear to be unnecessary for enjoying the good life; in fact to emphasise the need for thought would make difficulties for the egalitarian since only some people are capable of leading intellectually satisfying lives, or morally good lives. This makes it difficult to see what Frankena's principle of equality has to do with simply being *human*. Surely every sentient being is capable of leading a life that is happier or less miserable than some alternative life, and hence has a claim to be taken into account. In this respect the distinction between humans and non-humans is not a sharp division, but rather a continuum along which we move gradually, and with overlaps between the species, from simple capacities for enjoyment and satisfaction, or pain and suffering, to more complex ones.

Faced with a situation in which they see a need for some basis for the moral gulf that is commonly thought to separate humans and animals, but can find no concrete difference that will do the job without undermining the equality of humans, philosophers tend to waffle. They resort to high-sounding phrases like "the intrinsic dignity of the human individual."[11] They talk of the "intrinsic worth of all men" as if men (humans?) had some worth that other beings did not,[12] or they say that humans, and only humans, are "ends in themselves" while "everything other than a person can only have value for a person."[13]

This idea of a distinctive human dignity and worth has a long history; it can be traced back directly to the Renaissance humanists, for instance to Pico della Mirandola's *Oration on the Dignity of Man*. Pico and other humanists based their estimate of human dignity on the idea that man possessed the central, pivotal position in the "Great Chain of Being" the led from the lowliest forms of matter to God himself; this view of the universe, in turn, goes back to both classical and Judeo-Christian doctrines. Contemporary philosophers have cast off these metaphysical and religious shackles and freely invoke the dignity of mankind without needing to justify the idea at all. Why should we not attribute "intrinsic dignity" or "intrinsic worth" to ourselves? Fellow-humans are unlikely to reject the accolades we so generously bestow on them, and those to whom we deny the honor are unable to object. Indeed, when one thinks only of humans, it can be very liberal, very progressive, to talk of the dignity of all human beings. In so doing, we implicitly condemn slavery, racism, and other violations of human rights. We admit that we ourselves are in some fundamental sense on a par with the poorest, most ignorant members of our own species. It is only when we think of humans as no more than a small sub-group of all the beings that inhabit our planet that we may realize that in elevating our own species we are at the same time lowering the relative status of all other species.

The truth is that the appeal to the intrinsic dignity of human beings appears to solve the egalitarian's problems only as long as it goes unchallenged. Once we ask *why* it should be that all humans—including infants, mental defectives, psychopaths, Hitler, Stalin and the rest—have some kind of dignity or worth that no elephant, pig or chimpanzee can ever achieve, we see that this question is as difficult to answer as our original request for some relevant fact that justifies the inequality of humans and other animals. In fact, these two questions are really one: talk of intrinsic dignity or moral worth only takes the problem back one step, because any satisfactory defence of the claim that all and only humans have intrinsic dignity would need to refer to some relevant capacities or characteristics that all and only humans possess. Philosophers frequently introduce ideas of dignity, respect and worth at the point at which other reasons appear to be lacking, but this is hardly good enough. Fine phrases are the last resource of those who have run out of arguments.

In case there are those who still think it may be possible to find some relevant characteristic that distinguishes all humans from all members of other species, I shall refer again, before I conclude, to the existence of some humans who quite clearly are below the level of awareness, self-consciousness, intelligence, and sentience, of many non-humans. I am thinking of humans with severe and irreparable brain damage, and also of infant humans. To avoid the complication of the relevance of a being's potential, however, I shall henceforth concentrate on permanently retarded humans.

Philosophers who set out to find a characteristic that will distinguish humans from other animals rarely take the course of abandoning these groups of humans by lumping them in with the other animals. It is easy to see why they do not. To take this line without re-thinking our attitudes to other animals would entail that we have the right to perform painful experiments on retarded humans for trivial reasons; similarly it would follow that we had the right to rear and kill these humans for food. To most philosophers these consequences are as unacceptable as the view that we should stop treating non-humans in this way.

Of course, when discussing the problem of equality it is possible to ignore the problem of mental defectives, or brush it aside as if somehow insignificant.[14] This is the easiest way out. What else remains? My final example of speciesism in contemporary philosophy has been selected to show what happens when a writer is prepared to face the question of human equality and animal inequality without ignoring the existence of mental defectives, and without resorting to obscurantist mumbo-jumbo. Stanley Benn's clear and honest article "Egalitarianism and Equal Consideration of Interests"[15] fits this description.

Benn, after noting the usual "evident human inequalities" argues, correctly I think, for equality of consideration as the only possible basis for egalitarianism. Yet Benn, like other writers, is thinking only of "equal consideration of human interests." Benn is quite open in his defence of this restriction of equal consideration:

... not to possess human shape is a disqualifying condition. However faithful or intelligent a dog may be, it would be a monstrous sentimentality to attribute to him interests that could be weighed in an equal balance with those of human beings... if, for instance, one had to decide between feeding a hungry baby or a hungry dog, anyone who chose the dog would generally be reckoned morally defective, unable to recognize a fundamental inequality of claims.

This is what distinguishes our attitude to animals from our attitude to imbeciles. It would be odd to say that we ought to respect equally the dignity or personality of the imbecile and of the rational man... but there is nothing odd about saying that we should respect their interests equally, that is, that we should give to the interests of each the same serious consideration as claims to considerations necessary for some standard of well-being that we can recognize and endorse.

Benn's statement of the basis of the consideration we should have for imbeciles seems to me correct, but why should there be any fundamental inequality of claims between a dog and a human imbecile? Benn sees that if equal consideration depended on rationality, no reason could be given against using imbeciles for research purposes, as we now use dogs and guinea pigs. This will not do: "But of course we do distinguish imbeciles from animals in this regard," he says. That the common distinction is justifiable is something Benn does not question; his problem is how it is to be justified. The answer he gives is this:

... we respect the interests of men and give them priority over dogs not *insofar* as they are rational, but because rationality is the human norm. We say it is *unfair* to exploit the deficiencies of the imbecile who falls short of the norm, just as it would be unfair, and not just ordinarily dishonest, to steal from a blind man. If we do not think in this way about dogs, it is because we do not see the irrationality of the dog as a deficiency or a handicap, but as normal for the species. The characteristics, therefore, that distinguish the normal man from the normal dog make it intelligible for us to talk of other men having interests and capacities, and therefore claims, of precisely the same kind as we make on our own behalf. But although these characteristics may provide the point of the distinction between men and other species, they are not in fact the qualifying conditions for membership, or the distinguishing criteria of the class of morally considerable persons; and this is precisely because a man does not become a member of a different species, with its own standards of normality, by reason of not possessing these characteristics.

The final sentence of this passage gives the argument away. An imbecile, Benn concedes, may have no characteristics superior to those of a dog; nevertheless this does not make the imbecile a member of "a different species" as the dog is. *Therefore* it would be "unfair" to use the imbecile for medical research as we use the dog. But why? That the imbecile is not rational is just the way things have worked out, and the same is true of the dog—neither is any more responsible for their

mental level. If it is unfair to take advantage of an isolated defect, why is it fair to take advantage of a more general limitation? I find it hard to see anything in this argument except a defence of preferring the interests of members of our own species because they are members of our own species. To those who think there might be more to it, I suggest the following mental exercise. Assume that it has been proven that there is a difference in the average, or normal, intelligence quotient for two different races, say whites and blacks. Then substitute the term "white" for every occurrence of "men" and "black" for every occurrence of "dog" in the passage quoted; and substitute "high I.Q." for "rationality" and when Benn talks of "imbeciles" replace this term by "dumb whites"—that is, whites who fall well below the normal white I.Q. score. Finally, change "species" to "race." Now re-read the passage. It has become a defence of a rigid, no-exceptions division between whites and blacks, based on I.Q. scores, *notwithstanding an admitted overlap* between whites and blacks in this respect. The revised passage is, of course, outrageous, and this is not only because we have made fictitious assumptions in our substitutions. The point is that in the original passage Benn was defending a rigid division in the amount of consideration due to members of different species, despite admitted cases of overlap. If the original did not, at first reading, strike us as being as outrageous as the revised version does, this is largely because although we are not racists ourselves, most of us are speciesists. Like the other articles, Benn's stands as a warning of the ease with which the best minds can fall victim to a prevailing ideology.

NOTES

1. Passages of this article appeared in a review of *Animals, Men and Morals*, edited by S. and R. Godlovitch and J. Harris (Gollancz and Taplinger, London 1972) in *The New York Review of Books*, April 5, 1973. The whole direction of my thinking on this subject I owe to talks with a number of friends in Oxford in 1970–71, especially Richard Keshen, Stanley Godlovitch, and, above all, Roslind Godlovitch.
2. *The Methods of Ethics* (7th Ed.) p. 382.
3. For example, R.M. Hare, *Freedom and Reason* (Oxford, 1963) and J. Rawls, *A Theory of Justice* (Harvard, 1972); for a brief account of the essential agreement on this issue between these and other positions, see R.M. Hare, "Rules of War and Moral Reasoning," *Philosophy and Public Affairs*, vol. 1, no. 2 (1972).
4. *Introduction to the Principles of Morals and Legislation*, ch. XVII.

5. I owe the term "speciesism" to Dr. Richard Ryder.

6. In order to produce 1 lb. of protein in the form of beef or veal, we must feed 21 lbs. of protein to the animal. Other forms of livestock are slightly less inefficient, but the average ratio in the U.S. is still 1:8. It has been estimated that the amount of protein lost to humans in this way is equivalent to 90% of the annual world protein deficit. For a brief account, see Frances Moore Lappe, *Diet for a Small Planet* (Friends of The Earth/Ballantine, New York 1971) pp. 4–11.

7. Although one might think that killing a being is obviously the ultimate wrong one can do to it, I think that the infliction of suffering is a clearer indication of speciesism because it might be argued that at least part of what is wrong with killing a human is that most humans are conscious of their existence over time, and have desires and purposes that extend into the future—see, for instance, M. Tooley, "Abortion and Infanticide," *Philosophy and Public Affairs*, vol. 2, no. 1 (1972). Of course, if one took this view one would have to hold—as Tooley does—that killing a human infant or mental defective is not in itself wrong, and is less serious than killing certain higher mammals that probably do have a sense of their own existence over time.

8. Ruth Harrison, *Animal Machines* (Stuart, London, 1964). This book provides an eye-opening account of intensive farming methods for those unfamiliar with the subject.

9. *Journal of the Experimental Analysis of Behavior*, vol. 13, no. 1 (1970). Any recent volume of this journal, or of other journals in the field, like the *Journal of Comparative and Physiological Psychology*, will contain reports of equally cruel and trivial experiments. For a fuller account, see Richard Ryder, "Experiments oh Animals" in *Animals, Men and Morals.*

10. In R. Brandt (ed.) *Social Justice* (Prentice Hall, Englewood Cliffs, 1962); the passage quoted appears on p. 19.

11. Frankena, *op. cit.* p. 23.

12. H.A. Bedau, "Egalitarianism and the Idea of Equality" in *Nomos IX: Equality*, ed. J.R. Pennock and J.W. Chapman, New York 1967.

13. G. Vlastos, "Justice and Equality" in Brandt, *Social Justice*, p. 48.

14. E.G. Bernard Williams, "The Idea of Equality," in *Philosophy, Politics and Society* (second series) ed. P. Laslett and W. Runciman (Blackwell, Oxford, 1962) p. 118; J. Rawls, *A Theory of Justice*, pp. 509–10.

15. *Nomos IX: Equality;* the passages quoted are on pp. 62ff.

Answer Key

Progress Check 1.1

1. Academy 2. *The Republic* 3. harmonious balance 4. teleology 5. soul 6. physical 7. self-assertion 8. reason 9. ignorance 10. guardian 11. tyrannical 12. oligarchic 13. timarchic 14. auxiliaries 15. forms

Progress Check 2.1

1. Alexander the Great 2. Plato 3. teleologist 4. self-realization 5. entelechy 6. *eudaimonia* 7. intrinsic 8. means 9. successful 10. secondary 11. self-sufficient 12. hedonist 13. rational 14. cattle 15. insecure 16. complete 17. contemplative 18. divine 19. luck 20. intellectual 21. habit 22. deficiency 23. moderation 24. sake 25. modesty

Progress Check 3.1

1. nature 2. Jeremy Bentham 3. spirit of scientific objectivity 4. consequences 5. principle of utility 6. utility 7. psychological egoist 8. ethical egoist 9. is–ought 10. sanction 11. political 12. retributivist 13. private ethics 14. inefficacious 15. retroactive legislation 16. hedonic calculus 17. intensity 18. fecundity 19. extent 20. intrinsically

Progress Check 4.1

1. principle of utility 2. quality 3. intellect 4. sense of dignity 5. inferior type 6. infirmity of character 7. egoistic 8. disutility 9. incommensurable 10. entitlements 11. selfishness, mental cultivation 12. democracy

Progress Check 5.1

1. deontological 2. moral certainty 3. structure of reason 4. good will 5. conditionally 6. duty 7. prudential 8. nonmoral 9. immoral 10. inclination 11. motive 12. duties to oneself 13. maxim 14. categorical imperative 15. formalist 16. objects 17. impartial 18. prescriptive 19. hypothetical 20. autonomy of the will

Progress Check 6.1

1. utilitarianism 2. social contract theory 3. justice 4. inviolate 5. society 6. identity of interests 7. ideal observer 8. original position 9. veil of ignorance 10. mutually disinterested 11. principle of equal liberty 12. deontological ethics 13. difference principle 14. maximin principle 15. reciprocity

Progress Check 7.1

1. selfishness 2. ethics of altruism 3. beneficiary criterion of morality 4. beneficiary 5. cynicism/guilt 6. objectivist ethics 7. whim/fancy 8. neomysticism 9. life 10. nature 11. productivity 12. pride 13. happiness 14. traders 15. force

Progress Check 8.1

1. school of thought 2. Jean-Paul Sartre 3. Simone de Beauvoir 4. unorthodox methods 5. traditional philosophy 6. existence/essence 7. atheistic 8. nihilistic 9. artificially formulaic 10. systems 11. personal responsibility/bad faith 12. inauthentically 13. despairing quietism 14. content/form 15. free

Progress Check 9.1 ✳

1. reason 2. morality of care 3. male bias 4. Lawrence Kohlberg 5. conventional 6. Carol Gilligan/ moral dilemmas 7. identity formation 8. intimacy/separation 9. selfishness/responsibility 10. Nel Noddings 11. principled morality 12. justifying 13. relation 14. natural caring 15. joy

Reasoning Skills Assessment

Part One
1. N 2.C 3.N 4.N 5.N 6.F 7.F 8.C 9.C 10.F

Part Two
1. O 2.O 3.A 4.E 5.E 6.A 7.O 8.O 9.A 10.A

Part Three
1. Socrates is a Greek. 2. Trees have leaves. 3. Jean-Guy has a right to vote. 4. Interest rates are declining. 5. So, you did not do something wrong. 6. if p, then r. 7. not q.
8. Some C are A. 9. Mary is a cheater. 10. r is q.

Part Four
1.U 2.U 3.U 4.U 5.U

Progress Check 10.1 ✳

1. empirical study 2. prescribe 3. metaethical 4. justify 5. ultimate foundations 6. factual claim 7. normative 8. verification/justification 9. moral/nonmoral 10. conceptual claims 11. conceptual analysis 12. logically mysterious 13. necessary/sufficient 14. explanation 15. personal opinion 16. premise/conclusion/inference 17. relevance/acceptability/sufficiency 18 premise indicators 19. conclusion indicators 20. enthymeme 21. complex argument 22. standard form 23. conjoint premises 24. context 25. ethical case study analysis

Progress Check 11.1

1. interpersonal 2. form 3. modus ponens 4. consequent 5. affirms 6. denies 7. invalid 8. hypothetical 9. disjunct 10. value 11. judgment 12. probable 13. inductive generalization 14. worse 15. analogical 16. practical syllogisms 17. logical fallacies 18. sound 19. factual premise 20. role-exchange test 21. inconsistent 22. universalizability 23. new cases test 24. ad hominem 25. circular reasoning 26. two wrongs fallacy 27. appealing to authority 28. straw man 29. red herring 30. slippery slope

How to Write a Moral Position Paper

One of the hardest tasks facing you as a philosophical beginner is the writing of your first ethics paper. With this in mind, we will look at the process of structuring and organizing a "thesis defence." A thesis defence requires that you take a stand or position on some controversial moral issue. Let us go through the steps.

STEP ONE: PICK A MORAL ISSUE

When writing a "thesis defence" or "moral position paper," you must first pick an appropriate topic. What you *do not* want to do is to select an issue that may be better suited to psychology, sociology or anthropology, something philosophical beginners occasionally do. To ensure that your topic suits the course, be certain that it concerns matters of moral value and/or ethical principle. In your paper, you should be trying to conclude that something is good or bad, right or wrong, better or worse, praiseworthy or blameworthy. If your paper is about an action or policy decision, for instance, then you should state that it should or should not be enacted or that we ought or ought not do whatever is involved What you *do not* want to do is to pick an empirical topic—one that can be settled by scientific investigation or statistical analysis. Functional explanations, matters of cause and effect, as well as those pertaining to correlations between variables, are best dealt with by empirical researchers (see Chapter Ten's discussion of the kinds of claims about morality). Below are some sample topics and questions that are appropriate and inappropriate to the development of an ethical thesis.

Inappropriate Topics and Questions for a Moral Position Paper

1. The effects of child abuse on adult development
2. How caffeine works on memory

3. The relationship between income and family size
4. The correlation between intelligence and academic performance
5. Does watching violence on TV relieve stress?
6. How is personality related to birth order?
7. When will the world come to an end?
8. What is the function of morality in social organization?
9. How does moral conscience develop?
10. Why do some people choose to act immorally?

Appropriate Topics and Questions for a Moral Position Paper

1. Corporate Responsibility
   - Is a company's right to earn a profit absolute?
   - Is a company's sole responsibility to the shareholder?
   - What obligations do corporations have toward society in general?
2. Pornography
   - Should pornography be legal and easily available to the public?
   - Should minors have access to pornography?
   - Should pornographic material be banned on the Internet?
3. Capital Punishment
   - Should convicted murderers be executed?
   - Do convicted murderers deserve to die?
   - If all life is sacred, should murderers suffer capital punishment?

STEP TWO: MAKE SURE YOUR NORMATIVE ISSUE IS RELATED TO DISTINCTIVELY MORAL VALUES, NOT MERELY TO NONMORAL ONES

In Part Two of *Moral Philosophy for Modern Life*, Second Edition, a distinction was made between moral and non-moral values. Although it is sometimes difficult to distinguish between the two, let us say, for our purposes, that moral values are those that affect human interests in important ways (see Chapter 10). They tend to be tied to things like virtue, rights, justice, fairness, liberty, equality, happiness, freedom and duty. Some regard moral duties to be so important that they are binding on, or prescriptive for, all of us. By contrast, nonmoral values entail optional duties. They depend on our personal tastes, preferences, wants and desires, or those of others whom we wish to please. Nonmoral values are often related to prudential matters; that is, they pertain to what is good for us personally. They are not about what is dutiful and binding for all.

Examples of Nonmoral Value Statements

1. M&Ms are better than Smarties.
2. It is better to invest in stocks than to save your money in a bank.
3. Country music is terrible.
4. You should not buy an unreliable car.
5. Your choice in wallpaper was wrong.
6. It was good of you to share that useful information.

Examples of Moral Value Statements

1. We have an obligation to feed the world's hungry.
2. War is sometimes justifiable.
3. Affirmative action policies should be eliminated.
4. Criminals should not be punished, but rehabilitated.
5. Abortion is always wrong.
6. All people are created equal.

STEP THREE: STATE YOUR THESIS OR MORAL POSITION

Once you have selected your topic and identified the moral values involved, you need to express a position that is either positive or negative, for or against. Let us say, for instance, that you have decided to write a paper on biomedical ethics as it relates to the use of aborted fetal tissue in scientific research. Having picked your topic, you must eventually take a stand on it. Be careful, however, not to prejudge the issue before careful reflection, analysis, and evaluation. You do not want to decide in advance what you plan to justify in the end. This would be a form of "begging the question" (see Chapter Eleven). For practical purposes, nonetheless, you should state a tentative position up front, articulating arguments both for and against. For our intentions, I am going to assume that you have picked a topic, that you have already conducted a preliminary examination of the arguments on both sides of the issue and that you have decided where you stand. In other words, you have a moral position and are now prepared to formulate arguments in defense of your thesis. You are also prepared to criticize those arguments against the position you are taking.

STEP FOUR: PREPARE FORMAL ARGUMENTS ON BOTH SIDES OF THE ISSUE

In writing your thesis defense, it is not enough simply to pick an issue and argue one side of it. This, obviously, would make your argument "one-sided" and less persuasive than it could otherwise be. What you must do is produce arguments on both sides of the issue and demonstrate why those on the opposing side are inadequate. It is helpful to ask two basic questions when forming syllogistic arguments. They are (1) Why? and (2) So what?

By asking the "why" question, you can uncover those facts or empirical variables relevant to your argument. Suppose the issue is smoking in public places and your thesis is: "Smoking in public places should be prohibited"; you could then ask, "Why?" In response, you might claim that smoking in public places endangers the health of others. You could have some research evidence to support this empirical claim. Philosophically and ethically, however, the question would still remain, "So what?" What is it that you are suggesting that makes this empirical claim about smoking's harmful effects ethically relevant? The answer to the "So what?" question is the following: "That which endangers the health of others should be prohibited." By answering the "So what?" question, what you have formulated, in effect, is the value premise that gives your factual claim moral relevance, because together they lead to the conclusion that: "Smoking in public places should be prohibited." See how this argument can be expressed as a practical syllogism.

Value Premise: That which endangers the health of others (a) should be prohibited (b).

Factual Premise: Smoking in public places (c) endangers the health of others (a).

Value Conclusion: Therefore, smoking in public places (c) should be prohibited (b).

Formal Structure: A is B

                                 C is A   (valid syllogism)

                                 Therefore, C is B

In the example above, note that by asking the "why" question first, we initially arrived at our factual premise—actually the middle part of the syllogism. The second "So what" question gave us the value premise. Once we had the first two parts or statements in place, we could arrive at our conclusion and check for the validity of our argument by exposing its formal structure. This process of question asking can be used to produce practical syllogisms on both sides of the issue. Like before, we could ask ourselves what reasons could be given for opposing our thesis. If someone were opposed to banning smoking in public places, we might ask, "Why?" Once an answer to this question was provided, then we could ask, "So what?" Again, our two answers could be pieced together to form a valid syllogism—in this case, in opposition to our thesis. This method will help to produce arguments in the form of practical syllogisms; of course, not all arguments are structured this way. Don't feel you must limit yourself to this form. If you prefer, come up with *modus ponens* arguments, *modus tollens* arguments and so on.

STEP FIVE: CRITICIZE OPPOSING ARGUMENTS

In defence of your moral thesis, it is not enough simply to offer arguments on both sides of the issue. To convince others that your position is correct, you must show why opposing arguments are unjustified, inadequate or unacceptable. Why are *your* arguments better than your opponent's? Given the skills you mastered in Part Two of *Moral Philosophy for Modern Life*, you can evaluate opposing arguments in the following fashion:

a. First, look at the conclusions of the opposing arguments. Do they follow from preceding premises? If not, then the arguments are invalid and may be rejected.

b. Second, are the factual claims in the opposing arguments acceptable? Are they based on sufficient evidence, appropriate statistical analysis or acceptable inductive conclusions? If the factual claims embedded in opposing arguments are unacceptable, then, again, the arguments can be rejected.

c. Third, do the value premises in the opposing arguments hold up under rational scrutiny? Do they pass the tests of adequacy (i.e., new cases, role exchange, higher-order principle, consistency and universalizability—see Chapter Eleven? If the value premise of a particular syllogism is not defensible, then the conclusion deriving from it can be rejected.

d. Fourth, look for informal fallacies (see Chapter Eleven). Are any diversionary or intimidation tactics used? If so, then the counter-arguments based on them are weak and, likely, need not be accepted.

e. Fifth, are there any conceptual questions that need to be raised? Is there any ambiguity or vagueness on the opposing side?

STEP SIX: BE SURE THAT ALL OF *YOUR* SUPPORTING ARGUMENTS HOLD UP UNDER RATIONAL SCRUTINY AND CRITICAL EVALUATION

As the saying goes, "What's good for the goose is good for the gander." Be sure that your own conclusions follow from preceding premises and that you have adequate support for your factual claims. Be sure, as well, that your value premises are justifiable and that you have not included any informal fallacies in arguments supporting your side of the issue. In addition, you want to try to eliminate any vagueness and ambiguity in your position. Depending on how you have put your arguments together, some fine tuning may be required.

OTHER HELPFUL HINTS

The process of writing a thesis defence, as described above, can be simplified into structural elements. You might find it helpful to conceptualize its structure in the following fashion.

Topic Introduction and Thesis Statement

Supporting Arguments	Opposing Arguments

Criticisms of Opposing Arguments

A paper containing this structural organization would begin with an introduction to the moral topic to be discussed. Then, its position or thesis would be stated, explained and clarified in a few sentences. After this, the strongest arguments in favour of the thesis could be given, followed by arguments against. The paper would conclude, in this case, with criticisms of opposing arguments.

Alternatively, what you could do is

a. introduce the moral topic

b. state your position

c. describe opposing arguments

d. criticize and reject those opposing arguments, and

f. finish up with your strongest "arguments for"

Either format is acceptable; choosing between them is a matter of personal preference. If you are taking an unpopular position, however, the second alternative may be preferable. If you fairly and accurately state the opposing position and then give good reasons for rejecting it, greater openness to your own position can be created.

On page 426 is a sample "Argument Assembly Chart" containing all of the structural elements of a thesis defence. Specific arguments included in the chart are expressed in a kind of shorthand as practical syllogisms. An actual paper based on this chart would require that syllogisms be expanded and explained in proper written form. Fleshed out, each syllogism could comprise about one page of your paper, as could your introduction and explanation of your thesis. From the chart included here, I could imagine developing a five-to-eight-page paper. I mention this because length often seems to be a concern among students I have taught. They frequently worry that they will not write enough. Let me assure you that if you follow the "recipe" here, you will write more than enough in most cases. In fact, I predict you will surprise yourself with how much you actually have to say. Good luck!

ARGUMENT ASSEMBLY CHART
THESIS: Smoking in Public Places Should Be Prohibited

SUPPORTING ARGUMENTS

Value Premise	Factual Premise	Conclusion
Argument 1		
That which endangers the health of others should be prohibited.	Smoking in public places endangers the health of others.	Therefore, smoking in public places should be prohibited.
Argument 2		
That which increases health-care costs should be discouraged.	Smoking in public places increases health-care costs.	Smoking in public places should be discouraged.
Argument 3		
Violating the rights of others is wrong.	Smoking in public places violates the rights of others.	Smoking in public places is wrong.

OPPOSING ARGUMENTS

Value Premise	Factual Premise	Conclusion
Objection 1		
That which interferes with everyday business practices should not be enforced	Public smoking regulations interfere with everyday business practices.	Therefore, public smoking regulations should not be enforced.
Objection 2		
Limiting individual choice is wrong.	Public smoking regulations limit individual choice.	Public smoking regulations are wrong.

Criticisms of Opposing Arguments
Opposing Argument 1
a. Logic and Conclusion: *Acceptable.*
b. Factual Premise: *Correct.*
c. Value Premise: *Unacceptable.* Fails new-cases test (e.g., regulations governing industrial wastes and car emissions interfere with business and profit maximization, yet we are in favour of them).
d. Fallacies: *None.*
Opposing Argument 2
a. Logic and Conclusion: *Acceptable.*
b. Factual Premise: *Acceptable.*
c. Value Premise: *Unacceptable.* Individual choice is acceptable only insofar as other's rights are not violated.
d. Fallacies: *None.*

Source: Falikowski, *Moral Philosophy: Theories, Skills, and Applications*, p. 335.
Adapted from the Association of Values Education and Research, *Value Reasoning Series*, the University of British Columbia, 1978–1981.

Case Studies for Ethical Analysis

Instructions: Use the case-study method described in Chapter Ten to handle the following moral dilemmas.[1]

1. According to a certain hospital rule, nurses are required to have a physical examination every year. While conducting one such exam, a doctor discovers that a nurse has a low-grade infection he is supposed to report. However, he thinks there is little chance the nurse will spread the infection. She says she will have it treated and asks him not to report the case. Should he report it or not? Justify your answer.

2. A 73-year-old male patient has been suffering from lung cancer and there is virtually no prospect of recovery. Other organs are functioning poorly. The doctor warns of a possible heart attack. The patient's family asks that in the event of a heart attack, the patient be allowed to die. In that event, should the doctor write a "do not resuscitate" or "no code" order? Justify your answer after following the seven-step dilemma resolution process outlined in Chapter Ten.

3. Bob, who is 15 years old, wants to have his ear pierced so that he can wear an earring. But his mother and father are very upset at the prospect. They put a great deal of pressure on him, arguing that this will embarrass them among their friends and that he will encounter difficulties getting a job. They say he is morally obliged, as their son, to follow their strong wishes in this regard; if he wants to have an earring, he should wait, they say, until he is living on his own. What should Bob do? Why?

4. A psychiatrist is asked by the police to release information about one of his patients who is suspected of murder. The police believe that information about the patient's criminal background would be helpful to them in making their case. On the contrary, the doctor believes that psychiatric predictions are unreliable evidence. Should the doctor withhold the information? Justify your answer after analyzing the situation.

5. In its advertisements, a US automobile manufacturer tells people to "buy American" because the sale of foreign cars, it says, is putting Americans out of work. The same firm also lobbies Congress for higher tariffs so that foreign cars will cost more. Yet most of its parts are manufactured in other countries, and some of its cars are assembled in foreign plants where labour is cheaper, even though these cars bear an American name. The company tries to keep this information secret, but argues that it could not make a profit if it had to rely exclusively on higher-paid American workers. Is the automobile manufacturer doing anything morally wrong? Should Congress place higher tariffs on foreign cars, given the American manufacturer's position?

NOTE

These case studies are found in Richard M. Fox and Joseph P. DeMarco, *Moral Reasoning: A Philosophic Approach to Applied Ethics*, Fort Worth: Holt, Rinehart, Winston, 1990

Argument Analysis Worksheet

Instructions: Use the following worksheet as a tool for critically analyzing and evaluating the readings found in this book. Make copies if you intend to conduct more than one analysis.

Reading: _____

1. In general terms, what is the moral topic or issue addressed by this reading?

    _____

    _____

    _____

2. Specifically, what moral values, ideals or ethical principles are in conflict?

    _____

    _____

    _____

3. What position is taken by the author? What is the author's primary thesis?

    _____

    _____

    _____

4. List the major factual claims used by the author to defend the position taken.

    _____

    _____

    _____

5. How are the factual claims supported, if at all? What evidence is given for each one? Are there any statistics, surveys, experiences, examples, empirical studies or processes of inductive logic used to justify the factual claims? Illustrate and explain. Is the support for the major factual claims adequate? Why or why not? What, if anything, more is needed?

    _____

    _____

    _____

6. Are the ethical principles, values and normative assumptions embedded in the reading justifiable? Do they pass the tests of adequacy discussed in the logic portion of the book (e.g., role-exchange, new cases, higher-order principle, consistency and universalizability)?

    _____

    _____

    _____

7. Is the logic valid? Are the arguments sound? Do the moral/ethical/logical conclusions follow from the preceding premises? Are the premises relevant to the conclusion? Are they acceptable? Are they sufficient to prove the conclusion? Why?

    _____

    _____

    _____

8. Are any logical fallacies included in the argument? Do you find any diversionary tactics, emotional appeals or attempts to intimidate? If so, which ones (e.g., red herring, *ad hominem*)?

    _____

    _____

    _____

9. Is the moral position taken by the author adequately defended, given your earlier answers? What could strengthen the author's position? What is weakest about the position? Are you persuaded in the end by the author's arguments? Why or why not?

    _____

    _____

    _____

10. Finally, from what moral perspective are the arguments made (e.g., from a utilitarian, egoist, deontological or existential vantage point)? Explain.

    _____

    _____

    _____

Glossary

A priori: That which is not derived from experience, nor dependent upon it (e.g., *a priori* truths may be seen as necessary, certain and universally true, independent of all experience; nothing in experience can prove them false).

Altruistic utilitarianism: An ethical philosophy stressing the greatest happiness for the greatest number. It may require self-sacrifice and doing things for the sake of others.

Argument: A series of related statements (premises) leading to a conclusion.

Consequentialism: A type of ethical theory that determines the rightness or wrongness of any action on the basis of its consequences.

Consequentialist: One who evaluates the morality of an action by its consequences or results.

Contingencies: Conditional, varied or changing possibilities of what could happen.

Deontological ethics: An ethical perspective emphasizing the importance of doing your duty and adhering to rules and principles of right conduct.

Disinterestedness: A state that is free from personal interest or one not influenced by private advantage and selfish motivations.

Disutility: The opposite of utility; causing or increasing disadvantage, pain, misery, dissatisfaction and suffering.

Doctrine of Teleology: The theory that everything in the universe has a proper function to perform within a harmonious hierarchy of purposes.

Doctrine of the Mean: Applied to life, it implies choosing the mean point between excess and deficiency. This mean point is determined relative to particular individuals, not by some purely mathematical calculation.

Elucidations: Explanations to remove obscurity and to clarify.

Empirical study: An investigation of any phenomenon using experience, experiment and/or sensory observation for verification.

Entelechy: An inner urge within each living thing to become its unique self, e.g., an acorn's urge to become an oak.

Ethical egoism: A moral position maintaining that it is right and good to pursue pleasure and that this is what we ought to do even if we choose not to.

Ethics of altruism: a morality which defines good acts as those which benefit others (Rand).

Eudaimonia: The happiness achieved through well-living and well-acting; it is tied to the concept of successful living.

Factual statement: A claim or assertion that is true or false in principle.

Functional explanation of morality: According to Plato, the morally good life is based on the proper inner workings of the soul.

Happiness: The ultimate end of life or purpose for which things are done.

Hedonic calculus: Jeremy Bentham's method of calculating or measuring the painful and pleasurable consequences of particular actions; it is used to arrive at morally correct decisions.

Hedonist: Someone who sees the chief good as the pursuit of pleasure.

Higher faculties: The elevated mental, spiritual, and emotional capacities that add to human dignity.

Higher pleasures: Satisfactions related to the intellect, to our feelings and imagination, and to our sense of dignity.

Ideal observer: One who can see a situation from all perspectives and without bias.

Infirmity of character: A weakness in moral personality that leads people to opt for lower and inferior pleasures.

Inviolability: A quality that makes irreverent treatment of any person wrong; actions that injure, harm or hurt others may also infringe upon people's inviolability.

Is–ought fallacy: Arguing that something should be the case simply because it is.

Just society (Plato): A society in which different classes of people live and function harmoniously together under the enlightened guidance of the guardians or philosopher kings.

Logical fallacy: A rhetorical device used to win arguments through diversion, emotional appeal and/or intimidation.

Logical form: The structure of an argument.

Lower pleasures: Satisfactions derived from physical and bodily pleasures.

Maxim: The rule of conduct implicit in any voluntary action.

Metaethics: A nonnormative, philosophical approach to ethics and the study of its foundations.

Morality of care: A psychological logic of relationship which contrasts with the formal logic of fairness that informs the justice approach to morality.

Natural caring: A predisposition that can replace self-interested impersonal justice as a basis for morality.

Nonmoral value judgments: Normative statements not related to morality.

Nonnormative: Not value-laden, but factual, logical, empirical or verifiable by experience or sensory observation.

Objectivist ethics: Ayn Rand's conception of morality, which promotes rational selfishness or rational self-interest.

Normative: Value-laden or relating to values and value judgments.

Practical reason: Reason in its application to morality.

Premise: A previous statement from which another is inferred.

Pride: The moral equivalent of ambition.

Principle of utility: A general rule of conduct requiring us to maximize pleasure and minimize pain in situations where our actions impact on human interests.

Productivity: According to Ayn Rand, one of the highest qualities of man's character.

Prudence: The state or act of proceeding with caution or in the interests of oneself.

Psychological egoism: A behavioural theory stating that it is human nature to seek pleasure and to avoid pain.

Realm of forms: A realm beyond sensory experience knowable only by reason; permanent and immutable (unchanging); more real than perceived objects.

Retributivist: One who seeks retribution (punishment) for a wrong-doing and regards it as a proper response to mischievous acts; one who seeks payment in pain to reestablish the balance of justice.

Rhetorical: Designed to persuade or impress; artificial eloquence or flashy oratory.

Sanction: A source of pleasure and pain giving binding force to any law or rule of conduct; related also to reward and punishment.

Self-realization ethic: For Aristotle, a morality of self-fulfillment wherein the potential for moral conduct is actualized through the development of appropriate habits.

Society: A self-sufficient association of individuals who co-operate for mutual advantage under rules designed to promote the welfare of all.

Soul: A notion used by Plato to explain the main motives or impulses to action within any person; comprised of appetite, spirit, and reason; something akin to psyche, self or personality structure.

Tacit agreements: Understandings among people that are not spoken or explicitly stated; they are implied but are not expressed in words.

The categorical imperative: Immanuel Kant's supreme and unconditional principle of morality that serves as the basis for all other derivative moral commands.

The good life: A life of the intellect and rational activity in accordance with virtue.

Traders: People who earn what they get and refuse to take the undeserved; how moral relationships should be viewed in terms of Ayn Rand's objectivist ethics.

Utilitarianism: A moral theory based on the principle of utility; it holds that good actions are those producing pleasure or happiness and minimizing pain or suffering.

Valid reasoning: An acceptable form of rational argument leading to a necessary conclusion.

Veil of ignorance: An imaginary veil that, theoretically, prevents people from knowing anything about themselves.

Veracity: Truthfulness or honesty; the accuracy of a statement.

Index